THE NOVELS OF
WORLD WAR I

GARLAND REFERENCE LIBRARY
OF THE HUMANITIES
(VOL. 232)

THE NOVELS OF WORLD WAR I
An Annotated Bibliography

Philip E. Hager
Desmond Taylor

GARLAND PUBLISHING, INC. • NEW YORK & LONDON
1981

© 1981 Philip E. Hager and Desmond Taylor
All rights reserved

Library of Congress Cataloging in Publication Data
Hager, Philip E.
　The novels of World War I.

　(Garland reference library of the humanities ;
v. 232)
　　Includes indexes.
　　1. World War, 1914–1918—Fiction—Bibliography.
2. World War, 1914–1918—Juvenile fiction—
Bibliography.　I. Taylor, Desmond, 1930–
II. Series.
Z5917.W33H33　[PN3448.W3]　　808.83′9358　　80-8496
ISBN 0-8240-9491-3　　　　　　　　　　　　　　AACR2

Printed on acid free, 250-year-life paper
Manufactured in the United States of America

To Phyllis
for her willingness to read "just one more novel" after the scores of others
P.E.H.

For Erica, Onica & Ingeborg
with love
D.T.

CONTENTS

Foreword	ix
Acknowledgments	xv
The Adult Novels	
Introduction	3
Bibliography	9
The Juvenile Novels	
Introduction	313
Bibliography	317
Bibliography of Critical Materials	451
Indexes	
Author	469
Title	483

FOREWORD

This annotated bibliography of World War I novels was developed after the publication of Philip Hager's "A Checklist of Novels of the European War, 1914–1918" in the *Bulletin of Bibliography & Magazine Notes* (October-December, 1977). However, since the completion of the checklist, whose more than 800 entries have served as the basis for the present work, we have discovered a substantial number of additional titles that have escaped all of the useful subject lists and standard bibliographies. Thus, this listing grew steadily as we continued to search out all possible leads with both libraries and collectors throughout the United States and Canada.

This bibliography contains some 900 adult and 370 juvenile entries. Our aim was to include all novels published in English, including English translations of such foreign novels as *Life in the Tomb* by Stratis Myrivilis (item 869), translated into English more than 55 years after its publication in Greek. Some prose works which we have included may be better classified as novelettes or even short stories—some juvenile works contain as few as 30 pages—but if the titles were bound separately, we have treated them as novels. For example, James Hanley's *The German Prisoner* (item 609) is a short story published in book form.

Also, there are a few titles that do not qualify for any one genre, let alone that of the novel. In these few cases we have indicated their unusual status in the annotation. The example that readily comes to hand is *In Parenthesis* by David Jones (item 734), a curious mixture of poetry and prose in a form all its own. There are some critics (notably Fussell in his *The Great War and Modern Memory*, 1975) who challenge the autobiographical status of Robert Graves' *Goodbye to All That* and make a case for it as fiction. Although there may well be some merit to this argument, our investigation indicates that it is not a novel or even fiction, but rather an autobiography. Granted, Graves plays fast and loose with the facts, but this book is generally accepted by most critics as a war memoir. It is crucial to emphasize that Graves describes his experiences in the war directly, not through a fictional character or characters (which is a perfectly legitimate practice in a novel or a short story). In contrast, in Siegfried Sassoon's fictionalized memoirs, the character of George Sherston is used to relate Sassoon's own war experiences in considerable detail.

We selected those novels that use the World War I conflict either as a substantial part of the action or those whose plot is set wholly or in part against the 1914–1918 war period. We have rejected all war memoirs (even when a specific critic may characterize a particular work as largely fiction, e.g., *Goodbye to All That* by Robert Graves) and collections of short stories. The work of fiction must deal in some significant and substantial way with an aspect of the war, or with its impact on people on the battlefields and on the home fronts. Naturally, there is some subjectivity involved in the selection process.

We have not included novels that show the effect of the war on postwar life and activities. Novels which concentrate only on the Russian Revolution as distinct and apart from the involvement of Russia in World War I are also excluded. We have, however, included such works as the *Road to Calvary* trilogy of Alexis Tolstoi (items 481 and 776) since the first part clearly reflects the impact of the great war on the destiny of Russian society.

The following are examples of novels omitted from this bibliography. They are provided for the interested reader as specific and representative indicators of our selection criteria. *The Years* (1937) by Virginia Woolf consists of a number of chapters with all but one titled by the "years" beginning with 1880. The chapters "1917" and "1918" contain the only two brief references in the novel to the war. Chapter "1917" describes a dinner party in a basement residence in London which is interrupted for a few minutes by a German air raid. Chapter "1918" is only four pages long. Perhaps a hundred words in each of the two chapters deal with the war. *After War* (1931) by Ludwig Renn is set in postwar Germany. The plot describes how the protagonist is unable to find employment after the war and joins the German army. This leads to various adventures involving political intrigue. The scenes of barracks life are placed in the postwar period and the protagonist's attraction to Communist ideology is described. *Palimpsest* (1926) by H.D. has been characterized by at least one critic as a collection of stories rather than a novel. In any case, it is a prose work consisting of three parts, the first placed in ancient Rome, the second set in the postwar London of 1926, and the third placed in modern Egypt. The London story contains flashback memories of 1916 in London where Ermy, one of the female characters, "represents the war—her young husband [Freddie] was killed in it." There are no other references to the war. Ermy's musings and remembrances of her husband are devoted to their love relationship and banter. A final example is *England, Their England* (1933) by Archibald Macdonell. The first short chapter (16 pages) is directly concerned with the war. The narrator is wounded and shell-shocked. From Chapter 2 through the conclusion (pp. 17–299) he is described recuperating in England and as he endeavors to follow a literary career in postwar England. A publisher asks him to write a book which will be a series of episodes revealing the English character. The narrative contains an occasional reflection on the war, but the vast bulk of the plot and action is concerned with the postwar period in England.

The inclusion of juvenile novels created special problems in the verification of author and title entries. However, there are two bibliographies that were invaluable in identifying titles for this project. Of the two, Harry K. Hudson's *A Bibliography of Hard Cover Boys' Books* (revised edition; published by the author [Data Print], Inverness, Florida, 1977, 280 pages) is by far the more exhaustive, comprehensive, and valuable work. It is a labor of love by a longtime collector of juvenile books and the single best source (we are tempted to say the *only* source) for tracing the many title variations within and among series. Hudson also sorts out the confusing array of pseudonyms used by and for authors in many of these series. It is the basic bibliographic source for any collection or library specializing in boys' books in series.

Girls Series Books: A Checklist of Hardcover Books Published

1900–1975 (Children's Literature Research Collections, University of Minnesota; Minneapolis: University Libraries, 1978, 121 pages) is a simple listing with none of the elaborate bibliographical detail characteristic of the outstanding Hudson work.

We have obtained hundreds of novels from scores of libraries in the United States and Canada. However, some books have been unobtainable, and wherever possible we have tried to locate any available critical material on these titles (including reviews, plot summaries, etc.) in order to provide some annotation information, sketchy though it may be.

The publication information for the earliest edition of every title was determined by examination of the *National Union Catalog*, *Mansell's*, the *British Museum Catalog*, or, in a comparatively few instances, from the *Cumulative Book Index* and specialized bibliographies. Naturally, if the book itself had an earlier imprint, this was accepted as the most authorative information. Authors' names were taken from the title page of the books. In cases where a pseudonym was used, we have considered this the main author entry and have given the real name, if known, following in parentheses. In cases where the author used a shortened version of his actual name we added the missing elements in accordance with the Library of Congress author entry in the *National Union Catalog*. When the authors of anonymous works are known, their names are used as the main author entry but are placed in brackets.

Pagination is included for virtually all entries. In a small number of cases where we have been unable to obtain a novel from any source in the United States or Canada, and the standard bibliographic tools such as the *National Union Catalog*, the *British Museum Catalog*, or *Cumulative Book Index* have omitted pagination, the length of the text is not indicated. In a few instances, mainly juvenile works, we have estimated the pagination when pages were unnumbered.

Careful verification of all the titles in this bibliography was undertaken several times in the *National Union Catalog*, its cumulation, *Mansell's Pre 1956 Imprints*, and the *British Museum Catalog*. If a citation was not located in these sources then the *Cumulative Book Index* and the *United States Catalog 1928* and its preceding volumes were searched. In every entry we have cited

Foreword *xiii*

the earliest imprint located. In cases of translations from foreign languages the original foreign imprint information has also been listed if available. If there are variant English and American titles for novels published in England and the United States, the title used in the primary bibliographic entry is the one considered to be the first edition or the probable title of first publication based on the nationality of the author. No doubt there are some cases of simultaneous publication, but information to resolve this is unavailable.

In our search for all possible novels to include in this project, we examined the obvious indexes, lists, and bibliographies such as the H.W. Wilson *Fiction Catalog* and specialized library book catalogs, e.g., The Hoover Institution on War, Revolution and Peace at Stanford and the New York Public Library's *Subject Catalog of the World War I Collection*. Some of the titles in the New York Public Library catalog were unavailable for examination. As a means of identifying the basis of their inclusion in our bibliography we added the letters "NYPL" in the annotation location as a source reference for the reader. In a handful of entries (mainly juvenile) which we also have been unable to examine, there is some question as to one or more factors. The following letters in combination with an item number for a bibliographic entry indicates the question or questions: A = juvenile?; B = World War I?; C = fiction?; and D = adult? Some item number examples are: j11AB, j88B, and j344AB.

The author and title indexes have been provided for ease of location and verification by the collector, the researcher, the librarian, and the interested student.

ACKNOWLEDGMENTS

We are greatly in the debt of many librarians and libraries throughout the United States and Canada who have graciously provided us with assistance in the preparation of this bibliography. Most of the novels covered in this project were necessarily obtained through interlibrary loan due to their scarcity or unavailability in the Puget Sound area.

Our special thanks go to those libraries which graciously checked our want lists against their holdings: Appalachian State University, Ball State University, Boston Public Library, Bowling Green State University Popular Culture Library, Case Western Reserve University, Chicago Public Library, Detroit Public Library, Free Library of Philadelphia, Hoover Institution, Idaho State Library, Library of Congress, Louisiana State University, National Library of Canada, New York Public Library, New York State Library, St. Louis Public Library, Southern Illinois University at Carbondale, University of Minnesota Children's Literature Research Collections, University of North Carolina, University of South Florida, University of Virginia, and the Vancouver Public Library.

The Library of Congress and its remarkable book catalogs were an invaluable and absolutely essential resource. Kay Blair of the Loan Division extended to us every possible loan courtesy of this great collection. Indeed, the generous assistance and many suggestions of librarians such as Evva Larson of the Idaho State Library and Margaret O'Bryant at the University of Virginia were vital for the completion of this bibliographic project in its present form.

We are particularly grateful to J.B. Dobkin and Paul Eugen Camp, Special Collection Librarians at the University of South Florida, and Nancy Steen and Nancy White Lee of the Popular Culture Library at Bowling Green State University for their splendid cooperation in loaning us countless juvenile novels from their rare book collections. The completion of this bibliography in its present comprehensive form would have been impossible without their generous and understanding cooperation.

Our contacts with private collectors in the field of juvenile literature were more than just helpful. Harry K. Hudson not only shared the remaining volumes of his juvenile collection with us but also placed us in contact with the University of South Florida Library which had previously purchased the bulk of his sizable collection of juvenile books for boys. Other collectors who graciously loaned prized volumes from their private libraries were President Roland Dille of Morehead State University and Dr. Barrett Potter at the S.U.N.Y. Technical College. Richard Schneider in Bedford, New York, willingly undertook to check our want list against his personal collection and verified a number of crucial bibliographic questions.

A special appreciation is due Anthony S. Bliss, Rare Books Librarian at Northern Illinois University, who unexpectedly and graciously supplied a full-page annotation of a scarce juvenile title from his special collection. The cooperation of the staff of the Seattle Public Library and especially Ellen F. Buckley of the Children's Literature section at the University of Washington Library deserves special recognition and thanks. Indeed, the staff and catalogs of the Pacific Northwest Bibliographic Center were a priceless location resource as was their generous search of the WLN database.

The Faculty Research Grant awarded by the University of Puget Sound Enrichment Committee helped to cover the travel and interlibrary-loan expenses associated with this project. Our thanks go to our colleagues on this committee for their support. Special thanks also go to Mary Beth Baker, Collins Library Interlibrary Loan Assistant at the University of Puget Sound, who was ever helpful and cheerful with all our countless requests for books from other libraries.

Finally, one of our greatest debts is due to the diligent typing of much of our preliminary manuscript by the conscientious and highly competent Rebecca Duncan, now retired secretary to the Collins Library Director. Similar appreciation and thanks are also due to Kathryn Macpherson for her excellent typing assistance with the manuscript. The delightful Berdine Kulla, however, requires the highest praise for her determined and persistent efforts to completely retype the entire manuscript under the pressure of an ever-present deadline. The understanding and patience of these persons handling literally reams of notes and revisions preceding the final copy deserve our deepest gratitude and heartfelt thanks.

Philip E. Hager Desmond Taylor
Professor of English *Library Director*

Collins Library
University of Puget Sound

Adult Novels about World War I

INTRODUCTION

   The scope of this bibliography has been made as wide as
possible in order to reveal all aspects of the war--how the
bloody and terrible focus of the trenches diffused its impact
throughout the world in all walks of life--from juvenile literature and popular novels to the relatively few significant works
of adult fiction. While we finally identified some 900 adult
titles (and 370 juvenile stories), it was necessary to examine
many more, nearly four hundred.
   The Great War novels are especially interesting for the
views they provide of the nations and the participants; not
only the English, French, and Germans, but also the Turks,
Africans, Russians, and all the other nationalities, including,
of course, the Americans. This was the war that would end all
wars. It ended a period of prosperity and peace, particularly
in Europe, which such writers as Stefan Zweig (*The World of
Yesterday: an Autobiography*. New York: The Viking Press,
1943) nostalgically called "the Golden Age of Security." There
was then evident what we would now characterize as a Darwinian
idealism or optimism. It seemed that the world of the nineteenth century was "on the straight and unfailing path toward
being the best of all worlds." Past generations and eras had
had their wars, revolutions, and famines, but progress, seen
as a direct result of the discoveries of science and the inventions of technology, promised to better the world. The last
vestiges of human blunder, evil, greed, and intolerance seemed
well on the way to oblivion, especially by the extraordinarily
lovely spring and summer of 1914.
   This was the first war that would employ on a vast scale
such modern equipment as machine guns, poison gas, tanks, and
airplanes, some for the first time. It was the first war that
would forecast the uses of heavy weaponry and technology in
later years. Bernard Bergonzi, in his *Heroes' Twilight, a
Study of the Literature of the Great War* (New York: Coward-
McCann, 1966) describes the implications for the future by
declaring that World War I "started as a war to end wars, but
instead it pointed forward to the totalitarian state, to an
even greater war and a concept of unlimited conflict in which

not merely uniformed armies but whole populations, down to the smallest child, are regarded as appropriate victims for destruction on a scale that makes the slaughter on the Somme appear ordinary."

It is not just the stench and blood and horror of war as described in these novels that is of interest, but also the depiction of how war changes soldiers and noncombatants, and how civilians back home strive to maintain normality, perhaps to reaffirm traditions, in order to "keep the home fires burning" as a means to preserve as much as possible a way of life which they sense is in grave danger. It is also our aim in examining the fiction of this war to discover what people were like under the stress of the first major conflict in the twentieth century. In a sense, our annotations might well serve as their fictional "biography."

We discovered how much the people of this "Age of Security," who were in so many ways leading comfortable and idealistic lives, were unsophisticated about the degree to which men and nations could still become violent. Indeed, we learned how their responses would change year by year, even day by day, and how their experiences would affect them for years, if not forever.

The novels which treat war as glorious were far fewer than we anticipated. It is now apparent that the themes of the novels did not change from fervent patriotism or even jingoism to revulsion and outrage as the human casualties were recognized back home. A simple experiment can test this observation. The reader may choose at random a score of novels published in 1919 (the year in which 111 novels, the largest number, appeared) and observe how comfortably the dominant subject matter--life in war, the siege of capital cities, day-to-day activities, conversations, and even thoughts of draft-age youths in love with village girls--is similar to and, indeed, reflects so much of the same subject matter as the novels published between 1920 and 1950. The plot of many Great War novels often simply serves as an opportunity or even an excuse to introduce inept German spies who bungle their assignments or Allied secret service operatives who never fail to uncover enemy plots and change the course of the war. Quite often the war is merely a backdrop to the love interests of the chief characters, whether they be soldiers suddenly called up for duty or wives who marry again because their soldier husbands are presumed dead.

A considerable majority of World War I novels fall into the category of popular literature whose purpose is mainly to tell a story, to entertain, to divert the reader briefly from life about him. On the other hand, some titles appear to reflect the intention of the author to instruct the reader in

Introduction

the author's special view of human nature and the world "as it really is." Serious fiction, as many of our annotations indicate, constitutes a rather small part of the adult novels listed in this bibliography.

Many of the critical assessments of World War I literature suggest that the fiction written during the early part of the 1914-1918 period was pro-war; that later fiction was characterized by disenchantment, and finally, by revulsion and outrage at the waste of human life and the folly of war. How true this judgment may be of much of the nonfiction, poetry, and short stories we cannot say. However, our reading and examination of all the novels that deal with the war or some aspect of it reveal a different composite picture.

We do not intend to dismiss or overlook the superb critical examinations and assessments of World War I literature in Paul Fussell's *The Great War and Modern Memory* (New York and London: Oxford University Press, 1975) and in Bernard Bergonzi's *Heroes' Twilight* (or, for that matter, to ignore any of the other studies listed in our Bibliography of Critical Materials). For example, Bergonzi "examines the impact of World War I on England's poets and prose writers." Fussell's study concentrates on the "British experiences on the Western Front from 1914 to 1918" and is concerned with poetry, nonfiction, and fiction about the war, that is, the entire body of literature relating to the western front. Our investigation into the considerable body of imaginative literature about the war in all its theaters--in Africa, at Gallipoli, in Mesopotamia, in the Balkans and Russia, in all parts of the world--is not generally similar in character or theme to many areas discussed in the Fussell and Bergonzi studies. The serious fiction, on the other hand, does treat most if not all of the themes and objectives presented in these two important critical works. Moreover, it is this serious fiction that obviously will be of enduring reputation and interest to the literary scholar and student. Thus, for readers who wish to examine a representative and basic listing of the twenty most significant novels of the Great War that do treat the general themes discussed by Fussell and Bergonzi, we suggest the following:

Henri Barbusse. *Under Fire: The Story of a Squad.* 1917. (item 113)
Vicente Blasco Ibáñez. *The Four Horsemen of the Apocalypse.* 1918. (item 198)
Herman Broch. *The Sleepwalkers.* 1932. (item 663)
Louis-Ferdinand Celine. *Journey to the End of the Night.* 1934. (item 695)
Humphrey Cobb. *Paths of Glory.* 1935. (item 703)
John Dos Passos. *Three Soldiers.* 1921. (item 452)

Ford Madox Ford. *Some Do Not.* 1924. (item 485)
———. *No More Parades.* 1925. (item 493)
———. *A Man Could Stand Up.* 1926. (item 502)
Jaroslav Hasek. *The Good Soldier: Schweik.* 1930. (item 611)
Ernest Hemingway. *A Farewell to Arms.* 1929. (item 561)
Frederick Manning. *The Middle Parts of Fortune: Somme & Ancre, 1916.* 1929. (item 567)
William March. *Company K.* 1933. (item 686)
Stratis Myrivilis. *Life in the Tomb.* 1977. [1923-24] (item 869)
Erich Maria Remarque. *All Quiet on the Western Front.* 1929. (item 575)
Jules Romains. *Verdun.* 1940. (item 750)
Siegfried Sassoon. *Memoirs of an Infantry Officer.* 1930. (item 630)
Mikhail Sholokhov. *And Quiet Flows the Don.* 1934. (item 699)
Fritz Unruh. *The Way of Sacrifice.* 1928. (item 543)
Arnold Zweig. *The Case of Sergeant Grischa.* 1929. (item 547)

Passages of memorable description and power are found not only in the major novels. Some powerful sections occasionally appear in otherwise undistinguished novels. One short work in particular, *The German Prisoner* by James Hanley (item 609), manifests one of the most powerful and lasting impacts of any story about the war. The memory of Hanley's description of a brutal and appalling incident in no-man's-land conveys still, and better than most, the true horror and dehumanization that was a product of this war to end all wars.

Of all the varied topics, themes, and categories reflected in these many novels touching on the war, we wish especially to identify and to discuss briefly two. The first is the imaginary war and battle story. There are eight that have some direct connection with World War I. (Of these, four are juvenile and are discussed in that section of this bibliography.) Among the adult novels, Palmer's *The Last Shot* (item 8), written before the war began and published in 1914, imagines what would happen if two great adjoining nations whose armies are referred to only as the Grays and Browns should go to war. Giesy's *All for His Country* (item 33), published in 1915, is singular in being one of the very few that have any reference to Japan. In this case, the story imagines what might might have happened if the Japanese had invaded the United States. *Hindenburg's March into London* (item 90) by Paul Munch, published in 1916, relates in apocalyptic rhetoric the glorious invasion and defeat of England by Germany. This is an obvious propaganda piece. However, since it was published in the United States it is not entirely certain whether the intention was to alarm the Americans or to serve as support for the cause of the Central Powers. The fourth novel in this first category is a peculiar combination of fantasy, science fiction, and satiric spoof. Anthony Burgess in his 1962 title, *The Wanting Seed* (item 807), has placed his plot in the twenty-first century, in the England of George VI, about one hundred years from now. A major theme is that population growth can best be controlled by war, in which the real enemy is woman. World War I is used as the mythical and classical war for this bizarre final solution. The experiences, memories, attack plans, battlefield actions, and so forth of World War I provide the basic material for this fantasy of the future.

In Parenthesis by David Jones (item 734), a singular fantasy in a category all by itself, is a curious combination of prose, poetry, traditional Welsh heroes, and Arthurian legend. In this case, the experiences in the trenches in France combine with images of the past in a phantasmagoria of time and myth.

For the second category it is informative to apply our present consciousness of blacks in American society to the substantial body of World War I novels. Only five titles deal specifically with the experiences and the participation of blacks in the war and on the home front. *The Long Walk of Samba Diouf* (item 490), published in 1922 by Jérôme and Jean Tharaud, relates the participation of the Senegalese colonial troops from West Africa in the French front-line trenches. Written with careful attention to detail and to African customs, it is an almost anthropological study of a group of primitive men thrust into the violence of a European war completely foreign to their African experience. Extremely popular in France at the time of its publication, the book is especially notable for its sympathetic description of the men and its complete absence of race prejudice.

The four other titles were all published in the United States within fourteen years of each other. Charles Mack's *Two Black Crows in the A.E.F.* (item 535) appeared in 1928 and attempted to recreate in fictional form the comic exploits of two blackface vaudeville performers after they enlist in the army and are sent to the front lines in France. The plot is really a burlesque, and although they encounter a Senegalese soldier in France, the action is directed primarily toward the slapstick, which seldom if ever succeeds for the modern reader. *Wings on My Feet* by Howard Odum (item 573), published in 1929, is what we would now call an "Uncle Tom novel." In the attempt to describe the black in the war from the perspective of the ordinary black soldier, the author resorts to dialect and all of the associated elements such as blues and traditional negro song tunes, crap game contests, and the expected "darky" activities that now carry a strongly prejudicial ring to contemporary ears.

In considerable contrast to this "traditional" approach to blacks is *The Sister of a Certain Soldier* (item 256) by Stephen Maher. The first of the five titles to be published (in 1918), the basic message of this brief tale is that blacks are as human and as capable of sacrifice and patriotic fervor as whites. The plot used to accomplish this aim, however, concludes with considerable bathos as a consequence of the author's highly sentimental and melodramatic notions of character and action.

The one title which really strives to deal with the actual circumstances of the black in American society and military service during the war is Victor Daly's *Not Only War: A Story of Two Great Conflicts* (item 666), published in 1932. The conflicts of Daly's title are the war and the ingrained race prejudice in American society, especially in the South and in the army and its officer corps. The author reveals a series of discriminatory events befalling the hero, Montgomery Jason, that eventually culminates in a self-effacing humanitarian gesture in no-man's-land, with the consequential death of Jason for his efforts. Although the story at times is sentimental and the writing verges on the ordinary, the quiet sense of injustice reflected in the resolute integrity and honesty of Jason conveys even now a remarkable impression of what it must have been like to be a black during the Great War.

As we look back over the many novels about the war with their variety of plots and characters, it is highly surprising that only five present any discussion of the black in World War I. Ironically, the only other titles that make even a fleeting reference to black U.S. troops are a few of the juvenile stories. The interested reader is referred to the Ross Kay titles (especially item j188) and the introduction to the juvenile section of this bibliography.

1914

1   Byrne, Donn. *Through "Hell" to Peace; a Great Sensational Story of the Present War*. New York: John Adams Thayer Corp., 1914. 15p.

   A picture of the war as it did not happen. Kaiser Wilhelm has been assassinated by a Russian, the Germans have the upper hand in Europe and are winning. They have sunk the United States cruiser *Minneapolis* off Ireland, and the battleships *New York* and *Massachusetts* by airplane attacks off Newfoundland, though America seems not yet to have entered the war. The novel's main character, McCarthy, is a colonel in the United States aviation corps and a staff officer, "the most prominent military aviator in America...." He is the narrator of the novel and tells of the U.S. War Council which is meeting in New York City to plan strategy against the Huns. This War Council, comprising eight men, the President, "the explorer ex-President," a "great oil king," "the great Ironmaster," "the younger Morgan" (J.P.?), Brisbane, Debs, and Gompers, put into operation a naval encirclement of the German navy advancing toward America in the Atlantic. Oil-carrying vessels meet the enemy ships and incinerate the luckless Germans. A melodramatic fantasy.

2   Graves, Armgaard Karl (pseud.), and Edward Lyell Fox. *The Secrets of the German War Office*. New York: McBride, Nast & Co., 1914. 240p.; London: T. Werner Laurie, 1914. 182p.

   This material was first published serially in *Collier's Weekly* before the war and was treated as authentic spy information, although the question remains whether the material is fiction or the memoirs of an unidentified spy. It is included here as a curiosity. (The Library of Congress assigned it a history classification.) A revised edition with no co-author indicated and suppressed passages of the original edition included was published in London in 1915 by T.W. Laurie with 194 pages. This work is in the form of a memoir by a supposedly successful secret agent of the German spy system. (Graves claimed to be a distinguished professor at a major university in the U.S. with many other publications to his credit.) He relates his experiences over a twelve-year period and describes details of secret German missions designed to influence the conduct of the war predicted to be imminent. Graves and Fox write in a journalistic style but demonstrate little knowledge of the German language.

3   Hocking, Joseph. *All For a Scrap of Paper; a Romance.* London: Hodder & Stoughton, 1914. 255(?)p.

Not seen; NYPL.

4   Leblanc, Maurice. *The Bomb-Shell.* Translated by A. Texeira De Mattos. London: Hurst & Blackett, 1914. 320p.

A spy mystery melodrama revolving around the impersonations of a woman spy, the kidnapping of a son of the German Kaiser, and various murders.

5   Le Queux, William Tufnell. *The German Spy: A Present-day Story.* London: George Newnes, 1914. 251p.

The main character, Rupert Manton, 28 and unemployed, becomes involved in London with Ronald Whitmarsh, a spy for Germany and boss of "the clearing-house of the espionage of Europe" in a home known as the House of a Thousand Secrets. Secrecy, intrigue, and murder become Manton's companions, for Whitmarsh pays money for state secrets and battle plans, engages in deceit, and double-crosses spies, killing them in ingenious ways. Eventually Manton succeeds in exposing Whitmarsh, which results in the arrest of over 350 foreign agents.

6   [Meynell, Wilfrid]. *Aunt Sarah & the War: A Tale of Transformations.* London: Burns & Oates, 1914. 83p.

Written in the form of letters which attempt to show the war's effect on the social order in England. The basic concern of Aunt Sarah in her first letter is with her own personal difficulties when she is deprived of the services of her second footman, Henry, when he enlists. However, patriotism eventually develops, and by the end of the book she has turned her great house into a hospital, even devoting her time to nursing the wounded, Henry among them. Among the letters are some from her nephew, Owen Tudor, at the front, and her niece, Pauline Vandeleur, training with the Red Cross.

7 Newton, Wilfred Douglas. *War*. London: Methuen & Co.,
   1914. 236p.; New York: Dodd, Mead & Co., 1914. 236p.

   An imaginary invasion of England, observed through the
   eyes of a quiet civilian (in some obscure clerk's position)
   who hides and watches the entire invasion process beginning with the disembarkation of the first enemy troops
   and the first English deaths. Mainly through his eyes,
   but occasionally through those of his girl friend and her
   mother, appears a view of the war which ranges over the
   heaps of bodies and shrieking wounded, blood-soaked villages, sieges, sickness and filth, women violated, starving
   populations, and battles and guerilla fighting. At the
   conclusion his girl friend is taken by drunken enemy
   soldiers and he is shot. A grim and graphic view of war.
   Both the obvious propaganda purpose and the intent to
   create an anti-war spirit fail.

8 Palmer, Frederick. *The Last Shot*. New York: Charles
   Scribner's Sons, 1914. 517p.; London: Chapman & Hall,
   1914. 517p.

   Written before the start of the war, this novel attempts
   to answer the question "What would happen if two great adjoining nations should go to war tomorrow?" The chief
   character is a young woman who lives on the frontier of
   one of the two warring countries. She has two lovers, and
   each is of high rank in an opposing army. The author has
   developed the usual love and human interest features that
   tend at times to overshadow the war aspects of the story.
   Palmer creates a situation in which each country is perfectly equipped and organized in accordance with the most
   modern military techniques of the times. The scenes are
   not specifically identified as to location, and the
   author refers to the two opposing armies only as the Grays
   and the Browns. The individual soldiers are described
   as nameless cogs in a war machine that is developed to almost
   mathematical perfection. (The author was a war correspondent who had ample opportunity to observe the various conflicts of the previous twenty years. This vast eyewitness
   experience enabled him to create an accurate and fairly
   minute description of modern warfare techniques that give
   the novel a most convincing atmosphere and sense of reality.)

9 Sheehan, Perley Poore, and Robert Hobart Davis. *"We Are
   French!"* New York: George H. Doran Co., 1914. 127p.

   Anatole and Pierre, two old soldiers of the French Legion,
   are the chief characters. Anatole turns out to have been a

real hero in the war. He blows the Charge call when commanded to sound Retreat, and the troops go on to victory. His friend Pierre constantly tells the story in the village inn, the tale spreads eventually to Paris, and Anatole is summoned there to receive the Legion of Honor award. The two men go together, but rather than ride in a carriage they walk, like the foot soldiers they once were.

1915

10   Altsheler, Joseph Alexander. *The Forest of Swords; a Story of Paris and the Marne.* New York: D. Appleton & Co., 1915. 316p.

A sequel to Altsheler's *Guns of Europe* (item 11), the action continues and deals primarily with the resistance of the Allies to the German advance on Paris. The story follows the adventures of John Scott, a young American, and Philip Lannes, a Frenchman, as the Germans are finally forced back. Scott is captured by the Germans but is successfully rescued by his friend Philip in his airplane. Philip's sister, Julie, a Red Cross nurse, is introduced to Scott, and a future romantic interest is implied as the novel concludes.

11   ———. *The Guns of Europe.* New York: D. Appleton & Co., 1915. 319p.

The first novel of the author's World War I series. The chief protagonist and hero is a young American, John Scott, who is in Vienna with his uncle and a friend when war is declared. When he leaves Vienna he loses contact with his companions but soon becomes acquainted with Philip Lannes, French aviator and spy. Scott accompanies Lannes in his airplane across the border. On the way they encounter a German airplane and experience a "thrilling" midair flight. When they reach the French lines Scott decides to enlist in a company composed of young English and American adventurers who are fighting with the French. The story concludes with the Germans advancing on Paris. The novel provides a vivid view of Austrian and German mobilizations and the early period of fighting in France.

12   ———. *The Hosts of the Air; the Story of a Quest in the Great War.* New York: D. Appleton & Co., 1915. 326p.

The final novel of the author's trilogy. The plot now

centers on the young American, John Scott, and Julie Lannes, the Red Cross nurse. Julie, captured along with her maid, Susanne, is suspected of being a spy and is carried off by an Austrian prince. John learns of their whereabouts and finally escapes with both women in the limousine of the prince. However, when they are in danger of being recaptured, Julie's brother suddenly appears in his flying machine and rescues all of them from under the noses of the enemy soldiers.

13 Alvord, James Church. *The Iron Cross*. West Medford, Mass.: Christian Women's Peace Movement, 1915. 31p.

Not seen; NYPL.

14 Andrews, Mary Raymond (Shipman). *The Three Things; the Forge in Which the Soul of a Man was Tested*. Boston: Little, Brown & Co., 1915. 58p.

This story first appeared in the *Ladies' Home Journal* and describes how Philip Landicutt, a wealthy American snob, loses his class pride, dispels his race prejudice, and regains his belief in God when he enters the war in Belgium. The tale is obviously intended to be didactic and is characteristic of the journalistic medium in which it was first published.

15 Ayres, Ruby Mildred. *Richard Chatterton, V.C.* London: Hodder & Stoughton, 1915. 413p.

A very tangled and trite story, appearing to have been written to keep the reader on pins and needles from one issue to another. For example, the wealthy Sonia jilts the handsome Richard Chatterton as a slacker. He secretly departs for the French front as a private in the Black Brigade and performs a double deed of heroism which wins him the highest English decoration. Sonia in the meantime becomes involved with the false friend of Richard. When Richard is decorated and sent home wounded Sonia becomes insanely jealous because of the medal and the pretty nurse accompanying Richard. This sort of plot development continues at some length until the author is finally able to get her two chief characters together. So much for the plot. There are some graphic scenes of departing troops, trench warfare, and base hospitals as a contrast with various views of life in London and the English countryside.

16 Barney, John Stewart. *L.P.M.: the End of the Great War.*
    New York: G.P. Putnam's Sons, 1915. 419p.

   This novel has what we might now characterize as a
   political science fiction plot. An American millionaire
   scientist discovers the secret of gravity and how to
   counter its force and float any heavy object in midair.
   With credentials from the U.S. Secretary of State he travels
   to Europe to inform the heads of government of his discovery
   and to show them how this new power can be directed against
   them if they do not agree to his demands and make peace.
   Germany defies him and the scientist decides to bring what
   he calls his "little peace maker," a 907-foot steel dreadnought that rides on air as "lightly as a piece of thistle
   down," and compel the Germans by force to yield to the
   demands of civilized people. The author has dreamed up
   humorous caricatures of a number of well-known people and
   of various national characteristics of several of the
   major European powers.

17 Bell, John Joy. *Wee Macgreegor Enlists.* London: Hodder &
    Stoughton, 1915. 191p.; New York: Fleming H. Revell,
    1915. 213p.

   One in a series of popular Scottish dialect novels which
   relate the adventures of the young man Wee Macgreegor. On
   his nineteenth birthday he enlists in the "Glesca Hie-
   landers." He buys a ring for his girl friend, Christina,
   whom he persuades finally to wear it and goes into basic
   training with his friend Wullie Thomson. While at training
   camp Macgreegor falls under the influence of a local vamp
   called Maggie who is especially attracted to soldiers in
   kilts. This, of course, soon leads to a misunderstanding
   with Christina which is not resolved by the time Macgreegor
   leaves for the front. When Macgreegor is wounded, his
   life is saved by his friend Wullie, who then writes an
   eloquent letter to Christina, which convinces her to rush
   to the hospital, and the disagreement is soon over. Generally, this is an entertaining and cheerful sort of story
   with witty dialogue but cannot be taken seriously as a war
   novel.

18 Birmingham, George A. (pseud. of James Owen Hannay).
    Gossamer. London: Methuen & Co., 1915. 309p.

   Deals with complex financial activities in the world at
   the outbreak of the war. The novel constitutes a plea,
   as one reviewer put it, for "that under-dog of current

literature, the financier." High finance, the novel insists, is not octopus-like. It is the protective web or gossamer, with which finance embraces the world. The filament can be easily damaged by unthinking, impulsive individuals. Conversation among the novel's four characters, two Irishmen, a German-Englishman, and an American, makes this a novel of ideas, heavy in its consideration of egotism, altruism, and human failings. Ascher, an Irish financier and nationalist, may have some appealing qualities, but this cannot save the story from the banal and trite.

19 Bleneau, Adele. *The Nurse's Story in Which Reality Meets Romance*. Indianapolis: Bobbs-Merrill Co., 1915. 260p.

A Louisiana nurse, young, intelligent (speaks three languages), has a responsible job in a hospital near Paris. She is beset by the treachery of a German who wishes to involve her as an accomplice, and attracted to a wounded English officer whom she restores to health; love prevails, and the villain is reformed. The book offers some detail regarding hospitals, battlefields, and army conditions, but this is mainly a popular novel.

20 Bradley, Mary (Hastings). *The Splendid Chance*. New York: D. Appleton & Co., 1915. 328p.

The "splendid chance" is the descriptive phrase by the heroine, Katherine King, for what she expects in life from studying painting in France. (An earlier opportunity to marry a wealthy American, whom she did not love, was not her idea of the "splendid chance.") On her way to Europe the lighthearted Katherine meets an English serviceman, Captain Jeffrey Edgerton, and becomes engaged to him in France, but Germany's declaration of war interrupts the couple's marriage plans. The terror of the German drive toward Paris, starkly portrayed, dominates the last part of the novel.

21 Bridges, Victor. *A Rogue By Compulsion: an Affair of the Secret Service*. New York: G.P. Putnam's Sons, 1915. 354p.

A melodramatic spy adventure dealing with the British secret service and the German spy network. Neil Lyndon is sentenced to a three-year prison term for a crime he did not commit. He escapes from the Dartmoor prison and is saved from rearrest by two men who later prove to be German spies. One is a Russian whose daughter, Sonia, makes up the third member of their group. Lyndon is unable to understand their interest in him until it becomes apparent that they are counting on his resentment against the government for his unjust imprisonment. In turn, the German spies expect to use his inventive talents in the interest of "Kaiser Bill." But with the assistance of two of his good old friends, one of them a girl who has been loyal to Lyndon throughout his imprisonment, he is finally able to serve his government while demonstrating his innocence at the same time.

22 Buchan, John. *Greenmantle*. New York: George H. Doran Co., 1915. 345p.

A novel involving secret-agent activity. The hero is Major Richard Hannay, who is the hero also of John Buchan's *The Thirty-nine Steps*. Hannay has just recovered from being wounded at Loos and is offered an assignment in Turkey. Hannay is to go to Constantinople to investigate a holy war in the making there, organized by Germany to incite the Turks and other Islamic people against the Allies. He is also to uncover the individual who is the mastermind of the uprising, the "jehad." (The mastermind turns out to be a woman, Hilda von Einem.) One of Hannay's two partners is an English officer familiar with the East, Hon. Ludovick Gustavus Arbuthnot Cospatrick (called Sandy); the other, an American, John Scantlebury Blenkiron. The expedition is successful. Buchan wrote the novel while on active duty in World War I.

23 Campbell, R.W. *The Kangaroo Marines*. London: Cassell & Co., 1915. 127p.

Not seen; however, the action is placed mainly in the Dardanelles, Turkey, and near Eastern campaigns. NYPL.

24 ———. *Private Spud Tamson*. Edinburgh & London: W. Blackwood & Sons, 1915. 292p.

A loosely organized review of the steps in the life of a soldier in the British army who is from the Glasgow slums. Enlistment, basic training, and the inevitable combat are delineated. Spud Tamson enlists when the war breaks out, dies in combat, and receives the Victoria Cross. The author fought in the Boer War, and during World War I was a member of the British territorial force.

25 Castle, Agnes (Sweetman) and Egerton. *The Hope of the House*. London: Cassell & Co., 1915. 339p.; New York: D. Appleton & Co., 1915. 369p.

A view of the war by those on the home front. Unfortunately, the plot is conventional, with a happy ending which is unsupported by the previous story line. The protagonist is David Owen who at twenty finds himself the inheritor of Treowen, the home of his family for generations. But David has little money, so little that his solicitor advises him to sell the beautiful place. He accepts a lifetime of self-sacrifice to keep the house. When the war starts and Johnny, his younger brother, is killed, David is in despair. About this time Belgian refugees are sent to the Welsh countryside. Vivianne, a refugee girl, soon is noticed by David, and through an unusual chain of circumstances, the nearly despondent Belgian girl and the despairing Welshman "find one another." David's pity for the lonely girl ripens into love with incredible speed and she immediately marries him and both live happily ever after.

26 ———. *Little House in Wartime.* London: Constable, 1915. 275p.

The foreword describes this book as "the true record of an average family during the first year of the war of wars; ... how the quiet stay-at-home family felt and thought in the days of the titanic conflict ... the little things that happened in a little country house." The "little house" is a country villa in Surrey, England. Strictly a bit of patriotic pap.

27 Chambers, Robert William. *Who Goes There!* New York: D. Appleton & Co., 1915. 339p.

Written in the style of the adventure-historical romance. The World War I setting during the first days of the conflict seems only a convenience--probably any war would do just as well. Kervyn Guild, an American of Belgian background, is playing chess with the Yslemont mayor when the town is overrun by the enemy. Guild is taken prisoner but later released by the German commanding officer on condition that he go to England and bring back General von Reiter's daughter, who is being held there as an enemy national. Guild accepts and then begins "a series of stirring adventures." When Guild and Karen arrive safely in Belgium he discovers that she is not really the daughter of the general, but only a ward whom he expects to marry. The novel concludes with the hero, Guild, fighting on while Karen, the heroine, must wait until the war is over before she and Kervyn can at last be together forever. There are scarcely any war scenes--only the fight between the Germans and Belgians at the conclusion of the story.

28 Comfort, Will Levington. *Red Fleece.* New York: George H.
    Doran Co., 1915. 287p.

   The publishers described this novel as one which presented
   the author's "passionate vision of the idiocy and waste of
   war and its crime toward the peasants who are made cannon
   meat." The reviewer in *The Atlantic Monthly* labeled it
   "pacifist propaganda." The main character, an American
   war correspondent, viewing the European War from the
   Russian lines, comes under the influence of a woman revolutionary, Berthe Wyndham. This woman and grim hospital
   scenes change the hero from an impassive, "distant" observer of war into a fervent humanitarian, viewing war no
   longer as glorious but recognizing its senseless slaughter.
   The reviewer for *Outlook* praised the book as "the first
   novel of any real consequence dealing with the present war."

29 Crosland, Thomas William Hodgson. *Find the Angels. The
    Showmen; a Legend of the War.* London: T. Werner Laurie,
    1915. 95p.

   Not seen: contains two stories. NYPL.

30 Cule, W.E. *Thy Son Liveth; a Vision of the War.* London:
    Nisbet & Co., 1915. 28p.

   Not seen; NYPL.

31 Dodd, Frank W. *Hell Dock; a Romance Founded on Fact....
    German Submarine Trickery Exposed.* London: The Potter-
    Sarvent Pub. Co., 1915. 224p.

   Not seen; NYPL.

32 Gibbs, George Fort. *The Yellow Dove.* New York: D. Apple-
    ton & Co., 1915. 330p.

   The Yellow Dove is the name of an airplane used by the
   British secret service for special observation flights over
   the enemy. The author, however, doesn't make this completely clear for the first part of the novel, obviously
   for suspense purposes. This technique is characteristic of
   this glib and fast-paced adventure mystery. Cyril Hammersley refuses to enlist and offers only weak excuses to his
   friends and neighbors. Thus, even his closest friends in
   the story's super-patriotic atmosphere view him with doubt,
   and particularly as a result of his German family connections. Eventually, this suspicion is removed as it becomes
   apparent that Cyril is really a loyal British citizen.

But Doris Mather, an American girl who is a Red Cross worker in London, has never once doubted him. She too becomes deeply involved in all the secret projects in which Cyril is active. Indeed, she even saves his life in a crisis by flying the Yellow Dove out of danger. Lying, treachery, and deceit practiced in the interest of one's country become golden virtues. Most of the action takes place behind the scenes. Hardly any description of the fighting, hospitals, refugees, or the terrible destruction is ever given.

33 Giesy, John Ulrich. *All for His Country*. New York: The Macaulay Co., 1915. 320p.

The novel is about what might have happened if the United States had been invaded by Japan during the war. The hero of sorts is Meade Stillman who goes to Washington to offer the government his aero-destroyer, a special and unique aircraft. But political and commercial interests conspire against him, and his mission fails. Shortly after he returns home to Utah a Mexican force attempts to invade the U.S. and the U.S. Army rushes to the border. Simultaneously the Japanese forces invade the West Coast and then take over New York City. The Mexican invasion turns out to be a ruse but all is saved when a girl remembers Stillman and his invention, and the brave inventor responds to his country's service and the nefarious invaders are smashed. A sensational potboiler of little or no literary merit, included here as a curious and rather unique example of an imaginary account of the invasion of the United States during World War I.

34 Hocking, Joseph. *Dearer Than Life: a Romance of the Great War*. London: Hodder & Stoughton, 1915. 312p.

Not seen; NYPL.

35 Jeans, Thomas Tendron. *Gunboat and Gunrunners: a Tale of the Persian Gulf*. London: Blackie & Son, 1915(?). 384p.

Not seen; NYPL.

36 Le Queux, William Tufnell. *At the Sign of the Sword: A Story of Love and War in Belgium*. New York: Sully & Kleinteich, 1915. 187p.; London: T.C. & E.C. Jack, 1915. 187p.

The plot uses a romantic story to hook together a series of descriptions of the atrocities of the Germans in Belgium.

Aimee de Neuville, the daughter of the richest man in Belgium, falls in love with Edmund Valentin, a young lawyer. But her father has arranged a marriage for her with a business associate by the name of Arnaud Rigaux, whom she cannot stand. When the war comes, Edmond enlists and Rigaux is revealed in his true colors as a traitor to his country. Aimee is ultimately subjected to the rapes and horrors suffered by many other Belgium women. Rigaux offers to save her, at a price, but Aimee prefers death. Edmund, however, comes to her rescue and is seriously injured. Nonetheless, they both manage to escape to England.

37 Lowndes, Mrs. Belloc (Marie Adelaide [Belloc] Lowndes). *Good Old Anna*. London: Hutchinson & Co., 1915. 398p.

   This spy story concerns the experiences and emotions of naturalized Germans living in the cathedral town of Witanbury in England. One of the group is a secret agent for Germany; the others are not in sympathy with militarism. Anna Bauer, "good old Anna," a servant for an Englishwoman, is unwittingly snared as a conspirator by the secret agent's machinations.

38 Lynn, Escott. *In Khaki for the King, a Tale of the Great War*. London: W. & R. Chambers, 1915. 375p.

   A red-hot, action-filled war story packed full of all the typical adventures expected in such popular novels. For information on other World War I novels by Escott Lynn see items 85, 254, 371, 430 and 457.

39 MacLean, Charles Agnew, and Frank Harris Blighton. *"Here's to the Day!"* New York: George H. Doran Co., 1915. 314p.; London: Hodder & Stoughton, 1915. 314p.

   A novel of obsession. Count von Hollman of the German army, in a toast "to the Day" in the company of the American consul in Luxembourg and a friend, unconsciously reveals his military passion and that his words mean that war is imminent. A minor character refers to the German's obsession: "The only trouble with him was that you had to kill him to cure him of what was the matter with him." Aviation plays a large role in the plot, as the Germans move across Luxembourg to the Marne.

Adult Novels

40 Marshall, Archibald (pseud. of Arthur Hammond Marshall).
    Rank and Riches: a Novel. London: St. Paul & Co., 1915.
    429p. [Title in U.S.: *The Old Order Changeth, a Novel*.
    New York: Dodd, Mead & Co., 1915. 472p.]

   This story focuses on the family of Armitage Brown, a
   self-made millionaire and the changing social order in
   England. He has just purchased Kemsale, a great old
   English house, after its extravagant hereditary owner has
   frittered away the family fortune. Brown has theories
   about how to redeem the land and holds forth on the conflict between his basically sound ideas and the old, deep-
   rooted traditions. At this point the war breaks out and
   the novel poses the question "What is to come after?"
   Several critics have compared Marshall very favorably with
   Trollope--both as to his theme and as to his leisurely
   technique.

41 Oppenheim, Edward Phillips. *The Double Traitor*. Boston:
    Little, Brown & Co., 1915. 308p.

   Another spy adventure. A young Englishman, Francis
   Norgate, is attached to the British Embassy in Berlin.
   But after a confrontation with a German prince at a local
   restaurant, he is dismissed from his post. On his way
   back to England he travels next to a German crockery manufacturer who turns out to be a spy. Surprisingly, Norgate
   obtains a list of the German spies in England. He hurries
   to Scotland Yard and the Foreign Office with his information but he is not treated seriously. As a result, he
   does his own investigation teaming up with an Austrian
   baroness who is half English. Due to their efforts England
   is partially prepared when war begins.

42 "Q" (pseud. of Arthur Thomas Quiller-Couch). *Nicky-Nan,
    Reservist*. Edinburgh & London: W. Blackwood and Sons,
    1915. 314p.; New York: D. Appleton & Co., 1915. 314p.

   A story of village life in Cornwall, England, recounted
   by revealing the slow awakening to the war's vileness of
   an erstwhile opportunistic Cornish fisherman, Nicholas
   Nanjivell, known popularly as "Nicky-Nan." Two other
   characters, Miss Polsue and Miss Charity Oliver, the community's moral watch-dogs, add a note of grimness. The
   author's intention is to show the effect of the war on the
   various classes of citizens in the villages of England.

43 Reeve, Arthur Benjamin. *The War Terror; Further Adventures with Craig Kennedy, Scientific Detective.* New York: Harper & Brothers, 1915. 376p.

One of the Craig Kennedy series of detective stories which were popular in the early part of the century and now are largely forgotten. This novel is mainly a detective story with passing reference to the war. Professor Craig Kennedy, the incredible millionaire, scientist, and shrewd detective, now becomes entangled in the involved spy system of the warring European nations. America, although neutral, soon becomes infested with spies of all description and mission. The narrative is written in the first person singular of Walter, a reporter for the *Star* newspaper who chronicles the exploits of Kennedy in a series of remarkable adventures directly or indirectly connected with the war. The crafty detective covers an assassins group and their electromagnetic gun and foils their plans to murder a host of world-famous men in cities throughout the world. The plot embraces the usual detective-fiction-action: break-ins, mysterious clues, wire-tappers, poison and drugs, etc., which are intermixed with all sorts of scientific and technical devices and explanations both fact and fiction. The war serves mainly as a minor background against which the improbable adventures of Kennedy dominate.

44 Ruck, Berta. *The Lad with Wings.* London: Hutchinson & Co., 1915. 344p. [Title in U.S.: *The Boy with Wings.* New York: Dodd, Mead & Co., 1915. 387p.]

A sentimental love story placed against the summer and fall of 1914. Paul Dampier is an aviator who is in love with Gwenna Williams, a working girl. With the outbreak of the war they are quickly married before he flies off for his country. But Gwenna wants to be with her husband no matter what. Thus, she takes the first opportunity to do so and they both perish in mid-air, as it were.

45 Sladen, Douglas Brooke Wheelton. *His German Wife; The Romance of a British Officer.* London: Hutchinson & Co., 1915. 391p.

The hero of this rather melodramatic propaganda piece is Rene Isherwood, a young English army officer, created in the traditional mold of the manly, clean-cut, honorable Englishman. He marries a German girl and is on his honeymoon in Germany when the war begins. One of the main themes is the struggle of his wife between her devotion to her country and her love for her husband. Another is the comparison of German and English types and standards. The story also provides a good view of the people who left Germany after the declaration of war as well as the conditions within both countries during the first few months of the war.

46 Stevenson, Burton Egbert. *Little Comrade, A Tale of the Great War.* New York: Henry Holt & Co., 1915. 315p. Also published with the title: *Girl from Alsace.* New York: Grosset & Dunlap, 1915. [Title of edition in England: *Little Comrade: The Romance of a Lady Spy in the Great War.* London: Hutchinson & Co., 1915. 343p.]

Deals with the first few weeks of the war. Bradford Stewart, a surgeon from America, is just returning from a convention in Vienna when he is caught near the German border by the outbreak of war. In a hotel in Aix-la-Chapelle he is surprised by an effusive greeting from a lovely young woman who noisily proclaims him as her husband. When they are alone she reveals that she has been acting to allay the waiter's suspicions about her. She also reveals that she is a French spy who crosses the lines to deliver messages to General Joffre, which she can continue to do only if Stewart will act the part of her husband. He agrees and the story goes on to record their adventures.

47 Thorne, Guy (pseud. of Cyril Arthur Edward Ranger Gull). *The Secret Sea-plane.* London: Hodder & Stoughton, 1915. 243p.

A story of espionage and secret weapons as John Gregor Lothian seeks to recover his good name and uncover a German espionage ring operating in England. By means of a secret airship which can travel with equal ease and speed on land, sea, or in the air, he rescues his fiancee from German spies and simultaneously destroys the Germans. Then the remarkable ship is turned toward London to intercept five dirigibles which have been sent to bomb the city.

48 ————. *The Secret Service Submarine: A Story of the Present War.* London & Edinburgh: T.C. & E.C. Jack, 1915. 190p.; New York: Sully & Kleinteich, 1915. 190p.

At the start of the war John Carey tries to enlist, but is turned down because of an old lameness from a school-boy

accident. Greatly disappointed, he returns to the Norfolk
school where he has been an assistant master. Nevertheless,
he is soon able to serve his country in another way. Dr.
Upjelly, the head of the school, turns out to be a German
spy. John, with the assistance of his brother, a naval
officer, and two boys from school, captures the enemy sub,
thus preventing the spy from sending his information back
to the fatherland. This prevents an invasion of England.

49 Veer, Willem de. *An Emperor in the Dock*. London & New
York: John Lane Co., 1915. 320p.

This novel is a parable. The emperor is Kaiser Wilhelm
II who is ultimately "reduced to normal dimensions." When
a private yacht owned by a Dutch gentleman, on which the
Emperor is sailing, is destroyed by a mine, the Emperor is
rescued by another Dutch vessel, the *Cornelia*. On board
this vessel are an American, Pryston, two English cousins,
Douglas Gordon and Harry Tod, three Germans, and a Dutch
crew. The passengers form a court to try the Kaiser for
his transgressions.

50 Waddell, William Freeland. *The Patriot and the Spies; a
Tale*. Paisley: A. Gardner, 1915. 182p.

Not seen; NYPL.

51 Williamson, Charles Norris, and Alice Muriel (Livingston).
Secret History Revealed by Lady Peggy O'Malley. Garden
City, N.Y.: Doubleday, Page & Co., 1915. 319p. [Title
in England: *Secret History*. London: Methuen & Co., 1915.
313p.]

A superficial novel with a worldwide setting, including
an army post in Arizona and the battlegrounds of Europe.
The story connects a crisis in Mexico with World War I.
Lady Peggy O'Malley, 16 years old, meets and falls in love
with an American aviator, Captain Eagleston March. The
captain, his superior officer, Major Van Dyke, and Lady
O'Malley become involved with airplanes, submarines, and
state secrets. Captain March's air exploits change the
future of nations. One time he puts a German zeppelin out
of action. When he is badly wounded, he is nursed back to
health by the adolescent Lady O'Malley. The plot is thin
and the narrative far from convincing.

1916

52 Ammers-Jueller, Jo van. *A Young Leon of Flanders: A Tale of the Terror of War.* Translated by Carel Thieme. London: Headley Brothers, 1916. 320p. [*Een Jonge Leeuw van Vlaanderen; een Verhaal uit den Oorlog van 1914.* Harlem: H.D. Tjeenk Willink & Zoon, 1915. 246p.]

Takes place in Belgium during the early days of the German invasion. The primary character is Leon Casimir (the Leon of the title), a sixteen-year-old boy who is an expert motorcycle rider. With the start of the war he becomes a dispatch rider in the Belgian army and nobly distinguishes himself. Leon has many narrow escapes and adventures. The novel closely follows his activities as well as the violent impact of the war on the Casimir family, whose daughter married a German. The husband, Gustav Schnitzler, at first is able to conceal his true nature behind his presumably artistic interests. In reality he is a narrow-minded and arrogant man who comes to demonstrate a crass stupidity and insensitivity in all his relationships which, by implication, are German characteristics.

53 Bates, Sylvia Chatfield. *The Vintage.* New York: Duffield & Co., 1916. 55p.

Originally in the magazine *Woman's Home Companion* (July 1916), this story presents the regeneration of a young man, Henry Colbrooke. Beginning as a denunciator of respect for the flag and patriotism during World War I, he changes his attitude after being shown letters of his grandfather, who, at his age, was killed in the American Civil War.

54 Bell, John Joy. *Cupid in Oilskins.* London: Hodder & Stoughton, 1916. 187p.; New York: George H. Doran, 1916. 187p.

A trifling and heavy-handed attempt at war humor. The story describes the melodramatic romance of a gunner in the English Navy who has been informed that he must sink an enemy submarine in order to win a certain girl called Lydia with a "lovely pigtail."

55 Benjamin, René. *Private Gaspard, a Soldier of France*.
    Translated by Selmer Fougner. New York: Brentano's,
    1916. 300p. [Title in England: *Gaspard the Poilu*.
    London: Heinemann & Co., 1916. 284p.] [*Les Soldats de
    la Guerre*. Gaspard. Paris: A. Fayard, 1915. 319p.]

   Contemporary reports indicate that many French readers
considered this novel to be France's literary masterpiece
of the war. (The book was awarded the Goncourt prize for
1915.) The plot concerns Gaspard, a snail merchant and
genial, bourgeois Parisian, as typical a common soldier as
Kipling's Mulvaney. Though the irrepressible Gaspard is
disabled for life, losing a leg after two days of fighting,
his experiences, poignant and comic, reveal a France energized and "recreated" by the war. Now of only historical
interest.

56 Benson, Edward Frederic. *Mike*. London: Cassell & Co.,
    1916. 342p. [Title in U.S.: *Michael*. New York:
    George H. Doran Co., 1916. 370p.]

   Michael Comber, son of an English titled father, resigns
an army commission to pursue musical interests. Eventually he meets two German musicians, Hermann and Sylvia
Falbe, brother and sister. The love that develops between
Michael and Sylvia is tested by the outbreak of the war,
but survives even the later, tragic meeting of Michael
and Hermann on the battlefield.

57 ————. *Robin Linnet*. New York: George H. Doran & Co.,
    1916. 320p.

   The title of this novel is the name of the hero, nicknamed "Birds," though his mother, Lady Helen Grote, is the
principal character. She is eagerly pursued as a hostess
at her country house of Grote. The objective of the novel
is to reveal the effect of the war upon Robin's mother.
Robin enlists and Lady Grote, detesting the war and trying
to avoid it, considers turning her country house into a
Boccaccian hermitage safe from "the plague." The scheme
reveals how important the war was to individuals most
concerned with their financial interests.

58 [Berger, Marcel]. *In the Fire of the Furnace* by a Sergeant in the French Army. Translated by Mrs. Cecil
    Curtis. London: Smith, Elder & Co., 1916. 414p.

[Title in U.S.: *The Ordeal by Fire*. New York: G.P.
Putnam's Sons, 1916. 532p.] [*Le Miracle du Feu*.
Paris: Calmann-Levy, 1916. 494p.]

The time period is from August 1 to September 9 of 1914.
Michel Dreher, initially a cynic and sceptic, is eventually transformed by the war into a loyal and earnest patriot.
He is in Switzerland when the war breaks out and seriously
considers not returning to France. However, he does return, to become a sergeant in the army. As the war continues he slowly emerges from his initial cynicism and is
wounded in the battle of the Marne. With his newly found
values and devotion to his country he comes to think seriously also of a young French girl, Jeannine Landry, whom
he had not previously taken seriously. The epilogue which
takes his story into 1915 describes his return from the
war and marriage to Jeannine. The novel is an attempt at
a psychological study of war motives and attitudes. The
dialect reflects a curious cockney manifestation (dropping
"aitches" and so forth) that appears completely out of
place. Perhaps the original French version is superior.

59 Bindloss, Harold. *Johnstone of the Border*. New York:
F.A. Stokes Co., 1916. 339p. [Title in England: *The
Borderer*. London: Ward, Lock & Co., 1916. 320p.]

A story of a Scotsman, Andrew Johnstone, who though unable to continue his career as a soldier because of an
accident, is able to serve his country admirably as a
civilian by blocking the intrigue of two enemies of his
country.

60 Bishop, George Bernard Hamilton. *The Barbarian; a Tale of
the Russian Front*. London: Society of Saints Peter and
Paul, 1916. 16p.

Not seen; NYPL.

61 Bourget, Paul Charles Joseph. *The Night Cometh*. Translated from the French by G. Frederic Lees. New York:
G.P. Putnam's Sons, 1916. 312p.; London: Chatto &
Windus, 1916. 247p. [*Le Sens de la Mort*. Paris: Plon-
Nourrit, 1915. 328p.]

Questions the purpose and worth of France's involvement
in the war, by discussing mankind's spiritual and material
views of the world. Through analyzing the position of an

atheist army physician, and a young soldier's faith in God, the novel implies that if a country's role in the war possesses no eternal purpose, the sacrifice is absurd.

62   Campbell, R.W. *The Mixed Division*. London: Hutchinson & Co., 1916. 320p.

Not seen; NYPL.

63   Chambers, Robert William. *The Girl Philippa*. New York: D. Appleton & Co., 1916. 514p.

Replete with action during the two weeks covered by the plot. Eventually the novel becomes a love story, bringing together two young British secret service operatives, a counterspy, a Belgian artist, and a young girl cafe cashier. The story first appeared in the *Cosmopolitan* magazine and reflects its popular literature origin.

64   Cobb, Geoffrey Belton. *Stand to Arms*. London: Wells Gardner, Darton & Co., 1916. 182p.

Not seen; NYPL.

65   De Crespigny, Charles (pseud. of Charles Norris Williamson and Alice Murial [Livingston] Williamson). *Where the Path Breaks*. New York: Century Co., 1916. 275p. [Title in England: *The War Wedding*. London: Methuen & Co., 1916. 214p.]

Barbara Fay, an American, married to Sir John Denin the day he left for the front, assumes that Sir John has been killed when she hears nothing from him after many months. She remarries a brutish man with whom she had nothing in common. The truth about her first husband is that he had been severely wounded, was in a coma for eight months, and awoke in a hospital. Sir John takes a new name and establishes a new life in America, residing, because of sentiment, in the house in which Barbara had lived in California, which she had described to Sir John many times before their marriage. Sir John becomes a writer and publishes a book which becomes internationally popular. A letter from Barbara leads to further correspondence and a meeting between the two and a resolution of what fate had produced. The novel was described as sentimental and Victorian when it appeared and the years since have not altered this assessment.

66 De Selincourt, Hugh. *A Soldier of Life*. London: Constable, 1916. 308p.

   The central character is a British soldier, James Wood, who is wounded and sent home after spending months in the trenches. The experience has left him crippled in mind as well as in body and filled with hate for war. He sees no meaning in it, and it represents for him the worst kind of human stupidity. He has lost his faith both in God and mankind. At home he is literally smothered in admiration by his family, friends, and neighbors, which serves only to increase his contempt for the world. He yearns now for the ordinary, commonsense experiences of existence. He also contemplates marriage with an ordinary girl, Amy. But his subconscious interjects strange hallucinations consisting of prolonged dialogs with a ghostly young man and a lovely, sensuous woman called Corinna who attempts to re-inspire him to resist the blandishments of a comfortable, ordinary existence. After a prolonged period of doubt and debate, with various consultations with a doctor and others, he makes a desperate struggle for "normality," under tremendous pressure. Finally, Corinna convinces him that he must remain true to his real self. The book more or less concludes with James finally saved through the intuition and insight of Corinna. The primary theme appears to be the crisis in moral and spiritual life which the horrors of the battlefield can bring about.

67 Dix, Beulah Marie. *The Battle Months of George Daurella*. New York: Duffield & Co., 1916. 320p.

   A fantasy. The countries and setting are contrived, and the characters symbolic. George Daurella, an army lieutenant, protects a war nurse, Joyce Averill, in a burning village and places her in safety across the border. Later, as an escaped prisoner, he is to be executed, but is rescued by the nurse.

68 Edgar, George. *Honours of War*. London: Mills & Boon, 1916. 315p.

   Not seen; NYPL.

69 Fetterless, Arthur. *Gog, the Story of an Officer and Gentleman*. Edinburgh & London: W. Blackwood and Sons, 1916. 341p.

   Not seen; NYPL.

70 G., H.L. (Arthur Christopher Bensen). *Meanwhile, a Packet of Letters* by H.L.G. London: John Murray, 1916. 168p. [Title in U.S.: *Meanwhile, a Packet of War Letters*. New York: E.P. Dutton & Co., 1916. 168p.]

Not seen; NYPL.

71 Hale, Beatrice Forbes-Robertson. *The Nest-builder: A Novel*. New York: F.A. Stokes Co., 1916. 376p.

The story begins on board an Atlantic passenger ship coming to the U.S. Mary, an English girl, and a Bohemian American artist, Stefan Byrd, meet, have a whirlwind love affair, and marry as soon as they reach port. The theme is the marriage of two people of contrasting and diverse personalities. Stefan is the artist, devoted to life and love but only as they help him to express beauty in his forms of art. Mary symbolizes woman as the creator of the human race, holding all things subservient to the "nest-building" instinct which is vital in protecting and continuing the race. For a while they are happy, but when material success comes, they begin to see how far apart they are in their ideas. At one point he sees that he never really wanted a wife and all that it entails but rather wants to capture life and make it his own using her as "a vessel fit to carry it." It is only in his experience in the trenches in France that he sees what he feared. He has used his art to escape the ugliness, not of the world, but rather of his selfish and stubborn nature. The war is only a minor theme in this drama of marriage and is considered primarily as a maturing experience for emotional and mental growth.

72 Hamilton, Mary Agnes (Adamson). *Dead Yesterday*. New York: George H. Doran Co., 1916. 408p.

Focuses on reactions of educated people, specifically London intellectuals, toward the war, primarily through conversations in London occurring before and after August 4, 1914. The novel is a heady one about characters who are dedicated pacifists but seem tired of life.

73 Hannah, Ian Campbell. *Quaker-born: a Romance of the Great War*. New York: G. Arnold Shaw, 1916. 261p.

The Quaker-born protagonist, Edward Alexander, studying at Cambridge, enlists with his friends, despite his religious scruples, when he witnesses the enemy's bombardment

Adult Novels

of Scarborough. He serves with an ambulance group. His reported death changes the belief of his friends that he ignored his religious beliefs. His marriage follows closely on his return from the war.

74 Hellier, F. *Colonials in Khaki, a Tale*. London: Murray & Evenden, 1916. 127p.

   Not seen; NYPL.

75 Herrick, Robert. *The Conscript Mother*. London: Bickers & Son, 1916. 99p.; New York: Charles Scribner's Sons, 1916. 99p.

   World War I turns the happiness of an ordinary Italian family into tragedy. Meanwhile, an engaging picture of Italy at war is presented, through glimpses of sons and mothers involved in the conflict. The novel emphasizes D'Annunzio's appeal to Italian patriotism and Italy's rebuff of Giovanni Giolitti, who tried to keep Italy neutral during the war.

76 Kummer, Frederic Arnold, and Henry P. Janes. *The Second Coming; a Vision*. New York: Dodd, Mead & Co., 1916. 96p.

   The story starts on a Christmas eve sometime during the war and describes what might have happened if Christ were to appear to various people such as the foot soldier Noel Bonhomme, holding his icy rifle in the cold trenches, and the German Kaiser. The Kaiser, after conferring with his staff officers and stressing his displeasure with the progress of the war, emphasizes the urgent need to produce a much greater effort the next day to break through the French lines. He then goes to bed and Christ visits him and listens to the arguments of the Kaiser, before gently replying with the words and sentiments attributed to Christ in the New Testament. The Kaiser, however, is not influenced by this colloquy with the Savior. The next day, Christmas, sees furious fighting and then a great snowstorm that symbolizes the beginning of Germany's eventual defeat. The Kaiser from that day on is broken in spirit. He lies dying on the following Easter when Christ again visits him. The Kaiser expresses his repentance. The descriptions of the battle scenes are quite realistic, but the rest seems a fantasy dated by time.

77 L., C.E. *My-Man; Letters from a Wife to a Husband "Somewhere in France"* by C.E.L. New York: George H. Doran Co., 1916. 96p.

Not seen; NYPL.

78 Leblanc, Maurice. *The Woman of Mystery*. New York: The Macaulay Co., 1916. 352p.

The protagonist, Paul Delrose, joins one of the armed services immediately upon discovering, on the day of his marriage, that his father was murdered by the mother of Paul's wife. Through the rest of the story moves another woman, a woman of mystery, who is perhaps a German spy, and closely resembles the mother of his wife. Eventually Elizabeth, his wife, is abducted during the war, then rescued, and the mystery woman identified.

79 Le Queux, William Tufnell. *Annette of the Argonne; a Story of the French Front*. London: Hurst & Blackett, 1916. 256p.

Not seen.

80 ———. *Number 70, Berlin; a Story of Britain's Peril*. London: Hodder & Stoughton, 1916. 248p.

Not seen; NYPL.

81 Locke, William John. *The Wonderful Year*. London: John Lane, 1916. 345p.; New York: Dodd, Mead & Co., 1916. 364p.

The title refers to the year preceding the war and describes the enjoyable experiences of an Englishman, Martin Overshaw, a teacher of French to uninterested English schoolboys. Martin travels to a small town in France near Paris and eventually enlists in the French army. Upon being wounded, he returns to the village in France in which his wonderful year's experiences began. The book, published in *Harper's Bazaar,* presents an excellent description of French provincial life.

82 Lowndes, Mrs. Belloc (Marie Adelaide [Belloc] Lowndes). *Lilla: a Part of Her Life*. London: Hutchinson & Co., 1916. 360p.

The main character, Lilla, is a delicate and quiet woman whose marriage to Robert Singleton, although not unhappy, is basically colorless and prosaic. She and her husband make their home with his relatives, which causes Lilla to repress her own personality until she scarcely knows what strong emotion really is. In early 1914 she is informed of the death of her husband. She takes up war work and soon meets Dare Carteret. They are married within five weeks after their first meeting. Lilla now learns what love means. Then, in the midst of all her newfound happiness, her first husband suddenly returns, alive after all. The story concludes with Lilla in France and with one of the two men departing with Kitchener on his ill-fated voyage. The novel is chiefly notable for its many vivid pictures of London in wartime, especially the first zeppelin raid on the city.

83 ———. *The Red Cross Barge.* London: Smith, Elder & Co., 1916. 197p.

Recounts the story of the early period of the German invasion of northern France. A german surgeon, Dr. Max Keller, the chief character and hero, is a warmhearted and simple man who is convinced of the nobility and invincibility of Germany's imperial armies. As the Germans sweep on toward Paris, he is left behind in a small French village in charge of a wounded fellow officer. He shortly finds that the French injured are in charge of a young French girl, Jeanne Rouannes, and the doctor offers his services. He soon develops such a deep devotion and respect for Jeanne that he is even willing to impersonate one of the despised English soldiers so that he can be allowed to see her dying father and give him his professional care. When the German army returns in defeat, he protects her from them and eventually gives up his life to protect her.

84 Lucas, Edward Verrall. *The Vermilion Box.* London: Methuen & Co., 1916. 265p.; New York: George H. Doran Co., 1916. 346p.

An epistolary novel. The box refers to the English postbox (mailbox). Richard Haven, a fiftyish barrister and bachelor, and his sisters, brothers, and friends present a picture of the war through their letters. Some of the twenty or more correspondents were younger and some older than Haven, providing a multifaceted view of the war. Some contemporary records of the war are used in the novel.

85 Lynn, Escott. *Oliver Hastings, V.C.; a Realistic Story of the Great War*. London: W. & R. Chambers, 1916. 404p.

The two young heroes of the story are Oliver Hastings and Vivian Drummon. They are just about to join the Tenth Wessex Fusiliers Battalion commanded by Oliver's father, Colonel Hastings, in July of 1915. They have an exciting encounter with a German spy before leaving England for the front, and later encounter the same spy when their unit goes to Flanders. The novel describes their adventures not only in France but also in Greece and Serbia. The author provides plenty of war scenes ranging over the details of trench warfare, raiding parties, artillery duels, bombs, bayonet attacks, etc. The style of the author is somewhat crude and awkward, especially the dialog.

86 Macaulay, Rose. *Non-combatants and Others*. London: Hodder & Stoughton, 1916. 305p.

Focuses on the different attitudes in the mainstream of life in England during the war: those who make opposition to the war their cause; those whose patriotism makes them support it uncritically; those, the largest group, whose complacent lives are untouched by its actuality; and a very few sensitive, thinking people who realize its futility and tyranny and see war as a means by which the government consolidates its iron hold on the people.

87 MacGill, Patrick. *The Red Horizon*. London: Herbert Jenkins, 1916. 306p.; New York: George H. Doran Co., 1916. 304p.

Follows a group of newly trained British troops as they depart England for action on the battlefields of France. There is no special hero as such but rather the men as a group, although Bill the cockney stands out as a unique character study reminiscent of a Dickens novel. In any case, the narrative deals with the everyday life of the troops and especially the grim and realistic view of life and death in the trenches. The plot involves a wide range of front-line experiences such as souvenir hunting, the first exposure to battle, the physical torments and suffering of the men, the psychological strain of conflict, and so forth. A gripping and fairly graphic impression of the war, and somewhat journalistic.

Adult Novels

88 [Meynell, Wilfrid]. *Halt! Who's There?* by the author of *Aunt Sarah & the War*. New York: G.P. Putnam's Sons, 1916. 114p. [Title in England: *Who Goes There?* London: Burns & Oates, 1916. 94p.]

Consists of excerpts from the diary of Pauline Vandeleur, the heroine of Maynell's *Aunt Sarah and the War* (item 6). As a hospital nurse in London, Pauline reflects the pathos and other emotions produced in the English populace by the war.

89 Montague, Margaret Prescott. *Of Water and the Spirit*. New York: E.P. Dutton & Co., 1916. 56p.

Depicts how an American spinster aided the dying during a day and a night on a battlefield somewhere between Brussels and Paris. As a result, her life and outlook were forever changed. Originally appeared in the *Atlantic Monthly*, May 1916.

90 Münch, Paul Georg. *Hindenburg's March into London*.... London: J. Long, 1916. 253p.; Philadelphia; John C. Winston Co., 1916. 220p. [*Hindenburgs Einmarsch in London, von Einem Deutschen Dichter*. Leipzig: Grethlein, 1915. 260p.]

A fanciful story about the imaginary invasion and defeat of the English by the Germans. Written by a German author, apparently the work was intended to galvanize patriotic enthusiasm and to encourage support of the German masses for the war effort. The book, in favor of the German side, covers much of the political, social, and cultural ideologies of both countries in efforts to propagandize. The Germans are pictured as joyous Saxons who will liberate England from its mistaken notions and ill-conceived heritage. One incident describes what could well be called a blitzkrieg by a swarm of zeppelins, a gigantic fleet of submarines, and a massive German invasion of England using boats from the French ports on the English Channel. This invasion is followed by a series of battles in the south of England and the final glorious climax when the German troops march into a conquered London and pitch their tents around Buckingham Palace. The language is apocalyptic rhetoric that glorifies the German fatherland and its great mission with intense zeal. This novel is included as a unique and curious relic of propaganda of the First World War.

91 Mundy, Talbot. *King--of the Khyber Rifles: A Romance of Adventure*. Indianapolis: Bobbs-Merrill Co., 1916. 395p.

The protagonist, Athelstan King, is required to defuse a developing holy war in India purported to be fomented by Germany. His companion in the work is the heroine, an enigmatic Yasmini. India's native environment is well presented. The novel appeared in *Everybody's Magazine*, May 1916-January 1917.

92 ———. *The Winds of the World*. London: Cassell & Co., 1916. 307p.

A mystery story of adventure, intrigue, danger, and uncertainty that focuses on the loyalty of an Indian regiment and the failure of German diplomacy. The three chief characters are Kirby, an English colonel in a Sikh regiment, a trusted aide of Kirby called Risaldar-Major Ranjoor-Singh, and a dancer called Yasmini who is privy to all the activities going on behind the scenes in India. A devious group of German merchant spies are the counterpoint to the activities of the three main characters.

93 [Munthe, Axel Martin Fredrik]. *Red Cross & Iron Cross*, by a Doctor in France. New York: E.P. Dutton & Co., 1916. 142p.; London: John Murray, 1916. 142p.

A powerful fictional narrative of the experiences of a doctor in one of the front-line hospitals in France. The varied activities are described in explicit and minute detail, particularly the horrors and the fears present on the battlefields. The narrative is based on actual experiences and only thinly disguised as fiction. The book clearly condemns in powerful terms the German officers, but turns compassionate and understanding when speaking of the enemy privates. Moments of heroism, sacrifice, devotion, and even tenderness are fully described. On the other hand, there are graphic descriptions of the terrors and even the most gruesome incidents of warfare.

94 Oppenheim, Edward Phillips. *The Kingdom of the Blind*. Boston: Little, Brown & Co., 1916. 305p.

The phrase "kingdom of the blind" represents the England of the war years, oblivious of the danger of German spies. The plot of the novel, mainly a romance, concerns the efforts, ultimately successful, of the head of England's military intelligence service, Hugh Thomson, to identify

Captain Ronald Granet of the British army and a nephew of
an English financier, as a German spy. The novel is informative regarding the secret service as well as military
methods and tactics, submarine disasters, and zeppelin
forays, in one of which the villain is dispatched.

95 Palmer, Frederick. *The Old Blood; a Novel*. London: John
   Murray, 1916. 319p.; New York: Dodd, Mead & Co., 1916.
   390p.

An American from Massachusetts, Phil Sanford, travels
to England to become acquainted with family members distantly related to him, and visits one relative's French
chateau. When the war breaks out, he is captured by the
Germans but later rescued during the battle of the Marne.
He then enlists in the English artillery and is wounded,
with little of his face intact. Eventually plastic surgery
repairs much of the damage, and he is nursed to health by
one of his relatives. The novel is basically a romance
with a view of the day-to-day life of a French family who
live very near the front.

96 Palmer, John Leslie. *The King's Men*. New York: G.P.
   Putnam's Sons, 1916. 311p.; London: Martin Secker,
   Ltd., 1916. 303p.

The author, an assistant editor of the *Saturday Review*,
depicts the changes which war was producing in England.
"The war is not only a military event. It is, so far as
the English are concerned, a social revolution." Palmer's
approach is to introduce the effects of the war upon a
wide choice of people who are unified in serving king and
country, particularly the women and a group of artists and
workers. They all act differently. The novel's title is
taken from the patriotic appeal "Your king and your country need you." The action of the war occurs offstage.

97 Prevost, Marcel. *Benoit Castain*. Translated by Arthur C.
   Richmond. London: The Macmillan Co., 1916. 223p.

The story is placed in a small French village located
near where the frontiers of France, Luxemburg, and the
annexed portion of Lorraine converge. Benoit Castain is
a quartermaster in the French army. Young and handsome,
he has made a career out of military service. He is
stationed at Fort Cissey, a modern defense base claimed
to be invincible, which overlooks the main road to the
village. He meets the daughter of the caretaker of the

local chateau, and a love affair soon develops. But the war now begins and all of this idyllic life is over. The Germans invade, and the French forces retreat, leaving the village to the enemy. The retreat of both the army and the flight of the villagers are covered in detail. It is soon apparent that it is better for a woman to die than to fall into the hands of the Germans. Some attention is given to the wide network of German spies and especially how Castain is eventually duped by one because of his trusting nature. This is a tale of two "ill-starred lovers" that probably is a realistic and graphic description of the disasters and agonies of war.

98   Rickard, Mrs. Victor (Jessie Louisa [Moore] Rickard). *The Light Above the Crossroads*. London: Gerald Duckworth & Co., 1916. 310p.

The first half of the novel is a detailed account of the circumstances which led Marcus Janover, the hero, to become a spy. Unfortunately the author is unable to make either her character sympathetic or the justification for his decision convincing. This may well be due to the fondness of the author for German life and society. The protagonist, Marcus, is the son of an English father and an Irish mother. He is quite young when his father sends him to Germany to be educated for a diplomatic career. At his school he meets Eitel von Verlhof and they become close friends even after they both fall in love with the same girl. Marcus loses all of his money and is forced to leave his embassy position, but his chief asks him to become a secret agent in Berlin. This he does for the first ten months or so of the war. In spite of the efforts of the author, the story doesn't really come off: her characters never come alive.

99   Scott, John Reed. *The Cab of the Sleeping Horse*. New York: G.P. Putnam's Sons, 1916. 361p.

The title derives from the situation in which a coded letter has been left in an empty cab "guarded" by a sleeping horse. The letter's contents are important to the United States, England, France, and Germany. In the secret service office in Washington, D.C., two beautiful women and numerous men, including the American Secretary of State, plot to recover and keep the letter. A melodrama.

100 Sherwood, Margaret Pollock. *The Worn Doorstep.* Boston: Little, Brown & Co., 1916. 195p.

This story is told through letters from an American woman to her dead lover, an English scholar who was killed in France early in the war, but who remains alive in her memory. The woman dedicates herself to war work in England to deaden her grief. No doubt the story had considerable contemporary appeal. The description of English character and English life conveys some sociological interest.

101 Sinclair, May. *Tasker Jevons: the Real Story.* London: Hutchinson & Co., 1916. 336p. [Title in U.S.: *The Belfry.* New York: The Macmillan Co., 1916. 332p.]

James Tasker Jevons is an unrefined cockney who marries Viola Thesiger, against her family's wishes. They travel to Europe to see the belfry in Bruges, which represents for them friendship between countries and classes and is a symbol of romantic adventure. Tasker joins a Red Cross ambulance unit, becomes a family hero in saving the life of his brother-in-law, and wins Viola's devotion, which had been threatened throughout their marriage by the differences in their social class and temperament.

102 Sladen, Douglas Brooke Wheelton. *The Douglas Romance.* London: Hutchinson & Co., 1916. 399p.; New York: Brentano's, 1916. 399p.

A tale of a Scottish family called Douglas and a love story that uses the war as a convenient backdrop. The heroine, Miradel, is in reality Isabel Douglas, the daughter of an Italian nobleman. Her father, to her sorrow, had married a Scottish descendant of the Douglas family. Miradel dreams of nothing but love and lovers, and finally departs for London to seek romance and fortune. She answers an ad of the Babylon Theater and is hired by Oliver Gray, the manager, for the lead in the musical "Mary, Queen of Scots." Gray is a bit of a rake and falls in love with Miradel. He insists on a contract with her in which she must agree to marry him and be his wife for one month, after which she can have her complete freedom of thought and action. She agrees and soon creates a huge success on the stage with her role. However, now she meets Archie Douglas, the present son and heir of the Douglas family. Even though she is secretly married to Gray, she falls in love with Archie. Eventually both men go to the front and Archie is soon killed in the war. Gray loses his leg while saving many of his buddies. Several scenes describe the front in some detail.

103 Stilgebauer, Edward. *Love's Inferno*. Translated by C. Thieme. New York: Brentano's, 1916. 306p.; London: Stanley Paul, 1916. 306p.

This novel was published in Dutch in 1915, and in German (Basle: Frobenius, Ltd., 1916), but its sale was prohibited in Germany and possession was forbidden. Dr. Edward Stilgebauer, a well-known professor at Frankfort-on-the-Main, described the war critically from a German viewpoint. The *New York Times* reviewer declared that "spiritually the book is the agonized cry of a revolting conscience against what the author's own country has done...." The influence of Anatole France and Paul Bourget appears in the writing.

104 Taffrail (pseud. of Henry Taprell Dorling). *Pincher Martin, O.D.; A Story of the Inner Life of the Royal Navy*. London: W. & R. Chambers, 1916. 340p.

The story begins about a year or two before the start of World War I. Pincher Martin has just joined his first ship, the large battleship *Belligerent*. The plot relates his experiences on her until she is sunk by a torpedo. Pincher is then stationed on a torpedo-boat destroyer and he takes part in the battle of Jutland. An entertaining account of the experiences of the British sailor, Pincher Martin.

105 Tinayre, Marcelle. *Sacrifice*. Translated from the French by M. Harriet Capes. London: Andrew Melrose, 1916. 288p. [*La Veillée Des Armes. Le Départ: Août 1914*. Paris: Calmann-Lévy, 1915. 291p.]

The story begins on a partly modern and partly old-fashioned Left Bank street in Paris. The inhabitants are described from the point of view of Mme. Anselme, who operates a stationer's shop and whose idols are her only son Frechette, a sculptor, and the Davesnes couple, the two leading characters of the book. The novel tells the story of how the war affects life on this little typical French street from July 31 to August 2, 1914. Most of the action is viewed through the eyes of the young and lovely Simone Davesnes, who is very much in love with her husband, Francois. Her fear and agony and ultimate courage when he as a lieutenant in the reserves is called up to join his regiment are obviously related as a model for patriotic behavior. The theme is the self-sacrifice and heroism of the ordinary French people when called upon by the demands of the war and their country. Though written with some literary skill and style, the plot does not quite live up to the writing.

106 Tracy, Louis. *The Day of Wrath: A Story of 1914.* New York: E.J. Clode, 1916. 280p. [Title in England: *The Day of Wrath; a Romance of the Great War.* London: W. & R. Chambers, 1916. 251p.]

A story of two people, unacquainted but thrown together by happenstance in a Berlin train station. While they are traveling together toward the Belgian border, war is declared between Germany and England. They cross the Belgian border scarcely ahead of the German troops and are eventually rescued by British soldiers. The novel supposedly is based on official British, French, and Belgian factual data.

107 Walpole, Hugh Seymour. *The Dark Forest.* London: Martin Secker, Ltd., 1916. 316p.; New York: George H. Doran Co., 1916. 320p.

The "dark forest" in Russia shelters wounded soldiers, their attendants, soldiers preparing for battle, and symbolizes disaster, which must be surmounted. The novel traces the experiences of a couple of Englishmen with a Russian Red Cross unit ("Octroi") that follows the Russian army in its advances and retreats during the first campaign against the Austrians. Types of Russians and Englishmen are shown, highly individualized, revealing the different effects of war upon various participants. Amid acts of mercy by the Red Cross unit, many vivid pictures of war shatter any romantic notions of the men.

108 Warr, Charles Laing. *Echoes of Flanders.* London: Simpkin, Marshall, Hamilton, Kent, 1916. 307p.

Not seen; NYPL.

109 Wells, Herbert George. *Mr. Britling Sees It Through.* London: Cassell & Co., 1916. 433p.; New York: The Macmillan Co., 1916. 443p.

Through the character of Mr. Britling the influence of the war on England's population during the first two years is depicted, revealing the war's effects upon the inhabitants of the fictional village of Matching's Easy in Essex. Mr. Britling experiences the horror of the war first hand: his aunt is killed during a zeppelin air raid; his son, who lies about his age in order to enlist in the war, is killed in the trenches. Mr. Britling spends his days and energy constructing in his mind a world which makes sense and one which he understands. He eventually pieces together a meaning which rationalizes the sacrifice mankind is making: thus Mr. Britling "sees it through." The novel represents a commentary "on the sorrows, pains and consternations of that part of the war which is likely to leave the deepest mark on the memories of Englishmen."

110 Wilson, Theodora Wilson. *The Last Weapon; a Vision.* London: C.W. Daniel, 1916. 185p.

Not seen; NYPL.

111 Wyndham, Horace. *Ginger; Selected Passages in the Military Career of Pte. (Ginger) Jordan, B.E.F.* London: R. Scott, 1916. 154p.

Not seen; NYPL.

1917

112 Andreev, Leonid Nikolaevich. *The Confessions of a Little Man During Great Days.* Translated from the Russian by R.S. Townsend. New York: Alfred A. Knopf, 1917. 242p.; London: Gerald Duckworth & Co., 1917. 242p.

The diary of a Russian clerk of forty-five who revolts against the war but gradually experiences a patriotic awakening. He gets no nearer than Petrograd, however. The clerk relates with considerable candor his life with his wife and children, how his wife goes nursing, life in Petrograd, the city depot where the wounded arrive, and how he eventually decides to go to the front and serve with the ambulance corps. The author demonstrates a superior literary skill with a genius for analysis that at times can achieve a hypnotic intensity. Clearly, this is a superior novel.

113 Barbusse, Henri. *Under Fire: The Story of a Squad.* Translated by Fitzwater Wray. New York: E.P. Dutton & Co., 1917. 358p.; London: J.M. Dent & Sons, 1917. 344p. [*Le Feu (Journal d'une Escouade).* Paris: E. Flammarion, 1916. 386p.]

Considered one of the epics of the First World War.

Adult Novels 43

It is written from the point of view of the ordinary soldier. The story includes scenes of soldiers in masses as well as in individual circumstances. A varied and brilliant narrative that graphically describes the dirt, the vermin, the stench, and the sordidness of the battlefield conditions in the trenches, conveying at times the atmosphere of a charnel house. A tale of warfare in some of its grimmest aspects, forcing realities of the war upon the reader. Barbusse mixes the humorous moments and incidents of the fighting men with the horrors and human-interest incidents of the war.

114   Bartimeus (pseud. of Lewis Anselm Da Costa Ritchie). *The Long Trick*. London: Cassell & Co., 1917. 292p.; New York: George H. Doran Co., 1917. 278p.

The main theme of this very loosely knit novel is the Allied effort to destroy German U-boats. The author attempts to create an authentic description of the habits and the talk of the men who go to sea to fight, leaving their wives and sweethearts behind to suffer the uncertainties of their safe return. A portrait of Englishmen at sea and their spirit in wartime. The author attempts to contrast the characteristics of the British and the German naval officers, particularly in the account of the sinking of an ocean liner by the Germans and in "the battle of the mist." This story was obviously written in the heat of the war with all the advantages and disadvantages of such a commitment.

115   Benson, Stella. *This is the End*. New York: The Macmillan Co., 1917. 245p.

An English girl leaves home in wartime to become a London bus conductor. Her family starts a search for her by driving their car around the English coastal areas following whatever clues the girl gives them in her letters home. Her brother, home on leave from the war, is the only family member who knows that the "house by the sea" which she writes about is in reality only a fictitious spot. Both the girl and her brother have always had a very secret world of games. This all comes to an end with the news of the brother's death in France. The novel reflects a sense of complete hopelessness. The *Spectator* critic characterizes the novel as "a book ... kaleidoscopic in its change from mockery to tenderness, from realism to fantasy...."

116 Bottome, Phyllis. *The Second Fiddle.* New York: Century Co., 1917. 363p.

Deals with the business life and love affairs of Stella and especially her affair with Sir Julian Verny, who is sent home from the war front to recuperate from his injuries. Stella has been a secretary for seven years to her father, a great naturalist, and later the secretary to an expert accountant, Leslie Travers. Stella's father was a dreamy antiquarian and her mother a housewife who could not manage anything. When she was unhappy she would say she was in tune with the infinite. Hence, Stella and her sisters usually had to fend for themselves. The title refers to Stella's position as a secretary. The characters in the novel are basically caricatures of real life except for Stella, who seems to be the only one to convey a sense of reality.

117 Brown, George Rothwell. *My Country: A Story of Today.* Boston: Small Maynard & Co., 1917. 359p.

The plot and the manner in which this war story is developed are reminiscent of E. Phillips Oppenheim. Wilhelm Hartman, the hero, is known as Billy; his twin brother is Karl. Both are Prussians by birth although their father has become a loyal American citizen. After the death of the father, Karl returns to Germany for his education and becomes completely prussianized. Billy, through the influence of the Prussians, who also plan to make use of him later unbeknownst to him, is appointed to Annapolis and eventually promoted to an important position in the U.S. Navy. The crisis comes when Billy, because of his dual citizenship, suffers the distrust of his fellow officers. He then meets his twin brother, who has secretly returned by submarine as the official representative of the Kaiser to instruct Billy to spy for Germany. The novel concludes with Billy's successful dealing with his brother and his saving and ultimately winning the girl he loves.

118 Burke, Edward (pseud. of Winifred Boggs). *My Wife.* New York: E.P. Dutton & Co., 1917. 280p.; London: Herbert Jenkins, 1917. 315p.

A fictionalized autobiography of a middle-aged man during World War I. He dreams of his boyhood sweetheart although other male admirers show appreciation of his wife's good looks and qualities. When his former flame appears on the scene after twenty years, he finds himself completely disillusioned about her. Generally this is a clever and lighthearted tale that describes the mundane life on the home front.

119 Cable, Boyd (pseud. of Ernest Andrew Ewart). *Grapes of Wrath*. New York: E.P. Dutton & Co., 1917. 285p.; London: Smith, Elder & Co., 1917. 268p.

A story of the battle of the Somme from the point of view of "an ordinary average infantry private." Four close friends and fellow soldiers are the heroes of the tale. Larry Arundel is a well-educated Englishman from the wealthy class. Billy Simson was an errand boy for a small shop. "Pug" Sneath comes from the London streets. The American is called after his birthplace, Kentucky. They are traced as they go through wrecked villages and communication trenches pounded by German guns, crawling through no-man's-land to destroy a German firing position amidst the slimy mud, drizzling rain, and the cold, while wounded and surrounded by the dead and dying. The battlefield descriptions are quite graphic and convey a vivid sense of the horror of the war. The title comes from the hymn that beats in Kentucky's head as he witnesses the destruction of the war.

120 Campbell, R.W. *Donald and Helen; a Romance of the Old Army*. London: Hutchinson & Co., 1917. 351p.

Not seen; NYPL.

121 Chambers, Robert William. *Barbarians*. New York: D. Appleton & Co., 1917. 353p.

The plot consists of eight episodes with each relating the fate of one of eight men who set sail together for Europe on a mule-laden transport ship. Each man is characterized as in quest of something he could not find in America. They are all fed up with the isolationism of the U.S. from the European struggle. Several join the French army and their adventures are described until their deaths in battle. The author makes clear his contempt for and disapproval of the U.S. government because it did not enter the war at the very beginning. The novel is heavily colored by his views and tends toward the propaganda category more than literature.

122 ———. *The Dark Star*. New York: D. Appleton & Co., 1917. 421 p.

A well-written adventure story that appeared originally in *Cosmopolitan*. The main characters are Rue Carew, the young daughter of an American missionary; Jim Neeland, her friend; a Russian princess; and a German prima donna. As a child in Turkey, Rue Carew had played with the "wonder box" of Herr Conrad Wilner, which held, along with the figure of a Chinese god and other treasures, a series of maps and plans. Years afterwards when she went to study art in Paris, under the protection of her Russian princess friend, Rue learned how important the old sketches were. She cables her childhood friend, Jim Neeland, in America, and has him go to her old home in the Catskills to find the box and bring it to Paris. But someone else had been there before Jim. A German singer also knows of the sketches, which turn out to be plans of the Dardanelles fortifications. From then on Jim becomes involved in a series of adventures, but with his Irish blood and wits manages to survive.

123 Chartres, Annie (Vivanti). *Vae Victus*. London: Edward Arnold, 1917. 291p. [Title in the U.S.: *The Outrage*. New York: Alfred A. Knopf, 1918. 261p.] [*Vae Victis! Romanzo*. Milan: R. Quintieri, 1917. 349p.]

A grim and violent tale of the invasion of Belgium by the German army. The plot deals with three women who are victims of rape and brutality: Louise Brandes, her little daughter Mirelle, and her young sister-in-law Cherie. The child, Mirelle, becomes insane with fear, losing her power of speech and all comprehension after a night of terror. Cherie also is shocked into a total memory block after her brutal treatment. The child that is born to her months later, however, awakens her maternal instincts in spite of her outrage. Louise remembers clearly the violent and painful events. They go as refugees to England, but their return to Belgium provides little or no hope for any of them. However, the author has supplied a dramatic and sentimental conclusion: not only is Mirelle's speech restored but also her sense of peace and renewal. This story offers a vivid picture of the terror and violence of war, especially as it was visited upon innocent women by pillaging troops. In retrospect, its impact in 1918 must have been a powerful factor in stimulating patriotic hatred for the Germans. Now, however, its propaganda aspect is all too apparent.

124 Cholmondeley, Alice (pseud. of Mary Annette, Countess von Arnim, Countess Russell). *Christine*. New York: The Macmillan Co., 1917. 250p.

This novel is in epistolary form. Some doubt exists whether the letters are fiction. (Even the publisher could provide no certainty.) The letters, written from May to August of 1914, purport to be to a mother from a young Englishwoman with a talent for music who is in Germany to study the violin. Christine, the protagonist, initially believes all Germans are "simple and kindly." Her disillusionment soon begins at her boarding house where she becomes a target of the anti-English remarks of the other boarders. Christine becomes engaged to a young Prussian officer with a love of music. When the war starts, Christine's situation soon becomes impossible and she leaves to join her mother in Switzerland. Unfortunately, she contracts pneumonia on the way and dies in a hospital in Stuttgart. It would appear the letters were written by someone who knew German and the Germans fairly well. As one reviewer remarked: "It would be difficult to find a book in which the state of mind of the German people just before and at the very beginning of the war was pictured so clearly, with so much understanding and convincing detail."

125 Clouston, Joseph Storer. *The Spy in Black*. Edinburgh & London: W. Blackwood and Sons, 1917. 341p.

Although this novel is obviously a contribution to the cause of the Allies, the German spy is characterized as a man of reasonable decency and ordinary humanity. Lieutenant von Belke, a German naval spy, is sent to England to discover secrets of the British fleet. But as a consequence of an error in the German plans, and the cleverness and beauty of a patriotic Irish woman, he is captured, the German plan is foiled, and all their boats destroyed. The plot also involves a duped minister of the English government as well as the usual romantic interest. The novel is told partly in the form of a diary kept by von Belke which has chapters added later by the fictional editor of the spy's notes.

126 Connor, Ralph (pseud. of Charles William Gordon). *The Major*. New York: George H. Doran Co., 1917. 383p.; London: Hodder & Stoughton, 1917. 350p.

The hero is young Larry Gwynne who is of Quaker persuasion. The story begins a number of years before the

war when Larry is a small boy, and takes him through his
school and college days. His Quaker training has taught
him to despise war, and this religious training persists
even when he is a major in the Canadian army, "still a
pacifist, but, thank God, no longer a fool." The story
describes the effect of the war on a number of other characters as well and also recounts their various love stories. A number of Canadian women are characterized as
supremely loyal, patriotic, and courageous, although more
than a few tended toward pacifism before Belgium was invaded. Just as in England where very few people were
able to see the possibility of the coming war, Jack Ro-
mayne was one of the few in Canada, but any talk of a
possible German conflict was more often than not ridi-
culed. When the war does break out, the response to duty
and country is overwhelming. At the establishment of the
first volunteer Canadian army for which only 25,000 men
were needed, over 100,000 rushed to enlist for the cause.
The several German characters are described in stereotyped
fashion.

127 Copplestone, Bennet (pseud. of Frederick Harcourt Kitchin).
     The Lost Naval Papers. London: John Murray, 1917.
     293p.

Describes in a series of unrelated incidents of World
War I the espionage and sabotage investigations of Scotland Yard, whose chief officer, William Dawson, is reminiscent of Sherlock Holmes in attitude and parlance. An
account of naval papers which are lost comprise one of
the main incidents in the novel.

128 Dark, Sidney. *Afraid*. New York & London: John Lane
     Co., 1917. 310p.

A tale about a young man who seems to have been born
without any courage. Jasper Sedley has been fearful
since his earliest childhood. Although his moral courage and intellectual honesty are exemplary, the very
thought of physical suffering makes him weak and helpless.
As a consequence, his life at home and at school is miserable. He finds it impossible to make friends. Indeed,
he even lost the woman he loved because at a crucial
moment he failed to go to her aid. It is only when he
is forced into the war that those circumstances at last
drive him to draw upon his latent courage. It is obvious
that the proper and sympathetic treatment in his childhood
might have helped him to overcome the fears that have thus
far so adversely affected his life. The novel's propaganda meaning is obvious.

Adult Novels

129 Davis, Richard Harding. *The Deserter.* New York: Charles Scribner's Sons, 1917. 43p.

A story of a young soldier named Hamlin who attempted to desert at Salonika during the last weeks of 1915. The plot is based on an incident that happened to the author while he was in Salonika and represents his message to all soldiers and sailors, namely, to be true and honorable in their duty to their country. A didactic patriotic story that first appeared in the *Metropolitan Magazine* in 1916.

130 Diver, Katherine Helen Maud. *Unconquered: A Romance.* London: John Murray, 1917. 378p.; New York: G.P. Putnam's Sons, 1917. 433p.

A conventional war story about the infatuation of Sir Mark Forsyth for a selfish young beauty called Bel Alison. He returns from the war with an injured spine, and his erstwhile girl friend Bel quickly exits from his life. However, all is not lost, for Sheila Melrose, a sweet young thing who has always loved Sir Mark (and has always been his mother's choice for him), becomes the happy replacement for Bel. The story tends to be too long, with a theme that indicts democratic governments for their failures and blunders.

131 Erichsen, Erich Anton. *Forced to Fight; the Tale of a Schleswig Dane.* Translated from the Danish by Ingeborg Lund. London: Wm. Heinemann, 1917. 184p. [*Den Tavse Dansker; en Bog om Dem, der Gjorde Pligt*. Copenhagen: H. Hagerup's Forlag, 1916. 130p.]

A view of how Germany conducted the war as described by a 27-year-old Danish soldier who was in the German army at the front. He presents vivid, realistic accounts of hardship in the trenches, the attack on Liège, and life in Prussia and on the Russian front. The soldier makes it clear he fought without the least conviction in the cause of Germany. (The book was banned from sale in Germany.)

132 Ervine, St. John Greer. *Changing Winds, A Novel.* New York: The Macmillan Co., 1917. 571p.; Dublin: Maunsel, 1917. 571p.

Deals with the experiences of four young men who have been friends from their school days. The plot revolves about Henry Quinn, a young Irishman whose father, hating England, was determined to rear his son as an Irishman. The father-and-son relationship still has a strong basis of affection and confidence even though they are at odds in temperament. The son, however, has not inherited any of his father's rugged and direct personality, but tends to be a dreamer rather than a fighter. In fact, Henry appears to display a physical cowardice that is a mystery and a source of distress to them both. Henry becomes a writer and plans to marry Mary Graham, the sister of his friend. At this point the war breaks out and the three friends of Henry go to the front. All are killed. Henry would like to go also but is obsessed by his physical fear. He finally confesses all of this to Mary, and although she will still marry him, there is an element of contempt and dismay now present in her attitude toward him. Finally, when chance places him in the middle of the Sinn Fein Easter Rebellion, he finds that he is not a coward. As a result, he now decides to enlist for the front even though he is secretly convinced that he will not survive.

133 Ferguson, John Alexander. *Stealthy Terror*. London & New York: John Lane Co., 1917. 304p.

This story belongs to the genre of the German spy-mystery in which the enemy is pictured as capable of brutal methods to advance political intrigues. Hugh Abercromby, a medical student studying in Germany, suddenly finds himself called upon to help a man who is mysteriously beleaguered, in hiding, mortally wounded, and unable to speak. He gives Hugh the distinct impression that the materials in the packet are of extreme importance. After this incredible incident Hugh feels he is relentlessly followed by unknown persons, becoming so busy avoiding them and matching wits that he has little opportunity to look at the documents. Finally, he escapes to England where, after examining the packet, he thinks he is the victim of a joke and decides the matter is closed. But the action has just begun. His residence is attacked and he escapes to London where he continues to be hunted. He decides that the documents are secret German invasion plans for England. However, the English authorities do not treat him seriously at first until Hugh is able to convince them of the attacks on his life. The author has created a wildly sensational and involved tale that depends heavily on incredibly stupid German spies. Or, the hero is very lucky and brilliant à la James Bond.

134 Fleming, Guy. *Off with the Old Love; a War Story*. New York: Longmans, Green & Co., 1917. 324p.

The title derives from the proverb "It is well to be off with the old love before you are on with the new." Much of the action involves life at Ravenscroft, England, where most of the characters live. The plot depicts a number of love stories that are placed against the battlefield trenches and hospitals in France.

135 Fox, Edward Lyell. *The New Gethsemane*. New York: Robert M. McBride & Co., 1917. 73p.

This tale was first published in the *Woman's World* in 1916. Anhalt, the cobbler of Oberammergau and the Christus of the Passion play, is a pacifist who thinks it is wrong to kill. He refuses to join the army and is shot for his beliefs.

136 French, Allen. *At Plattsburg*. New York: Charles Scribner's Sons, 1917. 310p.

The story is told in the form of a series of letters from Private Godwin which describe the daily life of a Plattsburg recruit. The novel's strong didactic purpose gives a "general picture of the fun and work at a training camp." The author has based his story on his personal experiences. Love interest is introduced almost as an afterthought and in order, no doubt, to conform to the conventions of popular fiction, but the basic theme is the necessity of preparedness.

137 Géraldy, Paul (pseud. of Paul Lefèvre). *The War, Madame*.... Translated by Barton Blake. New York: Charles Scribner's Sons, 1917. 109p.; London: T.C. & E.C. Jack, 1917. 96p. [*La Guerre, Madame*.... Paris: G. Crés & Co., 1916. 108p.]

The story is an account of a young soldier's experiences in Paris on the last day of his leave before returning to the front where he is killed. The narrative describes his feelings on being with his sweetheart again, as well as his conversations with two of his women friends about his life and experiences at the front. The aim of the author is to make it apparent that it is possible to go through the horrible struggle and not come through completely embittered.

138 Gibbs, George Fort. *The Secret Witness.* New York: D. Appleton & Co., 1917. 403p.

A mystery, detective melodrama which unfolds against the background of Sarajevo and Vienna during the first few days of the war. The story relates the adventures of Hugh Renwick of the British diplomatic service and the Hungarian Countess Strahni, who attempt to warn the Archduke Ferdinand and his wife of the assassination-plot attempt. How the pair learn of the plot, their inability to warn the victims in time, and the escape into Russia when pursued by the finest of Germany's and Austria's secret agents are described with a heavy dose of suspense and technical detail.

139 Goldring, Douglas. *The Fortune: a Romance of Friendship.* Dublin: Maunsel, 1917. 332p.

The thesis of the author deals with a lost cause of socialist pacifism in England during the war. The story relates the influence of James Murdoch, an Anglo-Irishman, over Harold Firbank, the son of stuffy middle-class parents. Scenes cover life at a public school, at Oxford, and in a coastal area. When the war begins, the author personifies the pacifist argument in earnest and especially in the personage of James and his unusual influence on Harold and his wife, Petronella, or Peter, for short. In the end, however, the propaganda of the author's method is somewhat inept: Goldring so stacks his argument that the characters representing ideas opposed to pacifism are rendered as complete asses when they defend their point of view. Otherwise, the characters in the novel, especially Peter, Harold, and the minor ones, are drawn with care. The war seems only a remote cause for the extended arguments; the Germans are never mentioned.

140 Gould, Nat. *The Rider in Khaki, a Novel.* London: John Long, 1917. 319p.

The flimsiest bit of romantic fluff, and characteristic of what has been called by some, "typical women's magazine fiction." The war is mixed up with horse racing and romantic relationships. The tale begins in England in 1914 with five major characters. There are two plot lines. In one adventure, Alan Chesney is described as he goes off to the war but manages to survive an especially dangerous attack and return home just in time to ride in a famous horse race before he must return again to the trenches. The other story line covers the activities of Carl Meason, a road surveyor, before and after his marriage to Jane. The characters are wooden and the writing is poor. A regular soap opera.

141 Gratacap, Louis Pope. *The End: How the Great War was Stopped; A Novelistic Vagary.* New York: Thomas Benton, 1917. 274p.

A forecast of the end of World War I through heavenly intervention. The main characters, mediums for supernatural visitations, receive the announcement that they have been chosen to view and interpret for everyone the end of the war, an end resulting from the complete paralysis of the opposing armies. A world of enduring peace is prophesied. A fantasy.

142 Hales, Alfred Greenwood. *Ginger and McGlusky.* London: Hodder & Stoughton, 1917. 320p.

One of the long series of McGlusky stories. Most of the book is dialogue, in Scottish dialect. Ginger is the young, volatile, exaggerating sidekick of "Old Timer" McGlusky, the competent, sensible, but flamboyant army man, an inventor of useful mechanical tools and gadgets. Early in the novel McGlusky is inventing, from discarded spare parts, an improved airplane to fly against the Germans, and his contraption is successful. Ginger and McGlusky have the usual wartime experiences at the front, are captured by the Germans, McGlusky is wounded, and Ginger receives the Victoria Cross.

143 ———. *McGlusky's Great Adventure.* London: Hodder & Stoughton, 1917. 283p.

Another of the long series of McGlusky stories. At the beginning of the war McGlusky is in New Zealand. Too old to join the forces, he signs on as a deckhand on a ship leaving for England. In spite of his age, McGlusky travels in many of the war areas and is involved in exciting adventures. Employs the usual broad Scots dialect, as in the author's *Ginger and McGlusky* (item 142).

144 Hamilton, Robert W. *Belinda of the Red Cross.* New York: Sully & Kleinteich, 1917. 342p.

At the beginning the heroine is in nurse's training in a large New York hospital. Although she was born in this

country, she is the granddaughter on one side of French
and, on the other, of German ancestors. As she nears
the conclusion of her training, a young flyer who has
crashed is brought in with a smashed shoulder. He turns
out to be her final patient in training, and they find
each other attractive. After her graduation, however,
she joins the Red Cross service in France, and the young
flyer offers his talents to the French army, although
neither knows the other's intentions. Belinda works in
the field hospitals, and the flyer ends up crossing the
battle lines. Both are eventually captured by the Germans.
The two German cousins of Belinda play a significant role
in the story at this point and many of the incidents
appear rather improbable. An entertaining war story,
if the reader is not especially critical or discriminating.

145   Hay-Newton, F. *Somewhere in Scotland: August to December, 1914.* London: John Murray, 1917. 299p.

Not seen; NYPL.

146   Hemenway, Hetty (Hetty Lawrence [Hemenway] Richard).
Four Days: the Story of a War Marriage. Boston:
Little, Brown & Co., 1917. 57p.

A story of a wartime marriage of a serviceman during
a 96-hour leave from the front. Before being granted
leave, however, the young soldier learns he will be
transferred from the Flanders front to the Dardanelles.
After his marriage and short leave, as the couple are
saying farewell at the train station, a remark is overheard that the average life of an officer in the Dardanelles is only eleven days.

147   Hocking, Joseph. *Tommy and the Maid of Athens.* London:
Hodder & Stoughton, 1917. 187p.

Not seen; NYPL.

148   Hopkins, William John. *The Clammer and the Submarine.*
Boston: Houghton Mifflin Co., 1917. 346p.

Adam and Eve, the chief characters of this tale, are
figures in a number of the author's other stories dealing with the Massachusetts coastal area. In this sentimental story, Adam awakens to the call of patriotism
and leaves his amiable clam-bed shore and his beachcombing

and loitering to enlist in the navy. The author shows a
sense of humor with this trifle, but often tends to soap-
opera sentimentality.

149 Howard, Keble (pseud. of John Keble Bell). *The Smiths in War Time*. London & New York: John Lane Co., 1917. 307p.

Deals with the home front in England during the war.
Written in a light vein, it relates how a Mr. Smith,
seventy-three years old, and his devoted wife, try to do
their utmost for their country. They rent out their
villa and move to a cottage where they dismiss one of the
three maids who previously kept them so comfortable.
Smith tries to observe a meatless day and even drill for
the home service. As close as we ever get to warfare is
when the Smith grandson is reported missing in action
but finally is returned home alive by airplane. Very
clearly this is a tale that attempts to make attractive
the home-front sacrifices and to cultivate a determination to support the war.

150 Jeans, Thomas Tendron. *A Naval Venture; the War Story of an Armoured Cruiser*. London: Blackie & Son, 1917(?). 416p.

Not seen; NYPL.

151 King, Basil (pseud. of William Benjamin Basil King). *The High Heart*. New York: Harper & Brothers, 1917. 420p.

The story of a proud, young Canadian woman, Alexandra
Adare, who becomes a governess in an American household
dominated by the arrogant, domineering father and financier, J. Howard Brokenshire. Her engagement to the
youngest son High results in a battle of wills, and it
isn't until the father capitulates that Alexandra realizes
that she does not love the son, but another American,
Larry Strangeways, who enlists in the Canadian Army and
is invalided out in 1917. The story also details the
reluctance of the United States to enter the war.

152 Leblanc, Maurice. *The Golden Triangle: the Return of Arsene Lupin*. Translated by Alexander Teixeira De Mattos. London: Hurst & Blackett, 1917. 312p.; New York: The Macaulay Co., 1917. 362p.

The time is April of 1915. Paris is filled with

injured and crippled soldiers as well as spies and plotters. The story concerns one of these soldiers, Captain Patrice Belval, who tries to free the woman he loves from the fate which confronts her. However, the circumstances are too complicated for the honest Captain to comprehend. The "Little Mother Coralie" of the hospital wards is the wife of Essares Bey, a Turkish scoundrel financier who is posing as an Egyptian and naturalized French citizen. Seemingly, the very wealth of France is at stake. Fortunately, the famed detective, Arsene Lupin, appears on the scene, under an assumed name of course, and uses his incredible skill to untangle the web of mystery. The story is filled with suspense but so confused at various moments that there is difficulty in figuring out just what is what and who is who.

153 [Le Queux, William]. *Behind the German Lines; Amazing Confessions of Col.-Lieut. Otto von Heynitz....* London: London Mail, 1917. 190p.

Not seen.

154 [————]. *Hushed up at German Headquarters; Amazing Confessions of Col.-Lieut. Otto von Heynitz....* London: London Mail, 1917. 188p.

Not seen.

155 Locke, William John. *The Red Planet*. New York: John Lane Co., 1917. 349p.; London: John Lane, 1917. 312p.

The story is narrated by Major Meredyth, a crippled veteran of the Boer War who is in a position to observe all activities in a small town in the south of England: scenes of the dramas of love affairs and the everyday life of the people. The Major acts as the father confessor to everybody in the little village when war comes to affect its normal life. The Major relates the story of the death of Althea Fenimore, the daughter of the local nobleman. This is tied to the account of Captain Leonard Boyce of the British army. Boyce is on the surface an overpowering individual, huge, strong, with every indication of being a hero and a model soldier. Women adore him. But it appears he harbors a secret weakness--a fear that seems to paralyze him whenever there is a sudden crisis on the battlefield. Indeed, he is an involuntary coward and also a liar and a hypocrite who eventually commits suicide. Betty Fairfax, a beautiful and sensitive woman, is the chief female character in the novel. Her character and qualities qualify her for the comment by the Major that she is "the embodiment of the Woman of the Great War." The book covers a number of general themes but especially emphasizes duty, the major theme of the book. Originally appeared in several issues of *Good Housekeeping*.

156 ――――. *Rough Road*. New York: Grosset & Dunlap, 1917. 308p.

The major theme is how a man can find his soul through service in the war. The protagonist is James Marmaduke Trevor who has been overly protected by his mother since birth. Convinced that he is of a delicate nature, he leads a toy-Pomeranian sort of existence in luxurious surroundings. As a consequence, he has been contemptuously nicknamed "Doggie." He becomes engaged to a very proper girl. When the war begins, "Doggie" is persuaded to enlist, but he experiences considerable fear. He visits a doctor who pronounces him "absolutely horse-strong." Now that he has no reasonable excuse, he reluctantly accepts a commission, but is rather quickly dismissed because of his incompetency. He now perceives some bitter truths about his character and determinedly resolves to make himself a real man. He enlists as a Tommy, becomes a good soldier, and at last finds himself. However, in his newfound manhood he is not the same "Doggie" as when he was engaged to Peggy. As it turns out neither one is any longer especially interested in marriage. Thus, as a result of this and subsequent events, the issue is gradually resolved to everyone's benefit. The author has devised a well-developed plot with moments of humor and human understanding. Nonetheless, it is difficult to understand just how the effeminate "Doggie" is able to become a real man, war or no war. The novel appeared serially in *Good Housekeeping*.

157 MacGill, Patrick. *The Brown Brethren*. London: Herbert Jenkins, 1917. 296p.; New York: George H. Doran Co., 1917. 296p.

An autobiographical novel of comic and serious incidents of war. Though individuals like Fitzgerald, Reynolds, Snogger and Bowdy Benners, who receives a D.C.M., appear prominently in the book, war is the main character, and death is the ever-present companion. The author served in the war from its outset, as a stretcher bearer, until wounded at Loos.

158 Machen, Arthur Llewelyn Jones. *The Terror: A Fantasy.*
London: Gerald Duckworth & Co., 1917. 190p. [Title in
U.S.: *The Terror: A Mystery.* New York: Robert M. McBride
& Co., 1917. 227p.]

The scene is placed in rural Wales, where strange deaths
have occurred. Workers in munition factories, miners,
farmers, laborers, and even tourists are stricken, some
apparently asphyxiated, and others are victims of unex-
plained violence. It is thought that the Germans before
the war started constructing underground hidden vantage
points from which they are now projecting deadly rays to
destroy the English people. Ultimately, however, it is
discovered that the "terror" is due to the uprising of all
the animals against their human masters who in waging war
have descended lower than beasts. Mankind has therefore
lost its spiritual dominance, with the result that the
hatred of man is contagious. The animals under this spell
have turned on all men to destroy them. Not until the
animals' revolt is ended are the English enabled to over-
whelm the enemy. An ingenious fantasy of some originality
with descriptive passages of considerable beauty about
the Welsh countryside.

159 Mansfield, Charlotte. *The Dupe: A British and South
African Story of the Years 1914 and 1915.* London:
Simpkin, Marshall, Hamilton, Kent, 1917. 394p.

A spy story. The main character, the dupe, is female,
the American widow of an inventor whose death gave her
possession of specifications for a flying gun. Her next
marriage is to a ruthless German, though Dawn Mather, the
dupe's close friend, turns out to be a remarkable counter-
plotter in the marriage. The novel describes in detail
the effect of the sinking of the *Lusitania* upon the inhabitants of Durban, Africa.

160 McKenna, Stephen. *Ninety-six Hours' Leave.* London:
Methuen, 1917. 299p.; New York: George H. Doran Co.,
1917. 305p.

Three young army officers arrive in London on leave for
96 hours. After they arrive they pick up a congenial
navy man to join their party. One of the group, Kit
Markham, decides to impersonate Prince Christoforo of
Catania. They all enthusiastically go along with the
gag, and all enter the Hotel Semiramis where they carry
off the affair so well that even the hotel orchestra

plays the Italian national anthem in honor of the distinguished prince. The impersonation very nearly succeeds but for Kit's interest in a girl. This lighthearted, comic plot is further complicated by two German spies who become interested in the movements of the so-called Italian prince and provide some moments of excitement and possible danger to the four men.

161 ———. *Sonia; Between Two Worlds*. London: Methuen & Co., 1917. 404p.; New York: George H. Doran Co., 1917. 475p.

Sonia Dainton, the namesake of the novel, plays a very small part in the plot, which deals mainly with the activities and development of George Oakleigh, the narrator, and his two friends, Lord Loring and David O'Rane. This is a typical English novel of school and college life, a large portion of which deals mainly with the action and thoughts of the English people in the years preceding the war as well as with some descriptions of the changes that the war imposed on English life.

162 Molesworth, Guilford Lindsey. *A Spy of the Huns*. London: R. Scott, 1917. 166p.

Not seen; NYPL.

163 P., K.S. *Records of a Rectory Garden* by K.S.P. London: Longmans, Green & Co., 1917. 75p.

Not seen; NYPL.

164 Parry, D.H. *With Haig on the Somme*. London: Cassell & Co., 1917. 301p.

Not seen.

165 Pennell, Elizabeth (Robins) (pseud.: N.N.). *The Lovers*. London: Wm. Heinemann, 1917. 170p.; Philadelphia: J.B. Lippincott Co., 1917. 170p.

The scenes of the story range from the heart of London to the battlefields of France. It is largely an autobiographical tale and is taken from a short story of the author called "Les Amoureaux" (*Century*, June 1911), which forms the first chapter of the four that make up the book. It is one of the better descriptions of life under training in England and of the various military activities at the front. One of the aims of the author is to show the incredible and wasteful tragedy of war.

166 Phillpotts, Eden (pseud.: Hext [Harrington]). *The Nursery (Banks of Colne)*. London: Wm. Heinemann, 1917. 300p. [Title in U.S.: *The Banks of Colne (The Nursery)*. New York: The Macmillan Co., 1917. 343p.]

The novel is placed mainly among the flower nurseries of Colchester and the nearby oyster fisheries. An unsuccessful blacksheep brother deeply resents his smug and prosperous relative. He murders his brother's employee after tricking the man into believing that any injury to his employer is a favor to the older brother. The favor turns out to be the seduction of his brother's sensuous but rather simple wife. Mixed up with this is the life story of Aveline, supposedly a widow and artist, who remarries without letting her lover know that her first husband is still alive. When her new husband finally discovers the truth he enlists for the front and is killed. The war enters the plot as a device to remove conveniently one of the characters from the story. A somewhat turgid and old-fashioned melodrama.

167 Pierson, Jane Susanna (Anderson). *The Coming of the Dawn*. Cincinnati: The Standard Publishing Co., 1917. 299p.

Not seen; NYPL.

168 Pope, Narion Manville. *Between Two Gods*. Buenos Aires: Kidd & Co., 1917. 150p.

Not seen.

169 Reynés-Monlaur, Marie. *Sister Clare*. Translated from the French by M.E. Arendrup. London: Burns & Oates, 1917. 191p.; New York: Robert M. McBride & Co., 1917. 191p.

Details the plight of a group of French Franciscan nuns fleeing from the advance of the German army. The nuns travel through Belgium from Dinant on the Meuse to the relative safety of Rheims where they watch the burning of the cathedral. The story follows specifically the flight of Sister Clare, the most spiritual, simple, and revered of these followers of St. Francis.

Adult Novels

170 Richards, Harold Grahame. *Shadows; a Love Story*. New York: Dodd, Mead & Co., 1917. 393p.

   The story takes place in a quiet neighborhood in Wales. A small group of children with Hilda and Gwaine Brennan and Ronald Clinton are the chief focus. Hilda is the loveliest of the two girls but Ronald remains devoted to Gwaine. Ronald, however, has a dispute with his grandfather and leaves for London to make a living as a writer. During this long separation from Gwaine the war begins, Ronald enlists as a private, effects a reconciliation with his grandfather, and returns to Gwaine after his experiences in the first months of the conflict. The war scenes are vividly described. The fate of Hilda, although a minor incident in the plot, indicates the far-reaching consequences of the war.

171 Ridge, William Pett. *The Amazing Years*. London: Hodder & Stoughton, 1917. 274p.

   Details life in London during the war years through the eyes of a family retainer. She describes the family after the fall of their fortune and covers how the two family sons enlist in the British Army, see action, and are invalided home.

172 Rutledge, Marice (pseud. of Marice Rutledge [Gibson] Hale). *Children of Fate*. New York: F.A. Stokes & Co., 1917. 281p.

   The plot is set in Paris in wartime. Two lovers, a young French architect, Pierre, and his American girl friend, Natalie, are parted soon after the first call to mobilization. Pierre is described as a high-strung, sensitive young man who finds the idea of killing repulsive. To nerve himself to fight, he convinces himself that he is involved in a war between good and evil and is literally battling for the survival of civilization. Although encouraging his argument, Natalie has already begun to doubt the patriotic claims. She eventually comes to feel more and more that war cannot solve anything. If Germany is defeated, another enemy will appear eventually. Her visit to the wounded Pierre brings on a crisis in which she is forced to tell him her true convictions. The author seems to lay the ruin of war at the feet of women, implying that without their sanction the world would not again and again return to the "maleness run riot" which is war. Pacifism is the chief theme in this sexist novel.

173 Sheehan, Perley Poore. *The Passport Invisible.* New York: George H. Doran Co., 1917. 241p.

An improbable wartime spy mystery. Just before the U.S. enters the war an eighty-year-old American woman is leaving Germany for home after a two-year visit. She brings with her three love letters, two from her past. Because of her age and motherly appearance, her letters were not examined by the German customs officials. She later meets a young American man who has several strategic documents that must get to Washington. But he is cornered by German agents and is unable to leave the country. When she learns of his desperate plight, she decides to accept the mission in spite of witnessing his death. With her brave and patriotic heart and "sweet motherliness," she successfully brings the papers back to the States and gives them directly to the President. A fearless "Mary Worth" melodrama.

174 Sidgwick, Cecily (Ullmann). *Salt of the Earth.* New York: W.J. Watt, 1917. 313p.

A typical propaganda novel designed to encourage hate for prussianism whether military or civilian. Brenda Müller, the heroine of the story, is of German background but with English training and sympathies. She has visited her German relatives a number of times and eventually marries her cousin, Lothar Erdmann, who is a typical Prussian officer. Brenda, however, soon becomes unhappy because of the arrogance of Lothar's friends and relatives who consider themselves the supreme examples of mankind or "the salt of the earth." To complicate matters her husband proves unfaithful. When war comes Lothar, of course, is off to serve the fatherland, but forces Brenda to stay in Berlin with his parents. Later she follows him to Belgium and eventually escapes to her parents' home in London. Lothar also ends up in London, as a German spy to secretly direct zeppelin raids. He is caught finally and shot. A strictly good-guys and bad-guys plot.

175 Sinclair, May. *The Tree of Heaven.* London: Cassell, & Co., 1917. 358p.; New York: The Macmillan Co., 1917. 408p.

A novel of English life, society, and fortitude as represented in one family and symbolized by their sacrifice in the war. The novel examines the psychological effect of the war on the home front, social relationships, suffering, patriotism, sacrifice, etc. The story begins about 1910 and traces the development of the Harrison family from the nursery days of the children to their school and college days. The primary characters are Frances Harrison and her four children: Dorothea, Michael, Nicholas, and John. She is a successful wife and mother who has achieved all she ever wanted in life, a good and loving husband, children, and confidence in the future of England. Thus life seems very full when 1914 arrives and the war soon calls her children one after the other to their death. The basic theme is the courage with which Frances paid the price of being a mother of sons during the war. The novel explores many of the issues of English society from about 1910 to 1918. A brief but vivid account of Belgian refugees arriving in London is memorable. The novel is written with ability and style.

176 Snaith, John Collis. *The Coming*. London: Chatto & Windus, 1917. 311p.; New York: D. Appleton & Co., 1917. 370p.

The question posed by this story is "What would Christ do in wartime England?" The scene is a small village. John Smith, a young carpenter, is somewhat a puzzle to the villagers. He is seemingly harmless but doesn't conform to the present standards of patriotism and religion. Also, since he doesn't enter the army, he is under suspicion; and since he doesn't go to church, he is obviously an unbeliever. Thus, he becomes an affront to the stiff-necked local vicar. Smith is also an epileptic and often hears inner voices from such figures as Goethe. This so shocks the vicar that he has Smith committed to an asylum. While there Smith imagines he is a new Messiah and writes a drama called "The Door" which is promoted by an American Jewish theater agent who forgoes any profit from the play, which is a phenomenal success. The drama so impresses all the nations of the world that they soon realize the error of their ways. John Smith is even awarded the Nobel Peace Prize, but he dies before it can be presented. A fantasy.

177 Spurr, Jack. *Conscript 'Tich.'* London: W. & R. Chambers, 1917. 223p.

Not seen; NYPL.

178 Stead, Francis Herbert. *No More War! "Truth Embodied in a Tale."* London: Simpkin, Marshall, Kent, 1917. 424p.

Not seen: NYPL.

179 Thanet, Octave (pseud. of Alice French). *And the Captain Answered.* Indianapolis: Bobbs-Merrill Co., 1917. 84p.

The plot of this patriotic pap is centered on the struggle of a mother to keep her son, Victor Hardy, a young guardsman, from taking a federal oath. The mother has been reared in a military family tradition. As a result, her present pacifism is primarily emotional. (Her father was a soldier in the Civil War; her husband died of fever during the Spanish-American war; her father-in-law was a career officer in the army.) Her father-in-law exercised a strong influence on young Hardy, and it is to be expected that she will see the patriotic light sooner rather than later, which is precisely the case. The story is a superficial pretense of a psychological examination of human motives.

180 Tracy, Louis. *The Revellers.* New York: E.J. Clode, 1917. 339p.

The story begins in a small English village. Martin Bolland, one of the village boys, is the chief character. He encounters curious adventures through taking care of Angele, a small, capricious girl who is a stranger to the area. Her mother, a Mrs. Saumares, is of German birth and has suddenly turned up with her daughter on a summer visit to the village. Martin becomes involved in a sensational murder trial, and the consequent publicity reveals that he is of noble birth and not the son of farmer Bolland. His father now comes to claim him. He is trained to be a soldier and eventually achieves a high rank in the war. The author throws in a love interest and the entanglements of a sinister German spy network. A very loosely constructed novel.

181 Tremaine, Herbert. *The Feet of the Young Men; A Domestic War-novel.* London: The C.W. Daniel Co., 1917. 239p.

Describes life on the home front during the war. The novel observes typical men and women "on the street," particularly those of the middle and lower classes having pacifist and socialist inclinations. These English citizens consider the conflict on the Continent to be a matter

of great concern only to England's rulers and bosses, but
of little significance until they are called up and involved
in the war. Then, of course, it is an entirely different
matter.

182 Vallotton, Benjamin. *Potterat and the War*. London: Wm.
 Heinemann, 1917. 326p.; New York: Dodd, Mead & Co.,
 1917. 326p. [*De la Pais à la Guerre. Ce qu'en Pense
 Potterat*. Paris: n.p., 1915. 383p.]

 This is the third novel in the author's series featuring
 David Potterat, a retired police superintendent. (Apparently this is the only Potterat novel translated into
 English.) The story reveals how the news of the war came
 to Switzerland and how David Potterat, whose support was
 all for the French, chafed at the neutrality of his country. In order to do something for the cause, Potterat
 and his wife open their home to Belgian refugees. At the
 end Potterat writes three letters expressing his support
 of the Allied cause: one to Joffre, one to King Albert,
 and one to the supreme council of his country. It becomes
 the final act of his life, for he then dies. His friends
 believe that the frustrations of the war are the cause of
 his death. The purpose of the novel is to show that there
 are firm supporters of the Allies even in neutral countries.

183 [Ward, Mary Augusta (Arnold)]. *"Missing"* by Mrs. Humphry
 Ward. London: W. Collins Sons, 1917. 345p.; New York:
 Dodd, Mead & Co., 1917. 398p.

 The main figure is Nelly Sarratt, a war bride, whose
 brief honeymoon displays her innocent and beautiful nature
 through her love for her soldier husband, George. Shortly
 after he leaves for the front, word arrives that he is not
 only wounded but missing. Nelly becomes ill with worry
 and weeks pass while her friends care for her in her
 anguish. But Nelly's sister is a vicious and small-minded
 female who watches with silent approval all the travail of
 her sister. She thinks everything about the war is ridiculous and especially cannot forgive Nelly for marrying a
 poor soldier. Thus, when the sister goes to a French
 hospital to identify a man who has lost his memory but
 who might be George, she ends up denying his existence
 because it would spoil Nelly's future opportunities. Later
 George's memory returns and he asks for his wife. Nelly
 rushes to his bedside and they are together during his
 last moments. Happily, her sorrow is now able to turn her
 weaknesses into strength and she becomes a nurse. The

novel is not about the war so much as it is a picture of the pain and anguish of a woman at home. The story tends too often toward the pedestrian and qualifies as a melodrama.

184   Wells, Herbert George. *The Soul of a Bishop*. London: Cassell & Co., 1917. 320p.; New York: The Macmillan Co., 1917. 341p.

This story deals lightly with the war. It just happens to be placed at a time when the war breaks out. For the purposes of the plot any other catastrophe would work just as well, maybe even better. The book is really about the spiritual troubles of the Bishop of Princhester who up to now has had a happy married life and whose religious duties have never disturbed his conventional faith. Now that he has left his former life in London to settle in Princhester, he develops all kinds of doubts about himself and his life; in a word, he has a spiritual crisis. The start of the war temporarily steadies him but he soon grows worse. He visits a doctor who gives him a mysterious drug. He has visions, talks with an angel, sees God, etc., and returns to London to live in somewhat ascetic circumstances. There he meets Lay Sunderbund, an impossible American woman who wants to build him a temple. He finally rejects her offers and devotes himself to his new creed and the kingdom of God. One of Wells' lesser novels.

1918

185   Anderson, Robert Gordon. *The Cross of Fire: a Romance of Love and War To-day*. Boston: Houghton Mifflin Co., 1918. 381p.

Garrison Owen, the chief protagonist, has just completed his enlistment on the Mexican border and decides to go to New York for fame and fortune. (The war in Europe has been going on for about one year.) Upon his arrival in New York, Owen learns of the sinking of the *Lusitania*, and he immediately volunteers for the British army. Later, wounded and temporarily disabled, he returns to New York to recuperate. The U.S. has now entered the conflict and Garry does his bit by helping with military recruitment. At his first speech he meets a young woman, and the novel's love interest is established. The story eventually involves German spies and narrow escapes on two continents. At the conclusion, Garry is pictured as a steadfast fighter in the cause of freedom.

186 Andrews, Mary Raymond (Shipman). *Her Country [a Story of the Liberty Loans]*. New York: Charles Scribner's Sons, 1918. 81p.

A reprint of a patriotic story that was first published in the May 1918 issue of the *Delineator*. The plot concerns a young woman singer who at first is exclusively concerned with her career. Gradually, she decides to lend her best singing talent to the promotion of the wartime Liberty Loan program. A typical bit of patriotic propaganda fluff.

187 Angellotti, Marion Polk. *The Firefly of France*. New York: Century Co., 1918. 363p.

A standard cream-puff love story of the war. The U.S. has not yet entered the war but Devereux Baynes, who was born in France, decides to become an ambulance driver for the French. Although many of his adventures are described, he is never pictured in action as a driver. He eventually receives the French Croix de Guerre as well as the girl of his dreams.

188 Atherton, Gertrude Franklin (Horn). *The White Morning: A Novel of the Power of the German Women in Wartime*. New York: F.A. Stokes Co., 1918. 195p.

A tale to inspire contemporary feminists. Millions of German women represented by the intelligent and perceptive Gisela von Niebuhr have become disillusioned with the German war effort. Determined to rise against the system, their single-minded commitment provides the power for them to succeed in their lofty goals with grim determination. The reader is told that when the tools of Prussian efficiency are used in the hands of the democratic process to oppose tyrannical German autocracy, the latter will ultimately be vanquished. The novel is obviously a tribute to German women and the revolution they are potentially capable of creating. Combined with this didactic theme is a passionate love story. We are shown Germany both in peace and in war. The book concludes with the author's argument that it is quite possible to "believe that a revolution conceived and engineered by women is possible in Germany."

189 Bacheller, Irving Addison. *Keeping Up with William, in Which the Honorable Socrates Potter Talks of the Relative*

Merits of Sense, Common and Preferred. Indianapolis: Bobbs-Merrill Co., 1918. 114p.

A spirited fictional monologue on the Great War by the Honorable Socrates Potter who also appears in the author's companion volume, *Keeping up with Lizzie*. Potter is full of wise sayings and common sense touched with sentiment and livened often with humorous anecdotes to illustrate a point. Another theme represents what William (the German Kaiser) stands for and the impact and spread of "the German Leprosy" in our midst. Potter also engages in a didactic excoriation of the German influences in American life. A clear example of the "hate the Hun" hysteria of the period.

190 Bailey, Irene Temple. *The Tin Soldier*. Philadelphia: Penn. Pub. Co., 1918. 456p.

The "tin soldier" in this novel is a young millionaire, who is considered a slacker during the war because he is not involved in the war effort though he is above draft age and wishes to fight. Two women play major roles in the tin soldier's life: Jean, his fiancée, who helps him bear the humiliation caused by those accusing him of a lack of patriotism, and a manipulating woman who wishes to marry either Jean's father or, failing that, the father of the tin soldier. Though this novel was a best seller in 1919, it tends to be overly sentimental and unduly long. A popular melodrama.

191 Baskerville, Beatrice C. *The Playground of Satan*. New York: W.J. Watt, 1918. 308p.

The title refers to Poland, despoiled by war. A Polish noble family, living in Russian Poland in a house 800 years old, is first touched by the war when the sister of one of the servants is murdered by Prussians. Subsequent events make life grim for the family, which at first refuses to leave when threatened by the advancing Prussians. The eventual flight from their house brings even greater terror. A love story runs through the plot.

192 Bennet, Robert Ames. *The Blond Beast*. Chicago: Reilly & Britton, 1918. 416p.

A young American, Allan Thorpe, is in Germany as a student. He admires all things German. Welcomed into a German family where he becomes a "heart friend" with the son, he falls in love with the beautiful daughter. After a year's study and residence with the German family, he is joined by a wealthy, independent girl friend from the States. She shows a profound ignorance of German life and customs and soon develops a haughty contempt for their manners. Her attitude soon gives her a reputation as a possible "spy woman." When war is suddenly declared, her daring and frank dislike for various German officials soon involves her, and Thorpe, and his German friend in a number of dangerous incidents, and they are arrested and rearrested as spies. They manage to escape execution innumerable times. Against this backdrop develops a love and counter-love romance. The novel attempts to reveal the standards of patriotic wartime German thought, morality, and family dignity, as well as obvious examples of fanatic German brutality and aggression.

193 Bennett, Arnold. *The Pretty Lady*. London: Cassell & Co., 1918. 327p.; New York: George H. Doran Co., 1918. 352p.

G.J. Hoape, the central character, is a wealthy, experienced, and successful man of fifty who becomes rejuvenated by the lovely young French courtesan, Christine. At the same time he is greatly influenced by the sophisticated and cultivated Lady Paulle and Concepcion, both women from his own background. Much of the plot is placed in the West End of wartime London. G.J. seems mainly a privileged pleasure seeker and a bit of a cad who is gradually drawn into usefulness as an organizer and a member of war committees. The novel examines the impact of the war upon the nature of human relationships among the sexes. The characters, particularly Lady Paulle, may symbolize society during the war years in England.

194 ———. *Roll-call*. London: Hutchinson & Co., 1918. 300p.; New York: George H. Doran Co., 1918. 417p.

The protagonist is George Edwin Cannon, familiar to readers of other Bennett novels as Hilda Lessway's son. At seventeen George becomes an apprentice in an architect's firm and at twenty-two wins the competition for the design of a town hall. When war begins, he leaves his wife Lois and their three children and enlists. The novelist vividly describes the new artillery lieutenant's initial war experience. The moral of the story is that the shock of the war can often shake up an individual for the better, regardless of what may happen later.

195 Benson, Edward Frederic. *Up and Down*. London: Hutchinson & Co., 1918. 333p.

A novel of the years 1914 to 1917, in the form of a record of conversations between the two principal characters about patriotism and life and death as affected by the war. The character of one principal, Francis, because of his wisdom and personality, appears to be modeled on St. Francis of Assisi.

196 Berger, Marcel and Maude. *The Secret of the Marne: How Sergeant Fritsch Saved France*. New York: G.P. Putnam's Sons, 1918. 361p.

This husband-and-wife team sets out to respond in fictional form to the question "Why did General von Kluck, on September 2, 1914, order his vanguard to deflect to the south-east, instead of continuing their rush towards Paris?" The novel proceeds to answer through an account of the adventures of Henry Fritsch, a teacher of languages before the war. Fluent in German, he is able to penetrate to the very center of the German forces. Once there and by skillful planning he is able to influence the course of events so that Paris is saved. The assistance of two French girls turns out to be a significant factor in his success. Naturally a good adventure story also can use a love interest, so the story concludes with the prospect of a double wedding at which General Joffre promises to appear.

197 Blasco Ibáñez, Vicente. *The Enemies of Women*. Translated from the Spanish by Irving Brown. New York: E.P. Dutton & Co., 1918. 547p. [*Los Enemigos de la Mujer (Novela)*... Valencia: Prometeo, 1919. 447p.]

The story is placed in wartime Monte Carlo which is filled with wounded soldiers. The great resort hotels have been converted into military hospitals; yet the gambling halls still operate. The main character is Prince Michael Fedor Lubimoff who has organized a group called "The Enemies of Women." (His female counterpart is Alicia, the Duchess de Delille.) He consorts with a motley group of nobility who revel in luxury and sensuality, especially on the yacht of the Prince. When the war arrives this sybaritic group of men decide to live in the villa of the Prince and ignore the conflict--with women excluded. A crazy quilt of quasi-philosophic nonsense permeates vast portions of this peculiar novel.

Adult Novels

Apparently one theme is that no one can insulate himself, no matter how privileged, whether wealthy or noble, from the main currents of his times—in this case, the war. The closing section of the book relates the entrance of America into the war and the meaning of this event to those in the artificial world of Prince Lubimoff. One of the lingering messages of the author is that now that the war is over with its innumerable dead, the aim of life is to live, ignorant of sorrow, and pass triumphant over all the forgotten graves. The novel has beautifully written passages, especially the descriptions of scenery. The war is handled mainly as an abstract concept affecting human thought and behavior.

198 ———. *The Four Horsemen of the Apocalypse.* New York: E.P. Dutton & Co., 1918. 489p. [*Los Cuatro Jinetes del Apocalipsis (Novela)*.... Valencia: Prometeo, 1916. 396p.]

Marcelo Desnoyers leaves France in 1890 to escape military duty when he reaches nineteen. He travels to Argentina where he eventually marries one of the two daughters of his employer. Marcelo later becomes rich and returns with his wife and two children to France. But with the outbreak of the war, he feels regret for his former disloyalty. Too old to serve his country, he looks to his son, Julio, to redeem his guilt. His son, however, lacks any sense of duty to France and prefers such things as the tango and the pleasures of the flesh. He is carrying on a love affair with a married woman at the time, but when her husband is wounded at the front she leaves him and again becomes the devoted wife. Julio is now left footloose and eventually enlists and gives his life for the cause. A very strong anti-German hate permeates the novel, reflecting the virulence of the author's hatred of Germans. The four horsemen, of course, refer to war, conquest, famine, and death.

199 [Bond, Aimée]. *My Airman Over There, by his Wife.* New York: Moffat, Yard, 1918. 288p. [Title in England: *An Airman's Wife.* London: Herbert Jenkins, 1918. 302p.]

Told mainly through a series of letters, this novel poignantly describes the close relationship between a husband and wife. Bill, the husband and British airman, has just been sent to France. His wife writes the narrative connecting the letters which recount the story of their reactions to the agony of wartime separation. She describes her life at home and the everyday activities on the home front. Bill's letters relate the fighting at the front, the air battles, the crashes, the deaths and dying of the front-line soldiers. The book concludes with the response of the wife, Aimée, to Bill's death through a series of epistle-like short chapters addressed to her now dead husband.

200   Bowes, Joseph. *The Young Anzacs: A Tale of the Great War.* London: Oxford University Press, 1918. 276p.

Not seen.

201   Boylesve, René (pseud. of René Marie Auguste Tardiveau). *You No Longer Count (Tu N'es Plus Rien!).* Translated from the French by Louise Seymour Houghton. New York: Charles Scribner's Sons, 1918. 270p. [*Tu N'es Plus Rien.* Paris: A. Michel, 1917. 324p.]

A novel that drives home relentlessly the point that service to the cause of war is all that counts in the end. The highest goal is self-sacrifice. The story is a study of the mental development of a young French wife, Odette, whose husband was one of the first to be killed in the war. She is at first literally prostrated by his death. For her the war is seemingly over and she devotes her hours and days to her grief. The war, however, soon crowds in upon her. Deaths of friends and acquaintances are announced almost daily, and slowly her sympathy for the wounded induces her to devote her time to nursing. Odette learns that the individual no longer counts, but it is the war that is the only reality, and she gives her utmost to the common need.

202   Buckrose, J.E. (pseud. of Annie Edith [Foster] Jameson). *The Silent Legion.* London: Hodder & Stoughton, 1918. 311p.; New York: George H. Doran Co., 1918. 312p.

The story of the Simpson family, especially Barbara, a nurse, and her lovers; also a portrait of the English middle class as symbolized by the Simpsons. The father is characterized as an unknowing hero of the times. The death of his only son in the war, the loss of his business, and the discovery of the heart problems of his wife cause him to represent "the great banner of the middle class." He sends for his daughter Barbara to leave her hospital nursing and come home to help with her mother. Barbara, having functioned for such a long time in an atmosphere of

Adult Novels

sacrifice, begins to see sacrifice as an end in itself, so she finds a peculiar sort of joy in breaking off with her Canadian lover to go to care for her ill mother. The mother, however, readily sees through her daughter's situation and refuses to accept Barbara's blind gesture of martyrdom. A soap-opera melodrama.

203 Campbell, R.W. *Dorothy V.A.D. and the Doctor.* London & Edinburgh: W. & R. Chambers, 1918. 96p.

Not seen.

204 ————. *Sergt. Spud Tamson, v.c.* London: Hutchinson & Co., 1918. 255p.

Not seen.

205 Castle, Agnes (Sweetman) and Egerton. *Minniglen.* London: John Murray, 1918. 348p.; New York: D. Appleton & Co., 1918. 389p.

First and foremost a sentimental love story with the war mainly as a backdrop. Visiting in the Scottish Highlands, Ann Joscelyn becomes lost on the moors and is rescued by a young Highlander. In the darkness she was never able to see clearly his face, but the impression of his personality and remarks are not forgotten. Sometime later in London she meets a young Scotsman whom she believes was her rescuer. She never mentions the incident, but it greatly influences her relationship with him. Consequently, they are eventually married and soon after she learns that her assumption was inaccurate. Her husband now grows extremely jealous over this "affair" and leaves her to enlist for the front. They do not meet again until he is sent home from France wounded and blinded. A happy reconciliation follows and they live happily ever after.

206 Chambers, Robert William. *The Laughing Girl, a Novel.* New York: D. Appleton & Co., 1918. 360p.

The protagonist is Michael O'Ryan, a Chilean by birth. As a citizen of neutral Chile, he has evaded war service, though he is pro-United States. An uncle has left him a business fortune, including a chalet in Switzerland. Arriving in Switzerland to examine the property, he learns that he must live in the chalet for a year before he may sell it. Since many enemy aliens are residing in Switzerland, he soon discovers that the friends he makes and the servants who work for him turn out to be a "bunch of royal crooks" or "a bunch of dips trying it on each other."

207 Clouston, Joseph Storer. *The Man From the Clouds*. Edinburgh and London: W. Blackwood and Sons, 1918. 338p.

Roger Merton, presently sub-lieutenant in His Majesty's Navy, lands on Ransay Island in the North Sea. Certain that the first person he encounters there is a German spy, he proceeds to try to outwit him by acting as a German spy himself. Arrested and removed from duty for "inefficiency," Lieutenant Merton later returns as an official British spy, able to justify his earlier actions by revealing that the individual he earlier met was a German agent.

208 Cobb, Thomas. *Captain Marraday's Marriage*. London & New York: John Lane Co., 1918. 311p.

Recounts details in the wartime experiences of Captain Dick Marraday, who is wounded in the war and invalided home. A routine war novel undistinguished by either characterization, plot, or style.

209 "Commander" (pseud.). *Clear the Decks! A Tale of the American Navy To-day*. Philadelphia: J.B. Lippincott Co., 1918. 302p.

John Miggs, just out of high school and too poor to continue his formal education, enlists in the navy and is sent to the United States Naval Academy. Ultimately he is promoted to the high rank of admiral. The novel presents an account of navy life and duty and realistically describes one of the sea battles of the war. No doubt the story had some recruiting appeal when first published.

210 Cooke, Marjorie Benton. *The Clutch of Circumstance*. New York: George H. Doran Co., 1918. 230p.

A spy novel. The principal character is the gorgeous wife of a very patriotic citizen. She is highly regarded and also on personal terms with many high officials. Although born and brought up in the United States (her grandfather was a German) Lady Roberta Trask becomes a secret agent for the Germans in spite of her husband and all her friends. She later becomes infatuated with Lord Kendrick, a member of the British War Council, but he scorns her love. As a result, she betrays Kendrick and all the others on his ship by passing on the departure date and hour of the boat he takes to leave for France. Her act of treason is discovered by a young girl, and Lady Trask and her accomplice, an Irish officer, are forced to face the death penalty. The lady, however, because of her husband's status, is allowed the privilege of committing suicide rather than facing the firing squad. The reader is assuaged by the triumph of her love for her husband at the end. Lady Trask rediscovers that she has loved her husband after all. She also forgives all of her accusers and expires "in the odor of sanctity," as it were.

211 Dane, Clemence (pseud. of Winifred Ashton). *First the Blade: A Comedy of Growth*. London: Heinemann & Co., 1918. 288p.; New York: The Macmillan Co., 1918. 317p.

Justin is the type of Englishman, the snob with the public-school manner but with no real manners, that English fiction has created effectively. This is the story of Laura Valentin and Justin Cloud, who grow up together and drift into an engagement. Justin views his marriage as more of a social achievement than anything else. He seems still wrapped up in collecting birds' eggs and tends to ignore the needs of Laura. Ultimately, the situation is brought to a head when Coral, the abrasive little sister-in-law, advises Laura to smash Justin's valuable collection of eggs. The implication is that Justin needs a shock to jar him into reality and to act like a man. The start of the war is another shock and Justin decides to go off to the front. The novel concludes with the impression that Justin is at last growing up.

212 Davignon, Henri. *The Two Crossings of Madge Swalue*. Translated from the French by Tita Brand Cammaerts. London & New York: John Lane Co., 1918. 230p.

The two principals are Jean Swalue, a Belgian, and Madge, his English wife. Madge has persuaded her husband to live in England. As the war continues, he becomes more the Belgian in every way, ultimately dying for Belgium. Madge returns to Bruges and gives birth to their son. A patriotic melodrama.

213 Dawson, William James. *The War Eagle, a Contemporary Novel*. London & New York: John Lane Co., 1918. 313p.

Although the hero, George Waller, is of English birth, he had been taken to America as a young boy to live in New York. He decides to devote his life to literature and writing, and spends the summer of 1914 by a small lake in British Columbia living the primitive life. When the war breaks out he does not leave for England but returns to New York in order to finish a novel, until the *Lusitania* tragedy. While he is disturbed because the U.S. does not join in the war on the Allied side, he all the same becomes involved in a love affair. The thread of the story depends for interest primarily on the reactions of the many characters to the war. The first third of the book is placed in western Canada, and the rest deals with the attitudes of the people in New York to the war, combined with the author's ruminations on their opinions which may or may not have been representative. This is strictly a home-front scene before the U.S. actively joined the Allies.

214 Deeping, Warwick. *Valour*. London: Cassell & Co., 1918. 339p.

The major theme is the conquest of fear by means of the insight that the aftereffects of cowardice can be far worse than death. The protagonist is Pierce Hammersley, a spoiled and temperamental young man, who is the son of a rich manufacturer. He finds himself unable to face the harsh realities of war as an officer, is branded as a coward, and dismissed from the service. He returns home disgraced, but eventually love conquers all because he is able to rehabilitate himself through the inspiration of his new love for Janet Yorke. He pulls himself together, decides to enlist as a private, and covers himself with glory on the battlefield. The war scenes are in Gallipoli and the front-line trenches in France. A slight effort.

215 Dehan, Richard (pseud. of Clotilde Inez Mary Graves). *That Which Hath Wings; a Novel of the Day*. London: Wm. Heinemann, 1918. 492p.; New York: G.P. Putnam's Sons, 1918. 625p.

Another novel that promotes the thesis that war can bring regeneration to a decadent and foolish society. The plot is a long affair with a multitude of characters and scenes very much in the tradition of Victorian literature. Dr. Owen Saxham and his wife and son reappear from the author's previous novel. Of the many characters it seems to be Patrine, the niece of Dr. Saxham, who comes closest to being the heroine of the story. In the confused days before the war Patrine is involved in a love affair with a German count and, for those times, apparently allowed it to go far beyond the bounds of discretion. Later, when the affair is finished and she comes to love Alan Sherbrand, a pilot in the British Flying Corps, she realizes that by the conventional standards of her society she has rendered herself totally unfit to be his wife. However, in accordance with the thesis of the novel, under the stress of the war, the stain on her character is literally washed away. Later Alan is wounded and is blinded, but in the end his sight is mercifully restored. Baune, the young son of Dr. Saxham, is an exemplary model of the ideals of the Boy Scouts, especially in wartime. He had been kidnapped by the malevolent German count but is eventually returned to his parents by the peculiar fortunes of war (and the turns of the author's plot). Many scenes describe the Allies' military activities. The scenes and characters are tied together in a story of verbose detail and loose construction.

216 Delafield, E.M. (pseud. of Edmée Elizabeth Monica De La Pasture). *The War-Workers*. London: Wm. Heinemann, 1918. 272p.

A satiric novel that describes the incredible sense of self-importance generated by some civilians on the home front. In this case, a Miss Charmion Vivian is the primary character and butt of the author's malicious humor. As the director of the Midland Supply Depot, she has ample opportunity to exercise her snobbery and instinct to domineer. Her portrait is extremely well done, and the author has created a small gem which is unfortunately now very dated as to topic, although not as to character. Charmion's mother, Lady Vivian, is the type who refused to have hysterics when her husband had a paralytic stroke. The author has authentically captured the special accents of the workers while introducing comic incidents at appropriate intervals in the narrative. The story is a pleasant and delightful interlude in a heap of generally undistinguished novels of the period.

217 Dillon, Mary C. (Johnson). *Comrades*. New York: Century Co., 1918. 396p.

A story of romance with its share of sentimentality. A lovely young American girl journeys to study in Germany about a year before the war breaks out. She soon has suitors of many nationalities but especially Hugh Hatfield, of a long-established English family of the nobility. The rivalries among the various young men are described in some

detail and with a sense of humor. Rumors of war soon
appear, however, closely followed by the war itself.
Hugh Hatfield goes from one adventure to another, to
higher deeds of honor. He falls madly in love with Beatrice and makes sure to stay in contact with her until he
finally learns that he is the one she really loves.
Shortly after the sinking of the *Lusitania,* Hugh decides
to present her to his father as his future wife. During
the course of this love story, the author reveals a
special knowledge of the German national character and
the pathos and irrational folly of warfare.

218   Diver, Katherine Helen Maud (Marshall). *The Strong Hours.*
       Boston: Houghton Mifflin Co., 1918. 497p.

The two principal characters, Derek Blount and Van
Blount, are brothers. Van is the prospective Lord Avonleigh, but the elder Lord Avonleigh has second thoughts
about Van's reliability. Van's love of the easy road
makes him a simple mark for the aliens abounding in the
novel, and the war is an unsettling tragedy in the intimate
life of the Blount family. Upon the elder Lord's death,
Van inherits and Derek wins the woman who has turned
against Van. A soap opera.

219   Dodge, Henry Irving. *The Yellow Dog.* New York: Harper
       & Brothers, 1918. 77p.

A tale of how one man in a small suburban town not far
from New York decided to develop a way to offset the in-
sidious German propaganda sweeping the country and to make
his town 100% American in opinion. He decides that the
way to inspire the townspeople to resist the blandishments
of the Germans is to organize "The Boy Detectives of America" with all the boys in the town. The boys would then
corner any citizen who questioned U.S. policy and hand a
yellow card to the offending individual as a means of
shaming his or her thoughtless and ignorant opinion of
the war. As a result, the atmosphere of the town gets so
patriotic and pure that the "resident German agent" must
cease business and move elsewhere. The thoughtlessness of
many Americans during the war offers plenty of opportunities for instruction on the errors of their ways. We see
the spread of "Yellow Dog" societies in many towns and
cities throughout the land in order to combat the American
false conceptions of the war as a result of German propaganda.

Adult Novels

220 Eddis, F.E. *"That Goldheim" a Spy Story Exposing a Special Danger Resulting from Alien Immigration*. London: Selwyn and Blount, 1918. 286p.

Not seen; NYPL.

221 Fetterless, Arthur. *Battle Days*. Edinburgh & London: W. Blackwood and Sons, 1918. 313p.

Not seen.

222 Flatau, Dorota. *Yellow English*. London: Hutchinson & Co., 1918. 256p. [Title in U.S.: *Yellow Souls*. New York: George H. Doran Co., 1918. 343p.]

Another German spy story that illustrates an especially malevolent German infiltration of English family life and society. Otto Friedrich Schultz as a poor boy of seventeen came to England from Germany. With incredible persistence he worked his way up until he became successful as a rich banker and was honored with a peerage for services rendered to the crown. Now known as Lord Wellrock, he has become completely a citizen of his adopted country and marries Lady Mary Cranleigh. Lord Wellrock becomes the father of a son, Freddie, who is brought up to hate the English and plot for Kaiser Bill. It now turns out that the good Lord Wellrock was a secret German spy sent to England years before the war began. When the war begins a series of disasters occur to the English army which are eventually traced back to information supplied by the spy, Lord Wellrock and his son, Freddie. As a consequence, Lady Mary is forced to reject both her husband and her son for their devious and nefarious plotting. While the overblown plot seems to be reasonably worked out, the writing is often incredibly bad.

223 Frothingham, Eugenia Brooks. *The Finding of Norah*. Boston: Houghton Mifflin Co., 1918. 93p.

Although couched as a love story, this book appears to fall more in the category of disguised political pamphleteering. The plot is placed in the time between President Wilson's election in November 1916 and his declaration of war in April 1917. The story ostensibly deals with two lovers separated by the conflicting currents of opinion created by the war. Henry and Norah disagree on President Wilson's foreign policy. Henry rejects the President's vacillating course of action;

Norah's support of the President's policy is explicable to Henry only as pro-Germanism. The outbreak of war does not improve matters, and their engagement is broken. Meanwhile another man has come to understand Norah and share her beliefs, and the story concludes with a faint promise that these two will eventually get together.

224 Gatlin, Dana. *The Full Measure of Devotion*. Garden City, N.Y.: Doubleday, Page & Co., 1918. 56p.

In a quiet little village in the United States in 1915, the prospect of war seems extremely remote to everyone. A quiet older couple live with their cherished son (just out of his teens) who begs for permission to enlist. The parents refuse, until they see that he is determined to serve his country, especially after the *Lusitania* disaster. Little by little they become used to the absence of the son, so that when the news of his death arrives they are able to accept it with touching and brave stoicism. At the time of publication, this slight novel was probably a tearjerker. Now, however, it only impresses one as unduly contrived and sentimental. First published in *McClure's Magazine*.

225 Gibbon, John Murray. *Drums Afar: An International Romance*. London & New York: John Lane Co., 1918. 352p.

This is a love story of Charles Fitzmorris, an Oxford man who enters the University at the age of nineteen. While there, he makes a number of permanent friendships and enjoys the leisurely life. On his long vacations he travels throughout much of western Europe improving his knowledge of European history. On one of his trips he meets Madeleine Raymond, a pleasant American girl, whom he later comes to know intimately when he completes his education and becomes a newspaper man in Fleet Street. He becomes so attracted to her that he travels to America, and it is there that he realizes his true feelings for her. War, however, breaks out, temporarily separating the two, and he returns to England. Later when they meet again, it is in radically altered circumstances. He is now permanently crippled. This, however, leads to their complete happiness, as this dramatic circumstance creates the opportunity for their mutual love to be declared at last. The novel also attempts to picture the Americans as the British perceive them.

226 Giesy, John Ulrich. *Mimi: A Story of the Latin Quarter in War-time.* New York: Harper & Brothers, 1918. 87p.

   A story whose thesis seems to be that war can ennoble human character and activity. The novel is placed in the Latin Quarter of Paris. Mimi and her artist-lover learn that war is declared and that he must go to the front. She bravely faces his departure and her inevitable struggle for a livelihood and shortly learns that she is with child. Her girl friends give her some practical advice, which she rejects. Indeed, Mimi in her own way will also be a soldier; she will raise her child for France. When her artist-lover returns from the front and learns of the coming child, he immediately marries her, and only a short while later both are in a happy delirium over their baby. Descriptions of the life and people of the Latin Quarter form the background of this tale in which Mimi is called "Madonna" as a result of her tranfiguring love for her baby about to be born.

227 Gilbreath, Olive. *Miss Amerikanka, a Story.* New York: Harper & Brothers, 1918. 296p.

   A war romance. Miss Amerikanka is the name given by her Russian friends to the American girl who is the narrator of this tale. A girl of breeding and sensitivity, she displays a love of Russian literature and wishes to visit that country. Against all advice she decides to take the difficult winter journey on the Siberian railroad. It turns out to be possible only because she is able to go in the suite of a Russian general who is traveling to the front. She is repelled by the general who is a most forbidding military type and exhibits a scorn for the Russian people. He eventually turns out to be a secret supporter of Prussia. On the other hand, she is attracted to the other traveling companion, Dmitri Nikolaievitch, who turns out to be a patriotic young man of character. Obviously, there develops a deep liking and sympathy almost immediately between the two. Dmitri is eventually assigned a dangerous mission involving the exposure and conviction of traitorous men in high government places (this includes the general) who are exploiting the people for their own gain and for the Germans. He succeeds and returns to finally acknowledge his love for Miss Amerikanka.

228 Gilson, Charles James Louis. *In Arms for Russia*. London: H. Milford, 1918. 284p.

Not seen; NYPL.

229 Grey, Zane. *The Desert of Wheat, a Novel*. New York: Grosset & Dunlap, 1918. 376p.

The protagonist is Kurt Dorn who is of half German and half American family background. Kurt is a patriotic American who despises his German blood. His father remains loyal to the fatherland. On his wheat ranch Kurt is happy to produce grain that can be sent as food for the American troops in France. However, his harvest is ruined by the I.W.W. (International Workers of the World). The author takes great pains to castigate everything about the I.W.W. and the dangers it represents to the nation. With the harvest ruined, Kurt decides to join the war and purge his guilt at having German blood. The old father is eventually converted to the right side; the wheat farm meanwhile is temporarily a desert (hence, the title). When Kurt returns home from the war half dead from his terrible experiences, life soon returns to him and his farm. A formula novel with a melodramatic story of make-believe that was extremely popular in its day. The characters seem to be stereotypes. Of interest primarily for the picture of anti-German spirit on the home front.

230 Grierson, Francis Durham. *The Single Star*. New York: George H. Doran Co., 1918. 93p.

The story of how an officer can be produced from an enlisted man. (The title refers to the rank insignia of second lieutenant.) The plot relates how John Martin enlisted and came to realize "the difference between the cast-iron system of blind obedience and the British method of live intelligence." His experiences as a recruit, private soldier, and lance corporal are described in realistic and authentic terms. The story gives an excellent idea of the routine of the British soldier in training. The usual love interest is combined with the illustration of the devoted parents of the patriotic hero. The book concludes just as Martin receives his commission and is about to leave for France and the front.

231 Guiches, Gustave. Translated by Frederic Taber Cooper. *Soldiers Both: a Novel*. New York: F.A. Stokes Co.,

1918. 321p. [*Les Deux Soldats; Roman*. Paris: E. Fasquelle, 1917. 354p.]

This patriotic story glorifies not only soldiers but also those men who must remain at home and tend the necessary and vital affairs of civilian life. Julien Farjol, a hitherto successful novelist and playwright, has failed miserably with his last play. Sensing that he has lost a vital element of the self he used to be, he returns to his native land, hoping to "find himself" there. War breaks out after he reaches France. He is deeply disappointed when he is rejected for military service because of his physical condition. Julien's copartner is Henri Massaguel, a peasant farmer and a man Julien has grown to love during his stay in France. Henri is obliged to join the army immediately but is frantic with worry because he must leave the heavy farm work to his wife and his old parents. Farjol decides this is his opportunity. He offers himself as the substitute for Massaguel, promising to maintain the farm and protect his wife and parents. Since Massaguel is secretly eager to do his part for France, he now can leave for the army, confident that all will be well. Though Farjol has a hard and difficult struggle ahead of him as he begins the physical toil he is not used to performing, eventually he comes to relish the beauty and fertility of the earth. He finds he must force a stern discipline on his heart to honor his commitment to Henri. When Massaguel returns home on furlough, Julien can proudly yield to him a flourishing farm and a faithful, happy wife. The novel emphasizes the joys of the bucolic life, selflessness, and personal integrity.

232 Harradan, Beatrice. *Where Your Treasure Is*. London: Hutchinson & Co., 1918. 255p. [Title in U.S.: *Where Your Heart Is*. New York: Dodd, Mead & Co., 1918. 367p.]

The chief character is Tamar Scott, a London dealer in precious stones and antique jewelry. Although the war is raging in Europe and homes are desolated in England, Tamar is oblivious, for her interest in the beauty of gems is consuming. She is asked to appraise a group of precious stones of a Yorkshire archaeologist. This project leads her into a friendship with the family who inherited them. This is followed by a trip to Holland which brings her into association with Belgian refugees and volunteer war workers, who ultimately enlarge her perspective. As a result, justice, service to others, and love slowly become a part of her world view. Elements of the story seem more than improbable, especially when the author appears to abandon her major character by the conclusion of this rather tedious and artificially constructed novel.

233 Harris, Credo Fitch. *Where the Souls of Men Are Calling; a Love Story Out of the War Zone.* New York: A.L. Burt, 1918. 298p.

The story begins in April of 1917 in a small town called Hillsdale somewhere in the U.S. The chief character, Jeb Tumpson, aged 26, is tall, strong, handsome, but extremely vain and also very much of a coward. But as the author makes it clear this last factor is something that even Jeb is not aware of. In fact, Jeb talks a great deal of just what he would do if the U.S. should ever enter the war. As a result, he is generally considered a fervent patriot. However, when the U.S. does enter the war, Jeb soon becomes very depressed and spends most of his time trying to avoid any possibility of military service. Ultimately, under the impression that hospital duty means he would be far from the front, Jeb decides to enlist in a hospital unit. He is assigned stretcher-bearer responsibility which turns out to be one of the most dangerous tasks. The scenes range from the small town, to a steamship which is sunk, and finally to the battlefield in France. Various graphic descriptions, such as the murder of the little Red Cross nurse by the German U-boat captain, the experience of Jeb in no-man's-land, and the scenes of the starving and tortured French children, generate considerable patriotic hate and emotion. A young woman, a brave sergeant, and a heroic doctor provide a contrast of honor and duty to the cowardly Jeb.

234 Holt, Lee. *Green and Gay.* London & New York: John Lane Co., 1918. 313p.

A seriously wounded soldier has just been brought into a little convent hospital near the front lines in France. There is some question among the staff about his nationality, for it is clear he is not French. He has received a skull fracture that has caused total amnesia as well as a complete loss of speech. His cheerful and pleasant personality soon causes everyone to regard him with considerable affection, especially Jacqueline, the young daughter of Madame de Sarigny. At this point there is some feeling that he might just possibly be German, although he is generally regarded as English. Madame de Sarigny, who is in charge of the hospital, decides to call him their Barbe Blonde. Eventually he slowly learns to write and read and begins to recover his perceptive intelligence. In a nearly fatal accident, the memory and speech of the Barbe Blonde are miraculously regained. Soon after he is well enough to go home to his family and his country. He later returns, however, and he and Jacqueline realize together their mutual happiness and love.

235 Hughes, Rupert. *The Unpardonable Sin, a Novel*. New York: Harper & Brothers, 1918. 326p.

The story starts with an emotional incident of war that generates probably the most fascination and revulsion: the mother and sister of Dimny Parcot have been raped by German troops during the invasion of Belgium. When news of their pregnancies reaches Dimny, she quickly rushes to Belgium to bring them home. One difficulty after another, however, interferes with her attempts to locate them. But with the help of an American who ultimately falls in love with Dimny, she eventually finds her sister and mother. It is very hard to help them once they are found, as their sense of shame and innate pride make it extremely difficult for them to face their family and friends. At last Dimny's love and persuasion prevail and they all travel homeward. Dimny's sister and her hated German baby are drowned during a submarine attack, but Dimny is able at last to return her mother to her father, who accepts his wife and her baby with a sympathetic and paternal love. Dimny, with the horrors of war left behind, finally yields to the claim of love and all is well in a melodramatic and flamboyant conclusion.

236 Hurrell, Francis Gordon. *A Dreamer Under Arms*. New York: E.P. Dutton & Co., 1918. 306p.

The author has based his story on personal experiences. The protagonist is a thoughtful man of books who can scarcely conceive of himself as a soldier, let alone a man of bold action. Indeed, he thinks of himself much as a dreamer or one who is given to speculation. But when war breaks out he is strangely compelled to enlist. In the training camp he is soon a part of a larger group of men with whom he feels he can have nothing in common. However, he soon comes to see them as friends all the same. One of them, a heavy-drinking Welshman "with the voice of an angel" soon becomes his special buddy. The author has created a slow-paced and reflective novel of individual experiences in time of war.

237 Isham, Frederic Stewart. *Three Live Ghosts*. Indianapolis: Bobbs-Merrill Co., 1918. 250p.

After three prisoners of war in Germany escape and return home to London, they discover that they are considered officially dead. Each one for his own reasons decides to remain so. The English lord is separated from his wife, and believes his homecoming would hardly be welcomed. The cockney discovers his gin-ridden mother all too happy with his insurance money. The American has family troubles and doubts whether his homecoming would be welcomed at all. The three men have become close friends and the American and the cockney decide to do what they can to help their English friend in his personal affairs.

238 James, William R. *Corp'ral Kelly of the Fightin' Fifth*. New York: Platt & Nourse, 1918. 298p.

Begins with Brooklyn's Emerson High School graduate Danny Kelly and his introduction as a National Guardsman into the army life of the Fighting Fifth Company. His squad is nicknamed the Wurra-Wurra squad. After months of training, the men embark on a somewhat uneventful journey to France. At their destination near the front, they undergo intensive training. Their participation in the war begins with a German counterattack. Going over the top becomes a way of life for the Americans of the Fighting Fifth. At the end the company is decimated, with only two survivors.

239 Jenkins, Burris Atkins. *It Happened "Over There."* Chicago: Fleming H. Revell, 1918. 192p.

Another run-of-the-mill war romance. The principal characters are the Lady Mary Shoreham and an American captain. The story begins on a transatlantic liner and quickly switches to include scenes in a munitions factory, air raids in London, Red Cross activity, and submarine attacks. The plot shows little if any character development, and the writing style is prosaic.

240 Jones, Doris Egerton. *The Year Between*. London: Cassell & Co., 1918. 324p.; Philadelphia: George W. Jacobs, 1919. 372p.

Begins as a bit of a love story between John Beresford and January ("Jan") Ellice, whose dissolute husband has recently died. The love story becomes involved with the war when Beresford takes January from the Australian bush where she has lived, to his family and civilization. Beresford fights in the disastrous Gallipoli campaign with the Anzacs and is invalided home. The novel's title refers to a year between a parting and a meeting.

241 Kaye-Smith, Sheila. *Little England*. London: Nisbet & Co., 1918. 300p. [Title in U.S.: *The Four Roads*. New York: George H. Doran Co., 1919. 320p.]

Treats the effect of the war upon a Sussex, England, farming community called Sunday Street. The book is divided into seven parts, individually named for separate characters and involving the particular individual's point of view. A graphic picture of the English countryside develops from the events. The novelist explains why the inhabitants of this corner of England sacrificed their lives: They "had not died for England--what did they know of England and the British Empire? They had died for a little corner of ground which was England to them, and the sprinkling of poor, common folk who lived in it. Before their dying eyes had risen not the vision of England's glory, but just these fields, with the ponds and the woods and the red roofs."

242 [Kehoe, Thomas Joseph]. *The Fighting Mascot, the True Story of a Boy Soldier,* by the Boy Soldier Himself. New York: Dodd, Mead & Co., 1918. 237p.

A novel about a 16-year-old English boy in the 5th King's Liverpool regiment, who participates in the battles at Ypres and Arras. He is wounded and returned home to England. The story is told in his words, though he says that he needed and sought the help of a competent writer. (This is one of several books which the *National Union Catalog* and/or other bibliographic references labeled "personal narrative" or "sketches" or "nonfiction," but which the New York Public Library later classified as fiction.)

243 Kelley, Ethel May. *Over Here, the Story of a War Bride*. Indianapolis: Bobbs-Merrill Co., 1918. 259p.

A supreme example of the super-patriotic war story about the home front. Elizabeth, the heroine, a young woman of eighteen, is sweet, gay, fun-loving, not very mature, and dislikes the war or even thinking about it. In a short time she falls in love with an ardent young soldier and begins to see the war's purpose in a new perspective. The author's theme is clear—how the great war made a woman of her. She immediately insists that her "Tommy" volunteer for front-line duty and that he marry her before leaving. For her husband's peace of mind, she does not tell him about their forthcoming child. When her husband is killed before the birth, she bears the sad news with "sweet fortitude." As a character, of course, she exemplifies the strong-willed, resolute, and courageous young women on the home front.

244 Klaxon (pseud. of John Graham Bower). *H.M.S.* Edinburgh and London: W. Blackwood and Sons, 1918. 327p.

Not seen; NYPL.

245 Laing, Janet. *Before the Wind*. London: J.M. Dent & Sons, 1918. 344p.; New York: E.P. Dutton & Co., 1918. 352p.

Set in the first year of the war, the plot combines a detective story with a humorous and light satire of the home front in Scotland. The chief character is Ann Charteris who has developed from a careless adolescent of seventeen into a rather lonely young woman left to make her own way in the world. She obtains a job as companion to rich, lovable, but eccentric old ladies in Scotland. Ann soon is able to make herself invaluable to them. Her sincerity and seriousness so impress the old ladies that they decide to follow her advice: to open their house as a special hostelry for the "wrack-straws," those relatively useless but privileged folks who, with their large retinues of servants, withhold labor from the war effort. Each wrack-straw will pay his own way, but the same group of servants will care for them all. Thus, the elderly Misses Barton of Bartonsmuir invite a dozen such people to join them in their capacious house by the sea. For mystery and excitement, a jewel thief and his partner enter the household, followed by an amateur detective who has received a V.C. at the first battles of Ypres. Mysteries are solved during a zeppelin raid, and a double romance is brought to an extraordinary climax.

246 Leake, R.E. *Letters of a V.A.D.* London: A. Melrose, 1918. 313p.

Not seen; NYPL.

247 Lee, Jennette Barbour (Perry). *The Air-man and the Tramp*. New York: Charles Scribner's Sons, 1918. 134p.

A frankly sentimental and artificial tale. Gabrielle Eaton, a young woman, inherited a valuable but woefully neglected old estate. The picturesque old place would, by rights, have gone to the son of the former owner. The son, a pilot in France, was killed scarcely two months before Gabrielle learned the estate was hers. Since the former owner had no other relatives, he left the place to the orphaned daughter of the woman he once loved. The orphan, of course, is Gabrielle. On impulse Gabrielle hires a tramp to serve as her gardener. It is soon apparent that there is a mysterious aspect to his presence. As the story progresses, it is clear that although the heroine was at first basically indifferent to the war effort, she eventually experienced a patriotic awakening as well as a romance with the mystery tramp.

248 Le Roux, Hugues. *On the Field of Honor (Au Champ d'Honneur)*. Translated by Mrs. John Van Vorst. Boston: Houghton Mifflin Co., 1918. 281p. [*Au Champ d'Honneur*. Paris: Plon-Nourrit, 1916. 297p.]

This is a novel narrated by the father of the hero, Robert Le Roux, a French lieutenant who died in action at the front. The father was able to reach his son when he was dying in the hospital, and wrote down the story of his son. Through his son's diary and the letters to and from his son, the father vividly reveals the effect of the war upon French life. (This book is one of several which the *National Union Catalog* and/or other bibliographic references labeled "personal narrative" or "sketches" or "non-fiction," but which the New York Public Library has later classified as fiction.)

249 Lincoln, Natalie Sumner. *The Three Strings*. New York: A.L. Burt, 1918. 321p.

A murder-mystery story placed in Washington, D.C., during the war. The war, however, is only a convenient plot element to provide contemporary interest to what is now a prosaic and forgotten tale. Chess-game diagrams sent in letters to and from Europe figure as the secret intelligence medium. Evelyn Preston, daughter of a wealthy mother and new step-father, returns home a day early, to discover a dead man in the library of the house. This produces suspicion among the members and friends of the family. The dead man turns out to be a notorious German spy as well as the ex-husband of a close friend of Evelyn. A Dr. Hayden is eventually revealed as a spy in disguise. A love interest develops between Evelyn and a dashing French ace pilot, Captain René La Montagne.

250 Long, Helen Beecher. *The Girl He Left Behind*. New York: George Sully & Co., 1918. 272p.

Not seen.

251 *The Love of an Unknown Soldier: Found in a Dug Out*. London & New York: John Lane Co., 1918. 195p.

This story is related in a series of letters by a young British officer to an American girl whom he had met in New York City. She eventually comes to France for war work, and one or two chance meetings occur between them. The acquaintance is only slight, however, and the girl seems never to realize just what she has come to mean to the young Englishman. In his loneliness and isolation he pours out his heart to her in his letters. The manuscript, supposedly found in an abandoned dugout at the front, vividly depicts the feelings and sufferings of men in the trenches. In a note of explanation, the publisher relates how it arrived in his hands and remarks "I was from the first impressed with its literary value, but as I read on I became more and more deeply absorbed in its poignant human importance to some particular American girl, who, all unknowingly, had quickened the last days of this unknown soldier's life with romance."

252 Lowndes, Mrs. Belloc (Marie Adelaide [Belloc] Lowndes). *Out of the War?* London: Chapman and Hall, 1918. 284p.

A spy story in which a German, a Captain Horatio Drake, poses as an officer in the British Navy. The novel reveals some of the captain's activity as a lady's man, specifically concerning a Betty Felbrigge, recently married to a British naval officer away on service. Rather contrived.

253 Lutes, Della (Thompson). *My Boy in Khaki, a Mother's Story*. New York: Harper & Brothers, 1918. 194p.

A sentimental little novel that is primarily concerned with the home front. It relates the emotions and concerns of a mother when she must see her son go off to serve his country. The narrative is sprinkled liberally with spontaneous letters home from him describing his various training exercises. Also there are letters from a budding girl friend, and the reader is exposed to the beginnings of young love. The novel illustrates the efforts of the mother, son, and girl friend to do their best to keep up their spirits.

254 Lynn, Escott. *Knights of the Air*. London: W. & R. Chambers, 1918. 384p.

Not seen.

255 MacGill, Patrick. *The Dough Boys*. New York: George H. Doran Co., 1918. 306p.

A chronicle of the friendship and adventures of three young friends in wartime. As members of the American Expeditionary Force in France, they meet for the first time in a little French village which they call "Mud Wallow." Murtagh Sullivan, a red-haired giant of an Irishman and ex-bartender of Kelly's Saloon in New York City, is in his early twenties and is the oldest of the three friends. Corporal "Stiffy," born a cockney and only nineteen, has a mighty hankering for women. Burke, the young American, a lover of poetry, is under age, and lies about his age in order to enlist. Through the mishaps and adventures of these three the author describes the daily life of the average soldier. At first the men are stationed many miles from the front and are kept busy cleaning streets and cesspools and moving dung heaps, not especially engaging activities for the three friends. They eventually are placed in an engineer's company up north just behind the front lines. Eager to participate in the battle, they get into a hand-to-hand fight with the enemy, using spades and other tools since they had not yet been issued weapons. The novel recounts exciting front-line trench warfare and the battle for a church in which the Germans have placed a machine-gun nest. The three friends are particularly well-developed characters, but the dialogue moves generally at an awkward pace. An unexceptional novel, with scarcely a plot, but the author appears to know front-line conditions at first hand.

256 Maher, Stephen John. *The Sister of a Certain Soldier*. New Haven, Conn.: Morehouse & Taylor, 1918. 48p.

A short melodramatic story related by an older doctor. The heroine is a young girl, Lucy Morphy, the daughter of

a prosperous farmer. Lucy is one of the most successful
students in her high school but differs from all of the
other girls in her class because "her blood was largely
negro." She reveals her strong pacifist convictions as
a result of her religious belief and the deep sense of
race prejudice stemming from the petty everyday cruelties
she is subjected to by the whites. A polio epidemic
strikes the surrounding area and Lucy goes to offer her
services to a stricken farm family who are blatant bigots.
The narrator now loses contact with Lucy for nearly a year,
then suddenly one day learns that she also was seriously
ill with polio but eventually managed to pull through although now afflicted with a heart condition. The old
doctor is invited to visit Lucy at a special celebration.
Lucy has managed to organize a company of Negro troops
to leave for the front in France. A parade is planned
with a special song composed for this event. The entire
countryside now venerates Lucy for her selflessness and
patriotism. On a horse Lucy leads the black troops, almost as a Joan of Arc symbol, and then sings a stirring
patriotic song in the emotional climax of the story. The
narrator meanwhile learns of the events in her life during
the last year, her deep patriotism and her sacrifice. As
he and the rest of the people from the town and area go to
the station to bid goodbye to the black troops, Lucy suddenly dies of a heart attack on the platform. An emotional
and melodramatic tale that seeks to demonstrate that blacks
are human and are just as capable of self-sacrifice and
love of country as any white person. Strictly of historical interest now and one of the very few stories that deal
with blacks during the time of the great war.

257 Marbo, Camille (pseud. of Marguerite [Appell] Borel).
The Man Who Survived. Translated by Frank Hunter Potter.
New York: Harper & Brothers, 1918. 190p.

When two French soldiers who are old school friends are
hit by the same bullet, one dies and the other survives.
However, the soul of the virtuous young husband, Jacques
Breton, lives on in the body of the lusty, free-living
bachelor, Marcel Lauret. A battle occurs for supremacy
between Jacques and Marcel's body. Meanwhile, the widow
of Jacques has undertaken to nurse the wounded body of
Marcel. She is a child-like woman for whom Jacques had a
deep but placid love, but Jacques in the body of his
friend sees it would be fatal to try to tell her the truth
of his altered circumstances. Instead, he tries to woo
her under the name of the other. He eventually wins and

Adult Novels

marries her, but his very success brings him pain and suffering. She has developed a selfish and consuming passion considerably different from and lower than her former love for him. Jacques, soon betrayed by his "new" body with old habits, welcomes his eventual return to perfect health and the battlefield as the only possible solution to this hopeless impasse. As he returns to the front (and his probable death), he muses that "I am not this one or that."

258 Margerison, John S. *Destroyer Doings*. London: C.A. Pearson, 1918. 114p.

   Not seen; NYPL.

259 ———. *The Hungry Hundred (Royal Naval Reserve)*. London: C.A. Pearson, 1918. 189p.

   Not seen; NYPL.

260 McCutcheon, George Barr. *Shot with Crimson*. New York: Dodd, Mead & Co., 1918. 161p.

   A sensational spy story dealing with the devious and treacherous presence of German spies in our midst--even in the hearts of American homes. The action takes place in New York City in the house of Mrs. Carstairs, the beautiful wife of a wealthy and prominent citizen. She is an intelligent woman, well-loved and respected by her family and friends. An explosion at a munitions factory, the sudden and mysterious death of a servant, disastrous leaks of vital information from official files all lead, through the efforts of a young U.S. Army captain, to a surprising revelation and ultimately to tragedy for Mrs. Carstairs. The book appears to be a piece of wartime propaganda that warns the unwary reader of the grave spy peril and to keep mum on any important military or national issue.

261 Morris, Gouverneur. *His Daughter*. New York: Charles Scribner's Sons, 1918. 326p.

   This rather sentimental and mediocre story demonstrates the cleansing effect that war can have on an individual. The novel begins with the meeting of Frederick Dayton with Dorothy Grandison, a girl just fifteen. In love with the idea of being in love, they become engaged. However, this is no obstacle to Frederick, for when he leaves to study art in Paris, he meets Clair D'Avril and she comes to live in his studio. Later returning to the United States, he and Dorothy are married, but Frederick, inconstant by nature, follows one woman after another with no pretence of faithfulness to his wife. His one true love is his daughter Ella, who dies. Somewhat later, however, Frederick learns he has had another daughter by Clair, but when he attempts to locate her, it is made clear that he will not be permitted to act as her father. With the start of the war he becomes at first an ambulance driver and then a pilot, while his long-suffering and forgiving wife becomes a nurse in a military hospital. Presumably Frederick will now become the steadfast, honest, and faithful fellow he previously was unable to be under other circumstances.

262 Morton, Guy Eugene. *The Enemy Within*. Baltimore, Md.: Saulsbury Publishing, 1918. 315p.

   Not seen; NYPL.

263 Mundy, Talbot. *Hira Singh's Tale*. London: Cassell & Co., 1918. 298p. [Title in U.S.: *Hira Singh: When India Came to Fight in Flanders*. Indianapolis: Bobbs-Merrill Co., 1918. 308p.]

   According to the author this story is based on actual happenings. The narration is in the words and expresses the viewpoint of an Indian Sikh, Hira Singh, a non-commissioned cavalry officer in the first regiment to leave India for the military service with the British in France. The story traces the regiment's journey from Delhi to Marseilles and then to the battlefield where the regiment was eventually captured and imprisoned by the Germans. Most of the novel deals with the escape of the surviving soldiers of the regiment led by their chief surviving officer, Hira Singh. The escape route takes them across Asia, Persia, Afghanistan, and finally back to India after a series of exciting and narrow escapes involving treacherous acts and attacks by Turks and Kurds. This is mainly an old-fashioned adventure story very much in the Kipling manner.

264 Nadaud, Marcel. *The Flying Poilu: A Story of Aerial Warfare*. Translated by Frances Wilson Huard. New York: George H. Doran Co., 1918. 217p; London: Hodder & Stoughton, 1918. 216p. [*En Plein Vol, Souvenirs de Guerre Aérienne*. Paris: Hachette, 1916. 207p.]

   Rather than being a novel in the strict conventional

Adult Novels

sense with a plot and primary characters, the story presents a vivid series of pictures of French fliers, their work, their talk, their friends, and their loves. Chignole is the character who serves to hold all of the various scenes together throughout the book. A boy from the streets of Paris, he grows up with a passion for mechanics and becomes expert with bicycles and then automobiles. When the war begins, his talents are soon in demand. However, he also wants to fly and his steadfast and dependable nature so impresses those about him that he gets the opportunity. The story is narrated by "Old Charles," Chignole's friend, who comes to have an almost brotherly relationship with Chignole even though "old Charles" is in command and the social superior of Chignole. We observe Chignole in the aircraft, facing the ever-present dangers in the skies and refusing ever to surrender to the enemy. For the same exploit he wins the Military Medal--a courageous endeavor but contrary to regulations--and is expelled from the Flying Corps. The book was probably written as a favorable view of our determined and courageous French allies.

265 Newton, Wilfrid Douglas. *The War Cache*. London: Sampson, Low, Marston, 1918. 246p.; New York: D. Appleton & Co., 1918. 304p.

A superficial war-mystery story written in a breezy, almost flippant tone. Cicely Baistain, a nurse in an English hospital, receives from one of her patients a mysterious paper along with the confession that he has been a German spy. As a result, she and two of her friends, one, a government chemist and the other, a junior staff officer, decide to investigate the information they decipher from the paper. This produces several days and nights of adventure, close shaves with death, pursuits of and hand-to-hand conflicts with German spies. They finally uncover the hidden cache of over 500,000 francs of money and treasure to be used for the enemy war effort. The plot liberally mixes the usual conventional elements of love, war, and adventure in what was for the time a popular "thriller diller."

266 Oppenheim, Edward Phillips. *The Pawns Count*. Boston: Little, Brown, 1918. 315p.; London: Hodder & Stoughton, 1918. 316p.

The plot is set during the first years of the war, principally in the U.S. although the opening scene is in London. The chief characters are the "brave and beautiful American girl" Pamela Van Teyl; John Lutchester, a British secret service officer in love with Pamela; Oscar Fischer, supposedly a patriotic American but in reality a pro-German leader in the U.S., who is also in love with Pamela; and a Japanese prince, pretending to be a valet, who represents Japanese imperialist ambitions. The story focuses on three crucial documents, one of which is a formula for a new explosive. This is another of Oppenheim's formula stories of international intrigue and adventure.

267 ———. *The Zeppelin's Passenger*. Boston: Little, Brown & Co., 1918. 314p.

A spy novel. The hero is a Swede who is the son of a German mother and has become a spy in the service of the Germans. The story opens with the Swede dropped by a zeppelin on the English North Sea coast. His ploy is to bring letters from Major Felstead, a German prisoner of war, to his sister, Philippa Cranston, and the major's sweetheart, Helen Fairclough. The women are forced by threats to keep secret the mission of the Swede, although Philippa feels no qualms at all about cooperating. All in all the story turns on a trite plot filled with artificial and wooden characters. A distinctly pacifist tone in a mediocre war-spy tale.

268 Pier, Arthur Stanwood. *The Son Decides; The Story of a Young German-American*. Boston: Houghton Mifflin Co., 1918. 222p.

Consists largely of a series of arguments in favor of the Allies' participation in the war, with only a very thin story line. The plot is the account of the reaction of Rudolf Hertz to the war during his school days and through his freshman year at Harvard. His father as well as his mother and sister, and at first Rudolf, support the German cause. Once war is declared by the United States, all of their neighbors support American involvement. For a while the family stands united in support of the Germans, but as the separation of the two countries becomes more obvious, the Hertz family begins to experience a similar fate. Rudolf eventually rejects his father support for Germany and joins the "Harvard Regiment." When Rudolf enlists his father virtually disowns him, but before he leaves for France, a reconciliation is arranged between the two.

Adult Novels

269 Putnam, Nina (Wilcox), and Norman Jacobsen. *Esmeralda: or, Every Little Bit Helps*. Philadelphia: J.B. Lippincott Co., 1918. 172p.

Another home-front story, placed in an exclusive Long Island community. A Mrs. DeWynt is overwhelmed with bridge luncheons, Red Cross teas, and other exhausting forms of war work when her niece Esmeralda Sprunt from California comes to visit. Esmeralda's ideas for war work differ drastically from her aunt's, and the exclusive household and its servants get plenty of shocks from the "Western" style of the heroine. The purpose of the novel is to satirize many of the wartime fads and social pretensions of some of those who volunteered for war-work activities. Inconsequential fiction.

270 Richmond, Grace Louise (Smith). *The Enlisting Wife*. Garden City, N.Y.: Doubleday, Page & Co., 1918. 39p.

The heroine, Judith Taine, is married to Lieutenant Kirke Wendell, Jr., just before he leaves for France. She keeps a journal of her activities and Kirke's letters from France. Described in the journal are the departure of Kirke's troop train from his hometown, Judith's work with the Red Cross, and an inspirational gathering of wives of enlisted men.

271 Rickard, Jessie Louise (Moore). *The Fire of Green Boughs*. London: Gerald Duckworth & Co., 1918. 311p.

"Green boughs" represent Europe's young men and women who are fired by the war, "offered up," and cheated by the older generation. Sylvia Tracy, finding herself a misfit occupationally, goes to Ireland on a friend's advice and while there rescues a German naval officer and shields him from capture while he peacefully dies. Returning to London, Sylvia discovers that the story of the incident follows her and hounds her. The novel contains a dramatic description of London in an air raid.

272 Rinehart, Mary (Roberts). *The Amazing Interlude*. New York: George H. Doran Co., 1918. 317p.; London: John Murray, 1918. 291p.

An early Rinehart novel. No mystery story, this tale is about a nineteen-year-old, small-town girl, Sara Lee Kennedy, contributing to the war effort. Believing that her only suitable talent is cooking, she goes to Belgium, in spite of the protests of her fiancé, Harvey, and establishes a soup kitchen behind the lines, financed by the Ladies Aid. Sara succeeds with the aid of Henri, a young Belgian who is serving his country as a spy. Eventually Sara returns home out of loyalty to Harvey, but discovers that her feelings have changed too drastically, and she returns to her house of mercy in Belgium and, of course, to Henri. The character of Sara is probably the least convincing in the story. However, the author provides a graphic description of life in the small kitchen behind the lines and of the soldiers who rest there from the rigors of front-line action.

273 ————. *Twenty-three and a Half Hours' Leave*. New York: George H. Doran Co., 1918. 86p.

Sergeant Gray, through a series of unfortunate incidents, makes a seemingly impossible-to-win bet with his squad to have breakfast with the general. He loses his uniform during inspection and, sans uniform but covered with a long slicker which he subsequently loses, keeps a date with a pretty girl who turns out to be the general's niece. She inveigles him into taking part in a plan to expose an espionage agent. As a consequence the general invites Sergeant Gray to breakfast.

274 Ruck, Berta. *The Years for Rachel*. London: Hodder & Stoughton, 1918. 305p.; New York: Dodd, Mead & Co., 1918. 345p.

The title refers to the Biblical story of Jacob and Rachel. (Jacob served Rachel's father for fourteen years which to him passed almost as if they were a few days.) The plot deals with the nearly ten-year, on-again, off-again engagement of Gwen Brook who at eighteen was matched with Selby Henderson, a bank clerk. Initially she looked forward to her marriage, but for one reason or another the ceremony was postponed for ten years. Then the war broke out and served to postpone the matter once again. Gwen now finds herself in London and in the process discovers that Selby is not necessary to her life. Indeed, she now meets the man who is just right for her. A singularly unimaginative and banal tale.

275 Shepherd, William Gunn. *The Scar That Tripled: A True Story of the Great War*. New York: Harper & Brothers, 1918. 47p.

The hero of this war story is a young American volunteer

with the British army in Salonica. He is wounded while saving another's life under nearly impossible conditions. Homesick, disgusted, and discouraged because of the hardship and dirt of the battlefield and lacking recognition of his bravery, he decides to desert and go home. He is persuaded not to do so by his American acquaintances and returns to his unit only to be severely reprimanded and to lose his rank. He then becomes sick and his wound is discovered. As a result, he is decorated for his bravery and is publicly honored. Now nothing can stop him from staying in the army until the war is over. Richard Harding Davis based his story *The Deserter* (item 129) on the first part of this actual incident, thinking that the man was a coward. (Davis died before the facts were revealed.)

276 Sidgwick, Mrs. Alfred (Cecily Ullmann Sidgwick). *Karen*. London: W. Collins Sons, 1918. 300p. [Title in U.S.: *The Devil's Cradle*. New York: W.J. Watt, 1918. 301p.]

Karen Gilfoy, a young Englishwoman, travels to Germany to attend the wedding of a German girl she knew at school. While there she meets a German count who is a widower with a twelve-year-old son. They fall in love and are married in a very short time. The novel begins in 1913, but with the start of the war her husband, the count, is killed in a duel. From that moment on, her life becomes increasingly perilous. She manages, with the help of an American friend, to avoid disaster and escapes from Germany into Switzerland to England in a series of adventures. This fairly interesting adventure story conveys an undercurrent of strong propaganda.

277 Sidgwick, Ethel. *Jamesie*. London: Sidgwick & Jackson, 1918. 255p.; Boston: Small, Maynard & Co., 1918. 358p.

Jamesie is the small son of the eccentric Lord Iveagh Suir, whose activities were described in an earlier novel, *Hatchways*. Jamesie is created as a touchstone and as a symbol of the new hope of England beyond the agony of the war and the old traditional constraints of English society. At the start, the aristocratic family circle is busy with the usual ordinary social activities. The war serves mainly as the background for the story, which covers a two-year period from 1914 to 1916. Although the war enters profoundly into everyone's life (several family members are killed at the front) the main focus is on everyone's personal affairs. At the conclusion Jamesie meets death suddenly when the *Sussex* is torpedoed in the

English Channel. A sense of fatalism pervades the author's view of life and the action of her characters. Sketched in the form of letters, this relatively slight novel is written with considerable literary flair.

278 Smith, Arthur Douglas Howden (pseud.: Allan Grant). *The Audacious Adventures of Miles McConaughy; an Epic of the Merchant Marine*. New York: George H. Doran Co., 1918. 354p.

A jocular tale of three merchant seamen and their experiences on the high seas during the war. Captain Miles McConaughy, from Ulster, is the leader of a trio of sailors who are distinguished in the narrative by their various dialects. Jock Grant, a Scotsman, is the first officer; Evan Apgar, the chief engineer, is a Welshman. There are also varying religious backgrounds, Presbyterian and Methodist, which are used for quasi-didactic as well as humorous purposes. Thus, although they may disagree on some religious matters, the three heroes still agree on the basics and they make no undertaking without the appropriate prayers and hymns. They sink a German sub, later take charge of another ship, and capture a German sub and tow it into port. They then sail a troop transport to the Dardanelles where they land and indulge in a number of victorious skirmishes with the Turks. This seems almost on a juvenile level. The emphasis is on humor and heroism in a rather heavy-handed manner. The story may have qualified for light entertainment in its day but now is clearly out-of-date.

279 Sproul, Albert Cliff. *Behind the Enemy's Lines*. Elgin, Illinois: David C. Cook, 1918. 40p.

Not seen; NYPL.

280 ———. *Spies*. Elgin, Illinois: David C. Cook, 1918. 37p.

Not seen.

281 [Stanley, Dorothy (Tennant)]. *Miss Pim's Camouflage by Lady Stanley*. Boston: Houghton Mifflin Co., 1918. 321p.

A most improbable war fantasy. Miss Pim, a very respectable and solid English old maid of fifty, discovers her extraordinary gift on a day when she is doing her kind of war work in the garden, weeding her onion bed. Overcome by the heat she returns to the house to discover that she has become invisible. She looks in the mirror and discovers she cannot see herself. She masters the ability to become invisible or visible at will and decides to offer herself to the War Office. Her fantastic services are accepted and she is sent to the front. The story follows her improbable and strange adventures within the German lines. The author has combined humor and horror in a curious blend. One wonders if readers were really diverted by this "cute" tale in 1918.

282 Sterrett, Frances Roberta. *Jimmie the Sixth*. New York: D. Appleton & Co., 1918. 322p.

This curious story begins in a small town in Virginia. The residents are surprised and aghast to learn that James Capen, one of their local boys, has decided to become a fashion designer. In spite of the talk and objections in the town and in his own family, he firmly persists in his chosen calling regardless of family feelings or traditions. Even though seven years bring him fame, wealth, and success, the pride of his childhood sweetheart, Mary Louise, keeps her from admitting her love for him. But the war now provides him with the great opportunity of vindicating himself and his manhood as well as his profession from the snickering and the snide objections. His bravery in the Foreign Legion wins him the French military medal and the Croix de Guerre. His fashion knowledge of line and color, especially valuable in the art of wartime camouflage, finally gives Jimmie the respectability that enables Mary Louise to overcome her objections and her own discomfort and marry him at last.

283 Stillgebauer, Edward. *The Ship of Death: A Novel of the War*. Translated from the German by M.T.H. Sadler. London: Constable, 1918. 280p. [*Das Schiff des Todes; Roman aus dem Weltkrieg*.... Olten: Trösch, 1917, 326p.]

The author, a journalist and professor of philosophy in Tübingen, Germany, was forced to leave Germany early in the war and settle in Switzerland because his descriptions of the war in his book, *Love's Inferno* (item 103), discredit Germany. (Neither he nor the book was permitted in Germany.) His present book is similarly strong. It concerns a large passenger ship, the *Gigantic*, rumored to be carrying munitions, which is torpedoed by a German submarine. (This account is reminiscent of the story of the

Lusitania.) About halfway through the novel we are taken aboard the submarine, meet its captain, who is crazed, and follow his removal from the submarine and his incarceration in an insane asylum.

284 Stone, A. *American Pep; A Tale of America's Efficiency.* New York: R.J. Shores, 1918. 336p.

A tense romantic spy mystery that takes place on the American home front. German spies are out to ruin a picturesque munitions plant deep in one of the valleys of Appalachia. The hero and heroine undertake risks and adventures to protect the production of the plant. The most thrilling adventure is about an engineless train filled with munitions rolling on a wild ride down a mountain railroad siding with every jar threatening to blow the train and the hero to bits. The obvious theme is the courage and daring patriotism of the hero and his girl friend contrasted with the shifty and treacherous German spies.

285 Strunsky, Simeon. *Professor Latimer's Progress: A Novel of Contemporaneous Adventure.* New York: Henry Holt & Co., 1918. 347p.

This novel seems a light, satiric American equivalent of *Mr. Britling Sees It Through* (item 109) reflecting America's temperament and attitude toward the war. When Professor Latimer finds that the war gets on his nerves, his doctor orders him to take a month's vacation, which takes the form of a walk throughout the countryside, during which he meets these individuals: a movie queen; an industrialist; an efficiency expert; a medical specialist; a factory inspector; a teacher of "spontaneous self-expression"; the radical Grimsbys who are attracted to odd people; and an ex-journalist who now has decided to understand things rather than just write them up. This cross section supposedly reveals to the good professor the innate wisdom in the country and is meant to impress the reader.

286 Thurston, Ernest Temple. *The Nature of the Beast.* New York: Harper & Brothers, Bazaar, 1918. 20p.

A story that endeavors to reveal "German character" and ruthless attitudes, as personified in Ernst Kleinenberg, a representative of a Berlin engineering firm who becomes acquainted with a Belgian family of St. Trond prior to the

war. As a German officer in charge of the occupying forces
during the war, he violates the daughter Anna just prior
to her escape with her family to England. Eventually Anna
meets an aviator who, after the war, obtains a position of
high government responsibility. Anna agonizes over her
new love and whether to tell him her story. (When she
does so in a letter, her mother secretly destroys it.)
She marries, is supremely happy, and has a child. When
one day her husband invites a Belgian houseguest for the
weekend, he turns out to be Kleinenberg. Anna eventually
tells her husband the entire story. The story is written
matter-of-factly and without strident propagandist rhetoric.
The anti-German tone clearly shows the depth of feeling
created by incidents such as Anna's rape.

287 Tilden, Freeman. *Khaki: How Tredick Got into the War.*
New York: The Macmillan Co., 1918. 220p.

A story about Tredick, a small ordinary American town,
and its inhabitants in wartime. At the beginning of 1917
all of the residents have little use for the war and generally feel that peace is the highest good. Even the sinking
of the *Lusitania* does not disturb their love of peace.
When the U.S. formally declares war, a recruiting officer
comes to Tredick and only after considerable effort is he
finally able to get one man to enlist. The birth of the
town's patriotism stems from a respected maiden lady's
disgust about the complacent attitude of the town. When
she suddenly leaves and later is reported to be a victim
in a German U-boat attack on a Red Cross ship, all of the
town's citizens become aroused: the young men enlist, the
young women volunteer as nurses, and the old men donate
their money to war activities. This is an obvious propaganda piece written to whip up any laggardly spirits in
the land.

288 Train, Arthur Cheney. *The Earthquake.* New York: Charles
Scribner's Sons, 1918. 307p.

More of a didactic patriotic tract for the times than a
novel. In any case, the plot takes a typical American
family of the upper class and describes the effect of the
war on them and their friends. When overwork causes John
Stanton, successful bond merchant in New York, to break
down, he, his wife, and daughter Margery spend ten months
wandering in the Far East. It is only when they get a
letter from their son Jack saying he is going to apply for
a commission in the armed forces that the war comes to mean

much to them. When they return, they discover New York
is no longer the same. Their feelings and experiences
and what they learn in wartime America constitute the
major point of the book. This novel is obviously a call
to patriotic concern and service on the part of all
citizens.

289 Vachell, Horace Annesley. *The Soul of Susan Yellam*.
London: Cassell & Co., 1918. 300p.; New York: George
H. Doran Co., 1918. 309p.

Another story which deals with the impact of the war on
a small village, in this case in England. The book deals
primarily with Susan Yellam, who cannot reconcile herself
to her only son's marriage and to his departure for the
war front. From the time he leaves, she decides no longer
to occupy her pew in the local church. The news of her
son's death at the front is shortly followed by the death
of his young wife. The baby is left to Susan's care,
which finally causes Susan to soften her stubborn views
of English village life and character during the war years.

290 Valentine, Douglas (pseud. of George Valentine Williams).
The Man with the Clubfoot. London: Herbert Jenkins,
1918. 311p.; New York: Robert M. McBride & Co., 1918.
323p.

Another war mystery. The main theme is the need of an
English officer, Captain Desmond Okewood, to rescue his
brother Francis from the clutches of the German secret
service. Much of the action takes place inside Germany,
and there are interesting descriptions of the internal life
in that highly regimented society. The story starts before the U.S. enters the war. The heroine of the novel,
an American woman, is married to a despicable German snob.
She figures in the somewhat improbable rescue of Captain
Okewood in the Hotel Esplanade. The heroine just happens
to be in the right place at the right time for the plot to
work out properly. Francis eventually becomes her new love
interest, as a consequence of her continuing distaste for
her marriage. The Germans are viewed as stereotypes in
this effort to whip up patriotic sentiment against the
Huns.

291 Vallotton, Benjamin. *The Heart of Alsace*. London: Wm.
Heinemann, 1918. 244p.; New York: Dodd, Mead & Co.,
1918. 311p. [*On Changerait Plutôt le Coeur de Place*....
Paris: Lausanne, 1917. 319p.]

The theme of this novel deals with the Alsace-Lorraine

question of loyalties. The story begins with a young
Swiss tutor who comes to take charge of the education of
a small group of Alsatian boys. At first he is puzzled
by the things he sees and hears, for he came expecting
that the Alsatians would be French patriots. After a
while he begins to understand that their feeling is not
expressed in these overt ways. He finds that there are
two courses open to the people there: to become exiles;
or to remain, submitting to but never accepting German
control. Two of his pupils accept the first position, and
the other two accept the second way. When war comes they
are divided and the letters written by these young men,
now soldiers, to their former tutor conclude the book.
The author's preface leads the reader to conclude that
this novel is at least partly autobiographical.

292 Vance, Louis Joseph. *The False Faces: Further Adventures from the History of the Lone Wolf*. Garden City, N.Y.: Doubleday, Page & Co., 1918. 331p.

Another impossible war-spy adventure tale. The Lone
Wolf (a master thief in an earlier story by the author)
helps the Allied cause by breaking up a German spy plot.
On a ship headed for port he is drawn into an intrigue
by an English girl who desperately needs help in safely
getting a tiny cylinder of white paper into the hands of
the American secret service. But on board the same ship
is a trio of Germans who know about the cylinder and do
not hesitate to murder to get it. When they succeed,
they signal a waiting U-boat to blow up the ship in order
to hide their nefarious misdeeds. However, they fail to
reckon with the adventurous hero. He is rescued and
reaches New York City just in time to foil their efforts.
Naturally, the reader gets excitement aplenty in the one-
upmanship by the Lone Wolf. A touch of romance and the
eventual reform of our man indicate better days ahead for
him.

293 Waldo, Nigel. *Wallflowers*. New York: The Hannis Jordan Co., 1918. 60p.

A brief and inconsequential tale about Robert Whitney,
a young manager of one of the major industrial plants in
the Midwest. The story begins with a brief dialogue between Whitney and two other men about his collection of
photographs from lovely young women he has dated. One
especially, of a Betty Andrews, is pointed out which
causes pangs of jealousy in Whitney. He next is on a

train traveling to his enlistment training camp. As he
rides to camp he muses on the farewell of his factory
workers and his relationship with Betty, and concludes
that his work and his leadership at the plant will be
readily assumed by others, especially his father. He
exhibits a strong patriotic sense of duty and of serving
his time for the good of all. While at camp he and a
number of his associates are invited to the Hunter estate
to a dinner dance. Betty turns out to be there, and after
an allegation of graft because of the government contracts
held by his industrial plant, she defends him and both
finally admit their love. She will wait for him until he
returns. This is a short, saccharine. and sentimental
tale built on the merest bit of plot.

294 Ward, Mary August (Arnold). *The War and Elizabeth*.
London: W. Collins Sons, 1918. 329p. [Title in U.S.:
Elizabeth's Campaign by Mrs. Humphry Ward. New York:
Dodd, Mead & Co., 1918. 327p.]

A story of English country life and how the people reacted to the war. Elizabeth, a practical and capable young
woman who has won honors at Oxford as a Greek scholar, is
engaged by Squire Mannering to be his secretary. The
squire is opposed to the war, for it has interrupted his
classical studies and interfered with his private business
activities. He quarrels with his neighbor and best friend
and estranges his children, all of whom heartily support
their country. Under the influence of Elizabeth the
squire soon decides not to disinherit his oldest son and
agrees to plow up his park for agriculture. When his
youngest son is killed at the front, he becomes a complete
supporter of the war effort. At the same time he begins
to fall in love with Elizabeth, but this relationship must
take a backseat until the war is won. *The New York Times*
critic dismissed the novel in these words: "A great deal
of the novel is perfunctory, full of repetitions, and
drags so badly as to become extremely wearisome." There
is no reason to change this assessment.

295 Watts, Mary (Stanbery). *The Boardman Family*. New York:
The Macmillan Co., 1918. 352p.

The outbreak of the war alters the life of the heroine,
Alexandra ("Sandra") Boardman, the daughter of an upper-
class Ohio family, trained in the Matson Dancing-School
and now dancing in New York City. She is engaged to
marry Max Levison, her manager, but on their trip to

Europe on the ill-fated *Lusitania* Max is drowned. Sandra marries an earlier flame and dances to provide entertainment for the troops in an army camp.

296 West, Rebecca. *The Return of the Soldier*. London: Nisbet & Co., 1918. 188p.; New York: Century Co., 1918. 185p.

The protagonist is a British officer, allegedly dead, but actually a victim of shell shock and amnesia. His consciousness eventually returns in an English hospital, but he has lost much of his orientation. He now thinks of himself as the young man of fifteen years ago who is still deeply in love with an innkeeper's daughter. Both are now married, but he insists on once again seeing his former love. This confused situation is resolved eventually when he regains his memory completely and returns to the front. The war then serves as a solution for his dilemma at home, his unfortunate marriage, and his faded former sweetheart.

297 Wharton, Edith Newbold (Jones). *The Marne: A Story of the War*. New York: D. Appleton & Co., 1918. 128p.

A tale of the attitude of Troy Belknap to the war. Since the age of six, Troy has sailed to France every June on one of the most expensive steamers. When the war begins, he is just fifteen. His great love is France and his high regard is for his former Alsatian tutor, M. Gautier. When he finds his tutor's grave while visiting the battlefield of the Marne, the discovery creates within him a deep desire to get into the war and help "to save France." However, Troy is too young and must return to his American school in New York. Later, when he reaches eighteen, he returns to France as an ambulance driver. Involved in the second battle of the Marne, he is wounded, but saved, he believes, by the watchful spirit of his old friend and tutor, M. Gautier. The author also pictures the initial patronizing attitude of some of the American women volunteers and how they altered their mistaken impressions when they came to know the real France. The story is nicely written with the grace and simple style typical of the author.

298 Williamson, Charles Norris, and Alice Muriel (Livingston) (pseud.: Capt. Charles de Crespigny). *Everyman's Land*. Garden City, N.Y.: Doubleday, Page & Co., 1918. 370p.

An effusive chronicle of the war written from the perspective of a young woman who promotes a white lie.

The female protagonist is Molly O'Mally. Her only relative is her twin brother, who has been blinded in the war and whom she must somehow support. In desperation she concocts a fanciful scheme to convince a Mr. and Mrs. Beckett, American millionaires, that she is the fiancée of their son Jim, who has been reported killed in action. Because she had once been romantically involved with their son before the war, Molly is able to pull off her audacious plan with ease. The Becketts virtually adopt her and her brother and they all end up on a tour through the devastated countryside and begin to plan for its reconstruction as a memorial to Jim. In spite of her growing guilty conscience, Molly is still able to enjoy the journey. Suddenly it turns out that Jim is alive and has been a prisoner. But all comes out well, and both the happiness of Molly and her brother are assured. Prosaic plot and style.

299 Witwer, Harry Charles. *From Baseball to Boches*. Boston: Small Maynard & Co., 1918. 366p.

One of those utterly unbelievable stories of the war. The narrative is in the form of a series of letters from Ed Harmon, formerly a baseball star, to his pal Joe. The book is filled with baseball slang applied to Ed's wartime experience, i.e., the nine "innings." Ed, having enlisted as a "doughboy," is sent to England and then to France where he meets Jeanne who temporarily causes him to forget why he enlisted. Quickly married, she serves as not only his wife but as his lady luck. He is sent to the front, and, although he is wounded and captured by the Germans, all comes out well. He later becomes a special confidential courier, has a meeting with General Pershing, and is sent on an official mission to England where we see him carrying off the honors in a baseball game between the Army and the Navy. As one critic phrased it, "Its picturesque baseball slang reads like a sporting editor's prize story of the world's series now being played in France."

300 Wylie, Ida Alexa Ross. *Towards Morning*. London: Cassell & Co., 1918. 317p.; New York: John Lane Co., 1918. 318p.

The plight of the Germans is symbolized in this story of Helmut Felde. The story begins when Helmut is only ten. His mother teaches him that life is no game and that one must advance for the honor of one's parents and the glory of the fatherland. Helmut is of a delicate and dreamy temperament and is unable to endure the German gymnasium training. He fails three times. Confused by a system of ideals and precepts he cannot understand, he finally is sent to serve in the army as an ordinary soldier. The military system slowly destroys his sensitive nature. Continually goaded by his mother, relatives, and companions, his better nature is eventually sacrificed until he becomes morose. Ordered by "them" to do a "foul and evil thing" for the fatherland, he reverts to his honest nature and better instincts, but this costs him his life and the disgrace and ruin of his parents. In this honorable death he is finally able to assert a spiritual victory over the system, and of course restores himself in the eyes of the woman who loves him. This is supposed to be an inside view of the making of a German soldier; however, the melodramatic conclusion is a letdown from an otherwise well-written tale.

301 Young, Florence Ethel Mills. *Beatrice Ashleigh*. London: Hodder & Stoughton, 1918. 312p.; New York: George H. Doran Co., 1918. 314p.

A poorly crafted and rather clumsy novel about the emotional and spiritual growth of a woman as a result of her lover's war wounds. Beatrice Ashleigh, the protagonist, once had complete freedom before the death of her father, an atheist, but after his death she is placed in a completely different situation with her uncle, a country clergyman in a small English parish. She becomes involved in the activities of the parish, activities she would never have considered previously. Although she comes to admire her cousin James, she is unable to return his love, for earlier another man, Fred Hurst, had laid claim to her. But Fred had committed an act in his past that Beatrice is still unable to forgive even though he is deeply ashamed. When he returns from the front terribly disfigured as a result of his war wounds, she overlooks his scars and forgives the past. The essential message is that true love can finally conquer everything.

1919

302 Abdullah, Achmed. *The Man on Horseback*. New York: James A. McCann, 1919. 340p.

The story begins in Berlin shortly before the war starts. Tom Graves is "the Man on Horseback" and the plot is seen mainly through his perspective. Tom is a naive and rather simple-minded American who was a cowboy before the "Yankee Doodle Glory" gold mine changed his fortunes. Once the joke of Spokane, the success of his mine has given him not only plenty of money but also a mysterious quality that eventually causes the German government to start a web of intrigue and treachery to gain control of his mine. Finally, Tom is persuaded to accept a commission in the German army and to swear allegiance to the German Emperor. However, he does wake up eventually to the evil plot and acts with amazing dispatch and energy. The story presents a fairly good picture of German life, particularly in Berlin at the outbreak of the war. The descriptions of the German patriotic "blood-lust" is vividly portrayed. Contains an interesting series of observations on how the Germans viewed and supported the development and declaration of the war. There is clearly a strong anti-German bias that may tend to classify this banal novel as propaganda fiction.

303 ———. *The Trail of the Beast*. New York: James A. McCann, 1919. 343p.

The story of a young American detective in Paris. The action begins in January of 1914 with the murder of a much beloved member of the French Chamber of Deputies. The murdered deputy was also a powerful political figure of ultraradical socialist persuasion as well as a hard-nosed pacifist who constantly attacked any support of the army. Another murder follows, obviously connected to the first, and before long there develops a maze of secret diplomacy and behind-the-scenes manipulations. It is eventually discovered that the two murdered men were basically pawns of the power-mad and corrupt national ambitions of imperial Germany. Basically this is a strong propaganda novel on the diabolical nature of the Germans, especially when it comes to corrupting the internal affairs of France.

304 Adams, Samuel Hopkins. *Common Cause: A Novel of the War in America*. Boston: Houghton Mifflin Co., 1919. 468p.

This story, by a well-known newspaperman, delineates the attempt of a young newspaper reporter, Jeremy Robson, and ultimately his confederate, Marcia Ames, to resist individuals who wish to make the newspaper serve partisan interests, and particularly dangerous German propagandists. The plot develops in a "half-Germanized" American state ("Centralia") as war approaches. Marcia is to be married

Adult Novels   111

       to a Prussian officer, but she sides in the love and ro-
       mance part of the plot with Jeremy and his "new ideal of
       Americanism."

305   Allain, Marcel. *The Yellow Document: or, "Fantômas of
          Berlin."* New York: Brentano's, 1919. 344p.

       The French possess top-secret material (the "yellow
       document") which the German secret service must recover.
       The fidelity of the French colonel in whose hands the
       document rests and the double-crossing tactics of the
       German authorities keep the document in French control.
       The hero and heroine engage in rather unbelievable experi-
       ences with German agents, and the personal involvement of
       the Kaiser strains belief. The novel is one of the Fantô-
       mas detective stories.

306   Aumonier, Stacy. *The Querrils.* London: Methuen & Co.,
          1919. 272p.; New York: Century Co., 1919. 354p.

       "Querril" is the name of a folksy, liberal English
       family. "It was a tradition of the family to discuss
       flippantly the things that mattered, and seriously the
       things that didn't matter." Half-heartedly pacifist, the
       unity of the family is tested by the war, by the unjust
       imprisonment of one member, Peter, and the death of an
       older son. The author's theme seems to be "to show the
       world of reality taking its revenge upon this delicate
       and artificial bit of civilization," and to reveal the
       essential weakness of the Querrils' method of life. The
       novel shows equivalent weaknesses as literature.

307   Barbusse, Henri. *Light.* Translated by Fitzwater Wray.
          New York: E.P. Dutton & Co., 1919. 309p.; London:
          J.M. Dent & Sons, 1919. 308p. [*Clarté; Roman.* Paris:
          E. Flammarion, 1919. 290p.]

       An account of the experiences of a French worker, Simon
       Paulin, who has always attempted to conform to society's
       views in such matters as patriotism. Inducted and ordered
       onto the battlefield, Paulin is horrified by what he
       experiences and dismayed by the meaninglessness of the
       war he sees. Returned home from hospitalization and
       baffled by the delusions he recognizes among the civilians,
       Paulin spends his life isolated from them. Major themes
       are the delusion of patriotism, religion, and false moral-
       ity and the economic and territorial imperialism of the
       master classes.

308 Barton, George. *The Ambassador's Trunk*. Boston: Page Co., 1919. 310p.

A story of espionage, set in Washington, D.C., during World War I. The novel concerns the theft and recovery of an important state document relative to a Mexican-American contract giving the United States Army exclusive claim to Mexico's oil reserves.

309 Battersby, Henry Francis Prevost. *The Edge of Doom*. London & New York: John Lane Co., 1919. 350p.

The more interesting part of this novel is the second part, which deals with the war. The story takes place in England, East Africa, and at the front in France. Rumors of the death of Julian Abingdon, an official in central Africa, reaches his friends and family in London. His fiancée, Cyllene Moriston, in an effort to find the truth, insists on searching for him. His cousin, Jim Chayton, decides to take charge of her expedition even though he has never had any liking for Julian. When Cyllene becomes ill with fever, she stays with some German missionaries while Jim goes on to find out about Julian, who is discovered alive and even well but living with native women. Julian wishes to stay officially dead so he can remain in Africa. Jim does not tell Cyllene the truth and eventually marries her. The war now breaks out and he is sent to the front. In the meantime Julian turns up and once again meets Cyllene, but she now discovers that she no longer has any love for Julian and devotes herself exclusively to her husband still off in France.

310 Beach, Rex Ellingwood. *Too Fat to Fight*. New York: Harper & Brothers, 1919. 55p.

Norman and his friend Shipp decide to enlist in the army but when they are sent to the training camp at Plattsburgh, Norman, known to his friends as "Dimples," is turned down because he is far too fat to fight. However, "Dimples," with the "pull" of an influential friend manages to be sent as a Y.M.C.A. worker to France where he distinguishes himself in aiding and cheering the troops until he is caught in a gas attack and has his leg amputated. Shipp visits him in the hospital where he has lost much of his fat and cheers him on to his eventual recovery and the return to his former self. "Dimples" is a fat Falstaffian figure in this amusing but otherwise insignificant novel.

Adult Novels

311 Begbie, Harold. *Mr. Sterling Sticks it Out, a Novel*. London: Headly Bros., 1919. 324p. [Title in U.S.: *The Convictions of Christopher Sterling; a Novel*. New York: Robert M. McBride & Co., 1919. 267p.]

A novel about Quaker opposition to war. The story examines the differences of viewpoint about the war in four brothers of one family. Though largely a protest of the breach of faith of His Majesty's Government with the Quakers, and the cruel treatment of conscientious objectors in prison, the novel is also an examination of contrasting positions on patriotism and religion. The protagonist, Christopher Sterling, had settled in London's East End and become a Quaker, many years before the war. He vehemently resists the order to join the military, and instead makes speeches against conscription. He is ultimately imprisoned and dies from the incarceration.

312 Berger, Marcel. *A Life at Stake*. Translated from the French by Fitzwater Wray. New York: G.P. Putnam's Sons, 1919. 464p.

The hero, artist Jean Darboise, now a soldier, is bitter over the unfairness of his military superiors. From despair and possible suicide he is retrieved by a man whom he has accidentally wronged. The novel holds a brief for forgiveness. The reviewer for *Outlook* regarded the novel as "a war story which describes realistically and rather drearily the discomforts and unpleasing life of a French *poilu* who, after being wounded, is forced to serve in the 'auxiliaries.' The thing is well done, but hardly seems worth doing." Our reading does not alter this assessment.

313 Bertrand, Adrien. *The Call of the Soil*. Translated by J. Lewis May. London & New York: John Lane Co., 1919. 227p. [*L'Appel du Sol*. Paris: Calmann-Lévy, 1916. 302p.]

Traces a French regiment's first march and baptism under fire in the first battle of the Marne. Three comrades, Captain de Quéré, Lieutenant Lucien Fabre, and Sergeant (later Lieutenant) Vaissette, are the principal characters who, between battles, discuss what causes them to fight and willingly die. They conclude it is the "call of the soil." Ultimately only Vaissette survives, and it is he who summarizes what impels the soldiers to sacrifice: "But France lives on!" The novel provides a graphic picture of the early days of the war. (*The Call of the Soil* received the Goncourt prize for 1916.)

314 Black, Alexander. *The Great Desire*. New York: Harper & Brothers, 1919. 396p.

Primarily the story of Anson Grayl, an intelligent man of philosophic bent who tries to understand the "great desire" which he believes is "indwelling in the heart of humanity." His pursuit, if successful, is to be the subject of a book. The novel reviews conditions in the city of New York during wartime.

315 Blasco Ibáñez, Vicente. *Mare Nostrum (Our Sea), a Novel*. Translated from the Spanish by Charlotte Brewster Jordan. New York: E.P. Dutton & Co., 1919. 518p. [*Mare Nostrum*.... Valencia: Prometeo, 1916. 422p.]

Concerns the voyages of a Spanish sea captain, Ulysses Ferragut, persuaded by Frau Freya Talbert to work for the Germans, transporting oil to German submarines which have slipped into the Mediterranean. After the death of his son on a boat torpedoed by a German submarine, Captain Ferragut defects from his erstwhile German friends and seeks revenge, ultimately dying in this endeavor. The *Publishers Weekly* reviewer praised Ibáñez' ability to "achieve the impression of the impotence of human arrogance to escape the slow grinding of the almighty windmills."

316 Bond, Aimée. *A pair of Vagabonds*. London: Herbert Jenkins, 1919. 310p.

Not seen; NYPL.

317 Botsford, Charles Alexander. *Fighting with the U.S. Army*. Philadelphia: Penn. Pub. Co., 1919. 320p.

Presents conditions in the European theater of World War I. The book may be viewed as an instruction manual around which the story of two young Americans, Lieutenant Rodman Van Horne and Lieutenant Ralph Storm, is woven. Actual strategies and diagrams are presented, such as the plan for the destruction of the entrance to the canal linking Zeebrugge with Bruges, home bases for the German U-boats.

318 Bottome, Phyllis. *A Servant of Reality*. London: Hodder & Stoughton, 1919. 268p.; New York: Century Co., 1919. 454p.

A military surgeon, Captain Anthony Arden, is

incarcerated in a German prisoner camp. When released, as the eldest living son of his family, he has duties to the family, one of which is to marry. A frivolous girl, Kitty, appears on the scene, and Captain Arden succumbs to her. Kitty faces death from cancer, the doctor discovers, and he must decide between the choices of saving Kitty for a short while or letting her die mercifully. The author demonstrates considerable insight about the emotions and thoughts of a man just recently released from a prisoner-of-war camp.

319 Bower, B.M. (pseud.of Bertha Muzzy Sinclair). *The Thunder Bird*. Boston: Little, Brown & Co., 1919. 317p.

Johnny Jewel, a daredevil flyer who owns an airplane, has been rejected by the American aviation corps. While on a flight into Mexico for the International News Syndicate, he discovers a spy, delivers him to the American government, returns to Mexico for another spy, and then is accepted in the service and made second lieutenant.

320 Bowes, Joseph. *The Anzac War Trail with the Light Horse in Sinai*. London: H. Milford, 1919. 281p.

Not seen; NYPL.

321 Brown, Alice. *The Black Drop*. New York: The Macmillan Co., 1919. 392p.

Recounts the history of the American Tracy family during the war. Charles Tracy, a Boston journalist, is the black sheep. A comment near the end of the novel refers to Charles: "He had a black drop in his blood. God knows where he got it!" Initially Charles is merely neutral about America's concern with the war, but eventually the family discovers that Charles is a paid propagandist for Germany. The family is faced with the choice of exposing Charles or sharing his guilt. A typical American melodrama whose theme is the need to adopt a high moral tone.

322 Brown, Demetra (Vaka) and Kenneth. *In Pawn to a Throne*. New York: John Lane Co., 1919. 326p.

A love story between an American, Elihu Peabody, secretary to the Athens legation, and a Greek girl, Artemis Byzas. Intrigue in Greek political affairs abounds. Artemis, of a Greek royal family, and duty-bound against her will to marry a royal designate, discovers that Greece's royal family is betraying their country to the Germans. Elihu frustrates the plotters and changes Artemis' position from pawn to free agent in affairs of the heart. Reasonably accurate descriptions of Athens during the war.

* Buchan, John. *Adventures of Richard Hannay.* Boston: Houghton Mifflin Co., 1919.

Contains the author's three novels: *Thirty-nine Steps* (1915), *Greenmantle* (item 22), and *Mr. Standfast* (item 323). Only the last two are novels of the war. Refer to the separate annotations of these two works. (The first title is a collection of spy stories about the war.)

323 ———. *Mr. Standfast.* London: Hodder & Stoughton, 1919. 412p.; New York: George H. Doran Co., 1919. 374p.

The last and third volume of Buchan's Greenmantle series (see item 22). The main character, Mr. Standfast, is Peter Pienaar, who is assigned by the British intelligence service to uncover the masterminds of a group of German spies. Another character is Dick Hannay, who appeared in Buchan's *Thirty-nine Steps* and *Greenmantle*. Mr. Standfast and Hannay who has now become a brigadier general and has seen service at the Somme and other battles, frustrate the main German secret-service agent, who has been directing the German submarine offensive from the shores of England. The action areas of the novel include Scotland and Asia as well as the western front. The main German mastermind is apprehended, taken into the Allied trenches. There he is executed as a spy by being pushed over the top of a trench to be killed by the Germans firing from their trenches, who suspect that the German-language shouts for rescue are a ruse.

324 Campbell, R.W. *John Brown: Confession of a New Army Cadet.* London & Edinburgh: W. & R. Chambers, 1919. 260p.

Not seen.

325 Cannan, Gilbert. *Pink Roses.* London: T. Fisher Unwin, 1919. 284p.; New York: George H. Doran Co., 1919. 335p.

Trevor Mathew is a London clerk rejected for military service. He courts Cora, who wears artificial pink roses when they first meet, and she introduces him to her pink rose-bowered flat. Eventually Trevor meets a Ruth Hobday, whom he associates with "real" dew-petaled pink roses. Artificiality is replaced by reality. The novel is basically an account of the mind of English youth who have begun to think deeply about the war.

326 Chambers, Robert William. *In Secret*. New York: George H. Doran Co., 1919. 322p.

One of the main characters, Evelyn Erith, a censor for the United States government, hears about Kay McKay, who is wanted by the Germans because of his knowledge of a most important military secret. The two band together, go to Switzerland to obtain the remainder of Germany's "great secret." Switzerland swarms with enemy spies, but the two foil Germany's plan for conquest and strengthen their romantic interest in each other.

327 ———. *The Moonlit Way; a Novel*. New York: D. Appleton & Co., 1919. 412p.

This spy story, opening in pre-1914 Constantinople, shifts to Paris, then later to America, and involves many German and American agents operating in Europe during the war. The climax comes with the discovery that the Welland Canal is in danger of being dynamited.

328 Connor, Ralph (pseud. of Charles William Gordon). *The Sky Pilot in No Man's Land*. New York: George H. Doran Co., 1919. 349p.

The protagonist is a sincere and high-minded Canadian missionary preacher named Barry Dunbar who enlists in the Canadian army as a chaplain. The plot traces Dunbar's experiences through his military life, ranging from a mere "sky pilot" or minister to his battalion, to a strong and inspired spiritual leader and comrade. The personal relationships of Barry and Phyllis carry through the themes of spiritual growth, love, and comradeship. In terms of technique and plot the novel is very conventional, with huge doses of sentimentality sprinkled liberally throughout the story.

329 Cook, William Victor. *Grey Fish*. London: W. & R. Chambers, 1919. 303p.

Deals with the search for German submarines off the coast of Spain during the war. The grey fish of the title is taken from the Shetland Islands toast: "Health to man and death to the grey fish." The story consists of twelve connected episodes in which two of the characters are the main focus of interest. One is a young Scot who is ostensibly employed by an English wine-merchant firm with offices in a number of Spanish ports. The other is a Spanish middle-aged stevedore who is from the peasant class and once was a smuggler. Mainly a popular adventure story with shipwrecks, torpedoed boats, gasoline explosions, and featuring an Italian woman captain who rams U-boats, it has plenty of the usual German-spy activities and daring exploits.

330 Copplestone, Bennet (pseud. of Frederick Harcourt Kitchin). *The Last of the Grenvilles*. London: John Murray, 1919. 308p.

A curious adventure tale of naval activities during the war that presumably provides "a true and amusing picture of the British sailor in wartime." The story relates the life of Richard Grenville from his childhood until he enters the navy and experiences the war. The plot has the usual war romance as well as the activities of spies and their detection by the British. The hero is the elder Grenville, formerly a career man in the navy who loses his life in a sea battle against von Spee, the German commander. The description of this battle is one of the high points of the novel. The major theme seems to be the glory of English history and England's tradition as a maritime power. The plot is pedestrian.

331 Darlington, William Aubrey. *Alf's Button*. London: Herbert Jenkins, 1919. 320p.

The button in the title refers to the article on British soldier's undress coats or tunics. In this fanciful novel the metal used to make a particular button on a tunic was partly from Aladdin's lamp, melted down. A soldier, Private Alfred ("Alf") Higgins, while polishing his buttons, is suddenly unnerved by the appearance of the genie of Aladdin's lamp. Alf and his fellow soldier, Bill Grant, dub the genie "Eustace" and give him the most mundane orders and involve him in inconsequential projects. (One reviewer opined that Alf should have ordered the genie to stop the war.)

332 Dawson, Coningsby William. *The Test of Scarlet, A Romance of Reality.* New York: John Lane Co., 1919. 313p.

Concerns the last days of the war, presenting graphic scenes of Canadian artillery soldiers just before battle and during the engagement with the enemy. The novel consists of three parts: the indignity of not dying, the march to conquest, and "into the blue."

333 Dillon, Mary C. (Johnson). *The American.* New York: Century Co., 1919. 300p.

The novel's heroine, Helen Seymour, is a settlement worker. "Reddy" Paschal, a gang leader, and Ted Jarvis, a rich idler, fall in love with Helen. When both suitors enlist in the military service, Helen accompanies them as a nurse's aide. In battle Ted is wounded, and as "Reddy" maneuvers Ted to medical help, he is himself wounded. Helen nurses "Reddy" until his death from the wound and then becomes engaged to Jarvis. A typical popular novel.

334 Dorling, Henry Taprell (pseud.: Taffrail). *The Curtain of Steel.* New York: George H. Doran Co., 1919. 249p.

Not seen.

335 Dunbar, Ruth. *The Swallow: A Novel Based upon the Actual Experiences of One of the Survivors of the Famous Lafayette Escadrille.* New York: Boni & Liveright, 1919. 246p.

Upon the outbreak of war Richard Byrd impetuously leaves his home in Texas for England in order to enlist. Not permitted to join the English forces, he departs for Paris, where he is able to join a flying squad. Nicknamed "the Swallow," he is severely wounded, almost fatally, while fighting over Hill No. 304, but is nursed back to health in a French hospital by an English-speaking Red Cross nurse.

336 Ferraro, Agnese (pseud. of Mary Agnes Sullivan). *Private Angelo Ferraro, U.S.N.G.* Pittsburgh: Pittsburgh Printing Company, 1919. 176p.

Written mostly in the form of breezy letters from a young Italian American in the hospital corps of the American Army to his mother, who serves as the narrator and commentator. Nearly two-thirds of the book deals with the military training of Private Ferraro, beginning with his first day of service in New York City. The letters describe the famous "White Way" of the city, reaction to the presence of the soldiers, the attitude of people toward the war, and such topics as patriotism, war slackers, troop entertainments, and military training experiences. The last third of the book deals with the impressions of Private Ferraro about the French countryside, field hospital experiences, spy intrigues, and German prisoners of war. This book may well have had its origin in a series of letters actually written during the war and assembled by the author in the format of a novel.

337 Foote, Mary (Hallock). *The Ground-swell*. Boston: Houghton Mifflin Co., 1919. 283p.

A mother, wife of a retired army officer, recounts the wartime experiences of her children, one of whom dies a heroine's death in the war. Insignificant.

338 Frooks, Dorothy. *The American Heart*. Kansas City, Mo.: Burton Publishing Co., 1919. 218p.

Not seen; NYPL.

339 [Galsworthy, John]. *The Burning Spear: Being the Experiences of Mr. John Lavender in Time of War*. Recorded by A.R. P-M. London: Chatto & Windus, 1919. 248p.

Originally published anonymously during the last few months of the war and republished in this version with the acknowledgment of the author. Galsworthy has devised a comic little satire on the incredible propaganda used by the government and the press to arouse mass emotions in wartime. John Lavender, a kindly and peaceable old gent who is literally intoxicated by all the propaganda, asks for and receives a commission from the Propaganda Ministry to travel about the country to stimulate devotion and support for the great cause. Lavender is described by the author as a descendant of Don Quixote and Pickwick. Joe Petty, his associate, is dubbed Sancho Panza. Accompanied by Blink, an irrepressible sheep dog, Lavender soon earns his reputation as a harmless crank. All his speeches and adventures serve to satirize the home-front propaganda. A slight novel completely unlike Galsworthy's other, more serious, fiction.

340 Gambier, Kenyon (pseud. of Lorin Andrews Lathrop). *The White Horse and the Red-haired Girl.* New York: George H. Doran Co., 1919. 290p.

The time of this novel is 1914. A young, persistent English girl, Peggy Travers, single-handedly attempts to rescue her brother, wounded and in prison in Belgium. Her success, which constitutes the novel's plot, is recounted by one of the novel's characters in the following long catalog: "You went into Belgium with a suitcase in your hand and a small hope in your heart. You have come out with more loot than a German could snatch--a bag of diamonds, a dog, four children, a Belgian maidservant, a Belgian great lady, a sweetheart for your brother, an American citizen dressed as a German lieutenant, a Prussian officer who will be interned for all the war because he tried to murder a girl--and an airman, an American-French airman; a wonderman!"

341 George, Walter Lionel. *Blind Alley....* Boston: Little, Brown & Co., 1919. 431p.

The lengthy sub-title of this novel suggests the book's theme: "Being the picture of a very gallant gentleman; the adventures of his spirit in war and peace; the tale of his daughters, his son, their friends; of their loves and miseries; of the way of the world through the great war into the unexplored regions of peace--." The novel is an examination of a typical English upper-middle-class family during the war, particularly the war emotions of Sir Hugh Oakley, and of the sensualism that the war has induced in many women, particularly in Sir Hugh's daughter Monica, as if, one character puts it, "the war had pulled out some safety pin, and her emotions had begun to act beyond her government." England, and the rest of the world, are, in Sir Hugh's view, left in a blind alley.

342 Gibbs, George Fort. *The Black Stone.* New York: D. Appleton & Co., 1919. 358p.

The millionaire Alan Jessup, on a safari to Africa, has unknowingly transported a German spy, von Hengel, on his yacht. At Gibraltar von Hengel obtains the Kaaba, the sacred Black Stone of Mecca, and is going to use it to provoke an East African uprising when he leaves the ship. The rest of the plot concerns Jessup's search for von Hengel and his capture. The romance aspect of the novel involves Jessup and a girl called Constance, who is training to become a nurse. A melodramatic popular novel.

343 Glasgow, Ellen Anderson Gholson. *The Builders*. Garden City, N.Y.: Doubleday, Page & Co., 1919. 379p.

In this novel the old, traditional culture of Virginia and the demands of wartime America blend. This blending is "an earnest and patriotic effort to show to the South of today that it has now the best possible chance to become an active rather than a passive power in National life and National politics, and that the welding of this country through its war effort is one of the best results of the war." This view is expressed by David Blackburn, one of the chief characters, when he mails from France a long letter to Caroline Meade, after America has entered the war. A secondary theme is the study of the personality of a woman whose selfishness causes her to charm others in order to impose her will upon them.

344 Haines, Donal Hamilton. *The Dragon-flies: A Tale of the Flying Service*. Boston: Houghton Mifflin Co., 1919. 299p.

The story of a young American aviator, Dick Allen, and his friends, their training in the United States, and their daring escapades along the battlefront in Europe. The story tells of Allen's encounters with spies, both Allied and enemy, his attacks on German balloons and German transport lines, and of many engagements in the air with German aircraft.

345 Hamilton, Cicely Mary. *William--an Englishman*. London: Skeffington & Son, 1919. 250p.; New York: F.A. Stokes Co., 1919. 277p.

Relates what happened to a honeymoon couple who were caught in the fast-moving events of the first stages of the war. They are two ordinary middle-class people. William Tully, a London clerk, is an ignorant, conscientious, undersized but well-meaning man whose life before the war was mainly in "service." The social and revolutionary movements of the time led him to become a socialist and a pacifist. His wife Griselda was of a similar political persuasion and was active in the suffrage movement as well. Married in July of 1914, they travel to the forest of Ardennes in Belgium for their honeymoon. It is there that the full initial shock and fury of the war catch them unawares. They see the shooting of hostages by the Germans and are themselves beaten and abused. William is forced to work like a slave while Griselda is is considered a fortune of the war by the German troops. The novel is obviously somewhat of an after-the-fact propaganda piece that attempts to show the weakness of the socialist/pacifist ideology in the face of the ruthless terror of war. The novel is written in an earnest and realistic manner calculated to cause the appropriate emotions, at least in readers then.

346 Herbert, Alan Patrick. *The Secret Battle*. London: Methuen & Co., 1919. 243p.

The first half of the novel describes the campaign at Gallipoli. Harry Penrose is the protagonist whose moral energy enables him to reach the heights of heroism. All the same, he finally is overcome by his nerves to the point that his inner resources are all but exhausted. At first Harry views his experiences with romantic vision, but all too soon the flies, corruption, crushing weariness, and disease are all too apparent. However, in spite of his Gallipoli experience he enlists for France, where he is able to become a highly efficient scout officer. Eventually the terrible experiences he has undergone cause his final collapse into disgrace. He is court-martialed for cowardice in the face of the enemy and shot. The story provides considerable reflections on man and his nature during wartime.

347 Hill, Grace Livingston (Grace Livingston Hill Lutz). *The Red Signal*. New York: Grosset & Dunlap, 1919. 304p.

The heroine, Hilda Lessing, a hired girl on a truck farm, foils the schemes of German spies whose plans she overhears at the farm. Hilda's patriotism is responsible for other services to the United States government, and they eventually bring her the president's commendation. The love interest involves Hilda and Dan Stevens, a young engineer.

348 ———. *The Search*. Philadelphia: J.B. Lippincott Co., 1919. 317p.

A young American soldier, John Cameron, is involved in romance and religious experiences. A school chum, Ruth Macdonald, develops a more mature outlook on the war and life from her relationship with John. Young officers who are opportunistic and girls who are frivolous are loathsome to Ruth. John finds solace in the Y.M.C.A. and the Salvation Army. On the battlefield he also saves the life of an officer whom he detests, which makes him feel closer to God. Ruth becomes a nurse and arrives in France at the end.

349 Hogue, Oliver. *The Cameliers*. London: Andrew Melrose, 1919. 279p.

Not seen; NYPL.

350 Howard, Berthyl. *War's Rosary*. Kansas City: Burton Pub. Co., 1919.

Not seen.

351 Howard, Keble (pseud. of John Keble Bell). *The Peculiar Major; an Almost Incredible Story*. London: Hutchinson & Co., 1919. 246p.; New York: George H. Doran Co., 1919. 246p.

An amusing or somewhat comic fantasy about Major Aubrey Cloudsdale who is given a flashy ring by an old Turkish priest in Palestine. While alone in his camp one day the major decides to try on the ring and through a series of incredible adventures determines that the ring makes him invisible when he wears it. When the major tells his commanding officer about the mysterious ring, he orders the major to report forthwith to a London hospital. There the whimsical plot gets going. We see how the major gets arrested, how he makes history in the House of Lords, and how he has other marvelous adventures with the ring. One chapter relates how the major planned to settle the fate of the Kaiser. The book is a light-hearted farce of passing interest.

352 Huard, Frances (Wilson). *Lilies. White and Red*. New York: George H. Doran Co., 1919. 268p.

This book uses a collective title to cover two novelettes. The first, "Mademoiselle Prune," refers to a benevolent, old maid who exerts her generous and Christian spirit upon everyone she encounters. A seemingly respectable German officer is billeted in her home. She nurses him during an illness, and friends begin to despise her. Later, the German officer, torn between patriotism and duty, and morality, causes her death. The story provides a moving description of the humble and faithful old French woman. The second, "The Cockerel," refers to a 12-year-old orphan boy, Victor Lenoir, nicknamed Toto, who is abandoned by his foster parents. However, he becomes a war hero and receives the Croix de Guerre. The story emphasizes French steadfastness in suffering and sorrow.

353 Hughes, Rupert. *The Cup of Fury; a Novel of Cities and Shipyards*. New York: Harper & Brothers, 1919. 350p.

Describes America in the war through shipyard activity near Washington, D.C. The main character, Marie Louise Webling, an American citizen but the adopted daughter of a German couple who used her while all of them were in Germany to promote Germany's war aims, foils the plans of German spies in America. The love interest draws Marie and the owner of the shipyard together. A realistic portrait of the wartime atmosphere of Washington in an otherwise melodramatic popular novel.

354 Jenkin, A.M.N. *The End of a Dream*. London & New York: John Lane Co., 1919. 292p.

The major theme is shell shock and its terrible consequences. Arnold Cheyne, the protagonist, had been deeply in love with Nadina, a gorgeous dancer, before he went to war. When Nadina refused to marry him because she was not yet ready to abandon her career, Arnold rebounds into a loveless marriage with Sheila Maclaren. But under the effect of shell shock he no longer recognizes Sheila and believes Nadina is his wife. The hospital doctor advises Nadina to humor him in his hallucination. Arnold shortly escapes from the hospital and ends up in Cornwall with Nadina. When a man follows them, Arnold spots him and eventually murders the pursuer. Then when Arnold experiences a terrifying dream about the horrors of trench warfare, he kills Nadina. An amateurish and poorly constructed plot.

355 Jenkins, Herbert George. *John Dene of Toronto: A Comedy of Whitehall*. New York: George H. Doran Co., 1919. 322 p.

John Dene, Canadian millionaire and "inventor of the naval destroyer" has caused the elimination of all German U-boats by his invention. In this remarkable accomplishment Dene has been protected by Department "Z" of the British secret service. Suddenly two Denes appear on the scene, one of whom is eventually discovered to be Jim Dene, John's brother and double. The far-fetched plot is unfolded with some verve.

356 Jerome, Jerome Klapka. *All Roads Lead to Calvary*. London: Hutchinson & Co., 1919. 287p.; New York: Dodd, Mead & Co., 1919. 348p.

In this novel by the author of *The Passing of the Third Floor Back,* the outbreak of the war leads the altruistic Joan Allway, a journalist, to realize more fully that the world's hope lies in loving God. The novel presents a brief but sharp defense of the position of the conscientious objector. A popular novel of the time.

357 Johnston, William Andrew. *The Apartment Next Door*. Boston: Little, Brown & Co., 1919. 301p.

Jane Strong, a Riverside Drive society girl, and several United States secret service men apprehend several German spies in New York City. The love interest of the novel involves Jane and two of the American agents.

358 Kauffman, Reginald Wright. *Victorious: a Novel*. Indianapolis: Bobbs-Merrill Co., 1919. 407p.

Concerns America's part in the war between April 2, 1917, and the Armistice. The day-to-day routine of Pennsylvania villagers reveals the effect of the war upon people in the United States. The hero is Andy, a newspaper reporter who becomes a correspondent in France and dies on the battlefield.

359 Kelland, Clarence Budington. *The Highflyers*. New York: Harper & Brothers, 1919. 360p.

Potter Waite, son of one of the wealthiest Detroit automobile manufacturers, is a daredevil car driver. His female counterpart is Hildegarde von Essen, daughter of a wealthy German-American and an equally reckless driver. The two have an automobile accident. While Potter is in the hospital, America enters the war, and when he is released from the hospital, he joins the war effort. The plot becomes a collage of pro-German machinations. Love between Potter and Hildegarde triumphs over the complications and frustrations stemming from the war.

360 ———. *The Little Moment of Happiness*. New York: Harper & Brothers, 1919. 400p.

Captain Kendall Ware, an American on military duty in Paris, meets a French girl, Andrée, of rather free morality.

Kendall succumbs to her, then feels guilty, thinking of his mother's letters and of his American girl friend, Maude Knox, who is presently in Paris. A war story that compares French and American moral standards.

361 Kennedy, William Antony. *The Invader's Son*. New York: George Sully & Co., 1919. 387p.

The major theme is the social problem of the German-fathered children born in the German occupied regions. The rather complex plot suggests that France does not need to fear these children's future if the people of France care for their upbringing. About a third of the story occurs during and at the end of the war. The novel begins on the day before the scheduled wedding of a young couple in a small village in northern France. After the hurried wedding ceremony the new husband must immediately leave for the front. The Germans soon invade the village, and the new bride is raped by a German officer. About a year later the young husband slips behind the lines to his village only to discover his wife has a baby. He then secretly leaves (as he arrived) now believing his wife has been unfaithful. When the war is over he decides to leave France instead of going home, thinking his family will believe him dead. But the village doctor tells him the truth about the child, entreats his loyalty and compassion for his wife and the child, and convinces the husband to take the child for his own. The rest of the story proceeds to relate the subsequent life and prosperity of this family. The narrative tends to be rather crude at points, but the plot has a number of genuinely dramatic moments scattered throughout.

362 King, Basil. *The City of Comrades*. New York: Harper & Brothers, 1919. 405p.

While this novel deals only incidentally with World War I combat, it attributes the regeneration of a "down and out" club member to his wartime experience and concludes with his ardent recruiting of men for military service on the United States home front.

363 ———. *Going West*. New York: Harper & Brothers, 1919. 48p.

A love story involving an American boy, Charles Lester, who married, against the wishes of his parents who disapproved of the girl. Charles enters the service and is killed in the war. ("Going west" was a British term for dying in battle.) The novel describes how Charles, after his death, "communicated" with his wife, whom he persuaded to patch up the ill feeling between her and his parents.

364   Kreutz, Rudolf Jeremias. *Captain Zillner: A Human Document.* Translated by W.J. Alexander Worster. London: Hodder & Stoughton, 1919. 326p.

Simultaneously a picture of Austria as it attacks Russia in 1914 and the story of the development of the psyche of Zillmer, an impeccable soldier and officer. Zillner is aghast at the slothful, incompetent, contemptible Austrian general staff and the waste of military personnel which results. He learns that his sacrifice in the war is worse than useless; that war is not glorious but a "monstrous, criminal insanity." He is touched by the ordinary soldiers, the "simple ones: the common men, the last and the least of all: souls that do not count...." Hope is thinkable and possible for Zillner only with the coming of the children of a new generation, "the little saviours of the world...." The novel contains some brilliant front-line combat descriptions.

365   Kummer, Frederic Arnold (pseud.: Fredericks Arnold). *The Web: A Novel.* New York: Century Co., 1919. 280p.

The story of Bob Hoffman, an American spy of German descent in the British service, and how he brings to nought the scheming of the German Secret Service, thus insuring a naval victory for Britain. The publisher reported that the novel was founded on the actual work of the British Secret Service which resulted in the destruction of the German fleet off South America.

366   Laing, Janet. *The Man With the Lamp.* London: J.M. Dent & Sons, 1919. 287p.; New York: Dutton, 1919. 287p.

Concerns the relationship of people temperamentally akin though politically opposite. The novel is more or less a case study in the conflicting claims of patriotism and the artistic temperament. Martin Ascher, a German reared in England and a close friend of a James Carruthers, escapes near the English Rathness coast from a sinking U-boat on which he has been serving. The area is one in which he and James had rambled together years before. While searching for Carruthers, Ascher meets Andy Kinross, who is interested, like Ascher, in music, and they discover through much discussion that they are kindred souls. Although the novel is melodramatic, the climax is unexpected.

367 Lang, William. *A Sea-Lawyer's Log*. London: Methuen & Co., 1919. 257p.

Not seen; NYPL.

368 Lathrop, William Addison. *Love Time in Picardy*. New York: Britton Publishing Co., 1919. 347p.

The novel's foreword discloses that "It is the purpose of this story to show a small composite picture that shall, in a measure, typify a hundred thousand similar cases." The outbreak of the war breaks up the blossoming of love between a French boy and girl, Anatole and Yvonne, in Picardy, who are meant to symbolize all youth. Anatole goes into the army and Yvonne's grandfather, Père Gerome, is carried off to Germany as a prisoner. The novel represents an unsettling picture of German fiendishness and cruelty involving French and Belgian women.

369 Latzkó, Adolf Andreas. *The Judgment of Peace: A Novel*. Translated by Ludwig Lewisohn. New York: Boni & Liveright, 1919. 280p. [*Friedensgericht*. Zürich: Max Rascher Verlag, 1918. 278p.]

Qualifies more as a polemic against war than a novel. (The author has repeated the arguments already presented in his earlier collection of short stories entitled *Men in War*.) His thesis is that war is a game for diplomats. The hero is George Gadsky, a pianist who has enlisted and submitted to the arbitrary military discipline. George comes to feel "crushed, torn out of his real self, degraded to the level of a shabby, beaten sneak." The author describes the absurdities that the war and its monstrous demands have created in a bitter though brilliant exercise that dwells almost hopelessly on all of the disreputable aspects of mankind. It can well be compared with Barbusse's *Under Fire* (item 113).

370 Lewys, Georges (pseud. of Gladys Adelina Lewis). *The Charmed American: A Story of the Iron Division of France*. Translated by Georges Lewys. New York: John Lane Co., 1919. 328p.

Recounts the "horrible realities of war" at Verdun,

Ypres, Arras, the Somme, the Aisne, Maison de Champagne, and Lorraine. The narrator is François Xavier, a native of Alsace, who went to live in San Francisco after serving in the French military before the war. The war breaks out the day he is to be naturalized an American citizen, and he rejoins his earlier military unit, the Iron Division of France. For almost three years he fights, receiving the Croix de Guerre and becoming the only soldier in his company of 250 who survived. Since Xavier survived battle after battle, his French comrades believe "l'Américain" to possess a charmed life. (This book is one of several which the *National Union Catalog* and/or other bibliographic references labeled "personal narrative," "sketches" or "nonfiction," but which the New York Public Library later classified as fiction.)

371 Lynn, Escott. *Tommy of the Tanks*. London: W. & R. Chambers, 1919. 415p.

Describes the personal part played by Lieutenant Thomas Dacre ("Tommy"), his devoted aide Private Herring, and Sergeant Bull, a hard-headed veteran of the war. They are together in the tank "Glengarry" during the bloody campaigns of 1918. Details of the war are realistically described, such as the use of tanks to smash through barbed-wire entanglements and machine-gun nests. The book is similar to a diary in its minute detail and matter-of-fact style. The novel covers the Allies' final push against the Germans after their futile drive for Paris and the English Channel. The story is presented from the point of view of an actual English participant and tends to emphasize the role of the English troops in the 1918 campaign almost exclusively.

372 Lyons, Albert Michael Neil. *A London Lot*. London & New York: John Lane Co., 1919. 279p.

Based on *London Pride,* a play by Lyons and Gladys Unger, this novel is in large part a love story during the war involving Cuthbert Tunks, an English volunteer fighting in France, and Cherry Walters. Recuperating in an English hospital from a leg wound, Cuthbert discovers that Cherry is one of the ward maids. The novel ends with a happy reunion of the couple in their London neighborhood.

373 MacGrath, Harold. *The Private Wire to Washington, the Inside Story of the Great Long Island Spy Mystery that*

Baffled the Secret Service. New York: Harper & Brothers, 1919. 236p.

A swank residence on Long Island, where guests are assembled, serves as the setting for this novel which involves a German spy plot. The host's private telephone line to the nation's capitol is tapped, and one of the guests, Bob Winthrop, is suspected of being an important enemy agent. Ultimately Winthrop is revealed to have been helping the United States secret agents, and the actual enemy spies are apprehended and punished. The *Ladies' Home Journal* published this novel serially in 1918 and it exhibits the expected characteristics of such popular literature.

374 Mackenzie, Compton. *Sylvia and Michael: The Later Adventures of Sylvia Scarlett*. London: Martin Secker, Ltd., 1919. 504p.; New York: Harper & Brothers, 1919. 323p.

This novel is Book Three of the series on the character Sylvia Scarlett. This story describes the adventures of Sylvia in Russia, Serbia, Bulgaria, and Rumania during the war. Upon arriving in Russia, Sylvia experiences the war at first hand by surviving a bombardment. The two characters of the title meet only at the end of the story on the island of Samothrace. The novel disappointed readers then, and the passage of time has not altered this assessment.

375 Maher, Richard Aumerle. *The Hills of Desire*. New York: The Macmillan Co., 1919. 257p.

A young married couple traveling about in a gypsy wagon primarily to speed the husband's recovery from a lung condition, part company after a falling out. He enlists in the war and she becomes a Red Cross nurse. They are reunited, in person and emotionally, during an air raid on a hospital in which the husband is recuperating, when the wife drags him from the flames, saving his life.

376 Marshall, Archibald (pseud. of Arthur Hammond Marshall). *Sir Harry: A Love Story*. New York: Dodd, Mead & Co., 1919. 375p.

The setting is Royd Castle. The characters are the Brents, a family now having dwindled to only three persons, the sixteen-year-old Sir Harry, his mother, and his grandmother, Lady Brent. Lady Brent, as an exotic experiment, has kept her grandson in seclusion through half the war, carefully registering his emotional development in respect to the two subjects of love and war. Sir Harry becomes enamored of a girl, Viola, goes to war, and soon dies in action. Lady Brent's experiment is inconclusive, as is the novel.

377   Mason, Grace (Sartwell). *His Wife's Job*. New York: D. Appleton & Co., 1919. 238p.

The title refers to the position the wife, Anne, obtains with the organization employing her husband, Roger Henderson. A New York businessman, Roger has grown tired of the daily business routine and with his wife. In 1917 he leaves for Plattsburg for military training. After he goes to France, Anne opens a shop on Fifth Avenue in New York, called "The Shop of Precious Things." The shop is not a success, and when her wounded husband returns to America and later is sent back to France on a civilian assignment with the American Committee after the Armistice, Anne returns with him to work for the same organization. The novel ends with the couple's recognizing each other's abilities and appreciating each other far more than ever before. The *Woman's Home Companion* published this novel in installments.

378   ———. *The Shadow of Rosalie Byrnes*. New York: D. Appleton & Co., 1919. 235p.

Rosalie marries Lieutenant Gerald Cromwell after an acquaintance of less than a week. The husband leaves for duty in France after entrusting, by letter, his wife to his mother's care. Other family members keep the letter from the mother. Lieutenant Cromwell is wounded in his first battle, recovers after the Armistice has been declared, and returns home to America to discover the machinations of the members of his family who wish to have his marriage annulled.

379   Maurois, André (pseud. of Emile [Salomon Wilhelm] Herzog). *The Silence of Colonel Bramble*. Translated by Ronald Boswell (London edition) and Thurfrida Wake (New York edition). London & New York: John Lane Co., 1919. 207p. [*Les Silences du Colonel Bramble*. Paris: B. Grasset, 1918. 250p.]

A light-hearted, much of the time hilarious, picture of British officers at mess and at various staff and brigade

Adult Novels

headquarters in Poperinghe, Belgium, and at the front. The group described in the novel are a doctor, a chaplain, a French interpreter, and a colonel. Considered a bit risqué at times--or at least in 1919. A superb description of British, Scottish, and Irish speech by a Frenchman. During the war Maurois served as an interpreter with a Scottish division, and his character Aurelle is based on this experience. A minor effort of an important French writer.

380 Maxwell, William Babington. *A Man and His Lesson*. London: Hutchinson & Co., 1919. 256p. [Title in U.S.: *Glamour*. Indianapolis: Bobbs-Merrill Co., 1919. 306p.]

The hero of this tale is Bryan, a writer of popular plays. He finds himself jilted by his socially prominent girl friend, who decides she prefers a duke. Bryan then marries a fairly ordinary young woman and discovers he has made a happy and comfortable choice. However, his former girl friend now decides she wants him back, and his unfaithfulness so disturbs him that he considers suicide. The war begins and he decides to enlist and let the front accomplish what he planned to do himself. The story offers some very good battlefield descriptions, especially of the Somme battles. Otherwise, the novel traces Bryan's progress from selfishness to altruism which eventually becomes a war-weariness. The moralistic tone of the plot cannot provide the saving grace for this otherwise pedestrian effort.

381 McCarthy, Justin Huntly. *Nurse Benson*. London: Hurst & Blackett, 1919. 255p.; New York: John Lane Co., 1919. 336p.

Basically a love story with a war setting, this novel was based on a play by McCarthy and R.C. Carton. Impetuously eager to meet Captain Tibbenham, a holder of the Victoria Cross who has been invalided home, the spoiled Lady Gillian Dunsmore impersonates Nurse Benson who has been employed to care for the captain. The novel describes the many humorous situations which beset Lady Dunsmore.

382 McKenna, Stephen. *Sonia Married: A Novel*. London: Hutchinson & Co., 1919. 335p.; New York: George H. Doran Co., 1919. 370p.

Many of the characters in this melodramatic tale appeared in Stephen McKenna's *Sonia: Between Two Worlds* (item 161). The author considered the present novel to be an epilogue to the earlier one. In this story Sonia has married David O'Rane who was blinded in the war. The marriage collapses during the first year and Sonia falls in love with another man, whom she later leaves before ending up homeless and pregnant. O'Rane, however, finds Sonia and accepts her and the baby. Motherhood transforms Sonia, and her early marriage is revitalized. This banal melodrama is accompanied by a running commentary on the political situation in England and on the war, which reveals the prevalence of radical idealism that promises to transform the postwar world. Nonetheless, a horrendous melodramatic tale.

383   Montague, Margaret Prescott. *The Gift*. New York: E.P. Dutton & Co., 1919. 59p.

The story of a clergyman who, having lost his faith in God when his son died in France during World War I, rediscovers his faith when a woman, facing death, appeals to him for strength and inspiration. In helping her he regains his faith. Appeared originally in the *Atlantic Monthly* of March 1919. Basically a moralistic tract.

384   Morton, John Bingham. *The Barber of Putney*. London: Philip Allan, 1919. 334p.

About World War I from the point of view of men in the ranks. It is a story with a moral, extolling the simple virtues of the men who fight unquestioningly because of duty and honor. Tim Himrick leaves his wife and barber shop to enlist for the front but manages to survive and return home.

385   Nadaud, Marcel. *Birds of a Feather*. Translated from the French by Florence Converse. Garden City, N.Y.: Doubleday, Page & Co., 1919. 192p.

A further account of the experiences of Chignole, the happy-go-lucky, roguish youngster who grows serious through his war experiences in Nadaud's novel of the preceding year, *The Flying Poilu: A Story of Aerial Warfare* (item 264). The present novel comprises four sections and recounts Chignole's exploits in the air with three other aviators. The four sections of the novel appeared in the *Atlantic Monthly* between November 1918 and March 1919. (Nadaud was a French aviator, wounded three times in the war and demobilized.)

386 Oppenheim, Edward Phillips. *The Box with Broken Seals*. Boston: Little, Brown & Co., 1919. 300p.

Another spy story involving the war. An English detective, Crawshay, suspects another character, Jocelyn Thew, of transmitting propaganda documents to Germany. In their opposing efforts the two characters checkmate each other in a battle of wits.

387 Richmond, Grace Louise (Smith). *Red and Black*. Garden City, N.Y.: Doubleday, Page & Co., 1919. 381p.

"Red" is Dr. "Red Pepper" Burns, redheaded and possessing a "redheaded" temper. He is the physician who appears in several of the author's previous novels. "Black" is the minister of the community's principal church. "Black" courts the friendship of the reluctant "Red" and is eventually successful. The novel contains much about the war in England and in France, including information on entertainment in the American Expeditionary Force camps. Otherwise banal.

388 Rickard, Jessie Louisa (Moore). *The House of Courage*. London: Gerald Duckworth & Co., 1919. 375p.; New York: Dodd, Mead & Co., 1919. 394p.

Chiefly concerns women and their courage in time of war. One character, Hilda, decides to leave the quiet and pleasant life of her Irish country home and go to France to nurse her wounded husband. Another incident shows how a mother who is half French and half German had the courage to kill herself rather than permit her German soldier son to inform on the British fugitive whom she had hidden. In another story almost superhuman courage is demonstrated by a wife when she puts on a cheerful face and is misjudged as heartless when her husband is killed. Although the novel describes some of the circumstances of soldiers in wartime and the conditions in a German prison camp, the major emphasis is on how women reacted to the pressures and personal tragedies of wartime. This can be considered one of the first attempts in World War I fiction to describe some of the psychological effects of captivity in a German prison camp.

389 Rinehart, Mary (Roberts). *Dangerous Days*. New York: George H. Doran Co., 1919. 400p.

A novel of American wartime society between 1916 and 1918. The setting is supposedly the Midwest, and the characters are mostly the "fast, new-rich set." Clayton Spencer, strongly pro-Allies, manufactures munitions. Natalie, his wife, regards the war as simply a disturber of her comfort. The stereotyped German spy appears plotting to destroy Clayton's steel mill.

390 Robins, Elizabeth (pseud.: C.E. Raimond). *The Messenger: A Novel*. London: Hodder & Stoughton, 1919. 305p.; New York: Century Co., 1919. 426p.

The time is 1914. Greta von Schwarzenburg, a German woman spy, poses as a governess in the household of Sir William, an English government official. A young American girl, Nan Ellis, comes under the domination of the governess, but the innocence of the girl, free of guile, becomes a match for the spy. A romance involving Nan and two of Sir William's friends embellishes the plot to a very limited extent.

391 Roche, Arthur Somers. *The Eyes of the Blind*. New York: George H. Doran Co., 1919. 322p.

A detective mystery story, set immediately after America has entered the war. A newspaper owner, Stephen Gryce, is pro-German and anti-American. By the time he changes his position, a German spy ring is exposed and punished and Stephen has become a patriot of his country.

392 Roth, Amelia M.A. *An Heiress in Name Only; or, The Adventures of Gwendolyn*. Baltimore, Md.: Saulsbury Publishing Co., 1919. 106p.

Not seen; NYPL.

393 Ruck, Berta. *The Land-girl's Love Story*. London: Hodder & Stoughton, 1919. 344p.; New York: Dodd, Mead & Co., 1919. 353p.

Describes conditions in England which, because of the war, forced many English women to become "land-girls," the English term for "farmerettes." Two officers stationed near the girls' farms provide romantic relationships among the four characters. A melodramatic farce.

394 Rudolf, Robert de Montjoie. *The Wiltons in War Time*. London: Society for Promoting Christian Knowledge, 1919. 158p.

Not seen; NYPL.

Adult Novels

395 Sapper (pseud. of Herman Cyril McNeile). *Mufti*. New York: George H. Doran Co., 1919. 303p.

The setting is at the front and later in London. Derek Vane, on sick leave in London, questions the war's significance as he contemplates England's economic situation. Romance involves Derek and two women, Joan and Margaret Trent, the latter a nurse in France. From the review in the London *Spectator*: "The description of the bombing of a hospital in France is perhaps the most exciting thing in the book." An understatement.

396 Shanks, Edward Buxton. *The Old Indispensables, a Romance of Whitehall*. London: Martin Secker, Ltd., 1919. 255p.

A story that is either absurdly ridiculous or is a low-keyed satire of the stuffy prigs of English wartime officialdom. It seems that the Circumvention Branch of the Circumlocution Office has just outgrown its space and now must move elsewhere, but some functionary now suddenly discovers the prospects of hotels as a solution for their office-space dilemma. The novel relates with a quasi-flamboyant style the activities of the typical English bureaucracy: its loves, frustrations, and mundane concerns in wartime. The author has provided a list of the "dramatis personae." The novel is a curiosity of little interest and less importance.

397 Sinclair, Upton. *Jimmie Higgins: A Story*. New York: Boni & Liveright, 1919. 282p.

Socialism during the war, described through events in the life of Jimmie Higgins, who was a machinist and socialist worker in a small American town and served at Chateau-Thierry. The novel is an indictment of the army and tends to be a vehicle mainly for the author's socialist propagandizing.

398 Sleath, Frederick. *Sniper Jackson: A First Novel*. London: Herbert Jenkins, 1919. 303p.; Boston: Houghton Mifflin Co., 1919. 283p.

Depicts the life of a sharpshooter at the front, in the person of Lieutenant Ronald Jackson and other battalion members, such as "Cissie" Rankine, Big Bill Brown, and Old Dan Haggerty. Many aspects of a sniper's life are revealed, in no-man's-land, in the billets, and on leave. The novel presents a vivid description of winter in Flanders.

399 Snaith, John Collis. *Love Lane.* London: W. Collins Sons, 1919. 277p.

Tells the story of how the war affected an ordinary, at times vulgar, middle-class English family. Combat duty in the war served to rescue one member from obscurity and gave him a position of respect and honor. Much of this change was influenced by conversation with one of his buddies in the trenches. A disintegrating marriage began to be repaired when the couple took pride in the husband's war service. The novel also reveals how the wife's father mellowed under the influence of the war.

400 ―――――. *The Undefeated.* New York: D. Appleton & Co., 1919. 339p.

Wartime England is depicted through the part Blackhampton, the exact geographical center of England, played in the war and the changes war effected in the character of the people. Especially well drawn are the individuals Josiah Munt, magnate and mayor of Blackhampton, and William Hollis, his greengrocer son-in-law, who enlists and fights in the trenches.

401 Stern, Gladys Bronwyn. *Children of No Man's Land.* London: Gerald Duckworth & Co., 1919. 353p. [Title in U.S.: *Debatable Ground.* New York: Alfred A. Knopf, 1921. 402p.]

Another novel that uses its plot mainly as a device to present various ideas rather than any depth of characterization or literary accomplishment. The story is far too often marked by verbose and endless repetition of the same ideas or points. The story deals with a group of young women involved in the women's rights movement, as well as the Jew-without-a-country theme. Deborah Marcus is the chief protagonist, whose indulgent parents have given her a completely unrestricted opportunity to seek and find her own happiness. Ultimately, she marries a young, family-dominated Jewish boy who has long loved her. Her experimentation serves only to develop a reactionary influence in her personality. The effect of the war in England has created some disruption among the English Jewish families, which have one foot on English soil and the other, by and large, on German. This split is exemplified in Deborah's brother Richard when he discovers he was born in Germany during his mother's visit there and before his father became a naturalized English citizen. This situation helps to reveal the "enemy alien" hysteria so prevalent then in England and America.

402 Tarbell, Ida Minerva. *The Rising of the Tide; the Story of Sabinsport*. New York: The Macmillan Co., 1919. 277p.

An account of the history of the United States during the war, through the story of the fictional western town of Sabinsport. The events of the war help to imbue the town with patriotism and efficiency as a counter to the cruelty, arrogance, and ambition of the Germans.

403 Trent, Paul (pseud. of Edward Platt). *"Blue Peter": A Romance of the Navy in the Great War*. London: Odhams, 1919. 224p.

A naval spy story set in northern England during the war. It concerns Lieutenant Commander Peter Barr, captain of a destroyer which is sunk by a German submarine. His young officer, York Darley, is killed in action, but Darley's sister Janet impersonates her brother and provides the Admiralty with incriminating evidence against another officer, Guy Loder, with German connections, as well as against a beautiful young actress, Lucie Mair, also of German background. Guy and Lucie, whom Janet incriminates, try to escape in a submarine but are lost as the sub is captured under fire.

404 ———. *A Naval Adventuress; a Story of the British Navy in the Great War*. London: Ward, Lock & Co., 1919. 308p.

Not seen.

405 Ulrich, Charles Kenmore. *Fires of Faith: The Romance of a Salvation Army Lassie*. New York: Grosset & Dunlap, 1919. 270p.

Tells the story of the Salvation Army at work in the bowery of New York City and on the battlefields of Europe during World War I. The novel is illustrated with scenes from the photoplay produced by the Players-Lasky Corporation.

406 Valentine, Douglas (pseud. of Valentine Williams). *Okewood of the Secret Service*. New York: Robert M. McBride & Co., 1919. 374p.

The main character is the British army's Major Desmond Okewood, who appears in at least one other book by the author. Purposely having his death at the front publicized, the major disguises himself as Basil Bellward, one of Germany's top spy officials, and involves himself in action and about London. The enemy is Captain Maurice Strangwise, also in disguise. Major Okewood manages ultimately to destroy the Prussian spy organization.

407 ———. *The Secret Hand: Some Further Adventures by Desmond Okewood of the British Secret Service*. London: Herbert Jenkins, 1919. 320p.

A mystery novel concerning the murder of an aging vaudevillian actor who surprises foreign agents attempting to obtain the Star of Poland, a jewel from the Polish coronation sword. Major Desmond Okewood, on leave from the Western front, becomes involved when the chief of the British secret service sends for him after the murder and informs him that he is the only man who can handle the case, which has international scope, involving German and Polish espionage.

408 Van Dyke, Henry. *The Broken Soldier and the Maid of France*. New York: Harper & Brothers, 1919. 65p.

Relates the unusual experience of a young French soldier, Pierre Duval, who, after fighting in the battles of the Marne, the Aisne, and Verdun, and after being decorated with the Croix de Guerre, receives a month's leave to return to his farm and his wife. On the way home, toying with the idea of deserting in order to avoid the battleground, he encounters the reincarnation of Jeanne d'Arc in a French forest, which persuades him to return to battle and, consequently, to his death. First appeared in *Harper's Magazine* (December 1918).

409 Van Zandt, Earl Christian. *Yank--The Crusader*. Denver: W.C. Erickson, 1919. 245p.

Follows the fortunes of two idealistic and Christian young recruits as they grow up. Fred Sheldon on a ranch in Oklahoma, and Christy Strong in Denver, are recruited into the American Army where they meet and become fast friends in Y.M.C.A. work. The story follows them to the battlefields of Europe where they continue to carry the word of God to their companions.

410 Vassili, Paul (pseud. of Catherine Radziwill). *The Firebrand of Bolshevism, the True Story....* Boston: Small, Maynard & Co., 1919. 293p.

Captain Rustenberg, a German spy, travels extensively in Russia in the line of duty, both before and after the czar's fall. Soon he defects, disgusted by the dishonest methods of the men whom he considered to be honest. The Russian anarchists appear to be financially supported by Germany and greatly responsible for the Brest-Litovsk treaty. The author asserts that the basis of much of the captain's experience with bribery and corruption is based on fact.

411 Warner, William Henry, and De Witte Kaplan. *Mothers of Men.* New York: T. Scott, 1919. 317p.

An Austrian girl becomes a victim and the mistress of an Austrian army officer. She escapes from him to Paris, marries a French soldier, and, later in the war again meets the Austrian, whom she discovers to be a spy. While trying to defend herself from him, he is killed. Proverbial sayings and moralizing appear throughout the novel.

412 Witwer, Harry Charles. *"A Smile a Minute."* Boston: Small, Maynard & Co., 1919. 378p.

Not seen; NYPL.

413 Yver, Collette (pseud. of Antoinette [de Bergevin] Huzard). *Mirabelle of Pampeluna.* New York: Charles Scribner's Sons, 1919. 177p. [*Mirabelle de Pampelune.* Paris: Calmann-Lévy, 1917. 314p.]

When Louise, a young French girl, reads the story of Mirabelle of Pampeluna, it becomes for her an accompaniment or a "running parallel" to the news from the war front. The love story aspect of Mirabelle's romance becomes an analogy for the romantic involvement of Louise with Henri and her marriage to him, before he goes to war and is blinded. Medieval chivalry and gallantry are revived in twentieth-century terms.

1920

414 Baxter, Arthur Beverley. *The Parts Men Play.* London: W. & R. Chambers, 1920. 444p.; New York: D. Appleton & Co., 1920. 331p.

The major theme is the rigidity and uselessness of the English aristocracy. The plot deals with an American writer, Austin Selwyn, who has the opportunity to meet the family of Lord Durwent. The daughter, Elise Durwent, possesses a colorful personality and shares Austin's feelings about the uselessness of her class. He soon begins to fall in love with her. When the war breaks out, Austin perceives it as a terrible mistake in which all the people of the West have been trapped by their ignorance. He soon starts a crusade against the war and writes pacifist literature, which causes a break between himself and Elise. She glories in and supports the war effort. Of course, Austin is gradually convinced of his mistaken ideas, ends up in France at the front, and wins Elise.

415 Bazin, René François Nicolas Marie. *Pierre & Joseph.* Translated by Frank Hunter Potter. New York: Harper & Brothers, 1920. 436p.

Concerns a small village in Alsace-Lorraine at the start of the war. Although all of the residents are German subjects, they have still remained completely French. Joseph, the younger of two brothers, decides to flee to France and enlist in the French army. Pierre, the older, decides it would be better for him to enlist in his German regiment in order to protect the family factory and estate from confiscation by the Germans. Joseph is sent to the eastern front and develops an increasing hatred for the German side. Later when he is sent to the western front and is required to kill French soldiers, he instead kills his superior officer and then deserts to the French army. One of the more interesting efforts to oppose the German invaders is the description of opening the sea sluices around Nieuport in order to flood the land. The narrative covers this and other such events of the war in a serious and convincing fashion characteristic of the better historical fiction of the war.

416 Bowes, Joseph. *The Aussie Crusaders With Allenby in Palestine.* London: H. Milford, 1920. 270p.

Not seen; NYPL.

417 Bunker, Annie Crosby. *Crowning an Ideal, a Story of the World War.* Boston: Christopher Publishing House, 1920. 95p.

Not seen; NYPL.

418 Dorgelés, Roland [Adopted name of Rolland Maurice Lecavele]. *Wooden Crosses.* London: Wm. Heinemann, 1920. 295p. [*Les Croix de Bois.* Paris: A. Michel, 1919. 319p.]

This story is similar to Barbusse's *Under Fire.* It is

the tale of a squad whose activities are portrayed with
almost photographic realism that vividly shows the powerful reality of what Malcolm Cowley called "mud and brutality." The book is in the form of the reminiscences of
a young and pampered Frenchman, Gilbert Demachy. The
story attempts to reveal the spirit of sportsmanship, the
light-hearted laughter in the face of hardship, and other
such efforts geared to prevent breaking under the strain
of the brutal conditions of the front. Gilbert is an
example of the casual way in which many of the squad take
upon themselves every burden and difficulty. Indeed, when
Gilbert is eventually fatally wounded, he dies with "a
song on his lips." The author wrote this novel in 1916
but the French censor refused its publication until after
the Armistice in 1918.

419 Dos Passos, John Roderigo, Jr. *One Man's Initiation--
     1917.* [*A Tale of the European War*]. London: George
     Allen & Unwin, 1920. 128p. [Republished in 1945 as
     First Encounter.]

The protagonist is Martin Howe who has enlisted in the
ambulance corps. He is overjoyed to be on the ship that
is taking him to France and feels he has turned a new
leaf in his life. Some of his experiences with their
psychological reactions are related in a series of dis-
connected scenes. They turn out to be drab pictures of
disillusionment with the war and of everything the conflict represents--the artificial hatreds and the insanity
of the battlefields. Martin is pictured as someone who
is struggling to save himself from a spiritual death by
developing a vision of a better way. This is Dos Passos'
first novel and exhibits most if not all of the faults of
a first effort--fragmentary, ill-formed, and awkwardly
written. The preface to the retitled reissue attempts to
contrast the attitudes of the generations who fought in
both world wars. The novel is now only of historical
interest.

420 Frankau, Gilbert. *Peter Jackson, a Cigar Merchant: Ro-
     mance of Married Life.* London: Hutchinson & Co., 1920.
     399p. [Title in U.S.: *Peter Jameson: A Modern Romance.*
     New York: Alfred A. Knopf, 1920. 431p.]

When we first meet the protagonist, Peter Jameson, he
is a business man, married and with two small daughters,
who is pictured as successful in every way and satisfied
with his circumstances. At first the beginning of the
war does not especially stir him, although within the

first three months he finds himself thrust into the midst
of the conflict. The story from this point on follows
his activities and experiences at the front, which are
interspersed with his homecomings to see his wife. Intermixed with many vivid battle descriptions is "a lively
criticism of our military authorities and ... a vivid impression of the Battle of Loos." Peter is twice wounded
and is finally sent home with shell shock from which, with
his wife's care and understanding, he recovers. This new
dimension in their relationship deepens their love to a
maturity far beyond their prewar relationship. The story
concludes with the Armistice.

421   Gibbs, George Fort. *The Splendid Outcast*. New York:
      D. Appleton & Co., 1920. 352p.

Jim Horton, an American, encounters his brother, Harry,
an army officer, whom he has not seen or heard from for
nearly five years. Harry is the family's coward and black
sheep. Jim discovers his brother hiding behind the lines,
avoiding his major's orders, paralyzed by fright. The
brothers agree to exchange uniforms and "dog-tags," and
have Jim carry out the orders. This he does, so well that
he earns the Croix de Guerre, for his brother. Seriously
wounded and reviving in a hospital, Jim discovers that no
one believes the bizarre incident, so that he plays out
the ruse. Jim discovers in the letters in Harry's pockets
that his brother is married to a beautiful girl, Moira,
who is involved in a blackmail scheme. The novels' characters are wooden creations; the plot is poor, contrived,
unconvincing, and most improbable.

422   Gibbs, Philip Hamilton. *Wounded Souls*. New York: George
      H. Doran Co., 1920. 320p.

This book might well be considered a collection of the
author's war experiences with which he has constructed a
rather thin plot for fictional purposes. Wickham Brand
marries a German girl "as proclamation to the world" that
he affirms the brotherhood of all people in spite of the
war. He is disgusted and upset when his friends cold-
shoulder him. His family and relatives in England refuse
to accept his wife when he takes her there after the war.
She soon dies and he eventually will probably marry Eileen
O'Connor. Enough of the plot. The most interesting and
valuable portion of the novel is not the plot but rather
the detailed and vivid view of the effect of the German
occupation on civilian life and attitudes. The most

interesting sections deal with the entrance of the English into Lille, shortly after the Armistice. The people swarm out of their houses to celebrate the return of the Allies and the departure of the hated Germans. There are descriptions of what happened to the French women who fraternized with the German troops and activities of the French underground. The author manages to describe not only the German treatment of civilians in their occupied lands but also the attitudes, experiences, and anti-German activities of the civilian populations. One of the more fascinating scenes deals with the return of the German soldiers to their homeland and what the author refers to as the "boot-licking" welcome given by the German population to their defeated armies. Armistice night with its celebrations and tragic memories is vividly described.

423 Hays, Harold Melvin. *Blighty*. New York: Communal Printing Co., 1920. 19p.

Not seen; NYPL.

424 Imbrie, Walter McLaren. *Legends*. Glennie, Michigan: Midland Press, 1920. 55p.

Not seen.

425 Inchbold, A. Cunnick. *Love and the Crescent: A Tale of the Near East*. New York: F.A. Stokes Co., 1920. 316p.

Set in Armenia during the war, this novel recounts the horrifying tribulations of Veronica, daughter of an Armenian physician, and her family, as they escape to France. Other characters are a motley group of Russian, French, Greek, Turkish, Arab, and Bedouin nationals.

426 Jepson, Edgar. *Pollyooly Dances*. New York: Duffield & Co., 1920. 266p.

The young heroine is a successful dancer on her way to New York when the story begins. Her guardian, the Honorable John Ruffin, is also on the same boat but traveling on different business. Because he has successfully avoided military service, he is scorned by all the patriotic English on the ship. Secretly, he is in the service of the government and on a special mission concerning German spies. The plot turns out to be involved primarily with German spy plots rather than dancing or Pollyooly. This is a mediocre detective war mystery.

427 Kelly, Thomas Howard. *What Outfit Buddy?* New York: Harper & Brothers, 1920. 211p.

   A tale about Jimmy McGee and his buddy, O.D. Front-line fighting involves Jimmy and more or less represents the American soldier's role in France. O.D. is killed and Jimmy must break this sad news to O.D.'s mother and Mary, his girl.

428 Kubinyi, Victor von. *Mr. Man.* New York: Weidner Printing and Publishing, 1920. 160p.

   Not seen; NYPL.

429 Locke, William John. *The House of Baltazar.* London & New York: John Lane Co., 1920. 311p.

   The action begins at Churton Towers, once the country seat of a great family, and now a convalescent hospital for British officers. The main character, John Baltazar, a mathematician who has lived in China for eighteen years, is now living in England. Cut off from the day-to-day affairs of the world, Baltazar is unaware even that a war is in progress. The war makes its impression upon him when some German bombs from a zeppelin land on his home and destroy his research materials. He now offers himself for service in political activity. For the benefit of his son's career as an officer in the war--his son had lost a foot, and received the Military Cross--Baltazar makes a sacrifice which forces him to return to China.

430 Lynn, Escott. *Lads of the Lothians: With the Royal Scots in Gallipoli.* London: W. & R. Chambers, 1920. 381p.

   Describes the siege of Gallipoli by the British Mediterranean Expeditionary Force and a French force. The siege lasts more than eight months with heavy casualties, and the campaign ends in retreat. The story concerns the courageous exploits of several men of the Royal Scottish Guards. The author notes that he "has freely drawn" on Lieutenant-Colonel A.H. Mure's book, *With the Incomparable 29th*, "in depicting many of the scenes."

431 Mason, Alfred Edward Woodley. *The Summons.* New York: George H. Doran Co., 1920. 308p.

   Contains a mishmash of subplots which qualifies it as a melodramatic quasi-detective story. It is based on the experiences of the author in such places as England, Spain and Egypt. Harry Luttrell, the protagonist, has a strong sense of honor and self-discipline which impells him to join the army. He must leave his sweetheart Stella when he accepts a post in Egypt. His friend, Martin, becomes a secret service agent in Spain. When Harry comes home on leave he discovers he no longer cares for Stella. At the same time he meets and falls in love with Joan Whitworth. Stella in despair soon commits suicide under conditions that cause Joan to be suspected, but all comes out well when Martin clears up the confusion. The war assumes an increasingly less significant role as this nondescript novel proceeds on its prosaic way.

432 Montague, Margaret Prescott. *England to America*. Garden City, N.Y.: Doubleday & Co., 1920. 56p.

A story about an American soldier on leave who visits his English buddy's family. He is puzzled over their peculiar reserve during his visit and does not learn until the last day that they had heard just before his arrival of the death of his friend. The story first appeared in the *Atlantic Monthly* of September 1919 and received the O. Henry Memorial Prize for 1919.

433 ———. *Uncle Sam of Freedom Ridge*. Garden City, N.Y.: Doubleday, Page & Co., 1920. 60p.

Recounts as a parable the story of the patriotism of an old man, nicknamed Uncle Sam because of his physical similarity to the national figure. His patriotism carries him through his sorrow over the death of an only son in France. Pained when the United States Senate failed to ratify the League of Nations plan and his country was disgraced and dishonored before the world, he commits suicide as reparation for his country's shame. Appeared in the *Atlantic Monthly* (June 1920). President Wilson in an interview recommended that this story be read by all Americans.

434 Nylen, Irene. *Man's Highest Duty, a Story and a Message*. New York: A.L. Schmoeger, 1920. 127p.

Not seen.

435 O'Donovan, Gerald. *How They Did It*. London: Methuen & Co., 1920. 304p.

The pronoun "they" in the title refers to the civilians on the home front during the war. The novel satirizes the British Government, especially the Ministry of Munitions at Whitehall.

436 Oppenheim, Edward Phillips. *The Devil's Paw, A Novel.* Boston: Little, Brown & Co., 1920. 295p.

Oppenheim was one of the more popular mystery-adventure novelists of his day. This tends to be a typical and average example of his type of adventure story. The heroine, Miss Catherine Abbeway, half-Russian and half-English, is an aristocrat whose sympathies are entirely with the workers and the oppressed. She belongs to a secret labor council whose aim is to bring about an early peace with the Central Powers. All but two on the council are upright and honest people; these two are secretly in the pay of Germany. Catherine at great risk intercepts the messages from the two socialists on the council. She is discovered by Julian Orden, the son of a peer, but he decides to protect her effort by claiming her as his fiancée. It turns out that she saves England and the Allies from disaster, and true love now blooms with Julian.

437 ———. *The Great Impersonation.* London: Hodder & Stoughton, 1920. 318p.; Boston: Little, Brown & Co., 1920. 322p.

An improbable impersonation mystery is more the subject of this novel than is the war. Sir Everard Dommey is the real hero after an incredible character change and exchange with Baron Leopold von Ragastein, the perfect model of German fitness and efficiency as well as the physical double of Sir Everard. The plot begins shortly before the war in the German colony in East Africa where these two men meet. Von Ragastein is involved in a secret mission to England for the German government. When the war begins, he enlists in a Norfolk regiment. At the end the reader discovers that Sir Everard is not quite the drunken bounder he at first appeared to be in Africa. The remarkable character change and alteration of identities makes for a surprise denouement that is unconvincing.

438 Poole, Ernest. *Blind; A Story of These Times.* New York: The Macmillan Co., 1920. 416p.

The basic theme is that the blindness of the narrator is no different from that of the leaders of the world who permit the insanity of war to occur. This sketchy story tends to be more of a tract than fiction. Larry Hart, the narrator, describes his happy childhood and college years in New England. After college he goes to New York as a newspaper man and lives with a doctor friend in the slums. He becomes interested in reform movements, mixes with radicals, writes plays, and goes to Berlin in 1914 as a correspondent and later to Russia. When the U.S. enters the war, he enlists and is eventually blinded at the front. The closing chapters are mainly the observations of the author on America's part in the war.

439 Poore, Ida Margaret (Graves). *Rachel Fitzpatrick*. London: John Lane Co., 1920. 312p.

A run-of-the-mill novel that tends to use the war mainly as a vehicle to create a story for the heroine of the title. Rachel is an Irish girl who, after spending two years with wealthy relatives in London, is sent to Germany for her education. After the start of the war her aunt's German husband takes advantage of her isolated situation to make love to her. She runs away and eventually manages to reach Ireland. The novel touches upon the course of the war and the Irish attitudes and problems of that time.

440 Robinson, Eliot Harlow. *The Maid of Mirabelle, a Romance of Lorraine*. Boston: Page Co., 1920. 304p.

A sentimental novel of the final days of the war and the immediate postwar period. The story occurs in a small village in Lorraine. Daniel Steele, an American who has come to do war-relief work, soon falls for Joan le Jeune. For a while she makes Daniel forget his promise to marry Faith, the girl back home. Indeed, Joan forgets her own boy friend, Jean, in this brief infatuation, but by the end of the novel both return to their original relationships and all is well. A melodramatic tale of Lorraine in wartime with the focus almost exclusively on the boy-meets-girl situation.

441 Schem, Lida Clara (pseud.: Margaret Blake). *The Hyphen*. New York: E.P. Dutton & Co., 1920. 1052p.

A curious novel of extreme length. It seems to be more of a prolonged essay than fiction, for it really is an analysis of the basic character and state of mind of the German population in the United States, especially as they appear to an author of non-English background. The hero is the son of a nihilist Russian princess and a Prussian-American father, who represents a synthesis of these backgrounds. He is raised in the German ethnic community of Hoboken (called Anasquoit in the book). The son aspires to become an authentic American. The war especially

disillusions him about Germany and he decides that the
only way out for those like himself of German blood and
heritage is to enlist and fight the Huns. A prolix and
thoroughly prosaic novel of little or no artistry.

442   Sinclair, May. *The Romantic*. London: W. Collins Sons,
      1920. 249p.; New York: The Macmillan Co., 1920. 203p.

Set in the first few weeks of the war, this is a psychological study of cowardice. Charlotte Redhead has just
broken off her love affair with Gibson Herbert, her boss.
She is now attracted to John Conway who appears to be a
clean and upright man of strength. They work together as
farm laborers but in a strictly platonic relationship.
After the start of the war they join the ambulance corps.
Under the threat and experience of danger, Charlotte sees
John go to pieces. Under this tension and strain he also
develops a streak of cruel behavior. Charlotte is able to
accept the truth only gradually. After he has been killed,
a psychiatrist gives her the probable explanation of John's
weakness, and she is able to understand and forgive John.

443   Sleath, Frederick. *The Seventh Vial*. London: Herbert
      Jenkins, 1920. 312p.

Describes the adventures of a British flyer during the
war and covers the usual flying experiences against the
German aviators. A rehash of countless other similar war-
story descriptions.

444   [Sturgis, Granville Forbes]. *Mildmay Park; Episodes of
      a Doughboy in a London Hospital*, by My Sergeant.
      Boston: Richard G. Badger, 1920. 149p.

Mildmay Park is a very lovely park in suburban London
that is considered an ideal spot for romantic meetings;
a park made for love according to the author. But now in
wartime it tends to be filled also with many soldiers,
many of whom have been wounded at the front and are home
in London on hospital leave. The story begins with the
meeting of a young wounded soldier of eighteen and a pretty
young English woman in the park. He is from the Lake Washington area of Washington State. The novel is a series
of his experiences in London as he recuperates at one of
the military hospitals. The novel paints a fairly graphic
and sensitive portrait of wartime London from the perspective of a young American soldier. An interesting view of
the social life available to a young and lonely American
G.I. in London during World War I. Written with some style

445 Vane, George. *The Waters of Strife*. London: John Lane Co., 1920. 287p.

The activities and heroism of an American boy and girl of Belgian descent are the central focus. The story begins in prewar England with a taste of the intrigues of a German count who is exiled to England, and the bulk of the novel describes the ruthlessness of the Germans in Belgium. *The New York Times* reviewer remarked, "The book is very badly constructed and the character drawing amateurish, but the account of Aline's experiences in Belgium is interesting and occasionally dramatic." This assessment is far more kind than the novel deserves.

446 Watson, Frederick. *Pandora's Young Men*. London: W. Collins Sons, 1920. 291p.

A comic satire directed at the British Government during the war. Decidedly inferior to the efforts of Edward Shanks (item 396) and Rose Macaulay (item 86) who have dealt with the same subject.

1921

447 Borden, Mary. *The Tortoise, A Novel*. New York: Alfred A. Knopf, 1921. 280p.

An emotional love story that will outdo all but the most banal and melodramatic soap operas of radio or television. Helen Chudd is a beautiful and extremely proud creature. Her husband is an Englishman of distinction, character, and considerable strength who, however, lacks finesse and tends not to be demonstrative in his great love for her. Indeed, it is a peculiar relationship for he has not yet, as the author so quaintly phrases it, possessed her. And so he knows he has more or less taken his chances on permanently keeping her. As the story commences, it is apparent that he will lose her to a charming French fellow who, of course, has all the supposed attributes that the poor husband so sadly lacks. The husband seizes the coming of the war as a way of easing his loss of her and goes to the front. Ironically, she also goes to the front as a nurse after the suave Frenchman ultimately fails her. Thus, in their respective disillusionments the couple give their utmost to the war effort. At the end of the war, however, they "find" and appreciate each other with maturity that could only have been tempered by the noble conflict.

448 Botsford, Charles Alexander. *At the Front*. Philadelphia: Penn. Pub. Co., 1921. 304p.

    Not seen.

449 Burr, Anna Robeson (Brown). *The House on Charles Street*. New York: Duffield & Co., 1921. 283p.

    Two young American women on a holiday trip in Europe are stranded in France near Mount Blanc at the outbreak of the war. They manage to travel to Geneva where eventually they secure railroad passage to London via Paris. They meet an Englishwoman, Miss Violand, who is also going to London. Elizabeth returns to the U.S. but the other girl, Sydney, decides to remain in London and help out in the war effort. At first she is a volunteer typist at a small hospital but eventually becomes the personal secretary to Sir Thomas Easterly, M.P. This position places her in a unique position to observe the nature of English society at the highest levels and especially the operation of the government during the years 1914-1917. Her friend Elizabeth returns to London as an American volunteer to France in 1917. The novel concludes with Sydney cheering the U.S. troops as they enter London upon the official entrance of America into the war. This is an interesting story of how the English see an American servicewoman and how their social structure begins to undergo some long-term changes as a result of the wartime pressures. The action takes place mainly in London.

450 Cannan, Gilbert. *Pugs and Peacocks*. London: Hutchinson & Co., 1921. 288p.

    Pugs and Peacocks (the title symbolizes upper-class life) deals with the upheaval caused by the war in the life of a middle-aged Cambridge professor who, desiring only to stand apart from the war-caused madness, is engulfed by it and eventually imprisoned, not for his participation in the conscientious objectors' movement he espouses, but for his letter to a German colleague clandestinely sent to avoid the censor during the war. The novel's action occurs largely in a country house located between Newmarket and Cambridge.

451 Dawson, Francis Warrington. *The Gift of Paul Clermont*. London: Wm. Heinemann, 1921. 332p.; Garden City, N.Y.: Doubleday, Page & Co., 1921. 332p.

    Paul represents the spirit of France and is a symbol of

the thousands of talented young men who fought the great
war to the bitter end. Paul's friendship for an American
buddy symbolizes the relations between the two countries.
The story begins with a description of Paul's life, beginning with his poverty-stricken childhood in a small drab
French village before the war. When war finally comes,
we observe his struggles with his emotions, his experiences at the front, his prison life, his stay in the hospital, and his eventual death on the battlefield. (Republished in 1928 with a long introduction under the title
Paul Clermont's Story and My Own, followed by *The Gift of
Paul Clermont.*)

452 Dos Passos, John Roderigo, Jr. *Three Soldiers.* New York:
George H. Doran Co., 1921. 433p.

One of the more significant novels of any war. The
story is a devastating indictment of militarism. The plot
deals with three young men of very different personality,
mentality, and social background and begins with their
basic training experiences in the U.S. John Andrews, a
Harvard graduate and aspiring musician, tends to be the
chief protagonist and his story concludes the book. From
the beginning of his military experience John resents being
forced into the army, for which he had no use and was thoroughly unfitted. After action at the front he becomes
even more convinced that it all is absurd butchery. He
is eventually wounded, ends up in a hospital, and is sent
back to his unit just as the Armistice is signed. Shortly
after he is sent with a school detachment to Paris where
he meets Genevieve Rod, a young attractive Frenchwoman who
admires and appreciates his nature and artistic talents.
On an unauthorized outing into the countryside with her he
is apprehended by the M.P.'s and sent to a labor battalion.
At this point he deserts and eventually makes his way to
the country house of Genevieve where he stays at the nearby
inn. He is eventually informed on by the innkeeper and is
taken prisoner again. The second young man, Dan Fuselli
of Italian background, makes every effort to avoid any
difficulty with the military system and advances in rank.
Chrisfield is a high-strung farm boy from Indiana with a
quick temper, who is court-martialed when he announces he
intends to kill Sergeant Anderson when the war is over.
He eventually kills Anderson, and a rumor leaks out that
he did it. Chrisfield deserts and becomes a refugee in
France, forever on the move. The novel attempts to destroy
the myth of the glamour and the glory of war. In this it
succeeds very effectively. It is a sensitive story and a

highly vivid document of the social realities at that
time. It presents the pervasive tedium, the dehumanizing
regimentation, and the physical terrors of war with power
and authority.

453   Ewart, Wilfrid Herbert Gore. *Way of Revelation; A Novel
      of Five Years*. New York: G.P. Putnam's Sons, 1921.
      534p.

A perceptive if somewhat sentimental novel that describes
the effect of war on various types of men. The story begins in the midsummer of 1914 in London with a description
of the rising generation involved in the pleasures of the
time. The plot focuses on four young people in this society, Adrian Knoyle and Eric Sinclair and the two women
they are interested in, Rosemary Meynell and Faith Daventry. When the war begins Adrian and Eric are among the
very first to leave for the front, while the stay-at-homes
are pictured as they react to the conditions and influences of the war. Eric marries Faith shortly before he
is killed. Adrian, who comes home to marry Rosemary,
finds her more interested in a group of society types.
The novel concludes with Faith and Adrian left to build a
life together after the destruction of five years of war.
There are some excellent descriptions of battle scenes and
behind-the-lines activities, including hospital conditions.
Scenes of life in the trenches alternate with those of
London society. The book vividly reveals the glory, tragedy, and squalor of war.

454   Hay, Ian (pseud. of John Hay Beith). *The Willing Horse;
      A Novel*. London: Hodder & Stoughton, 1921. 318p.;
      Boston: Houghton Mifflin Co., 1921. 283p.

A war novel that tends to use the great war as a backdrop to a love story. The story is related with characteristic Scottish humor and generally describes the
effect of the war on Scottish people with occasional
scenes at the front. Through the novel runs the romance
of two young people, barely of age, and both starting out
in disobedience of their rather narrow-minded Scottish
parents. Roy enlists while Marjorie goes to London for war
work. In London, Marjorie has an assorted career as a
canteen girl, driver, and chorus girl, which is the last
straw for her parents who now cut off her allowance. Marjorie is soon nearly penniless and in danger of starving.
On one of Roy's leaves from France they are married and
later when Marjorie has just become a mother Roy is almost
fatally wounded.

455 Johnson, Owen McMahon. *The Wasted Generation*. Boston: Little, Brown & Co., 1921. 343p.

For the most part this is a conventional and melodramatic war novel told in diary form with chunks of sociological debate inserted into a rather sensational plot. It is the diary of a young American who enlisted in the Foreign Legion at the outbreak of the war. He describes the horror and waste of the war and conveys his sense of disillusionment with the failure of the social order, especially the methods of education that permit such a catastrophe to come about. Combined with this social thesis is the story of his hopeless love for a young French woman. He is prevented from marrying her by an insurmountable obstacle which she refuses to describe, and which is revealed only at the conclusion of the book.

456 Keable, Robert. *Simon Called Peter*. London: Constable, 1921. 347p.; New York: E.P. Dutton & Co., 1921. 332p.

The theme is how the experiences of the war in France affected Peter Graham, a Church of England curate, and how they eventually turned him to the Roman Catholic faith. Most of the characters seem only interested in a good time--eating, drinking, loving. Into this earthy life comes Peter as a military chaplain in France. Peter never experiences any military action and has no special desire to do so. As chaplain he has little or no impact on the troops. He soon, however, accepts the moral laxity of the wartime atmosphere and joins in the carefree and dissolute life with Julie, the female heroine. Originally from South Africa, she is a woman of bitter experience but of considerable charm and vitality. The story is primarily a view of the so-called dissolute life up behind the fighting lines when all know that death is only a moment away.

457 Lynn, Escott. *Comrades Ever!* London: W. & R. Chambers, 1921. 351p.; Philadelphia: J.B. Lippincott Co., 1921. 351p.

An account of the adventures of Cecil Barrington, British civil servant and officer in the British Volunteer Force in British Nyasaland. This is a story of military operations which ended in the loss of Germany's colonies in East Africa. The plot is in the form of a diary, portions of which were (supposedly) periodically sent to the author while the African conflict was in progress. Cecil becomes a close friend to Mwele, a huge and powerful Masai warrior

who once had saved Cecil from a crocodile. The story
traces the adventures of these two through innumerable
fights, night attacks, and struggles in the bush. The
tale is told from the English point of view, with great
emphasis on German atrocities.

458 Maurois, André. *General Bramble*. Translated from the
French by Jules Castier and Ronald Boswell. London:
John Lane Co., 1921. 188p. [*Le Général Bramble*, 1918;
revised edition published as *Les Discours du Docteur
O'Grady*. Paris: B. Grasset, 1922. 236p.]

The sequel to the *Silence of General Bramble* (item 379)
using the same characters such as the Irish Doctor O'Grady,
the caustic Colonel Parker, the Roman Catholic padre, the
French interpreter Aurelle, and, of course, General Bramble.
The narrative is a witty series of conversations which comment on and describe everyday life in the camps. The purpose of these extended conversations is to display with
wit and humor the friendship and goodwill which exist among
the personnel of the Allied armies, with particular emphasis on the French and English soldiers and their special
relationships.

459 Rolland, Romain. *Clerambault; the Story of an Independent
Spirit During the War*. Translated by Katherine Miller.
New York: Henry Holt & Co., 1921. 286p. [*Clerambault;
Histoire d'une Conscience Libre Pendant la Guerre*.
Paris: A. Michel, 1920. 318p.]

This novel might best be characterized as an essay in
novel form. It is the record of Clerambault's thoughts
and activities regarding the war and its various issues.
The fictional story is subservient to the various ideas
developed and presented by the author through his characters. Indeed, the many characters represent the different points of view which Clerambault encounters. Clerambault is described as a poet who is filled with love of
humanity but with vague and generous theories which are
more emotional than precisely logical. The story opens
with Clerambault reading to his family an ode to peace
and brotherhood. When the war starts, he is stunned at
first and then becomes enthusiastic with patriotism. Later when his son is killed his anguish changes his perspective completely. He is described as he passes through
various emotional or psychological states which represent
what every sincere spirit in similar circumstances experienced during the war. At one time he is exalted, then

depressed, isolated, deserted by his family, and even persecuted. Eventually when he succumbs to his detractors, it appears to his few remaining friends that here, indeed, is another crucifixion. Rolland, in effect, has quietly but unsparingly revealed that those who have lost a son, husband, or brother to their country, cannot bear to admit that their country might have been mistaken, for fear that their sacrifice was all in vain.

460 Sedgwick, Anne Douglas. *Adrienne Toner*. London: Edward Arnold, 1921. 316p.

Adrienne is an American woman who generously uses her large fortune from a toothpaste company to indulge her bizarre spiritual ideas and language based on an unnamed cult. She bestows her assistance upon the problems and affairs of her friends, cures their headaches by laying hands on them, dominates nearly everyone she meets, and includes among her supporters youthful innocents and even cynics. She soon captivates a young Englishman, Barney Chadwick, and all of his family. But his friend, Roger Oldmeadow, who is older, more perceptive, and more skeptical, is resistant to Adrienne's appeal. Roger wants Barney to marry his nice young cousin who is much more suited to him. Barney, however, marries Adrienne, with disastrous results. She is the type who makes everyone suffer who comes near her even though she wants to promote happiness. Thus, when Barney leaves her, Roger from a sense of fair play takes her part and is her only friend. It is with the start of the war that Adrienne is really able to prove her faith and love for others. She ultimately takes on an unusual beauty and radiance while Roger comes to love her, although the reader is left with the impression that Roger's love will be hopeless. This is strictly a homefront story that might have occurred during any period of recent history.

1922

461 Andrews, Mary Raymond (Shipman). *His Soul Goes Marching On*. New York: Charles Scribner's Sons, 1922. 84p.

The plot is simple enough. On a trip to the Middle West, Theodore Roosevelt by chance meets a little boy who is intent on bass fishing. Roosevelt befriends the youngster for a brief time and when he departs has so impressed the boy with the motto and inspiration of his life that the boy never forgets the experience. The memorable event later provides the inspiration for the young man and his buddies of the Rainbow Division to fight heroically on the battlefields of France.

462 Cather, Willa Sibert. *One of Ours*. New York: Alfred A. Knopf, 1922. 459p.

An exceptionally well-written novel. The doomed hero, Claude Wheeler, is "one of ours" who eventually leaves his Nebraska farm to fight and ultimately to die in the war. An eager, sensitive young man, he feels inarticulate longings for which his life has so far brought no resolution. Even in the peaceful and satisfying world around him in Nebraska he never really feels at home. All his relationships have been a disappointment except with the dependable old Mahailey and his mother, though his mother's rather narrow religious beliefs have now created a barrier of sorts between them. His marriage proved to be the greatest disappointment of all. Amidst his prosperous farm and in the middle of so much material plenty, he still feels unfulfilled and longs to do something with his life. When war comes, it provides a release for him, and he goes gladly, never questioning its purpose. Once in France he finds the youth he believes he never had experienced as well as the companionship which now gives meaning to his life. He dies before any disillusionment with the war might affect him. Claude is clearly a misfit, a quasi-tragic figure who seems to illustrate the thesis that this world has no place for an idealist; that possibly the best that can be wished for is death. Although the war scenes are vivid and based on authentic knowledge of the war, the great conflict serves more as the process to reveal the solution for the personal problems of Claude.

463 Cogswell, A.M. *Ermytage and the Curate*. London: Edward Arnold, 1922. 304p.

Ermytage, a schoolmaster, and Seymour, a curate, are friends at a hospital and convalescent center and afterwards at the Boulogne English labor base. Both are afflicted by shell shock, which prevents their return to the front. The author relates his story with an ample spooning of humor which softens the implicit indictment of war and all of its stupidities and waste, especially behind the lines. Lightly superimposed on this are the love affairs of the two protagonists. In general, the writing is very poor and the story lacks any serious quality.

Adult Novels

464 Cohn, Clara (Viebig). *Daughters of Hecuba: A Tale of Our Times*. Translated from the German by Anna Barwell. London: George Allen & Unwin, 1922. 308p. [*Tochter der Hekuba; Ein Roman aus Unserer Zeit*. Berlin: E. Fleischel, 1917. 347p.]

Set in Berlin and its environs, this novel describes the war from a woman's point of view. Like the Grecian Hecuba, the women in the novel face loneliness, hope, and isolation in the loss of husbands, lovers, and sons. Love of their homeland vies with their hate of the war. The novel ends as peace is being discussed.

465 Cummings, Edward Estlin. *The Enormous Room*. New York: Boni and Liveright, 1922. 271p.

Originally considered to be a memoir of the war (and, indeed, still so classified by many libraries) this is now generally categorized as a documentary or autobiographical novel based on the experiences of the author while in the Norton-Harjes Ambulance Service in France. The action is placed during three months in 1917 after the arrest of Cummings by the French military police for some undisclosed transgression. Cummings ends up in the huge dark room of a provincial prison, hence the name, *The Enormous Room*. During his three months in prison he meets three unusual men with personalities that add a very particular meaning to his prison experience. *The Enormous Room* is created as a metaphor for Bunyan's *Pilgrim's Progress*, e.g., the Delectable Mountains represent the Wanderer; Zoo-loo, a Polish farmer; and Surplice. Cummings has transformed his French prison-camp experiences by means of his very personal and creative interpretation of the actual events and personages encountered, to produce one of the most perceptive and artistic contributions of great war literature. This is a very personalized view and vindication of the nature of man in spite of the insanity and brutality associated with the war.

466 Dana, Mercedes. *According to Her Light*. Philadelphia: Dorrance & Co., 1922. 298p.

Not seen; NYPL.

467 Goodridge Roberts, George Edward Theodore. *The Fighting Starkleys; or, The Test of Courage*. Boston: Page Co., 1922. 250p.

Concerns a family of New Brunswick Canadians and their

neighbors and friends whose sons enlist in the 26th Infantry Battalion in 1914. Describes many examples of the bravery of these men in action on the Belgian front.

468 Harrison, Henry Sydnor. *Saint Teresa, A Novel.* Boston: Houghton Mifflin Co., 1922. 455p.

A novel set mostly in the confused and difficult period before the participation of the U.S. in the war. Various themes are introduced, from patriotism to pacifism, with an interesting view of the battle of the sexes. Teresa De Silver, the courageous and gutsy heroine, is a veritable superwoman, possessing everything--beauty, intelligence, youth, and an amazing business ability--coupled with a quixotic nature and social independence. She acquires a controlling interest in a steel company and in spite of great opposition refuses to let it become a munitions factory. She hires as her efficiency manager Dean Masury, a young man who turns out to have just as strong a will as hers but also the opposite point of view. He soon makes no bones about what he thinks of her pacifist policy and does not hide his attempt to turn the output of the company into shells. An incredible battle of wills results (but naturally observing all proprieties on both sides). This creates a deep mutual respect in both of them. However, eventually this results in an actual knock-out fight, with Saint Teresa the winner. Nevertheless, their previous extreme dislike reverses completely and love develops between them. One critic called it a novel of Wall Street, another a good yarn with a strong underlying current of cynicism. In any case, it uses wartime America principally as a setting for an incredible duel of the sexes.

469 Laughlin, Clara Elizabeth. *Jeanne-Marie's Triumph.* New York: Fleming H. Revell, 1922. 160p.

The story of a young girl, Jeanne-Marie, growing up in Paris in the pre-war years, and of her father's death at Verdun. Her father had taught her to see much history in the streets of Paris during the war, and Jeanne-Marie recalls memories of him along the streets he so loved. She instructs others to "find" their lost ones as she did in the places they loved. The novel tells of Jeanne-Marie's loyalty to France and her denunciation of those who so soon forgot the sacrifice so many paid that France might remain free. Jeanne-Marie becomes a Jeanne d'Arc in her single-minded devotion to her country.

Adult Novels 161

470 McFee, William Morley Punshon. *Command*. Garden City, N.Y.: Doubleday, Page, 1922. 337p.; London: Martin Secker Ltd., 1922. 317p.

Deals with a young officer who never secures a position of supreme command. The author spends considerable time analyzing the nature and psychology of his characters, especially the nature and talents required to be a commander. The most interesting parts of the book are the scenes and actions at sea which seem to be greatly influenced by Joseph Conrad.

471 Raymond, Ernest. *Tell England: A Study in a Generation*. London: Cassell & Co., 1922. 320p.; New York: George H. Doran Co., 1922. 342p.

A tale of the lives of three young men from their earliest school days to their death in the war. The story covers their five adolescent years at Kensingtowe, an English boy's school. When the war begins they are all of fighting age. Archie is soon killed in France at the beginning of the war, while Rupert and Edgar are transferred to the Dardanelles where they serve in the Gallipoli conflict. On their troopship they become friends with Padre Monty, the chaplain, who converts them and sends them into the battle with a sense of mission. Edgar dies at Cape Helles and Rupert later returns to France where he is killed during the final days of the war. The story is constructed as if it were written by Rupert with a prologue by Padre Monty.

472 Rolland, Romain. *Pierre and Luce*. Translated by Charles De Kay. New York: Henry Holt & Co., 1922. 136p. [*Pierre et Luce*. Geneva: n.p., 1920. 176p.]

The story takes place in Paris in the early months of 1918. Pierre has been called up for military service, but has a six-month wait before the military can use his services. During this period Pierre has plenty of time to consider the futility and madness of war. He also meets Luce and they fall deeply in love, spending every possible moment together and discussing the problems of life, love, and death which face them. They are supremely happy during these few days together. The Germans soon begin a new military advance which reaches its height during Easter. When Pierre and Luce enter the church on Good Friday, a bomb completely destroys the church and they are killed. This is a simple, well-fashioned story

of youthful love which attempts to grasp a moment of
happiness and life amidst the insanity of the times and
the ever-present prospect of death.

473 Rosner, Karl Peter. *The King*. Translated by Agnes Blake.
     London: Methuen & Co., 1922, 245p. [*Der König; Weg und
     Wende*. Stuttgart & Berlin: Cotta, 1921. 299p.]

   Not seen; however, the novel is about the German Emperor,
William II; NYPL.

474 Washburn, Claude Carlos. *The Lonely Warrior*. New York:
     Harcourt, Brace & Co., 1922. 345p.

   Stacey Carrol, the protagonist, returns to his home in
Illinois after four years on the battlefields of Europe.
He is obsessed with the idea that his mind has now been
totally distorted out of all harmony with his past life;
he feels his old self has been completely destroyed. The
story deals mainly with the period at home when he gradually comes to realize that no part of his life or personality can ever be destroyed. The novel is fairly crude
and demonstrates a notable lack of literary style.

475 Woolf, Virginia (Stephen). *Jacob's Room*. London: L. & V.
     Woolf at the Hogarth Press, 1922. 290p.

   A lyrical novel from one of the major women novelists
of the twentieth century. The story traces the brief
life of Jacob Flanders from boyhood through Cambridge
University and ultimately to his death at Flanders. A
silent but lovable English youth, Jacob is viewed through
a series of impressions as revealed by his room, by glimpses of him through the eyes of his friends, and by a number of character-revealing incidents. In a very real
sense, Jacob is only a reflection mirrored in his surroundings. Woolf demonstrates her unusual style and innovative
techniques with a strong sense of literary consciousness;
unfortunately, her technique weakens the plot structure
so that the novel's point tends to be lost to the reader.

1923

476 Berger, Marcel. *The House of Death*. Translated from the
     French by Marcel Berger. London: A.M. Philpot, 1923,

250p. [*Les Dieux Tremblent, Roman*. Paris: A. Michel, 1921. 318p.]

Not seen.

477 Borgese, Giuseppe Antonio. *Rubè*. Translated by Isaac Goldberg. New York: Harcourt, Brace & Co., 1923. 394p. [*Rubè, Romanzo*. Milan: Fratelli Treves, 1921. 421p.]

Filippo Rubè is given to paralyzing introspective musings. He is thirty and although an unsuccessful lawyer, possesses a logical mind capable of hairsplitting arguments that he believes eventually capable of extraordinary accomplishments. However, his present failure and lack of zest for life cause him to welcome the excitement of the war. He enlists at once, but at the first indication of danger goes to pieces in fear. This causes him to indulge in prolonged introspective orgies, during which he alternately characterizes himself as a hero and then as a craven coward. Eventually all his principles become confused and his career declines through one impossible situation after another. The story ends with him in an insane delirium which is broken occasionally by lucid moments. This is a superior novel that captures an epoch and portrays the decline of a man. The war and the years immediately following are described with remarkable verisimilitude.

478 Boyd, Thomas Alexander. *Through the Wheat*. New York: Charles Scribner's Sons, 1923. 266p.

A candid acount of what it meant to be a hero in the Marines, from the perspective of the ordinary enlistee. The story relates the experience of William Hicks who never hesitated or fled from any action or responsibility and never thought of glory or heroism as such. He accepted whatever happened as unavoidable. The novel follows him as he performs his duties on or about the front line. He is the good, if not the perfect, soldier that all generals would devoutly hope to have available. But during an extremely heavy attack and after all the accumulated experiences and tragedies of the battlefield, his senses become completely deadened. He is thought to be mad, for he would now wander about under heavy fire with perfect composure. The story is a straightforward narrative of the physical and spiritual progress and decline of a normal man under battlefield conditions. A major theme is the tragedy and horror of war.

479 Caine, Thomas Henry Hall. *The Woman of Knockaloe; a Parable*. London: Cassell & Co., 1923. 209p.

The setting is an enemy-civilian internment camp on the Isle of Man. One of the main characters, Mona Craine, and her father supply the camp with food from their farm, Knockaloe. Mona falls in love with one of the internees, a German called Oskar. This is considered treasonous, and Mona must leave Knockaloe. When the internment camp is abandoned, Oskar's English employer will not accept him back in his employ, and his German mother refuses to welcome the couple into her home and life. A pacifist novel presenting an intense picture of national hatred.

480 Lawrence, David Herbert. *Kangaroo*. London: Martin Secker Ltd., 1923. 403p.; New York: Thomas Seltzer, 1923. 421p.

The plot is based on the psychic experiences of Richard Lovatt Somers, which are produced not only by the war but also by the chaotic postwar period. Richard is a writer and a lonely, isolated individual who is prone to introspection. With his wife Harriet, he has been in voluntary exile from England since the start of the war. They have wandered about Europe and India and eventually reach Australia where the story takes place. Although he avoids most human contact, he usually attempts to involve himself in some project concerning others. On two occasions in Australia he has such an opportunity, but each time he does not follow through. This, of course, estranges the few friends he has, and especially Kangaroo, a passionate lover of mankind who wants to redeem the world with love. (Kangaroo would even institute a so-called dictatorship of love and, as a consequence, has become the leader of an association of ex-soldiers.) When Kangaroo dies, Richard retreats even further into his isolation, and his sense of frustration causes him to contemplate death. The story seems primarily an occasion for the author to indulge in frequent reflections on civilization, freedom, and democracy in their widest sense and in their specifically Australian manifestation. All of this speculation is a result of the impact of the war on the postwar world and probably represents Lawrence's own struggle to sort out in his mind all of the complex issues of the times. The novel seems at times to wander on with little or no direction. This is very much autobiographical and with strong didactic purpose. Nevertheless, a very tedious novel.

481 Tolstoi, Aleksei Nikolaevich. *The Road to Calvary*. Translated by R.S. Townsend. New York: Boni & Liveright, 1923. 451p. [*Khozhdenie po Mukam 1921-1922*.]

A panoramic view of Russian life from early 1914 to the beginning of the revolution in 1917. The main theme is the collapse and disintegration of a society. In some ways it is reminiscent of *War and Peace*. The sketchy plot concerns the interests and interrelationships of an upper-middle-class family from St. Petersburg. The narrative captures the confused intellectual life and progressive moral decline of Russian society in the activities and experiences of two sisters, Katia and Dasha.

Katia, the older sister, married to a lawyer of reputation becomes disenchanted with her marriage and flirts with the more radical intellectual and artistic isms. The younger sister, Dasha, is a law student and musician who exhibits a far more level-headed nature. Much of the plot is based on her love affair with a young radical electrical engineer, Teliegin, their subsequent separation by the war, and his service on the Austrian front.

When the war begins the two sisters enter hospital work in Moscow where Katia meets a young Marxist theoretician whom she eventually marries after the death of her husband in the revolution. The story is filled with considerable detail and a large cast of characters. There are scenes of the initial advance of the Russian army and the enthusiasm of the first days of the war followed by the defeats and succeeding retreats. The disorganization, ineptitude, and confusion of the Russian army are vividly presented as well as the havoc and terror of the civilian populations affected by the bloody battles and troop movements. Teliegin is taken prisoner by the Austrians, with a grim description of prison camp life.

The narrative reflects the growing discontent in Russia as it inevitably progresses to the revolution of 1917. Some of the most powerful sections deal with the course of events in St. Petersburg and Moscow as the revolution becomes a reality. The novel seems to be especially useful as a view of how the war influenced the eventual dissolution of human society.

This is the first volume of what finally became a trilogy of novels. The first one, titled "The Sisters," originally appeared in a Russian émigré journal in Paris in 1921-1922. The second one, titled "Nineteen-Eighteen," was probably written in Russia and completed in 1925. Both volumes were published together in English in 1935 under the title *Darkness and Dawn* (see entry under the author in 1935 for the full bibliographic description). The second part continues the narrative from the end of 1917 through 1919.

Part two is primarily concerned with the fate of Russia during the revolution. The husbands of Katia and Dasha take opposite sides but without any clear idea of where they will end up. While the husbands fight at cross-purposes in the civil war the two sisters are immersed in their immediate and dismaying circumstances. The scenes of revolution make up the major portions of this part. The World War is only a very distant event amidst the confusions of a nation involved in a cataclysmic civil war. (See item 776 for the annotation of the complete trilogy.)

482 Wharton, Edith Newbold (Jones). *A Son at the Front*. New York: Charles Scribner's Sons, 1923. 426p.

Deals with Campton, a great American painter whose only son, John, born in France, is subject to French military service. The father, his divorced wife, and her banker husband all try to help the son avoid dangerous service. But the son does not wish to be protected and while presumably on headquarters staff work quietly returns to his regiment at the front. The novel concentrates on the participation of the Americans in the war and especially the conversion of John Campton from neutrality to conviction that no civilized man can afford to remain aloof from such a conflict. The plot traces Campton as he encounters all sorts of people, humble French servants, Parisian friends, and fellow Americans, all of whom represent various attitudes toward the conflict. He suffers a number of wounds and eventually is killed at the front. The author demonstrates her characteristic literary style and ability, but the plot is never really able to grapple with the realities of war in an authentic manner. This is a novel that focuses primarily on character and manner but is stronger in intent than in accomplishment.

1924

483 Cahill, James Semple. *Behind the Scenes of Destiny*. Philadelphia: Dorrance & Co., 1924. 393p.

Relates the early wartime adventures of an American citizen in Germany. Escaping in disguise, he also assists British citizens to escape, and travels to Britain to enlist as a British air force officer. He engages in espionage for the Allies and his adventures take him from Britain to France, Italy, and Germany.

484 Cowan, Louise Henry. *Trapped*. Boston: Christopher Publishing House, 1924. 260p.

Not seen; NYPL.

485 Ford, Ford Madox. *Some Do Not; a Novel*. London: Gerald Duckworth & Co., 1924. 352p.

The first novel of a series (*Parade's End*) originally composed and conceived as a unit by the author. The chief character is Christopher Tietjens; the other major characters are his wife, Sylvia, and his true love, Valentine. These novels can be considered as parts of an allegory which feature one man, Christopher, as a species of individual long since died out, representing the stability and order of a long-gone age. Christopher, then, is doomed to be destroyed by the disruptive times in which he lives. Although he is involved in the early battles of the war, and suffers mild shell shock, his most important battle is his relationship with his wife, affected by the war's influence upon his character and outlook. This is a sophisticated novel of interpersonal relationships set against the background of the war. We know the war is going on somewhere, but the focus is primarily on the three principal characters and their personalities. (See items 493, 502, & 532.)

486 Miller, Patrick (pseud). *The Natural Man*. New York: Brentano's, 1924. 318p.

The hero is a young artillery officer named Blaven. The story reveals the psychology of many of the fighting men in the war by specifically tracing the process by which the hero comes to find himself. This is basically a very sober approach with no recourse to heroics or glorification by combat activity. The story is a sustained description of the wartime routine of dirt, duty, drudgery, and death as it is reflected in the daily activities of the average soldier, or "natural man." Without deliberately doing so the novel unconsciously, it seems, creates a definite anti-militaristic impression. It is written with ability and some power.

Adult Novels

487   Montague, Margaret Prescott. *The Man from God's Country*.
      New York: E.P. Dutton & Co., 1924. 44p.

   Richard Webb, journalist, is facing up to the unsettling
recognition that he has been the inspiration for many
young men to join the military, to fight a war in which
Webb no longer believes. The recognition was traumatic
when Webb confronted the body of the unknown soldier in
England, certain that it was a young American whom he had
met briefly during the war, and who had assured Webb that
it was his writing that had inspired the young man to enlist in the British Army. This work appeared in *North
American Review* (November 1922).

488   Mottram, Ralph Hale. *The Spanish Farm*. London: Chatto &
      Windus, 1924. 233p.; New York: Dial Press, 1924. 275p.

   The first volume of Mottram's *Spanish Farm* trilogy (see
items 498 & 508). It is a chronicle of French rural life.
The setting is a large farm in French Flanders within
hearing distance of the guns at the front. Its nearness
causes the farm building to be used by the British troops
for billeting. The chief character is the farmer's daughter, Madeleine Vanderlynden, a capable young French peasant girl. She captures the respect of a series of army
officers and enlisted men who are only too glad to pay
liberally for her assistance and supplies. The story
turns out to be a character study of Madeleine and an
authentic view of everyday life in the war zone. The
dominating love interest is her affair with a well-bred
English lieutenant, Geoffrey Skene. The author also
obviously intends Madeleine to represent the resolute
character and spirit of the people living on the French
borderlands. The novel is a simple and unpretentious
minor masterpiece of the war.

489   Stallings, Laurence. *Plumes*. New York: Harcourt, Brace
      & Co., 1924. 348p.

   The protagonist is Lieutenant Richard Plume who comes
from a family of fighters harking back to 1865. When
the U.S. enters the war in 1918, Richard leaves his
instructorship in a small college in the South and his
wife Esme and child to enlist for the front in France.
He returns seriously wounded. After six months in the
hospital and the loss of his leg he is able to get about
but only with the use of canes and a metal brace. He
finds a job in a Washington laboratory and is able to have

his wife and his son join him. Through all his suffering, and obviously that of his wife as well, he comes to reject the fighting creed of his family tradition. He now despises war and believes that his body represents a searing protest against its folly, futility, and suffering. A cripple and in pain most of the time, he knows he has been a fool. Indeed, life for Richard under these handicaps is sheer torture. The author vividly describes how he feels and how he exists with the constant pain. His friend Gary, who is also crippled, is the spokesman of some of the bitterest and most devastating cursing of war imaginable. This is a graphic record of personal anguish that is also a single-minded indictment of war and of the mistaken patriotism that gives it unthinking support.

490 Tharaud, Jérôme and Jean. *The Long Walk of Samba Diouf*. Translated by Willis Steell. New York: Duffield & Co., 1924. 201p. [*La Randonnée de Samba Diouf*. Paris: Plon-Nourrit, 1922. 313p.]

An unusual novel that describes the life of the Senegalese blacks in West Africa as well as later in their colonial regiment sent to fight for France in the war. The author describes the men in their barracks life where many are plagued by fears caused by their unfamiliarity with what was happening, as well as the fighting among themselves about inherited race feuds. They are seen in the promiscuous life of the training camps, in the trenches, in the hospital, and receiving medals for their bravery. The authors use their character of Samba Diouf as the focus for the long journey of the Senegalese from Africa to France and back again to Africa. The novel is constructed with a simplicity that eloquently captures the nature of the men. It is a serious and sympathetic anthropological view of a primitive people and their customs when they are propelled into the midst of World War I and the twentieth century. The story is told with an absence of race prejudice. A most interesting novel both in subject and in approach.

1925

491 Cocteau, Jean. *Thomas the Impostor*. Translated by Lewis Galantiere. New York: D. Appleton & Co., 1925. 154p.; reprinted as *The Impostor*. London: Peter Owen, 1947, 132p. [*Thomas l'Imposteur*. Paris: Gallimard, 1923. 154p.]

The imposter is a French youngster who passes himself

off as a soldier by donning a borrowed uniform and assuming another name. Eventually the youngster is adopted as a mascot of a detachment of marines, and ultimately dies a brave and gallant death.

492 Deane, Peter. *The Victors....* London: Constable, 1925. 118p.

The main character is a young soldier who saw service on the western front and continued in the service for a rather long time after the Armistice. As a civilian he was unable to find employment, so that after being jobless for three years, he committed suicide. An ordinary novel, though harrowing.

493 Ford, Ford Madox. *No More Parades; a Novel.* London: Gerald Duckworth & Co., 1925. 319p.; New York: A. & C. Boni, 1925. 309p.

A sequel to Ford's *Some Do Not* (item 485). The hero, Christopher Tietjens, is in command now of a draft battalion in a base camp in France. The action of the novel involves only about three days. Tietjens has left England after his farewell to Valentine Wannop, whom he now loves, thinking that his despised wife Sylvia has separated from him for good. Against this personal drama the author has provided a considerable amount of detail of life in an English base camp--the continual worry, incredible detail, endless duties, dirt, work, air raids, suspicion, and multiplicity of human personalities examined under the stressful conditions of wartime. Ford has described with great skill a fairly common theme in many novels of this period, namely, the conclusion of an age and of a tradition in England. With considerable skill and subtlety, Ford describes the complicated emotional relationships of his characters. A superior novel.

494 Gibbs, Philip Hamilton. *Unchanging Quest: A Novel.* London: Hutchinson & Co., 1925. 320p.

A historical novel covering about thirty years of European history. It begins in the early 1890's and continues through World War I, the Russian revolution, and the occupation of Germany following the Armistice. The central focus that holds the various elements of the story together is the narrator and his life-long passion for Katherine, who eventually marries a radical Russian prince. The plot tends to be sketchy and generally covers the thirty years in the lives of six people, their inter-relationships, and the impact of the events in history upon them. The character of Katherine is used by the author to dwell in some detail upon the Russian revolution and its events. The nature of the novel makes it obvious that the author harbors a deep hatred for war and all that it stands for. His scenes of the war and especially of Russia before and after the revolution are exceptional. Unfortunately, most of the characters seem to lack any vitality and appear to serve mainly as devices with which to describe the sweep of recent European history.

495 Kellermann, Bernhard. *The Ninth of November*. Translated from the German by Caroline V. Kerr. New York: Robert M. McBride & Co., 1925. 443p. [*Der 9. November; roman*. Berlin: S. Fischer, 1921. 474p.]

A picture of Germany during the last days of the European war. Specifically, we are shown Berlin on the eve of November 9, 1918, a city reduced in power and strength. General von Hecht-Babenberg is the chief protagonist. He is a vain and egotistical creature who appears more concerned about the whims of a pretty female than the issues of war. His family is also described--the son Otto who, having disabled himself by a self-inflicted wound, is barred from trench duty; Ruth, the daughter, who works in the soup kitchens in the city. We are shown graphic scenes of the political and social life of Berlin, the frenzy of front-line fighting, and the fear and terror of the German people as the empire is slowly destroyed. The thesis of the author is that the Germans are not malignant or deliberately cruel, but, in a sense, victims of fate or circumstance against which they are either too weak or powerless to react. The war is seen not as some heroic or grand adventure but rather as it actually was, filled with paradoxes, contrasts, and confusion. The author's style is similar to a cinema montage, for the scenes tend to change far too rapidly, as do the characters.

496 Kinross, Albert. *God and Tony Hewitt; a Novel*. London: R. Holden & Co., 1925. 280p.

A mediocre and conventional love story in a war setting. Tony, an English captain in the army, returns home on leave to discover his wife has become lazy, avoiding all responsibilities, and stupefying herself with liberal quantities of booze. He returns to the war disillusioned with his marriage. However, he soon encounters Violet Carter, a surgeon and war worker who offers her friendship. Later when his marriage finally is dissolved and Violet's engagement falls through, they discover their mutual love.

497 MacNichol, Shaw. *Between the Days, Being the Writing of Jean Bruyard: a Story of Franche Comté*. Edinburgh and London: W. Blackwood and Sons, 1925. 400p.

Not seen; NYPL.

498 Mottram, Ralph Hale. *Sixty-four, Ninety-four!* London: Chatto & Windus, 1925. 300p.; New York: Dial Press, 1925. 365p.

The plot of this novel is based on the same story described in his first novel, *The Spanish Farm* (item 488). The first novel examined the psychology of the people of devastated France by a close-up view of Madeleine Vanderlynden, the peasant farmer girl of Flanders who has a wartime love affair with an English lieutenant. The second novel relates precisely the same story, but from the point of view of Geoffrey Skene, the lieutenant. Thus, the same incidents are repeated in both novels, but this time involving the psychology of a well-bred English officer. The author has created a realistic novel that is a rich and sensitive record of the war. The book is notable for the view it offers of the deteriorating and war-torn civilization of Europe.

499 Wassermann, Jakob. *Faber: or, The Lost Years*. Translated by Harry Hansen. New York: Harcourt, Brace & Co., 1925. 347p. [*Faber; oder, Die verlorenen jahr, roman*. Berlin: S. Fischer, 1924. 264p.]

Describes the return of a young German architect to his native city after nearly six years as a prisoner of war. He finally escapes through Siberia, but when he eventually reaches home, he is unable to resume his married life. The story details this crisis and the corresponding problems of his wife, Martina. Their problems are examined not only in terms of their individual relationships but also in terms of the forces in society that have formed their personalities. The author has created a dramatic tale that becomes an examination and a criticism of central European life at that time. The novel is a craftsmanlike narrative with a dramatic plot and sharp characterization. The author demonstrates considerable literary style and technique. A psychological novel.

1926

500 Bennett, Enoch Arnold. *Lord Raingo*. London: Cassell & Co., 1926. 409p.; New York: Doran & Co., 1926. 393p.

It is London in the middle months of 1918. There is some suggestion that the author has created a political satire of the home front and of the British government. The pettiness, vanity, ineptitude, and jealousies of all the bureaucrats are shown as they blithely deal in lives and money. On a more personal level the novel examines the character of the hero, Lord Raingo, a retired business man of considerable wealth. He is appointed by the Prime Minister to a seat in the cabinet and at the same time is given a peerage as payment for the job of directing British propaganda and publicity. The identities of some of the principal political figures are thinly veiled in this satire. There is a suggestion of a love affair, and the novel concludes with a graphic and detailed account of Raingo's illness, hospital stay and treatment, and eventual death that extends over nearly the last hundred pages.

501 Faulkner, William. *Soldiers' Pay*. New York: Boni & Liveright, 1926. 319p.

Faulkner's first novel and very much a product of the "lost generation" literary tradition. Donald Mahon is traveling home by train from the war. Not only is his face terribly disfigured, but he has also lost much of his memory. Two passengers on the train, Joe Gilligan and Margaret Powers, decide to help him after speculating what his reception home will be like. They can imagine his father's shock, who up to now has thought him dead. They also sense his pretty fiancée's likely reaction. The story relates the poignant story of Donald's homecoming against the backdrop of a small southern town. Faulkner has created his characters with considerable skill and care, and the novel shows all the signs of the major literary talent that the author later developed.

502 Ford, Ford Madox. *A Man Could Stand up--Novel*. London: Gerald Duckworth & Co., 1926. 275p.; New York: A. & C. Boni, 1926. 347p.

The third novel following *No More Parades* (item 493) and *Some Do Not* (item 485). The story begins with a telephone call for Valentine Wannop exactly at the moment of the wild Armistice celebration. The call informs Valentine that Christopher is back from the war. Now with the war over and with some assurance that Sylvia Tietjens has indeed left him for good (however, with no intentions of divorce), Christopher and Valentine decide to "stand up" for whatever happiness the future can bring them under these circumstances. There are penetrating scenes of the war in the trenches as observed by Christopher, which create a remarkable mosaic of those nightmarish experiences. Ford is a master of the traditional English novel which in this series explores not only the psychology of the three principals with unusual detail and perception but also the mental and physical effect of the war in the trenches. A novel of skill and substance.

503 Gibbs, Arthur Hamilton. *Labels: A Novel*. London: Hutchinson & Co., 1926. 280p.; Boston: Little, Brown & Co., 1926. 295p.

Although this novel deals with the consequences of the war, it is more of a postwar story than a war story. The setting is the upper-middle-class home of Sir Thomas Wickens, a well-meaning but rather fatuous London stockbroker who has been knighted for his financial patriotism. Being a zealot for the great cause, Sir Wickens has amply surrounded himself with all of the official propaganda trappings of the war effort. The author uses him and his family as a general symbol of this level of society after the Armistice. His children all return home from the war: Thomas, who never starved to death in a prison camp; Dick, a captain in an artillery group; and Madge, who has been a nurse in the field hospitals. The novel is primarily a tale of the readjustment of the parents and their children to a world of peace. The characters tend to represent various points of view about the war and the nature of man. The author makes it especially clear that he is strongly opposed to all the stupidity, hypocrisy, and cruelty which are the cornerstones of the mass slaughter just concluded.

504 Jameson, Margaret Storm. *Three Kingdoms*. New York: Alfred A. Knopf, 1926. 365p.

The war plays only a minor and somewhat incidental part in this rather traditional "slice of life" novel. The major theme deals with the conflict of domestic and marital obligations with the appeal of a professional life for a wife and mother. Laurence Story marries Dysart Ford, a young lawyer, just beginning her career before the war. She soon becomes a mother and he is sent off to the war. While he is gone she achieves a high executive position with an advertising firm and has what the author refers to as a wholly platonic affair with a cousin. All this sooner or later comes to the attention of her husband and so alters his sensibilities that their relaionship seems to be permanently changed into a semi-detached marriage in which each one lives his own life. But all comes out well in the end. They are eventually reunited over a divorce case involving a vituperative woman.

505 Mackenzie, Compton. *Fairy Gold*. London: Cassell & Co., 1926, 469p.; New York: Doran & Co., 1926. 447p.

Mainly a love story of the young Lieutenant Richard Deverell and Vivien, the daughter of the owner of the small private island of Roon off the coast of Cornwall. Richard is sent to the island in charge of a small garrison of soldiers. The antipathy of Vivien's father toward the military interlopers is solidified by the death of his son in combat. He contrives to have Lieutenant Deverell sent into combat and then is persuaded to commercialize his island. His death prevents the island's development, and Roon and its companion island are inherited by Vivien.

506 McClure, Robert E. *Some Found Adventure*. Garden City, N.Y.: Doubleday, Page & Co., 1926. 335p.

The main character, Martin Riley, enlisted in the army, but would have liked to avoid joining the service, though hesitating to admit this to himself. He could not pass the physical examination for officers' training, but is made a corporal on the staff of a general in a National Guard division; while overseas he becomes commissioned. At the war's end he is garrisoned in the north of France, falls in love with a cultured French war-widow, Mme. Laurent, and plans to enroll in the four-months' course available to American soldiers at the University of Paris.

507 Montague, Charles Edward. *Rough Justice, a Novel*. London: Chatto & Windus, 1926. 383p.; Garden City, N.Y.: Doubleday, Page & Co., 1926. 336p.

A love story placed against a picture of English country life and society and contrasted with the brutality of the war. Auberon and Molly Garth, two cousins, are brought up by Thomas Garth, a junior English cabinet minister, who is the uncle of the boy and the father of the girl. Thomas is filled with a foreboding that all is not well with either the country or the world. Auberon goes to prep school and Oxford with his close friend, Victor Nevin, who is a symbol of the crumbling English upper class that has never been required to compete to achieve a place in society. All the same, Victor is greatly admired for his intelligence and handsome appearance. Auberon, on the other hand, is pictured as tending to athletics. His early imaginativeness has been lost in the mill of the English public schools. A detailed picture of college life, its glamor and friendships, is captured with considerable impact. All of this peaceful world comes to an end with the start of the war. Victor is now engaged to Molly who has turned into a lovely and intelligent woman. Even this test of friendship still results in Auberon's worship of Victor, although he too has grown to love Molly. Auberon with his physique and determination soon masters the rigors of military training and front-line strife. Victor, however, with his finer and yet more fragile spirit, cannot take the inanities of military routine. Confused and stunned after a night artillery attack, he wanders back behind his lines to a peasant's cottage where a young peasant woman traps him, burns his clothes, and keeps him in place of her slain husband through the years of the conflict. An English provost marshal hears of Victor's circumstances and "shell shock," searches him out as a coward and a deserter, and blows out Victor's brains in a French courtyard. One of the main themes of this novel is the series of brutal military executions which later proved to be one of the more disgraceful and inhuman activities of the war. *Paths of Glory* (item 703) is another, more powerful, novel which pursues this theme even further into the absurdities of military justice.

508 Mottram, Ralph Hale. *Crime at Vanderlynden's*. London: Chatto & Windus, 1926. 219p.; New York: Dial Press, 1926. 265p.

The third novel of the author's trilogy dealing with life on a Flemish farm during the war. The other two novels are *The Spanish Farm* (item 488) and *Sixty-Four, Ninety-Four* (item 498). The crime mentioned in the title refers to the destruction of a shrine by an English soldier who only wanted shelter for his mule. As the shrine was located on the Spanish farm, Madeleine feels she is due compensation for the damage. Dormer, an English soldier and the army investigator on the case, spends months attempting to locate the guilty soldier but never succeeds. Meanwhile he attempts to keep headquarters quiet and to

calm the stubborn Madeleine and her family. The entire
story is seen through the eyes of young Dormer, who is as
much caught up in the machinery of the war as any French
civilian. He is shown working and quietly thinking as he
moves to and from the front in his various responsibilities.

509 Nason, Leonard Hastings. *Chevrons*. New York: George H.
Doran Co., 1926. 339p.

Deals especially with the participation of the American
forces in the war. The chief protagonists are Jake and
Sergeant Eadie who are described as they fight their way
into the battles of Mont Sec and Montfaucon. The author
makes a special effort to reveal the total picture of men
and armies at war--the advance of the exhausted infantry,
artillery in action, soldiers sweating as they drag their
equipment and weapons into the lines, airplane dogfights,
and a town literally pounded to death. The novel makes a
strong effort to capture the authentic slang of the troops
and the emotional moods that resulted in special or characteristic expressions of the war, and creates with remarkable fidelity the conditions and behavior of the men and
officers as well as their states of mind.

510 Pollock, Channing. *The Enemy; Novelized from the Play by
Channing Pollock*.... New York: Brentano's, 1926. 275p.

The *Enemy* presents the war from the point of view of a
Viennese family and their friends, between June 1914 and
June 1919. The hope and belief are expressed that a new
day of peace is dawning. The story presents the lives of
a pacifist professor and his daughter, whose husband is
killed in the war and whose baby dies; her rapacious and
opportunist father-in-law whose fortune is made from pro-
fits of war; and a young Englishman who, loving the young
widow, returns to Vienna after the war and looks forward
to a better world with her.

511 Thompson, Sylvia Elizabeth. *Hounds of Spring*. London:
Wm. Heinemann, 1926. 339p.; Boston: Little, Brown &
Co., 1926. 366p.

The story of Zina Renner, the well-bred daughter of an
English baronet of Austrian-English background. She is
about to marry Colin Russell, a brilliant young Oxford
idealist, when he is called up in the first draft of the
war. He is very shortly reported to be missing in action
and probably killed. This is the first harsh reality of

life that Zina has ever faced. She becomes toughened by
her experience, but all the same suffers a psychic shock
that in its own way is as tragic as Colin's case of shell
shock. Zina and the family are unaware that he has recovered his memory after four years when he is found by
Zina's father in a hospital in Paris. In the meantime
Zina has permitted herself to drift into marriage with a
man who offers her a life of wide interests but for whom
she has no real love. Now that Colin is found, the family
problem is whether to tell Zina of Colin's return. All
have a great reluctance to do so except her little sister,
Wendy, who faces life and facts squarely, without sentimentality, and finally decides to deal with her sister in
full frankness.

1927

512   Divine, Charles. *Cognac Hill*. New York: Payson & Clarke, 1927. 382p.

A behind-the-lines story of army life and loves in
France. Allen Proctor falls in love with Marjorie Lothrop,
a war worker in the Cognac Hill camp, but she feels that
their relationship may only be a result of the special
stress and excitement of the times and decides to hold
Allen off while experimenting with Gordon. Allen and
Gordon are friends but of contrasting personalities. The
story, according to one reviewer, is about a "group of
fire-eating young hospital orderlies and man-eating nurses"
in a dialogue no soldier ever heard in or out of the trenches. This is a rather hackneyed tale, but it does give
some sense of the confusion and mess of the war.

513   Empey, Arthur Guy. *A Helluva War*. New York: D. Appleton & Co., 1927. 323p.

Ostensibly, a humorous novel about the antics of Terrence
X. O'Leary, a brawny Irish-American private, who is forever
getting in and out of awkward situations. The novel makes
ample use of Scottish and Irish dialects, but the entire
story is rather crudely drawn slapstick comedy that more
often than not is simply insipid in effect.

514   Gristwood, Arthur Donald. *The Somme, Including also The Coward*. London: Jonathan Cape, 1927. 189p.

Two short novels comprise this book. *The Somme* covers
a brief time span which recounts the horror of trench

warfare on the Somme battlefield. The narrator, Tom
Everitt, and his platoon in "C" Company of the Loamshires
are involved in an offensive operation to defend their
sector. Everitt is wounded and given medical aid aboard
a hospital train. The other story, *The Coward,* takes
place after the Armistice and stresses the theme of pacifism. In the introduction H.G. Wells especially recom-
mends the novel to boys for this reason. However, the
hero is so unattractive, even disgusting, as a pacifist
that Wells' objective could have scarcely had any hope of
success. The hero deliberately shoots himself in order to
escape being sent to the front lines and manages to avoid
any punishment. The author's sympathies are apparently
with the cowardly protagonist.

515 Ingram, Archibald Kenneth. *Out of Darkness: A Drama of
Flanders.* London: Chatto & Windus, 1927. 312p.

After a notorious affair in England an English artist,
Faversham, has at last settled down in Flanders with his
French wife and their two children. When the war begins,
an English colonel, an old enemy of the artist, discovers
him in his Flanders retreat. The colonel sneeringly forces
Faversham into war service. Meanwhile, his French wife,
enraged and bitter, finally obtains her vengeance on the
colonel when the war ultimately forces him into her hands.
The war scenes are rather well done, but are mainly the
setting against which the author exposes the relationships
of his characters.

516 Kimber, Hugh. *San Fairy Ann; Ça ne fait rien: A Love Story
of the Great War.* New York: J.H. Sears & Co., 1927.
321p.; London: R. Holden & Co., 1927. 312p.

A commonplace tale of the loves of Richard Steele, who
exemplifies the soldier's philosophy that "it doesn't
matter." Steele thinks he loves April Rue, and while April
remains faithful to him he falls in love with Joan Morley
and marries her. The story describes Steele and his friends
during and after the war in France. Steele fails to make
a living for Joan and their new child, and the mother and
child eventually die. The only merit in this otherwise
prosaic novel is its vivid and convincing account of the
hardships of military and civilian life during and immediately after the war.

517 Kyne, Peter Bernard. *They Also Serve*. New York: Cosmopolitan Book Corp., 1927. 344p.

A view of the war from the point of view of Professor, a three-quarter thoroughbred horse. Professor, the pride and joy of his cowboy master, tells his stable mates the story of his adventures in France with his master, Private Ern Givens of the artillery.

518 MacDonald, Philip (pseud.: Anthony Lawless). *Patrol*. London: W. Collins Sons, 1927. 245p.

A realistic story of the bloody adventures of an English patrol fighting the Arabs in Mesopotamia during the war. It relates the experiences and daily activities of a small group of cavalrymen who are accidentally isolated from their main army when the officer who has their orders is killed before he is able to reveal them. Much of the dialog is written in the quasi-slang of the British army. The cavalrymen wander across the hot desert and finally make a permanent camp at an oasis, but the Arabs soon surround them and slowly proceed to shoot them one by one as the days go by. The story is a tension-filled ordeal of death and frustration that only concludes with the death of the last English soldier as he manages to kill all of the four Arabs who have hounded his patrol in the desert for so long.

519 Martin, Mabel. *The Lingering Faun: A Novel*. New York: F.A. Stokes Co., 1927. 312p.

A story of postwar refugees in Paris. The chief characters are the Russian Prince Petanoff and Barbara, his American wife. Her family is very much against her marriage, and even she has been made to feel an outsider by her husband, who now that nearly all of their financial resources are spent is ready to sell his wife to the envoy of a sultan in order to aid his sister. In many ways this is a very bad novel, but it does indicate the hysteria of postwar Paris, if the reader can manage to finish it.

* Mottram, Ralph Hale. *The Spanish Farm Trilogy, 1914-1918*. New York: Dial Press, 1927. 550p.

This book contains the three novels entitled *The Spanish Farm* (item 488), *Sixty-four, Ninety-four* (item 498), and *The Crime at Vanderlynden's* (item 508). See each of the separate titles for annotations.

520 Newberry, Perry. *Forward Ho! A Story of the Argonne*.
New York: F.A. Stokes Co., 1927. 284p.

Relates the war experiences of a sixteen-year-old French-American youth. The action begins when he escapes from a town held by the Germans and finally makes his way to the American lines in the Argonne. There, in spite of an order to the contrary, he takes part in the fighting and performs bravely. The style of the author tends to be awkward and stilted, and the characterization tends toward caricature. One critic called the novel "Little Rollo in the Great War," an observation that seems to have stood the test of time.

521 Noble, Edward. *Moving Waters: A Story of the Two Sea Services*.... London: Jarrolds, 1927. 287p.

The two sea services of the title are represented by the two brothers in the story. Jag Haines is a captain in the British merchant marine, and his brother Jimmy is an officer in the regular navy. Both are in love with the same woman, Dorothea Nesbit, their childhood playmate. Recognition is conferred on Jag when his ship sinks a German sub. Later, when his ship is also sunk, he is captured and imprisoned on a German submarine. Jimmy is ordered out to find and destroy the U-boat. Eventually he locates the sub and his nearly half-dead brother and brings him home to recuperate with Dorothea.

522 Pulleyne, Douglas. *This, My Son*. London: Chapman & Hall, 1927. 306p.

A story about a young gypsy, one of twin boys, in England. When war breaks out, one boy will not accept England as his country; rather, because of his memories of days of happiness there, he fights for Germany. During the war he captures his brother who, having been operating as a spy, is condemned to death by a firing squad. The twin fighting under Germany's banner changes places with his brother and sacrifices his life for his twin.

523 Rolland, Romain. *Mother and Son*.... Translated from the French by Van Wyck Brooks. New York: Henry Holt & Co., 1927. 415p. [*Mère et Fils*. Paris: Michel, 1927. 2 vols.]

This volume forms the third part of the author's tetralogy, *The Soul Enchanted*. The story takes place during the

war years and presents the pacifist ideas of the author
in fictional form. The character of the heroine, Annette
Riviere, is described as she experiences the war. The
novel concludes as she and her son Marc have come to a
profound understanding and deep love. The novel tends
toward the sentimental and serves more as a tract for the
author's notions than as any significant work of fiction.
Unfortunately, it is not up to the preceding two volumes
in the series, or on the level of his splendid novel *Jean
Christophe*.

524   Saunders, John Monk. *Wings: Based on the Paramount Picture*. New York: Grosset & Dunlap, 1927. 249p.

Two boys in love with the same girl enlist in the Army
Air Corps and are assigned to the same basic-training camp.
After their flight training is over, they are sent to France
and help to down a German fighter plane. Later one of the
flyers is shot down in enemy territory and reported dead.
His friend tries to seek revenge by downing a German plane,
which turns out to be piloted by his friend who had managed
to steal it at a German airfield.

525   Stevens, James. *Mattock*. New York and London: Alfred A. Knopf, 1927. 320p.

Deals with the story of Private Marvin Mattock, a son of
a Kansas farmer, told in the local vernacular. Mattock
serves as a symbol of the average American man in the war.
The novel describes his reactions and experience when he
must leave all of the familiar surroundings of civilian
life and is forced into military life and routines. The
story also serves as a chronicle of Company F from a midwestern division, ranging from the time it undergoes its
first training period in France to its first convention
with the American Legion. The book is filled with much of
the commonplace routines so characteristic of military life
and doesn't attempt to create any false romantic notion of
wartime life.

526   Thompson, Edward John. *These Men, Thy Friends*. London: Alfred A. Knopf Co., 1927. 285p.; New York: Harcourt, Brace & Co., 1928. 319p.

A historical novel based on the 1916 campaign in Mesopotamia. The experiences of a group of ordinary soldiers
are described in considerable detail. The characters indulge in extended conversations which at times represent

various points of view of the author on the issues of the war and army life. The story deals with the everyday trivia of an army in an unfriendly country and with the fact that its leadership often verges on the incompetent. The author's satire is often heavy-handed.

527 Venable, Clarke (pseud.: Covington Clarke). *"Aw Hell."* New York: Reilly & Lee Co., 1927. 329p.

Traces the war exploits of Jeptha Montgomery Brice, an almost illiterate, mountain-dwelling man of Tennessee. After numerous rejections for army service, Jeptha finally arrives in France to fight under the name of an A.W.O.L. American soldier. The story documents his simple bravery and devotion to his comrades as they prepare and engage in the battle for the Argonne Forest. ("Aw Hell" was an expression used by an inarticulate comrade when under emotional stress.)

1928

528 Ball, Eustace Hale. *The Legion of the Condemned.* New York: Grosset & Dunlap, 1928. 256p.

A melodramatic story based on the Paramount film of the same name (screenplay by John Monk Saunders) featuring Gary Cooper as the hero, Gale Price. The story deals with the daredevil men of the famous Lafayette Escadrille. Gale Price joins the French pilots after he finds his sweetheart Christine in the arms of a German officer. One of the duties of the men of the Lafayette Escadrille is to drop and pick up Allied spies behind the German lines. Price discovers that Christine is the female spy he has been ordered to drop behind enemy lines. Later the two are reconciled, captured by the Germans, and eventually rescued by the Lafayette Escadrille amidst dropping bombs and enemy troops dashing for cover.

529 Bellah, James Warner. *The Sons of Cain.* New York: D. Appleton & Co., 1928. 247p.

The action is placed in London at the time of the Armistice. An American major, Murray Petching, while celebrating with his friends, meets Frederika Seleyce who also served in France during the war. Unfortunately, she is married to a man who is a cad and an ass. Although she does not love him, he will neither divorce her nor let her divorce him. The novel attempts to deal with the disintegration of social and moral standards during those days. Murray represents rectitude and probity and although he comes to love Frederika greatly, he refuses to accept a less than honorable relationship with her. But eventually all is well, for an appropriate way is finally possible for them to be together and, of course, with honor.

530   Brophy, John. *The Bitter End*. New York: E.P. Dutton & Co., 1928. 252p.

A story about the development and even forced maturity of a sensitive but naive and sex-scared young man. Donald Foster enlists at sixteen, partly to show his manhood to his family and friends. He is basically an innocent in the ways of the world and afflicted by all the disadvantages of Victorian prudery. Indeed, he is totally unprepared for the brutality and vice connected with the war. But his friends give him a standard of behavior and values he can hold to at last. Wounded and sent home to England to recuperate, he meets a girl who soon offers him a new ideal of love and affection. Unfortunately, when his leave is over, he has a disastrous misunderstanding with her. The main purpose of the plot is to show the evolution of Donald Foster against the backdrop and influence of the war. A happy ending is implied at the conclusion, when the Armistice seems to promise a reunion with his former love. There is also an attempt to criticize the inequities of military life and to reveal the futility of war as a method of resolving differences.

531   Chack, Paul. *The Entente Upon the Seas; Historical Romance*. Translated from the French by ... L.B. Denman. Liège: Vaillant-Carmanne, 1928. 321p. [Title of edition in England(?): *Sea Fights, 1914-1918, Historical Romance*. London: Simpkin, Marshall, Hamilton, Kent & Co., 1929. 322p.]

Not seen; NYPL.

532   Ford, Ford Madox. *The Last Post*. New York: A. & C. Boni, 1928. 285p. [Title of edition in England: *Last Post*. London: Gerald Duckworth & Co., 1928. 292p.]

Although this is the final novel of the four Tietjens family titles of World War I, it technically does not qualify for this bibliography since it deals with the postwar world and circumstances of the several characters. It is this story that resolves the fate of the Tietjens family and their estate as an anachronism that inevitably must die as, indeed, is the case at the conclusion of the novel.

533 Guest, Carmel (Goldsmid). *The Yellow Pigeon*. London: George G. Harrap & Co., 1928. 294p.; New York: Dial Press, 1929. 307p.

A series of episodes involving nurses and several women of various nationalities doing war work in Belgium, only a few miles from the front. Crystal Heath, the wife of a physician, is the principal character.

534 Kessel, Joseph. "Pilot and Observer" in *The Pure in Heart*. New York: Dodd, Mead & Co., 1928. 288p. [The title page carries the statement: "Comprising the novel published in Paris under the title *L'Equipage* here rendered *Pilot and Observer* and the three stories published in Paris under the title *Les Coeurs Purs*." This volume contains 157 pages devoted to *Pilot and Observer; L'équipage*. Paris: Nouvelle Revue Francaise, 1923. 217p.].

Concentrates on the lives of two French airmen, Lieutenant Claud Maury and Cadet Jean Herbillon, who have met at the front and become close friends, not realizing that one is the husband and one is the lover of the same woman. The novel describes the day-to-day life of airmen at a French air base close to the front. (The French version appeared in no less than 114 editions.)

535 Mack, Charles E. *Two Black Crows in the A.E.F.* Indianapolis: Bobbs-Merrill Co., 1928. 339p.

This is an attempt to create a humorous burlesque of a war story set in France. The two characters are based on the vaudeville circuit performers of those days called "The Two Black Crows," a blackface team consisting of the spry Willie and the lazy Amos. The author was one of the original members of the team. The plot, such as it is, serves mainly as a shadowy background for the exploits of the two characters. As members of a Pioneer Infantry regiment in France, the Crows have not had a dull moment since they enlisted in Tennessee. A chance encounter with Tongo Bok, a Senegalese soldier of France, starts them on their adventures which include experiences on the front lines, capture by the Germans, and an incredible escape. Seeing the Crows on the stage may well have been satisfactory slapstick entertainment; but reading of them and their comedy exploits tends to be another matter, for their humor depends upon facial expressions, the spoken word, and body movements. It is clear that current programs such as M.A.S.H. (the successful movie and TV series) are not the sole or only attempts to introduce comedy into the grim realities of war. Hasek's novel, *The Good Soldier: Schweik* (item 611) is probably the supreme artistic comic novel dealing with the Great War.

536 Mackenzie, Compton. *Extremes Meet*. London: Cassell & Co., 1928. 318p.; Garden City, N.Y.: Doubleday Doran & Co., 1928. 316p.

This appears to be the first authentic novel about the British secret service during the war. Milton Waterlow is an agent on duty in southeast Europe. He soon finds himself harassed by his superiors and his subordinates as well as distracted by a flirtatious wife of a legation official. To top it all off he also assumes responsibility for an attractive little local dancer called Queenie Walters. Nevertheless, in almost 007 style he so nearly succeeds in catching a German spy that he is awarded the coveted command of a Q-boat. It is obvious that this bit of spy-fluff does not demand all the literary powers of the author. However, the book does exhibit entertaining humor and even satire with an obvious sense of literary style.

537 Maugham, William Somerset. *Ashenden: or, The British Agent*. London: Wm. Heinemann, 1928. 304p.

A partly autobiographical novel composed of eight or ten entertaining stories of the experiences of a British secret agent, Ashenden, engaged in the diplomatic sphere of activity. Ashenden is a novelist and playwright, but was made a lieutenant in Britain's secret service in 1914. Ashenden was told that his new profession would provide him with much interesting material for his writing career. His first assignment was in Geneva, where he was in charge of several minor spies working for England. In Geneva he meets, as one reviewer put it, "the inevitable lady of the snares," as well as Prince Ali, a pasha, and the Hairless Mexican, who constantly changes wigs for his assassination jobs. The novel is inferior to Maugham's best works.

Adult Novels

538 Nason, Leonard Hastings. *Sergeant Eadie*. Garden City, N.Y.: Doubleday, Doran & Co., 1928. 374p.

The story of one man's experiences in the war. Sergeant Eadie of the American Expeditionary Forces is seen in nearly all of the activities of the war, from being in a torpedoed transport ship to experiencing shell shock followed by his eventual recovery. The narrative is amply filled with brutal and yet poignant humor. It is probably as honest a view as is available of the A.E.F. in the war.

539 Sassoon, Siegfried Lorraine. *Memoirs of a Fox-Hunting Man*. London: Faber & Gwyer, 1928. 395p.

The first part of this autobiographical novel deals with fox hunting. The last part concerns the war in France, with impressive war scenes. The fox-hunting man, George Sherston, carries into the war a sense of nostalgia and security which he so highly valued in the English countryside that he left for the war, though he realizes that after the war, hunting in England's "garden" will not be the same. The book first appeared in England anonymously. It is now considered to be one of the more significant novels written about the Great War.

540 Schickele, Rene. *Maria Capponi*. Translated from the German by Hannah Waller. New York: Alfred A. Knopf, 1928. 332p. [*Maria Capponi*. München: Kurt Wolff, 1925. 483p.]

The novel is a broad mosaic of European society and life covering the years immediately before, during, and after the war. The narrative has a Proust-like aspect in its detailed concern with the sensations of the two protagonists. The principal character is Claus von Breuschheim, an ex-German officer who has just lost his wife under tragic circumstances in a glacier crevasse. As a result, he now decides to write his memoirs in order to remove his thoughts as much as possible from his personal loss. The woman who stands out in the story is Maria Capponi, an Italian marchesa who was his first love. She introduced him to the mysteries of love at the age of fourteen. Now that his beloved wife is dead, he tries to turn again to Maria. Aside from this theme of love, the book carefully explores the death and rebirth of an entire social structure in Europe. We see European society through the eyes of Claus as a fourteen-year-old boy and then at various ages and stages of his development. The novel captures the ambience of this erstwhile gay and carefree life with brief, revealing passages of artistry. The effect of the war and its aftermath on European society is seen through the experienced and responsible eyes of a Claus who has become "a care-laden" man. Claus, then, is a representative example of not only the primary observer of European life through this period but also a recipient of its upheavals. This is a well-written and sensitive novel and the first volume of a trilogy.

541 Thurston, Ernest Temple. *Portrait of a Spy: A Novel*. London and New York: G.P. Putnam's Sons, 1928. 300p.

The life of the Oriental dancer-spy Mata Hari provides the basis for this novel. The spy in the novel is Mada Garass, who uses the war as a means to gain revenge. The plot departs but little from the known facts of Mata Hari, who was executed by the French for her connection with the Germans.

542 Tomlinson, Henry Major. *Illusion: 1915*. New York: Harper & Brothers, 1928. 25p.

A surrealistic portrayal of wartime during a few hours in June of 1915. The narrator comes upon a French house which he had been seeking, with the sense of being lost in another age in an unreal world. The countryside is peaceful, but "it was not accurately fitted to the earth, it was not quite firm on its base." It was "as though the narrator stood in the June of one year and saw distantly the pale ghost of the old chateau in a silent June of the past." The narrator is conducted to his battalion near Neuve Chapelle where nobody seems to believe in the reality of the war although evidence of it is all around. The story was first published in the *New Adelphi* (1927) and reprinted from *Harpers Magazine* (September 1927).

543 Unruh, Fritz Wilhelm Ernst von. *The Way of Sacrifice*. Translated from the German by C.A. Macartney. New York: Alfred A. Knopf, 1928. 181p. [*Opfergang*.... Berlin: Reiss, 1919. 204p.]

Views the war from a German perspective. According to the publisher the book was originally written in the spring of 1916 at the behest of the German General Staff as a propaganda effort to spur the troops. But the book turned out to be a very different work and was suppressed by the censor until 1918. The publisher also indicates that it was possibly smuggled in manuscript from among the German soldiers and could have "done much toward undermining German morale during the last months of the war." Be that as it may, it is a story of a storm-troop company and its fate at Verdun. Various individuals are described in a highly emotional style at times. There is Captain von Werner who secretly writes in his diary about his serious doubts concerning the purpose of the war; Sergeant Hillbrand, a German of the old school; Clemens, an ex-schoolmaster; the cadet who carries a wounded bird in his shirt front until the morning of the disastrous assault; Preis, the drummer who dreams of glory but in the end is attacked by diarrhea in the midst of the advance; and the shell-shocked exwaiter who goes mad. The book concludes with the company going into its final insane and hopeless assault on the French forts at Verdun. This is an unusual and powerful perspective from the German side and joins with Dos Passos, Rolland, and others in creating a corpus of outstanding anti-war literature.

544 Vring, Georg von der. *Private Suhren: The Story of a German Rifleman*. Translated by Fred Hall. New York: Harper & Brothers, 1928. 327p. [*Soldat Suhren, Roman*. Zurich: P. Zsolnay, 1927. 383p.]

The novel is autobiographical, rather like a diary in form, presenting detailed pictures of life behind the German lines. Private Suhren is a German soldier who believes strongly in the righteousness of the war, even though he is little more than a pawn moved by his officers as he moves through Germany, France, and Russia.

545 Wharton, James B. *Squad*. New York: Coward-McCann, 1928. 300p.

An account of the experiences of eight men of the American Expeditionary Force in France. It is apparent that the major characters are types rather than individual and full-dimensioned personalities. The author has created all eight as dissimilar as possible apparently for better contrast and point of view. For example, there is a Philadelphia Italian, a New York East Side Jew, an Irishman, a Serbian miner from Pennsylvania, a high-school boy from San Francisco, a Swede from Texas, and a corporal from Ohio. The story is a hard-boiled, vivid, and realistic account of the war. It seems an especially good description of what war was like for the average soldier.

546 Wiley, Hugh. *"Here's Luck!"* New York: J.H. Sears & Co., 1928. 297p.

Focuses on an American engineer-regiment platoon erecting barracks and warehouses in France during the war. The platoon, nicknamed "The Gang," is a group of hard-drinkers who, as one reviewer put it, soon discover that the foreign "inhabitants are strange, the trains are queer and liquor is plentiful. Something must be done about establishing an Entente Cordiale.... The Entente is maintained by rum and riot."

547 Zweig, Arnold. *The Case of Sergeant Grischa*. Translated from the German by Eric Sutton. New York: Viking Press, 1928. 449p. [*Der Streit um den Sergeanten Grischa, Roman*. Potsdam: G. Kiepenheuer, 1928. 552p.]

A novel about the competition for the life of a peasant Russian prisoner of war in the eastern front, who escapes from his incarceration in a timber camp, filches the papers of a dead Russian deserter, Bjuscheff, who was judged a spy after his death. Grischa is apprehended with the stolen identification papers, and he is sentenced to death and executed. Grischa had corroborated his acknowledged identity, but a German general made an issue of the matter and insisted on a sentence of death. "When once a man is caught in the machine, he comes out a corpse." (On the German battlefields, many deserters were considered to be agents of Bolshevism and were feared as such; they were informed that they could be executed if they did not surrender by a certain date.) This novel is a parable of the conflict between might and right and a passionate novel of man's inhumanity to man. One of the finest novels of World War I.

1929

548 Acland, Peregrine. *All Else is Folly: A Tale of War and Passion*. London: Constable, 1929. 273p.; New York: Coward-McCann, 1929. 345p.

This novel concludes with the question "Does man fight only because he hasn't yet learned to love?" The background to this query involves the passionate love of Canadian line officer Alexander Falcon for Adair Hollister, wife of a war prisoner in Germany. When Falcon is severely wounded in battle, his features nearly shot away, he is,

after a long while, visited by Adair, who no longer cares
for him. Ford Madox Ford, in a prefatory note, claimed
that the novel was "the first really authentic work of
imaginative writing dealing with the War to come out of
the great British Dominions."

549 Aldington, Richard. *Death of a Hero: A Novel*. London:
Chatto & Windus, 1929. 440p.; New York: Covici, Friede,
1929. 398p.

A flashback examines the life of Captain George Winterbourne of the British army who, shell-shocked by his experiences of war's destruction, kills himself on the eve
of the Armistice by stepping into a line of fire at the
front. His friend the narrator (Aldington?) reveals what
he knows of the hero, in order to give value to what George
Winterbourne did. The narrator considered that the "unrealistic" culture of middle-class England in which Winterbourne grew up was ultimately responsible for his death.
A savage debunking of the entire concept of heroism.
(Aldington began writing the novel in 1918 in Belgium
"almost immediately after the Armistice" but began it all
over again a decade later.)

550 Alverdes, Paul. *The Whistlers' Room*. Translated from
the German by Basil Creighton. London: Martin Secker,
Ltd., 1929. 99p. [*Die Pfeiferstube: Bericht aus einem
Lazarett*. Leipzig: 1928. Pp. 30-55.]

Whistling is a basic element in this novel. The novel's
three characters, German soldiers in a military hospital,
had received throat wounds from enemy bullets, and, while
undergoing therapy, must use silver pipes, inserted by
their physician, for breathing. "When they breathed a
soft piping note like the squeaking of mice came from the
silver mouth ... hence they were called the whistlers."
A fourth "whistler" who joins them is an Englishman, a
war prisoner, and the common disability of the quartet
binds them as friends. The suffering which war produces
becomes the agent for breaking down barriers between
enemies and developing friendship.

551 Barretto, Laurence Brevoort. *Horses in the Sky*. New
York: John Day Co., 1929. 338p.

An analysis of four young men's psychological reactions
to the war. The four, Bender, Hitchcock, Holmburg, and
Tower, all Americans, are ambulance drivers in the Aisne

region of France. One of the men, Jerry Tower, dismissing the preferred love of a French girl, yearns to find his "dream sweetheart," Allison Porter, who appeared to him, dream-like, in a hospital where he was virtually dying, and caused him to recover.

552 Bertram, Cyril Anthony George. *The Sword Falls*. London: George Allen & Unwin, 1929. 280p.

A novel about Albert Robinson, an elderly cockney clerk who lives with his wife Victoria ("Dot") in the suburbs. The novel presents convincing descriptions of London during the war, training camp life, and other military experiences of Robinson. Specifically the novel presents, as a result of the war, the disintegration of Robinson's family and the loss of what he holds dear, and his stoical reconstruction of his world. Robinson must cope with the following events: his cowardly son is shot down by his comrades; his wife experiences a form of insanity and dies from pneumonia; his daughter leaves home; the family's house is demolished by German bombing; and Robinson receives a serious abdominal wound in war service. A melodrama almost reminiscent of "As the World Turns."

553 Blake, George. *The Path of Glory*. London: Constable, 1929. 224p.; New York: Harper & Brothers, 1929. 224p.

Two friends, Clydeside shipyard workers, Col Macaulay and John Macleod, enlist in a Highland regiment as pipers. When Col marries Kirsty, who almost immediately deceives him, John gives Kirsty and her lover a thrashing. Soon after, the two pipers are sent to war, and both die at Gallipoli. The novel presents a realistic account of the wartime life of Scottish soldiers and of the trench fighting at Gallipoli, where disease was as threatening as bullets.

554 Chamson, André Jules Louis. *Roux the Bandit*. Translated from the French by Van Wyck Brooks. New York: Charles Scribner's Sons, 1929. 198p.

A novel of a young French peasant and a conscientious objector, whose attitude and action against the war made him a legend while he was yet alive. After hiding out for three years and suffering much privation, he was caught by the authorities, jailed by the gendarmes, and sentenced for twenty years. The novel was the second of Chamson's trilogy of mountaineers of the Cevennes Mountains.

Adult Novels 193

555 Daviot, Gordon (pseud. of Elizabeth Mackintosh). *Kif: An Unvarnished History*. London: Ernest Benn, Ltd., 1929. 286p.; New York: D. Appleton & Co., 1929. 353p.

Only the first half of this story concerns the war. Nineteen-year-old Archibald Vicar ("Kif") is described through his four years of war experiences in France. After the war he returns to London and seeks a job. The second half of the novel concerns his postwar success before fate turns against him and his world comes crashing down in final disgrace and he is executed. A popular melodrama.

556 Dawson, Coningsby William. *The Unknown Soldier*. Garden City, N.Y.: Doubleday, Doran & Co., 1929. 60p.

The plot suggests that Christ lived and died anew within the person of each nation's Unknown Soldier. A somewhat sentimental religious parable of only historical interest. It was originally published in the *Delineator* magazine.

557 Forester, Cecil Scott. *Brown on Resolution*. London: John Lane Co., 1929. 272p. [Title in U.S.: *Single-Handed*. New York: G.P. Putnam's Sons, 1929. 273p.]

An early historical thriller by the writer of the Hornblower series of historical novels. In this case, the plot concerns the heroic career of Albert Brown, a sailor in the Royal Navy. The story traces his life from the time of his birth to Agatha Brown, his spinster mother, as a result of her romance with a handsome naval officer. As a consequence, Albert is brought up to be a sailor. His chief exploit is the defeat of the *Ziethen*, a German cruiser on which he had been a prisoner. By himself and armed only with a rifle he manages to hold up the ship for twenty-four hours at Resolution in the Galapagos Islands. According to the *London Times*: "It is an ingenious piece of might-be-true naval history in which the unit of interest is the ship, not the man."

558 Frank, Leonhard. *Carl and Anna*. Translated by Cyrus Brooks. London: Peter Davies, 1929. 117p.; Published under the title *Beloved Stranger* in 1946. [*Karl und Anna*. Berlin: Propyläen-verlag, 1926. 174p.]

While two brothers, Carl and Richard, are together in a prison camp, Richard describes his wife Anna so engagingly to his brother that when Carl escapes from prison he finds

Anna and courts her. When Richard is released, he discovers that he has lost his wife to his brother. The novel was praised for its "psychological believability." Classed as a war novel because of the account of the four years the brothers spent in a prison camp in Russia.

559 Glaeser, Ernst. *Class of 1902*. Translated by Willa and Edwin Muir. New York: Viking Press, 1929. 397p.; London: Martin Secker, 1929. 316p. [*Jahrgang 1902*. Potsdam: G. Kiepenheuer, 1928. 354p.]

Evokes the experiences of middle-class German youth in the school class of 1902, who though they received military training in school, were too young to enlist. Reviewers praised the author's presentation of youth at odds with the adult world and preoccupied with sex. The novel is a commentary on young Germans who were soon to become a part of the "lost generation."

560 Grabenhorst, Georg. *Zero Hour*. Translated from the German. Boston: Little, Brown & Co., 1929. 306p. [*Fahnenjunker Volkenborn*. Leipzig: Hase & Koehler, 1928. 245p.]

Hans Volkenborn, the protagonist, enters officers' training in order to lead a much more pleasant and varied life than that of the common soldier. Essentially an upper-class view of the war which tells how a sensitive group of young Germans went to fight, how they suffered and endured, and how they became disillusioned. A good deal of immature and amateurish philosophizing. Strongly autobiographical, the story is far from a direct or compelling document on the war. Although similar to Remarque's *All Quiet on the Western Front* in subject matter, it falls far short in quality.

561 Hemingway, Ernest. *A Farewell to Arms*. New York: Charles Scribner's Sons, 1929. 355p.

A novel which makes a statement of disaffection, but not revulsion, about the war and what is defined as military glory, along with the blossoming of a poignant love story, both themes managed with literary confidence. Hemingway's respect for physical force, shown in his fascination with boxing, bullfighting, and hunting, made him appreciate the exhilaration which the war could cause among comrades. In the novel, the hero, Lieutenant Frederick Henry, an American ambulance officer, is fighting with the Italian army at Isonzo on the Italian-Austrian border, before the Unite

States entered the war. When Henry is severely wounded, he is nursed by Catherine Barkley, a Scottish nurse. Though frequent movements of the troops often separate the two, they eventually fall in love. When the Italian army retreats from Caporetto, the troops disintegrate, and Henry decides that to remain with the army would be senseless. He gives his farewell to arms and escapes with the pregnant Catherine to Switzerland. Their child is born dead in Switzerland and Catherine's death occurs but a few hours later. This novel, partly autobiographical--in World War I, Hemingway served in the Italian army and was badly wounded--is Hemingway at his best in reflecting on the war a decade after it ended.

562 Hodson, James Lansdale. *Grey Dawn--Red Night*. London: Victor Gollancz, 1929. 287p.

A recital of much of the life of the main character, John Hardcastle, a young Englishman, but especially his war experiences until his death from a German shell. Apparently much of the novel is autobiographical. The phrase "grey dawn" repesents the main character's childhood and youth under the smog of Manchester; "red night" symbolizes the war. Considerable detail is provided about the training procedure for soldiers at home and in the European field in 1916. This part of the novel has been highly praised. The war scenes are vivid.

563 Lee, Mary. *"It's a Great War!"* Boston: Houghton Mifflin Co., 1929. 574p.

The war at the front from 1917 to 1920, described through the experiences of Anne Wentworth, a noncombatant. The scenes include canteens, barracks, hospitals, and the army of occupation in Germany. Since the author was with a hospital unit in France and also served near the front, the novel is probably partly autobiographical. It shared the $25,000 price for the best war novel presented by Houghton Mifflin and the *American Legion Monthly* with W. T. Scanlon's *God Have Mercy on Us! A Story of 1918* (item 577).

564 Löhrke, Eugene William. *Overshadowed*. Jonathan Cape & Harrison Smith, 1929. 235p.

A novel of the breakdown of a sensitive young man, Darrow, by the horrible brutality he witnesses in the war, specifically along the western front and the Rhineland. Darrow was a "mamma's boy" who was impelled to enlist by his mother, for reasons of her own. He served in the infantry where his experiences were a hell on earth. Several reviewers commented on the novel's Conradian style.

565 Mackenzie, Compton. *The Three Couriers*. London: Cassell & Co., 1929. 314p.; Garden City, N.Y.: Doubleday, Doran, 1929. 295p.

A novel in the author's series begun in 1928 with *Extremes Meet* (item 536). The main character again is Commander Roger Waterlow, British secret service agent. In this novel Waterlow is attempting, with French and Italian diplomat officials, to intercept enemy couriers. The setting is the Balkans. Seems partly autobiographical.

566 Mahon, Terence. *Cold Feet*. London: Chapman & Hall, 1929. 249p.; New York: Coward-McCann, 1929. 249p.

A partly autobiographical novel of a British army captain who is executed for cowardice during battle. The story traces the captain's life back to elementary school and the root of his cowardice. The army chaplain accepts the body after the execution, and describes an event in the captain's life immediately prior to the execution which clearly makes it apparent that the captain is a hero after all.

567 [Manning, Frederic]. *The Middle Parts of Fortune; Somme & Ancre, 1916*. London: Piazza Press; Peter Davies, 1929. 2 vols. [Published in 1930 with the title: *Her Privates We* by Private 19022.]

First published anonymously, the book was republished the next year under the title *Her Privates We* with the pseudonym Private 19022. The original version contains all of the language of the trenches and battlefields, both profane and otherwise, that was characteristic of the men who served. Hemingway once said that this novel was "the finest and noblest book of men in war that I have ever read." The story begins with the return of a unit from action and concludes with an attack in which nearly all of the characters described by the author are killed. There are scenes of the trivial and boring minutes and hours spent between the attacks and in the rest periods away from the front lines. The banality of military life and warfare is all too apparent. The point of view is that of the ordinary soldier in the war. The central character and narrator is referred to only as Bourne. There is no plot, no important female character, and nothing much happens except in the realm of the war. This is a heavily autobiographical novel. It is now considered to be one of the most outstanding works of fiction on World War I. (St. Martin's Press republished the original version in 1977.)

568 Markovits, Rodion. *Siberian Garrison*. Translated from the Hungarian by George Halasz. London: Peter Davies, 1929. 387p.; New York: Liveright, 1929. 407p. [*Sziberiai garnizon, kollektiv riportregény*. Budapest: Genius, 1929. 503p.]

The story of a Hungarian from Budapest who is drafted into the Hungarian army, sent to the eastern front, taken prisoner by the Russians in 1915, and held for nearly six years in Siberian prison camps. The novel depicts the prisoners' adaptation to prison life, of the society which evolves among the prisoners, and of their eventual release three years after the Armistice. The novel is characterized by a graphic realism that is relentlessly applied.

569 Morris, Walter Frederick. *Bretherton: Khaki or Fieldgrey?* London: Geoffrey Bles, 1929. 319p. [Title in U.S.: *"G.B.": A Story of the Great War*. New York: Dodd, Mead & Co., 1929. 306p.]

A psychological war story. Gerard Bretherton ("G.B."), a leader of a British company of soldiers, is discovered dead in a chateau behind the German lines, dressed in the uniform of a German general. The dead body of the Duchess of Wittelsberg lies nearby. A flashback to 1915 provides the explanation of this enigma. Concurrent with this mystery story, the reactions of Allied and German officers to many of the war's important battles are presented.

570 Nason, Leonard Hastings. *The Man in the White Slicker*. Garden City, N.Y.: Doubleday, Doran & Co., 1929. 290p.

An account of a mysterious experience during the war. An officer in a white raincoat walks out of the woods in the Argonne toward a machine-gun crew that became separated from their unit, and orders the crew to fire on their troops. The crew knock out the strange man and he presently disappears, but more mystery develops in his wake.

571 Nazhivin, Ivan Fedorovich. *Rasputin*. Translated from the Russian by C.J. Hogarth. New York: Alfred A. Knopf, 1929. 2 vols. [*Rasputin, Roman*. Leipzig: F. Fikentscher, 1923. 3 vols. in one.]

An account of Russian life before, during, and after the war, with the evil spirit of Rasputin hovering throughout the scenes. The Mother Russia described is not "Holy Russia" but a horrid and an ugly Russia. The novel has been compared to Tolstoy's *War and Peace*.

572 Nordhoff, Charles Bernard, and James Norman Hall. *Falcons of France: A Tale of Youth and the Air*. Boston: Little, Brown & Co., 1929. 332p.

This novel describes experiences of two very young (seventeen) Lafayette Escadrille members, particularly Charlie Seldon, on his reconnaissance missions and air battles, his capture by the enemy, and so forth. Both authors were members of the Lafayette Escadrille during the war.

573 Odum, Howard Washington. *Wings on My Feet: Black Ulysses at the Wars*. Indianapolis: Bobbs-Merrill Co., 1929. 309p.

The story is related in the form of a monologue in which the rhythms of black speech are interrupted by brief bits of song that turn out to be new words to old and traditional tunes ranging from the blues to the songs blacks sang in the fields, camps, on the road, and over crap games in the U.S. Army. It is a tale of the typical black soldier and his reactions to the war. One critic referred to it as the "black parallel to 'All Quiet on the Western Front,'" but it is obvious now that this is a gross exaggeration. This is one of the very few novels depicting the black in World War I and from the point of view of a black. The dialect now seems almost coy and today appears to be a vestige that has an artificial if not prejudicial ring to contemporary ears.

574 O'Flaherty, Liam. *Return of the Brute*. London: Mandrake Press, 1929. 187p.

This study of nine soldiers, victims of the war, made brutish by the conflict, traces their life at the front in France in 1917. After being continuously subjected to fear and suffering and hunger, all but one of them die.

Adult Novels

Some of the men who are psychologically studied in this novel are George Appleby, fanatically religious; Michael Friel, policeman; Gunn, a simple soldier; Simon Jennings, dubbed "The Gent" by his comrades; Lamond, a young student; Jeremiah McDonald, doltish, a victim of pranks by his mates; James Shaw, most respected by the others; and Daniel Reilly, an excellent soldier who survives. The descriptions are earthy. One critic epitomized the book with a popular description of similar novels of the time: "After all, the entire war was not fought in the latrines."

575 Remarque, Erich Maria. *All Quiet on the Western Front.* Translated from the German by Arthur Wesley Wheen. Boston: Little, Brown, 1929. 291p.; London: G.P. Putnam's Sons, 1929. 319p. [*Im Westen Nichst Neues.* Berlin: Kiepenheuer & Witsch, 1928. 287p.]

Presumably an autobiographical account of a young soldier and three friends who were pulled out of school and pressed into duty in the trenches. The main character is Paul Bäumer, a private, who survives the war physically but is emotionally destroyed by his experiences in filth and meanness while searching for some light to survive the traumatic nightmare of the war. Seen through Paul are the rank-and-file soldiers' response to fear, sickness, and the danger of the shelling at the front lines. A tragic story of comrades too young to have formed any roots. In Paul's squad Corporal Himmelstoss devises disgusting jobs and penalties for the recruits under him. Paul says, "We learned that a bright button is more important than four volumes of Schopenhauer." Paul's friends, Katcyinsky, Muller, and Kemmerich die in Flanders. The novel's power rests in its passionate hatred of war, as it exhibits the disillusionment provoked by the conflict. After the novel was published, hatred in Germany and abuse from the German right-wing press forced Remarque to move to Switzerland. (During World War II Remarque came to the United States, where he wrote *Arch of Triumph.*)

576 Renn, Ludwig (pseud. of Arnold Friedrich Vieth von Golssenau). *War.* Translated by Willa and Edwin Muir. London: Martin Secker, Ltd., 1929. 364p.; New York: Dodd, Mead & Co., 1929. 342p. [*Krieg.* Frankfurt am Main: Frankfurter Societäts-Druckerie, 1929. 413p.]

An autobiographical novel, written as a diary, recounting the story told by a German army private who is promoted to corporal. He relates his experiences in an unemotional tone, characterized by unusual detachment and realism. The story begins with the first day of the German mobilization and concludes with the Armistice. Many details of life in the trenches are vividly captured with considerable impact. An episodic and exceedingly impressionistic account which achieves its unusual impact through abrupt, staccato, narrative technique. The war is depicted without the least trace of glamor or romanticism and only occasionally relieved by moments of grim humor.

577 Scanlon, William T. *God Have Mercy on Us! A Story of 1918*. Boston: Houghton Mifflin Co., 1929. 337p.

An informative account of United States Marines fighting at Verdun, in the Meuse-Argonne, Chateau-Thierry, Belleau Wood, Soissons, ending with the Armistice. Autobiographical basis: Scanlon was a sergeant in the Marine's Sixth Regiment. The book was co-winner of the prize of $25,000 presented by the Houghton Mifflin Company and the *American Legion Monthly* for the best World War I novel. Mary Lee's novel "*It's a Great War!*" (item 563) shared the prize.

578 Schauwecker, Franz. *The Fiery Way*. Translated by Thonald Holland. London: J.M. Dent & Sons, 1929. 252p. [*Der Feurige Weg*. Leipzig: Der Aufmarsch Verlagsgesellschaft, 1926. 231p.]

Begins with the introduction of raw recruits into military life and training. The story relates the everyday trivia of the military life--drill, barracks activity, exercises, etc. The fictional narrator is never identified by name, but obviously represents the author. Interspersed throughout the story are many observations and commentaries on the circumstances of war, national ideologies, and military doctrine. The war scenes are rendered especially vivid and horrifying by the cinema-verité technique of the author. Pictures of agonizing death, shell shock, and the other agonies of the front lines are painted with searing reality. The novel presents an intense, impressionistic view of German war experiences and defeat, but concludes on a strong note of militaristic nationalism.

579 Schindel, Bayard. *Golden Pilgrimage*. Garden City, N.Y.: Doubleday, Doran & Co., 1929. 324p.

Relates the awareness of a young boy, Peter Longman, and the effect of the war upon him from 1914 to 1918. Peter's father is a captain in an American training camp, and he and Peter travel extensively about the United States to military duty assignments. Peter's view of the war changes from enthusiasm for the conflict to disillusionment.

580 [Schulz, Emil]. *Schlump: The Story of an Unknown Soldier*. London: Martin Secker, Ltd., 1929. 309p. [Title in U.S.: *Schlump: The Story of a German Soldier; Told by Himself*. Translated from the German by Maurice Samuel. New York: Harcourt, Brace & Co., 1929. 299p.; *Schlump; Geschichten und Abenteuer aus dem Leben des Unbekannten Musketiers Emil Schulz....* Munchen: Kurt Wolff, 1928. 279p.]

Schlump is a very simple sixteen-year-old German youth when the war begins. The conflict seems mainly a matter of dirt, starvation, love, and horseplay. Schlump is created as an outgoing, even manic roughneck who goes through the fighting without any spiritual agony or suffering, and without ever questioning the war or its purpose. The story is almost picaresque with Schlump's fighting, eating, lovemaking, money-making scheming, selling military supplies, etc. He and his fellows are characterized by a rowdy camaraderie. This is a picture of the uncomplicated animal fighting-man for whom guilt and remorse are clearly foreign in most instances. The novel surveys four years of fighting from the perspective of what the war was like for the ordinary and uncomplicated soldier. When the war is over, Schlump remains the same simple person he was when it started. Although the novel presents a vivid account of the German retreat preceding the Armistice, the writing is prosaic.

581 Seton, Graham (pseud. of Graham Seton Hutchison). *The W Plan*. London: T. Butterworth, 1929. 301p.

A spy story involving a Scottish colonel, Duncan Grant, who, disguised as a German officer in uniform, is dropped from a plane behind the German lines to learn about Germany's secret "W" plan. Grant, of course, obtains the documents, saving the English from a possibly devastating attack.

582 Stowell, Gordon. *The History of Button Hill*. London: Victor Gollancz, 1929. 431p.

Button Hill is a suburban town in Yorkshire, England. The main character, Eric Ellersby, has grown up in the community, and along with other boys in the town goes to war. The novel deals with the boys' activity in the war and the influence of the conflict upon them. An autobiographical novel by an ex-soldier.

583 Trites, William Budd. *A Modern Girl*. New York: F.A. Stokes, Co., 1929. 286p.

Provides many pictures of French urban scenes in 1918. (The author lived most of his life in France.) The novel is primarily a love story set in France involving a young, beautiful American girl, Hilda March, and an aviator, Jack Stafford.

584 Weston, George. *Wings of Destiny*. New York: Dodd, Mead & Co., 1929. 312p.

Discharged from the military unjustly, Lieutenant Millard Delvan is sent to Switzerland to gather data for the American secret service. Through his meeting Baroness Seidler, a passenger on the same ship to Europe, Lieutenant Delavan gains entrance into the German secret-service world. After many hair-raising adventures, including sentencing to be shot as a spy, Delavan ends the novel safely, and in love.

585 Wheen, Arthur Wesley. *Two Masters*. London: Faber & Faber, 1929. 32p.

The narrator is a young recruit, Carter, who is a member of the remnants of the Australian Expeditionary Force which fought at Gallipoli. The force is being reorganized in Egypt; the time is December 1915. The novel's subject is a philosophical discussion between Carter and Ralston, a battle-tried intellectual and idealist. While the expeditionary force is later on duty in France, Carter's association with Ralston becomes firmer, as Carter works at fusing his emotional view of the war with a pragmatic attitude toward the seemingly worthlessness of life in the war around them. Ralston, seemingly serene and imperturbable, becomes "the rallying-point" for all the men. When Carter is sent to the officers' training school in England, the association between the two men is maintained, in a very long letter from Ralston, which arrives in Carter's hands after Ralston has been killed in no-man's-land.

1930

586 Aldington, Richard. *At All Costs*. London: Wm. Heinemann, 1930. 45p.

A brief account of a military engagement in which undermanned Allied forces are charged with holding off twenty to thirty German divisions for 12 hours until additional Allied reserve divisions arrive. The plot focuses on the destiny of "B" Company and its ultimate annihilation.

587 Bartlett, Vernon. *No Man's Land*. London: Allen & Unwin, 1930. 329p. [Title in U.S.: *The Unknown Soldier*. New York: F.A. Stokes, Co., 1930. 329p.]

Relates the thoughts of Stevenson, an Englishman who is the only character in the book. He is near death from enemy gunfire and mentally relives his experiences in a shell hole in no-man's-land while painfully waiting for nightfall to crawl back to safety. He is killed by his comrades who mistake him for a German soldier. The book presents a clear account of the conflict in the Ypres Salient. Early in his life a gypsy had forecast that Stevenson would be given homage by distinguished men in the world. The prediction comes true when Stevenson's body is honored as the "unknown soldier" in a special ceremony in England.

588 Benoit, Pierre. *Axelle*. New York: Dial Press (Lincoln MacVeagh), 1930. 316p. [*Axelle, Roman*. Paris: A. Michel, 1928. 351p.]

A psychological love story with its setting in a German prison camp near Königsberg and the nearby castle of General Count von Reichendorf. A French prisoner and former electrician, Sergeant Dumaine, while repairing the castle's electric wiring, meets Axelle, a relative of the Count. Repeated meetings develop the novel's love interest and produce the conflict between a love of country and a love of the enemy. Contains some general descriptions of prison camp life.

589 Benstead, Charles Richard. *Retreat: A Story of 1918*. London: Methuen & Co., 1930. 317p. [Title in U.S.: *Retreat: A Novel of 1918*. New York: Century Co., 1930. 355p.]

An account of the deterioration of a middle-aged regimental English priest, Elliot Warne. He succumbs to madness and death from influenza as a result of his horrible experiences at the front and the loss of confidence in the effectiveness of his "divine mission." Contains vivid scenes of Ludendorff's effective push of March 1918 and the retreat of the British Fifth Army, with special attention given to Gough's army and the effect upon the soldiers of an artillery unit in the retreat from St. Quentin.

590   Blaker, Richard. *Medal Without Bar*. London: Hodder & Stoughton, 1930. 638p.; Garden City, N.Y.: Doubleday, Doran & Co., 1930. 663p.

The life of the main character, Charles Cartwright, a middle-aged, British lieutenant of artillery, is examined from the outset of the war through his years of service as a gunnery officer. Describes the part which the large field guns and their operators played in the war.

591   Boileau, Ethel (Ethel Mary [Young] Boileau). *The Arches of the Years*. London: Hutchinson & Co., 1930. 288p. [Title in U.S.: *The Map of Days, a Novel*. New York: E.P. Dutton & Co., 1935. 283p.]

Relates the life story throughout World War I of Jock Chisholm, a Scots Highlander, who is a born fighter and a professional soldier who has been an officer in the Boer War. His life is filled with plenty of drama, action, and, of course, romance. He is created as a character with a fateful personality which enables him to exercise an unusual power and influence over women as well as to command men. His powerful second-sight ability enables him to see the reality of all those things involved in the Great War that are not obvious to most men. His personal vision ultimately results in his disillusionment and the decision that all war is devastating. In spite of his successful career as a general and soldier, Jock abandons his profession at the age of forty to enter the ministry. He is the big, blue-eyed, red-haired, fighting hero who is also a romantic lover with a mysterious power over others. The combat scenes are perhaps the best and most believable portions of a highly melodramatic novel. The author has been greatly influenced by Kipling. The plot tends to be an artificial romance that is unable to support the serious intentions of the author.

592   Bröger, Karl. *Pillbox 17: The Story of a Comradeship-in-Arms*. Translated by Oakley Williams. London: T.

Butterworth, 1930. 219p. [*Bunker 17, Geschichte einer Kameradschaft*. Jena: E. Diederichs, 1929. 186p.]

The story of a German fortification outflanked by the enemy. The personnel suffocate when bombs bury the fortification's entrance. The one survivor, Corporal Schmalz, who had been sent for help, is judged mad and takes his own life.

592a Burrage, Alfred McLelland. *War Is War*, by Ex-private X. London: Victor Gollancz, Ltd., 1930. 288p.; New York: E.P. Dutton, 1930. 288p.

Not seen; NYPL.

593 Canfield, Dorothy [Dorothea Frances (Canfield) Fisher]. *The Deepening Stream*. New York: Harcourt, Brace & Co., 1930. 393p.

Details the life of Matey Gilbert whose father, an American college professor, and his family divide their time between his several American college posts and France. Matey grows to adulthood feeling closer to a French family, the Vinets, than she does to her self-engrossed parents. After marriage Matey and her husband, with their two children, determine to lend their efforts to the war by going to France in 1915. During the next four years, the realism of the war impinges on the romantic impulse which brought them to Europe, and a much sobered, more mature, and disillusioned couple returns home in 1919. (The novel recounts an attack by the German Big Berthas on Paris.)

594 Colette (pseud. of Sidonie Gabrielle Colette). *Mitsou; or, How Girls Grow Wise*. Translated from the French by Jane Terry. New York: Albert & Charles Boni, 1930. 162p.; London: Victor Gollancz, 1930. 159p. [*Mitsou; ou, Comment l'Esprit Vient aux Filles*. Paris: A. Fayard & Cie., 1919. 167p.]

One of those hazy sentimental-sensual fantasies of a woman in love. Mitsou is a dancer in a Paris music hall during the war. She meets her "Lieutenant in Blue" and they fall in love. In the process she comes to learn a number of things about herself and life in general. Mitsou is the only character given a name in the story. Part of the action is presented through letters between Mitsou and her lieutenant lover. The novel is of little significance to the literature of the war.

595 Dawson, Coningsby William. *Fugitives from Passion.*
Garden City, N.Y.: Doubleday, Doran & Co., 1930. 373p.;
London: Hutchinson & Co., 1930. 336p.

Gordon Fithian and Gay Dolores are childhood sweethearts who grew up and lived in a rugged Canadian area. When war came, Gordon entered the service and Gay left Canada to live with titled relatives in England. Gay marries an officer whom her guardians approved, but upon the officer's death, she returns to Gordon. Much of the action of this novel deals with Gordon's officer-training experiences, life in the trenches, and his incarceration in a German prison camp during the war.

596 Dent, Walter Redvers. *Show Me Death!* New York: Harper & Brothers, 1930. 375p.

A sixteen-year-old Canadian boy is sent to France and becomes a gunner in the Canadian "suicide corps." This autobiographical novel recounts this boy's life at the front, the disfiguring injuries he received in the fighting, and the moral struggle and spiritual suffering of a typical young combatant.

597 Deval, Jacques (pseud. of Jacques Boularan). *Wooden Swords.* Translated by Lawrence S. Morris. New York: Viking Press, 1930. 270p. [*Sabres de Bois*.... Paris: A. Michel, 1929. 253p.]

A comical account of war service by a hopelessly near-sighted Frenchman. His eyesight keeps him out of the trenches and places him safely in a supply unit, but he fights the foe with typewriter, spittoon, broom, and mop. An ironic comedy, poking fun at militarism and viewing the war and the world as farce.

598 Erskine, Laurie York. *Comrades of the Clouds.* New York: D. Appleton & Co., 1930. 256p.

A novel of the day-to-day life of a highly competent group of airmen of the Allied Expeditionary Forces.

599 Federn, Karl. *Baron Fritz.* Translated from the German by Donald Douglas. New York: Farrar & Rinehart, 1930. 296p. [*Haupmann Latour, nach den Aufzeichnungen eines Offiziers.* Hanover: A. Sponholz, 1929. n.p.]

A humorous cycle of yarns about the war. Baron Fritz Talbot Latour von Saint-Aubin is an artillery officer

Adult Novels

commanding a regiment in eastern Germany. He is young, a Don Juan, and a resolute fighter. He extricates himself and his men from military difficulties through laughter. The story is loaded with accounts of life in and behind the German front from the point of view of German army officers. Describes a few atrocities committed by the Allies.

600 Fowler, Guy. *The Dawn Patrol, Novelized by*.... New York: Grosset & Dunlap, 1930. 241p.; London: Readers Library, 1930. 188p.

Tells the story of the men of Squadron 31 of the Royal Air Force. The main character is Captain Dick Courtney, a fighter pilot and leader of the air patrols on their morning missions against the German lines. His final mission takes him on a one-way flight deep into German territory to bomb a munitions dump vital to the success of the expected German assault. A novel based on the motion picture of the same name which was originally taken from a story by John Monk Saunders.

601 Fredenburgh, Theodore. *Soldiers March!* New York: Harcourt, Brace & Co., 1930. 314p.

The main character, young Zorn, is a corporal at twenty, goes to France and becomes a first sergeant at twenty-one. By then he is a courageous, hard-bitten soldier. Authentic pictures of regimental life of the A.E.F., specifically of the 101st Field Artillery, 26th Division, and also of the ill-feeling of the regular soldiers toward drafted troops and National Guard soldiers. (The author served eighteen months in France.)

602 Frenssen, Gustav. *Otto Babendiek*. London: George G. Harrap, 1930. 553p. [Title in U.S.: *The Anvil*. Translated from the German by Huntley Paterson. Boston: Houghton Mifflin Co., 1930. 553p.; *Otto Babendiek, Roman*. Berlin: G. Grote, 1926. 1291p.]

An autobiographical novel. The second half of the story presents moving descriptions of Otto Babendiek's war experiences. The canvas describing the war is large, providing details of the effect of the war upon a large circle, particularly upon the generation older than the soldiers.

603 Frey, Alexander Moriz. *The Cross Bearers: A Story of the Medical Corps*. Translated by Herbert Palmer and Leslie W. Charley. New York: Viking Press, 1930. 306p. [*Die Pflasterkaesten, ein Feldsanitatsroman*. Berlin: G. Kiepenheuer, 1929. 350p.]

Describes the life of surgeons, stretcher bearers, and clerks in the German Medical Corps during four years of war, through the experiences of Private Funk, a clerk. "I'm done!" he shrieks one time, and adds "No more, sick or well. I want to tell the truth. I want to say: War and soldiering are the craziest, stupidest, most shameful and degrading things in the whole world."

604 Fulcher, Paul Milton. *Guests of Summer*. New York: The Macmillan Co., 1930. 420p.

The novel revolves about the character of Jack, born in Ebineezer, a town near the Blue Ridge Mountains. Jack is the illegitimate son of Ellen Trey, an artist. He runs away and lives with his foster parents, the Amory family. Upon America's entrance into the war in 1917 he joins the ambulance corps in France. After the war Jack becomes restless in his American small town and returns to his wartime sweetheart in France. A realistic account of small-town life during the war.

605 Gibbs, Arthur Hamilton. *Chances: A Novel*. Boston: Little, Brown & Co., 1930. 285p.

A story of two brothers, Tom and Jack Ingleside, one an engineer, the other a lawyer. When the war came the brothers discovered that they loved the same girl. Both men go off to the war, and Tom's sacrificial death in action permits Jack, the lawyer, to have the girl both loved. The first part of the novel recounts the school life of the brothers at the College de St. Malo. The second part of the novel deals with the war experiences. The description of trench warfare is photographic in its realism.

606 Godwin, George Stanley. *Why Stay We Here?* New York: D. Appleton & Co., 1930. 332p.

A story of the war from a Canadian viewpoint. The main character is Stephen Craig, from British Columbia, who is sent to France as an infantryman. He survives the war only to succumb to tuberculosis.

Adult Novels

607 Gurner, Ronald. *Pass Guard at Ypres*. London: J.M. Dent & Sons, 1930. 241p.

Recounts the psychological disintegration of a young British platoon leader, Freddy Mann, and his company, the 1st Battalion of Loyal Southshires, from their arrival in France through the siege of Ypres. The story reveals Freddy's change in attitude about the war--from acceptance to questioning its morality and his increasing disillusionment. The time is reached when nothing matters to Freddy. He is beyond hope, beyond caring, and all he can hear is the siren call of Ypres compelling him forward to a miserable death.

608 Hamilton, Mary Agnes (Adamson) (pseud.: Iconoclast). *Special Providence*. London: George Allen & Unwin, 1930. 324p. [Title in U.S.: *Three Against Fate: A Tale of 1917*. Boston: Houghton Mifflin Co., 1930. 287p.]

A psychological novel, presenting events via the thoughts and mental reactions of Jean Claviger. She is married to Harold, fighting at the front; Stephen, a pacifist, is in love with her. Harold's horrible experiences in the war make a telling impression on Jean, as does Stephen's love for her. When Harold returns, he shoots Stephen and is brought to trial. Thus the war has "killed" three people. The novel presents an impressive picture of the misery of war as it affected London's home sector.

609 Hanley, James. *The German Prisoner*. Muswell Hill: The author, 1930. 36p.

The following words from the introduction hardly begin to express the power of this short novel: "a mixture of realism and symbolism in an exposure of human nature in its most abject and terrible circumstances." This work eloquently depicts the terrifying quality of the incredible war in a way that no other work has quite managed to capture. The story describes the long dragging march up the line, the assembly in the jumping-off trenches, the awful attacks, head-splitting flashes of artillery and shells, the smoke, the horror, and the ultimate death. Superimposed on all of this terrible violence is the dialog of realistic language containing the dirty words, the curses, and the humor of the trenches. Peter O'Garra, forty-four years old and from Dublin, arrives with a British battalion near Boves, France, after a hot and dirty march. Later, O'Garra and Elston in foggy no-man's-land find themselves in a shell hole where they accidentally run into a young and terrorized German prisoner whom they kick and beat to a pulp until he is dead. This appalling action culminates with the two English soldiers dancing on the lifeless body after their unspeakable acts; and a shell blows all three to pieces. Only a handful of works convey the utter horror of the war in quite the same powerful manner. Manning's *The Middle Parts of Fortune* republished in its original version is one of these select few (item 567).

610 Harrison, Charles Yale. *Generals Die in Bed*. New York: William Morrow & Co., 1930. 269p.; London: Noel Douglas, 1930. 249p.

A gruesome narrative of trench warfare, told by a Canadian buck private who is a shock trooper on the front line with British troops. A stark book, it describes the hungry, drunken Canadian soldiers looting Arras--driving away the English Military Police with machine guns--and "avenging" the barbarism of the enemy by bayoneting hundreds of unarmed German soldiers rather than taking them prisoner. (The author served as a private in the Fourteenth Battalion of the Royal Montreal Regiment.)

611 Hasek, Jaroslav. *The Good Soldier: Schweik*. Translated by Paul Selver. Garden City, N.Y.: Doubleday, Doran & Co., 1930. 447p. [New and unabridged translation by Cecil Parrott with original illustrations by Joseph Lada. New York: Thomas Y. Crowell, 1974. 752p.; *Osudy Dobrého Vojáka Svejka za Světové Valky*. V. Praze: J. Hasek, expeduje A. Synek, 1920-22. 3 v. in 1.]

A narrative of a so-called feeble-minded and gullible Czech soldier. Schweik is an orderly who "fights the war" in detention camps and hospitals, everywhere but on the front lines. "Deliciously Rabelaisian in spots--a true satire" according to one critic and the "nearest thing to Bardolph and Falstaff that this war produced." A great episodic comic novel that more effectively than any other war novel applies the incisive cut of the surgeon's scalpel to all of the puffery and absurd cant of the military, the politicians, and the war. Schweik also has the happy knack of making fools of inflated authorities with his simpleminded solutions and inane behavior. The 1974 translation is greatly superior to the incomplete and bowdlerized English version of 1930. Hasek died while composing the further adventures of Schweik on the Russian front.

612 Heinz, Max. *Loretto, Sketches of a German War Volunteer.*
Translated by Charles Ashleigh. New York: Liveright,
1930. 316p. [*Loretto, Aufzeichnungen eines Kriegsfreiwilligen.* Berlin: Rembrandt-Verlag, 1919(?). 334p.]

Vivid account of years of trench battle, concentrating
on violence, ghastly bloodshed, and defeat. The reviewer
for the *New York Times* declared that "In no book on the
war has the psychology of defeat been so carefully analyzed
at first hand...."

613 Hueffer, Oliver Madox. *"Cousins German."* London: Ernest
Benn Ltd., 1930. 284p.

A war novel of some suspense. The involved romantic
plot starts with Anthony Paget, at the outbreak of the
war. As Paget and all the English and German nationals
return to Europe, Paget meets his friend Herbert Neal,
who is terribly excited over the prospect of going to war.
Paget ends up in London where he falls in love with Elizabeth, Herbert's sister. She is the central love focus of
Paget, Captain Lampart (who turns out to be a highly
placed German spy), and Franz Ernstausen. Paget is traced
in his war experiences to the trenches of France. There
is an honest attempt to portray both the English and the
Germans as complex individuals subject to all of the unhappy pressures and circumstances of the war and military
necessity. As the author states in his Apologia introduction, "I have chosen the title 'Cousins German' because
I ... firmly believe that our former enemies were just as
sinning and sinned against as were we; that they too
fought, perhaps mistakenly, for a high ideal; that they
too died, and very gallantly...."

614 Johannsen, Ernst. *Four Infantrymen on the Western Front,
1918.* London: Methuen & Co., 1930. 181p. [*Vier von
der Infanterie Imre Letzten Tage an der West Front 1918.*
Hamburg-Bergedorf: Fackelreiter-Verlag, 1929. 108p.]
[Title in U.S.: *Four Infantrymen.* Translated from the
German by A.W. Wheen. New York: Alfred H. King, 1930.
220p.]

Describes the summer of 1918 when the Germans continued
to fight although they probably realized they had lost
the war. The narrative is cast in the form of a German
private's impressions of these last days. He covers such
events as the retreat after the Hindenburg line was crushed,
and an attack from the air and from the Allies' guns

standing wheel-to-wheel for miles along the front. The
author has graphically captured the stark horror of the
German retreat, the bravery of the rear-guard action, and
the final disintegration of German discipline. The conversations of the private and his three friends tend to be
somewhat philosophical, cynical, and even witty, but in
essence cheerless. Indeed, that seems the point. The
characters can no longer even look forward to the dubious
pleasure of ultimate victory.

615 Keel, Frederick Bolton. *Seven Days in the Line; an Uncon-
ventional Record of a Week of War*. London: Simpkin,
Marshall, Hamilton, Kent, 1930. 181p.

Not seen; NYPL.

616 Kirk, Laurence (pseud. of Eric Andrew Simson). *Flight
Errant: A Story of Two Young People in the Years of
Transition*. London: Hutchinson & Co., 1930. 288p.

The story of a pilot, Simon Carme, in the British Air
Force, who has been assigned to training new pilots in an
aerodrome in England after his war duty in France. With
the Armistice, Simon tries a desk job in the Air Ministry
to please his wife, but cannot forget the joy he found in
flying and decides to return to duty at the aerodrome.

617 Leslie, Henrietta (pseud. of Gladys Henrietta [Raphael]
Schutze). *Mrs. Fischer's War*. London: Jarrolds, 1930.
287p.

The plot relates the point of view of an English-born
son. With the outbreak of the war Janet Fischer, the
wife, is placed in an impossible position. Carl, her husband, is fighting in the German trenches while John, her
son, has enlisted in the British army. As a consequence,
Janet is subjected to considerable emotional torment and
even social ostracism. The essence of the author's story
is of great poignancy. Unfortunately, the style and the
character development are poorly done. Nevertheless, as
a record of a very special type of anguish caused by the
war, namely, the fate of "alien enemies" and their families in both America and England, it is distinctive.

618 Lorenz, Helmut. *The Sunken Fleet*. Translated from the
German by Samuel H. Cross. Boston: Little, Brown & Co.,
1930. 342p. [*Die Versunkene Flotte, Roman*. Berlin:
M. Warneck, 1926. 385p.]

An autobiographical novel that traces the naval

experiences of the chief character, Commander Hans Barnow, aboard a high-seas flagship in the German submarine service. The Germans demonstrate their tactic of sinking their own ships when the Allies corner them in naval engagements. When Barnow is cornered by the French, he sinks his submarine outside the three-mile limit off the coast of Spain. The narrative provides numerous details on the naval war from the perspective of the Germans. The Zeebrugge submarine base and the Jutland victory are given particular attention.

619 McFee, William Morley Punshon. *North of Suez*. Garden City, N.Y.: Doubleday, Doran & Co., 1930. 309p.; London: Wm. Heinemann, 1930. 341p.

The setting of this novel is Port Said, where the hero, Lieutenant Stephan Rumford of the British Royal Naval Reserve, is stationed as the chief Neutral Transport Officer. While attempting to track down the source of hashish which is corrupting English servicemen, Rumford succumbs to the wiles of Anastasia Calisthenes, a beautiful Greek woman. He dies in an attempt to dump overboard all the ammunition on a burning vessel before it explodes. A popular formula novel of the day.

620 Morris, Walter Frederick. *Behind the Lines*. London: Geoffrey Bles, 1930. 313p. [Title in U.S.: *The Strange Case of Gunner Rawley*. New York: Dodd, Mead & Co., 1930. 312p.]

An interesting story about Peter Rawley, an officer with an artillery battery in France. He and his two friends and fellow officers, Piddock and Rumbald, figure in the first third of this story. Their unit is on a rest leave behind the front lines. The author provides a clear description of civilian activities, but especially the recreational and social pursuits of the British troops. Peter meets a woman ambulance driver and a romance soon develops, but soon thereafter his unit moves up to the front. Scenes of the devastated French countryside are graphic. Peter is forced into desertion by the accidental death of Rumbald (he believes that his unit thinks he has killed his commanding officer), and the bulk of the book traces his adventures with a gang of deserters directed by the ruthless Kelly. Later Peter forms a partnership with Alf, a cockney deserter. Their life behind the British lines is described with considerable drama and interest. Eventually Peter is able to impersonate a chaplain and then an artillery officer and inadvertently finds himself back with his original unit where he is wounded in a bombardment. The novel concludes with his return to England to recuperate and with the promise of his eventual reunion with his wartime love. The author has created a plot of some drama and human interest beyond the typical novel dealing with the war.

621 Moulton, Hugh Fletcher. *Urgent Private Affairs*. London: J.W. Arrowsmith, 1930. 320p.

A story of espionage and counter-espionage in England, played by desperate German professionals countered by amateur British sleuths. In the story Captain James McCarthy, having been invalided out of the service and having reenlisted under a false name for "C3" duty (postal duty, noncombatant) goes A.W.O.L. when he receives an anonymous letter concerning the unfaithfulness of his wife. On his return to London he discovers that in his absence his woolen-trade business has been taken over by German agents, and determines to reveal this with the aid of a young woman, a secretary in his business. The story from this point on is a series of chases, confrontations, and escapes until native British intelligence succeeds in outwitting duller German intelligence.

622 Nason, Leonard Hastings. *A Corporal Once*. Garden City, N.Y.: Doubleday, Doran, & Co., 1930. 312p.

A novel of the "typical American doughboy," presented through the life of buck private John L. ("Johnell") Sullivan. The title refers to Johnell, who previously served in the army on the Mexican border and almost became a corporal. When Johnell is shipped to France, he continues by choice to be a buck private, to enjoy life more, he reasons. The reviewer for *Bookman* summarized Johnell's army career: "Johnell had a time for himself; he went through the Allied Army drives, cleaned up machine-gun nests, kept his tongue in his cheek and saw the whole business through the eyes of a born humorist." The story portrays mistakes of green American soldiers in France.

623 Newman, Bernard Charles (pseud.: Don Betteridge). *The Cavalry Went Through*. London: Victor Gollancz, 1930. 288p. [Title in U.S.: *The Cavalry Goes Through!* New York: Henry Holt & Co., 1930. 276p.]

A British military officer succeeds in ending the war in victory for Britain in 1917 before America enters the conflict. The main character, Duncan, has been a successful strategist in British East Africa, and his techniques on the western front are just as successful, especially involving shellproof artillery and a group of super soldiers. Efficiency was the name of his game. This is a "pretend" novel, an "as it might have been" history of the war, which insists that the reader suspend disbelief. Several of the top, well-known Allied commanders are parodied.

624 Olden, Balder. *On Virgin Soil: A Novel of Exotic Africa*. Translated from the German by Lorna Dietz. New York: The Macaulay Co., 1930. 316p. [*Kilimandscharo; ein Roman aus Deutsch-Ost*. Berlin: Gyldendal, 1922. 243p.]

The war is viewed through the progressive mental deterioration of Lieutenant Huessen, commander of a nondescript group of planters and of other demoralized civilians-- "drunkards and heroes through necessity" pressed into duty--in German East Africa. Although Lieutenant Huessen is a young, correct military officer, he also is a sentimentalist and somewhat idealistic. Ultimately Huessen goes insane, and the other characters in the novel are either killed or wounded. The novel provides an arresting view of life in Africa during four war years, particularly in a colony Germany was losing.

625 Paul, Elliot Harold. *The Amazon*. New York: Liveright, 1930. 339p.

Describes the experiences of four women who, chiefly by accident, managed to get themselves sent up to the Argonne front in the Army Signal Corps to fight alongside men. A German officer is unnerved and loses his reason when faced by what he assumes may be a battalion of women and children. The novel makes use of the popular war rumor that somewhere on the western front a company of women is on active service in the trenches. The women are rough-and-tumble creatures and neurotic, though the term "amazon" of the title refers specifically to "Lieutenant Albert Snyder" who despised her father and thus felt she despised all men.

626 Pertwee, Roland. *Pursuit, a Novel*. London: Wm. Heinemann, 1930. 333p.

The first half of this novel concerns activity in the front-line trenches of France; the novel is in large part

a wartime love story involving two men, Major Fawlk and
Harley Trevelyan, and a girl, Joan Miller. Harley and
Joan's romance begins on a London housetop while a zeppelin
raid is progressing. The major becomes the villain, but
Trevelyan obtains revenge finally, after pursuing him all
the way into Africa.

* Private 19022 (pseud. of Frederic Manning). *Her Privates
We*. London: Peter Davies, 1930. 453p.; New York:
G.P. Putnam's Sons, 1930. 344p.

See item 567.

627 Raymond, Ernest. *The Jesting Army*. London: Cassell & Co.,
1930. 448p.

The action ranges from Gallipoli to the front-line
trenches of France, viewed through the eyes of Tony
O'Grogan, the hero, and his buddies in the British Legion--
the "jesting army" of the title. The author offers a
sentimmental view of the war emphasized in the singing,
joking, and the occasional praying of the British soldiers
rather than just the blood-and-guts realism which is usually the more typical approach in such novels. The story
tends toward the overly sentimental and moralistic at
times, which very often creates an unnecessary artificiality.

628 Rebreanu, Liviu. *The Forest of the Hanged: A Novel*.
Translated from the Rumanian by A.V. Wise. New York:
Duffield & Green, 1930. 406p.; London: George Allen &
Unwin, 1930. 350p. [*Pădureau Spânzuratilor; Roman*.
Bucharest: Cartea, Rômanească, 1922. 323p.]

The title of this novel refers to the execution of military deserters who have been apprehended and court-
martialled. The main character of the novel is Apostol
Bologa, a young Rumanian student and lieutenant in the
Hungarian Army, fighting on the Russian front. He has
been promoted and decorated twice. When Rumania throws
in her lot with the Allies, Apostol faces a dilemma: he
desires to stay with his Austro-Hungarian compatriots but
respects his duty to his native Rumania. He must desert,
while realizing that his destination may be the "forest
of the hanged" where others he has court-martialled have
been sent, particularly a brother officer who had attempted
desertion. A serious illness makes this fearful choice
unnecessary.

Adult Novels

629 Roberts, Leslie. *When the Gods Laughed*. Toronto: Musson Book Company, 1930. 282p.

An officer of the Canadian infantry gets drunk when he is supposed to lead a raid into no-man's-land at the front. As a result, he is court-martialled and stripped of his rank. All the same, he re-enlists as a private and literally fights his way back to a commission and the woman he loves. Told with almost a cheery sentimentality, the story relies heavily on the trite, and ultimately suffers accordingly.

630 Sassoon, Siegfried Lorraine. *Memoirs of an Infantry Officer*. London: Faber & Faber, 1930. 334p.; New York: Coward-McCann, 1930. 334p.

This is the sequel to *Memoirs of a Fox-Hunting Man* (item 539) as well as a companion piece to Robert Graves' book *Good-bye to All That*. The story begins where it left off in his previous novel, the trenches of Flanders in the dismal spring of 1916. The character of George Sherston is a thinly disguised representation of Sassoon himself. A number of wartime incidents are described, such as the single-handed charge of Sherston on a German position and the retreat of the Germans; Sherston's lone mutiny; and countless observations on the war experience. The setting of the novel ranges from the front in France to England where Sherston recovers from his wounds in a shell-shock hospital. The novel is strongly autobiographical and some of the events are covered from another perspective in the Robert Graves book cited above.

631 Schauwecker, Franz. *The Furnace: An Epic of the War*. Translated by R.T. Clark. London: Methuen & Co., 1930. 344p. [*Aufbruch der Nation*. Berlin: Deutsche Buch-Gemeinschaft, 1929. 381p.]

A very personal and sensitive novel written from the point of view of a German soldier. The character Albrecht is a student at the University of Göttingen when the war begins. He volunteers in the first mass enthusiasm for the war and leaves his family and new-found sweetheart, Grete, for the eastern front. This is a long and at times impressionistic story of his experiences--the day-to-day routine of trivial events and conversations among the soldiers, the prosaic incidents and ingredients of military life intermixed with the horrors of war, the devastating attacks, shellings, and agonies of front-line trench warfare. Albrecht is wounded and later sent to the French front at Verdun and then back again to the Russian front. A personal and honest chronicle written with grace and power.

632   Sherriff, Robert Cedric, and Vernon Bartlett. *Journey's End: A Novel*. London: Victor Gollancz, 1930. 286p.; New York: F.A. Stokes Co., 1930. 308p.

Based on the play of the same name (1928) the novel closely follows the outline, action, and dialogue of the drama. (One reviewer thought the novel version was sentimental; another remarked that "the play is greater than the novel.") The main characters are Jimmy Raleigh and Dennis Stanhope. Captain Stanhope, twenty-one, has succumbed to drink while serving at the front for three years. Raleigh, the brother of Stanhope's girl friend, joins Captain Stanhope's company. Stanhope, aware of his drinking problem, fears that his drinking will ruin Raleigh's opinion of him, though another friend, "Uncle" Osborne, assures him that his concern is groundless. Eventually Osborne is killed and Raleigh, wounded, dies as Stanhope takes care of him. A melodramatic popular novel.

633   Smith, Helen Zenna (i.e., Evadne Price). *"Not So Quiet ...' Stepdaughters of War*. London: Albert E. Marriott, 1930. 239p. [Title in U.S.: *Stepdaughters of War*. New York: E.P. Dutton & Co., 1930. 250p.]

The main character is a middle-class English girl, twenty years old, who drives an ambulance in Flanders during the war. She is in charge of a group of girls of a higher social class than her own, and her position makes for strained feelings. Later she becomes a member of the W.A.A.C. The sordidness of trench life and brutality at the front witnessed by the girls are vividly portrayed. The *Nation* reviewer declared that the "book was obviously written as a deterrent to future eager young women...." The book jacket describes the novel as "Savage, unsentimental, pitifully true, and profoundly compassionate."

634   Springs, Elliott White. *Contact: A Romance of the Air*. New York: J.H. Sears & Co., 1930. 308p.

About wartime flying. The main character is Winnie, an aviator trained in the United States and sent to England for final flying preparation. Winnie becomes an ace flyer in the war. The novel describes his flying experiences, his responses to battle incidents and death. Several wartime scenes of Paris. The girl Winnie left behind holds him together mentally and spiritually until the Armistice, though then he considers himself too grown up--he says "unworthy"--for his young fiancée. A popular novel.

635 Thompson, Edward John. *In Araby Orion*. London: Ernest Benn, Ltd., 1930. 82p.; New York: Farrar & Rinehart, 1930. 92p.

Describes a part of the world virtually untouched by writers of World War I novels. The story takes place in the Jordan area during the war and recounts the story of British soldiers campaigning in the Holy Land. The title concerns the main character, Corporal Henry Bateman, who dies in the novel, but only after he is able to say that he saw "in Araby Orion." A pedestrian novel.

636 Tomlinson, Henry Major. *All Our Yesterdays*. London: Wm. Heinemann, 1930. 539p.; New York: Harper & Brothers, 1930. 445p.

A survey of British historical events, beginning with the Boer War. The last half of the novel deals with the World War and draws on the author's experiences in Britain's intelligence service. (Some of the material is patently memoir, which makes the work a semi-autobiographical novel.) The novel analyzes Britain's historical panorama, reflecting the waste, stupidity, greed, and corruption which the author considers to have made the European War inevitable and which continued to exist in the conflict itself.

637 *War Nurse: The True Story of a Woman Who Lived, Loved, and Suffered on the Western Front*. New York: Cosmopolitan Book Corp., 1930. 264p.

The main character of this anonymously written novel is Corinne Andrews, of a well-to-do New York family and educated abroad. Corinne volunteers for war service as a nurse, serves during the four years of the war in French hospitals. The novel relates the demoralizing effects of war experiences which altered many individuals' moral standards. In the novel Corinne has a love affair and lives in France with a married American ambulance driver. The novel appears to be autobiographical.

638 Wendler, Otto Bernhard. *Soldiers' Women*. Translated from the German by Ian F.D. Morrow. New York: Harper & Brothers, 1930. 302p. [Title of edition in England: *Soldiers--and Women*. Translated by Ian F.D. Morrow. London: Allen & Unwin, 1931. 271p.] [*Soldaten Marieen, Roman*. Leipzig & Vienna: E.P. Tal, 1929. 238p.]

Depicts the consequences of the separation of five German soldiers from wives, mistresses, and girl friends during the war. Emotional wrenching and the destruction of homes are typical results. The setting of the novel is the Russian front and Germany.

639 Williamson, Henry. *The Patriot's Progress: Being the Vicissitudes of Private John Bullock*.... London: Geoffrey Bles, 1930. 194p.; New York: E.P. Dutton & Co., 1930. 194p.

World War I as witnessed by a British soldier, from his enlistment to the Armistice. Private John Bullock is wounded in a battle in which every soldier is killed or maimed. His leg is amputated in the field, and he is returned to England. Contains a forceful description of the horrors experienced in trench warfare, seemingly not to shock but to convince.

640 Winder, Francis Arnold. *Behind the Barrage*. London: Gerald Duckworth & Co., 1930. 288p.

Not seen; NYPL.

641 Wise, Jennings Cropper. *The Great Crusade: A Chronicle of the Late War*. New York: Dial Press, 1930. 319p.

The author has turned his observations of the war into a novel. Written in diary form by a fictional officer in the conflict, the novel is a forthright and candid recital of the tragic errors of American staff personnel which resulted in the loss of many men.

642 Young, Francis Brett. *Jim Redlake*. London: Wm. Heinemann, 1930. 787p. [Title in U.S.: *The Redlakes*. New York: Harper & Brothers, 1930. 617p.]

Chronicles the life, from boyhood to war service and marriage after the Armistice, of Jim Redlake, son and grandson of an English family on the fringe of the upper class. Jim "finds his maturity" in Africa, which is the setting of war action. The campaign between Smuts and von Lettow-Vorbeck is compellingly described.

Adult Novels 221

1931

643 Botcharsky, Sophie, and Florida Pier. *They Knew How to Die*. Peter Davies, 1931. 311p. [Title in U.S.: *The Kinsmen Knew How to Die*. New York: William Morrow & Co., 1931. 306p.]

An autobiographical novel described as "imaginative novelization" by Alexander Nazaroof, reviewer for the *Saturday Review of Literature*. As an unusually young girl, Sophie Botcharsky managed to become a Red Cross "Sister" on the Russian front very close to the fighting in makeshift field hospitals and aboard "sanitary trains." Offering considerable detail about the wounded soldiers and the suffering Russian peasants in the war, the novel recounts the experiences of a war nurse between 1914 and the Russian revolution. The narrative clearly explains the relationship between World War I and the Russian revolution.

644 Chambe, René. *Still a Woman, a Novel from the French*. New York: J.H. Sears & Co., 1931. 303p.

Not seen; NYPL.

645 Ellsberg, Edward. *Pigboats*. New York: Dodd, Mead & Co., 1931. 329p.

Written by a former naval commander, this is a novel based on the author's submarine-warfare experiences. Most of the book seems more like a manual of wartime submarine techniques, which range from an analysis of tactics to the effectiveness of torpedoes and depth-bomb construction data. The plot is so flimsy and sketchy that the book makes a much better instruction manual than a work of fiction. The authenticity of the information is without question.

646 Godfrey, George L. *Bonds in Common*. Columbus, Ohio: F.J. Heer Printing, 1931. 306p.

Not seen; NYPL.

647 Havens, Allen (pseud. of Alice Maud Allen). *The Trap*. London: L. & V. Woolf, 1931. 655p.

A historical novel employing such historical figures as Woodrow Wilson, Lenin, Trotsky, Sir Edward Grey, etc., as a part of the large roster of characters. The story line

uses two contrasting groups of people in different parts
of England connected with Germany and Russia by marriage
or interests and, with interesting implications, through
blood or friendship. The middle-class Butterworth family
in Lancashire is connected by the marriage of an insurgent
daughter Ray to the artist Ian Fisher who in turn is linked
to a group of intellectuals (writers, socialists, artists)
in the London area. As a result, through the Butterworths
and then through the Fishers, the author describes nearly
every stratum of English national life. For example, the
Butterworth men are turned into soldiers or profiteers by
the pressure of the war. The younger members of the
Fisher family and friends, male and female, enlist or become involved in various women's war activities. These
relationships and their connections with others are relatively complex. One of the major themes is the tragedy of
the breakdown of the bonds that link man to man due to the
war. One of the most powerful passages (reminiscent of
Faulkner's *The Fable*) is the author's description and
establishment of the significance of the spontaneous, and
quickly suppressed, fraternizing of the enemy troops during the first Christmas of the war.

648 Köppen, Edlef. *Higher Command*. New York: Jonathan Cape
& Harrison Smith, 1931. 427p.; London: Faber & Faber,
1931. 427p. [*Herresbericht*. Berlin: Gruenwald, Horen-
Verlag, 1930. 460p.]

Traces the experiences of Adolf Reisiger from August
1914 to September of 1918. Reisiger is an example of the
effect that conflict has on the individual soldier caught
up in the madness of the war zone. We see Reisiger's
personality begin to disintegrate under the pressure of
trench-life hysteria, front-line fighting, the loss of
close friends, the temptation of cowardice, and the mad
fear of dying. Ever present is the vision of tortured
minds and mangled bodies. In the end, Reisiger is completely unhinged by his disastrous experiences and ends
up in a mental hospital. Though the translation is poor
and leaves much to be desired, some of the battle scenes
are especially good. The author has applied a heavy-
handed dose of satire to his well-told story.

649 Leigh, James (pseud. of James Cumberbirch). *Nomads in
Flanders; the Romance of an M.T. Column*. London:
Houghton Pub. Co., 1931. 200p.

Not seen; NYPL.

650 Lengyel, Emil. *Cattle Car Express: A Prisoner of War in Siberia*. New York: Ralph Beaver Strassburger Foundation, 1931. 228p.

A view of the war from the perspective of the prisoners in the Russian prisoner-of-war camps in Siberia. The prisoners consist of a group of Hungarian soldiers, privates and officers, who were captured in the early part of the war on the eastern front. Most of the story deals with prison camp life and the struggle of the prisoners against lice, filth, starvation, and their ruthless and inhumane treatment. An interesting and exceptionally vivid account of the lot of prisoners of war on the eastern front.

651 Nason, Leonard Hastings. *The Fighting Livingstons*. Garden City, N.Y.: Doubleday, Doran & Co., 1931. 332p.

The war experiences of two American brothers, Rupert and John Livingston, related in the author's typical breezy manner. Rupert, the older and efficient one, is commissioned a captain at the start of the conflict. Although he is extremely anxious to get to the front, he is sent instead to a French instruction camp, which disgusts him greatly. Tired of such inaction he eventually escapes to the front lines as a private. The other brother John is basically a lighthearted individual who originally joined the militia to escape the draft, and now gets sent immediately to the front lines. Rupert's exploits in the crucial last days of the war when he gathers together a small band of soldiers into a platoon with himself as the self-appointed commander, provide the best sections of the novel.

652 Owen, Walter. *The Cross of Carl....* Boston: Little, Brown & Co., 1931. 99p.; London: Grant Richards, 1931. 120p.

An allegorical story of the war and its horrors. The tale is presumably written by a man who never experienced any war activity but does experience a vision of what happened to his *alter ego*, Carl, during and after an especially bloody attack on a heavily defended hill. The origin of the story is a cruel and fantastic bit of propaganda spread during the war and known as the "Kadaver" lie. A soldier by necessity, Carl was terribly wounded in his first battle and was thought to be dead. Thus he is stripped, tied in a bundle with three other corpses,

and sent to the Utilization Factory of the Tenth Army
Section to be converted into commercially profitable products for the profit of the shareholders of the factory.
Left dying on the platform at the end of the day, he awakens and escapes into the fields where he seeks rest in
a shallow trench in the ground he scoops out for shelter.
At dawn two brutal and bureaucratic officers come across
Carl in his "grave." As they observe him he jumps up and
berates them with an eloquent and resounding anathema.
The officers then kill him. Several descriptions might
well be called some of the more cruelly realistic in the
literature of this war, even more so, according to one
critic, than Barbusse or Remarque managed to accomplish.

653 Plivier, Theodor. *The Kaiser's Coolies*. Translated from
the German by Margaret Green. New York: Alfred A.
Knopf, 1931. 308p. [*Des Kaisers Kulis, Roman der
Deutschen Kriegsflotte*. Berlin: Malik Verlag, 1930.
397p.]

This novel is cast in the form of an autobiographical
narrative by a German sailor who served for four years
on minesweepers, patrol boats, and the famous privateer,
Woolf. The primary theme is the growing spirit of insub-
ordination among the enlisted men of the German fleet,
beginning with the minor incidents in 1917 and concluding
with the general mutiny which inaugurated the revolution
attempt in 1918. Written from the point of view of the
average sailor. The description of the Battle of Jutland
is probably the most interesting portion of an otherwise
weak novel. The prose tends to be crude and downright
poor at times.

654 Springs, Elliott White. *War Birds and Lady Birds*. London:
John Hamilton, 1931. 308p. [Title in U.S.: *The Rise
and Fall of Carol Banks*. Garden City, N.Y.: Doubleday,
Doran & Co., 1931. 307p.]

The adventures, both in battle and in love, in war and
in peace, of a young American sky pilot. The plot consists
mainly of a series of episodes loosely connected. The
story is basically a lighthearted recital of the activities
of Carol Banks in war and in peace until he is finally
snared by a woman. The best parts are his war adventures,
such as the time he fights the German ace von Koch and
wins.

655 Steele, Daniel Howard. *Snow Trenches*. Chicago: A.C. McClurg & Co., 1931. 361p.

The novel is based on the experiences of the author with the American Expeditionary Force in northern Russia and offers a graphic description of warfare in the Arctic Circle. The otherwise grim tale is relieved by the usual romantic interest, in this case an American soldier and a Russian woman, a refugee. The author's description of the region, its conditions, and the battles of the Allied troops against the Reds is accomplished with obvious journalistic ability. However, as literature the story leaves much to be desired.

656 Thomas, Adrienne. *Catherine Joins Up*. Translated by Margaret Goldsmith. London: Elkin Mathews & Marrot, 1931. 308p. [Title in U.S.: *Katrin Becomes a Soldier*. Translated from the German by Margaret Goldsmith. Boston: Little, Brown & Co., 1931. 321p.] [*Die Katrin Wird Soldat; ein Roman aus Elsass-Lothringen*. Berlin: Propyläen-Verlag, 1930. 325p.]

Deals with the life experiences of the young girl Katrin from her fourteenth birthday in 1911 to her death at nineteen in late 1916. The story is placed in Metz in Alsace-Lorraine. The author demonstrates a sensitive and delicate style in relating an unusual experience. The story is told in diary form by Katrin. An especially notable section records her day-by-day account of what occurred in Metz during August of 1914. The novel seems to be the story of a naive, loyal, and dutiful young woman who is faithful to the memory of her sweetheart killed in 1915. The book describes her long hours of bitter work as a kitchen worker for the Red Cross and later as a nurse when she is killed.

657 Tilsley, W.V. *Other Ranks*. London: R. Cobden-Sanderson, 1931. 269p.

Presents a picture of World War I as seen by an East Lancashire soldier, Dick Bradshaw, who never believes himself to be a soldier, but an "impostor" in the war. A participant in the bloody siege at Ypres, he always regarded himself as an interloper, flung unwillingly into an arena. With his comrades he suffers the indignities of vermin-infested clothing, short rations, and water-filled dugouts, but an unreality pervades his senses. For him the only reality is home.

658 Wilke, Karl. *Prisoner Halm.* Translated from the German. Indianapolis: Bobbs-Merrill, 1931. 317p.; London: Hutchinson & Co., 1931. 288p. [*Prisonnier Halm; die Geschichte Einer Gefangenschaft.* Leipzig: Koehler & Amelang, 1929. 296p.]

An autobiographical novel that has the terrible ring of truth in its description of the grim horrors of the front lines. Corporal Halm is taken prisoner by the French on the Belgian border during the days of the German retreat from the Siegfried line. He is first marched to a temporary camp just behind the front and from there to the prison camp at Candor where he spends several months. His sensitive and artistic nature makes the filth, cold, starvation rations, and cruelty an experience he can scarcely endure. He promises his fellow German prisoners that someday he will describe their prison camp horrors to the world. The story tends to be a grim and detailed catalog of the dreadful conditions and revolting activities. This may not be great fiction, but it conveys with honesty one of the less familiar aspects of the war. Obviously, not all the Huns were Germans.

659 Zilahy, Lajos. *Two Prisoners.* Translated by Joseph Collins and Ida Zeitlin. Garden City, N.Y.: Doubleday, Doran & Co., 1931. 504p.; London: Wm. Heinemann, 1931. 504p. [Translated and revised by the author. Harrisburg, Pa.; Stackpole Books, 1968. 468p.]

Describes eight years in the lives of two young upper-middle-class Hungarians of Budapest, Miette (Mariette) Almady and Peter Takacs. After a marriage of only four months, Peter is mobilized when war breaks out and sent to the eastern front. From this point the two stories of Peter and Miette parallel one another in separate chapters: Peter becomes a war prisoner in Siberia and Miette waits for him in Budapest.

1932

660 Bazin, René François Nicolas Marie. *Magnificat.* New York: The Macmillan Co., 1932. 244p.; London: Burns, Oates and Washbourne Ltd., 1932. 244p. [*Magnificat.* Paris: Calmann-Lévy, 1931. 286p.]

A simple, sincere, and dignified story on the theme of spirituality among Britanny peasants. Gildos Maguern is

the hero who lives in Catholic Brittany. As a boy he had
a strong urge to become a priest, which he mentioned only
to his mother. Years later while a soldier at the front
he is inspired by the behavior and actions of a chaplain.
He now resolves to pursue his long-neglected wish. Contrasted with his newfound resolve is his age (years beyond
the time when most men go into the priesthood), the poverty
of the family, and the obstinate opposition of his father
who needs his son to help on the farm. Another complicating factor is the love of Gildos for his cousin Anna
and hers for him. Ultimately, Gildos rejects the girl he
loves for his spiritual vocation, while Anna in her simple
but pious way understands the sacrifice he and she must
make. The war figures as a device to bring about the
spiritual crisis of Gildos.

661 Brandau, Hermann. *The Great Destroyer*. Chicago: The Carl
Schurz Publishing Co., 1932. 190p.

Not seen; NYPL.

662 Brehm, Bruno. *They Call It Patriotism*. Translated from
the German by Margaret Leland Goldsmith. Boston: Little,
Brown & Co., 1932. 373p. [*Apis und Este; ein Franz
Ferdinand-Roman*. Munich: R. Piper, 1931. 556p.]

A historical novel that concentrates on a number of
dramatic incidents in the lives of three historical figures. The first is Dragutin Dimitrijivic, nicknamed
Apis, the strong leader of the Union of Death, a Serbian
nationalistic society. The second is the Archduke Francis
Joseph, the Austrian heir designate whose assassination
at Sarajevo was the spark that started World War I. The
third individual is Gavrilo Princip, the peasant whose
two shots killed the archduke and his wife. The novel
begins with an account of the assassination of King
Alexander and Queen Draga in 1903, goes on to include
the murder at Sarajevo, and concludes with the execution
of Apis in 1917. This is generally a most successful
fictional re-creation of historical events and personages.

663 Broch, Hermann. *The Sleepwalkers: A Trilogy*. Translated
from the German by Willa and Edwin Muir. Boston: Little,
Brown & Co., 1932. 648p.; London: Martin Secker Ltd.,
1932. 648p. [*Die Schlafwandler*.... 3 vols. Munich &
Zurich: Rhein-Verlag, 1931-1932.]

This novel falls in the category of the most significant
fiction of the twentieth century. It is on a par with

Musil's *Man Without Qualities* and Mann's best novels. It
is a long and involved story of Germany during the thirty
years from 1888 to 1918. In three parts; each part is
devoted to the story of a different man, but all of the
parts are connected. The first-part protagonist is Joachim
von Pasenow, a romantic, who falls in love with a Bohemian
girl but marries the woman his father has chosen for him.
In part two the loves and business dealings of the anar-
chist, August Esch, are described. Finally, the third
part describes the last months of the war, with Wilhelm
Huguenan, a realist, as the chief protagonist. Portions
of the text, especially part three, are interpolated with
elaborate philosophical sections. The novel is representative of our time and civilization as a period groping
in ignorance and hubris. A remarkable philosophical novel.

664 Capy, Marcelle. *Men Pass*. Translated from the French by
Victor A. Yakhontoff. New York: Liveright, 1932. 273p.
[*Des Hommes Passèrent*.... Paris: Editions du Tambourin,
1930. 339p.]

A simple tale of a French village during the war. It
describes in detail the disintegration which slowly under-
mines all of the inhabitants. The novel begins as the
men of the village leave for the front and the women take
over the work in the fields. There is no plot in the
normal sense. Indeed, this seems almost a case study in
the breakdown of a small community. It is clear that the
war is incomprehensible to the peasants. The climax comes
when the women threaten a passive revolt unless they can
get help in the fields. The government sends first German
prisoners and then Russians to help the women. As a
result, the French peasants and the enemy join together
in the harvest while the war rages on. The implication
is that the same thing may be happening behind the enemy
lines as well. Obviously the message is that war is bad,
in fact, very bad.

665 [Childs, James Rives]. *Before the Curtain Falls*. Indianapolis: Bobbs-Merrill Co., 1932. 333p.

The chief character is a young American, Henry Filmer.
The time period is from 1914 to the late 1920's. The
story describes his service in the war and his postwar
life in Paris as well as relief work in Serbia and a visit
to Russia. Henry becomes disillusioned with life in the
West. The novel concludes with Henry reflecting on the
present chaos of the world while waiting for the crash

which will end the capitalistic system in America and the West. The author echoes most of what has already been said by Dos Passos, Edmund Wilson, and others. The descriptions of the war add nothing of significance to this genre. The bulk of the novel is concerned with postwar life and conditions.

666 Daly, Victor Reginald. *Not Only War: A Story of Two Great Conflicts*. Boston: Christopher Publishing House, 1932. 106p. [Reprinted 1969.]

An unusual story since it deals with some power and drama about race prejudice during World War I. The novel starts with a description of the southern family heritage of Bob Casper, who comes from a long line of South Carolinian ancestors. Bob arrives home from college to take his physical for officers' training since the U.S. has just entered the war. He meets a very pretty black girl and travels with her by train to Spartanburg. The other major character is Montgomery Jason, a black college man, who also wishes to try out for officers' training but is rejected. The plot obviously contrasts and compares these two young men in order to illustrate the deep and senseless injustice of race prejudice. Casper becomes a lieutenant and Montie just a private. They meet in France where Lieutenant Casper, unknown to Montie, does him a favor in recommending his promotion. The novel then follows Montie as he participates in a number of fighting adventures at the front. Later, during a rest period, Montie is billeted at the large house of a young French woman and her grandmother. Since Montie can speak French, they eventually come to talk and she asks him to help her with her English. Lieutenant Casper accidentally comes to see her and discovers Montie there. Casper's innate southern race prejudice comes rapidly to the fore and Casper forces the court-martial of Montie. Montie then loses all of his well-deserved promotions and bitterly reflects on the injustice of life, especially for blacks even when fighting for their country. Ironically, all of this time Lieutenant Casper has been writing to and going with Miriam, the pretty young black girl back in South Carolina. The novel concludes with Montie discovering Lieutenant Casper very seriously wounded in a trench under fire by the Germans. It is obvious that if Montie stays put he can return safely under cover of darkness to his lines. But Lieutenant Casper is so seriously wounded that it is certain he will not survive that long without medical treatment. Montie swallows his resentment and bitterness and decides to help Casper back to their lines. In the effort both are killed by the machine-gun fire of the Germans.

667   Dos Passos, John Roderigo, Jr. *1919.* New York: Harcourt, Brace & Co., 1932. 473p.

This is the second novel of the trilogy called *U.S.A.*, presenting a slice-of-life or cross-section chronicle of life in America during the war years through glimpses into the lives and characters of five young American men and women--a young poet, a radical Jew, a daughter of a Chicago minister, a working-class sailor, and a girl from Texas. Three techniques are used to make this novelistic survey as representative as possible: (1) biographies of various public figures, (2) brief impressionistic reflections from the life of the author, and (3) the newsreel, which involves quotations from newspapers, speeches, popular songs, and so forth. The novel includes brief scenes of ambulance and Red Cross service in France and Italy, battlefield scenes, etc., but the main picture is a mosaic of life in America during the war years, rather than the battlefronts of Europe.

668   Dwinger, Edwin Erich. *Between White and Red.* Translated from the German by Marion Saunders. New York: Charles Scribner's Sons, 1932. 492p. [*Zwischen Weiss und Rot; Die Russische Tragödie, 1919-1920.* Jena: E. Diederichs, 1930. 503p.]

A fictionalized narrative of the experiences of the author in the struggle between the Red and White armies in Russia during the revolution. Dwinger was a German officer who was captured by the Russians and compelled to join the White Russian forces for about six years. The book is a minor epic of the German war prisoners in Russia who are unable to return to their homeland and become trapped in the Russian revolution. The German prisoners are pictured enduring the most incredible treatment and sufferings such as torture, hunger, intense cold, etc. It is a long narrative that creates the impression of a huge nightmare, of mass insanity occasionally relieved by poignant moments of pathos, pity, and even love. This is a grim and horrifying view of war and revolution which indicts the Allied diplomats and generals who decided that European intervention in Russia was ever necessary.

669 Ellsberg, Edward. *Submerged; A Novel*. London: Hurst & Blackett, 1932. 286p.

   Not seen.

670 Hinkson, Pamela. *The Ladies' Road*. London: Victor Gollancz, 1932. 320p.

   Describes the war years both in England and in Ireland. The plot deals with the heartbreak that the war brought to the large English Mannering family and their Irish cousins, the Creaghs. Although there is little actual description of the war front, it still pervades the novel. The author makes the point that the women of the families, all of whom lose some person each loves, are as much the victims of the conflict as if they had been in the war zone in France. The topic of section one is the profound changes in the lives of all the members of the families, beginning with August 1914. The next section describes the home-front conditions, the agony of awaiting news, the undercurrents beneath the surface patriotism. Lastly, we see the return of the survivors and the postwar aftermath. The chief value of the book is its picture of the average person's war with the intensely small-scale, day-to-day anxieties that often tend to be more difficult to bear than the war-front experience itself.

671 Johns, William Earl. *The Camels are Coming*. London: John Hamilton, 1932. 259p.

   Not seen; NYPL.

672 Mann, Francis Oscar. *Grope Carries On: Being the Further Adventures of Albert Grope During the Great War*. London: Faber and Faber, 1932. 318p.

   A sequel to a previous novel of the author. In this book the character Albert Grope has reached middle age. In a chance meeting with a pompous member of Parliament he becomes involved in the war effort as an unpaid official of the Department of Minor Equipment in the War Office. Grope is a symbol for all of the incompetent and self-important government bureaucrats involved in the war effort. Basically a satire on the subject of bureaucratic inefficiency during wartime. The office love affair of Grope results in an unwanted pregnancy for the unfortunate girl, while Grope's wife is in France.

673 Mann, Leonard. *Flesh in Armour; a Novel.* Melbourne: Phaedrus, 1932. 349p.

   Not seen; NYPL.

674 Padover, Saul Kussiel. *Let the Day Perish.* New York: Robert O. Ballou, 1932. 226p.

   A bitter story of the persecution and terrible indignities suffered by Polish Jews during the war and in the pogrom years immediately thereafter. There is some indication that the story has an autobiographical basis. The narrative is a dramatic exposé of the cruelties, brutalities, and agonies of families that were separated and the tragedy of the children whose lives were filled with fear, revenge, insults, and starvation. The action ranges from the war years through the pogrom period commencing at the start of Poland's liberation, the Cossack invasion, the flight to Vienna and back again to Poland. This is one unrelieved series of distressing experiences arising out of the war. The novel is very much overwritten and sketchy in plot, but this in no way diminishes its powerful cry of injustice.

675 Rathbone, Irene. *We That Were Young.* London: Chatto & Windus, 1932. 466p.

   Not seen; NYPL.

676 Roberts, Cecil Edric Mornington. *Spears Against Us.* London: Hutchinson & Co., 1932. 285p.; New York: D. Appleton & Co., 1932. 353p.

   Relates the story of two families, one English and the other Austrian, whose relationships and romances are affected by the start of the war and the long years of alienation that result. The first part of the novel is a youthful idyll in the incredibly lovely Austrian Alps involving the mistress and the illegitimate son of the master of the house. When the war starts, the families are separated for four years but manage by secret letters to continue their relationships. Placed mostly in Austria we see the Crawleys welcomed by the Edelsteins at their Tyrol castle. After the Armistice the Crawleys return to succor their devastated friends with food and money. The story is notable because it is free of nationalistic propaganda and anti-war bitterness. The novel, however, is straightforward and prosaic. The sequel to this story is is called *Pamela's Spring* (published the year before) and deals with the various family members and their relationships following the war.

677 Seton, Graham (pseud. of Graham Seton Hutchison). *Life Without End*. London: T. Thornton Butterworth Ltd., 1932. 282p.

The story of the search by a young vicar, Hugh Richmond, for meaning in his life after being wounded in his first battle in the Sommer River Valley at Bazentin. He returns home and marries Margaret, who had nursed him during his hospitalization. He takes up his calling once again, only to become convinced that "life was not one far-off divine event to which the whole of creation moves but just one damn thing after another, life without end." Denouncing the Church from his pulpit, he disappeared and made a pilgrimage to the battlefields of France to find his lost faith and innocence, and there, as he prayed beside the grave of a dead comrade, received the revelation—the sign of the cross in the sky, a phenomenon seen years before just prior to his first battle. He now resolves to return home again, content.

678 Snow, Francis. *No Names, No Pack-Drill*. London: Cecil Palmer, 1932. 563p.

Not seen; NYPL.

679 Streatfeild, Noel. *Parson's Nine*. London: Wm. Heinemann, 1932. 339p.

The story of a family of nine children growing up in a vicarage in an English village and of its decimation by the war. At the end of the war three of the four sons are dead.

680 Strong, Charles Stanley. *The Spectre of Masuria*. Caldwell, Idaho: Caxton Printers, 1932. 322p.

A historical romance dealing with the Russian participation in World War I. The story is based mainly on a single campaign called "The Masurian Lakes" in which Hindenburg outmaneuvered the Grand Duke Nicholas and the Russian army was destroyed. The romance part of the plot deals with Prince Boris Petrovitch, a colonel of the Tsaritsyn Black Cossacks. This is an all-around action story that combines military espionage with tragedy.

681 Szabo, Pal. *People of the Plains*. Translated from the Hungarian by George Halasz. Boston: Little, Brown & Co., 1932. 287p. [*Emberek*. Budapest: Franklin-Társulat, 1931(?). 207p.]

An autobiographical novel of peasant life on the plains of Hungary. The hero is Bertalan who, first introduced as a boy, suddenly becomes aware of the realities of life by the death of his father. Life appears to be only a situation in which one must slave forever just as the countless other generations of peasants who have lived the same dreary and toilsome lives before him. He has an adolescent's affair with an older woman but later falls in love and becomes engaged to a nice young village girl when the war starts. He is sent off to the front to experience the harsh realities of the war zone. He finally returns to the village only to learn his girl has married another man. Indeed, life in the village seems to have changed so much (or he has) that everything now appears strange except the solid reality of the land. He eventually finds another girl and now begins to write of his experiences and impressions, especially life in the village. Much of the novel is devoted to Bertalan's descriptions of peasant life and peasant nature. The plot is placed against the great Hungarian plain and the mountain front above Trieste. A first novel, this is a mixture of occasionally awkward and incoherent language combined with freshness, humor, and some style in the writing.

682 Thompson, Edward John. *Lament for Adonis*. London: Ernest Benn Ltd., 1932. 315p. [Title in U.S.: *Damascus Lies North*. New York: Alfred A. Knopf, 1933. 315p.]

A peculiarly English novel that traces the love stories of two American Relief Force girls and two young English officers during the closing days of Allenby's 1919 campaign in Palestine. The story is heavily larded with the God-and-Country attitude of the British Army and the superpatriotic sentiments of the young. The author promotes the thesis that all courage, faith, and happiness died with the signing of the Armistice. This novel also seems a curious reversion to a typical nineteenth-century romanticism in which the war assumes importance primarily as an obstacle to true love.

683 Zweig, Arnold. *Young Woman of 1914*. Translated from the German by Eric Sutton. New York: Viking Press, 1932. 346p.; London: Martin Secker Ltd., 1932. 383p.

[*Junge Frau von 1914*. Roman. Berlin: G. Kiepenheuer, 1931. 465p.]

The young heroine is a German woman named Lenore Wahl. The story deals with her and her lover, Werner Bertin, during the early years of the war. The novel is part of a tetralogy, of which the first volume is the famous *The Case of Sergeant Grischa* (item 547). This novel deals especially with the war in the Verdun sector. The war scenes are vivid front-line descriptions of some detail. Unfortunately, the somewhat sentimental affair of the two lovers and their rather precious aesthetic indulgences occasionally leave one unsympathetic, when contrasted with the terrible suffering and horrors of the war. The two are separated when young Werner is called up for service to become a cog in the giant war machine. Meanwhile, Lenore has had their unborn child taken from her because marriage at that time seemed impossible. But eventually she determines that they will be married on the first twenty-four-hour leave he obtains. They experience the joys of this brief respite from the war before Werner must return to the front. The novel ends as she returns home with a prayer for her husband's safe return. The theme of the book combines a view of the pettinesses and irony behind the facade of the military machine with the life that goes on behind the housefronts and in the hearts and minds of those left at home. The author has also created an everpresent undercurrent of atmosphere that reveals the futility and hatefulness of war as a solution for anything. As one critic wrote: "The novel has breadth and nobility, no less than intimate understanding and tenderness." This still applies today.

1933

684 Boot, Douglas. *Frogs Die in Earnest*. London: Eyre & Spottiswoode, 1933. 350p.

The chief character of this adventure novel is Lieutenant Frederick Tyax of the Royal Navy who is known affectionately to his friends as "Rat," because of his thin face and dark lively eyes and his "dental exuberance." Rat takes life very casually until he meets Pauline, an ambulance driver. The account of their love story and adventures begins in 1916 and continues to 1925 when they both finally achieve some degree of fame and fortune. There is a fairly interesting account of

life on board Rat's light cruiser, the *Cauldron*, which
participates in the Battle of Jutland. These are probably
the liveliest and most interesting pages in the novel.
By and large this is a standard adventure-formula novel--
plenty of action, straight narrative, and with the usual
love story.

685   Buchan, John. *A Prince of the Captivity*. London: Hodder
         & Stoughton, 1933. 383p.; Boston: Houghton Mifflin Co.,
         1933. 357p.

A story of the war and its aftermath that relates the
adventures of Adam Melfort as a spy in the war and as a
fighter for a peaceful world afterwards. A man of considerable ability and vast accomplishments, Melfort is
forced by the disgrace of a wrongful forgery conviction
and imprisonment to give up his personal ambitions.
Realizing that his former career is no longer possible,
he sets out to develop his top physical condition, to
study languages and geography, and to perfect his ability
to disguise himself. He leaves prison in 1914 to become
a key agent in the English intelligence service, spending
most of the war years as a spy behind the German lines.
After the war he becomes involved in various adventures
such as an expedition to the Arctic to rescue a wealthy
American explorer, an assassination plot against a German
chancellor, etc. The adventure concludes with Melfort's
death after he escapes from Communist assassins with an
English financier. The novel tends to pack a multitude
of events and activities into its limited framework. It
should be considered mainly a mystery and adventure tale.

686   March, William (pseud. of William Edward March Campbell).
         Company K. New York: Harrison Smith & Robert Haas,
         1933. 260p.

One of the more significant and unique works of fiction
about the war. The novel is composed of 113 brief sketches, each of which carries the name of one of the members
of Company K. Each man relates his experience in the
first person. A number of episodes are viewed by several
of the participants from their different perspectives.
Although there is no direct continuity between the sketches there is a rough sequence of events that begins with
the training camp in America, then through the months of
front-line conflict, and back again to the States. The
unique structure enables the author to relate masterfully
both sides of a feud between an officer and a private

soldier as well as describe from six different perspectives the killing of German prisoners of war. This is a novel of protest against war. Written in a subdued and low-key style, it quietly but powerfully covers nearly every war situation from suicide, the murder of prisoners, and the killing of an officer, to a vision of Christ. It is written with a strangely impressionistic atmosphere that creates a far more powerful impact than a strictly factual and realistic account. The quality of the writing is superior.

687 Nexo, Martin Andersen. *In God's Land.* Translated by Thomas Seltzer. New York: Peter Smith, 1933. 343p. [*Midt i en Jaerntid.* Copenhagen: A. Aschehoug, 1929. 2 vols.]

The plot is set in a small Danish farming community immediately before and during the war. A new generation of get-rich-quick profiteering farmers who take advantage of Denmark's neutrality are contrasted with the old-style peasantry who have maintained a simple and more affectionate relation to the land under the enlightened and humane influence of Bishop Grundtvig. The main theme deals with a social system based on privilege. The novel is more didactic than a work of imaginative literature in any substantial sense.

688 Paletta, Filippo. *The Power of Love in the World War; Notes from the Diary of a Common Soldier Named Filippo Paletta.* New York: The Author, 1933, 421(?)p. ["*L'Angelo Della Guerra*" e "*Fanciulla del Piave*," dal *Diario di Guerra di Filippo Paletta*. Mount Vernon, N.Y.: n.p., 1933. 421p.]

Not seen; NYPL.

689 Plivier, Theodor. *The Kaiser Goes: The Generals Remain.* Translated from the German by A.W. Wheen. New York: The Macmillan Co., 1933. 368p.; London: Faber & Faber, 1933. 368p. [*Der Kaiser Ging, die Generäle Blieben; ein Deutscher Roman....* Berlin: Malik-Verlag, 1933, 347p.]

Though much of this novel is devoted to the November 1918 revolution in Germany, two chapters of the novel depict the closing weeks of the retreat of the German army, the breakup of the German navy--the High Seas Fleet sailors at Kiel refused to sail out of the harbor to engage the British--and the grim lot of the disheartened German civilians. Louis Kronenberger's tribute to the novel in reviewing it for *The New York Times* summarizes the dislocation of the German people in the closing days of the war: "Plivier's picture is vividly and accurately revealing: the crowds in the streets, the spreading revolutionary spirit, the pandemonium in high political circles are things we can all but join in, so clearly do we see them."

690 Taffrail (pseud. of Henry Taprell Dorling). *The Man from Scapa Flow*. London: Hodder & Stoughton, 1933. 320p.

Not seen.

691 Zander, Harry William. *Thirteen Years in Hell*. Boston: Meador Publishing Co., 1933. 307p.

Not seen; NYPL.

1934

692 Abdullah, Achmed. *Never Without You*. New York: Farrar & Rinehart, 1934. 296p.; London: Hurst & Blackett, 1934. 287p.

Mainly a love story fashioned into a historical romance. The hero is Hugh Gray, a typical American boy from Virginia whose mother had been a Russian singer. Hugh goes to study music at the Moscow Conservatory. Through the efforts and connections of an old friend of his mother, he becomes imbued with the revolutionary spirit of the times and is expelled from Russia. A cousin lives in the palace of a south German duchy and Hugh travels there and is engaged as the music teacher of the beautiful young duchess Victoria; of course, love blooms. Amid the issue of a commoner attempting to marry royalty, the war commences and quickly postpones the marriage. Victoria heeds the patrioic call of her country, and when the United States finally enters the conflict, Hugh becomes an army captain. Love eventually prevails, however.

693 Brehm, Bruno. *That Was the End*. Translated from the German by Geoffrey Dunlop. London: Hurst & Blackett, 1934. 333p. [*Das War das Ende*. Munich: R. Piper, 1933. 505p.]

Presents a shifting scene of the final year of the war

and its aftermath, from the Brest-Litovsk Conference of
December 20, 1917, to the signing of the Treaty of Versailles on June 28, 1919. It is a story of the machinations, manipulations, maneuverings, and secret treaties
consummated prior to the signing of the treaty. The
contradictions between the postwar aims of the European
Allies and the "peace without victories" idealism of President Wilson are contrasted.

694 Brophy, John. *The World Went Mad: A Novel*. London:
Jonathan Cape, 1934, 286p.; New York: The Macmillan
Co., 1934. 286p.

The main focus is on the members of the Crellen family
during the war. Rather than any battle scenes, the plot
is made up of a series of related incidents in various
places such as England, France, Germany, Egypt, and Mesopotamia, with isolated sketches of soldiers and civilians
on both sides. One of the basic messages of the book is
the essential stupidity and basic depravity involved in
the act of war. The plot demonstrates, however, an exaggerated coincidence when the son-in-law of Mr. Crellen
is consoled by a German who is then killed at his feet.
When the son-in-law brings home a photo of the dead German,
Mr. Creelen recognizes him as probably being his own illegitimate son, the product of Crellen's student days in
Germany. Although the novel attempts to be a panoramic
view of the war, it is far from successful, both in plot
and style.

695 Celine, Louis-Ferdinand (pseud. of Louis Ferdinand
Destouches). *Journey to the End of the Night*. Translated from the French by John H.P. Marks. Boston:
Little, Brown & Co., 1934. 509p.; London: Chatto &
Windus, 1934. 543p. [*Voyage au Bout de la Nuit, Roman*.
Paris: Denoël et Steele, 1932. 623p.]

Bardamu, the narrator, relates his adventures from the
outbreak of war to about 1933. He escapes from the front
and ends up in a hospital for the insane. Later, he embarks for French Colonial Africa and then for America,
but eventually ends up as a doctor in a rundown suburb
of Paris where he seems to relish the disgust with which
life and all its activities fill him. A notable and significent work of literature that obviously is not everyone's cup of tea. It is a sardonic, even lyrical display
of the modern world with its obscene gestures and activities emphasized all the more by the author in order to

indicate their doom. We see the war and its absurdities as well as business, industry, crowds, soldiers, colonial backwaters, whorehouses, factories, slums, and the fetid and stagnant cesspools of civilization pass in the assorted and even nihilistic views of the author. Bardamu is basically an autobiographical character. The story is a shocking exploration into all that is mean and pinched in life. This is the world viewed by an articulate underdog, a spokesman for the dispossessed, who possesses a vast knowledge of human anatomy and illness.

696 Cowen, William Joyce. *Man with Four Lives*. New York: Farrar and Rinehart, 1934. 277p.

A psychological war mystery that charts the gradual mental disintegration of young John Fenton who, after he kills his first German, a man named Hartman, later comes to believe he is responsible for the same man's death on yet two other occasions during the conflict. Quite obviously, Fenton develops a war-neurosis that eventually destroys his sanity. This process is dramatically brought to a climax after the war when Fenton's life is saved in the Alps by the young Baron von Hartman whom Fenton perceives as the wartime soldier he has already killed several times. Fenton again attempts to kill this new manifestation of Hartman and in the process becomes completely deranged. A brisk, action-packed narrative, the novel is written with considerable suspense and horror.

697 Gorman, Herbert Sherman. *Suzy*. New York: Farrar & Rinehart, 1934. 434p.

The war is used as a backdrop for this improbable novel. Susan Dillworthy, although born in the United States, went to London in 1914 with a variety stage act which soon failed. She then fled to Paris to become a dancer in a Left Bank cabaret. There she is nicknamed Suzy and in this new guise experiences a number of adventures involving spies and a marriage to a man who once was in love with the infamous female spy, Mata Hari. Suzy is a naturally intelligent but naive young woman who is shaped by her wartime experiences in Paris. This is a personal view of the war through the character of Suzy whose career is made to parallel the progress of the war. The novel is written in a compelling style which even today holds interest.

Adult Novels 241

698 Lazo, Hector. *Taps; a Novel of War and Peace*. Boston: Bruce Humphries, 1934. 125p.

Not seen; NYPL.

699 Sholokhov, Mikhail Aleksandrovich. *And Quiet Flows the Don*. Translated from the Russian by Stephen Garry. New York: Alfred A. Knopf, 1934. 755p.; London: G.P. Putnam's Sons, 1934. 755p. [*Tikhii Don; Roman*. Moscow: Moskovskii Rabochii, 1928. 2 vols.]

A historical chronicle of cossack life which starts before the war and ranges through World War I and the Russian Revolution. In spite of its origin in Stalinist Russia, it is basically free of propaganda and is a successful historical novel. The story begins with the Melekhov family in the small village of Tartosk in the Don basin of Tsarist Russia. Gregor, the elder son of the family, has an affair with the wife of his neighbor, which continues even after Gregor is married. As a consequence of this scandal Gregor leaves home and eventually enters the army. Complicated by family and village problems and unhappinesses, the plot ultimately follows Gregor into the eastern front against Germany and its allies. Gregor distinguishes himself in battle, is wounded, and is awarded the Cross of St. George, the first one in his village to be so honored. The novel provides a clear view of the eastern front through the experiences and eyes of Gregor. We see the discontent growing among the soldiers as Bolshevik agitators help to whip up the masses. The author carries his story through the revolution and the overthrow of the provisional government to the establishment of the Soviet Republic. But the point of view of the novel is strictly from the perspective of the strongly nationalistic cossacks. Although by the end Gregor and the others in his village have successfully resisted the revolutionary troops in their area and return to their homes, the revolutionaries die prophesying that the revolution will succeed. This is an enormous historical novel which portrays in great detail the primitive and legendary life of the Don cossacks in a period of great social and political upheaval. Its size and scope result in a lack of form that weakens the action. Passages tend to drag at times, but the overall effect is impressive both as a view of history and as a rich fictional portrait of the time.

700 Yardley, Herbert Osborn. *The Blonde Countess*. New York & London: Longmans, Green & Co., 1934. 314p.

Greenleaf is the chief of a special World War I American secret-service group referred to as The American Black Chamber. It is disguised as the Department of Chemical Supervision and located in Washington. A typical spy-mystery story, this novel charts the adventures of Greenleaf and his clever young secretary, Joel Carter, and their success in exposing the beautiful German spy otherwise known as the Blonde Countess. The author employs some reasonable and fairly authentic secret-service (what we would nowadays call "the company" or C.I.A.-method) techniques in tracking suspects of wartime espionage. Probably a typical (and mediocre) suspense and spy mystery novel of the period.

701 Yeates, Victor M. *Winged Victory*. New York: H. Harrison Smith & Robert Haas, 1934. 456p.; London: Jonathan Cape, 1934. 456p.

Deals with just six months of the war in 1918. The chief character is Tom Cundall, a fighter pilot with a British air unit on the western front, but the story has no hero. The squadron is depicted, with descriptions of the men arriving, talking, fighting, and dying. Tom survives more by good luck than skill as an aviator. His friend Williamson is killed the day before they are to return to England. The novel approaches the stature of *All Quiet On the Western Front* and similar quality novels. It is a long, authentic, and frequently bitter story of aerial action in the war, related with literary power and skill.

1935

702 Boyd, James. *Roll River*. New York: Charles Scribner's Sons, 1935. 603p.

A fifty-year account of four generations of the Rand family in Pennsylvania. An excellent portrayal of community life at the end of the last century. The second part of this two-part novel vividly recounts the experiences of one family member in the war.

703 Cobb, Humphrey. *Paths of Glory*. New York: Viking Press, 1935. 265p.

One of the more significant novels of the war which was made into a powerful motion picture in the late 1950's. The plot deals with an incident in the French army on the western front. A main theme describes the wide gulf between the officers and their men, which is unbridgeable even by the conscientious efforts of Colonel Dax. It is also a story of vicious ambition and duplicity on the part of a monstrous commander. Colonel Dax attempts to defend three men against blatantly unjust court-martial charges. But in the end the villainous commander, Assolant, sentences all three to be shot: Ferol, the tough ex-legionnaire; the courageous and intelligent Didier; and Langlois, a resigned soldier whose only wish is to see his unborn child. It is a powerful story that progresses in the logical and inevitable manner of a Greek tragedy. All the familiar war scenes are incorporated into the story. Petty military politics, battlefield butchery, and the stupidities of war form the hideous background for the execution of the three innocent men. A strong, anti-militaristic novel written with great skill and power.

704 Crocker, Arthur. *Australia Hops In*. Sydney: Shakespeare Head Press, 1935. 266p.

Not seen; NYPL.

705 Forester, Cecil Scott. *The African Queen*. London: Wm. Heinemann, 1935. 283p.; Boston: Little, Brown & Co., 1935. 275p.

Begins with Rose Sayer, an English spinster, resolving to carry on against the German commander who has rounded up all of her brother's black converts at his Central African mission after he dies. She is soon aided by the fearless and gallant Charlie Allnutt, who comes to her aid with a dilapidated steam launch called "The African Queen." Together they decide to blow up the German gunboat on the lake down river, and so they begin the long and perilous trip on the Uganda. This journey occupies a large portion of the novel and involves hardships and a constant fight against malaria. The novel is a study of the diverse personalities and bravery exhibited under the rigors of the jungle and the climate in German East Africa shortly after the outbreak of the war. This improbable adventure-romance was improved when adapted for the 1952 motion picture featuring Katharine Hepburn and Humphrey Bogart, who won his only Academy Award for this performance.

706 Frankau, Gilbert. *Three Englishmen: A Romance of Married Lives.* New York: E.P. Dutton & Co., 1935. 640p.; London: Hutchinson & Co., 1935. 640p.

The novel represents an exploration of English life and spirit from the days of the Boer War through World War I and the postwar adjustment years. The plot concerns about thirty years in the lives of three men who were schoolmates at Eton at the start of the story: Andrew Curie becomes a professional soldier; Jeremy Wainwright goes into politics and becomes a promoter; and Maxwell Benton becomes a surgeon. Curie seems to be the most important figure of the three. His life and experiences have the greater depth and attention in the book. He is created as a blunt, forthright, and somewhat stubborn British officer whose adventures in the war appear to be the highlight of the story. Curie is with the first 100,000 British soldiers of the "Contemptibles," as the British troops were called who knew only how to fight and die. Some subdued but powerful passages describe how a handful of the British manage to hold back wave after wave of German attacks in the British retreat from Mons. The remainder of the book deals with the adjustment of all three men to peacetime and its problems.

707 Gibbs, Philip Hamilton. *Blood Relations: A Novel.* London: Hutchinson & Co., 1935. 477p.; Garden City, N.Y.: Doubleday, Doran & Co., 1935. 477p.

The story of Audrey, an English girl who marries Paul, a German nobleman, just before the war. The novel follows her through the war years and beyond, describing her feelings as she is torn between her two loyalties. Her German husband, after his war experiences as an officer and as a prisoner, has a change of heart about the entire enterprise and purpose of Germany. The novel can be considered a useful interpretation of what went on in Germany in those years. The characters, however, tend to be two-dimensional although the plot is well thought out.

708 Graham, Stephen. *Balkan Monastery.* London: Nicholson & Watson, 1935. 344p.

A desperate tale about the impact of the war on a small group of children in the Balkans. The major character is

Desa Georgevitch, a ten-year-old Bosnian child, who is in a Belgrade school in 1914 when the war begins. When Belgrade is evacuated, the eighty small girls in the school are all sent to a mountain monastery for safekeeping. They remain there through the next four years. However, they experience considerable privation and are subjected to starvation conditions as they become an isolated group of homeless wanderers. Desa, however, has a happier fate. This is a heart-rending story, but the plot too often tends to be shallow and sketchy.

709 Hardy, Jocelyn Lee. *Everything Is Thunder*. Garden City, N.Y.: Doubleday, Doran & Co., 1935. 306p.; London: John Lane Co., 1935. 308p.

An adventure story that traces the activities of an English officer who escapes from a German prison camp during the war and ends up in Berlin with a young prostitute who becomes his friend. The descriptions of life in a German prison camp are realistically captured. (The author escaped from one during the war.) A romantic melodrama, the novel lacks any sense of honest literary style.

710 Jacob, Naomi Ellington. *"Honour Come Back--."* London: Hutchinson & Co., 1935. 351p.; New York: The Macmillan Co., 1935. 431p.

The theme is the flight and successful fight of a man against fear. Michael Benham is the son of an aristocratic family with a strong military tradition. However, as long as he can remember he could never bear the sight of pain whether it was experienced by an animal or a human. He comes to loathe and fear the tradition fostered by his family. Despite the publisher's disclaimer that this is not a war novel, the war is used throughout the story to demonstrate its disastrous impact on Michael's sensitive nature and values. The plot takes Michael from boyhood and shows how at the age of sixteen when the war starts he falsifies his age and joins up to escape his home conditions. But his father insists he take a commission and later wrangles him a soft job. His military training is described, as well as his leaves and his adolescent love affairs. The dialogue is most effective, however, when the author describes Michael at the French front and later on the Piave front in Italy. The novel traces his gradual mental disintegration as a result of the war. He finally deserts, thinking that he alone is responsible for the conflict still continuing. But two days later he learns that the war has ended. He now wanders, disoriented and without food, until he eventually reaches Sirmione on the southern shore of a lake in northern Italy. Here he meets a young Italian peasant girl and begins his mental and spiritual recuperation. He marries her, starts a family, becomes a fruit farmer in that pastoral land, and ultimately reaps contentment and happiness. A happy, melodramatic bromide.

711   McKenna, Marthe (Cnokaert). *A Spy Was Born*. London: Jarrolds, 1935. 255p.; New York: Robert M. McBride & Co., 1935. 255p.

The story is placed in Belgium during and after the German invasion. A German soldier who has a Belgian mother is the spy of the title. Dismayed and revolted by what he sees and must do, he decides to give critical information to the Allied forces. In conjunction there is also the theme of his loyal friendship with a Prussian who is responsible for a particularly revolting rape. This tragically causes the victim, who turns out to be a relative, to lose her sanity. The style is extremely prosaic.

712   Newman, Bernard Charles. *Spy*. London: Victor Gollancz, 1935. 288p.; New York: D. Appleton & Co., 1935. 282p.

The narrator represents himself as a British spy who during the war kept the British authorities informed about important German military plans. He enters Germany for the British in 1915 and gets himself appointed to the German General Staff headquarters on the western front. He is able to serve as an intelligence officer under the brilliant Colonel Nicolai, head of the German secret service. Through his false reports to the Germans he is finally able to destroy the morale of no less a personage than General Ludendorff himself. Many scenes of battlefield horrors appear in this spy-adventure thriller. The supreme impact is still apparent today, although when this book was first published, it was supposed to be the actual records of a British spy. A year later the author admitted that it was a creation of his imagination, although he again attempted to hoodwink the public with his *German Spy* (item 724).

*   Tolstoi, Aleksei Nikolaevich. *Darkness and Dawn*. Translated by Edith Bone and Emile Burns. London: Victor

Gollancz, 1935. 584p.; New York: Longmans, Green
and Co., 1936. 570p. [*Khozhdemie po Mukam*. Moscow:
1925. 2 vols. in one.]

Contains the first two novels of a trilogy completed in
1941. Refer to items 481 and 776 for annotations.

713 Turiánski, Osyp. *Lost Shadows*. Translated from the
Ukranian by Andrew Mykytiak. New York: Phoenix Press,
1935. 246p.

Appears to be an autobiographical novel based on the
"Road of Death" incident which occurred in 1915 in the
Albanian mountains. With the Austro-German offensive
pressuring the Serbs, the Central Powers forced some sixty
thousand prisoners of war to travel by foot on a trail
across the Albanian mountains from Galicia to the Italian
prisoner camps. Although it was only autumn in the valleys,
winter had already arrived at the higher elevations. Within three weeks of the start of the forced march, nearly
forty-five thousand prisoners died from either the cold
and starvation, or the bullets of the guards who shot any
who stumbled and fell. (The author was one of the prisoners who survived this grim march.) The plot centers on
seven prisoners who become lost in the mountains and
describes the greed, cruelty, and butchery involved in
this harrowing incident. The story is recreated with a
style that one critic referred to as "lovely and oddly
moving lyricism."

714 Vercel, Roger (pseud. of Roger Auguste Crétin). *Captain
Conan*. Translated from the French by Warre Bradley
Wells. New York: Henry Holt & Co., 1935. 296p.; London:
Constable, 1935. 319p. [*Capitaine Conan*. Lausanne:
Éditions Recontre, 1934. 280p.]

The chief character is Captain Conan, a former draper
from a small Breton town in France. The war has created
in him (falsely as it turns out) such a sense of courage
and recklessness that he becomes the leader of a group of
tough storm-trooper types. This novel tends to be a vivid
description of French army activities in the Balkans, with
the climax of the story occurring in a marsh battlefield.
The style of the author stresses harsh realism and distinct
pessimism. The novel deals primarily with character rather
than events. In this case, the men who have survived four
and one-half years of fighting and killing suddenly are
confronted by the Armistice and peace--a situation long

unfamiliar and now confusing. For some like Conan who felt alive only during the war, "Peace is the time when shirkers and rotters have the right to trample on the real men...." Perhaps the most memorable and moving moment in the novel occurs at the trial and conviction of the coward, René Erlane, a symbol of the protected mother's boy—helpless, terrified—who is in so many ways an innocent victim and finally is destroyed by the inhumane and inflexible war machine.

1936

715 Brittain, Vera Mary. *Honourable Estate: A Novel of Transition*. London: Victor Gollancz, 1936. 637p.; New York: The Macmillan Co., 1936. 601p.

The foreword notes that the novel "purports to show how the women's revolution—one of the greatest in all history—combined with the struggle for other democratic ideals and the cataclysm of the War to alter the private destinies of individuals." The title derives from the phrase in the Protestant marriage service. Marriage is one of the main subjects of the novel, with three marriages depicted in detail. The son of Janet Rutherston, the wife in the first marriage, marries Ruth Alleyndene, whose graduation with a first in history from Oxford had been followed soon by the announcement of her brother's death at Gallipoli. Ruth becomes a Red Cross nurse in France and falls in love with an American who is later killed in the Argonne battle. This part of the novel is chiefly about the nursing of wounded and dying soldiers in hospitals.

716 Cowen, William Joyce. *They Gave Him a Gun*. New York: H. Harrison Smith & Robert Haas, 1936. 275p.; London: Wm. Heinemann, 1936. 266p.

The thesis is an indictment of war instead of the usual patriotic propaganda and heroism. It is the story of Jimmy Golden who is sent to war with a gun. War transforms a timid and undersized young bookkeeper from a small town into a wartime killer and, eventually, a fugitive. Unfortunately, the anti-war messages have so preoccupied the author that the novel suffers greatly as literature. Many situations end up being neither exciting nor convincing, and the characters are poorly developed.

717 Deeping, George Warwick. *No Hero--This*. London: Cassell & Co., 1936. 436p.; New York: Alfred A. Knopf, 1936. 395p.

The narrative is in the form of a journal kept by Stephen Brent, an English doctor who served first in the Near East and then in France during the war. Basically this is an account of his war experiences and his hopes and fears. The doctor describes the great fear that underlies his experiences, beginning with the fiasco of Gallipoli, and continuing later with his participation in the Fifth Army in France. He also was involved in such conflicts as the Haig offensive that broke the Hindenberg line as well as the advance of the victorious Allies through the former German-occupied zone of France. There is abundant detail on conditions in the war zone, but the novel covers in a very conventional way much of the same material already written about in many other books on the war.

718 Forester, Cecil Scott. *The General*. London: Michael Joseph, 1936. 283p.; Boston: Little, Brown & Co., 1936. 305p.

A satirical novel that recounts the career of an English professional soldier from the Boer War through World War I, when he achieves the rank of lieutenant general and an elevated social position. The novel seems to be mainly a character study of Sir Herbert Curzon, who is described as a ruthless and ambitious Sandhurst prig who does his duty as he sees it. The perfect manner of this hero tends to reveal him in black and white terms--either as a savior, or as a perfect devil. In some ways the story seems to be a tract or thesis novel, but it is not clear whether it is an attack on the military caste system or not. General Curzon is portrayed as the type of leader who sends thousands and thousands of men to their deaths without a qualm. Basically a weak plot.

719 Guilloux, Louis. *Bitter Victory*. Translated from the French by Samuel Putnam. New York: Robert M. McBride & Co., 1936. 574p. [*Le Sang Noir*. Roman. Paris: Gallimard, 1935. 433p.]

Describes life in a provincial French town during the war. The main character is a teacher of philosophy, a professor Merlin, who has the nickname Cripure. The plot reveals the repercussions of the war on the daily routine of the local school and its staff, and especially Merlin.

The cast of characters includes the pompous schoolmaster who has composed a poem to a deputy's wife. She has just received the Legion of Honor and at the same time learns her son has been killed at the front. A third character is a dull-witted general surrounded by female Hun-haters, and a fourth group of characters are French troops who mutiny upon learning they are leaving for the front.

720 Hill, Herbert. *Retreat from Death*. London: Hutchinson & Co., 1936. 480p.

Tells the story of an 18-year-old British soldier in the front-line trenches during the last year of the War. After his battalion is decimated at St. Quentin, the young soldier and the remnants of his battalion retreat, never knowing where they are or where they are going, being shunted from one series of trenches to another while constantly under fire. The soldier's only respites from combat are a six-week period when he attends signal corps school and a stay in a military hospital after he has been badly gassed at the end of the war. His only thought is to survive when he observes his nineteenth birthday in a water-soaked tent on Armistice Day. A dreary and depressing view of the war from the perspective of an ordinary enlisted man.

721 Hyde, Robin (pseud. of Iris Guiver Wilkinson). *Passport to Hell; the Story of James Douglas Stark, Bomber, Fifth Regiment, New Zealand Expeditionary Forces*. London: Hurst & Blackett, 1936. 288p.

Not seen; NYPL.

722 Lernet-Holenia, Alexander Maria. *The Standard*. Translated by Alan Harris. London: Wm. Heinemann, 1936. 304p. [Title in U.S.: *The Glory Is Departed*. Translated from the German by Alan Harris. New York: Harper & Brothers, 1936. 304p.] [*Die Standarte; Roman*. Berlin: Deutsche Buch-Gemeinschaft, 1934. 295p.]

A novel written by an Austrian ex-cavalry officer about his experiences in the Balkans during the last weeks of the war. The main focus of the narrative is his vivid account of the annihilation of his regiment during a mutiny. The story describes the complete collapse of the Austrian fighting force and the destruction of its military tradition.

Adult Novels

723 Millholland, Ray. *The Splinter Fleet of the Otranto Barrage*. New York: Grosset & Dunlap, 1936. 307p.

Relates the story of submarine chasers manned by Americans as they seek to enclose the enemy submarines in the Adriatic, thereby curtailing their attacks on Allied shipping in the Mediterranean. The novel also recounts the submariners' participation in the Battle of Durazzo against a seemingly impregnable fortress, a battle which turned the tide of victory to the Allies on October 2, 1918.

724 Newman, Bernard Charles. *German Spy*. London: Victor Gollancz, 1936. 320p.; New York: Hillman-Curl, 1936. 317p.

The author pretends that he is writing the memoirs of a German agent, just as he claimed he did for a British spy in the book *Spy* (item 712). These are, nonetheless, the fictional memoirs of one Ludwig Grein who served as Louis Green in the British Army for nearly the entire war. As a spy story the novel is fairly exciting and not overly romanticized. It shows accurately the type of preparation a spy must make even before war begins in order to be most effective in the enemy country. The narrative relates the usual tricks and techniques employed by secret agents in sending their information back to their own country. The spy featured in this tale is eventually caught, after a number of the usual improbable circumstances to amuse the fancy of the casual reader. The point of view is interesting since it includes a description of British customs and manners from the German perspective.

725 Sassoon, Siegfried Lorraine. *Sherston's Progress*. London: Faber & Faber, 1936. 280p.; Garden City, N.Y.: Doubleday, Doran & Co., 1936. 245p.

The third volume of the author's biographical trilogy of novels. The first is *Memoirs of a Fox-Hunting Man* (item 539) and the second is *Memoirs of an Infantry Officer* (item 630). Shell-shocked during a bombardment, Sherston is sent to a hospital specifically for shell-shocked officers. Eventually brought back to normality by Doctor Rivers, he travels to Ireland for a short leave before returning to his regiment which is now in Egypt. Later the regiment is transferred to France where Sherston receives a head wound that causes him to be sent home. The story is related without exaggeration or sensationalism but tends toward an awkwardness of style. The description of the natural surroundings in Palestine and in France is rendered with some ability. The plot reveals with some vividness both the active and passive aspects of military life as well as a contrast between a pacifism that despises war and a pacifism which results in a refusal to fight.

726 Schultz, Walter C. *Double Duty; a Novel*. Chicago: Daniel Ryerson, 1936. 183p.

Not seen; NYPL.

727 Slade, Gurney (pseud. of Stephen Bartlett). *Lawrence in the Blue*. New York: F.A. Stokes Co., 1936. 269p.; London: Frederick Warne, 1936. 288p.

The story of two young men who enlist in the cavalry in Australia and are sent to Egypt to fight against the Turks in Sinai and in Palestine, where they meet T.E. Lawrence (Lawrence of Arabia) and learn of his exploits against the Turks.

728 Zweig, Arnold. *Education Before Verdun*. Translated from the German by Eric Sutton. New York: Viking Press, 1936. 447p.; London: Martin Secker & Warburg, 1936. 527p. [*Erziehung vor Verdun, Roman*. Amsterdam: Querido, Verlag, 1935. 627p.]

The novel is the third in the author's series of war tales which began with his *The Case of Sergeant Grischa* (item 547) and continued with his second, *Young Woman of 1914* (item 683). The hero of the second title, Private Werner Bertin, is also the chief character of this third story. The scene is placed in the countryside around Verdun in 1916 and concerns the friendship of Bertin with the two young German officers, the Kroysing brothers. When the youngest brother Christoph is killed, with implications of legalized murder, Eberhard, the older brother, develops a fierce desire for justice. The story provides not only a dramatic picture of one of the deadliest battles of the war but also a vivid picture of the thoughts and actions of the men on the battlefield. Although this is a view of the German forces, it creates a remarkable portrait of the circumstances and thoughts that were common to the troops of both sides. The style of the author tends toward the turgid and obscure at times and is not on a par with the first novel of the tetralogy, *The Case of Sergeant*

Grischa, especially in the characterization of Werner Bertin. A major theme is the cheapness of human life during one of the most devastating battles of the war.

1937

729 Blankfort, Michael. *I Met a Man*. Indianapolis: Bobbs-Merrill Co., 1937. 277p.

The story takes place behind the German lines in 1915 and is an account of the friendship between two men leading to an inevitable and tragic conclusion. Curtis, an American in German disguise, is an agent in the British secret service. The other is a German officer, Franz von Lehring. The travels of Curtis from England through Holland into occupied Belgium, disguised as a German private soldier, are related in some detail. Curtis meets Lehring on a crowded German troop train and they strike up a deep friendship based on common interests and values. Their association is traced until Curtis completes his spy mission, with tragic consequences. This is a fast-paced psychological adventure story with considerable suspense. However, an underlying theme is the question of integrity and morality when men of high principles are faced with serious ethical problems in wartime. A novel of some power and poignancy.

730 Briffault, Robert Stephen. *Europa in Limbo*. London: Robert Hale, 1937. 512p.; New York: Charles Scribner's Sons, 1937. 476p.

A sequel to *Europa* (1935), this novel continues the story of Julian Bern and Princess Zena through the war years and the Russian revolution. The author demonstrates a strong anti-capitalist bias throughout by combining the qualities of Marx and Christ in the character of Julian as he pursues his doomed love relationship with the Russian Princess Zena. A very personal view of the breakdown of Europe and the Communist education of the protagonist. The story provides a grand tour of European philosophy, politics, morals, science, and sex. The chief characters get into nearly every troublesome incident that occurred in Europe in all the disastrous years of the war. This includes air raids in London, trenches on the western front, prisoner-of-war camps, Petrograd, Moscow, and the strife of the Russian revolution. The author has sprinkled his plot liberally with sex and Marxist-socialist cant about the corruption of the classes in power in Europe and the future rise of a new society. One critic summed up the plot fairly well: "Briffault's sequel ... seems to be constructed on the theory that rape multiplied by murder equals history."

731 Child, Philip. *God's Sparrows*. London: T. Butterworth, 1937. 319p.

A story about the military service of the men from the Thatcher and Burnet families as typified by the life of Daniel Thatcher, born in Ontario in the 1890's. The time covered is 1915 through the winter of 1917-1918, involving the last big German push.

732 Crosby, Barbara (pseud. of Alan Corby). *Deep Soundings*. Caldwell, Idaho: Caxton Printers, 1937. 405p.

Relates with realism the convoying of merchant ships through the U-boat-infested North Atlantic during the war. The hero is Rex Dean, a young petty officer from Texas. The usual attempt at a love interest hardly distinguishes the story in any way. During his spare time the hero writes adventure tales for magazines and attempts to win the one woman who seems always to resist his advances. Eventually, of course, he marries her.

733 Heth, Edward Harris. *Told with a Drum*. Boston: Houghton-Mifflin Co., 1937. 250p.

The theme is the home front in Wisconsin and what happened to the German-American Tellinger family. The narrator is Leo, the small boy in the family. The basic conflict occurs between the austere old-line German father and his Americanized daughter. Unfortunately, the book never grapples with the far larger issue of war hysteria and persecution so evident throughout the country. Herta, the daughter, has married Francis, a passionate propagandist for the Allied side, while Tellinger follows the Hindenburg line. The relationship of the daughter and her pro-German father is never restored even after Herta's husband and the father's German son and grandson are killed in battle.

734 Jones, David Michael. *In Parenthesis; Seinnyessit e Gledyf ym Penn Mameu*. London: Faber & Faber, 1937. 224p.

A curious and extraordinary tour de force about the Great War. Not exactly a novel or a poem, the author has created a remarkable collage of language impressions and of fact, superimposed on traditional Welsh heroes and Arthurian legend. The bock is based on the experiences of the author in the trenches of France with the Welsh Fusileers from December 1915 to July of 1916 when he was wounded. The title refers to the war as it was fought by the amateur soldiers of a Welsh regiment. The protagonist, Private John Ball, survives six months in the trenches until he is wounded in the thigh. The narrative is a remarkable concoction of poetry and prose in a number of combinations. While Private Bell nervously waits in the trenches, the author explores with his language in an incredible combination of words and sounds, and, as a result, creates an innovative and spectacular and very personal impression of the war and its ironies. Jones uses the detailed military procedures and locations of the western front to admit a wide-ranging and freewheeling exploration of time and myth in combination with the present tensions and horrors of the war. Obviously this is not a novel in any conventional sense, but is included here because of its unusual nature as literature and fiction.

735 Klareich, Lee. *Through Blazes for Love*; edited by Joseph Lasky. New York: Printed by Ginsberg Linotyping Co., 1937. 132p.

Not seen; NYPL.

736 Lee, John Alexander. *Civilian Into Soldier*. London: T. Werner Laurie, 1937. 294p.

A picture of trench warfare viewed by John Guy, a New Zealand enlisted man. The novel presents war in its depravity, dehumanization, brutality, butchery, and barbarity, as the hysteria of battle turns thinking men into automatons. A compilation of the obscenities and crudities of battle humor as soldiers gloss over the ugliness of the war with trench wit.

737 Mackenzie, Compton. *South Wind of Love*. New York: Dodd, Mead & Co., 1937. 758p.

The second novel in the author's series of four entitled *The Four Winds of Love*. The story describes the travels of John Ogilvie from England to America, where he is an intelligence officer during the war. Ogilvie has a love affair with an Athenian girl who is referred to as the "south wind," hence the title. A large portion of the story describes military red tape, presumably based on the author's life.

738 Meersch, Maxence van der. *Invasion '14. Translated from the French by Gerard Hopkins.* London: Constable, 1937. 519p. [Title in U.S.: *Invasion.* New York: Viking Press, 1937. 707p.] [*Invasion 14. Roman....* Paris: A. Michel, 1935. 499p.]

The plot deals with what the war was like behind the German lines in occupied territory. The setting is an industrial area in northern France where the author grew up. The novel relates the effect of four years of German occupation upon fifty civilians such as Jean Sennevilliers, a quarry man, whose wife took a German lover; Hennedyck, an industrialist sent to a German prison; Guare, a chemistry professor involved in a spy plot; and Judith Lacombe, who loved a German soldier but became a prostitute after he deserted her. This novel's broad indictment of war maintains a remarkable objectivity of view and lack of animus toward the Germans. A deep sympathy for the Germans as well as the French is conveyed in the tale. The story has no main characters but is primarily a series of vignettes about the lives and homes disorganized by the invasion. There is little or no effort to explicate, only a rather realistic description of the mad impact of the war in almost minute detail. The sense of historical verisimilitude is exemplary and characterizes the novel as one of the better efforts of its kind.

* Sassoon, Siegfried Lorraine. *The Complete Memoirs of George Sherston.* London: Faber & Faber, 1937. 804p.

This title covers all three of the Sassoon novels previously published separately. See each individual title for annotation, i.e., *Memoirs of a Fox-hunting Man* (item 539), *Memoirs of an Infantry Officer* (item 630), and *Sherston's Progress* (item 725).

739 Sitwell, Edith. *I Live Under a Black Sun: A Novel.* London: Victor Gollancz, 1937. 400p.

A novel written as an allegory. The author's note in her Foreword suggests the use made of the historical background: "This novel is founded upon the story of Jonathan Swift, Stella and Vanessa. But not only the details of that story, but also the framework, have been changed. I have drawn copiously upon the works and letters of Jonathan Swift; in some cases the language of the latter has been modernized." Susan Daw, the daughter of a gardener, leaves home when her lover is killed in the war. Ultimately she marries the German who killed her lover. (Forced to fight men whom he did not hate, the German has travelled to pray at the grave of the man he killed, and by chance meets Susan at the gravesite.) The novel reproduces the misery that war pours on Susan and the thousands of plain, humble people like her.

740 Vercel, Roger. *Lena*. Translated from the French by Warre Bradley Wells. New York: Random House, 1937. 276p. [*Léna, Roman*. Paris: A. Michel, 1936. 253p.]

The novel commences with the death of De Queslain, a French officer, in a duel with a Servian officer in Sofia and then tells De Queslain's story which he had related to a friend the night before his duel. De Queslain, wounded and taken prisoner, is placed under the care of Lena, a Bulgarian doctor. A cruel kind of love develops between the two. This reaches a climax in an incident in which Lena pretends that he is about to rape her since that alone will make them safe from looters. However, De Queslain is carried away by the spirit of the occasion. The novel describes the final months of fighting in the Balkans at the end of the war and attempts to describe some of the effects of the war--the brutalization of De Queslain--and the consequences of the hatred and inhumanity of adversaries.

741 Wilson, Theodora Wilson. *Those Strange Years*. London: The C.W. Daniel Co., 1937. 306p.

Not seen; NYPL

1938

742 De Pourtalés, Guy (Guido James de Pourtalés). *Shadows Around the Lake*. Translated from the French by Geoffrey Sainsbury. New York: Alfred A. Knopf, 1938. 480p. [*La Pêche Miraculeuse; Roman*. Paris: Gallimard, 1937. 432p.]

Set in Geneva before and during World War I, the novel details the vicissitudes in the lives of the de Villars and the Galland families. It pictures the dark currents that lie beneath the quiet lives of these bourgeois families and the changes that the war and its fortunes bring into their lives. Written with grace and sensitivity.

743 Hanley, James. *Hollow Sea: A Novel*. London: John Lane Co., 1938. 499p.

Depicts the lives of sailors aboard a troop transport bound for a landing in Africa, and then on to Alexandria to transport more troops. The ship becomes a small isolated world, and the isolation works upon the personalities and relationships of the men. A landing on the wrong beach results in a massacre of the landed troops, and the ship, now a floating hospital and morgue, is denied a berth in Alexandria and ordered to return to its port of registry. Although the ship, with its cargo of dead and wounded, seems destined to sail forever, it arrives eventually in England, where the men disembark, relieved to abandon the ship which had been their prison on a voyage of horror.

744 Hutchinson, Ray Coryton. *Testament: A Novel*. New York: Farrar & Rinehart, 1938. 696p.; London: Cassell & Co., 1938. 732p.

The story of Anton Scheffler, a Russian count, seriously wounded early in the war and captured by the Austrians. While incarcerated, the count meets Captain Alexi Alexeivitch Otraveskov, a revolutionist. Repatriated together, they are shipped to the Russian rehabilitation center at Mariki-Matesk. Otraveskov becomes fascinated by the Christ-like character of Count Scheffler and, as the novel's narrator, recounts the lives of both men, their many psychological and spiritual experiences. In one instance Count Scheffler refused to lead a group of unfit soldiers back to battle duty; in another instance during the Russian revolution the count refused to sign a spurious confession and was sentenced by the Bolsheviks and executed. A letter which Count Scheffler leaves behind is his "testament" and the basis of this novel.

745 McKee, Ruth Eleanor, and Alice Fleenor Sturgis. *Three Daughters*. New York: Doubleday, Doran & Co., 1938. 504p.

Attempts to tell the story of the war activities of American women in France through the persons of three sisters, daughters of a wealthy Pennsylvania industrialist who manufactures weapons for the cause. All three sisters are in their twenties at the start of the war and all decide to go to France and donate their services to the war effort. The personal career and experiences of each sister are described. Candida (or Candy), the youngest, ends up in a "Y" hut and eventually as a telephone operator with the Signal Corps, close to the front. She is killed by an exploding shell after the Armistice. Camilla, just out of college, eagerly becomes involved in the Red Cross Appeals campaign, but is afflicted by mental problems and eventually ends up in a Catholic sisterhood. Elizabeth, the oldest, is pictured as a saint, a person for whom no task it too difficult or horrible to endure. She is the symbol of the selfless woman (and presumably the American woman). She eventually marries the man she helped bring back to sanity after the end of the war. It is apparent that the author holds firm pacifist opinions, but they do not prevent the story from dealing with most of the war issues in a manner that shows restraint and perspective. The descriptions of field-hospital conditions are stark with horrors seen and experienced under hectic conditions.

746 Sabsay, Nahum. *Through Tunnels and Canyons Roared a Train*. San Francisco: Printed by T.W. McDonald, 1938. 23p.

Not seen; NYPL.

747 Schauwecker, Franz. *The Armoured Cruiser: A Naval Romance of the Great War*. Translated by A. Katherine Barlow. London: Massie Pub. Co., 1938. 318p.

The story of an encounter between several ships of the Imperial German Navy and a numerically superior British fleet. Leading the German ships is a new fast cruiser, the flagship for the squadron and the pride of the German navy. Its invulnerability is tested by English shells. The resulting engagement provides a description of the destruction of the ship and its crew before its eventual sinking.

748 Zweig, Arnold. *The Crowning of a King*. Translated by Eric Sutton. New York: Viking Press, 1938. 458p.; London: Martin Secker & Warburg, 1938. 524p. [*Einsetzung eines Königs: Roman*. Amsterdam: Querido Verlag, 1937. 574p.]

The book constitutes the third part of the author's "Trilogy of Transition" novels (the first was *Education*

Before Verdun [item 728] and the second was *The Case of Sergeant Grischa* [item 547]). The story takes place on the eastern front in German general staff headquarters, at a time when it seems still possible the Germans might win on both the eastern and western fronts. The plot revolves around the struggle between the two major groups in Germany: the Pan-Germans with General Clauss as the chief exponent urging conquest and supported by the professional officers, and the group of Germans who have come to look on an honorable peace with reasonable terms as the best solution. Captain Paul Winfried can be considered the hero of the story. Bitterly disenchanted with the aims of German leadership and the ruling class, Winfried comes to represent those Germans who look for an honorable peace. This is a novel of ideas which offers some thoughtful observations on the nature of Germany then and in the 1930's. The novel seems weak, however, in character development.

1939

749   Lucas, Anna M.   *Amnesia, a Novel in Three Parts*.   Belleville, Ill.: Buechler Publishing, 1939.   279p.

Not seen; NYPL.

750   Romains, Jules (pseud. of Louis Farigoule).   *Verdun*.   Translated from the French by Gerard Hopkins.   New York: Alfred A. Knopf, 1939.   500p.   [*Les Hommes de Bonne Volonté*.   New York: Éditions de la Maison Française, 1932-.]

The Battle of Verdun is described in great detail both as military strategy and action and as it is viewed by a group of French soldiers. This is mainly the account of those men who took the brunt of the German attack, how they felt and thought, and how they managed to live through it. They are represented especially by such perceptive characters as the former school teachers Lieutenant Clanricard and Lieutenant Jerphanion, who give not only their personal reactions but serve to reflect the point of view of the ordinary fighting man. This is probably the most objective, faithful, and complete account of the battle in any novel on the war. The point of view of the author, however, is astringent and quite bitter with an intensive sense of the injustice of war. The novel tends to be didactic, for it is clear that the characters seem to be the mouthpieces of the author's views on a host of subjects about the war and the times.

751 Tousseul, Jean (pseud. of Olivier Degée). *Jean Clarambeaux: A Novel.* Translated by Elisabeth Abbott. Philadelphia: J.B. Lippincott Co., 1939. 715p. [*Jean Clarambaux.* Paris: Rieder, 1930-1936. 5 vols.]

A partly autobiographical novel of the life of a Belgian during several decades. The main character, Jean, the illegitimate son of a peasant girl, is a schoolmaster and noncombatant during the war. The fourth section of the novel realistically describes the German invasion and occupation of Belgium in 1914-1918. This portion offers a very good record of what the Belgian villagers experienced during this period.

752 Trumbo, Dalton. *Johnny Got His Gun.* Philadelphia: J.B. Lippincott Co., 1939. 309p.

Relates the mental experiences of a man who carries out his "idea of trapping time and getting himself back into the world." The Johnny of the title is Joe Bonham, a soldier who is a basket case, having lost his legs, arms, and face. A hole is where his mouth was, and his nose and eyes are masked. Joe is also deaf, dumb, and blind. In the hospital he gradually and painstakingly comes to recognize his condition. He can think, and this enables him to survive, he tells himself. "If you can keep track of time you can get a hold on yourself and keep yourself in the world but if you lose it why then you are lost too. The last thing that ties in with other people is gone and you are all alone." Joe reviews his early life and his outlook for the future. An uncompromising, unsettling, and gruesome novel, hammering relentlessly on the futility of war and its monstrous casualties.

753 Wittlin, Jozef. *Salt of the Earth!* Translated from the Polish by Pauline De Chary. London: Methuen & Co., 1939. 271p. [*Sól Ziemi....* Warsaw: "Rój," 1936. n.p.]

The first volume of a planned trilogy. The novel concerns the first six weeks of the war, and specifically the experiences of a Ruthenian peasant, Peter Neviadomski. (In Polish this surname means "son of an unknown father.") Peter can be viewed as a symbol of the "Polish Everyman, the eternal fall guy" in the Emperor Franz Josef's army. The author was an infantryman in the Austrian army during the war. The novel appeared in Polish in 1935 and was translated into nine languages.

754 Wren, Percival Christopher. *Paper Prison*. London: J.
    Murray, 1939. 480p. [Title in U.S.: *The Man the Devil
    Didn't Want*. Philadelphia: Macrae Smith, 1940. 393p.]

A melodramatic romance of two English brothers, and of
the girl they both loved. The story ranges from the English countryside to the Verdun trenches and the men of
the French Foreign Legion. The novel is in three parts,
each one related by one of the principal characters--the
first by Mark Tuyler, the next by his twin brother Luke,
and the last by Rosanne Van Daten. The plot ranges over
blackmail, an imposture, kidnapping, murder, and is highly
involved as well as highly improbable. However, the adventure seems to have plenty of suspense for an evening's
light entertainment. Some of the war scenes convey the
grim reality of the stench, mud, shell shock, and disillusionment of trench warfare.

1940

755 Anand, Mulk Raj. *Across the Black Waters: A Novel*.
    London: Jonathan Cape, 1940. 357p.

The story of Lal Singh (nicknamed "Lalu") who serves in
a division of Indian troops sent to fight in Europe. The
novel details their indoctrination into the war, the cultural assault upon their sensibilities, and their attempt
at "Europeanization." Lal Singh sees many of his comrades
die, and at the end of the novel becomes a prisoner of the
Germans.

756 Bruce, Keith. *Digger Tourists*. South Melbourne, Australia: Popular Pubs., 1940. 249p.

Relates the adventures and activities of Australian
troops in the trenches and behind the lines in France.
A prosaic popular tale that adds little or nothing to the
literature of the Great War, and only serves to duplicate
what has been far more capably described in many other
World War I novels.

757 Coles, Manning (pseud. of Adelaide Frances Oke Manning
    and Cyril Henry Coles). *Drink to Yesterday*. London:
    Hodder & Stoughton, 1940. 319p.

Another spy story of the war but featuring a double
agent. Michael Kingston, the English secret agent, is

in Germany during the war. He so impresses a German intelligence officer with his hatred of England and his devotion to Germany that he is sent to England as a German spy, thus making it easy for him to pass information to the British War Office. On one of his trips to England he marries the girl he met and fell in love with before the war. She now thinks he is simply in the army, hence Michael is compelled to live a double life as well as be a double agent. When the Armistice is settled he is a changed man and now finds that he cannot take up his old life in England. He also cannot forget the girl he met and loved in Germany but who was killed during the last days of the war. His wife now seems like a stranger to him. This aspect of the spy game rings reasonably true as an indication of what such activities can do to a normal individual who is sensitive enough not to be completely brutalized by his undercover experiences. One of the authors served in the British War Office during the war; the other, in the infantry and in British Intelligence.

758 Conkling, Roscow S. *"That Damn Jew."* New York: Falcon Press, 1940. 197p.

Not seen; NYPL.

759 Hudson, Alec (pseud. of Wilfred Jay Holmes). *Battle Stations!* New York: The Macmillan Co., 1940. 71p.

The plot is based on the personal experiences of the author in submarine warfare. The story is an exceptionally realistic adventure tale of a squadron of five subs during the war. Although highly technical in its detail of how subs are handled, it dramatically holds one's interest.

760 King, Rufus Gunn. *The Ambulance Driver*. Boston: Meador Publishing Co., 1940. 221p.

Not seen; NYPL.

761 Lebedeff, Ivan. *Legion of Dishonor*. New York: Liveright, 1940. 314p.

The chief character is an earnest young American, Harry O'Brien, who quits his newspaper job to enlist in the French army. On a night raid in no-man's-land he loses his way in the fog and is knocked out. After regaining consciousness he eventually ends up in the cellar of a

ruined chateau between the lines. The cellar is inhabited
by a motley group of disreputable French, German, and
British deserters who are led by a ruthless former German
butcher, Sergeant Steinicke. They raid the dead for whatever supplies or food they can find. On one such foray
they bring back a wounded young German Red Cross nurse
who has had her legs broken by a shell blast. O'Brien
soon finds himself falling in love with the nurse and his
patriotic spirit reviving. There is some skill in the
narrative development and a sense of suspense to the very
conclusion of the story. However, the plot seems a cross
between a pulp novel and a third-rate movie. Some of the
language is highly stilted; whether this is due to the
translation is not entirely certain. The author is a
former Czarist officer.

762 Malone, Paul Bernard. *Barbed Wire Entanglements*. Harrisburg, Pennsylvania: Stackpole Sons, 1940. 397p.

An account of American participation in the war. Douglas
Atwell, the hero who figures in the author's series of
West Point stories, is an officer in an American regiment
at the French front. The last chapter in particular is
the vehicle for the author's argument against American
involvement in any foreign war and, as a consequence, our
need to avoid "barbed-wire entanglements." The plot adds
nothing of any significance to the literature of the war.

763 Martin du Gard, Roger. *Summer 1914*. Translated from the
French by Stuart Gilbert. London: John Lane Co., 1940.
1078p. [*L'Été 1914*. Paris: Gallimard, 1936. 3 vols.]

Traces the evolution of the war from the points of view
of the two Thibault brothers. Antoine is a doctor, who
represents the forces of tradition and the bourgeoisie.
The other brother is Jacques, a professional revolutionary,
whose sole purpose is to struggle against the war. The
novel is not only an account of the events and activities
of the chief characters, but also a representation of the
moral problems facing the Thibaults and their generation.
The first part of the book describes the revolutionary
circles of Geneva where Jacques attempts to realize his
mission as a man of action who commits himself to fight to
his utmost against the war. Indeed, when all the others
desert their ideals, he decides to plan a last suicidal
attempt to prevent the war. Jacques will fly over the
front lines in an airplane, scattering leaflets that call
upon the troops on both sides to lay down their arms. But

the plane crashes and Jacques is horribly mutilated. He
then is carried along in the chaos of the French retreat
until a policeman puts a bullet through his head. The
epilogue ties in all of the twelve volumes of the series
by uniting the two major themes of war and family. This
is a well-written novel that can stand independently of
the first part. In the French-language edition the volumes
were called *Les Thibaults*. The title of the series in
English is *The World of the Thibaults*; this is also the
title of volume I. (Part II, published as volume II in
English, has the title *Summer 1914*.)

764 Rixon, Annie Louisa. *Yesterday and Today*. Sydney, Australia: G.M. Dash, 1940. 247p.

Not seen; NYPL.

765 Sinclair, Upton Beall. *World's End*. New York: Viking Press, 1940. 740p.; London: T. Werner Laurie, 1940. 627p.

The first of the Lanny Budd series. The plot covers
the period from 1913 to 1919, during which the gay, insouciant, and complacent pre-World War I population lost
its innocence in a bloody war. The novel relates the story
of the intrigues of big industry and the machinations of
the members of the Peace Conference and ends with Lanny
Budd's remark to his munition-making father that he would
"leave for the Côte d'Azur ... and watch the world come
to an end."

1941

766 Haskell, Edward Forelich. *Lance, a Novel about Multicultural Men*. New York: John Day, 1941. 359p.

"Lance" is the nickname of the novel's main character,
Lancelot Tenorton. His parents are English, though Lance
was reared in Germany. The story depicts Lance's life
during the closing months of the war when he is imprisoned
in a German prison camp in Bulgaria. Much of the novel
contains philosophical ruminations about the unnecessary
and absurd positions into which nationalistic considerations in every European country place its citizens. The
novel describes the little known war between the Allies
and the Bulgarians. The novel seems partly autobiographical, since the author (the son of an American father and

a Swiss mother who were both missionaries) spent much of his childhood in various countries for long periods of time.

767   Hilton, James. *Random Harvest*. London: The Macmillan Co., 1941. 351p.

Charles Rainier, the chief character, has been struck by a shell in a crater while on a reconnaissance mission at the front. The injury has caused a loss of memory about the events of the preceding three years. Rainier eventually regains his memory as he reconstructs his war experiences, though his memory does not return in one piece chronologically. Nearly a year after the onset of the shell shock, a sudden accident on the street restores his memory up to the shelling; but not until the outbreak of World War II does Rainier regain another vital missing part of his past. In recounting his traumatic war experiences, Rainier is forced to piece his memory together from his fragmented recollections. His experiences are narrated by his secretary, a Mr. Harrison.

768   Hutchinson, Arthur Stuart-Menteth. *He Looked for a City*. London: Michael Joseph, 1941. 425p.

Concerns the period from the 1890's to the 1930's. The war section relates the ordeal of a low-church Anglican priest, Gordon Brecque, and his wife regarding their elder son John, a conscientious objector. John is called a slacker by the parishioners and he is imprisoned. His parents are also suspiciously regarded for sheltering their long-time German maid, Minna, considered to be sympathetic to Germany. The vicar's younger son is a naval hero; his daughters are V.A.D. (Voluntary Air Detachment) workers. John's punishment by the government to hard labor produces pneumonia and eventually his death. Minna later commits suicide to free the vicar from the village persecution.

769   MacLennan, John Hugh. *Barometer Rising*. New York: Grosset & Dunlap, 1941. 326p.

Set in Halifax, Nova Scotia, the novel relates the intrigue of Colonel Wain, lately returned from the war, to place the responsibility for a disastrous undertaking in France upon his subordinate officer and nephew. The story covers eight fateful days in December 1917, culminating in the ramming of the *Mont Blanc*, loaded with TNT and picric acid, by the Belgian relief ship *Imo*, in the harbor of Halifax. The resulting explosion from the fire destroys a great portion of the city of Halifax.

770 Parker, Ellanore J. *The Flower of the Land (A Tapestry of the Great War)*. Los Angeles: DeVorss & Co., 1941. 180p.

The war through the eyes of a Canadian nurse, Sheila Bishop. A story of injured and dying men in hospitals with explicit descriptions of war injuries combined with air raids, ruined villages, refugees, and the endless weary tending of the doomed wounded by the devoted nurses.

771 Thorndike, Jeanie Paine. *Not to the Strong*. New York: Thomas Y. Crowell, 1941. 346p.

A romantic story placed in East Africa during the war. The plot is conventional and revolves around the usual boy-meets-girl-and-gets-his-girl formula. He is a handsome, dashing, but useless wonder who has failed in life so far. He is dying in the forest but is found by the girl, the daughter of an idealized Englishman type (stiff upper lip and all that). He recovers, falls in love with her but decides to give her up as an unattainable goal. When she is captured by the Germans, she is inevitably rescued by the now courageous hero and all is well. They live happily ever after.

772 Tucker, William J. *Not All Ashes*. Dallas, Texas: Southwest Press, 1941. 318p.

Not seen; NYPL.

1942

773 Davis, Clyde Brion. *Follow the Leader*. New York: Farrar & Rinehart, 1942. 525p.

The story of Charles Martel's childhood in Pabuloma, Missouri, his year in Europe as an infantryman (1917-1918), his return to the United States as a decorated hero, and his rise to relative wealth and position in his hometown. The most memorable section of the novel (chapters 21 and 22) deals with the condition of the soldiers aboard a transport ship during World War I.

1944

774 Shneur, Zalman. *Downfall*. New York: Roy Publishers, 1944. 252p.

Deals with the fate of the Jews in German-occupied Poland in 1915. The Shatz family, owners of a leather business in Warsaw and other Polish towns, represents the highest model of orthodox Jewry. The head of the family is Reb Jacob Shatz, a benevolent and very humane man. It is in the person of the German Lieutenant Lamke that military requisition and economic pressure soon come to bear heavily on the Shatz family and their business. The novel describes the disastrous course of action that befalls each member of the family under this vicious occupation. By the time the Germans retreat, little is left to Reb of all his life's work. This story seems a precursor to events that took place in World War II.

1945

* Dos Passos, John Roderigo, Jr. *First Encounter.* New York: Philosophical Library, 1945. 160p.

This novel was originally published with the title *One Man's Initiation--1917.* See item 419.

775 Sergeev-TSenskii, Sergeo Nikolaevich. *Brusilov's Breakthrough: A Novel of the First World War.* Translated from the Russian by Helen Altschuler. London: Hutchinson & Co., 1945. 336p. [*Brusilovskii Proryv; Istoricheskii Roman.* Moscow: Sovetskii pisatel', 1943-44. 2 vols.]

A novel of the Russian southwestern front, covering the period from March to July 21, 1916. Chiefly concerned with describing the tactical shifting of the battle lines, the story also reveals the graft and corruption among business-as-usual bureaucrats and industrialists.

776 Tolstoi, Aleksei Nikolaevich. *Road to Calvary.* Translated by Edith Bone. London, New York: Hutchinson, 1945. 680p.; New York: Alfred A. Knopf, 1946. 885p. [*Khozhdenie po Mukam.* Moscow: 1941. 3 vols. in one.]

Contains the three novels which constitute the trilogy *Road to Calvary.* The first two were published in English in 1923 and 1935, respectively (see item 481 and the *Darkness and Dawn* entry under the author's name in 1935 for annotations). The first part, "The Sisters," is the novel which deals primarily with World War I. The other two, "Nineteen Eighteen" and "Bleak Morning," are principally concerned with the Russian revolution and its effects on the chief characters, Katia, Dasha, their lovers and subsequent husbands as well as Russian society. The time period ranges from 1914 to the early days of 1920.

A vast panoramic romance, the main characters are separated by the war and repeatedly by the revolution and its aftereffects. Except for the third part where the diabolical treacheries of Trotsky are featured, most of the other historical events and characters that are included appear to be fairly and realistically presented. This is especially apparent in the author's sympathetic description of the White and Red armies. The first two parts were extensively revised to conform with Communist Party ideology when combined with the final section, "Bleak Morning." The entire trilogy occupied the author for about twenty-two years until its completion in 1941. The novel received the Stalin Prize and was a huge success, selling over six million copies. The novel concludes with a typical Communist upbeat propaganda view of the future.

1946

777 Hutter, Catherine. *On Some Fair Morning*. New York: Dodd, Mead & Co., 1946. 403p.

The main character is a rich, American woman, Elsa von Zeiritz, the wife of a half-Jewish German nobleman, who owns a large piece of property in Poland. The plot concentrates on Polish-German relationships. During the war Elsa attempts to convey to her husband and to her daughter her concept, superficial though it is, of American democracy. The intense patriotism of her German family and friends continually frustrates her well-meaning efforts.

1947

778 Thane, Elswyth (pseud. of Elswythe Thane [Ricker] Beebe). *The Light Heart*. New York: Duell, Sloan and Pearce, 1947. 341p.

Covering the period 1902-1917, this is the story of Phoebe Sprague of Williamsburg, Virginia. Her life becomes inextricably involved in European affairs leading up to the war, when she visits her British relatives in 1902. From this date she divides her time between New York, where she pursues a writing career, her home in Williamsburg, and her family in London, where she spends the war years after surviving the sinking of the *Lusitania*. The novel presents the anticipations, expectations, fears, and hopes of Europeans on the verge of involvement as well as in the first years of the war.

1948

779 Lister, Frederick William. *Wind That Blows*. London: Frederick Muller, 1948. 280p.

Not seen.

780 Thane, Elswyth (pseud. of Elswyth Thane [Ricker] Beebe). *Kissing Kin*. New York: Duell, Sloan & Pearce, 1948. 374p.

This novel, the fifth in the author's series about the Sprague family of Williamsburg, Virginia, describes the connections and fortunes of a score or more characters related by blood or marriage or mutual circumstances during the years 1916 to 1919. Much of the plot focuses on the events surrounding an army hospital in what had been an English country house and which is now staffed by English and American volunteer personnel. The story also presents in considerable detail action involving the United States Air Corps.

1949

781 Pakington, Humphrey Arthur. *Young William Washbourne, a Novel*. London: Chatto & Windus, 1949. 247p.; New York: Norton, 1949. 274p.

A sequel to the author's *The Washbournes of Otterley* (1948), this novel reviews the life of an Englishman of class from his youth at the turn of the century to the Armistice. As a child Washbourne had witnessed the ceremonial departure of the funeral yacht of Queen Victoria from the Isle of Wight. The experience made him long for a naval career. In time he was able to join the British Navy as an officer and participate in the action of the fleet in the North Sea during the war.

1950

* Ford, Ford Madox. *Parade's End*. New York: Alfred A. Knopf, 1950. 836p.

A reprint under a collective title of the four novels of the Tietjens family: *Some Do Not* (item 485), *No More Parades* (item 493), *A Man Could Stand Up* (item 502), and *The Last Post* (item 532), which see for annotations.

782 Forester, Cecil Scott. *Randall and the River of Time*. Boston: Little, Brown & Co., 1950. 341p.

Adult Novels 271

An account of a young Englishman's dilemma and tensions in the war and thereafter. The author has said that the novel was to describe the influence of fate on a person "who has lived through the wars and the depressions." The Englishman, Randall, is an infantry officer who has been in the thick of the war in one of the forward salient trenches of Ypres. While back in England on leave, he supplies the know-how for improving the Phillips flare used on the battlefield at night. Also while on leave he falls for the wiles of an unprincipled woman and marries her. This novel is the first of a projected series about Randall's experiences along the "river of time."

782a White, Antonia. *The Lost Traveller*. London: Eyre & Spottiswoode, 1950. 314p.; New York: Viking Press, 1950. 312p.

Not seen. A story of adolescence during the war.

1951

783 Butler, Eliza Marian. *Daylight in a Dream*. London: Hogarth Press, 1951. 125p.

Begins by introducing a Miss Rawlinson, spinster and teacher of educational methods in Arcady (an elementary training school for teachers), who uses her position as an escape from life. The only period in her life when she had felt alive were her years during the war while serving as an ambulance driver with a group of other young women. A strange dream sequence follows, in which events earlier in her day mingle with those of her ambulance-corps days. Following the dream, she meets again one of the ambulance drivers with whom she had worked, who brings her up-to-date on the activities of her co-workers in the ambulance corps. As a consequence, Miss Rawlinson perceives the emptiness of her own life.

1952

784 Bridge, Ann (pseud. of Mary Dolling [Sanders] O'Malley). *The Dark Moment, a Novel*. London: Chatto & Windus, 1952. 376p.; New York: The Macmillan Co., 1952. 337p.

The story of Feride, a Turkish girl of the governing class, her life of luxury before the war, and her hardships as she accompanies her husband in the revolution which freed Turkey from its traditional past and opened the country up to the twentieth century. A run-of-the-mill historical novel based on the participation of Turkey in World War I as a member of the Entente and the subsequent revolution leading to the overthrow of the repressive Ottoman rule.

785 Malraux, André. *The Walnut Trees of Altenburg.* Translated from the French by A.W. Fielding. London: John Lehmann, 1952. 224p. [*Les Noyers de l'Altenbourg.* Geneve: Skira, 1945. 194p.]

Compares the experiences of a soldier in World War II with those of his father in World War I. While the first and last chapters recount the son's experiences, the main story consists of the experiences of the father, Vincent Berger, an Alsatian and a university professor of oriental languages in Constantinople. There the father becomes attached to the German embassy during the uprising of the young Turks prior to World War I. With peace restored in Turkey, Berger returns to his home in Reichbach just in time to become involved in World War I on the Russian front. He is assigned to the intelligence service but during an experiment in chemical warfare is inadvertently gassed and invalided out of the service. The chemical warfare episode is dramatically described. The writing is felicitous.

1953

786 Merrill, Lewis C. *Whom the Gods Love: A Novel.* New York: Pageant Press, 1953. 267p.

An action-packed account of the annihilation of the entire D. Flight section of the 221st British Royal Flying Squadron over the western front. The plot provides vivid descriptions of the British aerial dogfights against Baron von Richthofen's notorious Flying Circus aces.

1954

787 Celine, Louis-Ferdinand (pseud. of Louis Ferdinand Destouches). *Guignol's Band.* Translated from the French b Bernard Frechtman and Jack T. Nile. Norfolk, Conn.: New Directions, 1954. 287p.; London: Vision Press, 1954. 256p. [*Guignol's Band; Roman.* Paris: Les Éditions Denoël, 1944-.]

The so-called hero, Ferdinand, is the victim of a German

strafing attack, as a result of which he has a hearing
problem, migraines, and a stump of a left arm. Discharged
from the French army, he goes to the French underworld
colony in London where he teams up with Boro, a sleazy
French musician. The novel is an extremely fast-paced and
bizarre rampage through the underworld life of London. The
main connection with the war is that the action of the
story takes place during that time and throughout the narrative the author interjects his brand of excoriation against
the war and especially the Allied side. This is vintage
Celine and demonstrates his unique style and bitterness.
This novel was intended to be the first section of a four-
part novel the author planned to publish. However, since
the other sections were lost in 1944 during his escape from
France, they have never been published.

788   Fallas, Carl Ronald. *Saint Mary's Village Through the Eyes
      of an Unknown Soldier Who Lived On*. London: Hodder &
      Stoughton, 1954. 256p.

A story of trench warfare, described by a writer who
served in World War I. The reviewer in the *London Times*
described the novel: "To a younger generation, with only
the experience of a very different war, there is something
a shade unreal in the romantic, idealistic, almost ethereal
quality that hovers over Mr. Fallas's gallant battalion.
The officers all seem to be blessed with both the depth
and sensitivity of Mr. Charles Morgan's heroes and the
chivalry and grace of John Buchan's Olympian world."

789   Faulkner, William. *A Fable*. New York: Random House, 1954.
      437p.

The setting of this novel is the western battlefield of
the war in the early part of 1918. The novel concerns the
zero-hour mutiny of a French regiment which had been ordered
to make a futile attack. The masterminds of the mutiny are
a corporal and his twelve comrades. The enemy is grateful
for the suppression of fighting, which they had been alerted
to expect, and the lull in the conflict is gradually taken
to be a kind of armistice. Analogies between the end of
this part of the war and the Passion of Jesus Christ are
numerous. Faulkner deals with his powerful and provocative
theme in a narrative and language that seem almost a parody
of his distinctive writing style. One reviewer succinctly
summed it up as "a compendium of a word-drunk mind."

790 Marshall, Bruce. *Only Fade Away; a Novel.* London: Constable, 1954. 333p.

Recounts the biography of Strang Nairne Methuen, a Scottish army officer who served in the British Regular Army in World War I and World War II. The first war is viewed through the witty and ironic perspective of Strang, who is accused, falsely, of cowardice in this war, by a bully, Claude Hermiston, who bedevils Strang for years. (This is one of several books which the *National Union Catalog* and/or other bibliographic references labeled "personal narrative" or "sketches" or "nonfiction," but which the New York Public Library later classified as fiction.)

791 Williamson, Henry. *How Dear Is Life.* London: Macdonald & Co., 1954. 335p.

The novel concerns the initiation of an immature eighteen-year-old English boy in the war when his Scottish Highland regiment is mobilized and fights at Ypres. The author's prefatory note reveals the source of much of the action and description:

The characters in this book are imagined, although several of them had an existence, for one man at least, in a world which has passed away. Most of the events, including the scenes in France and Belgium, are based on actuality but are not to be attributed to any particular unit of the British Army.

For some of the details of scenes in war-time London, the author gratefully acknowledges his debt to the authors of two books: The Home Front (by E. Sylvia Pankhurst), and In London During the Great War (by Michael MacDonagh).

1955

792 Hodson, James Lansdale. *Return to the Wood: A Novel.* New York: William Morrow & Co., 1955. 250p.

A novel about a survivor of World War I, Hargreaves, for whom the experiences at the Somme and Passchendaele and other events of 1914-1918 made him a pacifist. His wife shares his pacifism. When the Second World War occurs, Hargreaves attempts to understand the new war by recalling in some detail his World War I experiences. The evil of Hitler's rise, however, convinces him that he must fight again, although his new conviction wrecks his marriage.

793 Parker, Ellanore J. *The Land Lay Waiting*. New York: Pageant Press, 1955. 236p.

A love story and a search for self that uses the war as a backdrop for the development of the three main characters. Bob Dormer who works as a London newspaperman, marries Beth when she is only sixteen. They have two children and live in virtual poverty on his low pay. When his small son dies, Bob's ambition and desire to keep his marriage do also. He abandons his family and returns eventually to a farm in Canada. Meanwhile Beth is taken under the protective wing of Charles Ashly, a successful journalist friend of Bob. When the war begins, she becomes an army nurse, Bob enlists, and Charles becomes a mysterious secret agent. The love triangle aspect tends to dominate the plot. The war seems secondary to the personal destinies of the three major characters. There are some good descriptions of London in the frenzy of the first weeks of the war. Otherwise, this is a prosaic and pedestrian novel of limited literary quality.

794 Williamson, Henry. *A Fox Under My Cloak*. London: Macdonald & Co., 1955. 415p.

Traces the fortunes of Phillip Maddison, the hero of several previous novels by Williamson. Maddison is part of the now long-gone world composed of temporary English gentlemen who hold their World War I officer commissions from the King. The action follows Maddison through the battles of 1915 including an especially appalling description of the battle of Loos. The novel contains some particularly bloody and horrible war brutalities. There is a rather detailed account of the Christmas truce that was never reported back in England. The narrative clearly reveals the deep fear of death and the reluctance to die that existed just under the surface of the highly popular patriotism common among the military. Although the writing tends to be ordinary and even clumsy at times, the author reveals a strong compassion for his characters, especially those who were able to endure the daily grind and terrible conditions of the front lines.

1957

795 Osmond, Robert William. *The Glory and the Dream*. New York: Vantage Press, 1957. 245p.

Approximately half of the novel is placed in Australia at Glen Eidol, a bucolic mansion in the "out back" country

of New South Wales. This story can be considered a short
family saga of one generation of the Orde family. The
principal characters are Jeremy Orde and his sister Varna,
Eric Stensland, and the German brother and sister, Karl and
Frieda Kettering. The first portion of the book describes
the love affairs and activities of life at Glen Eidol.
William Orde, the father, strongly disapproves of Jeremy's
wish to marry Frieda, and Jeremy leaves home to marry her,
never to see his father and sister again. When the war
begins, Eric, Jeremy, Karl, and various others associated
with them, including Jeremy's father, all eventually wind
up at the front in France. There are some front-line trench
scenes at Ypres as well as activities behind the lines.
Jeremy and Karl (now a captured German soldier and the
brother of Jeremy's wife Frieda) briefly meet for the last
time as Karl is brought in as a prisoner. A short time
later Jeremy is killed and only his father and Eric survive
to return to Australia. A minor theme is the suspicion
generated by being a German in Australia during the war.

796 Troyat, Henri (pseud. of Lev Tarassov). *Amelie and Pierre:
A Novel*. Translated from the French by Mary V. Dodge.
New York: Simon & Schuster, 1957. 338p.

The second novel of a series, *The Seed and the Fruit*,
dealing with forty or more years of French family life.
(The first novel of the series appeared in 1956, the last
in 1962.) *Amelie and Pierre* recounts events which occurred
early in the war. Pierre is an infantry corporal who is
wounded at the front, returns home, and is nursed by
Amelie, who has been running the family business (a work-
men's cafe) and caring for their young daughter, Elizabeth.
The effect of the war upon the humble, devoted, and petty
bourgeois citizens at home is meticulously described.

797 Williamson, Henry. *The Golden Virgin*. London: Macdonald
& Co., 1957. 448p.

Concerns the four years of the war and specifically the
Battle of the Somme on July 1, 1916, as it touched the main
character, Phillip Maddison, the hero of Williamson's
earlier novel, *A Fox Under My Cloak* (item 794). Phillip
is traced through his military activities and experiences
in the front-line trenches. This is followed by contrasting chapters which chronicle his drinking at his South
London home while overawed by his social superiors. He
is the classic English example of the acutely class- and
self-conscious individual, devoid of humor, gauche, and,

Adult Novels

in spite of his courage and sensitivity, very difficult to like. The story seems mainly a character study and an examination of the English social system.

1958

798 Raymond, Ernest. *The Quiet Shore*. London: Cassell & Co., 1958. 256p.

A novel of the Dardanelles campaign at Gallipoli to secure the strait and enable the British navy to besiege Constantinople. The story recounts the story of the impasse and the retreat of the Allied forces. Woven into the battle is the devotion of two British officers, Gerry Browning and Colin Dester. The story is written as the reminiscences of Gerry Browning who, with his wife, is making a return pilgrimage to the battle scenes forty years after the war.

799 Williamson, Henry. *Love and the Loveless: A Soldier's Tale*. London: Macdonald & Co., 1958. 384p.

One of a series of novels about Phillip Maddison. This novel recounts the events in Maddison's life as a young, naive British transport officer in France during 1917, a year of widespread mutiny among the ranks of the French Army. Maddison's well-intended but impulsive actions arouse the suspicions of his superiors, endangering his career and threatening him with a court-martial. Through sheer luck and a few high-placed friends, Maddison survives the war unscathed.

1960

800 Doolittle, Hilda (Aldington). *Bid Me to Live: (A Madrigal)*. New York: Grove Press, 1960. 184p.

The author called the novel (whose title comes from Robert Herrick's poem "To Anthea") a madrigal of "war time love and death." The story is a brief account of "lost generation" characters in London and throughout England in 1917. The madcap lives of various individuals are revealed through the experiences of Julia Ashton, whose marriage to Rafe, home on leave from the western front, is disintegrating. Appears to be an artistic rendition of the atmosphere and spirit of the time. D.H. Lawrence and his wife Frieda are fictionalized in the novel.

801 Johnson, David. *Promenade in Champagne: A Novel.* London: Hodder & Stoughton, 1960. 255p.

A nostalgic, fast-paced, historical adventure story of the French army, narrated by the young Captain Charles Aiguillon. He and other members of the Angevin Regiment have only a brief exposure to the rigors of trench warfare when they are involved in the disastrous offensive of the French General Nivelle in 1917. The story is concerned mainly with the friendships and valor of a group of young officers who have trained together, many of whom will eventually die in the conflict. The novel stresses patriotic duty, devotion, and self-sacrifice for the fatherland. Contains the usual love affair.

802 Williamson, Henry. *A Test to Destruction.* London: Macdonald & Co., 1960. 461p.

In this eighth novel about the Maddison family during World War I, Phillip Maddison returns to battlefield duty. This novel appears to be closely modelled on the actual history of the period. The names used for some of the generals seem to be the only fictitious aspect of much of the narrative. Actual history thinly veiled as fiction.

1961

803 Elliot, Robert. *The Eagle's Height.* Letchworth, Hertfordshire: Air Review Press, 1961. 256p.

The story of a young English subaltern's adventures as a pilot in the Royal Air Force. Arriving in France as a "pink-cheeked boy of twenty" he becomes "a killing machine--a flying automaton devoid of nerves or conscience" as he sees his friends cut down in flames by the Germans. Killing becomes so much a part of his life that he cannot envision a future beyond the war. Contains vivid descriptions of aerial battles.

804 Harris, John. *Covenant with Death.* London: Hutchinson & Co., 1961. 447p.; New York: William Sloane and Associates, 1961. 442p.

The first half of this novel is a detailed examination of Edwardian life in England--the clothes, the manners, etc.--as background for the departure of an English battalion for France and the rigors of the front. The story is told through the character of Mark Fenner who recounts the recruitment of a city battalion, its training, and eventual fate at the great slaughter on the Somme on July 1, 1916. The novel questions the point of it all, the human stupidity, the butchery, the utter waste of war and its senseless glory. The author obviously based his tale on historical facts. Characters are mainly stock and predictable types, and the novel's love story is of a soap-opera nature.

805 Youd, Christopher Samuel. *Messages of Love*. New York: Simon & Schuster, 1961. 378p.

Chronicles the Fanshawe family, in England and in their home in Switzerland, through World War I and World War II. The reviewer for the *Booklist* characterized the novel as "Reminiscent of Galsworthy in its excellent characterizations and the natural way the plot evolves from them, and also in its sharp vignettes of upper-middle-class social life, whose economic base in this case is the textile industry of northern England." The story describes a typical pilot's role in the air war, specifically in the Sopwith plane.

1962

806 Boyd, Martin. *When Blackbirds Sing: A Novel*. London: Abelard-Schuman, 1962. 187p.

The fourth volume in the series on the Langton family, which chronicles in fiction the author's own family. The plot describes the spiritual odyssey of a transplanted member of the British landed gentry, Dominic Langton, who leaves his farm in Australia to enlist in England's military. At first the war speaks to a violence within him, and he rejoices in the release of the violence which the war offers. At the moment he kills a man, both he and his victim recognize each other's humanity. He now realizes he has violated everything good that he has known, and his integrity refuses to let him continue. An embarrassment to the military establishment, he is first invalided to a hospital where he recovers physically, then to an institution for the shell-shocked, and finally home to Australia where he hopes to receive the understanding of his wife.

807 Burgess, Anthony (pseud. of John Burgess Wilson). *The Wanting Seed*. London: Wm. Heinemann, 1962. 285p.

Best described as a collage of fantasy, science fiction, and satiric spoof. The setting is England of George VI's time, at least a hundred years from now. The novel engages a host of characters, all involved in the world of Tristram Foxe, schoolmaster, and his wife Beatrice-Joanna. The theme is apparently that population must at all costs be limited, either through contraception or, better as a final solution, war, in which the enemy is woman. World War I--the experiences, memories, attack plans, actions--provides the material for conducting effective war in the Foxes' futuristic, nightmarish world, and to satisfy the program of the infertility administrators. World War I was, in other words, "that pro-typical war," the "mythical" war, the "classic" war. "The organization, nomenclature, procedure, armament of this new British Army all seemed to have come out of old books, old films." Strictly speaking, this novel perhaps does not qualify as a World War I novel, but since the war figures so extensively in this fantasy of the future, it is included as a curiosity.

808 de Montherlant, Henry. *The Dream*. Translated from the French by Terence Kilmartin. London: Weidenfeld & Nicolson, 1962. 247p. [*Le Songe*. Paris: Gallimard, 1922. 255p.]

Focuses upon the fortunes of a single individual, the young French military officer Alban de Bricoule. The story details his relationships with the following: Prinet, his comrade in arms and French student turned soldier; Dominique, for whom Alban has formed a platonic adulation; and Douce, with whom he enjoys a love relationship. Alban's struggle for maturity is successful only when he is freed from each of the relationships. The war on the western front serves mainly as a background for the relationships of the major characters and an analysis of their temperaments.

809 Jack, Donald Lamont. *Three Cheers for Me: The Journals of Bartholomew Bandy, R.F.C....* New York: The Macmillan Co., 1962. 274p.

The protagonist and comic hero is Captain Bartholomew W. Bandy. He is a twenty-three-year-old Canadian from Beamington, Ontario, and the chief character in the Bandy series of novels. In this first story of the series Bandy is

pictured as an evangelical and prudish teetotaler who has
promised his mother and father that he will walk the
straight and narrow, resist all women, and avoid demon
rum while he is overseas. However, he falls from grace.
In 1916, Bandy is an infantry officer, but he is a misfit,
causing confusion among the ranks no matter what his
assignment. (On a reconnaissance detail to seize an
enemy soldier, he becomes confused in the dark and captures the colonel of his own outfit.) Embarrassed by his
ineptness, Bandy shifts to the Canadian Royal Flying Corps
and becomes an ace in his Sopwith Camel, downing ten enemy
aircraft in twelve days and winning the Croix de Guerre
plus the woman of his choice. Although the author provides
some very good descriptions of trench warfare and air combat, the story is written more as a comic farce, with some
scenes reminiscent of the silent movie comedies of the
Keystone Cops.

810 Sherman, Malcolm Clarke. *Shock Troops*. New York: Vantage Press, 1962. 132p.

   Not seen.

1963

811 Clevely, Hugh. *Garland of Valour*. London: Cassell & Co., 1963. 263p.

   Not seen.

812 Dilas, Milovan. *Montenegro*. Translated by Kenneth Johnstone. New York: Harcourt, Brace & World, 1963. 367p.

   A fictionalized chronicle of Montenegro during and immediately after World War I. The novel is divided into
three parts. The first describes the Austrian offensive
against Montenegro between December 25, 1915, and January
1916. Serbia has been overrun by the Central Powers, and
the ill-equipped and small group of Montenegrins are under
heavy attack from three sides. They fight superbly for a
week but corruption and lack of leadership have become so
rife that the army is ordered to surrender. In the second
part, "The Gallows," the country is subjected to the occupation. A long, harrowing episode describes the deathwatch of three men condemned to hanging for resisting the
occupying forces. The last section deals with the postwar
period of adjustment, through a handful of characters
reacting to political and social problems.

813   Jennings, John Edward, Jr. *The Raider, a Novel of World War I; the Chronicle of a Gallant Ship.* New York: William Morrow & Co., 1963. 272p. [Title of edition in England: *The Emden; a Novel of World War I; the Chronicle of a Gallant Ship.* London: Alvin Redman, 1964. 272p.]

   Appears to be mainly a fictional tribute to the officers and men on the German raider *Emden* which terrorized the waters of the Indian Ocean for about three months during 1914. (The *Emden* sank fifteen Allied ships before being destroyed by an Australian cruiser.) The author shows how the atrocity stories of the time had no reality: the German crew observed the letter of international law with fearlessness and chivalry. The novel tends to be wooden, especially in its character development.

814   Kessel, Joseph. *The Medici Fountain: A Novel.* Translated from the French by Herma Briffault. New York: St. Martin's Press, 1963. 375p.; London: Arthur Barker, 1963. 256p. [*La Fontaine Medicis.* Paris: Gallimard, 1950. 315p.]

   The chief character and hero is Richard Dalleau, a romantic adolescent student growing up under the cloud of war and all its pressures in France. The scale of the novel resembles *War and Peace.* The plot switches back and forth from the trenches to civilian life in Paris. Descriptions of the trenches, wartime Paris, and the pains of youth are realistically rendered. The novel is something of a *bildungsroman,* showing how adolescent youth turns worldly and learns about academic life, military life, and sex. This is the first volume of a projected tetralogy entitled *Le Tour de Malheur.*

815   Reeman, Douglas E. *The Last Raider.* London: Jarrolds, 1963. 381p.

   The Last Raider traces the course pursued by Captain Felix von Steiger, the German "Tiger of the Seas," from the time he became commanding officer of a German sea raider in Kiel, December 1917. The ship's mission was to destroy Allied shipping, and the narration recaps the log of the vessel. The story documents the emotions of men under the strain of an unceasing series of engagements with enemy warships, crisscrossing the Atlantic shipping lanes from Norway and Iceland to Brazil and the western coast of Africa. The crew realize that their release from pressure will come, in all probability, only in death. The ship is sunk by a British warship early in 1918 off the west coast of Africa. The plot generally is banal and the book seems alive only during the descriptions of the gun battles.

1964

816 Bee, David. *Our Fatal Shadows; a Novel of German East Africa and Tanganyika.* London: Geoffrey Bles, 1964. 414p.; [Title in U.S.: *Curse of Magira; a Novel of German East Africa and Tanganyika.* New York: Harper & Brothers, 1965. 414p.]

An engaging report of campaigns during the war in the two areas of Africa named in the title, as well as accounts of pioneer days in the same places. The author, an Englishman, tells the story of an English civil servant, Peter Disley, who goes to Tanganyika and attempts to solve a murder which took place while the Germans were there. The story also relates Peter's love for the land and for an alien woman, which serves as the connection between the contemporary world and the time of the Great War.

817 Hobson, Laura Keane (Zametkin). *First Papers.* New York: Random House, 1964. 502p.

Describes a Jewish family's life, especially the harrying of radicals and political liberals during the early years of the war. The main characters are the father, an intellectual; his wife, who is a teacher; Stefan Ivarin, editor of the *Jewish News*; and Evander Paige, a lawyer friend and Unitarian. The plot realistically describes the reaction of the educated European to the slow but certain approach of the war, and to the war as it continued for years.

818 Hunter, Jack D. *The Blue Max.* New York: E.P. Dutton & Co., 1964. 320p.

A novel about a German air squadron. The story concentrates on Bruno Stachel, an ace German fighter pilot who is brave, fatalistic, cold-blooded, and an alcoholic. Bruno is also viciously ambitious and tends to commit acts of violence and cruelty. However, his drinking inspires his flying abilities so well that in the closing months of the war he creates such an impressive record as to become a popular hero and win the coveted Blue Max, the German order of merit. Although the writing is ordinary, the character of the bizarre Stachel is fascinating.

819 Storm, Julie. *Madeleine*. Translated by Peter Wiles. London: William Collins Sons, 1964. 287p.

Not seen.

820 Wertenbaker, Lael Tucker. *The Eye of the Lion; a Novel Based on the Life of Mata Hari*. Boston: Little, Brown & Co., 1964. 379p.; London: Wm. Heinemann, 1964. 246p.

This novel is based on the life of Margaretha Geertruida Zelle McLeod, otherwise known during World War I as Mata Hari, the so-called glamorous female spy of the day. This is very much the typical spy story with such ingredients as marriage to an alcoholic British officer, dissolute life with and without him in the South Seas, a fantastic dancing career in the Paris of the Edwardian period, recruitment and war years as a spy for the Kaiser, and execution on October 15, 1917, by a French firing squad. The version of the author in this fictional recreation of the life of Mata Hari makes it difficult to understand what all the fuss was about. She turns out to be a relatively plain, ordinary, and not so bright female of little wit or ability. It is inconceivable how she could ever have been of much use as a spy by the Germans, or anyone else for that matter. (See item 876 for another attempt in fiction about the life of Mata Hari.)

1965

821 Blankfort, Michael. *Behold the Fire; A Novel Based on Events that Took Place Between 1914 and 1918 in London, Cairo, Constantinople, Jerusalem, and Some of the Villages of Palestine*. New York: New American Library, 1965. 397p.

The primary action is in Turkish-held Palestine during the war, dealing with a small band of Jews who were determined to realize the dream of "next year in Jerusalem." In exchange for the Zionist help against Turkish enemies in the war, the British agree to aid Judah Singer and his small band of zealots. The story relates the underground efforts of the Jewish saboteurs and spies in their joint efforts with the British against the Turkish authorities. The novel is based on events involving several historical figures.

Adult Novels

822 McCann, Hugh Wray. *"Utmost Fish!"* New York: Simon & Schuster, 1965. 384p.

Based on a historical incident called the Naval Africa Expedition of 1915-16. A small group of English soldiers and sailors have the task of pulling two heavy motorboats across incredibly rough terrain in order to sink the German fleet located on Lake Tanganyika. The object is to take the boats a thousand miles overland through jungles, mountains, swamps, wagering that they can be of use in destroying a vastly more powerful group of enemy boats. The story describes all the arduous difficulties, including the quarrels and jealousies between Commander Ian Frazer, a middle-aged Scotsman with a "flinty sense of duty," and his insuborinate second officer. The drama of the story is based on this personal conflict that nearly destroys all hope of success for the mission. The novel is reminiscent of *The African Queen* (item 705) by C.S. Forester. The title of the novel is a British submariner's term from World War I that meant "Fire all torpedoes!" Winston Churchill used this term on many of his plans and memoranda as an indicator of all due speed for a project. Churchill figures in the beginning of the novel as the principal figure who sets this military adventure in motion.

823 Millin, Sarah Gertrude (Liebson). *Goodbye, Dear England*. London: Wm. Heinemann, 1965. 326p.

Recounts the story of an English middle-class family caught up in the war, and traces the history of the various military conquests of Europe and their bearing upon the events which led to World War I. At the beginning of the war, King's Counsel Faraday belongs to a "Group" concerned with Germany's opposition to England, but the Group is unable to alert and motivate England's leaders. The war inevitably makes Britain, known for so long as "dear England," a thing of the past.

824 Raymond, Diana. *The Noonday Sword*. London: Cassell & Co., 1965. 229p.

Not seen.

825 Reeman, Douglas. *H.M.S. Saracen*. London: Jarrolds, 1965, 320p.

The story of a warship and her crew during two of the worst battles experienced by the Royal Navy: the ill-fated

Gallipoli campaign of World War I and the fight for the
control of the Mediterranean in World War II. The plot
is personalized through the eyes of Richard Chesnaye who
as a young midshipman first joins the ship in 1915. The
Gallipoli campaign is viewed in detail by the author
through the "business end of a U-boat's attack periscope."
Also described are the problems created by the construction and design of the *Saracen*. It was a ship with massive
guns created to support military landings, difficult to
handle at sea, very slow, and incredibly ugly. The crew,
and especially Chesnaye, grows fond of the "ugly duckling."
Later, in 1941, Chesnaye finds himself reassigned to the
ship. Love interest involves Chesnaye and a Red Cross girl.
A superior adventure story of the war, and historically
accurate.

826   Whitehouse, Arch (pseud. of Arthur George Joseph White-
      house). *Squadron Forty-four, A Novel about the Royal
      Flying Corps in the First World War.* Garden City, N.Y.:
      Doubleday & Co., 1965. 270p.

Based on the James Bellah short story "Fear," the two
principal characters are Flight Leader Captain Hoyt and
Paterson, a nineteen-year-old American replacement pilot
newly assigned to RFC Squadron 44. The main aircraft
duties in 1918 were ground support, escort duty, and the
very dangerous, low-level strafing and bombing missions
with the Sopwith Camels. The plot concerns the desperate
German spring offensive of 1918. Lieutenant Paterson at
first views the air war in romantic terms of aces and
"knights of the skies locked in mortal combat," but by
1918 scarcely any glamour is left and certainly no air
daredevil opportunities. The personal drama of the book
concerns Captain Hoyt's effort to restrain Paterson from
useless air heroics. The author writes with authority:
he was a Camel pilot with the RFC.

1966

827   Canaway, William Hamilton. *The Grey Seas of Jutland.*
      London: Hutchinson & Co., 1966. 256p.

The plot is sex-and-war melodrama. Lieutenant George
Wynne, with his American cousin Claire, and his German
cousin Werner, surprise two of the family servants in a
compromising act in a Bavarian forest. Claire follows
their example and freely copulates with the family gardener

and Werner. George, when he finds out, still endeavors to
regard his female cousin with affection. But when George
finds himself in the battle of Jutland, he seeks revenge
after all, disobeys orders, loses his ship, and uses his
last torpedo to sink Werner's ship. They both survive
together in the water because of Werner's heroic efforts.

828 Gann, Ernest Kellogg. *In the Company of Eagles*. New York:
Simon & Schuster, 1966. 342p.

A historical novel that describes the brutal and cursory
treatment of the wounded and the ghastly, endless, and
bloody spectacle of the terrible trench warfare. The two
briefly sketched characters, Paul Chamay, the French Escadrille pilot, and Sebastian Kupper, the German ace, are
scarcely more than puppets who utter the usual trite statement that war is hell, even when it is the gentlemen's war
of 1914-1918 daredevil, open-cockpit fliers. The central
story is about a minor battle in the first few weeks of the
horribly disastrous Allied offensive in the spring of 1917.
The novel adds nothing to the already vast amount of literature on the war. As the *New Yorker* reviewer remarked,
"The writing is stiff, precise and so cold and clipped that
the heartbeat, if there is one, cannot be heard or felt."

829 Hay, David. *No Through Road: A Story of the Last Assyrian
Campaign in Kurdistan: the Nation which Defied the Turkish Empire and Became Britain's Smallest Ally of the
1914-18 War*. Ipswich, England: Norman Adlard, 1966.
217p.

A historical novel of the last Assyrian campaign in
Kurdistan. The Assyrians succeed in defying the Turkish
troops and their Kurd allies after they join the cause of
Britain and Russia in World War I. The Assyrian cause
eventually became so hopeless that even the British and
the Russians gave little support to the impossible Assyrian
situation. The chief character and leader of the Assyrians
is the Archbishop Benjamin. The story begins in the autumn
of 1914 in a small Qutchanis mountain village. The Allies
contact the archbishop through his nephew in order to
encourage the Assyrian support in the war against the Turks.
As the weeks go by it becomes obvious that the Assyrian
tribes will eventually be rounded up by the Turks. In any
case, there is soon a flurry of behind-the-scenes preparations, negotiations, and soul-searching for the proper
course of action among the Assyrian tribes. The novel
concludes with the treacherous murder of the Archbishop

Benjamin and most of his small group of emissaries when they go to a negotiation meeting with a supposedly friendly Kurdish leader. When the war ends, there is the promise that the Allies' peace settlement will at last enable the Assyrians to return to their homeland. A curious and interesting view of a little-known incident in the vast canvas of the Great War. It obviously has little to do with the main theater of conflict but nonetheless draws attention to the great courage of a fearless people who became the victims of the war in an out-of-the-way corner of the Middle East.

830 Smith, Frederick Escreet. *A Killing for the Hawks*. New York: Ace Books, 1966. 253p.; London: George G. Harrap, 1966. 252p.

An account of the air war over France between the British S.E. 5 and German Albatross aircraft, through the eyes of one McConnell, an American volunteer pilot in the Royal Flying Corps. (The author fought with the Royal Air Force as a gunner and provides much aircraft lore in his novel.) Sex interest in the novel involves McConnell's squadron commander, John Seymour, a sadistic English aristocrat. On leave in London, McConnell meets, becomes infatuated with, and seduces Seymour's wife, though unaware of her identity.

831 Waring, Lily Florence. *Demons' Dawn: A Novel*. London: Johnson Publications, 1966. 254p.

Recounts the war experiences of several young Belgian patriots, soldiers, and espionage agents--their daring ventures, their successes, and their failures. The story ends with the Armistice, and the portent that the war just ended is but the beginning of a 100-year conflict.

1967

832 Coombs, Charles Ira. *Ace of the Argonne*. Cleveland: The World Publishing Co., 1967. 157p.

The hero, Tom Miller, a farmboy and college football player from the Midwest, joins the air force as a pilot. The horror of the conflict is increased when his girl friend, an army nurse, dies in an air raid. Vindictively Tom picks out the German flying ace Kurt von Hessel in the air and in a suicide action drives his plane into von Hessel's aircraft.

Adult Novels   289

833   Shedd, Margaret Cochran. *Hosannah Tree*. Garden City,
      N.Y.: Doubleday & Co., 1967. 391p.

      A tragedy involving missionaries Will and Phoebe Lucas
      in a remote area of northwest Persia (Kurdistan) near the
      Russian and Turkish frontiers, before and during the war.
      The novel places all of the war's belligerents in the town
      of Aliabad: Russians, Turks, Persians, Syrians, Kurds,
      Germans, English; even a French hospital for military
      personnel figures in the novel. Against overwhelming
      conditions--disease and the scheming of the Western powers,
      among other odds--the missionaries stick to their posts,
      attempting to help the impoverished Syrian plains people
      stave off the Turkish invasion threats and handle the
      marauding Kurdish tribesmen.

                                    1968

834   Gavin, Catherine Irvine. *The Devil in Harbour*. New York:
      William Morrow & Co., 1968. 310p.; London: Hodder &
      Stoughton, 1968. 310p.

      The war provides the backdrop for this historical romance
      involving German spies, British intelligence, the Russian
      ballet, and sea adventures culminating in the famous Battle
      of Jutland. The action commences in 1916 just before the
      Jutland encounter. A unit of the Imperial Russian Ballet
      is on tour in the Scandinavian countries, which offers an
      opportunity to the super spy Ritter, a German naval offi-
      cer, to impersonate a rich American munitions salesman.
      He uses one of the Russian ballerinas for his nefarious
      purposes, but is foiled when a gallant young Scottish
      sailor turns up and saves the ballerina from his evil
      clutches. The naval battle is described with considerable
      skill and vividness, but the rest of the plot is pale in
      comparison.

835   Smith, Wilbur A. *Shout at the Devil*. New York: Coward-
      McCann, 1968. 310p.; London: Wm. Heinemann, 1968. 310p.

      The story features a hard-drinking American Irishman
      named Glynn Patrick O'Flynn who makes a living poaching
      and smuggling ivory in German East Africa just before the
      war. O'Flynn's colleague and helper is Sebastian Oldsmith,
      a stranded young English wastrel. Both men make life
      miserable for Fleisher, the local German Commissioner, by
      hijacking his supply trains and killing his elephants.

When the war starts, a German cruiser is damaged in battle but manages to hide up a local river and make repairs. O'Flynn and Oldsmith now decide to work for the British Navy and attempt to destroy the cruiser. An action-packed, melodramatic adventure tale filled with guerrilla raids, sea battles, shark-filled waters, elephant hunts, etc., with substantial violence and humor.

836 Whitehouse, Arch (pseud. of Arthur George Joseph Whitehouse). *Squadron Shilling, a Novel of Aerial Combat Espionage in World War I*. Garden City, N.Y.: Doubleday & Co., 1968. 335p.

Based in part on Paul Bewsher's epic poem entitled *The Bombing of Bruges* and on the personal experiences of the author, who was an aerial gunner in the Royal Corps. The story deals with aerial combat and espionage involving two young American men. After graduation from Princeton, Ralph Macintosh travels to Canada to obtain a commission in the Canadian Royal Flying Corps. He eventually turns out to be a traitor to his country through his opportunistic and unprincipled nature. Bartley Crispin is the good guy who goes to Oxford to study architecture but soon enlists in the Royal Flying Corps and is trained as an aerial gunner. Both men end up in France in the same unit. Macintosh continues his espionage work with German spies, while Crispin is eventually put to work to track down Macintosh's dubious dealings even behind the German lines. The story describes the atmosphere of the training camps, a zeppelin bombing run over London, and the aerial fighting of Sopwith Camels and Bristol fighters. The descriptions of the air war have an authentic ring.

1969

837 Cloete, Stuart. *How Young They Died*. London: W. Collins Sons, 1969. 383p. [Title in U.S.: *How Young They Die: A Novel About the First World War*. New York: Trident Press, 1969. 416p.]

A skirmish-by-skirmish account of a portion of the war. The major character is the young nineteen-year-old lieutenant Jim Hilton who is described as he goes through the holocaust of the Somme, the Ypres Salient, and all the disastrous years of trench warfare. The novel is mainly Hilton's battle history, with brief glimpses into his personal life and activities during occasional leaves and rest periods. He is twice wounded, experiences shell shock, and survives to see the death of nearly all of his friends. The main focus of the book is on the grim battle scenes and conveys a perceptive view of the times and what it was that made so many Englishmen sacrifice their lives in a long and miserable war. The novel clearly has an autobiographical basis.

838   Giono, Jean. *To The Slaughterhouse: a Novel*. Translated from the French by Norman Glass. London: Peter Owen, 1969. 215p. [*Le Grand Troupeau*. Paris: Gallimard, 1931. 267p.]

The first group of men from Provence are called up to fight in the trenches to the north. Conscription literally decimates the mountain shepherds so that only a few old men watch after the animals. The narrative is devised about a parallelism of symbols: for example, when a man is brought home to the village from the trenches after deliberately having his hand shot through in order to be discharged, a fox's paw is brought in that the animal has bitten off in order to escape from a trap. The plot tells of the gradual disintegration of the pastoral way of life that existed before the war. None of the peasants can understand what is happening to their world. The author shows the horror and bestiality of the war as a gross exaggeration of the everyday aspects of life: the slaughter of an animal, envy of another's farm, etc. An obvious effort to compare human behavior with the non-human, natural world. The author is a committed pacifist whose back-to-nature theme is rendered with considerable skill in a powerful and ironic narrative that exposes the suffering caused by the madness of war and man's distortion of nature.

839   Hirst, George. *The Long Mountain*. London: Michael Joseph, 1969. 196p.

Appears to be a composite historical novel based on a combination of events that may have occurred at different times in the Balkans or eastern Europe during or before the war. The chief character and narrator is Ilya, a young man of eighteen. His mother, sisters, and close friend are all killed by a shell when the enemy, the Astanians, attack his village in the Strakolice valley. But Ilya and his Varslavian countrymen are unable to oppose the better-equipped enemy and they are ultimately overrun, the officers shot, and the rest marched off to work in the dismal coal mines. Ilya there meets Karel, and the two decide to escape or die in the attempt. They are successful and hide in one of the nearby farms with Karena, a young girl whose family has all been killed. Ilya joins the local partisan group while Karel leaves to fight the enemy in the south. Ilya's first crucial mission is to carry information on the southern resistance groups through the enemy lines to the capital city. He eventually reaches Czernovik and sees the commanding officer, only to learn he has been used as a decoy. Ilya, however, accepts another mission and returns to find that Karena now has joined the small partisan band. They declare their love. Now follows a series of adventures by the two lovers behind the enemy lines where they eventually team up with Karel. They witness the assassination of the Slovenian royal prince and princess by student sympathizers on the Astanian day of independence. The three escape the turmoil, and Ilya and Karena return to their resistance group only to learn it has been destroyed. The story ends as Karena decides she must search out her mother in Olszt but promises to wait for Ilya there until he returns. Written with some skill and drama, the plot may have some basis in fact.

840 Hunter, Evan. *Sons*. Garden City, N.Y.: Doubleday & Co., 1969. 396p.

A novel of three generations of a family connected with three wars: World War I, World War II, and the Vietnam conflict. Each of the three main characters is eighteen years old. The novel is a continuous flashback, each chapter shifting in time; it opens and closes with the Vietnam soldier's story. The object is to show that essentially the same situation faces each of the three generations during each of the three wars. A sensitive description of the dilemmas of American life as experienced by each of the chief characters.

841 Saxon, Peter. *Unfeeling Sky*. London: Howard Baker Pubs., 1969. 158p.

Not seen.

842 Stancu, Zaharia. *A Gamble With Death: a Novel*. Translated from the Romanian by Richard A. Hillard. London: Peter Owen, 1969. 201p. [*Jocul cu moartea*. Bucuresti: Editura Pentru Literatura, 1962. 253p.]

A picaresque novel set in the Balkans in 1917. The Germans have invaded the countryside and are everywhere feared and hated. A number of the inhabitants are rounded up to work as prisoners and are sent by train on a long journey through the Balkans to an undisclosed destination. The narrator is a young country boy who lives by his wits; the other major character is a disgraced aristocrat and ex-diplomat who is knifed when he attempts to rob the boy. The boy is ordered by the Germans to care for the man he has injured. Eventually when the train is blown up by partisans, the two escape. The remainder of the story describes their adventures as they find their way back to Bucharest. There are many artful descriptions of wartime conditions behind the lines, with a stark portrayal of the violence, poverty, and starvation that are so common in those circumstances.

1970

843 Marshall, William Leonard. *The Age of Death*. London: The Macmillan Co., 1970. 376p.; New York: Viking Press, 1970. 308p.

Encompasses World War I, the Spanish Civil War, and World War II, connected via the novel's characters. The minor character in one part of the novel becomes a major character in a succeeding section. The first 58 pages are devoted to World War I in Belgium and produce some of the most vivid pictures of battlefield action at Passchendaele, in which the front-line trenches are unceasingly bombarded by the Germans. Nicholas Arden and George Gilfallen, British soldiers, somehow survive the constant shelling only to relive the horror of their experience in the hospital to which they are evacuated. Nicholas is shell shocked and goes insane. Gilfallen, with a shattered arm, is invalided home to his wife and small son Anthony, an idealist who is destined to participate in the wars to come. A major theme is the conflict of generations, especially the contrast between the disillusioned older generation who are incapable of transferring their wisdom to the idealistic younger generation.

844 Plowman, Stephanie. *My Kingdom for a Grave*. London: Bodley Head, 1970. 240p.

This novel is the second and concluding part of *Three Lives for the Czar* (1970). The main character, Andrei Alexandrovitch Hamilton, is a Russian officer witnessing not only the demoralization of the Russian soldiers and the country but the fall of the Russian empire as well.

845 Trevor, Elleston. *Bury Him Among Kings*. London: Wm.
Heinemann, 1970. 343p.; New York: Doubleday & Co.,
1970. 374p.

The story tells how the war affected one English family,
the Talbots, whose two sons Aubrey and Victor, and the
family gardener and chauffeur, enlist with the Duke of
Lancaster's Light Infantry and participate in the big push
at Ypres. Around these main characters revolve hectic
and terrible front-line battles. Battle scenes are realistic and their impact is substantial. The author is
strongly anti-war in his comments about the conflict.

846 Whitehouse, Arch (pseud. of Arthur George Joseph Whitehouse). *Playboy Squadron, a Rollicking Novel of Young
Americans Flying and Fighting with the R.A.F. in World
War I*. Garden City, N.Y.: Doubleday & Co., 1970. 267p.

This novel, like others of the author, is based on his
war experiences. It is the tale of a group of American
college students who decided that flying would be an
adventurous way to fight in the war. They all think of
their adventure as a lark and look forward to returning
home in dashing uniforms covered with decorations in order
to impress their girl friends and families with their
wondrous exploits. Their trip to England is one long
party and their frivolous activities continue even on
land. When their orders are lost, Ellis Burdon, the
leader of Squadron 86, arranges to get them attached to
the Royal Flying Corps and they come to be known as
Burdon's Brigade, notorious for their escapades and tricks,
hence the title of the novel. The authenticity of the
author's description of the aerial fighting contrasts with
the high jinks of the Americans on the ground, particularly
in London.

1971

847 Hill, Susan. *Strange Meeting*. London: Hamish Hamilton,
1971. 224p.

A novel about emotional survival during the war, told
through the conversations and relationship of two young
British officers, John Hilliard and David Barton, who
meet for the first time in France during the first year
of the war. A photographically realistic description of
trench life during the great war.

848 Robinson, Derek. *Goshawk Squadron*. London: Wm. Heinemann, 1971. 218p.

A novel about a scout squadron of the Royal Flying Corps in France led by a martinet, Major Stanley Woolley, who is intent on preserving the lives of his flyers by forcing them to recognize that war is not a game but a murderous contest for survival. The author provides an exceptionally realistic description of battle scenes and such incidents as the repair of airplanes with baling wire.

1972

849 Delderfield, Ronald Frederick. *To Serve Them All My Days*. New York: Simon & Schuster, 1972. 638p.

Traces the life of a twenty-one-year-old Welshman, David Powlett-Jones (known affectionately as "P.J.") from the days of his service on the western front to his life as headmaster of an English public school, Bamfylde, until the end of World War II. "P.J." had spent three years in the trenches during World War I and returned from the war suffering shell shock. The novel, replete with characters of the English countryside, presents an engaging panorama of English life and history during the last years of World War I.

850 Harris, John. *The Mustering of the Hawks*. London: Hutchinson & Co., 1972. 256p.

Recounts the coming of age of aviation during the war years through the story of Ira Penaluna, British pilot, war ace, and hero. To himself he is a frightened, sometimes terrified boy, sickened by the carnage he creates and saddened by the continuing loss of his fellow combat fliers for whom the war has become essentially a routine fight for survival.

851 Levin, Meyer. *The Settlers: A Novel*. New York: Simon & Schuster, 1972. 832p.

A survey of Israeli history from the early 1900's to the end of World War I, as related by the experiences of the Chaimovitch family. An interesting description of the Zion Mule Corps, a little-known World War I auxiliary fighting unit.

852 Masters, John. *The Ravi Lancers: A Novel*. Garden City, N.Y.: Doubleday & Co., 1972. 447p.

    The latest (in 1972) of Masters' series of Indian novels, which began with his *Nightrunners of Bengal* (1951). Soldiers from India, the private regiment of Krishna Ram, prince of an Indian state, are fighting for England in the trenches on the western front. Their commanding officer in the British detachment is Warren Bateman, a captain in the Indian Army. Both Ram and Bateman accept and respect each other's country and way of life. Ram is deeply committed to preserving tradition, but recognizes values in the civilization of the West, though disturbed by the different moral standards of the two cultures. The soldiers adjust to the task of killing white Westerners as directed by the English, and the war becomes for the Ravi Lancers "a white man's war, and they'll learn to kill white men...." The horror of the warfare shatters the commonalities of East and West: Ram declares that Western civilization is "disease."

853 Solzhenitsyn, Alexander Isaevich. *August 1914*. Translated from the Russian by Michael Glenny. Vol. I. New York: Farrar, Straus & Giroux, 1972-. 622p. [*Avgust Chetyrnadtsatogo*. Vol. I. Paris: YMCA-Press, 1971-.

    August 1914 describes and evaluates the first two weeks of Russia's offensive into East Prussia and the defeat of Russia's Second Army while the First Army simply stood by and did nothing. The novel begins with descriptions of Russian rural life at the outbreak of the war. A very large number of characters is introduced, fictional and historical, from virtually every stratum of Russian life. The moral purpose of the novel is to determine and concentrate upon the cause of Russia's defeat in the battle of Tannenberg, in which over 90,000 Russian soldiers were encircled and killed or captured, and which sealed the doom of Imperial Russia. The responsibility for the crushing defeat was placed on the ineptness and lack of military skills of the Russian officers. Those responsible go unpunished, however, because of their influential position in the Tsar's court. Solzhenitsyn's insistent theme is that only a reconstructed Russia will eradicate Tsarism's rottenness, so that a new Russia can arise. Generally considered to be a major novel of power and distinction.

854 Stander, Siegfried. *The Fortress*. London: Victor Gollancz, 1972. 288p.

    A story of conflicting ideologies between the district

magistrate of a remote outpost in German West Africa and
the young German lieutenant who arrives with his squadron
to take military command of the post in the final months
of 1914. The magistrate wishes to be left in peace to
conduct the affairs of the small settlement; the impulsive
and overbearing lieutenant hopes to engage the settlement
in battle against the British enemy to further his own
ambitions. Ironically, when the British arrive, the lieutenant is off in the brush chasing a native who has stolen
the outpost's cattle, and it is the district magistrate
who must make the decision whether to hold the outpost or
capitulate.

1973

855 Jack, Donald Lamont. *That's Me in the Middle: The Journals of Bartholomew Bandy*. Vol. II. Garden City, N.Y.: Doubleday & Co., 1973. 300p.

The second of three volumes of the wartime misadventures
of Bartholomew Bandy, first introduced in *Three Cheers for Me* (item 809). This fearless World War I ace blunders
unwittingly and unwillingly into situations with hilarious
consequences which are infuriating to his superiors. However, Bandy always comes out on top.

856 Stanley, William. *One Spring in Picardy*. Cremorne, N.S.W., Australia: Angus & Robertson, 1973. 253p.

A realistic account of life among English aviators at an
air base in 1918. The main character, Robson, flies out-
moded FE-2b bombers at night and tries to dismiss his
wretched commanding officer from his thoughts by spending
time with a French girl, Madelaine, who is an ambulance
driver.

857 Strathern, Paul. *One Man's War*. London: Quartet Books, 1973. 186p.

The story of Peter Strang's life as a private in the
British front-line trenches, of his capture by the Germans
while a patient in a military hospital, and of his internment in and his eventual escape from a Bavarian castle
converted into a prisoner-of-war compound. Because of an
innocuous code he had devised while in the trenches to
overcome the monotonous life, the Germans suspect Peter
of intelligence operations, and attempt to break the code,

which is of no importance. Escaping through the sewers of the castle, Peter arrives finally in Munich to find the city in revolution, even though the Armistice has been declared. Here he lives in hiding with some rather improbable persons, fearing that the British will believe that he cooperated with the Germans. He eventually makes his way from the city still in revolt and prepares to escape to Switzerland and then home.

858   Whitehouse, Arch (pseud. of Arthur George Joseph Whitehouse). *Wings for the Chariots*. Garden City, N.Y.: Doubleday & Co., 1973. 256p.

British fighters of the Royal Flying Corps and of the new British weapon, the armored tank, join forces to break a stalemate in trench warfare prior to 1917. The combined aircraft-tank force is used in a daring rescue of a Swedish-American scientist and his wife, to keep a dangerous formula from the enemy. Introduced into the story are historical battlefield scenes and spectacular aerial dogfights. A melodrama.

1974

859   Johnston, Jennifer. *How Many Miles to Babylon? A Novel*. New York: Doubleday & Co., 1974. 156p.; London: Hamish Hamilton, 1974. 156p.

A story about two boys who grow up in Ireland just before the start of the war. One, Alexander Moore the narrator, is the son of a loveless marriage of landed gentry. The other is Jerry Crowe, a rough village boy who offers Alec genuine companionship and similar interests in spite of his grubby background and unpolished nature. Although this relationship constitutes a serious breach of the accepted class laws of that time, the two resolve to keep their friendship when they are sent to the trenches of Flanders. Alec, of course, is commissioned an officer, which further formalizes the class distinctions so painfully apparent in the larger society. The unsentimental description of life at the front with its damp, agonizing chilblains and exhaustion is very effective, especially by means of the author's technique of understatement. No battle scenes are described, only the conditions of the trenches and the inflexible structure of the military machine. The friendship between the two men is perforce clandestine, and is ultimately doomed with the apparent defection of Jerry and his death by firing squad. An underlying theme is the issue of Irish independence and social justice. On the whole this is a sensitive and well-written novel which realistically reveals the special tensions in Ireland and in the trenches of Flanders. Strongly reminiscent of writings of Robert Graves, Rupert Brooke, and Siegfried Sassoon.

860 Scholefield, Alan. *Lion in the Evening*. London: Wm. Heinemann, 1974. 175p.; New York: William Morrow & Co., 1974. 175p.

Set in British East Africa in 1916, this novel depicts the efforts of a young American engineer in building a railroad line for the British Army which will reach into the heart of the country as a means of better defending the area from the German army. By the time the railroad is near completion, it is urgently needed instead to evacuate the wounded and provide a means of retreat for the army. Paralleling this situation is the story of two lions whose physical disability compels them to prey on man, namely those building the railroad. With the successful evacuation of the army, the one remaining lion leaves the area, following the railroad, to which it is bound by its need to obtain prey easily.

1975

860a Gijsen, Marnix (pseud. of Jan Albert Goris). *Lament for Agnes*. Translated from the Netherlandic by W. James-Gerth. Boston: Twayne, 1975. 97p. [*Klaaglied om Agnes; Roman*. 's-Gravenhage: Nijgh & Van Ditmar, 196-.]

Not seen. A romance of Flemish lower-middle-class life during and after the war.

861 Jack, Donald Lamont. *It's Me Again*. Garden City, N.Y.: Doubleday & Co., 1975. 351p.

In this third volume of *The Journals of Bartholomew Bandy* the main character, Major Bartholomew Bandy, commander of a squadron of Sopwith Dolphins on his third tour of duty, is involved in his usual combination of accidental and comic escapades. Bartholomew is obsessed with the necessity of equipping all Royal Air Force pilots with parachutes, until he is designated the one to illustrate their function. His overzealousness in this endeavor makes him persona non grata with his superior officers, and in August 1918 he finds himself reassigned to northern Russia in charge of a White Russian training base.

862 Keneally, Thomas. *Gossip from the Forest*. London: W. Collins Sons, 1975. 222p.

A historical novel about the actions of the German and Allied signers of the Armistice on November 11, 1918, in the forest at Compiègne. The author reconstructs the event with considerable sympathetic depth. General Weygand, Marshal Foch, and Admiral Lord Wemyss represent the Allies. The Germans are represented by a major general, a flamboyant count, a naval captain, and the only civilian at the meeting, Matthias Erzberger, pacifist and Reichstag member. The plot concentrates on the efforts of the Allies to ram the Armistice down the throats of the Germans, and their efforts to negotiate the harsher provisions. The theme appears to be a study of the basically civilian and pacifist sensibility beleaguered by military power. Erzberger is a symbol of the humane and intelligent Weimar liberal who is doomed, both at the Armistice negotiations and later in 1921 when he is shot to death by two vengeful officers for his supposed crime against Germany in signing the Armistice. The reader sees the insanity controlling the opposing front lines through the eyes of Erzberger when he crosses them on his way to Compiègne, as well as the madness and fanaticism of the military both within Germany and at the forest clearing. This is a compelling novel, well-written and on a level with *August 1914* by Solzhenitsyn (item 853).

1976

* Jack, Donald Lamont. *Me Among the Ruins; The Journals of Bartholomew Bandy*. Vol. 4. Don Mills, Ontario: Paperjacks, 1976. 151p.

This title was first published as part two of the author's *It's Me Again* (which was originally issued as Bartholomew Bandy papers, Vol. 3). Refer to item 861 for annotation.

863 Mitchelson, Austin, and Nicholas Utechin. *Hellbirds*. New York: Belmont-Tower Books, 1976.

Not seen.

864 Scholefield, Alan. *The Alpha Raid*. London: Wm. Heinemann, 1976. 197p.

The German steamer *Afrika*, by controlling Lake Tanganyika, has been able to stymie the Belgian and British troops in East Africa. A plan is organized to have two small gunboats, the *Alpha* and the *Beta*, destroy the *Afrika*. To accomplish the mission, these vessels must be hauled over unbelievably rugged land. The "crew" of misfits who move the gunboats onto the lake are led by the psychotic Commander Bagley. All but one are from the British Navy. Other major characters are Lieutenant Ross, a playboy type who turns into a leader; Ward, a man who cannot face his adult responsibilities; Cristie, always the failure; and Sperry, an American deserter and adventurer whose ingenuity and shrewdness keep all on target. Tsetse flies, snakes, pitiless heat, and a typhoon almost ruin the operation, but it is crowned with success when Ross manages to ram his sinking *Alpha* into the paddle-wheel of the *Afrika*. The story is similar to *The African Queen* (item 705) by C.S. Forester. Although reasonably well written, the story adds little or nothing to the literature of the war.

1977

865 Cradock, Fanny (pseud. of Phyllis Cradock). *War Comes to Castle Rising*. London: W.H. Allen & Co., 1977. 337p.

The third novel in a series dealing with the Lorne family during the war. Gyles, the present Lord of Aynthorp, attempts to keep everything at his castle firmly under control, now that it is used also as a convalescent home for wounded officers. Although the younger members of the family are all in the war, the family life still goes on with its conflicts, births, tragedies, and deaths. The women of the castle serve as nurses to the wounded. Indeed, nearly every house in the village has a sign indicating a man is in service for "King and country." One of the convalescent men at the castle changes the total outlook of the family remaining at home. The author plans a sequel.

866 Findley, Timothy. *The Wars*. New York: Delacorte Press/ Seymour Lawrence, 1977. 226p.

A novel by a Canadian about artillery Lieutenant Robert Ross, a nineteen-year-old who enters the war in 1915 and

dies in 1922 after being crippled. Ross' experiences are
constructed from letters and snapshots—musty and yellowed
by age—and interviews with friends. This kaleidoscope
of scenes ranges from views of the prairies of central
Canada to the combat zone of Belgium. The misery of mud
and icy water on the battlefield and the horror of flame
throwers and poison gas are starkly portrayed as experienced by Ross who fights to survive while searching for
an understanding of the war's madness.

867   Hennessy, Max (pseud. of John Harris). *The Lion at Sea*.
London: Hamish Hamilton, 1977. 314p.

Recounts the flamboyant adventures of Lieutenant Kelly
Maguire (called "Ginger" by his shipmates), who is an
Anglo-Irish seaman in the British Royal Navy and has two
ships blown from under him. He rescues 180 British soldiers caught behind the German lines in Antwerp, is captured by the Turks from his faulty submarine in the Sea
of Marmosa after Gallipoli, and is finally rescued by the
Arabs and returned to the British lines. (*The Lion at Sea*
is to be the first volume of a trilogy.)

868   Lee, John Alexander. *Soldier*. Wellington, N.Z.: A.H. &
A.W. Reed, 1977. 148p.

Not seen.

869   Myrivilis, Stratis (Strates Myribeles). *Life in the Tomb*.
Translated from the modern Greek original by Peter Bien.
Hanover, N.H.: Published for Dartmouth College by the
University Press of New England, 1977. 325p.

A powerful Greek classic from the mid-1920's, now translated for the first time into English. The novel is constructed in the form of a series of letters written by
the hero, Sergeant Anthony Kostoulas, to his fiancée. He
tells of his experiences at the front in Serbian Macedonia
during 1917. Scattered through his accounts of trench
warfare covering the horrible deaths, mutilations, the
terrible shelling, and the mindless brutalities of everyday life at the front are his perceptive observations on
the total scope of the incredible world about him—from
the cruel to the ordinary. Life under these conditions
almost seems a living death at times. Sergeant Kostoulas,
the hero, is killed in action on the day of his last
letter home. The book is considered one of the master-
pieces of the literature on the war and belongs with

Frederick Manning's *The Middle Parts of Fortune* (item 567). It can be considered partly documentary, partly imaginative. The title of the novel is a reference to Christ in the tomb and carries an implication of resurrection from all of this hellish war, as well as the experience of crucifixion. One of the major themes is the notion that life emerges again and again from all of the death and destruction. Everything in nature is represented as being alive, as are all of the terrible artifacts of war, from bullets to artillery pieces. The author's style is poetic and sensitive. A major novel.

870   Stevens, Robert Tyler (pseud. of Reginald Thomas Staples). *Flight from Bucharest*. London: Souvenir Press, 1977. 318p.

As the German forces crumble before the Allied onslaught, two unlikely foes, one a captured English captain, Harry Phillips, the other, a German Major Carlsen, join forces to help a pro-German Rumanian princess to escape the socialist revolutionaries who would execute her. Many daring escapades later, safe in London, Captain Harry Phillips discovers the rescued princess is a commoner, whose escape permitted the real princess to evade capture.

1978

871   Cosic, Dobrica. *A Time of Death*. Translated by Muriel Heppell. New York: Harcourt Brace Jovanovich, 1978. 437p. [*Vreme smrti: Roman*. Beograd: Prosveta, 1972-1977.]

The story of the Serbian First Army's desperate attempt to hold their position against superior Austrian forces during the winter after the Sarajevo assassinations. The Serbian government pleads with the Allies for ammunition while exhorting its forces to maintain their positions and even push back the enemy with bayonets in lieu of ammunition. The Allies finally provide ammunition for a successful attack on the Austrians, but with considerable Serbian casualties. The bloody story of a little-known battle on the eastern front.

872   Edgar, Josephine (pseud. of Mary Howard). *Countess*. New York: St. Martin's Press, 1978. 343p.

The story of Viola Corbett, a turn-of-the-century English beauty who is a London shopgirl of common origin.

One of her boys, James-Carlo, is the illegitimate son of Lord James Staffray. Another son and two daughters are the children of her marriage to an Austrian count. The family is caught up in the turmoil of the war and of divided loyalties. James-Carlo, just seventeen, is marooned at school in England by the war and decides to enlist in the British Army. The novel describes the beginnings of the next world conflict, the rise of the National Socialists in Austria and the Fascists in Italy.

873 Evans, Alan (pseud. of Alan Stoker). *Thunder at Dawn*. London: Hodder & Stoughton, 1978. 253p.

A naval adventure set in a remote war theater in 1917. David Smith, an English navy commander, is off the west coast of South America in the HMS *Thunder*, an undermanned and slow ship with obsolete armor. When Smith learns that two modern German cruisers are on their way, the identical vessels that nearly sank him off Jutland, he tracks down their refueling supply ships and sinks them. The British and German ships then engage in a brief but violent battle and Smith manages to outsmart the Germans with his antiquated ship, before he is forced to withdraw to a port in Chile. A popular novel of some suspense, with vivid sea battles.

873a Malpass, Eric Lawson. *The Wind Brings Up the Rain*. London: Wm. Heinemann, 1978. 249p.

Not seen.

1979

874 Cameron, Ian (pseud. of Donald Gordon Payne). *The Young Eagles*. London: W.H. Allen, 1979. 249p.; New York: St. Martin's Press, 1980. 249p.?

Not seen.

875 Hepburne, Melissa. *Passion's Sweet Sacrifice*. Los Angeles: Pinnacle Books, 1979. 373p.

A spy mystery that uses the war as a foil against which the author appears to have great fun in constructing an absurd spoof. This tale begins with a melodramatic rape and a wedding at which the bride is drugged. The fast-paced action ranges from Tahiti to Marseilles, from Paris to the headquarters of the Germans in World War I where Sabrina, the female protagonist, is persuaded to offer her body in exchange for strategic secrets. She is rescued by two pilots enamoured with her beauty. Their plane is forced to land in North Africa where the English-speaking natives worship her as a sun goddess and fight to "fulfill" her and die. Sabrina and her two admirers escape, however, and she is soon forced back into spying in order to save Michael, one of her rescuers, from the evil manipulations of the German high command. A humorous joust with history in a non-serious, sex-adventure tale.

876 Huebsch, Edward. *The Last Summer of Mata Hari*. New York: Crown, 1979. 419p.

A fictional retelling of events in the life of Mata Hari, who was executed for her double-agent activities with the German and French secret services. In the novel her passion for one man involves her with munitions makers the world over, including the Krupp organization, before her arrest, trial, and execution. Much of the plot is based on poor or faulty history and written in a dull style that lacks the suspense and intrigue normally expected with such a topic. Falls in the category of a "popular" adventure story.

876a Jenkins, Robin. *Fergus Lamont*. Edinburgh: Canongate Pub., 1979. 293?p.; New York: Taplinger, 1979. 293p.

Not seen.

877 Masters, John. *Now God Be Thanked*. New York: McGraw-Hill, 1979. 589p.; London: Michael Joseph, 1979. 608p.

A first novel in what is to be a trilogy about the first World War called *Loss of Eden*. The plot deals with the first eighteen months of the war and concerns three generations of the Rowlands, an English family. Though the novel offers a fairly vivid picture of the horrors of the war in the trenches of France and on the high seas, one of the major themes is the great social change caused by the war as reflected in the relationships among the children and grandchildren and other members of the Rowlands family. The novel is mainly about the home front: those who support the war and those who see it as a way to make their fortunes. (Henry Rowland is the owner of an automobile factory that must switch from the production of expensive cars to the mass production of war material.) The story begins with a boat race on the Thames in July 1914, and ends at Christmas of 1915, when the war is in full swing. Actual historical characters such as Asquith, Lloyd George, and Churchill figure in the background. The plot has the standard contemporary emphasis on love and sex. The title comes from the Rupert Brooke sonnet entitled "Peace," written in 1914. A popular novel.

878   Morris, Suzanne. *Keeping Secrets*. Garden City, N.Y.: Doubleday & Co., 1979. 443p.

A novel of intrigue and romance set in Texas, involving a naive working girl and an upper-class matron who participate in surreptitious activities between munitions suppliers to the Mexican revolution and the German government. Many intricate subplots are involved in this long, romantic, and complicated novel. Reminiscent of those long nineteenth-century novels of Galsworthy and Dickens.

879   Paretti, Sandra. *The Magic Ship*. Translated from the German by Ruth Hein. New York: St. Martin's Press, 1979. 342p.

Relates a story far removed from the trenches of France. A German luxury liner with over 1,000 passengers aboard is en route to Germany from the United States. The ship reaches the mid-Atlantic only to receive a secret wireless message to turn back to the States. The war has just begun and the liner manages to slip back successfully to dock offshore near Bar Harbor, Maine. While the German crew and the dashing Captain Polack are forced to wait for the day they can safely return home, the hospitable Bar Harbor inhabitants welcome them with all the usual gestures of friendship and a round of parties. This all soon leads to a number of romances and various relationships. The bulk of the novel deals with these relationships while the liner remains anchored offshore. When the United States finally declares war on Germany, the romantic interlude is over. The war serves mainly as a vehicle to create a nostalgic atmosphere, as it were, for a minor romantic popular novel. The scope, depth, and literary ability, although similar, fall far short of such a novel as *Ship of Fools* by Katherine Anne Porter.

880   Pilpel, Robert H. *To the Honor of the Fleet*. New York: Atheneum, 1979. 384p.

A naval saga of the first two years of the war. Two

U.S. naval officers are assigned to the German and British fleets to learn as much as possible in preparation for the eventual entry of the U.S. in the war on one side or the other. The two spies, Gehlman, son of a wealthy Jewish-American, and Maltbie, naive and honorable, are involved in activities that seem dishonorable but are necessary for eventual victory. Several involved subplots, such as the affair between Gehlman and Maltbie's bride, add a bit of melodramatic puff to this popular novel.

881 Rock, Phillip. *The Passing Bells*. New York: Seaview Books, 1979. 433p.

A panoramic historical novel focusing on nearly a dozen major and interrelated characters with a supporting cast of literally thousands. It is a family saga that serves as a symbol of an end of an era in English life and society. The family members marry above and beneath themselves, witness the terrible slaughter of the Gallipoli campaign, and participate in the horrors of trench warfare in France. The novel provides a perceptive view of the emotional and social changes caused by the conflict. The battle scenes are realistic with considerable power and gruesome intensity. The novel is reminiscent of the television series "Upstairs, Downstairs." Although the plot and action are familiar to anyone who has read even a handful of the better novels of the Great War, the narrative is written with such skill and wit that the story still has fresh impact.

881a Roth, Joseph. *The Silent Prophet*. Translated by David LeVay. London: Peter Owen, 1979. 220p. [*Der Stumme Prophet. Roman.* Köln, Berlin: Kiepenheuer u. Witsch, 1966.]

882 Saffron, Robert. *The Demon Device by Sir Arthur Conan Doyle, as Communicated to ...: A Novel*. New York: G.P. Putnam's Sons, 1979. 287p.

Sir Arthur Conan Doyle posthumously relates his daring adventures in saving England, and perhaps the world, from destruction by the atomic bomb in 1917. Mysterious creatures dog his footsteps. A beautiful, mysterious woman is his accomplice, and Einstein and Lenin seek his assistance. The bomb, hidden in a golf bag in the House of Parliament, is at the very last moment thrown into the sea, after the subterranean munitions factory and all the workers and the secrets of the bomb were first destroyed. Sheer fantasy.

882a Shears, Sarah. *Annie's Boys*. London: Paul Elek, Ltd., 1979.

Not seen.

883 Stevens, Robert Tyler (pseud. of Reginald Thomas Staples). *My Enemy, My Love*. Garden City, N.Y.: Doubleday & Co., 1979. 360p.

A love story involving James Fraser, a Briton, and Sophie von Korvacs, an Austrian subject. The story begins in the summer of the assassination of Franz Ferdinand in Sarajevo and ends in Vienna at the end of the war. Book I, entitled "The Last Summer," is the story of Vienna before the war and of the band of assassins who pursue a group of young people through the mountains of Bosnia, believing that the young people recognize the assassins' purpose in Sarajevo. Book II, entitled "An Empire Lost," follows the fortunes of the von Korvacses through the war, particularly the son, Carl Korvacs, who for three years fought on the Italian front.

884 Welcome, John. *Bellary Bay*. New York: Atheneum, 1979. 328p.

The protagonist, Stephen Raymond, is the son of an English landholder residing in Ireland. At boarding school Stephen is abused by another student, Conway, who continues his bullying when both boys enlist in Britain's flying corps. Stephen's life is in danger when Conway becomes Stephen's commander and attempts to have Stephen killed, notwithstanding that Stephen has become a seasoned fighter pilot. When the war ends and Stephen returns to Bellary Bay, Conway is successful in causing Stephen's death. A major theme is the rise of *Sinn Fein* politics in Ireland.

1980

The following titles were either published or scheduled to be published in 1980. For example, although some bibliographic sources indicate 1979, Reach for Eternity *was published in 1980. The verso of the title page indicates that the English translation was copyrighted in 1980. Since we concluded our search in April of 1980 it is likely that*

Adult Novels

additional titles for 1980 appeared during the rest of the year, so this list is necessarily incomplete.

885   Bailey, Paul. *Old Soldiers*. London: Jonathan Cape, 1980. 120p.

886   Cosic, Dobrica. *Reach to Eternity*. Translated by Muriel Heppell. New York: Harcourt Brace Jovanovich, 1980. 410p. [A translation of volume 3 of *Vreme Smrti: Roman*. Beograd: Prosveta, 1972-1979. 4 vols.]

887   Ellis, Julie. *The Hampton Women*. New York: Simon and Schuster, 1980. 445p.

888   Harrison, Sarah. *The Flowers of the Field*. New York: Coward, McCann & Geoghegan, 1980. 492p.

889   Jones, J. *A Tree May Fall*. London: The Bodley Head, 1980.

890   McDonald, Roger. *1915*. New York: George Braziller, 1980. 425p.

891   Masters, John. *Heart of War*. New York: McGraw-Hill, 1980. 624p.

The second volume of his forthcoming trilogy. The first volume of the trilogy is *Now God Be Thanked* (item 877).

892   Palmer, Lilli. *A Time to Embrace*. Translated by Carey Harrison. New York: The Macmillan Co., 1980. [*Umarmen Hat Seine Zeit: Roman*. Locarno: Droemer Knaur Verlag, 1979. 422p.]

893   Smith, Gene. *Where Are My Legions*. New York: William Morrow & Co., 1980. 330p.

894   Stanley, W. *Cloud Nineteen*. London: Michael Joseph, 1980.

895   Stevenson, William. *The Ghosts of Africa*. New York: Harcourt Brace Jovanovich, 1980. 576p.

Juvenile Novels about World War I

INTRODUCTION

Juvenile stories is a genre that tends to be completely different from all other literature. The juvenile fiction dealing with the war years covers the preteen through the young adult years. Most of the literature produced during the war and on through the 1930's was written largely to formula and cranked out in a great number of series both for boys and for girls. Boy scout virtues and values are especially emphasized, and many books were endorsed by the Boy Scouts of America.

Aside from the expected bravery and heroism of the "all-American boy" and "girl" heroes and heroines in countless adventures, it is obvious that there was a clear didactic purpose to the vast majority of the 370 juvenile books about the Great War. Patriotic fervor, traditional family values, religious commitment, belief in God, and all of the solid American virtues of honesty, integrity, morality, etc., are constantly emphasized and rigorously accepted as a part of the natural order of things, and especially of American society.

It is interesting to note a rather remarkable effort in some juvenile stories to present Germany's side through the commonality of boy scout principles and activities. A good example is *The Boy Scouts Under the Kaiser; or Karl Adler's Devotion* by Robert Maitland (item j41), published in 1915. This tale illustrates the humane concern and support of the German military authorities by the rescue of two boy scout friends, one from America and the other from Germany, who are on a walking tour in France when the war begins.

The series stories for girls are largely attempts to duplicate the virtues and characteristics of the general run of heroes in the series for boys. One exception is the Red Cross Girls stories written by Margaret Vandercook (items j101, j102, j103, j104, j135, j136, j217, and j304) published from 1915 through 1919. This series often demonstrates a character, maturity of thought, and sophistication of plot relationships that most of the juvenile series books (especially those for boys) never approach.

There is one unusual series for boys, however, that deserves to be identified because of its slapstick humor and the outrageous antics of the two heroes. The twelve-volume Our Young Aeroplane Scouts series (items j49, j50, j51, j52, j93, j94, j125, j126, j195, j196, j282, and j283) is filled with so many clichés that the dialogue has come to achieve almost "camp" humor. While the vast majority of juvenile books emphasize patriotism, bravery, courage, mother, God, and country, these books by Horace Porter now appear to be almost a parody and a burlesque of their own genre. The plot action proceeds at nearly space-age speed. The two boy heroes work for the Central Powers as well as for the Allies while they dash madly through nearly all of the World War I war theaters. The inane dialogue is incredible. Although it is impossible to tell whether the author originally had a comic parody intention, it could be a conceivable explanation. A brief sample of dialogue from two of the titles follows:

> "What sort of hold-up is this?" cried Anglin, in startled recognition, "is it raining harumscarum aviators in Strasburg? By the great hornspoon, it's enough to make me believe I've got to see you under the roof."
> "I'll bet you know that we blew in with Rogue," proposed Billy, "for you have a way of seeing seven ways for Sunday."
> "You win, daddy-buck, on the first statement, but I'm still up a stump on the proposition of how you got into this house."
>
> (*Our Young Aeroplane Scouts in Germany*, 1915, item j50)

> "All right!" retorted the boy from Bangor, "don't give us any more of your beef, Stroganov!"
>
> (*Our Young Aeroplane Scouts in Russia*, 1915, item j51)

The generally wooden, formula plots and single-dimension characterizations are typical throughout the vast majority of juvenile series books for boys and girls, especially those published from 1914 through the 1930's. Moreover, they also incorporated a positive didactic purpose involving more than just the moral and ethical principles of scouting and the traditional values of country and home. Generally the war action, whether battles, dates, equipment, strategies, or conditions, etc., was historically accurate. One reader-collector of these books remarked that much of her detailed knowledge of the events and battles of World War I was based on many of the juvenile series stories she had read. She found that her later adult experiences and reading confirmed the historical accuracy

Introduction

of these juvenile stories of World War I. Indeed, they remain a fond reading experience for her.

In the Introduction to Adult Novels some comment was made about the place of blacks in World War I literature. Several of these juvenile stories have an occasional reference to negro troops. The Ross Kay titles that describe the heroic wartime adventures of the two Platt brothers are particularly good examples (see item j188). The same series (items j2, j3, j35, j36, j87, j121, j188, j278, and j326) also mention American Indian troops and actually feature two or three Indian soldiers who are the terrors of the battlefield. In those days the American Indian had an obvious mystique and prowess as a proficient and dangerous warrior in the juvenile books directed to boys and girls. In one case, (item j286) a fearless Indian soldier who collects the scalps of his German enemies causes great consternation in the German trenches, to the joy of his Allied comrades.

In 1916, Harrie Hancock published his juvenile Conquest of the United States series. The four series titles (items j81, j82, j83, and j84) describe the lack of military preparedness and inaction of the United States Congress that resulted in the invasion of the United States by Germany in the summer of 1920. The series traces the massive German sea armada, their shore invasion in Massachusetts, the capture of New York City, and the eventual American last stand at Pittsburgh. One interresting feature of this series is the support of Brazilian troops as a goodwill gesture from south of the border. The Germans are defeated by June of 1921 and accept a peace treaty on American terms. The series is obvious propaganda to spur American support of the war effort in Europe. The battlefield techniques and equipment are modeled on the Western Front in France.

Although some of this juvenile literature was a serious effort to instruct boys and girls in the elements of warfare--artillery placement and firing, submarine operation, military tactics, etc.--probably the main purpose was to offer reading entertainment and adventure. Now, however, this juvenile literature can serve as a measure of the present sophistication and technological knowledge of boys and girls. The juvenile stories of World War I (especially those published from 1914 into the 1930's) reflect a naiveté and relatively uncomplicated world view that today seems greatly out of date. This is a literature that describes a world far more innocent and simple than ours. Perhaps it is partly this sense of lost innocence, of the simple emotional response of the good against the bad, and of the unquestioned right of our side, that continues to convey such nostalgia today.

1914

j1   Brereton, Frederick Sadleir. *With French at the Front; a Story of the Great European War Down to the Battle of the Aisne.* London: Blackie & Son, 1914. 292p.

Not seen.

j2   Kay, Ross. *The Air Scout: An American Boy's Adventures when the Big War in Europe Began.* New York: Barse & Hopkins, 1914. 252p.

This companion story to *Search for the Spy* (item j3) relates the adventures of Earl Platt's twin brother, Leon. While visiting Paris, Leon encounters Jacques, a member of the French aviation corps, and the two boys quickly become friends. Shortly afterward as Leon begins a motorcycle tour of France, the war breaks out, and he makes his way to Brussels with an American friend. En route he has a series of daring adventures, and observes air battles and troop movements. When a French airplane lands in a field beside him, the pilot turns out to be Jacques, whereupon Leon decides to enlist and fly off with Jacques to join the French forces. From now on Leon and Jacques are together on missions and other harrowing adventures in enemy territory. They see the massive German advance through Belgium. Leon is wounded at the end of the novel in a foolhardy flag race across the trenches with Jacques. But all is well in the end with the promise that Leon will be back in the thick of the battle in a few days.

j3   ———. *The Search for the Spy: The Adventures of an American Boy at the Outbreak of the War.* New York: Barse & Hopkins, 1914. 253p.

The first title of the nine Big War Series of juvenile stories. Earl Platt and his twin brother Leon leave by boat for a summer vacation in Europe in 1914. While Leon goes on to London and Europe, Earl takes a bicycle trip from Liverpool to London. He runs into pigeon fanciers and several times encounters Philip Alden who uses Earl as an unknowing messenger for German spies. Earl is arrested when the English authorities mistake him for the spy Alden. Earl is soon released and becomes involved in a series of adventures with Captain Swain as they attempt to trip up Alden and his fellow conspirators. Naturally, they get their man and the story concludes as Earl decides to go to Paris to meet his brother. A juvenile story with a characteristic wooden plot that is typical of this series.

j4B   Lawton, Wilbur (pseud. of John H. Goldfrap). *The Ocean Wireless Boys on the Atlantic.* New York: Hurst & Co., 1914. 308p.

     Not seen.

j5   Strang, Herbert (pseud. of George Herbert Ely and C.J. L'Estrange). *A Hero of Liège; a Story of the Great War.* London: H. Frowde; Hodder & Stoughton, 1914. 250p.

     Not seen.

j6AB   Westerman, Percy Francis. *The Dreadnought of the Air.* London: S.W. Partridge, 1914. 382p.

     Not seen.

j7AB   ———. *The Sea-girt Fortress; a Story of Heligoland.* London: Blackie & Son, 1914. 296p.

     Not seen.

1915

j8   Ames, Franklin T. (pseud.). *Between the Lines in Belgium; a Boys' Story of the European War.* New York: Dodd, Mead & Co., 1915. 312p.

Two American brothers, Harvey and Martin Door, have gone to Europe in the summer of 1914 to visit their uncle on his farm near the Belgium border when the war starts. The uncle is immediately sent into the army and the two brothers decide to make their way to Brussels. The trains are so crowded that they must hike nearly all of the way. In the course of their journey they have numerous exciting adventures and close escapes. At one point they are held

Juvenile Novels

as prisoners in a German camp. They see a good deal of the fighting along the Meuse as well as the bombardment of Liège.

j9 ———. *Between the Lines in France; A Boys' Story of the Great European War.* New York: Dodd, Mead & Co., 1915. 306p.

This is more or less a sequel to his *Between the Lines in Belgium* (item j8). A group of young Americans go to Europe in the summer of 1914. Once there they become separated. The two who went to Belgium have their experiences in the title mentioned above, while this story follows the travels of two others from the group, Lucille and Tom Maillard. They are on a motor tour in France with their uncle. When the war starts, they are near the German border in northern France. The chauffeur of their uncle's car immediately leaves to join the army and Tom then takes over the driving. They are shown in their many adventures as they attempt to evade troop movements and dangers of the first weeks of the war. They are fortunate and finally reach the coast where they leave by boat for America. This is a juvenile story that has fairly accurate material on the conditions in France during the early days of the war.

j10 Arundel, Louis. *The Motorboat Boys Down the Danube; or, Caught in the Whirlpool of War* (also with variant subtitle: ... *or, Four Chums Abroad.*) Chicago: M.A. Donohue, 1915. 258p.

Volume three in the author's Boy Scout Series for boys and girls. Four young American boys, friends and scouts, are in Budapest waiting for a chartered powerboat to take them down the Danube River to the Black Sea. When the war breaks out they decide to continue with their trip in spite of the conflict. This eventually leads to a number of adventures with Hungarians, a refugee boy from Serbia, a bad thunder storm, artillery bombardments between the Austrians and Serbians along the river, and various other assorted and dangerous experiences on the way to Romania. Here the boys go by steamer to Constantinople and then home to the States.

j11AB Bennett, Rolf. *The Adventures of Lieut. Lawless, R.N.* 2nd ed. London: Hodder & Stoughton, 1915. 191p.

Not seen.

j12   Brereton, Frederick Sadleir. *Under French's Command; a Story of the Western Front from Neuve Chapell to Loos.* London: Blackie & Son, 1915.

Not seen.

j13A Bridges, Thomas Charles. *On Land and Sea at the Dardanelles.* London & Glasgow: Collins' Clear-type Press, 1915. 198p.

Not seen.

*   Cobb, Frank (pseud.). *Winning in the Air.* Akron, Ohio: Saalfield Pub. Co., 1915.

A reprint with different author and title of *The Boy Scouts with the Allies* ... by Robert Maitland (item j43).

j14   Crockett, Sherman. *Two American Boys with the Allied Armies.* New York: Hurst & Co., 1915. 305p.

The first title of this juvenile series of improbable war adventures. Jack Maxfield and his cousin, Amos Turner, are in Belgium on a special errand of mercy as the war begins. The plot is based on the search of Jack and Amos for Tom, Amos' brother, who has left home in a dispute with his father who is now dangerously ill. Tom has taken an assumed name and is reported to be an ace pilot for the British. The two boys search for Tom all over the main battlefronts of the war. They have plenty of opportunities to see the advance of the German armies through Belgium and the state and condition of the Belgian people in this desperate and uncertain time. There are the usual scenes of trench warfare, air battles, cavalry attacks, and artillery bombardments. The boys become involved with German spies and have a number of the usual narrow escapes characteristic of these single-dimensional and melodramatic juvenile series about the war. There is some effort in this story to describe the German soldiers in more balanced terms than most of the juvenile stories--as if they were human beings like everyone else.

j15   Drake, Robert L. (pseud. of Clair Wallace Hayes). *The Boy Allies on the North Sea Patrol; or, Striking the First Blow at the German Fleet.* New York: A.L. Burt, 1915. 235p.

The Boy Allies juvenile series dealing with naval operations covers the adventures of Jack Templeton, an English

boy, and Frank Chadwick, an American. Visiting Germany
when the war begins, Frank and his father escape to Italy,
but there they soon become separated. While searching
for his father in Naples, Frank rescues a sailor under
attack by a group of cutthroats. Frank, however, is
eventually shanghaied on a sloop through the devious efforts of the very sailor he rescued. A mutiny occurs and
the ship is directed to the coast of Africa. Here Frank
meets Jack who has spent most of his life there. Jack
overcomes the mutinous crew. As a result, Jack and Frank
decide to team up with the British agent who was also a
prisoner on the boat, and they travel to London and join
the British navy. The story describes how Jack and Frank
play an important part in the defeat of the German fleet
at Helgoland. It is through their clever strategy that
the Germans are lured into a battle which results in the
destruction of four of the large German warships.

j16 ———. *The Boy Allies Under The Sea; or, The Vanishing Submarines.* New York: A.L. Burt, 1915. 252p.

Now first lieutenants, Frank Chadwick and Jack Templeton
continue their wartime adventures on fast motorboat patrols
to destroy and capture German submarines in the Irish Sea
and the Atlantic. Their activities, as usual, involve
German spies and motorboat fights. The tale concludes
with their capture of a German sub, the U-16. In the
process, they sink three enemy battleships before entering
the German submarine port of Ostend where they track down
Davis, a secret agent working for the Germans. This all
leads to their capture by Davis, but this misfortune is
of short duration for they soon find a marvelous escape
ploy which is followed by further successful submarine
adventures against the enemy before they again return to
England. Another all-American-boy adventure so characteristic of this juvenile series.

j17 ———. *The Boy Allies Under Two Flags; or, Sweeping the Enemy from the Sea.* New York: A.L. Burt, 1915. 252p.

Jack and Frank continue their adventures by participating in a large naval battle in the Adriatic. After
the battle they join up with Lord Hastings, their mentor,
on the little scout cruiser *Sylph II* and are made the
first and second officers. A typical juvenile war story
of the period chock-full of improbable adventures. The
two heroes can do no wrong and, of course, always come
out on top over the "dirty Hun."

j18 ———. *The Boy Allies with the Flying Squadron; or, The Naval Raiders of the Great War*. New York: A.L. Burt, 1915. 254p.

Lieutenant Jack Templeton, an English boy of twenty-one, is first officer of the small scout cruiser *Sylph II*. His American friend, 2nd Lieutenant Frank Chadwick, age twenty, is the second officer. The story begins with their encounter with the German battle cruiser *Hanover* and its destruction. The two friends then travel to the Pacific to aid the Japanese against the Germans at Tsing-Tan. The plot describes the adventures of Jack and Frank both on water and ashore, in the Far East, Beirut, and through the Mediterranean. They also become involved in an airplane fight, resulting in their emergency landing in Germany. With their English pilots they eventually plot a daring escape from the Germans. All of this is capped by a special decoration of bravery bestowed by none other than King George V. A typical juvenile-series novel of the period.

j19 ———. *The Boy Allies with the Terror of the Seas; or, The Last Shot of Submarine D-16*. New York: A.L. Burt, 1915. 253p.

The sequel to *The Boy Allies with the Flying Squadron* (item j18). This time Jack and Frank are followed in their wartime submarine adventures against the Huns. A German spy mysteriously turns up on their sub but dies in his escape attempt. Further adventures deal with the capture of Frank by the Germans and his daring rescue. The action ranges from the North Sea and Baltic to the Mediterranean with plenty of adventures on land as well as on the sea. The story ends with the description of the mortal damage to the D-16 sub and the death defying escapes of the two heroes from a watery grave.

j20 Dyer, Walter Alden. *Pierrot, Dog of Belgium*. Garden City, N.Y.: Doubleday, Page & Co., 1915. 112p.; London: Curtis Brown, 1915. 112p.

Pierrot, a milk-cart dog, is pressed into military service to help, with another dog, to draw a machine gun. Pierrot comes under fire, is wounded, and eventually returns to his home outside Brussels. Much detail is presented about the importance of draft dogs in Belgium. Important during peacetime, the Belgian dogs are much more vital in wartime. The novel is not a sentimental

Juvenile Novels 323

animal story; its purpose was to encourage Belgian relief work. (The Pierrot Fund for Relief in Belgium was a reminder of the suffering of these dogs during the war.)

* Fiske, James (pseud.). *At the Fall of Warsaw*. Akron, Ohio: Saalfield Pub. Co., 1915.

A reprint with different author and title of *The Boy Scouts in Front of Warsaw* ... by George Durston (item j77).

* ———. *The Belgians to the Front*. Akron, Ohio: Saalfield Pub. Co., 1915. 233p.

A reprint with different author and title of *The Boy Scouts at Liège* ... by Robert Maitland (item j39).

* ———. *Facing the German Foe*. Akron, Ohio: Saalfield Pub. Co., 1915. 241p.

A reprint with different author and title of *The Boy Scouts with King George* ... by Robert Maitland (item j42).

* ———. *Fighting in the Alps*. Akron, Ohio: Saalfield Pub. Co., 1915.

A reprint with different author and title of *The Boy Scouts' Test* ... by George Durston (item j78).

* ———. *Fighting in the Clouds for France*. Akron, Ohio: Saalfield Pub. Co., 1915. 255p.

A reprint with different author and title of *The Boy Scouts with the Allies* ... by Robert Maitland (item j43).

* ———. *In Russian Trenches*. Akron, Ohio: Saalfield Pub. Co., 1915. 240p.

A reprint with different author and title of *The Boy Scouts with the Cossacks* ... by Robert Maitland (item j44).

* ———. *On Board the Mine-laying Cruiser*. Akron, Ohio: Saalfield Pub. Co., 1915. 244p.

A reprint with a different author and title of *The Boy Scouts Under the Kaiser* ... by Robert Maitland (item j41).

*   ———. *Under Fire for Serbia.* Akron, Ohio: Saalfield
      Pub. Co., 1915. 256p.

      A reprint with different author and title of *The Boy
      Scouts Before Belgrade* ... by Robert Maitland (item j40).

j21   Forward, Charles Walter. *Under the Blue Cross; a Story of
      Two Horses in the War.* London: Hodder & Stoughton,
      1915. 63p.

      Not seen.

j22   Garis, Howard Roger. *Larry Dexter in Belgium; or, A Young
      War Correspondent's Double Mission.* New York: Grosset
      & Dunlap, 1915. 208p.

      A juvenile story placed during the first few weeks of
      the war and mainly in Belgium. Larry Dexter is a star
      reporter for a large newspaper in the States. The wife
      and daughter (with their two friends) of Hampton Potter,
      millionaire and part owner of the paper, are caught in
      Belgium at the outbreak of the conflict. Larry is sent
      by his paper to report on the war and also search for the
      Potter women. As it turns out he searches mostly for the
      women. After an adventuresome sea voyage to England and
      a spy interlude in London, Larry ships off on an army
      transport from Dover to Ostend. Now his search for the
      Potter women and their friends begins in earnest. He
      meets Otto Dunder, a German-American boy with an old
      rickety taxicab, and they travel together through the
      Belgian cities of Bruges, Ghent, Brussels, and Louvain
      before reaching Liège. This and his subsequent travels
      give the young reporter plenty of opportunities to see
      not only the sights of war behind the front lines—wounded
      soldiers, troop trains, etc.—but also Belgian and German
      attacks and shellings. Eventually Larry accidentally
      encounters the Potter women at their overturned carriage
      in the countryside. They hire a wagon to Rotterdam where
      the Potters arrange safe passage to London and home, while
      the zealous reporter at last is able to send off several
      stories to his newspaper in the States. A typical boy's
      story of the period.

j23   Grant, Allan (pseud. of Arthur Douglas Howden Smith).
      *A Cadet of Belgium, an American Boy in The Great War;
      a Story of Cavalry Daring—Bicycle and Armored Auto-
      mobile Adventures.* New York: George H. Doran Co., 1915.
      286p.

      Jack Morton, an American boy, has been left with friends

in Liège while his father is away on a business trip. But when war breaks out he and his friend Raoul, both boy scouts, volunteer for messenger service. The plot is an account of their travels and adventures during the military campaign in Belgium from Liège to the fall of Antwerp.

j24 ———. *Fifty Feet Under the Sea*. New York: George H. Doran Co., 1915(?).

Not seen.

j25 ———. *Fighting the Zeppelins*. New York: George H. Doran Co., 1915(?).

Not seen.

j26 ———. *In defence of Paris, an American Boy in the Trenches; a Story of Infantry and the Big Guns*. New York: George H. Doran Co., 1915. 256p.

The author continues with the theme dealing with the part played in the war by boy scouts. In this case, the story deals with an American boy and a French boy. Ralph Gordon is visiting his sister who is married to a French cavalry officer when the war begins. With his friend François, he offers himself for messenger service. The plot relates the various and exciting adventures that the two boys encounter during the retreat of the French army and the advance of the Germans on Paris.

j27 Hale, Harry. *Jack Race Air Scout; or, Adventures in a War Aeroplane*. New York: Hearst's International Library Co., 1915. 241p.

Not seen.

j28 Hamilton, Frederick Spencer. *The Holiday Adventures of Mr. P.J. Davenant*. London: E. Nash, 1915. 160p.

The hero, a 16-year-old schoolboy on a skiing break, proves himself an able sleuth in revealing German plots to sabotage England's war effort during World War I. He works closely with his father's friend Cyril Ambrose who is attached to Scotland Yard. (This novel comprises the first four parts of the author's *Nine Holiday Adventures of Mr. P.J. Davenant in the Year 1915* [item j80].)

j29 ———. *Some Further Adventures of Mr. P.J. Davenant.* London: E. Nash, 1915. 309p.

Not seen.

j30 Hayes, Clair Wallace. *The Boy Allies at Liège; or, Through Lines of Steel.* New York: A.L. Burt, 1915. 256p.

Hal Paine and Chester Crawford, two American boys who have just graduated from high school, travel to Europe with Hal's mother. When they are in Berlin war is declared against Russia and France. Rather than sit out the war in the German capital, they decide to leave for Belgium by whatever means possible. They eventually meet two Allied officers also stranded in Berlin, Lieutenant Anderson and Captain Derevaux. All four now go through a series of incredible escapes from and captures by the Germans until the two boys finally are able to stage a dramatic escape by airship and crash land near a Belgian army outpost in the combat zone outside Liège. They seek and receive permission to join up with the Belgian army and again start a series of improbable adventures with German spies, captures, and battlefront activities during the battle at Liège. Another typical all-American-boy adventure calculated to inspire patriotic spasms and self-sacrifice. The further adventures of the two heroes are continued in *The Boy Allies on the Firing Line* (item j32).

j31 ———. *The Boy Allies in the Trenches; or, Midst Shot and Shell Along the Aisne.* New York: A.L. Burt, 1915. 256p.

The sequel to *The Boy Allies with the Cossacks* (item j33). After Hal Paine and Chester Crawford have returned from the eastern front carrying dispatches from the Grand Duke Nicholas to the French commander-in-chief, the two heroes then join up again with the British army. They soon are involved in several defeats of German forces in trench warfare and later successfully foil the plot to assassinate the French President Poincaré by the treacherous apaches in Paris. The next adventure of Hal and Chester is described in *The Boy Allies in Great Peril* ... (item j85).

Juvenile Novels

j32 ───────. *The Boy Allies on the Firing Line; or, Twelve Days Battle along the Marne.* New York: A.L. Burt, 1915. 253p.

This story, a sequel to *The Boy Allies at Liège* (item j30) continues the war adventures of Hal and Chester. The story starts just after the two are given commissions as lieutenants in the Belgian army for their bravery. They become involved in the fighting of the German advance through Belgium. The story relates their narrow escapes and battlefield adventures and concludes as they manage a clever escape in an airplane from German territory and fly off to Poland to safety.

j33 ───────. *The Boy Allies with the Cossacks; or, A Wild Dash over the Carpathian Mountains.* New York: A.L. Burt, 1915.

The story begins with Chester and Hal and their trusty dog, Marquis, in an airplane over the German lines. A sudden shot warns them to climb and there then appears a German aircraft in hot pursuit. Although only sixteen they have seen plenty of active service. Their experiences are the usual adventures such as being taken prisoners by the Germans and narrowly escaping death by firing squad through the intervention of the Emperor himself, and being sent back to Berlin. Naturally, they are both crack shots, with incredible skill with their fists and swords. They rush off to give a message to the Grand Duke Nicholas so that closer cooperation can occur between the Russians and the Allied forces in the west. The story traces their fantastic adventures through Poland to Russia and their meeting with the Grand Duke and subsequent experiences fighting with the cossacks against the Germans and Austrians. A typical all-American boy's tale of super patriotism and bravery so characteristic of the juvenile novels of this period and this series.

j34B Higgins, Aileen Cleveland. *A Little Princess of the Stars and Stripes.* Philadelphia: Penn. Pub. Co., 1915. 320p.

Not seen.

j35 Kay, Ross. *Dodging the North Sea Mines; the Adventures of an American Boy.* New York: Barse & Hopkins, 1915. 249p.

The time is August 1914 and England has been at war for two weeks. Earl Platt has arrived in London and received instructions from his father to go to find his twin brother Leon in France. Earl sees the American ambassador for assistance and is placed on a private yacht for France. But while crossing the channel during rough seas, Earl falls overboard and is left behind in the water where he is later rescued by a British torpedo-boat destroyer. Eventually Earl is put on board a presumably British trawler which later turns out to be a German minelayer in disguise. Earl is locked in the ship's cabin until the boat is forced into Yarmouth harbor. Now he is able to continue his journey to France. When Earl arrives in Paris he is unable to locate his uncle or his brother, but as the book concludes his uncle turns up with the news that Leon has been wounded and is in a hospital near the front lines. A chapter or two in the book offers a detailed discussion of the military operations of Germany up until the time of Earl's visit to Paris.

j36 ―――――. *With Joffre on the Battle Line: The Adventures of an American Boy in the Trenches*. New York: Barse & Hopkins, 1915. 249p.

Relates the continuing improbable adventures of Leon Platt, a 17-year-old American who enlisted in the French Army, and his new friend, Jacques Dineau, a French aviator. Both are caught behind the German lines in Mons, Belgium, as they endeavor to return to their regiment. From the Germans they commandeer at first horses, then a Benz limousine, and finally an airplane to reach their destination near Paris. They continue routing the Germans and finally receive the Medal of Honor from General Joffre for distinguished service and bravery on the field of battle.

j37B Lawton, Wilbur (pseud. of John H. Goldfrap). *The Ocean Wireless Boys and the Naval Code*. New York: Hurst & Co., 1915. 305p.

Not seen.

j38B ―――――. *The Ocean Wireless Boys of the Iceberg Patrol*. New York: Hurst & Co., 1915. 308p.

Not seen.

j39 Maitland, Robert (pseud. of William A. Wolff). *The Boy Scouts at Liège, or Paul Latour's Patriotism.* Akron, Saalfield Pub. Co., 1915. 152p.

The time is just before the invasion of Belgium by the Germans. A troop of Belgian boy scouts are just dispersing from their meeting in Liège. Two of them are the boy heroes of this defense of Liège story. Paul Latour and his close friend, Arthur Waller, are originally from Brussels but are now staying with an uncle in Liège. The two boys accidentally bump into a man on the street who drops a packet of sketches of the Liège fortifications. He turns out to be a German spy and the boys now begin a series of adventures involving secret German siege-gun mountings and arsenals. They eventually are able to turn over their information to the Belgian General Leman, the defender of Liège. The rest of the story describes their many and assorted adventures in the countryside around Liège both behind the German as well as the Belgian lines. Naturally, through their efforts the Germans are delayed sufficiently to allow the French to beef up their forces along the French border.

j40 ———. *The Boy Scouts Before Belgrade, or Dick Warner's Mission.* Akron, Saalfield Pub. Co., 1915. 157p.

Dick Warner, a boy scout from New York and the protagonist of this tale, has just arrived in Hungary to search out Mike Hallo who cheated his mother on the estate left after the death of Dick's father. Dick asks the American consul for permission to stay in Hungary after confronting Hallo in the town of Semlin. Dick's confrontation with the ex-partner of his father results in the attempt of the Hungarian authorities to arrest him. He escapes with the help of a young Serbian nationalist, Stephan Dushan. The story relates the adventures of Dick and Stephan in both Serbia and Hungary after the war breaks out. They are involved in bombing and spy plots against the Austro-Hungarian forces and are eventually successful in abducting Hallo. At one point the two boys fly a captured Austrian plane on a long scouting mission to verify Austrian troop movements. The plot has plenty of close escapes over water in boats, fighting in the streets of Belgrade, its occupation by the Austrians, and the eventual return of the city to the control of the Serbs after the retreat of the Austrians. By the end of the story Dick receives a large sum of money from Hallo and is sent back to America by the Serbs who are grateful for his courage and help in their cause.

J41 ───────. *The Boy Scouts Under the Kaiser, or Karl Adler's Devotion.* Akron, Ohio: Saalfield Pub. Co., 1915. 166p.

This is a surprising juvenile story to be published in America. It decidedly takes a reasonable and humane point of view in support of the German war effort. Karl Adler and his friend and fellow boy scout, Heinrich, from Düsseldorf, are on their long-planned walking tour of the battlefields of the last war in which Germany fought. It is late July of 1914 and the two boys suddenly are caught in France when the war starts. As obvious aliens they are soon threatened with capture and arrest but suddenly are rescued at night by a German zeppelin. They now are carried to the large German naval base on Helgoland where they soon are put to work as wireless operators on a German minelayer that steams off to the coast of England. The ship is torpedoed near the coast and the boys are saved, but by an English boat, and are sent to London as prisoners. They escape on the way and experience a number of the usual exciting and improbable adventures. There are further captures and dramatic escapes and the praise of the German Kaiser for their fearless bravery. Aside from the unique political point of view, this is a typical boy's wartime adventure story of the period.

j42 ───────. *The Boy Scouts with King George; or, Harry Fleming's Ordeal.* Akron, Ohio: Saalfield Pub. Co., 1915. 166p.

Relates the improbable adventures of Harry Fleming, a sixteen-year-old American boy scout, and his English chum, Dick Mercer, as they become motorcycle messengers for the British army in and about London at the outbreak of the war in 1914. A third boy scout, Jack Young, soon joins them as they find themselves caught up in a series of adventures with German spies.

j43 ───────. *The Boy Scouts with the Allies, or, Frank Barnes' Exploit.* Akron, Ohio: Saalfield Pub. Co., 1915. 167p.

The story begins with a brief description of French attitudes toward the Germans since 1870. Frank Barnes and his friend Henri Martin are enthusiastic over the prospect of war, and the two chums decide to go to Henri's home when the mobilization closes their school. Both decide to join the French boy scout troop at Amiens where they soon are engaged as dispatch messengers for the French army. Frank is also used as an air observer on a French aircraft at the front. The Germans soon occupy Amiens and the two heroes are used to carry messages about the city for the Germans but later are able to escape by the Somme River. When they return to the city, General Joffre decorates them both for their bravery. (This is the fourteenth story of the Boy Scout Series and the first tale that deals with World War I. The author makes some effort to introduce some historical background for instructional purposes, which is a rare feature in most of the juvenile stories of this type.)

j44 ———. *The Boy Scouts with the Cossacks; or, Fred Waring's Service*. Akron, Ohio: Saalfield Pub. Co., 1915. 163p.

The story begins at a border station between East Prussia and Russia. Frederick Waring, a young American boy scout, is expelled from Russia by the instigation of his vicious Russian uncle. Fred sets off walking into East Prussia to reach an American consul in Danzig, but some days later is attacked by villagers who think he is their English enemy. Fred is rescued by Boris who turns out to be Fred's cousin from Russia. The Germans detain Boris over the sudden disappearance of Fred; but when Fred attempts to rescue Boris, both are discovered and arrested. Just as Fred is to be executed the cossacks raid the Germans and save both boys. The story now describes the adventures of the two behind the German lines as they spy on troop movements and inform the cossacks of what they have seen. This is a typical juvenile adventure tale of close calls and courageous actions in the tradition of the Boy Scouts.

j45 Marlow, Ralph. *The Big Five Motorcycle Boys at the Front; or, Carrying Dispatches Through Belgium*. New York: A.L. Burt, 1915. 283p.

The five boys, Hanky Panky, Josh, Rooster, Elmer, and Rod, have come to Europe on business for a millionaire friend. Afterwards, they go on a vacation tour and are in Belgium east of Brussels near the German border when the war begins. Their goal is to reach Brussels, and this story is an account of their adventures in so doing. They observe the defense preparations in the Belgian countryside and are stopped by a group of Belgians as spies but are finally released by the mayor of the local village who speaks English. They experience a narrow escape from German cavalry, make friends with a Belgian family, witness a zeppelin bombing of roads and bridges, and volunteer to take an exhausted dispatch rider and his vital messages to Brussels. They finally arrive in the capital city where they have an interview with King Albert. A run-of-the-mill juvenile war story for boys.

j46 ———. *The Big Five Motorcycle Boys Under Fire; or, With the Allies in the War Zone.* New York: A.L. Burt, 1915. 256p.

The boys are still in Brussels waiting for one of the cycles to be repaired and expecting the Germans to attack the city at any time. When the cycle is ready, some Belgian soldiers nearly insist on expropriating it for the war effort. But the boys are finally able to keep the machine when a note from King Albert is presented. They watch the German troops enter the city in a huge almost endless procession before they slip away and head for Antwerp. They encounter many refugees fleeing from the invading enemy. The boys ford streams and rivers past bombed bridges while being chased by German cavalry. They even assist a wounded enemy soldier on their dash through the countryside to Antwerp. A typical juvenile war-series formula story written for boys and girls of the period.

j47 Payson, Howard (pseud. of John Henry Goldfrap). *The Boy Scouts on Belgian Battlefields.* New York: Hurst & Co., 1915. 312p.

Recounts the adventures of three American boy scouts in their search for a map of the location of a gold mine carried unknowingly by a German agent, a former resident of the United States. The search carries the boy scouts through villages destroyed by Germans and onto battle-fields where they help to bandage the wounded. The accomplishment of their mission is related in the next volume of the series, *The Boy Scouts with the Allies in France* ... (item j48).

j48 ———. *The Boy Scouts with the Allies in France; Raiding Uhlans, Spies, and Air-raids in War-wrecked France.* New York: Hurst & Co., 1915. 309p.

Not seen.

j49 Porter, Horace (pseud. of Horace Porter Biddle De Hart). *Our Young Aeroplane Scouts in France and Belgium; or,*

Saving the Fortune of the Trouvilles. New York: A.L. Burt, 1915. 247p.

The first of a twelve-volume juvenile series of war stories that appear to be written with tongue in cheek and in a breezy somewhat flippant style which at times seems a parody of all the standard juvenile war novels of the period. Not all of the series titles exhibit to the same degree the potpourri of clichés (see Introduction for examples). The two boy heroes are Billy Barry from Maine and Henri Trouville from France, close chums and experienced pilots. The boys are in Texas working in an airplane factory when the war begins and Henri is called home to protect the family château and its cache of gold and jewels. They both immediately leave for Dover and then for the coast of France in a seaplane. Attacked by a zeppelin, they run out of gas but manage to be dragged to the coast by a typically impossible hitch on a zeppelin anchor rope. Thus begins a number of typical and almost zany juvenile adventures across the battlefields of Belgium, France, and Germany. There are the standard plot elements ranging from the mission to save the valuables of the Trouvilles, spies, secret agents, armoured cars, narrow escapes on the ground and in the air, to the usual heroic and daring actions of the boy heroes who are invincible. This first story has a little of every war experience--air, trench, naval, and submarine--with the usual elbow-rubbing with the high and mighty, such as Generals Joffre and French. The tale ends with Billy and Henri in Germany with the devious master German spy, Herr Roque. A burlesque.

j50 ———. *Our Young Aeroplane Scouts in Germany; or, Winning the Iron Cross*. New York: A.L. Burt, 1915. 255p.

Henri and Billy, the boy heroes, are now in the service of the Germans. They are engaged to fly a military biplane over the great parade grounds in Hamburg as a demonstration of their incredible flying ability. But suddenly Germany's master spy, the fantastic Herr Roque, sends for them to come to his home to discuss another mission. Herr Roque is a master of disguise and reveals his vast storeroom of uniforms of all nations. The boys have no choice but to agree to his proposals and are disguised as students and taken on board a small steamer to Cuxhaven. During a bombing attack they take off in a seaplane with Roque for Helgoland where they spend

Christmas night. Roque is in a continual battle of wits
with the French super-secret agent, Ardelle. The action
rapidly switches from one place to another in almost
space-age speed. The action flashes off to Warsaw,
Przemysl, and points east. They are captured by the cossacks, rescued by Roque and his crew, and then go off to
the Russian lines at Lupkow and in and out of Russian-
held territory. This juvenile series is almost a parody,
filled with flippant, quasi-humorous, rapid-fire dialogue
and with a plot so packed with action that there is scarcely any connection with reality. No other series of juvenile stories quite compares with these chatty adventure-
mysteries.

j51 ———. *Our Young Aeroplane Scouts in Russia; or, Lost on the Frozen Steppes.* New York: A.L. Burt, 1915. 252p.

Billy and Henri arrive in Warsaw and are interviewed by
their aviation chief. The next mission is to observe the
German army movements nearby. They become involved in
more mysterious goings on with a silversmith while the
master spy Roque flits in and out of the narrative and a
huge cossack and his comrades from Petrograd persist in
their search for the two boys who are suspected by the
Russians of being spies. More zany adventures, a tracking
of spies with dogs toward Siberia, followed by their continued wild adventures across the Russian landscape with
brief interludes to look in on a battle here or there.
The story concludes as the two heroes receive the word
to travel to Turkey.

j52 ———. *Our Young Aeroplane Scouts in Turkey; or, Bringing the Light to Yusef.* New York: A.L. Burt, 1915. 256p.

Henri and Billy crash land in the desert. After a
sandstorm they are miraculously rescued by airplane and
taken to a cave by Yusef and learn of the Turkish plot
to start a holy war. In order to escape, the two boys
pretend they will fly for pay in the Turkish interests.
This leads to a series of adventures centering on their
relationship with the mysterious dual personality of
Yusef. All during the plot they are either the prisoners
of Yusef or he is theirs in a series of impossible escapades ranging from Cairo to Algiers and back to Cairo.
At one point the two boys are forced by the treacherous
Yusef to land on the head of the Sphinx. Billy and Henri
take Yusef back to Cairo, with a happy resolution to the
story. The dialogue continues in its flippant vein with

Juvenile Novels 335

rapid-fire plot action bearing little or no resemblance to reality, human nature, the Middle East, or the war. An impossible tale that qualifies as fantasy. More than any of the other juvenile series, this one truly qualifies as incredible.

j53 Ralphson, George Harvey. *Boy Scouts in Belgium; or,* (title page and running title) *Imperiled in a Trap* front cover: *Under Fire in Flanders*). Chicago: M.A. Donohue, 1915(?). 308p.

Almost qualifies as a fantasy-spy-adventure story for preadolescents. Harry, Jack, Jimmy, and Ned are completing their construction of an airplane they call the Grey Eagle. They are asked to trail a man who is suspected of stealing the construction plans of the Panama Canal. This spy they call the Rat. They follow him by steamer to France with their aircraft aboard. Once in Le Havre the plane is put together, and the four engage in a series of fantastic adventures chasing the Rat across France to Paris, Flanders, and then over the trenches where Ned is captured as a German spy. Then all four are captured by the Germans, along with the Rat, and imprisoned in a castle with secret tunnels, etc. The plans the Rat has carried turn out to be the harbor plans of Colon. The mission completed, the four boys return to the U.S. The narrative is strong on scout principles, but there is little or no connection with the war in this improbable juvenile story.

j54 ———. *Boy Scouts in the North Sea; or, "Mystery of U-13."* Chicago: M.A. Donohue, 1915. 252p. (Subtitle varies: in some printings it is worded *The Mystery of a Sub.*)

A juvenile wartime adventure tale of impossible incidents and incredible fantasy. Four American boy scouts, Ned, Jimmy, Jack, and Harry, are sent from Germany to a neutral port in Holland to return home to the U.S. The action takes place in the early days of the war when the U.S. is strictly neutral. A mysterious U-13 packet is discovered in the boys' baggage on the train. The package just as mysteriously disappears during the baggage inspection by border guards. The boys attempt to find any possible way to get passage home but are foiled by a mysterious man called Mackinder who periodically turns up throughout the story. Their ship is sunk by a storm and Frank, a fifth scout, joins them. Interned in Helgoland they escape in a German submarine with more adventures,

on the surface and underwater, when they encounter the
original U-13. This leads to an invitation to go underwater
treasure hunting with another Mackinder, but they
are eventually apprehended by a British warship and are
taken back to England for passage to the U.S. Of course,
all the mysteries are solved in the process.

j55 Sayler, H.L. (pseud. of Delysle F. Cass). *The Airship
Boys in the Great War; or, The Rescue of Bob Russell*.
Chicago: Reilly & Britton, 1915. 249p.

Another typical boys' series story with melodramatic
plot, heroic but improbable action, and wooden characterization.
This is the eighth and final story in this
series and the only one dealing with the war. Allan and
Ned (both under twenty-one) are the original Airship Boys.
Their good friend Bob Russell has been imprisoned as a
spy by the Germans although he is there as an American
newspaper reporter. In spite of the efforts of German
spies and their devious tricks, the boys manage to leave
America in their big airship, the *Ocean Flyer*, on their
rescue mission to Germany. Since the U.S. has not yet
entered the war, the time is probably about 1915. The
boys fly over Paris and then eventually to the town of
Mühlbrück where Bob is soon to be shot. Naturally, the
trip is filled with plenty of action-filled adventures
both on the ground and in the air. Bob is rescued and
they all take off to the east where they soon experience
a number of the more notable war incidents such as a
village massacre by the cossacks in East Prussia. They
soon turn up in Vienna on a humanitarian mission with the
wounded Lieutenant Racoszky. After an interesting description
of that wartime city, they foil an assassination
plot against the venerable Emperor Franz Joseph, reunite
Lieutenant Racoszky with his wife and decide to return
to America. But a desperate battle with German zeppelins
so damages the *Flyer* that they are forced to abandon it
over the ocean near England. They are picked up by an
English liner and head back to New York for, no doubt,
many more exciting adventures.

j56 Shaler, Robert. *Boy Scouts of the Field Hospital*. New
York: Hurst & Co., 1915.

Not seen.

* Sherman, V.T. *Boy Scouts with Joffre; or, In the Trenches
in Belgium*. Chicago: M.A. Donohue, 1915. 308p.

A reprint with a different author and title of *Boy Scouts*

in Belgium; or, Under Fire in Flanders by George H. Ralphson (item j53).

* ———. Scouting the Balkans in a Motor Boat; or, An Escape from the Dardanelles. Chicago: M.A. Donohue, 1915. 258p.

A reprint with a different author and title of the original story The Motorboat Boys Down the Danube; or, Caught in the Whirlpool of War by Louis Arundel (item j10).

* ———. The War Zone of the Kaiser; or, Boy Scouts in the North Sea. Chicago: M.A. Donohue, 1915.

A reprint with a different author and title of Boy Scouts in the North Sea; or, "Mystery of U-13" by George H. Ralphson (item j54).

j57 Strang, Herbert (pseud.). Fighting with French; a Tale of the New Army. London: H. Frowde; Hodder & Stoughton, 1915. 327p.

Not seen.

j58 ———. Frank Forester; a Story of the Dardanelles. London: H. Frowde; Hodder & Stoughton, 1915. 296p.

Not seen.

j59 Stuart, Gordon (pseud. of George Neser Madison). The Boy Scouts of the Air in Belgium. Chicago: Reilly & Britton, 1915. 224p.

Four young boy scouts from Ohio accompany their Professor Deane on a tour of Europe. The good professor is primarily interested in antiquities and artistic artifacts, and the scouts have plenty of time to themselves. The story begins when the four and their young guide Hans are at a refugee railroad station waiting for the last train to leave town. The Germans are nearly on the outskirts but since the professor does not show up, they decide to stay and wait for him. He is arrested as a spy and the boys hide in a handy nearby basement where they meet a mysterious boy called Loomp. Loomp arranges for them all to escape on a dirigible that night. Next follows a series of typical adventures during which they play hide and seek with the German troops over the Belgian countryside. At one point the boys run into a group of English scouts attached to a nearby British army outpost and soon are in the safety of the Allied lines. One of the scouts and Loomp decide to return to German territory to find the professor and regain Loomp's inheritance which a devious man has retained. This is primarily an adventure tale for preadolescents. A sketchy plot mainly based on an escape theme.

j60 Webster, Frank V. (pseud.; Stratemeyer Syndicate). *Two Boys of the Battleship; or, For the Honor of Uncle Sam.* New York: Cupples & Leon, 1915. 224p.

Not seen.

j61 Westerman, Percy Francis. *The Dispatch-Riders.* London: Blackie & Son, 1915. 288p.

Not seen.

j62A ————. *Sub of the R.N.R.: Story of the Great War.* London: S.W. Partridge, 1915. 384p. [Title in U.S.: *Sub of the Royal Navy; A Story of the Great War.* New York: Hubbell-Leavens Co., 1916. 384p.]

Not seen.

j63 Zerbe, James Slough. *Trench-mates in France: Adventures of Two Boys in the Great War.* New York: Harper & Brothers, 1915. 303p.

Another juvenile tale which follows in some detail the French troop movements during the first few months of the war, but exhibits only a very minor concern with creating a story. The book seems mainly a vehicle for a description of the technical side of war activity. Probably the main purpose is to provide a fairly accurate view of modern warfare for boys and girls. This it seems to do.

1916

j64B Appleton, Victor (pseud.; Stratemeyer Syndicate). *The Motion Picture Chums' War Spectacle; or, The Film that Won the Prize.* New York: Grosset & Dunlap, 1916. 224p.

Not seen.

j65 Baldwin, May. *Irene to the Rescue; the Story of an English Girl's Fight for the Right.* London & Edinburgh: W. & R. Chambers, 1916. 294p.

The plot is about a French family living in an old château near the border. One member of the family, now dead for some years before the story begins, had married a German woman. When the war breaks out and the château and the village are taken by the Germans, they are all considered spies and are put into prison. The heroine is Irene Mathers, an English girl, who believes completely in the innocence of her family and goes to Boulogne determined to save them. She has plenty of trials and unusual adventures, but her guts and considerable brass help her to persevere until she is finally successful. One contemporary reviewer complained that the author's conception of Irene displayed extremely bad manners and was hardly a model for young girls. The contrary seems to be the case.

j66AE Bennett, Rolf. *Captain Calamity.* London: Hodder & Stoughton, 1916. 254p.

Not seen.

j67A ———. *Commander Lawless, V.C.; Being the Further Adventures of Frank H. Lawless, Until Recently a Lieutenant in His Majesty's Navy.* London: Hodder & Stoughton, 1916. 175p.

Not seen.

j68A Bevan, Tom. *With Haig at the Front; a Story of the Great Fight.* London & Glasgow: Collins' Clear-type Press, 1916. 224p.

Not seen.

* Blaine, John (pseud.). *The Boy Scouts in England.* Akron, Ohio: Saalfield Pub. Co., 1916.

A reprint with a different author and title of *The Boy Scouts with King George* ... by Robert Maitland (item j42).

* ———. *The Boy Scouts in Europe.* Akron, Ohio: Saalfield Pub. 1916.

A reprint with a different author and title of *The Boy Scouts in Front of Warsaw* ... by George Durston (item j77).

*   ———. *The Boy Scouts in France.* Akron, Ohio: Saalfield Pub. 1916.

A reissue with a different author and title of *The Boy Scouts with the Allies* ... by Robert Maitland (item j43).

*   ———. *The Boy Scouts in Germany.* Akron, Ohio: Saalfield Pub. Co., 1916.

A reissue with a different author and title of *The Boy Scouts Under the Kaiser* ... by Robert Maitland (item j41).

*   ———. *The Boy Scouts in Italy.* Akron, Ohio: Saalfield Pub. Co., 1916. 226p.

A reprint with a different author and title of *The Boy Scouts' Test* ... by George Durston (item j78).

*   ———. *The Boy Scouts in Russia.* Akron, Ohio: Saalfield Pub. Co., 1916. 240p.

A reissue with a different author and title of *The Boy Scouts with the Cossacks* ... by Robert Maitland (item j44).

*   ———. *The Boy Scouts in Servia.* Akron, Ohio: Saalfield Pub. Co., 1916.

A reprint with a different author and title of *The Boy Scouts Before Belgrade* ... by Robert Maitland (item j40).

*   ———. *The Boy Scouts in the Netherlands.* Akron, Ohio: Saalfield Pub. Co., 1916.

A reprint with a different author and title of *The Boy Scouts at Liège* ... by Robert Maitland (item j39).

*   ———. *The Boy Scouts in Turkey.* Akron, Ohio: Saalfield Pub. Co., 1916.

A reprint with a different author and title of *The Boy Scouts Under the Red Cross* ... by George Durston (item j79).

j69   Brereton, Frederick Sadleir. *At Grips with the Turk; a Story of the Dardenelles Campaign.* London: Blackie & Son, 1916. 352p.

Not seen.

j70 ———. *With Joffre at Verdun; a Story of the Western Front.* London: Blackie & Son, 1916. 288p.

Not seen.

j71 ———. *With Our Russian Allies.* London: Blackie & Son, 1916. 376p.

Not seen.

j72 Carter, Herbert (pseud. of St. George Rathborne). *The Boy Scouts on War Trails in Belgium; or, Caught Between Hostile Armies.* New York: A.L. Burt, 1916. 256p.

Not seen.

* Cobb, Frank (pseud.). *Hunting Down the Spy.* Akron, Ohio: Saalfield Pub. Co., 1916.

A reprint with different author and title of *The Boy Scouts' Test* ... by George Durston (item j78).

* ———. *Winning the War Cross.* Akron, Ohio: Saalfield Pub. Co., 1916.

A reprint with different author and title of *The Boy Scouts with the Cossacks* ... by Robert Maitland (item j44).

j73 Copplestone, Bennet (pseud. of Frederick Harcourt Kitchin). *Jitny and the Boys.* London: Smith, Elder, 1916. 313p; New York: E.P. Dutton & Co., 1916. 305p.

It is 1913 and three boys are with their car on the Isle of Wight. They eventually end up with the capture of a German spy with the aid of their car, the jitny. It is the second part of this juvenile story which describes the mobilization, the camps, and the effects of the war on English life in rather faithful terms. There is no particular plot as such, and the humor is of a typical English variety. The main impact in this slight effort is the sense of duty among the English youth when the war begins.

j74 Crockett, Sherman. *Two American Boys in the French War Trenches.* New York: Hurst & Co., 1916. 314p.

In this second title of the Great War Series Amos and Jack continue their search for Amos' brother Frank, the noted air ace. The two boys are now with Joffre and the French forces. For plot purposes they have a number of special letters of introduction from retired Colonel Turner, Amos' father, which enables the fearless pair to obtain permission to go anywhere in the war zones with the complete cooperation and assistance of the Allied military. The quest for Frank brings the two boys in close contact with many pilots and Allied troops in the trenches and on the battlefields. Plenty of war adventures of all kinds cover most of the representative activities of the Allied war effort, especially trench warfare. The two boys, of course, perform their patriotic duties whenever the occasion demands, and that is fairly often. For example, they detect some German spies preparing to blow up a vital bridge of the Allies. They inform a nearby officer of their suspicions, help track the suspects, and save the bridge for the Allies. This and similar heroics are characteristic elements in most of these juvenile series for boys, e.g., Durston, Ralphson, Maitland.

j75 ———. *Two American Boys with the Dardanelles Battle Fleet.* New York: Hurst & Co., 1916. 314p.

The third story in the Two American Boys Series which follows the adventures of Amos Turner and his cousin, Jack Maxfield, in the search across European battlefields for Frank, the brother of Amos. The novel is a combination of history lesson and "gee whiz" juvenile adventure story for boys. At first the boys are on board a large Greek gunboat runner for the Turks. They soon and with typical derring-do manage to commandeer the craft and turn it over to the local British naval task force. For their extraordinary exploit they are taken to the vice admiral on his battleship, the *Thunderer*, and commended. They are then invited to stay aboard temporarily while the British bombard the Turkish outposts along the shores of the straits. After the battle they are assisted ashore in their project to locate a fabulous local flyer believed to be the long-sought-for Frank. In the process they witness a ferocious and bloody battle between the Turks and the Allied territorial troops in the invasion of Gallipoli. They ultimately are led by a Greek guide in the dead of night through the enemy lines to the Allied position where they finally locate the long lost brother, Frank. The story concludes with all three returning to the States to see the father, but with Frank promising to return soon to further aid the war effort.

j76 Drake, Robert L. (pseud. of Clair Wallace Hayes). *The Boy Allies in the Baltic; or, Through Fields of Ice to Aid the Czar*. New York: A.L. Burt, 1916. 252p.

Jack and Frank accompanied by Lord Hastings travel by the British sub D-17 to Helgoland, the strong German fortress, in order to sneak into the heavily guarded harbor and gather intelligence information. The war at this time is very much at a stalemate. The three heroes slip ashore at night, encounter the usual close calls and adventures before escaping back to their sub. Naturally, on the way out of the harbor they torpedo a German battleship before slipping through the Kiel Canal and the icy Baltic to Petrograd. Here they inform the Czar that he has a traitor among his closest advisors. Of course, Jack and Frank volunteer to stay to help trap the infamous Count Blowinski. The plot gets even more involved at this point, and both boys end up being wounded and Jack personally saves the Czar again when the Count attacks with a knife. The Count is shot, everything comes out well (as is typical), the Czar commends the boys, and Lord Hastings takes them back to good old England in the D-17.

j77 Durston, George (pseud. of Georgia Roberts Durston). *The Boy Scouts in Front of Warsaw; or, In the Wake of War*. Akron, Ohio: Saalfield Pub. Co., 1916. 159p.

Begins with a description of the defeated city under the impact of the German occupation: the refugees, the devastation, the circumstances of Poland as a country since 1770, and the conditions of life in Warsaw. The story tends to have a more complex plot and characterization than is the typical case in most juvenile novels such as this. The chief characters are the Morris family from America who are in Warsaw because the father, a professor, has received a three-year vacation to write a history of the city. Jack and Warren are the sons and Evelyn and Elinor are the daughters; the mother has been dead some time. Warren becomes close friends of the young boy Ivan, a Polish prince. They are in Warsaw when the Germans occupy the city and are soon arrested as spies because of the professor's book manuscript and notebooks. Meanwhile Elinor and a mysterious little girl named Rika (actually the daughter of a Polish princess) are kidnapped by a group of unscrupulous low-life gypsy types who intend to make beggars of the two children as a source of income. Warren and Ivan escape arrest and search for the two girls. The rest of the book details the adventures of the family and their escape from the Germans and eventual discovery of the missing children in Lodz through the miraculous assistance of Princess Olga and her family. The story has its didactic moments on the virtues of scouting, but for the most part the scouting angle is a minor element only in a family adventure tale in wartime.

j78 ———. *The Boy Scouts' Test; or, A Son of Italy*. Akron, Ohio: Saalfield Pub. Co., 1916. 152p.

A juvenile spy-adventure story placed in Italy behind the lines. Pietro Folea, a young Italian boy scout, accidentally encounters a spy for the Austrians when he finds a case of cigarettes in which there are notes on Italian military defenses. The spy turns out to be the infamous Bellini. Since Pietro is one of the few who can identify Bellini, the local Italian general asks him secretly to help in tracking the spy down before the Italian troops move up to the Austrian lines. Ultimately Pietro is the hero and Bellini is captured, although the boy is seriously wounded. Pietro is sent to a hospital where the king and queen of Italy commend him for his bravery and give Pietro an appointment to the King's guardsmen. Pietro's bravery and resourcefulness are, of course, correlated with his scout training.

j79 ———. *The Boy Scouts Under the Red Cross; or, Back of the Fighting Line*. Akron, Ohio: Saalfield Pub. Co., 1916. 164p.

News of the coming of the war reaches the students at a military school in New York. There is a great deal of excitement and several wish to go home. At the same time Zaidos, a young Greek student and the hero of this tale, receives word from home that his father is dying. He immediately departs, but when he arrives home he is impressed into the Greek army before he can see his sick father. However, he briefly goes A.W.O.L. at night in order to see his father. There he also meets his cousin Velo who turns out to be a villainous and dangerous rival for his inheritance. The rest of the story relates the experiences of Zaidos and Velo as recruits in the Greek army. The two are sent off as stokers in the engine room of a Greek transport ship which is soon torpedoed and sinks. But the two jump off in time to survive by swimming away while at the same time a sea battle surrounds them. They are later picked up by an English hospital ship. Velo repeatedly plots to kill Zaidos (who has had boy scout training in America) but never is successful. They both decide to join the Red Cross, and end up in the trenches of France. Eventually Velo screws up his courage and shoots Zaidos during a bombardment, but Velo is mortally wounded by a shell fragment. Zaidos is only stunned, and recovers. He now decides to become a doctor and travels to England with his new friends and eventually back to America to school, after arranging for a monthly donation from his father's estate to the field hospital in France.

* Fiske, James (pseud.). *Shelled by an Unseen Foe*. Akron, Ohio: Saalfield Pub. Co., 1916(?). 246p.

The ninth story in the author's so-called World's War Series. The story is identical to *The Boy Scouts Under the Red Cross* by George Durston (item j79).

j80 Hamilton, Frederick Spencer. *Nine Holiday Adventures of Mr. P.J. Davenant in the Year 1915*. London: George Newnes, 1916. 256p.

The first four parts comprise the author's previous novel, *The Holiday Adventures of Mr. P.J. Davenant* (item j28). This title continues the exploits of P.J. in various counties of England as he assists Cyril Ambrose of Scotland Yard to expose German espionage and sabotage in England during World War I. A typical mystery story for boys.

j81 Hancock, Harrie. *At the Defense of Pittsburgh; or, The Struggle to Save America's "Fighting Steel" Supply*. Philadelphia: Henry Altemus Co., 1916. 255p.

One of a series of novels dealing with the invasion of the United States by Germans in the World War I decade. Against well-trained German regulars, the Gridley High School cadet cavalry join the 38th Battalion to repulse the German advance and save Pittsburgh, America's steel capital. The story ends with the brave Americans still endeavoring to withstand the superior German forces.

j82 ─────. *In the Battle for New York: or, Uncle Sam's Boys in the Desperate Struggle for the Metropolis*. Philadelphia: Henry Altemus Co., 1916. 256p.

Traces the experiences of Captain Dick Prescott and Cadet Captain Bert Howard as the American forces rally to defend New York City against the German advance. The country is rapidly gearing up for the war effort. Training camps are set up along the Canadian and Mexican borders and munitions factories rebuilt in the interior of the country. A large number of U.S. troops are thrown into the trench fortifications near Yonkers as frantic preparations are made to resist the invaders on the ground and in the air. The American forces are in nearly continuous retreat. West Point is razed by the enemy. Philadelphia is captured and the Germans relentlessly invade New York City as the American Army withdraws from the now hopeless defense of the great city. The Germans demand billions of dollars in war reparations as the price of peace. The American Army regroups near Pittsburgh in what is termed as a last stand against the German foe, as the second volume in the Conquest of the United States Series ends.

j83 ———. *The Invasion of the United States; or, Uncle Sam's Boys at the Capture of Boston*. Philadelphia: Henry Altemus Co., 1916. 256p.

This is the first volume of the Conquest of the United States Series. It is quite clear from reading the four titles in the series that it is the intention of the author to alert the country to the dangers of the European war and the lack of preparedness of America. Although these four novels are juvenile stories to all intents and purposes, it is likely that they may also have had some adult appeal because of the subject matter and the developing anti-German hysteria in the country. The plot features Lieutenant Dick Prescott and his buddy, Cade Bert Howard, and their chums as they help to prepare against the probable invasion of the Massachusetts coast by the Germans. A huge enemy armada of warships and troop transports is massing just off the coast. American ground forces are actively preparing to resist the invasion by trench and fortification construction, military training, air observation sorties, etc. The American navy is drastically outnumbered by the German fleet and suffers a humiliating defeat after a ferocious sea battle. The terrible news sweeps the country as the enemy bombards the coastal areas and inflicts heavy damages. The story emphasizes that the Americans have a severe problem due to a lack of trained soldiers as a result of inadequate funding of the military and the general lack of preparedness of the country. Boston is captured and the Germans execute a number of bankers when the U.S. president

Juvenile Novels

refuses to exchange gold for their release. The Germans continue their relentless advance in the Northeast. The narrative is filled with plenty of blood and guts, with the cavalry charges and battle scenes obviously modeled on the war in France. The Americans suffer huge losses of men. Bert is captured and taken prisoner as the U.S. forces retreat, but he is exchanged for German prisoners of war and safely rejoins his chums as the story concludes on a pessimistic note.

j84 ———. *Making the Last Stand for Old Glory; or, Uncle Sam's Boys in the Last Frantic Drive*. Philadelphia: Henry Altemus Co., 1916. 256p.

The time is late January of 1921. The United States has been at war with Germany since the summer of 1920 and the Germans have invaded all of the northeastern states. The Americans are making a last-ditch stand about 25 miles from Pittsburgh. Cadet Captain Bert Howard and Lieutenant colonel Dick Prescott serve as the chief protagonists in this imaginary war and invasion of the U.S. modeled on the campaigns in France during World War I. Dick and Bert are transferred south to military headquarters at New Orleans where they are given a secret mission by their old chum and naval officer, Dave Darrin. This is a special strategy to destroy the German naval blockade of the eastern coast by a submarine offensive. The German ships are smashed and the tide begins to turn in favor of the U.S. The boys return to the Pittsburgh campaign and there is the usual trench warfare adventures involving scouting, air observation flights, cavalry attacks, bombardments, and German tanks. The ground war is finally turned in favor of the Americans when the food supply of the Germans is cut off and their army is surrounded. Brazilian troops join the Americans as a goodwill gesture from south of the border. A truce is attempted and although unsuccessful scarcely a few days pass before the German armies begin to surrender. A peace treaty is signed in June of 1921, on American terms.

j85 Hayes, Clair Wallace. *The Boy Allies in Great Peril; or, With the Italian Army in the Alps*. New York: A.L. Burt, 1916. 256p.

After their dangerous and exciting adventures on the continent fighting the Germans, Chester Crawford and Hal Paine are sent home by their parents. They stop off in Rome on their way when Italy declares war on Austria. As

they observe a demonstration in the streets, they are
suddenly involved in their next hair-raising caper by
being accused of being spies and arrested by Italian
troops. This leads to their Austrian spy hunt in Rome
and Venice. Chester, however, is captured by the Austrian
ambassador and his men and taken by train toward Trieste
where he is able finally to escape. He returns to Italy
to join his brother and their friends with the Italian
troops in the Alps in the campaign against the Austrians.
But things go badly and the two heroes and their friends
avoid Austrian capture only by a daring escape in one of
the enemy's aircraft.

j86 ―――――. *The Boy Allies ... in the Balkan Campaign; or, The Struggle to Save a Nation.* New York: A.L. Burt, 1916. 249p.

Hal and Chester with their friends have just escaped
from the Austrian troops in the Alps by flying a captured
airship across Austria toward the Balkans. They land in
Montenegro and soon are involved in their usual improbable
adventures with the Montenegrins and their King Nicholas
as they encounter and battle Austrian troops. They continue their hazardous journey through the other Balkan
countries with many wondrous and exciting experiences
until they reach at last the safety of the Greek frontier.

j87 Kay, Ross. *Fighting in France.* New York: Barse & Hopkins, 1916. 243p.

The continuation of the story of Leon and Earl Platt,
two American twin boys who have enlisted in the French
Army, and their friend Jacques Dineau, a French pilot.
All of these individuals are now attached to the infantry
and fight in the trenches where they continue to perform
their daring feats against the Germans.

j88B Lawton, Wilbur (pseud. of John Henry Goldfrap). *The Ocean Wireless Boys on the Pacific.* New York: Hurst & Co., 1916. 301p.

Not seen.

j89 Lee, Albert. *At His Country's Call: A Tale of the Great War.* London: Morgan & Scott, 1916. 343p.

A story of boy scout Maurice Millard of England who,
because of his service as a scout, was sent to the front

Juvenile Novels

to do first-aid work. He performs feats of bravery: rescuing his major from certain death, delivering messages deep in German-held territory, capturing a spy, and, when captured by the Germans, commandeering a German aircraft and flying back behind the British lines--after dropping the plane's bombs on German military facilities.

j90 Leighton, Robert. *Dreadnoughts of the Dogger; a Story of the War on the North Sea.* London: Ward, Lock & Co., 1916. 304p.

Not seen; NYPL.

j91 Marlow, Ralph. *The Big Five Motorcycle Boys on the Battle Line; or, With the Allies in France.* New York: A.L. Burt, 1916. 251p.

Two of the boys leave for home to visit the mother of one who has entered a hospital. The other three, Josh, Hanky Panky, and Rod, decide to continue their original travel plan and ride to Ostend and eventually Boulogne before leaving for home. But before they leave Antwerp and all its preparations for the war, they take pity on a distressed Belgian woman who must find her soldier husband André at the front lines in France and have him sign his inheritance papers. The boys immediately ride off to Dunkirk and Calais and head toward the great battle developing before Paris. Their chivalrous mission takes them through much of wartime France with a number of the usual kinds of experiences--close calls with the German cavalry and a shoot-out with some German troops, arrest as spies by French soldiers, a visit to a field hospital, and a chance to observe the battle for the Marne. They finally locate the wounded André, and he is able to sign his inheritance papers under the guidance of the local French general. Successful in their latest humanitarian mission, the three boys now depart for Paris and presumably the nearest French port and home.

j92 Moore, Henry Charles. *Under Jellicoe's Command; a Story of the North Sea.* London & Glasgow: Collins' Clear-type Press, 1916. 224p.

Not seen.

j93 Porter, Horace (pseud. of Horace Porter Biddle De Hart). *Our Young Aeroplane Scouts in England; or, Twin Stars*

in the London Sky Patrol. New York: A.L. Burt, 1916.
245p.

The airplane scouts Billy and Henri are now in England
under the sponsorship of Sir Charles as volunteers for
service in the Royal Flying Corps. A terrific zeppelin
bombing run occurs over London, and they take part in a
post-bombing survey of the city. They also become involved in a number of their typical adventure escapades
both in the air and on the ground, and on English and
European soil. The secret French master agent, Ardelle
Anglin, suddenly turns up again and encourages the two
to assist in tracking the chief secret agent of Germany,
the clever Herr Roque. There is the usual hunt for the
spy in London, followed by a seaplane trip to Dover
Castle, then a quick dash over the North Sea coast where
they spot a German sub. They now become thoroughly en-
meshed in spy activities in England for the Royal Air
Corps and Scotland Yard. The plot as usual is a series
of to-and-from dashes about England by car, train, and
plane. Roque takes them prisoner in a high apartment
building in London but they soon escape and team up with
two other airplane colleagues to destroy a captive balloon
behind German lines in France. There are the usual dogfights and then a special intelligence mission by cart to
Lille to locate the spy Ardelle. They slip out of Lille
in a nearly invisible French aeroplane made of aluminum
and transparent covering. Further adventures involve the
strafing and bombing of a German supply train, then off
to London and Paris and a narrow escape from disaster in
a passenger-train compartment before their safe arrival
in London. See the annotation for *Our Young Aeroplane
Scouts in Germany* ... for additional comment on this
series (item j50).

j94 ———. *Our Young Aeroplane Scouts in Italy; or, Flying
with the War Eagles of the Alps*. New York: A.L. Burt,
1916. 232p.

The Austrians are bombing the lovely city of Venice.
Billy and Henri are now in Venice to offer their ace
flying talents on behalf of the Italians. They immediately take off for the front at Gorizia, flying convoy
for a slow-moving dirigible. They see the appalling
sight of trench warfare and the heaps of Italian dead.
The boys now leave Trieste but are soon forced down on
the precipitous slope of a mountain by Austrian aviators.
They escape certain capture by literally climbing by

their fingers and toes over the gorge wall into a fissure which turns out to be a cave. They now encounter Antonio, a Tyrolean man of the mountains and free spirit who takes them back by foot and skis to the Italian lines. They now dash here and there; into the walled city of Cattaro in Montenegro, scouting for a U-boat, searching at the front for Antonio by horseback, capturing two Austrian pilots, having a near-disastrous car accident in a mountain river, etc. Flying off to San Pietro they finally locate Antonio who introduces them to the master who gives them each protective rings. There are more special missions--to Lyons by air, and as they return by steamer to Rome they are stopped by a British cruiser and learn that they are wanted in England for a special airplane construction project. They bid adieu to their Italian campaign, and thus conclude another fantastic, frenetic adventure.

j95   Ralphson, George Harvey. *Boy Scouts Under the Kaiser; or, The Uhlans in Peril*. Chicago: M.A. Donohue, 1916. 256p.

The sequel to *Boy Scouts with the Cossacks* ... (item j96). The four scouts are in Peremyshl when the Germans occupy that Russian-held Polish city. Jimmy is forced to enlist in the German uhlans (cavalry) while his friends escape into a rat-infested underground chamber where they are led to safety by a friendly stranger who also happens to be a scout. This is a crazy plot of improbable adventures in which one or more of the boys is either escaping or a prisoner of the Germans. Jimmy meets the Kaiser and explains his circumstances, but the Kaiser takes him on the German troop train leaving for the west. The others, Jack, Harry, Ned, and David, have their own zany experiences in and out of the Grey Eagle airplane in outwitting the Germans and locating Jimmy. Jimmy saves the Kaiser from a shell, but is imprisoned for the trouble anyway. But as one might expect, all of the boys escape to French-held territory where they meet General Joffre who assures them of safe conduct back to America. No relationship to the real war in this series of juvenile formula novels.

j96   ———. *Boy Scouts with the Cossacks; or, Poland Recaptured*. Chicago: M.A. Donohue, 1916. 258p.

Jimmy, Ned, Jack, and Harry are back home in New York City from Belgium. They attend a benefit concert to

raise funds for Polish war relief and are soon involved
in a complex series of improbable events including the
theft of the relief funds followed by their arrest. Jimmy
is shanghaied by Harvey, the gunrunner thief, and shipped
off as a crew member on a packet boat bound for the Russian
port of Riga. The other three boys are taken to the police
station where their secret service friend turns up to release them from the false charges. They learn of Jimmy's
fate and that the real thief intends to take information
to Russia that will help defeat the Germans. The three
boys immediately take the Grey Eagle airplane on a steamer
to Liverpool whence they fly to the eastern front, charged
with preventing the involvement of the U.S. in a contro-
versy with Germany. Meanwhile Jimmy is forced by Harvey
to join the cossacks and it turns out Harvey is also
forcefully impressed. They are involved in the usual
raids and attacks on the Germans by the cossacks as the
other three scouts arrive by plane at the fortress of
Peremyshl just as the Germans overrun Poland. A melodramatic juvenile action story.

j97 Ruck, Berta. *The Girls at His Billet, a Novel*. London:
Hutchinson & Co., 1916. 328p.; New York: Dodd, Mead
& Co., 1916. 344p.

Three sisters, their ages ranging from eighteen to
twenty-two, live in an isolated village on the bleakest
part of the east coast of England. Evelyn, Nancy, and
Elizabeth stay with their elderly aunt. Their daily lives
are as dull and prosaic as the village, for there are no
young men about. With the start of the war, a training
camp is established in the village, and a young officer
is billetted in their house. In a very short time two
fellow officers also arrive. The final result is three
wartime engagements. This slight literary effort falls
into the sentimental juvenile story for adolescent girls
category.

j98 Shaw, Frank Hubert. *With Jellicoe in the North Sea*.
London: Cassell & Co., 1916. 311p.; New York: Funk &
Wagnalls, 1916. 311p.

Not seen. A novel based on the life of Jellicoe, 1859-
1935; NYPL.

j99 Strang, Herbert (pseud. of George Herbert Ely and C.J.
L'Estrange). *Burton of the Flying Corps*. London:
H. Frowde; Hodder & Stoughton, 1916. 292p.

Not seen.

j100 ———. *Through the Enemy's Lines: a Story of Mesopotamia*. London: H. Frowde; Hodder & Stoughton, 1916. 279p.

Not seen.

j101 Vandercook, Margaret O'Bannon (Womack). *The Red Cross Girls in Belgium*. Philadelphia: John C. Winston Co., 1916. 269p.

Not seen.

j102 ———. *The Red Cross Girls in the British Trenches*. Philadelphia: John C. Winston Co., 1916. 287p.

The novel is the first in a series relating the adventures of four American girls who volunteer for hospital work in wartime Europe under the auspices of the Red Cross. This first volume finds the girls becoming accustomed to the rigorous life of the front lines and to the horrors of war. An espionage plot is also involved.

j103 ———. *The Red Cross Girls on the French Firing Line*. Philadelphia: John C. Winston Co., 1916. 264p.

The story finds the four American friends of the Red Cross Girls Series at their post in a French hospital, facing danger from the German shelling as they work tirelessly to save the lives of injured soldiers.

j104 ———. *The Red Cross Girls with the Russian Army*. Philadelphia: John C. Winston Co., 1916. 265p.

Three of the original four Red Cross girls decide to continue nursing the wounded soldiers of the Allied armies in Russia. The women, Nona, Barbara, and Mildred, are at the fortress of Grovno where the Russians make a last stand against the Germans. Nona discovers the mysterious Sonya, an old friend of her mother, living near the fortress. She learns that her own mother had originally come from Russia. The women discover a new sense of values from their war experiences. The months after the four arrive at Grovno turn out to be the darkest for Russia during the war. Russian troops are in constant retreat before the German army. There is a subplot on the relationship between Nona and Sonya. Sonya is imprisoned and sentenced to Siberia for her outspoken pacifist ideas. Meanwhile, the girls are to leave the fortress for Petrograd because of the coming German attack. Mildred remains to nurse the wounded General Alexis, while Nona and Barbara go on to Petrograd where they become ill and are near a breakdown from the rigours and exhaustion of the retreat. Mildred finally arrives and the three decide to return to France. General Alexis is able to have Sonya pardoned and she joins the women and travels with them to France where they have a reunion with their old friends. A curious story for girls. Russia is painted in mysterious and quasi-guidebook terms. The plot concentrates on behind-the-front activities of the American nurses. There also is a touch of love and romance. Better written and more thoughtful than the vast bulk of the juvenile series stories on the war.

j105A Westerman, Percy Francis. *Rounding up the Raider: A Naval Story of the Great War*. London: Blackie & Son, 1916. 255p.

Not seen.

j106AB ———. *The Secret Battleplane*. London: S.W. Partridge, 1916. 254p.

Not seen.

j107A Wynne, May (pseud. of Mabel Winifred Knowles). *An English Girl in Serbia; the Story of a Great Adventure*. London & Glasgow: Collins' Clear-type Press, 1916. 215p.

Not seen.

1917

j108 Austin, Oscar Phelps. *Uncle Sam's Boy at War; An American Boy Sees the European War: A Sequel to "Uncle Sam's Soldiers."* New York: D. Appleton & Co., 1917. 253p.

Follows the career of Dan Patterson, Jr., son of the main character in the author's other "Uncle Sam" books written twenty years earlier. The novel begins with Dan's enlistment in the National Guard and employs Dan's experiences to illustrate the advances made in warfare from the time of the Spanish-American War: the improvemen

Juvenile Novels

in the machine gun, the cannon which throws its projectile twenty miles, the airplane, zeppelin, observation balloons, armored cars, the periscope, the submarine, the telegraph, etc.

j109A Bevan, Tom. *With Cossack and Car in Galicia*. London & Glasgow: Collins' Clear-type Press, 1917. 220p.

Not seen.

j110 Brereton, Frederick Sadleir. *On the Road to Bagdad; a Story of the British Expeditionary Force in Mesopotamia*. London: Blackie & Son, 1917. 384p.

Presents a graphic view of the dangers and perils of an expeditionary force in the Mesopotamian desert and marsh. The protagonist as a boy was taken on a number of journeys to Mesopotamia by his guardian. As a consequence, his knowledge of the language and customs of the country is nearly equivalent to that of the natives. With the spread of the war to Mesopotamia, the hero of the story is included as a member of the expeditionary force because of his familiarity with that country. He is soon involved in all kinds of adventurous missions throughout the countryside. Written primarily as a story for boys.

j111 ———. *Under Haig in Flanders; a Story of Vimy, Messines and Ypres*. London: Blackie and Son, 1917. 286p.

Not seen.

j112A Bridges, Thomas Charles. *With Beatty in the North Sea; a Story of Our Gallant Navy*. London & Glasgow: Collins' Clear-type Press, 1917. 232p.

Not seen.

j113 Carter, Herbert (pseud. of St. George Rathborne). *The Boy Scouts Afoot in France; or, With the Red Cross at the Marne*. New York: A.L. Burt, 1917. 251p.

It is the first days of the war. The four scouts are in Antwerp preparing to visit Bumpus' mother who is in a hospital in Paris for medical treatment. The Germans have invaded Belgium and the boys are unable to travel directly to that city. They finally find a train to Calais at which point they switch to a horse cart and proceed to Paris. They have many opportunities to observe French military preparations, troop movements, and the reactions of the civilians to the war. They are caught between the opposing armies, and one chum is arrested as a spy. They experience plenty of exciting adventures, help out at a field hospital, drive ambulances, and witness a terrific artillery barrage. When they carry dispatches through a heavy bombardment to General Joffre, they receive the congratulations of the General for their bravery. They witness the battle of the Marne by Joffre's troops. The boys finally reach Paris after the usual narrow escapes. An adventure story that promotes the virtues and resourcefulness of scouting during wartime.

j114 Crockett, Sherman. *Two American Boys Aboard a Submersible.* New York: Hurst & Co., 1917. 305p.

The sequel to *Two American Boys with the Dardanelles Battle Fleet* (item j75). The two heroes have found Amos' brother Frank who has since returned home to the States to see his dying father. Amos has been sick and cared for by his good buddy Jack on a Greek island used by England and France as a base to force a passage through the Dardanelles to take Constantinople. Now that Amos has recovered, the two boys decide to go with a submarine-hunting patrol boat. The boys fall overboard during a gun duel with a Turkish boat and are picked up as prisoners by a Turkish destroyer and taken through a treacherous mine field and straits to the Turkish base at Maitos. The Turkish pasha pronounces them prisoners of war and imprisons them before sending them off to Constantinople on an arms transport. This is an old boat that breaks down and is intercepted by a British sub in the Marmara Sea. The boys are taken aboard the sub where they have their first opportunity to learn all about how the underwater craft operates. The sub heads for Constantinople, saves a Turkish boatload of women and children in the stormy seas, sinks a troop transport, narrowly escapes a destroyer before reaching Constantinople where the sub shells the vital docks, torpedoes a naval boat, shells the bridge on the *Golden Horn* before fleeing from the Turkish attack. They now experience the treacherous and highly dangerous return trip through the tightly guarded Dardanelles straits. This all occurs with the usual hazardous adventures before they safely reach their home base. The story ends as the two brave lads consider whether it now might not be a good time to return to the U.S. permanently.

Juvenile Novels 357

j115 Drake, Robert L. (pseud. of Clair Wallace Hayes). *The Boy Allies at Jutland, or, The Greatest Naval Battle of History*. New York: A.L. Burt, 1917. 255p.

Deals with the efforts of the British navy to keep the German fleet bottled up in Helgoland. The heroes are Lieutenants Frank Chadwick and Jack Templeton who are stationed on the heavy battleship *Queen Mary*. The story commences with the departure of the *Queen Mary* in late May of 1916 for patrol duty in the North Sea. The two heroes are traced through their various sea adventures with German zeppelins, crew rivalries, interludes on hydroplane scout missions, air battles, spy missions behind the German lines, and preparations before and during the Battle of Jutland. They eventually end up in Bremen where they hijack a German vessel and escape amid the usual improbable series of heroic actions before reaching the safety of England and their patron, Lord Hastings.

j116 Greene, Homer. *The Flag*. Philadelphia: G.W. Jacobs, 1917. 318p.

An incredibly sentimental tale of military patriotism. The plot begins with a school-boy snowball fight in which one of the two leaders covers himself with an American flag as a means of protest during one of the snowball assaults. But his opponent by the name of Penfield Butler jerks it from him. The flag is then trampled and torn under their feet. Penfield is then called a "Benedict Arnold" because of his unpardonable act and is ultimately forced to leave school. He leaves feeling almost branded for life because he is refused when he attempts to join the National Guard. Finally, he is able to join the fighting in Europe and thereby regains his good name and self-respect.

j117 Hayes, Clair Wallace. *The Boy Allies at Verdun; or, Saving France from the Enemy*. New York: A.L. Burt, 1917. 256p.

The American boys Hal Paine and Chester Crawford, in the uniforms of British cavalry lieutenants, are now attached to the French forces on the eve of the Battle of Verdun in 1916. With Stubbs, their war-correspondent friend, they have just delivered dispatches to General Petain. This juvenile tale describes the many heroic adventures of these three characters as the Germans attempt to storm the Verdun stronghold of the French. There is a bit of everything in this narrative--bayonet attacks, bombardments, sword battles, you name it--Hal and Chester are there. They encounter the fanatic French general Pombrey and his conspiracy to stop fighting and end the war. The boys are arrested as fellow conspirators but soon are exonerated. The French forces now turn the tide of the battle and Hal, Chester, and Stubbs are in the thick of it all with their usual incredible activities on both sides of the lines and up in the air. The French begin their advance and save Verdun. A characteristic juvenile-series story.

j118 ———. *The Boy Allies on the Somme; or, Courage and Bravery Rewarded.* New York: A.L. Burt, 1917. 249p.

Deals with the major offensive of the Allies under General Haig. The time is July of 1916. The British troops are on the offensive against the Germans. Lieutenants Hal Paine and Chester Crawford are now on the staff of Haig and are often used as his personal messengers and scouts on the battlefields. The narrative describes Hal and Chester as they participate in the advance and capture of the town of Combles and beyond. As is usual with the two heroes, there are plenty of close calls and fearless adventures ranging from being captured by the enemy to impersonating American newspaper correspondents behind the German lines in order to obtain intelligence information for Haig. They are involved in cavalry attacks, tank and armored-car battles, and a host of battlefield activities. They meet Stubbs, their newspaper acquaintance, and the tale concludes with typical heroics when all three escape their German captors by a dash for their hidden airplane. When Hal and Chester return to General Haig, he personally congratulates them and they both receive commissions as captains in the British army. Another juvenile story strong on heroics and patriotism.

j119 ———. *The Boy Allies under the Stars and Stripes; or, Leading the American Troops to the Firing Line.* New York: A.L. Burt, 1917. 228p.

This juvenile adventure commences with Hal and Chester learning that the U.S. has just declared war on Germany. The two boys are such brave figures that they are known by all of the top brass of the Allied forces and consort with the likes of Haig, Foch, and their associates. In

this story the two boys perform air reconnaissance over
the western front and participate with the Canadian
forces in the successful battle for Vimy Ridge before
they return home to the States for a brief leave. A few
chapters describe the attitudes of the people back home
to the war. The two friends naturally associate with all
the top officials of the U.S. and British governments in
Washington and soon become involved with Austrian and
German spies right in the nation's capital. Their reputations are such that they are invited to go to Fort
Niagara to help train American troops for overseas duty.
Indeed, they accompany the first group overseas with
General Pershing to the U.S. staging camp behind the
lines. The boys immediately zoom off in an aircraft and
spot a zeppelin. Immediately after this they enter the
front-line trenches as the Americans encounter the enemy
for the first time in the war.

j120A Horsley, Reginald Ernest. *Hunting the U Boats; a Tale*. London & Glasgow: Collins' Clear-type Press, 1917. 232p.

Not seen.

j121 Kay, Ross. *Battling on the Somme*. New York: Barse & Hopkins, 1917. 252p.

The sixth story of the Big War Series which continues
the story of Earl and Leon Platt, boy heroes. They are
now stationed along with their friend Jacques near the
small town of Albert and observe their first tank. They
are involved in an attack as the Allies' bombardment
pounds the positions of the Germans. There are descriptions of the battlefield activities of the boys, such
as hand-to-hand combat, in fairly graphic and bloody
terms. They encounter their first flamethrower. There
is a chapter or two on the Emperor Franz Joseph and the
recent history of the Hapsburgs. This story attempts
to describe more of the horror and death of the war than
most of the juvenile books of the period. The plot deals
exclusively with trench warfare and much of the blood
and guts of the battlefield. Indeed, this is in striking
contrast with most of the other stories by the author.
In spite of this more realistic attempt, the tale is still
typically juvenile in scope and character much like those
of the Stratemeyer Syndicate. The story concludes as
the wounded Jacques, who has been hospitalized, receives
a War Cross for his bravery.

j122 Lawton, Wilbur (pseud. of John H. Goldfrap). *The Ocean Wireless Boys on War Swept Seas*. New York: Hurst & Co., 1917. 309p.

  The story begins with Jack Ready and Bill Raynor, the Wireless Boys, leaving New York as passengers on a German liner to Europe. The war is declared a day or two after they depart. British cruisers attempt to capture the liner, but the captain decides to make a run back to the U.S. coast to evade capture. They encounter icebergs and are shelled by a British cruiser but escape in the fog to Bar Harbor. The boys are next asked to return to Europe to locate Tom Jukes, the son of a local magnate. They take a U.S. liner this time and go to Liège and arrive just as it appears the Germans are soon to invade. Tom Jukes is spotted in his auto and they all decide to drive out toward the front. They are forced to stop at a deserted farmhouse for repairs and are apprehended by German cavalry. Jack is arrested as a spy and sentenced to be shot at dawn. The Germans are all killed when a French aviator bombs the farmhouse. Jack escapes and is flown off to Louvain by the French pilot who turns out to be a friend. The three boys are reunited and return to America where there is a brief adventure involving illicit stock sales in New York. This is a formula juvenile story cranked out by the score, and similar to those of Durston and Ralphson, et al.

j123 Lyman, Edward Branch. *Me'ow Jones, Belgian Refugee Cat; His Own True Tale....* New York: George H. Doran Co., 1917. 91p.

  Not seen.

j124 Pier, Arthur Stanwood. *The Plattsburgers*. Boston: Houghton Mifflin Co., 1917. 184p.

  Chiefly the experiences of a number of college men at the Plattsburg training camp. The story is obviously based on actual conditions of the camp and describes how the men were not only drilled in the standard infantry techniques but also in the other military branches as well. The story is reprinted from the *Youth's Companion* and is basically a tale for boys.

j125 Porter, Horace (pseud. of Horace Porter Biddle De Hart). *Our Young Aeroplane Scouts at Verdun; or, Driving*

Armored Meteors over Flaming Battle Fronts. New
York: A.L. Burt, 1917. 242p.

Billy and Henri are flying in a special armored aircraft called a meteor over the Somme battlefront in northern France. The battle rages with terrific intensity. They decide to make a landing in a quiet zone and renew their acquaintance with a British officer friend from the campaign in Turkey. However, they quickly receive new orders and are off again in a constant seesaw of goings and comings over or on the battlefields of Verdun. In this story the two heroes get a closer look and taste of the carnage at the front, succor a wounded German soldier, and generally perform their typical humanitarian gestures regardless of the side of the lines they are on. Billy and Henri have served with the men of both sides, with spies, and generally rubbed noses and elbows with the high and mighty, important politicos, and just regular folks in their adventuresome winging over the various theatres of the war. In this tale they have considerably more ground activity involving the mechanical details of trench warfare than has been their customary lot heretofore. The story concludes as the two head for the English aviation base at Imbros to deliver message packets and to embark on yet another series of adventures.

j126 ———. *Our Young Aeroplane Scouts in the Balkans; or, Wearing the Red Badge of Courage*. New York: A.L. Burt, 1917. 240p.

The two scout heroes head north from the island of Imbros through the so-called Iron Gates of the Danube where the Austrians first launched their offensive against the Rumanians. In their usual rapid-fire adventure style they continue in the famous Kazan defile, above the Transylvanian peaks, and hither and yon over the Balkans, blessed by their usual good fortune in escapes and involved in many brave activities culminating in their final encounter with the "flying whale" that chases them into Wallachia. One of an incredible series of juvenile stories that uses an endless series of clichés in an endless series of rapid-fire actions à la the Three Stooges of movie fame. Simply unbelievable.

j127 Rolf-Wheeler, Francis William. *The Wonder of War in the Air*. Boston: Lothrop, Lee & Shepard, 1917. 347p.

The plot, such as it is, is primarily a vehicle to instruct young boys in what "an aviator must learn, how an aviator must live, in what appalling perils an aviator must risk his life," and to promote a high regard for this patriotic military duty. It is obvious too that another purpose of the book is to urge American boys to serve their country. That this is one of the highest and noblest purposes to devote one's life to is strongly emphasized. The book is instructive and accurate in its information. Probably the story was entertaining for boys when it was published.

j128 Sheppard, William Henry Crispin. *Don Hale in the War Zone*. Philadelphia: Penn. Pub. Co., 1917. 312p.

A juvenile story that traces the activities and adventures of Don Hale and his friend George Glenn after they leave their homes in Chicago intending to visit Don's father in Paris. Don works his way to France on a munitions boat which is attacked and sunk by a German submarine. Don and the crew drift in the lifeboats for several days before being picked up by a passing steamer and taken to England. Don hurries off to Paris where he unexpectedly runs into his friend George who tells him his father, a famous aviator, has disappeared. The boys travel to a Somme valley hamlet to stay with an eminent entomologist friend of Don's father, Monsieur Seunot. They observe plenty of troop and supply movements around the village before a heavy enemy bombardment forces them and Monsieur Seunot to flee into the countryside. There they are able to observe a major battle from a protected position. Then the two boys go through a series of chase-and-escape experiences with unknown soldiers who eventually turn out to be French. The boys are arrested, rearrested, and placed in prison when Don's father turns up and effects their release. The story ends as Don decides he will join the ambulance corps. The first story of several based on formula plots characteristic of this genre.

* Sherwood, Elmer (pseud. of Samuel Lewenkrohn). *Lucky on an Important Mission*. Racine: Whitman, 1917(?). Unpaged.

This story is included as part of the longer juvenile novel entitled *Lucky, the Young Soldier* (item j130).

j129 ———. *Lucky, the Young Navy Man*. Racine: Whitman, 1917. 213p.

Ted Marsh and his friend leave Arizona in November to

make their own personal contributions to the war effort.
Red Mack goes to join the air corps, Jim Arthur expects
to be conscripted, and Ted Marsh, the hero known as
Lucky, hopes soon to join the navy in New York. He meets
there John Strong who asks Ted to assist him in tracking
down a spy. Ted decides to team up with Strong instead
of trying to get into the navy. The two take passage on
a liner to Europe, acting as father and son. The liner
is soon torpedoed, and, as the liner sinks, Ted tries to
save the suspected spy but is knocked out for his trouble.
Ted is then rescued by a destroyer and the two spies are
arrested. Ted learns he can remain on board the destroyer,
as it is ordered to go to the Pacific Coast via the Panama
Canal to hunt for subs. A naval ensign and Ted go ashore
to a small town in Mexico to inquire secretly about any
German subs or supply depots in the area. Alberto, the
fishing-boat guide, is told all about the war and the
Germans when he seems sympathetic. They soon learn of
the location of the sub supply cache and arrange to make
off with the materials. The destroyer now travels to
San Francisco where Ted leaves the ship and takes Alberto
home with him to the ranch. There is plenty of Allied
war propaganda with great emphasis on the scheming and
devious Hun throughout the world. This is a standard
example of a juvenile series strongly reminiscent of
the Stratemeyer Syndicate productions.

j130 ———. *Lucky, the Young Soldier*. Racine: Whitman, 1917. 231p.

Although this formula story for boys qualifies for a
place in these annotations, it curiously includes a
number of the separately published tales of the author
with alternate titles that form a continuous narrative
to create this title, e.g., *Lucky, the Young Volunteer*
or *Ted Marsh, the Young Volunteer; Lucky Finds a Friend*
or *Ted Marsh and the Enemy; Lucky on an Important Mission*
or *Ted Marsh on an Important Mission*. Ted Marsh is the
boy hero. He leaves his friends at school for his summer
vacation in Arizona and New Mexico to take a horseback
camping trip with his father, brother, and Red Mack, a
family friend. They run into Mexican bandits connected
with General Villa. German spies enter the plot as
supporters of the Mexicans against the U.S. and Canada
and to arouse the blacks against the U.S. Government.
The U.S. declares war on the Central Powers and joins
the Allies. The Germans attempt to encourage the Mexicans and the blacks to help their cause. Ted and Red
Mack work for the secret service in foiling a good many
of the spy activities of the Germans. However, much of

the story emphasis is on the Mexicans. The level of this juvenile series is on a par with many of the Stratemeyer Syndicate works and tends to fall even below those stories in literary quality and plot construction.

j131 Smith, Bertha (Whitridge). *Only a Dog: A Story of the Great War.* New York: E.P. Dutton & Co., 1917. 111p.

A war story told from the point of view of an Irish terrier who has had a happy home life with a French family until the Germans invade. The dog escapes and is taken in by one of the British units and a kindly British soldier adopts the dog. The dog repays his new soldier master with his devotion even unto death. A note in the book asserts that the story is based on an actual incident.

j132 Strang, Herbert (pseud. of George Herbert Ely and C.J. L'Estrange). *Carry on! A Story of the Fight for Bagdad.* London: H. Milford, 1917. 277p.

Not seen.

j133 Taffrail (pseud. of Henry Taprell Dorling). *The Sub, Being the Autobiography of David Munro, Sub-Lieutenant, Royal Navy.* London: Hodder & Stoughton, 1917. 356p.

A fictitious autobiography of David Munro, a normal, wholesome young boy who has enlisted in the British navy. The first part of the book describes his naval training experiences with some humor. The latter half deals with his life on board a destroyer during the first months of the war. The author states that his principal aim has been "to give some idea of the life and training of the boy who enters the Royal Navy as a cadet through the colleges at Osbourne and Dartmouth." A story for boys.

j134 Tomlinson, Paul Greene. *Bob Cook and the German Spy.* New York: Barse & Hopkins, 1917. 251p.

The story of two boys, too young to enlist, who are able to do their bit for the war effort in their own hometown. Bob Cook and his best friend, Hugh Reith, become involved in a number of adventures ranging from foiling the efforts of a German spy gang to bombing the local railway bridge and their attempt to burn down the High Ridge Steel Company owned by Bob's father. This is another typical juvenile patriotic tale. It is somewhat unique, however, in its balanced treatment of the issue of the German citizens and German residents of the United States in time of war. In spite of the super patriotism, the story assumes that the German residents are loyal citizens. In view of the hysteric anti-German feelings during the war years this seems rather surprising.

j135 Vandercook, Margaret O'Bannon (Womack). *The Red Cross Girls with the Italian Army*. Philadelphia: John C. Winston Co., 1917. 261p.

Nona Davis, alone of the four Red Cross girls, serves in Italy. She becomes friends with the emigrant Russian noblewoman, Sonya Valesky, an Italian-American young man, Carlo Navarra, and the Italian brothers Paulo and Eugino Zoli, who are in the Italian army and eventually die in battle. Nona becomes involved in the lives of all of these individuals as well as with a traitor who reveals Italian army secrets to the Germans.

j136 ———. *The Red Cross Girls with the Stars and Stripes*. Philadelphia: John C. Winston Co., 1917. 263p.

Continues the lives and loves of four young American women in the Red Cross who had been close friends through the first three years of the war. One, Barbara, has since married and has come back to New York to rear a family. But now that the U.S. has entered the war, Barbara's husband decides he must enlist. Eugenia's husband is missing in action and Mildred's General Alexis has been arrested by the revolutionaries in Russia as a supporter of the old regime. Thus, Eugenia and Mildred have returned to France as nurses. Barbara and Nona now also return as Red Cross nurses and all four women are stationed together again. The story is mainly a description of the daily activities and routines, love problems, and interpersonal relationships of the four nurses at a hospital and training camp of the American army in France. This series of stories is clearly above the wooden plots and single-dimensional characterizations in the bulk of juvenile-series war novels. There is a sophistication of character development, a deliberate discussion of values and moral implications which, coupled with the maturity of the emotional level, establishes a tone considerably adult in interest and writing ability. A refreshing change from the typical juvenile literature of the period.

j137 Ward, Kenneth. *The Boy Volunteers on the Belgian Front*.
New York: New York Book Co., 1917. 180p.

Describes the adventures of Alfred and Ralph, two American boys who were in Europe when the war began. They soon enlist in the Belgian army and participate in most of the important battles, carry messages, catch a spy, fight the German cavalry, and otherwise go through the typical experiences characteristic of the run-of-the-mill juvenile stories about the war. The book contains maps and diagrams which attempt to lend an authentic quality to the military events described. At the conclusion, the boys march into Antwerp with the Belgian troops and have a brief reunion with Ralph's parents. The first volume of another standard war-story series for boys.

j138 ———. *The Boy Volunteers with the American Infantry*.
New York: New York Book Co., 1917. 174p.

Ralph and Alfred have returned to France after their submarine adventure. Their parents were also torpedoed on their rescue ship and now have vowed to stay in France until the war is over. The boys are free to slip away and join up with the first of the American Expeditionary Forces. They encounter some old friends in the American army and are soon involved in an auto chase with spies. They finally reach the American army camp where they are "attached" as messengers and aides by the commanding general. Further spy adventures by the pair, followed by their orders to the front, enable them soon to see the nature of trench construction and warfare. They are involved in the thick of the action. They experience shell shock in a huge bombardment and recover in an aid station near the front when their parents arrive and take them to the American Hospital in Paris as the story ends. This is the final tale of this five-volume juvenile series for boys. Aside from an occasional effort to instruct the reader in some aspect of military or war action and equipment, the stories are typical and undistinguished examples of this genre.

j139 ———. *The Boy Volunteers with the British Artillery*.
New York: New York Book Co., 1917. 163p.

The third story in this series of juvenile tales about various aspects of the great war. Ralph and Alfred, two American boys, are recovering in a hospital in Paris after

an air crash and resolve never to go back into flying.
After their recovery they intend to go home. However,
they now become interested in the artillery branch of
the army and end up participating in the first great
French drive in the Somme area. Later they join up with
British artillery units. Scattered through the text are
the usual instructional diagrams to aid in understanding
the principles of artillery operation in war. Alfred's
parents and Ralph's mother learn of the boys' whereabouts
and visit them at the battery where they are stationed.
The plot and characters are the usual stereotypes typical
of the vast majority of these juvenile war stories.

j140 ———. *The Boy Volunteers with the French Airmen.* New
York: New York Book Co., 1917. 167p.

The further adventures of Ralph and Alfred in the second
volume of this series. They now try to get into the flying service. They make their way to eastern France and
meet another American boy, Tom, who has been a pilot for
two years in France. They enlist and are stationed at
an air camp at Verdun. The story is filled with information about all aspects of the air war such as details on
different types of aircraft used by both sides, flying
tactics and techniques, plane insignia, and so forth.
The story concludes with the crash of their airplane and
the death of Lieutenant Guyon after a furious air battle.
Both boys are seriously wounded and sent to a hospital in
Paris. A typical story of heroics and adventure for young
boys.

j141 ———. *The Boy Volunteers with the Submarine Fleet.*
New York: New York Book Co., 1917. 170p.

After more than two years of action in the war, Ralph
and Alfred are reunited with their parents at the British
artillery station where they have served. Their parents
induce them to return home to the States and they reluctantly leave the front and sail home. Within a day
at sea they are torpedoed by a German U-boat and end up
in a lifeboat with the ship's captain. When the sub
surfaces it spots the captain and takes him and the boys
prisoner aboard the craft. The narrative contains instructions on compass use and fairly detailed descriptions
on the operations and interior layout of submarines. The
sub is caught in an anti-sub net of the Allies. Ralph is
wounded and the sub is captured by a French naval boat
and taken to a British port while the boys are transferred

to a subchaser and have further experiences in sub warfare. They reach Le Havre just as it is announced America has entered the war. The fourth title of a typical juvenile war series of stories. The plots are conventional formula affairs embellished with a bit of didactic information on various aspects of the military services and their weapons.

j142A Westerman, Percy Francis. *A Watch-Dog of the North Sea: a Naval Story of the Great War*. London: S.W. Partridge, 1917. 375p.

Not seen.

1918

j143 Appleton, Victor (pseud.; Stratemeyer Syndicate house name). *The Moving Picture Boys on the War Front: or the Hunt for the Stolen Army Films*. New York: Grosset & Dunlap, 1918. 218p.

Blake Stewart, Joe Duncan, and Charles Anderson take their movie equipment to Europe where they film fighting episodes for propaganda purposes back home. Aboard ship they meet a French lieutenant and a German traveler whose actions arouse the boys' suspicions. While retrieving their stolen films behind the German lines, the boys encounter the suspicious characters again. A cloak-and-dagger, "gee whiz" juvenile story.

j144 ———. *Tom Swift and His War Tank; or, Doing His Best for Uncle Sam*. New York: Grosset & Dunlap, 1918. 218p.

Not seen.

j145 Atkinson, Eleanor (Stackhouse). *"Poilu," A Dog of Roubaix*. New York: Harper & Brothers, 1918. 225p.

About a year or so before the war Madame Daulac buys a young puppy and trains him to become a cart dog when her old dog is no longer useful. When the war begins in France, Poilu, the young cart dog, is fully trained and possesses a natural intelligence that enables the animal to learn quickly. His value is soon perceived by the military and he is drafted to pull a machine gun. The dog serves faithfully until his master is killed in the war. He then is returned to his mistress who reluctantly has him put to death so that he will not be taken by the Germans who have now occupied her area of France. The story of the dog serves primarily as a vehicle to demonstrate the courage and faith of the occupied French people and especially Madame Daulac. At the end of the story she is left alone, and the dog, her grandfather, husband, and young son-in-law are all dead while her daughter is a Red Cross worker in a convent and her young son is a refugee in England. In spite of all adversity, she valiantly keeps "the home fires burning."

j146 Barbour, Ralph Henry. *For the Freedom of the Seas*. Philadelphia: D. Appleton & Co., 1918. 299p.

Nelson Troy is with his father, Captain Troy, aboard a merchant schooner carrying lubricating oil to France from Boston. On the return trip they are sunk by a U-boat. His father is lost but Nelson saves his dog, Pickles. We next see Nelson on coastal patrol duty off Cape Cod where he participates in the capture of German spies in their onshore radio dugout. After this he transfers to the navy cruiser, the *Gyandotte*, on patrol duty in the Atlantic. While on watch duty during a storm he is knocked overboard and picked up by the Allied submarine, the Q-4. The submarine operation is described and he is finally taken to the Irish port of Queenland where he rejoins his cruiser. He next travels on convoy duty to France and then off to Helgoland and the famous battle of the North Sea. There seems little or nothing to recomment the novel now.

j147 Bates, Gordon (pseud. of Josephine Chase). *The Khaki Boys at Camp Sterling: or Training for the Big Fight in France*. New York: Cupples & Leon, 1918. 206p.

Four rookies, Jimmy Blaise, Roger Barlow, Bob Dalton, and Ignace Pulinski, are introduced to army life at Camp Sterling before being sent abroad. While at camp the four boys become involved in a German plot to poison Company E's food. When their German-American friend, Franz Schnitzel, is accused, the boys determine to undertake their own investigation to establish Franz' innocence.

j148 ———. *The Khaki Boys at the Front; or Shoulder to Shoulder in the Trenches.* New York: Cupples & Leon, 1918. 202p.

Records the trench experiences of the four American friends (Jimmy Blaise, Bob Dalton, Roger Barlow, Ignace Pulinski) and a newer addition, Franz Schnitzel, of German-American parentage. Their enthusiasm is soon tempered somewhat by their introduction to the harsh realities of warfare.

j149 ———. *The Khaki Boys On The Way; or Doing Their Bit on Sea and Land.* New York: Cupples & Leon, 1918. 208p.

Follows the adventures of Sergeants Bob Dalton and Jimmy Blaise, Corporal Roger Barlow, and Private Ignace Pulinski who are close friends as they leave Camp Sterling for their embarkation point and from there to board the troop transport *Columbia*. The four friends encounter a German spy, who escapes, only to meet him later aboard the *Columbia* where he is discovered signalling a U-boat. After the *Columbia* is torpedoed, the men are rescued and landed in Ireland, to be transported to England and then across the Channel for eventual action on the battle-fields.

j150 Beach, Charles Amory. *Air Service Boys Flying for France; or, The Young Heroes of the Lafayette Escadrille.* New York: George Sully & Co., 1918. 218p.

The two heroes of this juvenile series are Tom Raymond, from a family of inventors and mechanics, and Jack Parmly, friends since childhood in a small town in Virginia. Tom especially is attracted by aviation and is determined to fly, so both boys are sent to a nearby airfield to learn. Meanwhile, Tom's father has invented a new and improved airplane stabilizer, but the plans are stolen by a suspected German spy. All of this eventually leads to the boys' volunteering as fliers in France. They go on to a French flying school for additional training and then join the famous Lafayette Escadrille group of daredevil pilots and soon become involved in bombing runs over the lines and later a special mission to destroy a German munitions plant. On the way back they run out of gas but manage to force a German car into a ditch and obtain a few gallons of gas from the tank to permit them to fly on to the French lines. Naturally, the driver of the

car turns out to be the spy Tuessig who stole the
stabilizer plans from Tom's father in the States. The
boys retrieve the plans before the devious spy expires
of his injuries, and the two daring heroes fly on to
France. An improbable story with simple dialogue.

j151 ———. *Air Service Boys Over the Enemy's Lines; or,
The German Spy's Secret.* New York: George Sully &
Co., 1918. Unpaged [approx. 218p.].

Tom and Jack soon become first-class combat pilots with
the famous Lafayette Escadrille. Their many dramatic
successes against the German aces provide plenty of
action for their talents. A melodramatic plot provides
them with the opportunity to prove their worth in the
rescue of young Bessie and her mother from an old château
in Lorraine where a German spy (who followed the boys to
London from the States) has imprisoned the two women.
One of an especially undistinguished series of juvenile
stories.

j152 ———. *Air Service Boys Over the Rhine; or, Fighting
Above the Clouds.* New York: George Sully & Co., 1918.
218p.

Tom and Jack, experienced and daring pilots with the
Lafayette Escadrille, have just received news of the
entrance of the U.S. into the war and that Tom's father
is due to arrive in Paris with another of his inventions.
When the boys go to Paris there is a mysterious bombardment of the city and Tom's father is among the missing.
It seems the shells are coming from a monster German gun
about eighty miles away. Jack and Tom are given the
mission to search out the location of the big guns. They
help to destroy them and then cross the Rhine on a special
bombing mission to destroy one of the largest German
factories and railroad sections. Forced by an emergency
to land, they are captured by the enemy and run into
Tom's father, also a prisoner. They all manage to escape
in their airplane back to France when the Germans are
under a heavy attack. This is a typical series of juvenile stories told on a simple level and with a melodramatic plot based on improbable coincidence.

j153 Bernard, Marguerite, and Edith Serrell. *Deer* [sic]
Godchild. New York: M.E. Demetre, 1918. 88p.

Published for "the fatherless children of France,"
this novel tells a tale through the amusing letters

(purported to be authentic) between a 12-year-old New York boy called James and a French orphan girl called Andrée for whose care he is contributing ten cents each day during the war. The tale is entertaining, and the letters of James are believable, though misspelled and slangy. The book demonstrates some understanding of the nature of children.

* Blaine, John (pseud. of Georgia Roberts Durston). *The Boy Scouts on a Submarine*. Akron, Ohio: Saalfield Publishing Co., 1918. 235p.

A later reprint with a different author and title of *The Boy Scouts Under the Stars and Stripes* ... by George Durston (item j175).

j154 Botsford, Charles Alexander. *Joining the Colors*. Philadelphia: Penn. Pub. Co., 1918. 347p.

The plot depicts the enlistment and progress of Rodman Van Horne from school boy to lieutenant in the Canadian Expeditionary Forces. The first third of the book deals with Van's life and activities in an eastern prep school near the Canadian border. He decides one day to go to Toronto for a short vacation trip from school and encounters suspected German agents on the train. He also becomes quite enthralled with the Canadian war effort and army recruitment, so much so that he soon enlists on the spur of the moment. We follow his introduction into Canadian military training with various asides on the nature of the war, design of the Canadian uniform and equipment for the various ranks, training-camp procedures, hierarchy, etc. The bulk of the book describes Van in his fairly quick advance to sergeant because of his leadership abilities. He is promoted to sergeant major just before embarkation to Europe, where he is sent with his regiment to the trenches of France. The author intersperses occasional diagrams illustrating trench layout, artillery strategy, military dress, and a smattering of military lore and customs of the Canadian Army as a didactic feature. The last three chapters describe the front-line warfare experiences of Van and his buddies. For his heroism he receives the rank of lieutenant and is awarded the Victoria Cross. This is a juvenile-series novel written by one who served with the Canadian forces during the war.

j155 Brereton, Frederick Sadleir. *The Armoured-car Scouts; a Tale of the Campaign in the Caucasus.* London: Blackie & Son, 1918. 384p.

The greater part of the action takes place in the area of Erzerum and the upper Armenian plateau in the Caucasus. The time is the spring and summer of 1916. The three principal characters and heroes are Jo Creedy, a crusty English sailor, Guy Grammond of English background (about eighteen), and his Russian friend, Nicholas (of a similar age). Guy's father is murdered by his German business partner of many years. Although English, Guy has been brought up mainly in Russia and knows the language well. Guy now decides to return to England since he no longer has any family in Russia. Since the war is in progress, he decides to return again to Russia with a British navy armoured-car detachment in order to help "crush the German menace." Jo, one of the sailors on the British boat, turns up with Nicholas, so the three soon become close buddies. The major part of the story details the hazardous experiences of all three as they scout for Turkish troops. They also see firsthand the results of the terrible Armenian village massacres carried out by the Turks (a relatively unique topic for the vast majority of novels on this war). They successfully defend one small Armenian village but eventually the three are captured by the Turks. However, all three finally escape into the safety of their approaching armoured-car detachment. This is a strong anti-German tale which contains occasional digressions on the political, social, and military events in the Caucasus. In spite of its obvious propaganda purposes, this is definitely a cut above the typical boys' story, i.e., *Tom Slade, Motorcycle Dispatchbearer* (item j178), and exhibits some fairly good narrative qualities.

j156 ————. *From the Nile to the Tigris; a Story of Campaigning from Western Eggpt to Mesopotamia.* London: Blackie & Son. 1918. 330p.

Not seen.

j157 ————. *Under Foch's Command; a Tale of the Americans in France.* London: Blackie & Son, 1918. 287p.

Not seen.

j158   Brooks, Edna. *The Khaki Girls Behind the Lines or Driving with the Ambulance Corps*. New York: Cupples & Leon, 1918. 204p.

Details the adventures of Joan Mason and Valerie Warde as they cross the Atlantic to become members of the American Ambulance Corps, in which they serve with distinction. They uncover a German espionage system involving a beautiful German noblewoman, daughter of a woman involved in the plot uncovered by Joan in *The Khaki Girls of the Motor Corps; or Finding Their Place in the Big War* (item j159).

j159   ———. *The Khaki Girls of the Motor Corps; or Finding Their Place in the Big War*. New York: Cupples & Leon, 1918. 208p.

Two upper-middle-class girls who are eager to take part in the war effort join the Woman's Motor Corps, an organization of women trained in driving, mechanics, and first aid, and who function as a chauffeuring service to the military. Anxious to prove themselves so that they may be accepted for ambulance service in France, the girls are influential in entrapping a group of espionage agents.

j160   Cammaerts, Emile and Tita. *A Boy of Bruges; a Story of Belgian Child Life*. New York: E.P. Dutton & Co., 1918. 190p.

A story involving two young boys who become close friends. Mathieu is a Walloon peasant who goes to Bruges to be a companion to Pieter who has lived a sheltered life. After the death of his mother, Pieter must stay at the Ardennes farm of Mathieu's grandfather. There Pieter also soon becomes friends with Annette, the sister of Mathieu. When the war starts the two boys are involved as messengers and the story concludes as they recuperate in London. Of couse, Annette is also there as a Red Cross nurse.

j161   Chapman, Allen (pseud.; Stratemeyer Syndicate). *Ralph on the Army Train; or, The Young Railroader's Most Daring Exploit*. New York: Grosset & Dunlap, 1918. 280p.

The time is the middle of 1917. Ralph Fairbanks is the chief dispatcher for the Great Northern Railroad in

Jenkins Junction. Many of the railroad employees are foreign-born and some exhibit great sympathy for the cause of the Kaiser. These German-Americans serve as the Kaiser-lover stereotype in America--thick accent, Teutonic mannerisms, etc. Ralph is soon in the center of a number of sabotage plots to destroy or wreck railway engines, troop and munitions trains, etc. He wishes to serve his country but cannot enlist or be drafted because of his heart condition. The German saboteurs attempt to dynamite railway bridges and generally cause all the kinds of mischief they can. The tale concludes after Ralph spots the spy ringleader in a passing Pullman car and is nearly killed in his attempt to alert the authorities of his discovery. Of course, Ralph is saved and the German sympathizers are all rounded up so that the army trains can get safely through Jenkins Junction and serve the war effort. A fair amount of railroad operating procedures and lore is included in this juvenile spy story. A typical boy's story characteristic of this genre and the productions of the Stratemeyer Syndicate.

* Cobb, Frank (pseud.). *The Potter Boys Under Old Glory*. Akron, Ohio: Saalfield Pub. Co., 1918.

A reprint with different author and title of *The Boy Scouts Under the Stars and Stripes* ... by George Durston (item j175).

j162 Crockett, Sherman. *Two American Boys with Pershing in France*. New York: Hurst & Co., 1918. 302p.

Jack Maxfield and his cousin Amos Turner are with the American Expeditionary Force in France. The two boys receive a new mission to search for little Pauline Winters, a distant relative of Jack's mother. (Pauline had been visiting relatives in France when the war began and no one has heard from her since.) Naturally in the course of the search for Pauline, the boys experience many perils--in the trenches, in the air, with German prisoners and spies, with General Pershing, in no-man's-land, you name it--Jack and Amos were there. Naturally they find the girl and arrange for her to return to Allied lines and home.

j163 Davidson, Halsey. *Navy Boys after the Submarines, or, Protecting the Giant Convoy*. New York: George Sully

& Co., 1918. 218p. [Republished as *Deep Sea Boys after a Submarine*.... New York: Equitable, 1930.]

The first of five volumes in the Navy Boys Series. The protagonists are a group of boys from the small New England town of Seacove who enlist in the Navy in early 1917 before the United States has entered the war. Philip Morgan and his chums, Ikey Rosenmeyer, Michael Donahue, and Alfred Torrance, take their basic training at the large naval camp of Sangarack and then set off on their first two cruises in the new destroyer *Colodia*. Among their adventures crossing the Atlantic to England are the sinking of a German U-boat, the capture of an enemy raider, the destruction of a German bomber, and so forth.

j164 ―――. *Navy Boys Behind the Big Guns, or, Sinking the German U-boats*. New York: George Sully & Co., 1918. 218p. [Republished as *Deep Sea Boys Behind the Big Guns*.... New York: Equitable, 1930.]

This third volume in the Navy Boys Series relates the continuing adventures of the four Seacove boys: Philip Morgan and his close friends, Alfred Torrance, Michael Donahue, and Ikey Rosenmeyer, aboard the super-dreadnaught *Kennebunk*. They take part in a short battle with the British fleet against some of the naval forces of Germany. Another run-of-the-mill example of a juvenile series popular during the early part of this century.

j165 ―――. *Navy Boys Chasing a Sea Raider, or, Landing a Million Dollar Prize*. New York: George Sully & Co., 1918. 218p. [Republished as *Deep Sea Boys Chasing a Sea Raider*.... New York: Equitable, 1930.]

The four friends in the second book of the series continue their adventures in the U.S. Navy on board the destroyer *Colodia*. They demonstrate their plucky nature and resourcefulness as members of the prize crew on the captured German raider *Graf von Posen*.

j166 Drake, Robert L. (pseud. of Clair Wallace Hayes). *The Boy Allies with the Submarine D-32; or, The Fall of the Russian Empire*. New York: A.L. Burt, 1918. 251p.

Frank and Jack are now on the English cruiser *Norwalk*. They go ashore in Calais and encounter three Russians who appear to have information on a coup to depose the Czar. The boys escape (Frank with a leg wound) back to the cruiser where their friend and patron, Lord Hastings, informs the British cabinet of the affair and it is decided to send a submarine fleet to aid the Czar in order to keep Russia in the war against Germany. Naturally Jack and Frank accompany the fleet. They counsel the Czar himself, engage in heroic efforts to protect the ruler and otherwise experience an incredible series of adventures in Russia and Finland. The two boys and Lord Hastings manage to save the Russian fleet from certain destruction by the Germans, but the Czar falls and they see the Kerensky government come to power. They now move on to Venice and the waters of the Italian campaign against the Austrian fleet. They end up being captured and unexpectedly meet up with Kaiser Wilhelm who because of his prewar friendship with Lord Hastings assures their safety as prisoners of war. Naturally, they finally all escape from the shore prison and are eventually picked up by an Italian cruiser.

j167 ————. *The Boy Allies with Uncle Sam's Cruisers; or, Convoying The American Army across the Atlantic.* New York: A.L. Burt, 1918. 252p.

Lord Hastings is notified of an enemy raider off the coast of South America, which the Allies are unable to capture. He plans a special mission to apprehend the elusive boat and sends Frank and Jack in disguise on an American liner to Buenos Aires. Naturally, they are captured by the raiders and the two heroes pretend to be German sympathizers. The German raider captures another American ship that is a plant, with the result that after all the prisoners are aboard they suddenly stage a surprise takeover after a fearful struggle and sail the ship back to New York to be turned into a transport. Jack and Frank now proceed to their next assignment on convoy duty aboard a British cruiser escorting the American troops to Europe. They are next on an armed merchant ship which is suddenly caught in a furious ocean storm that sinks the ship. They escape in lifeboats and wash up on an island off the coast of South America where they fall into the hands of pirates who have stolen a German submarine. After the usual adventures with the pirates in the jungle, they manage to convert the pirate captain to the Allied cause and to join them in an attempt to destroy the German sub base on the same island. Another characteristic juvenile-series novel filled with the usual simplistic characters.

j168 Driggs, Laurence La Tourette. *The Adventures of Arnold Adair, American Ace.* Boston: Little, Brown & Co., 1918. 335p.

A story that is written with a more obvious sense of literary style and construction than the bulk of the typical juvenile literature published during this period. Arnold Adair is a boy from New York who develops a love of flying while attending a famous school in Switzerland. With the outbreak of the war he enlists in the French Flying Corps where he, of course, performs heroically and has many thrilling adventures including his inadvertent capture by a former schoolmate who now is flying for the Germans. But all is well in the end since Captain Bunny Reinhardt honors his old school ties and friendship by managing to take Adair away from German territory to freedom in his Gotha three-seater.

j169 Driscoll, James R. *The Brighton Boys in the Radio Service.* Philadelphia: John C. Winston Co., 1918. 228p.

Joe Harned, Jerry Macklin, and Slim Goodwin, all Brighton Academy boys, foil a scheme of the Germans before reaching their assigned ship which was to become part of an armed convoy bound for Europe. Once aboard, Joe intercepts a German spy in the wireless room, who escapes to cause the wireless men more trouble. Once in France the signal corps' duty is to set up outposts close to the German trenches where the boys see much action. Following this, they are put in charge of a wireless tractor lodged in the mountains where they transmit advance information of an anticipated German advance. For meritorious service the boys then receive appointments to a newly established military college in the United States.

j170 ―――. *The Brighton Boys in the Submarine Fleet.* Philadelphia: John C. Winston Co., 1918. 256p.

Jack Hammond and Ted Wainwright, former Brighton Academy students, are assigned to the submarine *Dewey* with orders for escort service in the North Sea. The exploits of the boys include torpedoing German ships, razing a U-boat base, capturing a German U-boat, and engaging in the successful attack on the German-held U-boat base of Zeebrugge in Holland.

Juvenile Novels

j171 ———. *The Brighton Boys in the Trenches*. Philadelphia: John C. Winston Co., 1918. 228p.

This novel follows Herbert Whitcomb and Roy Flynn as they leave school to enlist in the infantry. Because of their ability as marksmen they are assigned to a platoon of snipers. While in camps they help to uncover a German sympathizer who tries to demoralize the troops. After reaching France, the two boys see much action, their platoon engaging in almost constant forays across no-man's-land. In the final chapter they are invalided back to the United States.

j172 ———. *The Brighton Boys with the Battle Fleet*. Philadelphia: John C. Winston Co., 1918. 219p.

This novel follows the adventures of Phil Martin, Tom Calvin, and Jed Harris, former Brighton Academy students now enlisted in the United States Navy, and John Sweeney, a veteran sailor. Their exploits include destroying a German wireless station in Mexico, searching for and attacking the German raider *Breslin*, and putting down a revolt on the captured *Breslin*. They end up on North Sea duty engaging in one of the biggest sea battles of the war.

j173 ———. *The Brighton Boys with the Flying Corps*. Philadelphia: John C. Winston Co., 1918. 233p.

The first of a series of novels, this finds eight students of Brighton Academy very much interested in the airdrome being built near their town. Having their services accepted at the airdrome, the boys lose little time in learning about aspects of flying, and seven are soon expert flyers and mechanics. Upon enlisting and being sent to France, they engage in many successful encounters with the German flyers.

j174 Durston, George (pseud. of Georgia Roberts Durston). *The Boy Scouts Under Fire in France; or, In the Field With Pershing*. Akron, Ohio: Saalfield Pub. Co., 1918. Unpaged.

Not seen.

j175 ———. *The Boy Scouts Under the Stars and Stripes; or, Serving on Land and Sea*. Akron, Ohio: Saalfield Pub. Co., 1918. 168p.

Lester Pomeroy invents a powerful gas that can put a

large number of men asleep without injury, as a substitute for the deadly gas the Germans are using at the battlefront. A group of German spies hear of his discovery and steal the only copy of the formula. The spy mastermind is a devious German called Wolf who poses as a horse buyer from Switzerland and plots a way to leave the U.S. and take the formula back to Germany. The spies lose the paper with the formula and this begins a series of dangerous adventures for Porky and Beany, the Potter twins. The German spy is killed when he tries to escape from the hospital after all his co-conspirators have either died or been captured. Porky and Beany are now informed by their mother and Colonel Bright that they can go to the front as messenger boys. They leave by boat for France, but their ship is sunk and the two boys disappear. They later turn up on a sub where they have been impressed to help man the shorthanded vessel. Naturally they save the day since they have secretly misadjusted all the torpedoes so none will fire in a straight line. After they arrive in France they are taken to meet General Pershing and commence their new messenger duties. The narrative of this juvenile story is interspersed with homilies and tract-like sayings calculated to encourage the simple virtues of scouting, parental respect, and patriotism.

j176 Emerson, Alice B. *Ruth Fielding at the War Front; or The Hunt for the Lost Soldier*. New York: Cupples & Leon, 1918. 204p.

At work in the field hospital in Clair, France, Ruth Fielding receives word that her friend, Tom Cameron, is being held by the Germans. Her determination to secure his release takes her behind the German lines.

j177 ————. *Ruth Fielding in the Red Cross; or Doing Her Best for Uncle Sam*. New York: Cupples & Leon, 1918. 204p.

Ruth serves in a hospital in France as a member of the supply department of the Red Cross and is instrumental in revealing a plot to defraud the Red Cross of its funds, a plot which began in her hometown and whose members accompanied her to France. The story is concerned chiefly with the wounded in the hospital and their care.

Juvenile Novels

*   Fiske, James (pseud.). *Fighting the U-Boat Menace.* Akron, Ohio: Saalfield Pub. Co., 1918.

A reprint with different author and title of *The Boy Scouts Under the Stars and Stripes* ... by George Durston (item j175).

j178   Fitzhugh, Percy Keese. *Tom Slade, Motorcycle Dispatch-bearer.* New York: Grosset & Dunlap, 1918. 206p.

Tom Slade, traveling on his trusty motorcycle named Uncle Sam, is on a dispatch errand west of Revigny in France when he takes a wounded German soldier prisoner. He continues on to his new assignment near the town of Cantigny. The American troops are on the verge of an offensive into Germany, led by General Pershing. Through Tom's eyes we view the preparations for the offensive, the tanks, the troops, etc. Tom volunteers to go over the top with his faithful cycle pulling a communications wire, but is saved from certain death by an expert sniper who later turns out to be his old friend, Roscow Bent. The story closes with Tom riding off on his dependable motorcycle to the war fronts in Picardy and Flanders. Although the scouting virtues are not emphasized quite as much as in *Tom Slade with the Colors* (item j181), the book is still filled with plenty of simplistic patriotism and the typical heroic actions of Tom.

j179   ———. *Tom Slade on a Transport.* New York: Grosset & Dunlap, 1918. 198p.

Tom has recently returned to his hometown after his steamer job (re *Tom Slade with the Colors,* item j181). He is now back working at the Temple Camp office. While helping out the local Red Cross women he discovers a German agent's documents hidden in a chimney. Tom decides to turn these over to his secret service friend, Mr. Conne, and Tom takes him up on a job offer in the war effort, as captain's mess boy on a transport to France. Tom falls overboard only to be rescued by a German U-boat. He is taken prisoner and sent to Germany to a prison camp near Alsace. His prisoner-of-war camp experiences are described in some detail and he soon meets Archie, an old friend from his hometown. They both decide to escape, and the story concludes with notice of their successful return to Pershing's forces in France. The Tom Slade series is about on a par with the Boy Allies Series of Hayes.

j180 ———. *Tom Slade with the Boys Over There.* New York: Grosset & Dunlap, 1918. 204p.

This sequel to *Tom Slade on a Transport* (item j179) begins with some background about old Pierre Leteur, his wife, and daughter Florette. It turns out that Tom's friend Armand is the brother of Florette. The Leteur family has lived always in Alsace but yearns for the day when it is once again a part of France. Tom and his friend Archer have escaped from a German prisoner-of-war camp and turn up at the Leteur house seeking shelter. They hide in the wine cellar. When they come out they discover that old Pierre has been killed and Florette and her mother have been taken away to a work camp. Tom and Archer continue their flight south to Switzerland in order to return to France. The major portion of the story is about their adventures on this journey. The story concludes with press releases on the success of their escape from Germany. There are many references to the benefits and techniques of scouting as well as the usual and expected patriotic sentiments.

j181 ———. *Tom Slade with the Colors.* New York: Grosset & Dunlap, 1918. 220p.

Most of this Tom Slade story occurs in and around Tom's hometown and is primarily a patriotic tale emphasizing the virtues and training of scouting. Tom and his scout buddies discuss with the local scoutmaster their eagerness to enlist in the Great War; but since they are too young, they agree to wait until they are eighteen. Tom meets and becomes a close friend of Roscoe Bent, a dapper young man who works at the local bank. Tom convinces Roscoe to return and register for the army when Roscoe goes off to the woods to stay. In the meantime, Tom decides to volunteer as a war transport ship's hand. He becomes a hero of sorts when he discovers a bomb in the storage room and helps in identifying the spy on board the vessel. Tom is then promoted to assistant wireless operator and shortly thereafter the ship is torpedoed and sinks, leaving Tom to be rescued by a passing schooner headed for South America. A scout story written in typical simplistic style and larded with the usual patriotic sentiments.

j182 Havard, Aline. *Captain Lucy and Lieutenant Bob.* Philadelphia: Penn. Pub. Co., 1918. 336p.

The story of one American family's contribution to the

Juvenile Novels 383

war effort. It involves the fourteen-year-old Lucy, who with her mother participated in Red Cross activities, her brother Bob, an American Air Force pilot on the French-German front, and her father, whose contribution was as a major in the Quartermaster Corps in the States.

j183 Hayes, Clair W. *The Boy Allies with Haig in Flanders; or, The Fighting Canadians of Vimy Ridge*. New York: A.L. Burt, 1918. 221p.

Lieutenants Hal and Chester are in the trenches in France with the American Expeditionary Forces. They serve as special aides with General Pershing. As usual they engage in all sorts of military missions, some at the personal request of Pershing because of their fearless reputations. The latest has them slip behind the German lines to Berlin to contact a woman secret agent who has a vital list of German spies and agents in the United States. They accompany a Canadian soldier as they journey to neutral Holland and pose as Dutch newspaper correspondents to get to Berlin. Their friend Stubbs has already preceded them, and they team up with him in Berlin. In a series of typical adventures, they get the list and escape back to Holland as McKenzie, their Canadian colleague and the best shot in the West, holds the Germans at bay. Hal and Chester are later off on a mission to General Haig and participate in the victorious advance against the Hindenburg line.

j184 Hornibrook, Isabel Katherine. *Scout Drake in Wartime*. Boston: Little, Brown & Co., 1918. 305p.

Not seen.

j185 Jackson, Charles Tenney. *The Call to the Colors*. New York: D. Appleton & Co., 1918. 324p.

Not seen.

j186 ———. *Jimmy May in the Fighting Line*. New York: D. Appleton & Co., 1918. 314p.

An adventure story for boys that deals with a soldier and his experiences with the first group of troops of the American Expeditionary Force to reach France. A typical example of patriotic juvenile literature written at the time.

j187   Johnston, Annie (Fellows). *Georgina's Service Stars.*
        New York: Grosset & Dunlap 1918. 313p.

A story for girls. The narrative is by Georgina Huntingdon, the granddaughter of a Kentucky editor who has the writing disease in her blood. She decides to write her memoirs and begins her story during the war but before the U.S. is actively involved. Her account is mainly a home front view of the U.S. She describes her present old Cape Cod home, ancestors, school, and family life through the eyes of a high school girl. War weddings, love affairs, news, and happenings to friends and relatives in the war, as well as her sacrifices for the war effort, are described.

j188   Kay, Ross. *With Pershing at the Front; America's Soldiers in the Trenches.* New York: Barse & Hopkins, 1918. 246p.

Relates the story of Earl Platt and his twin brother Leon after they join up with their countrymen in France. As they travel up to the front-line trenches on foot, their troop train is bombed and machine-gunned by a German airplane. Their day-to-day experiences are described in some detail: the hustle and bustle; the roads choked with refugees, troops, trucks, and tanks; bombardments; advances; German attacks; and hand-to-hand combat. The novel concludes with the Allies having turned back the German advance, and now pushing the Germans toward the Rhine with, of course, Leon and Earl in the midst of it all. The numerous realistic and graphic descriptions of front-line battle conditions are superior to many of those found in the other juvenile series books on the war. This is one of the few stories that briefly mentions the presence of Negro troops with the American forces in France.

j189   Parker, Thomas Drayton. *The Spy on the Submarine; or, Over and Under the Sea.* Boston: W.A. Wilde, 1918. 298p.

Not seen.

j190   Patchin, Frank Gee (i.e., Glines). *The Battleship Boys on the Sky Patrol: or Fighting the Hun Above the Clouds.* Philadelphia: Henry Altemus Co., 1918. 255p.

The battleship boys, Lieutenant Commander Dan Davis and Lieutenant Sam Hickey, are engaged in daring aerial

Juvenile Books

feats, first as they train in France, then in action against the German submarines, and finally in dirigibles and seaplanes. The book is a series of their exploits, their being shot down, and their rescue at sea. After Dan's plans for the blocking of the harbor at Zeebrugge are successful, and after valiant performances in that attack by both Dan and Sam, they are presented to and commended by King George of England.

j191 ———. *The Battleship Boys with the Adriatic Chasers.* Philadelphia: Henry Altemus Co., 1918. 255p.

Lieutenants Dan Davis and Sam Hickey participate in a desperate battle against the Germans after being rescued by the British when the Germans sink the American liner taking them to Europe. They keep the German fleet busy racing for home base. When a zeppelin is captured, the two lieutenants man it, but are cut adrift over German territory. Upon being rescued by an American battleship, they return to the *Cromwell* and their destination in the Adriatic, from where the Austrian and German ships prey on Allied shipping. The two boys evolve a plan to penetrate the harbor of Trieste and rid the area of hostile ships. After this success they receive well-deserved promotions and a leave in Paris.

j192 Perkins, Lucy (Fitch). *The French Twins.* New York: Houghton Mifflin Co., 1918. 201p.

The eighth volume in the author's The Twins Series, and intended as a story for both boys and girls. Purely and simply it is a super-patriotic tale placed in wartime Rheims. Pierre and Pierrette, the children of one of the cathedral caretakers, see their share of the events of war. However, they make friends in the Foreign Legion with the American relief unit and assist in the capture of two German spies.

j193 Perry, William B. (pseud. of William Perry Brown). *Our Jackies with the Fleet.* Akron, Ohio: Saalfield Pub. Co., 1918. 362p.

This juvenile story traces the activities and war experiences of a group of sailors or "jackies" after they graduate from the Great Lakes Naval Training Station. The dialogue is written in quasi-adolescent slang. The author is strong on nicknames for his single-dimensional characters: Ally, Snoddy, Telly, Solly, etc. After a

week's furlough they are sent on a troop train to New
York City for Atlantic sea duty on the destroyer *Perry*.
In a bomb plot to destroy the train the dynamiter is
caught by four of the "jackies." The narrative tends
at times to be a daily log of activities and life at
sea. The ship rescues steamers under attack by U-boats
and drops depth charges while the four friends discover
two traitors in the crew, and then go on shore leave in
England where they witness the bombing of London as well
as a zeppelin attack. The story concludes as the *Perry*
and its crew receive praise from the Secretary of the
Navy for their meritorious service.

j194 ———. *Our Pilots in the Air*. Akron, Ohio: Saalfield
Pub. Co., 1918. 311p.

A tale placed in eastern France at an Allied airport
near no-man's-land. Most of the action takes place
around the Appincourte Bluff area and describes the
various day-to-day activities of the men of a bombing
squadron--the social life, flight preparations, raids,
dogfights, and stunt flying. The main characters consist of several young men, primarily Orris Erwin, Lafe
Blaine, and Buck Bangs. The plot is a trite adventure
and action story for boys, covering most of the dramatic
aspects of the air war. Two of the heroes personally
receive decorations for their bravery from none other
than the generals Petain and Pershing. This is standard
juvenile war-literature fare.

j195 Porter, Horace (pseud. of Horace Porter Biddle De Hart).
*Our Young Aeroplane Scouts Fighting to the Finish; or,
Striking Hard Over the Sea for the Stars and Stripes*.
New York: A.L. Burt, 1918. 224p.

Billy Barry and Henri Trouville have just completed
another of their spectacular rescues, this time of the
top air ace of France after he was shot down in the
North Sea. Billy learns that he is one of the two heirs
of a millionaire uncle who manufactured airplanes, and
decides to head back to the States to claim his fortune.
But Billy and his chum are kidnapped by the noted German
secret agent, Herr Roque, and precipitated into another
incredible series of adventures. The boys escape Roque's
imprisonment and return to the home of the French ace
who arranges to take them by sea to their departed
steamer heading to the States. On the ship they participate in the unmasking of a German spy carrying new code

Juvenile Books 387

books for the spies in America. Billy collects his
inheritance, the two boys review the airplane factory,
visit Washington to demonstrate their mastery of the air,
and are tapped into the Allied air service and race back
to the front in Europe for duty.

j196 ―――. *Our Young Aeroplane Scouts in the War Zone; or,
Serving Uncle Sam in the Cause of the Allies*. New
York: A.L. Burt, 1918. 222p.

It is October and Billy Barry, the Bangor Boy, and
Henri Trouville are in northern France as the first shell
is fired by the American forces in the war. We see the
two in a tense air fight with the Huns over the battlefield trenches near St. Quentin and the Scarpe where the
boys catch their first view of General Pershing. They
are now part of what is known as the flying five. The
boys now dash off in air combat, experience a crash
landing, and are captured by none other than the German
lieutenant they worked for in Hamburg. They undertake
seaplane-scout-and-bombing duty against the new super
German subs in the channel followed by a medley of their
usual hectic actions. The story concludes on the usual
happy note when Billy is informed by London solicitors
that he is now a millionaire as a result of his uncle's
estate and interest in an American airplane factory. See
Our Young Aeroplane Scouts in Germany for critical comment
on this series (item j50).

j197 Randall, Homer. *The Army Boys in France; or, From Training Camp to Trenches*. New York: George Sully & Co.,
1918. 216p.

The story begins with Frank, Bart, and Tom employed at
the firm of Moore & Thomas before the United States has
entered the war. Rabig, another employee, is a bully as
well as sympathetic to the German cause. When the U.S.
declares war, everyone wants to go to fight including
the three friends. They enlist in the 37th Regiment and
are sent off to Camp Boone. A substantial portion of the
book describes their training-camp experiences before
they are shipped off to France. The overseas voyage is
an adventure-filled journey of spies, U-boat attacks,
and the defensive strategy of the convoy on the high
seas. At a French camp for advanced training, their
everyday life is described in some detail, including
recreational activities such as boxing matches. The
boys meet an old friend, Billy, who joins them in all

their future adventures. They see their first tank, and when a damaged German zeppelin lands near them, they capture the ship and the entire crew. Soon after they are sent to the front-line trenches of France and quickly become involved in their usual heroic activities in battle against the Huns. The story is strongly anti-German, with considerable emphasis on patriotic sentiment. Another breezy and basically superficial juvenile tale characterized by the usual unrealistic activities of four wonder boys who always come out on top.

j198 ―――. *The Army Boys in the French Trenches; or, Hand to Hand Fights with the Enemy*. New York: George Sully & Co., 1918. 214p.

This is the sequel to *The Army Boys in France* ... (item j197) continuing the adventures of Frank, Tom, Bart, and Billy in the front-line trenches of France. The boys are shown on night-scout missions in no-man's-land along with their impressions of tank warfare and the use of cavalry. Their daring escape from behind the German lines is made by the lucky appearance of an Allied airplane that swoops down to take them up and away from their German captors in the usual daring exhibition of coincidental happenings so characteristic of this series of juvenile stories.

j199 Rolt-Wheeler, Francis William. *The Wonder of War on Land*. Boston: Lothrop, Lee & Shepard, 1918. 372p.

Tells a thin story on which is hung military activities of the first part of the war. Horace Monroe, an American boy in school in Belgium, becomes a volunteer with the Belgians and the French when the Germans invade both countries. Horace accompanies the hunchback Croquier as he evades the Germans in a mission to carry the Captive Kaiser eagle mascot back to Paris. This is all symbolic of course and counts for little except to lend a bit of melodrama to the otherwise sketchy plot. Interspersed through the book are fairly detailed discussions of troop movements, strategy, weapons characteristics, and a host of related topics connected with land warfare, especially as these pertain to the German invasion. What we have is very nearly a blow-by-blow account of the German advance with appropriate details of their occupation and brutal treatment of civilians. The book describes the terror and the unspeakable acts of violence, against a grisly backdrop of heaps of dead bodies including women and children. Horace is used as a volunteer dispatch rider on several occasions, and this enables the story to describe with a fair degree of realism many of the land-war activities and conditions. This is a didactic story about the war and intended primarily for young readers.

j200 Shaler, Robert. *The Boy Scouts at Mobilization Camp.* New York: Hurst & Co., 1918.

Not seen.

j201 ———. *The Boy Scouts Call to Arms.* New York: Hurst & Co., 1918.

Not seen.

j202 Sheppard, William Henry Crispin. *Don Hale Over There.* Philadelphia: Penn. Pub. Co., 1918. 326p.

Mainly a juvenile adventure-mystery placed in the trappings of the war front in France. The stereotyped plot relates the experiences of Don and his friends serving as Red Cross ambulance drivers at the front. Aside from the standard descriptions of the war-torn countryside, the wounded, trips to an artillery installation and a trench complex, and the terrors of enemy bombardments, the narrative is concerned mainly with activities behind the front lines such as the mystery of Château de Morancourt. Don and his friends accidentally discover a secret underground chamber at the château filled with famous and valuable paintings.

j203 Strang, Herbert (pseud.). *With Haig on the Somme; a Story of the Great War.* London: H. Milford, 1918. 283p.

Not seen.

j204 Stratemeyer, Edward. *Dave Porter Under Fire; or, A Young Army Engineer in France.* Boston: Lothrop, Lee & Shepard, 1918. 308p.

The fourteenth volume of the Dave Porter Series and the first set during the war. Dave is still pursuing his occupation as a young civil engineer. When the war comes, he joins the American forces at first to spend some time in one of the many camps in the United States, then to be sent for service on the battlefields of France. There, as an army engineer, he faces numerous grave perils but, of course, does his duty unflinchingly and with outstanding courage. Better than half of the story describes the activities and experiences of Dave and his chums in their U.S. training camp. They then go by transport over the Atlantic, subject to the ever-present threat of German U-boat attacks. The last quarter of the novel relates Dave's adventures at the front with all the rhetoric and bravery so characteristic of these boys' stories. This is the typical juvenile story of super patriotism demonstrating all of the traditional American virtues of God, mother, and country.

j205 Stuart, Gordon (pseud. of George Neser Madison). *The Boy Scouts of the Air on the French Front*. Chicago: Reilly & Lee, 1918. 271p.

Tod Fulton and Jerry Ring, stalwart boy scouts eager to join the war effort overseas, travel to New York City to convince Tod's father, the inventor of an aircraft device, to allow them to enlist. All become involved in thwarting a spy plot to obtain Mr. Fulton's invention. There is the usual cops-and-robbers routine leading to Mr. Fulton's kidnapping. Hearing that Mr. Fulton may be among the survivors of a German sub sunk by a British gunboat, the boys immediately take passage to Le Havre to learn that he has probably been taken to Germany by foreign agents. The rest of the story consists of the air-combat adventures of the two boys over German lines followed by their daring and successful rescue of Mr. Fulton at Essen.

j206 Theiss, Lewis Edwin. *The Secret Wireless; or, The Spy Hunt of the Camp Brady Patrol*. Boston: W.A. Wilde, 1918. 310p.

Not seen.

j207 Tomlinson, Paul Greene. *Bob Cook and the German Air Fleet*. New York: Barse & Hopkins, 1918. 251p.

The U.S. has been at war with Germany for some time. Not yet eighteen, Bob Cook is eager to enlist. His father hears of a chance for Bob and his friend Hugh to join the famous Lafayette Escadrille. They enlist and leave for France aboard a troopship. The trip is filled with the usual spy alarms and submarine attacks before they reach France and travel to Paris. The boys are immediately sent to the Escadrille training camp for pilots and soon become full-fledged aviators. They are involved in all of the typical air-war adventures--dog fights, bombing runs, scouting and observation flights--with a crash landing behind the German lines. There is a spy incident at the Escadrille landing field with the exposure of a devious German sympathizer and saboteur.

j208 ──────. *Bob Cook's Brother in the Trenches*. New York: Barse & Hopkins, 1918. 253p.

Another patriotic boys' war story. The chief characters are Bob and Harold, both of whom are young men with the American forces in France. Harold is an officer in the trenches while Bob is in a flying squadron. Most of the story details the experiences of Harold and his buddies in trench warfare against the Germans. The book describes the usual day-to-day events, conversations amidst the bombardments, no-man's-land attacks, scout missions, sabotage, and espionage. As in many of these juvenile books there is only a very superficial involvement with the horror of the war.

j209 Trent, Martha. *Alice Blythe: Somewhere in England; A War Time Story*. New York: Barse & Hopkins, 1918. 215p.

One of a series of juvenile books by Martha Trent, this title depicts the exploits of a sixteen-year-old British girl in France and in England as she flies planes, drives an ambulance, saves a life, delivers a vital communique, and finally captures a German spy.

j210 ──────. *Helen Carey: Somewhere in America; A War Time Story*. New York: Barse & Hopkins, 1918. 217p.

The chief character and heroine is Helen Carey, a sixteen-year-old American girl who lives on a ranch in Wyoming. Although the United States is not yet in the war, Helen is corresponding with a Belgian soldier as a result of local war-relief activities. The story has the distinct American West atmosphere of sagebrush, gophers, horses, saddles, and cattle. When an Englishman comes to her father to buy horses for his country's war effort, the horses are stolen. Alone, Helen stops two horse thieves from murdering one of her father's ranch hands, and all of the horses are recovered. When the United States declares war on the Central Powers, many of the local boys volunteer for service. A Red Cross group is formed and Helen goes off by train to visit her aunt and to say goodbye to Allan (a mild romantic interest) before he sails for France with his military unit. On the train east she overhears a German plot to derail the troop train, and with a frantic car race and lasso trick she manages to stop the engine just in time. She is injured and sent to the hospital where she is celebrated as a heroic patriot. This is a simple girl's story of teenage social activities in an American Western setting during the war, with no pretense of literary quality.

j211 ———. *Lucia Rudini: Somewhere in Italy.* New York: Barse & Hopkins, 1918. 220p.

Most of the action occurs in the small Italian village of Cellino in the mountains near the Austrian border where Lucia, an extremely resourceful fourteen-year-old orphan, is the sole breadwinner for her younger brother and her grandmother. When the Austrians advance, Lucia helps to blow up a bridge and saves the village from the Austrian soldiers. She also helps a wounded soldier, Captain Riccardo, to escape. He turns out to be a wealthy officer. In gratitude he invites Lucia and her family to live with him in Naples. At the same time the king arrives, commends Lucia for her bravery, and awards her a medal. The story concludes in Naples as Lucia apprehends an Austrian spy while blissfully enjoying the new life provided by Captain Riccardo.

j212 ———. *Marieken de Bruin: Somewhere in Belgium.* New York: Barse & Hopkins, 1918. 224p.

The story begins in the little village of Zandre in September of 1915. Only a few villagers remain when the Germans invade. Little fourteen-year-old Marieken takes charge of the local inn and offers to cook for the German general and his staff if he lets her garden and farm animals alone. When a German lieutenant turns out to be an Englishman in disguise, she agrees to take his message to the Allied lines to warn them of an imminent German attack. She wades through mud, past sentries, through the forest and countryside at night, across no-man's-land and throws the message into the English trenches and then immediately heads back to the inn and arrives by sunrise, tired but unharmed. When war intensifies near the village, Marieken helps the English prisoners to escape. She receives two awards for her bravery, one from the Belgians and one from the English. The story concludes with the grand and happy reunion of Marieken and her family at the hospital in Fleurette where she is now working for the Allies.

j213 ———. *Valerie Duval: Somewhere in France*. New York: Barse & Hopkins, 1918. 213p.

A girls' story analogous to war-adventure stories for boys. Valerie is a sixteen-year-old French girl (with American relatives) from the small village of Vinon. The Duvals have a family tradition of service to their country. (Valerie's father was killed in the war and her brother is crippled.) When the Americans arrive in her village looking for billets, she decides to do her part. Dressed as a boy, she nearly reaches the front when an old French sergeant spots her. She is then permitted to work at an officers' inn in Riva near the front lines in an ambulance amidst heavy nighttime shelling. She captures a German machine gun and turns it against the Germans, forcing them to retreat. She returns home decorated by the commanding general with the Croix de Guerre and then goes off to help in a field hospital. Love now enters the plot and the story ends on a romantic note with Valerie and the American lieutenant Fielding in an embrace. Strictly a juvenile story for adolescent girls. The other similar stories of the author follow the same standardized pattern.

j214 Van Dyne, Edith (pseud. of Lyman Frank Baum). *Mary Louise and the Liberty Girls*. Chicago: Reilly & Lee, 1918. 255p.

Not seen.

j215 Vandercook, Margaret O'Bannon (Womack). *The Camp Fire Girls Behind the Lines*. Philadelphia: John C. Winston Co., 1918. 249p.

The Camp Fire Girls at Sunrise Hill Camp in California spend the summer entertaining the soldiers at a nearby camp and engaging in other wartime efforts. The plot also involves two conscientious objectors.

j216   ———. *The Camp Fire Girls on the Field of Honor.*
        Philadelphia: John C. Winston Co., 1918. 272p.

        The Camp Fire Girls are in France living on a French
        farm, doing whatever they can to assist their French
        neighbors in reconstructing their lives. They conduct
        a school for young children, work in the hospital, visit
        the nearby village to find those who need help, and even
        nurse a French soldier back to health.

j217   ———. *The Red Cross Girls Afloat with the Flag.*
        Philadelphia: John C. Winston Co., 1918.

        Not seen.

j218   Wells, Carolyn. *Patty-bride.* New York: Dodd, Mead &
        Co., 1918. 304p.

        A frothy novel for adolescent girls. Patty is the some-
        what scatterbrained young woman who, with her friends on
        the home front, tries to do her part for the war effort at
        "dinners and evening parties and little dances, all for the
        Khaki and the Blue!" The story begins with Patty's engage-
        ment to Captain Billie Farnsworth, who is soon sent on to
        duty in Washington, D.C. There is some intrigue involving
        spies in D.C. and Patty's projects, such as selling valen-
        tines to the soldiers in camp, Red Cross benefits, private
        charities, War Relief meetings, etc. Boys in their ro-
        mantic uniforms, spies, and talk of aviators and their
        adventures serve mainly as the furniture with which this
        trifling tale probably was designed to entertain girls
        and young ladies with harmless nonsense. This is one of
        the most egregious examples of this genre.

j219   Westerman, Percy Francis. *Billy Barcroft, R.N.A.S.: a
        Story of the Great War.* London: S.W. Partridge, 1918.
        416p.

        Not seen.

j220A   ———. *The Fritz Strafers: a Story of the Great War.*
        London: S.W. Partridge, 1918, 380p. [Reissued in 1931
        as *The Keepers of the Narrow Seas*.]

        Not seen.

j221AB ———. *A Lively Bit of the Front: a Tale.* London:
        Blackie & Son, 1918. 288p.

        Not seen.

Juvenile Novels

j222A ——. *The Submarine Hunters: a Story*. London: Blackie & Son, 1918. 288p.

Not seen.

j223AC ——. *To the Fore with the Tanks!* London: S.W. Partridge, 1918. 256p.

Not seen.

j224A ——. *Under the White Ensign; a Naval Story of the Great War*. London: Blackie & Son, 1918. 256p.

Not seen.

j225A ——. *Wilmshurst of the Frontier Force: a Story of the Conquest of German East Africa*. London: S.W. Partridge, 1918. 252p.

Not seen.

j226A ——. *With Beatty off Jutland: a Romance of the Great Sea Fight*. London: Blackie & Son, 1918. 284p.

Not seen.

j227 Whitehill, Dorothy. *Polly Sees the World at War*. New York: Barse & Hopkins, 1918. 256p.

Not seen.

j228 Widdemer, Margaret. *Winona's War Farm*. Philadelphia: Lippincott & Co., 1918. 318p.; London: J.B. Lippincott Co., 1918. 252p.

A troop of camp fire girls and one of boy scouts invest their funds in an old farm which they operate for a summer as their contribution to the war effort. Their discovery of a Civil War railroad tunnel leads to the capture of two saboteurs intent on blowing up a munitions powder plant.

j229 Young, Clarence (pseud.; Stratemeyer Syndicate). *The Motor Boys in the Army; or, Ned, Bob, and Jerry as Volunteers*. New York: Cupples & Leon, 1918.

Not seen.

1919

j230 Ames, Franklin T. (pseud.). *Between the Lines on the American Front: A Boys' Story of the Great European War*. New York: Dodd, Mead & Co., 1919. 315p.

This is the third novel of the author's series of war tales for boys (items j8 and j9), continuing the adventures of Tom Maillard and his Dorr cousins. After war is declared, they enlist and are sent to a basic training camp. Upon completion of their military training they ship off to France through submarine-infested waters. After a dramatic landing on French soil they receive further training before being sent into battle at Château-Thierry and St. Mihiel. The story is larded with patriotic fervor and enthusiasm. Also, the book clearly presents the idea that American soldiers are the peers of any other group of fighters in the world.

j231 Appleton, Victor (pseud.; Stratemeyer Syndicate). *The Moving Picture Boys on French Battlefields: or Taking Pictures for the U.S. Army*. New York: Grosset & Dunlap, 1919. 212p.

Continues the adventures of the American movie photographers Blake Stewart, Joe Duncan, and their assistant, Charlie Anderson, as they continue taking war pictures for American home consumption. Among the movies designed to inform and inflame the home front were those of battles, a German attack on a Red Cross hospital, a tank assault of the German trenches, and aerial dogfights, including one of the first uses of parachutes by German pilots. When they are given the assignment of photographing areas behind the German lines, they are captured and their films confiscated. However, they soon retrieve their films and dramatically escape.

j232 ———. *Tom Swift and His Air Scout; or, Uncle Sam's Mastery of the Sky*. New York: Grosset & Dunlap, 1919. 218p.

Not seen.

j233 Balmer, Edwin. *Ruth of the U.S.A.* Chicago: A.C. McClurg & Co., 1919. 361p.

The heroine, Ruth Alden, wishing to be a part of the war effort, goes to France, becomes involved with the popular aviator Gerry Hull, who flies for the French, and eventually finds herself confronting the German military situation at close quarters. Ruth's war work, in which she nearly loses her life, becomes a major contribution to the American war effort.

j234 Barbour, Ralph Henry, and H.P. Holt. *Fortunes of War*. New York: Century Co., 1919. 352p.

A juvenile story about Jerry Kendall who, after the death of his father, is left with a two-masted schooner. Jerry is inclined to sell the boat, but an older boy friend, Ben Duncan, convinces him to consider cargo hauling. The two set out with a load of lumber for France where the war has placed a high value on such products. In the process they make an unfortunate choice of a skipper and get mixed up with the Germans and a submarine. The two boys end up helping the U.S. government find a German sub base, in typical all-American boy-hero style.

j235 Barbour, Ralph Henry. *Under the Yankee Ensign*. New York: D. Appleton & Co., 1919. 335p.

Mainly a naval wartime story that occurs during August and September of 1917. David Garson, a young boy seaman of seventeen, is assigned his first sea duty on the converted submarine chaser 944 and becomes good friends with Pete Rooney. David is washed overboard in a terrific gale but luckily hauled back on board by his friend. The chaser is headed toward France on sea duty. On their way to Queenstown, Ireland, they are attacked by a sub and David is blown overboard by a shell. Pete jumps in to rescue him and both are later captured by a German sub. They are interrogated and when the sub attacks an Italian liner the two decide that escaping into the water is preferable to remaining on board the sub. A day or two later they are picked up by an American destroyer and returned to the 944 at Queenstown. One of the new crew members is Robert Dill who soon becomes a close friend of Pete and David. The rest of the story relates the experiences of the three friends after the 944 is sunk by a mine and they are assigned to a destroyer on duty in the waters between France and England. Life on the destroyer is described in some detail, as the ship chases subs and participates in gun battles. While on leave in England the three capture two German aviators who have secretly landed. After this coup they return to sea duty and the novel concludes as they avoid near-destruction at Helgoland. The narrative and writing are considerably better than the run-of-the-mill juvenile-series novels for boys and girls.

j236 Bates, Gordon (pseud. of Josephine Chase). *The Khaki Boys Fighting to Win; or Smashing the German Lines.* New York: Cupples & Leon, 1919. 210p.

The five friends of the Khaki Boys Series are in the midst of battle in the trenches, undaunted by the danger they face. In this volume they reveal an espionage plot concerning the U.S. Signal Corps and are captured by the Germans. Naturally, their pluck stands them in good stead and they soon escape.

j237 ————. *The Khaki Boys Over the Top; or Doing and Daring for Uncle Sam.* New York: Cupples & Leon, 1919. 210p.

The fourth book of the Khaki Boys Series finds the five comrades, Jimmy Blaise, Bob Dalton, Roger Barlow, Ignace Pulinski, and Franz Schnitzel in the front-line trenches going "over the top" in assault after assault. The story consists of attacks and counterattacks in which the five friends are cut off from their fellow soldiers behind German lines, escape, and then are captured, only to escape again.

j238 Beach, Charles Amory. *Air Service Boys Flying for Victory; or Bombing the Last German Stronghold.* New York: George Sully & Co., 1919. 218p.

Begins in the fall of 1918 with the American assault on the German forces in the Argonne Forest. The flying aces Tom Raymond, Harry Leroy, and Jack Parmly perform their typical feats, destroy the German command post, and rescue a six-year-old French child from her German uncle. The novel ends with the signing of the Armistice.

j239 ————. *Air Service Boys in the Big Battle; or, Silencing the Big Guns.* New York: George Sully & Co., 1919. unpaged (approx. 218p.).

The two heroes, Jack Parmly and Tom Raymond, demonstrate their daring and resourceful talent in the service of the American army under General Pershing. They are closely involved in many of the front-line battles in the American sector and especially in the events accompanying the

Juvenile Novels 399

      great German push against the Allied forces. Typical adventures involve their discovery and rescue of fellow pilots and friends shot down behind the German lines. A bit of romance develops over the interest of Tom in the sister of Harry, a fellow pilot and friend. She is serving as a Red Cross nurse in one of the American field hospitals during the Argonne drive.

j240   Bishop, Austin. *Bob Thorpe, Sky Fighter in the Lafayette Flying Corps.* New York: Harcourt, Brace & Co., 1919. 275p.

      A book of technical flying information about World War I airplanes, as well as a novel about two young Americans who, while serving with the French ambulance service, enlist in the French Air Force and serve as combat pilots for the French before the entrance of the United States into the war.

*   Blaine, John (pseud.). *The Boy Scouts on the Western Front.* Akron, Ohio: Saalfield Pub. Co., 1919.

      A later reprint with a different author and title of *The Boy Scouts Under Fire in France* ... by George Durston (item j174).

*   ———. *The Boy Scouts with Joffre.* Akron, Ohio: Saalfield Pub. Co., 1919.

      A later reprint with a different author and title of *The Boy Scouts in the War Zone* ... by George Durston (item j255).

j241   Brereton, Frederick Sadleir. *With Allenby in Palestine: A Story of the Latest Crusade.* London: Blackie & Son, 1919. 287p.

      Recounts the adventures of Lieutenant Donald Carruthers of the British army as he ventures behind the Turkish lines disguised as an Arab, on an espionage mission for the British. In the process he rescues his friend, Lieutenant Tom Masterman, who had been captured by the Turks and held in Jerusalem. One of the better series of juvenile stories.

j242   ———. *With the Allies to the Rhine; a Story of the Finish of the War.* London: Blackie & Son, 1919. 288p.

      Not seen.

j243   Brooks, Edna. *The Khaki Girls at Windsor Barracks*.
         New York: Cupples & Leon, 1919. 212p.

         Not seen.

j244   Burley, Andrew S. *Uncle Sam's Army Boys in Italy; or,
         Bob Hamilton Under Fire in the Piave District*. Chicago:
         M.A. Donohue, 1919. 253p.

         Bob and his friend Sid are in Italy near the Austrian
         Tyrol. It is spring and the U.S. has not yet entered the
         war. The boys have gone to Italy to have a tour of the
         front. Captain Borgia is their guardian and guide on
         their week or two tour of the Isonzo front. They observe
         a large air battle between the Austrians and the Italians.
         A large zeppelin bombs the small city they are in and
         they commiserate on the damage done. When they reach
         the front with their guide, there is a terrific Austrian
         barrage on the Italian positions. They climb to a high
         mountain observation point to witness the assault of the
         Italian mountain troops and there they meet the Italian
         king and his aides also touring the front lines. They
         visit a field hospital and become involved in an Austrian
         bomb plot, etc. They now decide it is time to return
         home to America, and travel by horseback to Rome. The
         story ends as they are apprehended by Italian soldiers
         who think they are Austrian spies.

j245   ———. *Uncle Sam's Army Boys in Khaki Under Canvas;
         or, Bob Hamilton and the Munition Plant Plot*. Chicago:
         M.A. Donohue, 1919. 250p.

         Bob Hamilton and Sid Oliphant, two friends from Rich-
         mond, Virginia, are ordered with their unit to stand
         guard against spies and saboteurs at various vital
         munitions factories along the U.S. east coast. They
         soon are closely associated with secret service agents
         and help devise various security measures to protect the
         war effort. The boys end up at a plant in Virginia near
         the coast. There soon develops a bombing attempt on the
         plant by an unknown spy plane thought to come from an
         offshore enemy war vessel. Tommy, a young boy employee
         at the plant, becomes friends with Bob and Sid but soon
         mysteriously disappears after he learns about a bomb
         plot to blow up the plant. Bob and Sid search for Tommy
         in a marsh near the coast and discover the hiding place
         of the spy seaplane. After a night and a day of observa-
         tion they capture the German spies and release their
         friend.

Juvenile Novels

j246 ———. *Uncle Sam's Army Boys on the Rhine: or, Bob Hamilton in the Argonne Death Trap.* Chicago: M.A. Donohue, 1919. 292p.

The American First Army is given the task of clearing out the Germans from the Argonne Forest, and Sergeant Bob Hamilton and Private Sid Oliphant are among those whose mission it is to destroy the machine-gun nests remaining in the Forest.

j247 Canfield, Flavia A. Camp. *The Refugee Family; A Story for Girls.* New York: Harcourt Brace & Co., 1919. 275p.

Deals with a refugee family in northern France. As the story begins, Marie and Paulette are two happy little school girls but the war forces them from their home. Their father goes into the army and their mother is deported to Germany. They go to live with their aunt and crippled cousin in a cellar in one of the bombed villages. Suddenly life becomes brighter when two American college girls doing relief work in France arrive in the ruined village. Eventually through their efforts the little girls have their home restored and their mother is permitted to return. Additional help is also sent by a group of little girls in America and all now seems well.

* Cobb, Frank (pseud.). *The Potter Boys in the Front Line Trenches.* Akron, Ohio: Saalfield Pub. Co., 1919.

A reprint with different author and title of *The Boy Scouts Under Fire in France* ... by George Durston (item j174).

* ———. *The Potter Boys with the Tanks.* Akron, Ohio: Saalfield Pub. Co., 1919.

A reprint with a different author and title of *The Boy Scouts in the War Zone* ... by George Durston (item j255).

j248 Davidson, Halsey. *Navy Boys at the Big Surrender, or, Rounding Up the German Fleet.* New York: George Sully & Co., 1919. 218p. [Republished as *Deep Sea Boys at the Big Surrender*.... New York: Equitable, 1930.]

The fifth and final volume of the Navy Boys Series. Once again the story details the experiences of the

Seacove chums as sailors aboard the escort destroyer *Colodia* on its mission across the Atlantic to England. The boys are involved in sinking a German U-boat, capturing a German raider, destroying an enemy bomber, and, finally, participating at the surrender of the German Navy following the Armistice. Naturally, they are all-American boys of exceptional bravery and responsibility and fulfill a didactic, patriotic purpose, a characteristic of most of these war-series tales for juveniles.

j249 ―――――. *Navy Boys to the Rescue, or, Answering the Wireless Call for Help*. New York: George Sully & Co., 1919. 216p. [Reprinted as *Deep Sea Boys to the Rescue*.... New York: Equitable, 1930.]

The four plucky heroes become involved in a number of adventures with Admiral Sims' flotilla on foreign service. They partake in the dangerous cruises of the destroyers and submarine chasers which were expected to defend the convoys of troops and supply ships through the German U-boat zones and mine fields. A fifth boy, George Fielding, joins the four Navy chums on board the *Colodia*, and their subsequent adventures involve a German spy, the patriotic actions of George's sister and family, and a race to rescue the *Redbird* and recapture it from German agents. After this climax they return to Hampton Roads for refitting their ship and shore leave.

j250 Drake, Robert L. (pseud. of Clair Wallace Hayes). *The Boy Allies with the Victorious Fleets; or, The Fall of the German Navy*. New York: A.L. Burt, 1919. 242p.

This is the final story in this series of juvenile war tales. Jack Templeton has been made the captain of his own vessel and Frank Chadwick, his buddy, is his first officer. The plot continues with the now familiar (and predictable) adventures of these exemplars of bravery in wartime. They are described on patrol duty with troop transports returning wounded to America and on convoys travelling to England. The story deals primarily with the participation of the two boys opposing the German U-boat attacks against Allied shipping. The two heroes eventually are sent to Washington, D.C., to receive the personal greeting of President Wilson for their gallant achievements on duty. The story concludes with the surrender of the last of the German fleet after the signing of the Armistice. A typical breezy juvenile story characteristic of the prolific children's book industry of the period.

Juvenile Novels

j251   Driscoll, James R. *The Brighton Boys at Château-Thierry*.
       Philadelphia: John C. Winston Co., 1919. 232p.

   Recounts the war experiences of two former Brighton
Academy classmates, initially competitors, who become
friends through their shared experiences on the battlefield at Château-Thierry. The classmates are Don Richards
of the Red Cross Ambulance Service and Clement Stapley,
a Marine. Together they capture one of two saboteurs
in their hometown. In France they capture the second
escapee. The friendship of the boys is securely established when they try to aid one another after both have
been wounded.

j252   ———. *The Brighton Boys at St. Mihiel*. Philadelphia:
       John C. Winston Co., 1919. 258p.

   Depicts the great concentration of Allied forces poised
for the final drive to regain the St. Mihiel salient held
for four years by the Germans. Many bloody battles are
fought, and the three former Brighton Academy students
acquit themselves well in the action. Among their exploits are the capturing of a spy, a German colonel, and
saving the town of Thiaucourt from destruction. The
story ends with the request of the Central Powers for an
armistice.

j253   ———. *The Brighton Boys with the Engineers at Cantigny*.
       Philadelphia: John C. Winston Co., 1919. 256p.

   Charlie ("Chick") Wharton and Bob Grier leave Brighton
Academy to enlist with the Third Regiment of Engineers
and are sent to the front to rebuild the railroad destroyed by the retreating Germans. When they are cut
off by a German advance, Chick and Bob make their way
back to their headquarters in Gouzeaucourt for additional
missions. When the boys are transferred to a newly arrived American troop train, they extinguish a fire in a
munitions car, discover a time bomb, and expose a German
saboteur who has travelled from the United States with
the Third Regiment.

j254   Du Bois, Mary Constance. *Comrade Rosalie*. New York:
       Century Co., 1919. 473p.

   The story is placed in the last months of the war in
northern France. The girl, Marie Rosalie, lives in a
château in the care of her governess. Her foster sister

Trinette is her principal playmate while her mother is serving in a French hospital. A number of airplane battles occur in the sky over the old château. A German spy who appears first disguised as a Belgian workman and later as a French curé, is finally foiled. Rosalie gets her special title from a young soldier and a young American pilot who call her "comrade." When an American pilot, Bertrand, is wounded, Rosalie corresponds with his sisters in America and soon becomes a good friend. Bertrand is awarded the Croix de Guerre for his valiant efforts. Thus, after the end of the war, Rosalie, Trinette, and the mother sail to America as guests of their American friends. The plot makes a point of revealing the feelings and actions of the French people in wartime in a sympathetic and realistic way.

j255 Durston, George (pseud. of Georgia Roberts Durston). *The Boy Scouts in the War Zone; or, On the Field of France*. Akron, Ohio: Saalfield Pub. Co., 1919. unpaged.

Young twins, Porky and Beany Potter, are permitted to visit the front in France in their boy scout uniforms as a result of their friendship with a general. They are able to see firsthand a dramatic dog fight in the sky between the Germans and the French and American planes. They also encounter a number of soldiers who are only too happy to relate their front-line experiences to the two young boys. Soon the twins are made messengers by General Joffre in the area just behind the front lines. Here the boys have the opportunity to observe the behavior and appearance of the German soldiers. At one point the twins are able to watch all of the military activities of a single day of heavy fighting on the front. They hear about the personal experiences of two American soldiers who had been held in a German prisoner-of-war camp. The book concludes with the boys preparing to return home after several exciting months in the thick of the war. The plot is most unlikely and the story line is obviously addressed to the preadolescent age group.

j256 Dyer, Walter Alden. *Ben, the Battle Horse; a Story of the Great War*. New York: Henry Holt & Co., 1919. 310p.

A book written for young boys about the history of a Kentucky horse named Buttercup. When war occurs Buttercup is taken to France, performs gallantly, and receives the Croix de Guerre.

j257 Emerson, Alice B. *Ruth Fielding Homeward Bound; or A Red Cross Worker's Ocean Perils*. New York: Cupples & Leon, 1919. 210p.

Ruth Fielding's transport ship is pirated by Germans, and her friend, Tom Cameron, is captured and held aboard a zeppelin on its way to bomb London. How Tom destroys the zeppelin, is cast adrift in a strange box, picked up by the pirated ship, and then takes control of the ship is the plot of this story for juvenile girls.

* Fiske, James (pseud.). *With Pershing in France*. Akron, Ohio: Saalfield Pub. Co., 1919.

A reprint with a different author and title of *The Boy Scouts Under Fire in France* ... by George Durston (item j174).

* ———. *With the Hero of the Marne*. Akron, Ohio: Saalfield Pub. Co., 1919.

A reprint with different author and title of *The Boy Scouts in the War Zone* ... by George Durston (item j255).

j258 Fitzhugh, Percy Keese. *Tom Slade with the Flying Corps: A Campfire Tale*. New York: Grosset & Dunlap, 1919. 244p.

A typical patriotic boys' story of the period. The novel begins with the announcement of the death in the war of Tom Slade, a good example of the "all-American boy hero" model used by many of the boys' stories of the period. Tom is an aviator in France. His life story is presented, starting from his orphan days in New Jersey when he became a boy scout and was imbued with all the ideals and values of scouting. Tom's adventures include being captured by the Germans from his torpedoed ship and sent to a prison camp. There he escapes to France where at first he became a motorcycle dispatch rider and later an aviator. The bulk of the story describes his wartime flying experiences in fighting the Germans. The narrator is a war correspondent who travels to Europe to dig out the details of Slade's exploits. The story is a combination mystery-adventure of the narrator's own wartime experiences as he attempts to trace the activities of

Tom Slade. In the process he discovers that Tom is still alive (a case of mistaken identity) and he relates the incredible tale of Slade's survival and return to the U.S. The story is a testament to scouting principles and values.

j259 Goss, Warren Lee. *Jed's Boy; a Story of Adventures in the Great World War.* New York: Thomas Y. Crowell, 1919. 235p.

The nephew of Jed, the author's character in an earlier novel about the Civil War, is the hero of this story. While on the farm the nephew is befriended by David, a boy his own age. The two boys enlist in the war. David is unnerved by his friend's apparent desertion to the Germans and joins the French secret service. However, the novel ends happily for all concerned when the nephew turns out to be a staunch patriot after all.

j260 Hancock, Harrie Irving. *Dave Darrin after the Mine Layers; or, Hitting the Enemy A Hard Naval Blow.* Philadelphia: Henry Altemus Co., 1919. 251p.

Another example of a typical series novel for boys and girls so characteristic of the first forty years of this century. The main characters of all the various series of the author (Grammar School Boys Series, High School Boys Series, West Point Series, Young Engineer Series, Annapolis Series, etc.) are based on his "famous" group of six school boys who were collectively known as Dick & Co. In the Dave Darrin series, Dave and Dan Dalzell are the two adventurous heroes who are created as super all-American boy types. They are officers in the U.S. Navy and in this adventure are stationed on a minesweeper that covers the waters off the coast of England. The plot records their adventures at sea, the icy storms, an encounter with a German U-boat, and the capture of Dave by the Germans, his interrogations with the other prisoners, and their eventual escape, etc. It is clear that the author is doing his best to whip up the appropriate patriotic emotions in the breasts of all his young readers. Dave Darrin is a paragon of strength, virtue, and altruism, who is clearly created as a model of behavior. Darrin even has a wife, Belle, who is in the Red Cross and who displays the same superhuman qualities of her husband. The plots of these novels are predictable formula stories with minimal literary qualities and style. Perhaps their chief value lies in their testimony to a time when boys and girls could not only believe in superpatriotic adventures but also read for recreation.

j261 ———. *Dave Darrin and the German Submarines; or, Making a Clean-up of the Hun Sea Monsters*. Akron, Ohio: Saalfield Pub. Co., 1919. 255p.

Dave is in charge of a U.S. torpedo boat destroyer near Ireland. The plot covers plenty of action with German subs. We follow the brave Dave as he is assigned duty on several ships, including a disguised merchant vessel with many hidden and powerful guns to entrap any enemy subs that think the ship defenseless. Dave is the usual resourceful hero who seldom makes a mistake and always manages to get the best of the enemy. The narrative explains convoy-defense strategy and techniques to outsmart and destroy enemy submarines. The plot has the usual dollop of traitors and spies, combined with plenty of sea fighting, including a 60-sub attack on Dave's troopship convoy. The story provides a liberal dose of patriotic messages and anti-German propaganda to encourage reader indignation and outrage. The tale ends with the appearance of Belle, Dave's wife, on board a passenger liner sunk by a German sub. This terrible news inspires Darrin to superhuman efforts to save her (which, of course he does just in the nick of time). The story concludes with the usual happy ending. Another typical juvenile-series novel with stereotyped plot and character.

j262 ———. *Dave Darrin on Mediterranean Service; or, With Dan Dalzell on European Duty*. Akron, Ohio: Saalfield Pub. Co., 1919. 255p.

Not seen.

j263 ———. *Uncle Sam's Boys Smash the Germans; or, Winding Up the Great War*. Philadelphia: Henry Altemus Co., 1919. 212p.

The action starts on the morning of July 18, 1919, in the trenches many miles west of Château-Thierry. Captains Dick Prescott and Greg Holmes and their men are in the midst of bullets, shells, dirt, and the blood and guts of the front lines. The Germans have just completed their last great push toward Paris, and the Allies are now starting their drive to the Rhine. There is constant rifle, machine gun, automatic, and grenade fire underscored by bloody bayonet and gas attacks. Several American Indians are in Dick's company. They soon are the terror of the front lines, volunteering to kill as many Germans as possible in retaliation for the torture-murder of a fellow soldier. Dick joins the Indians in a deadly raid. The bloody and horrible aspect of the war is well emphasized in this episode. The trenches literally begin to flow with blood as the Germans are forced back through their own trenches and across rivers and streams. Dick is seriously wounded and sent to a field hospital. There is the typical spy interlude when Dick's Indian troopers sight a spy in a German officer's uniform behind the enemy lines and bring him to the American lines where he is sentenced to be shot. The Armistice is signed and the American army becomes the Army of Occupation as Dick, Greg, and their friends arrive at the Rhine. This is a typical juvenile story of this genre except for the heavy stress on the bloody horrors of the war.

j264 ———. *Uncle Sam's Boys with Pershing's Troops at the Front; or, Dick Prescott Grips with the Boche.* Philadelphia: Henry Altemus Co., 1919. 212p.

It is a few months after the U.S. has declared war on Germany. The 99th Infantry Regiment is being formed in Georgia for basic training and recruitment. Captains Dick Prescott and Greg Holmes are assigned to the new regiment. The reader is given a glimpse of training-camp daily life, military procedures, disciplinary problems, etc. The issue of conscientious objectors is raised when three of the men declare this status. Dick, however, convinces two of them that their position is simply socialistic or some other "freak" talk and that they should fight for truth and justice. When Dick discovers the third soldier has a pointed head, he immediately grants his request to transfer to a non-combatant unit. The regiment now is sent by troopship to France. On the way, of course, the now standard U-boat attacks occur but the ships safely arrive in France and the boys are immediately taken off to the front as the Germans launch a heavy attack. The rest of the story has the usual battlefield adventures and excitement. After a daring mission behind the German lines, Dick and Greg are congratulated by none other than General Pershing.

j265 Havard, Aline. *Captain Lucy in France.* Philadelphia: Penn. Pub. Co., 1919. 377p.

Recounts the adventures of Lucy Gordon who is caught behind the German lines in France when Château-Plessis is taken. She is in the vicinity where her father, Colonel Gordon, lies wounded in a hospital waiting to be transferred as a prisoner to Germany. Captain Lucy escapes through the front lines to the Allied side with information which allows the Allied troops to recapture Château-Plessis and rescue her father.

j266 Hayes, Clair W. *The Boy Allies with Marshal Foch; or, The Closing Days of the Great World War.* New York: A.L. Burt, 1919. 251p.

Hal and Chester are now near Rheims in late July of 1918. The war has clearly turned in favor of the Allies and there are rumors of an armistice. Marshal Foch implements his plan for a decisive blow at the retreating Huns and the two boys are directed to undertake an expedition behind the lines to obtain intelligence information. They succeed and run into their foreign correspondent friend and the German General Knoff who inadvertently provides them with information they need. They return to their lines and the last great offensive of the Allies begins with the Germans in retreat. Details of the military action—snipers, barricades, artillery action, etc.—are followed through the eyes and experiences of the two chums as they pursue and fight the retreating Germans in a series of their usual "by the skin of the teeth" adventures. In the process they consort with Generals Pershing, Rhodes, and Foch and are invariably at the heart of the Allies' advance and negotiations for an armistice. The story ends with the well-known peace settlement, a German mob attack on American soldiers, to which the two brave friends repair, and a final friendly encounter with General Knoff and his family before they return home as colonels wearing the Distinguished Service Cross for their valor and bravery during four years in the war. The final title in this juvenile series.

j267 ———. *The Boy Allies with Pershing in France; or, Over the Top at Chateau Thierry.* New York: A.L. Burt, 1919. 248p.

Hal and Chester are in a shell hole in no-man's-land on March 20, 1918, just before the last desperate advance of the Germans. The enemy losses are horrendous as they attempt to take Ypres and push on a second time to Paris. But the Allies (principally the American infantry and the Marines) with Hal and Chester in the vanguard begin their counterattack and force the enemy

back again. All of this trench and battlefield warfare
is described through the usual heroic actions of the two
heroes and their buddies. There is also an episode of
tank warfare. Later the boys meet General Pershing and
are invited to be his temporary drivers to an important
conference with Marshals Foch and Haig. They next are
sent on a special spying mission behind the German lines,
which deliberately involves the capture of our two friends
and their subsequent placement by the Germans in a
prisoner-of-war mining camp near the Swiss border. They
eventually escape with vital intelligence information
which they successfully bring back to General Pershing.
This, of course, all leads up to the successful offensive
of the Americans at Château-Thierry and Belleau Woods
with Chester and Hal in the heart of the action.

j268 ———. *The Boy Allies with the Great Advance; or, Driving the Foe Through France and Belgium.* New York: A.L. Burt, 1919. 248p.

The two heroes, Captains Paine and Crawfield, are at
the American front east of Château-Thierry two days after
a major offensive in the Argonne. Chester and Hal are
sent out as scouts for intelligence in no-man's-land.
They move over the top late at night in a thick fog with
their war-correspondent friend at their heels. In another
adventure, involving Irish conspirators, they encounter
the Irish liberation question when a fellow soldier
brings them his red shamrock. Chester investigates and
is nearly killed in a secret meeting of the Irish conspirators. This leads to their court-martial and death
sentence, but one decides to confess to avoid that fate.
This leads Hal and Chester to travel to Rheims and inform
the commanding general of the secret meeting of the chief
Irish conspirators. Hal and Chester are now assigned to
the staff of Pershing and assist in the dramatic capture
of the Irish supporters. This is followed by more battlefield adventures and escapes at the Argonne. Hal and
Chester later end up in the very heart of the American
attack in the St. Mihiel sector. At the conclusion of
the story they receive commissions as majors for their
courageous service.

j269 Hornibrook, Isabel Katherine. *Campfire Girls in War and Peace.* Boston: Lothrop, Lee & Shepard, 1919. 292p.

Not seen.

j270 James, William R. *Barbed-wire Grant of the Engineers*.
New York: Platt & Nourse, 1919. unpaged.

Not seen.

j271 ———. *Barrage Fire Barnes of the Field Artillery*.
New York: Platt & Nourse, 1919. 281p.

Ray Barnes of Brooklyn responds to his former professor's appeal for Emerson High School graduates to enlist in some branch of the armed services. Ray enlists in the field artillery, made up of National Guardsmen. His training begins at Plattsburgh with hours of practice and instruction in artillery through the summer. When orders come, the soldiers go aboard transports for an uneventful voyage to France and are soon at their encampment where the "finishing" training is undertaken. The men receive orders to relieve a British battery at the front. Forced to retreat, Ray and his friends, Chet Warren and Buck Cassidy, are injured and hospitalized. After their recovery, the decimated battery is brought up to full strength and sent to the front. The final American push entraps the Germans in a pincer movement in which Ray and another American seize a German 77 gun and turn it on the Germans as the Germans retreat.

j272 ———. *Gunpointer Stewart of the Naval Militia*. New York: Platt & Nourse, 1919. 287p.

Follows the fortunes of Les Stewart of Emerson High School in Brooklyn as he enlists in the Naval Militia, trains and becomes a crew member of the American destroyer *Pixie* as it sets out for patrol duty in the North Sea. On the Atlantic voyage, the *Pixie* receives calls for help from ships which have been attacked by a giant submarine. When the giant submarine attacks the *Pixie*, Les is thrown overboard by an explosion and is picked up by the German sub. Aboard the ship is an impressed American, brother of one of Les Stewart's shipmates. Together they escape when the submarine is attacked, and in swimming to an island discover a secret German wireless station, served by carrier pigeon. They impart their discovery to the British Secret Service and regain their ship.

j273 ———. *Trooper Sharpe of the First Cavalry*. New York: Platt & Nourse, 1919. unpaged.

Not seen.

j274 Jasper, Philip. *Uncle Sam's Navy Boys Afloat: or The Raid along the Atlantic Seaboard.* Chicago: M.A. Donohue, 1919. 276p.

This story finds Jack Warren and Toby Jucklin, as newly enlisted sailors, aboard the destroyer *Prentice* going to the rescue of a passenger liner torpedoed by a German U-boat. A former classmate, Heinrich Dietrich, has boarded a German U-boat for Germany, only to turn up later in Guantánamo where the *Prentice* is on winter maneuvers. The boys interrupt a plan of Heinrich's to mine a United States battleship, but Heinrich escapes to capture Jack at a later date. With the end of winter maneuvers the ships leave the harbor for Newport, certain that war is near.

j275 ―――. *Uncle Sam's Navy Boys in Action: or Running Down Enemy Commerce Destroyers.* Chicago: M.A. Donohue, 1919. 256p.

Opens with Jack Warren and Toby Jucklin locating a secret wireless which the Germans are operating on the coast of Maine. The boys overcome the operator and send a false message to effect a rendezvous. On returning to their ship, the officers make arrangements and the rendezvous is carried out, but the German ship is warned and escapes, leaving the *Prentice* with a captured German yacht. Other adventures involve intercepting a German raider and searching for floating mines off the coast of Florida. After the area is rid of a number of mines, the German raider is sighted and the story ends with the *Prentice* closing in on the raider.

j276 ―――. *Uncle Sam's Navy Boys with the Marines: or Standing Like a Rock at Chateau Thierry.* Chicago: M.A. Donohue, 1919. 254p.

Begins in the north of France shortly after the United States has entered the war, and describes the fighting in the Belleau Woods and at Château-Thierry. The Navy boys are Marine sergeant Elmer Ketcham and Marine corporal Amos Flagg, whose exploits include foiling a German espionage plot, rescuing their captain on the battlefield, and much hard fighting against the Germans.

j277 ―――. *Uncle Sam's Navy Boys with the Submarine Chasers: or, On Patrol Duty in the North Sea.* Chicago: M.A. Donohue, 1919. 251p.

Andy Jennings and Caleb Green, New Englanders, are on

submarine-patrol duty in the North Sea on Andy Jenning's former yacht, the *Argus*. They perform their duties valiantly, sinking a 300-foot German U-boat, rescuing sailors in lifeboats, ridding the British fishing fleet of a troublesome U-boat, and capturing a German spy.

j278 Kay, Ross. *Smashing the Hindenburg Line; The Adventures of Two American Boys in the Last Drive*. New York: Barse & Hopkins, 1919. 241p.

Lieutenants Earl and Leon Pratt are somewhere in France in the last days of the war. They are now with the American forces and their friend Jacques is stationed with a nearby French brigade. The narrative makes a point of emphasizing the coarseness and brutality of the Germans. Earl, Jessie Tiger, a full-blooded American Indian, and several other troopers go on a special scout mission into the German lines. Meanwhile, Jacques and Leon take a night flight behind the German lines to destroy a strategic bridge. What follows is a series of action-filled adventures in German-held territory. Leon captures a German colonel, Jacques is wounded, and Jessie and Earl go in search of them. The plot becomes a trifle confusing by the end, when Earl and Jessie finally locate Leon and Jacques just as a terrific bombardment begins. All four appear to be in a desperate situation but the Indian scout leads them to safety just as the Armistice is signed and the war ends.

j279 Knipe, Emilie Benson, and Alden Arthur Knipe. *Vive la France; a Narrative Founded on the Diary of Jeannette de Martigny*. New York: Century Co., 1919. 364p.

The story begins in Rheims, France, in 1914. Fifteen-year-old Jeannette de Martigny is the heroine, who is inspired by the life of Jeanne d'Arc when the war begins. She is forced out of Rheims and goes to Paris where she makes friends with the personnel of an American ambulance corps and helps in the American hospital. Later when it seems her father is killed, she returns to her home in stricken Rheims and devotes herself to the care of the orphaned children. However, by the conclusion of the novel her father returns alive and she receives a decoration for bravery.

j280 Margerison, John S. *Midshipman Rex Carew, V.C.* London: Thomas Nelson & Sons, 1919. 346p.

Not seen.

j281 Perry, William B. (pseud. of William Perry Brown). *Our Sammies in the Trenches*. Akron, Ohio: Saalfield Pub. Co., 1919.

Not seen.

j282 Porter, Horace (pseud. of Horace Porter Biddle De Hart). *Our Young Aeroplane Scouts at the Marne; or, Harrying the Huns from Allied Battleplanes*. New York: A.L. Burt, 1919. 248p.

Begins with the Germans smashing past Rheims and Soissons to the Marne for the second time in the war. Paris is in danger and the Allies fight fiercely to stop the German drive. Billy and Henri join the Allied air forces and lend their expert weight and talent to the cause. American troop transports pour men into the battle as more and more Americans enter the fray. Meanwhile, the two brave air scouts are involved in their typical air adventures including an interlude with tanks, action in the battle of St. Mihiel, a mission to Metz, capture by the Germans, etc., intermixed with the mystery of an old mansion with secret passages. All this, of course, is combined with their usual juvenile high jinks as a counterpoint to a fast-paced round of action air adventures demonstrating the continued resourcefulness of the two boys. Part of a juvenile series.

j283 ———. *Our Young Aeroplane Scouts In at the Victory; or, Speedy High Flyers Smashing the Hindenburg Line*. New York: A.L. Burt, 1919. 228p.

The last title in this action-packed fantasy series about the air war. This is the twelfth title featuring Billy Barry, the boy from Bangor, and Henri Trouville, his French chum and so-called twin. The narrative begins with Billy and Henri selected to fly a protective mission over the headquarters train of General Pershing. The boys then are sent off to assist "a lost battalion" under fire by the Germans in the Argonne Forest. They bomb the enemy positions with deadly accuracy before the German air support is able to begin the belated attack on the meteor aircraft of the two chums. In the process, the boys spot a crashed airplane near the trenches and apply a daring landing to lend succor in the face of rifle fire from the German trenches. This all leads eventually to a hair-raising gun battle with the enemy followed by a typically daring escape back into

Juvenile Novels

the blue. The boys race through a number of their characteristic and incredible happenings both in the air and on the sod in a plot and action that bears only a remote resemblance to reality. Involves the usual interludes with spies, captures, and escapes. The two boys with the super French spy, Ardelle, wrap up their last sleuth activity, bid adieu to the redoubtable Madame Chaulnes, and fly off to Paris, gladly anticipating the end of the war and their departure from Brest. This series is a veritable riot of every cliché in the book hung on a round of zany adventures that compare with those of the Marx Brothers or even the Three Stooges. The only series quite like this in all the juvenile literature of the war. Simply incredible.

j284 Ralphson, George Harvey. *Over There with Pershing's Heroes at Cantigny*. Chicago: M.A. Donohue, 1919. 213p.

The story of the 337th Machine Gun Battalion, the Bearcats, and their famous Sergeant Red Top. The battalion has just completed its training at Camp Union and is now sent off to the embarkation port for transport to the battlefields of France. The book abounds with German spies both in the States and in France. The transport is nearly torpedoed before the troops' arrival on French soil. They soon end up at the front where bombardments, attacks, and hand-to-hand fighting soon engage their attention. Red Top and his men rescue two French girls under brutal attack by a German soldier and go on to capture and kill a number of German spies. The story concludes with the Bearcats' successful participation in the Battle of Cantigny. A typical propaganda story of the period with the Germans all pictured as cowardly, treacherous, devious, and brutal savages. The American and Allied troops are all clearly good guys. This is strictly a black-and-white, "us against them" juvenile novel.

j285 ———. *Over There with the Canadians at Vimy Ridge*. Chicago: M.A. Donohue, 1919. 221p.

An example of the war fiction for boys so characteristic of the period. The story begins in a camouflaged pit in no-man's-land on the western front in France. Private Irving Ellis is the young Canadian hero and protagonist of the adventure. There is an interesting encounter in the trenches with a Lieutenant Tourtelle who exhibits an unwarranted malice toward Ellis. Tourtelle turns out to be a secret spy for the Germans. He has a tattoo on his arm in a cubist style that contains a secret code message for the Germans. Tourtelle is wounded and his arm is amputated to save his life. His tattoo is discovered and his spy effort is slowly revealed when he wishes to save the tattooed skin on his severed arm. Ellis is called upon to impersonate Tourtelle by having a similar tattoo on his arm and by being sent behind the German lines to contact their spy system. He finally winds up working in the Berlin records office of the German espionage system where he eventually learns all the secret information he has been sent after. Naturally he comes out the hero.

j286 ————. *Over There with the Doughboys at St. Mihiel*. Chicago: M.A. Donohue, 1919. 214p.

Another unlikely juvenile war-adventure tale of Sergeant Red Top, Corporal Hawley, and their "Bearcat" buddies of the 337th Machine Gun Battalion on front-line duty in the French trenches. The most improbable part of the tale concerns Flying Fox and Jumping Bear, two American Indian soldiers, who collect German scalps as trophies to take home. Once again they rescue two French canteen girls from the Huns before participating in the Battle of St. Mihiel, after which the "Bearcat" battalion is awarded the Croix de Guerre. The story exhibits the usual black-and-white propaganda plot techniques and characterization.

j287 ————. *Over There with the Engineers at Cambrai*. Chicago: M.A. Donohue, 1919. 250p.

Sergeant Walter Beach, while serving with Company H of the United States Army Engineers, is commissioned to investigate a member of his crew suspected of spying for the Germans. Until the final chapter, the spy eludes the investigator, who has many other encounters with the Germans in the course of this juvenile spy mystery.

j288 ————. *Over There with the Marines at Chateau Thierry*. Chicago: M.A. Donohue, 1919. 224p.

Relates the adventures of two American Marines, Phil Speed and Jim Turner, as they engage in battle, capture several Germans, and are in turn captured by the enemy. They escape, only to be recaptured, but eventually are rescued by American Marines.

Juvenile Novels

j289 Randall, Homer. *The Army Boys in the Big Drive; or, Smashing Forward to Victory.* New York: George Sully & Co., 1919. 216p.

Frank, Tom, Billy, and Bart are with the very front-rank troops involved in the push to drive the Germans back to the Rhine. This is all part of the great counterattack of Foch in July of 1918 to stop once and for all the enemy advance and conclude the war. The Army Boys perform their usual heroics in the Battle of St. Mihiel and in the Allied drive against the retreating Germans. At one point Frank is mistakenly mixed up with a robbery of the paymaster's messenger. However, all turns out well in the end and the bully Rabig is discovered to be the culprit.

j290 ———. *The Army Boys Marching into Germany; or, Over the Rhine with the Stars and Stripes.* New York: George Sully & Co., 1919. 214p.

The four Army Boys are in a bayonet charge against the Germans. They perform their usual feats of bravery, but Bart is seriously wounded and hospitalized. Frank, Tom, and Billy foil a false order to retreat and are then sent out on a special night-scout mission. They are nearly captured but escape, using a canal tunnel and return to Allied lines carrying a vital German-fortification document snitched by Frank. They now are involved in the major preparations for the Argonne Forest battle which turns out to be the last stand of the enemy. The three Army Boys are among the first wave of the advancing American troops as they slowly inch their way through the Argonne Forest and its maze of German tunnels and fortifications. The story is one of the few that describes the use of liquid fire. The Germans initiate Armistice inquiries with Marshal Foch as the battle rages on, until the official announcement of November 11, 1918. The Army Boys continue their advance into Germany as part of the Army of Occupation. They receive the DSC for their heroic feats, and as a grand finale, quash a treacherous German attempt to blow up the Ehrenbreitstein Fortress now filled with American troops. The next title in this representative juvenile series is *Army Boys on German Soil* ... (1920). It is not included, as it describes the postwar occupation conditions such as the 1918 revolution attempt and thus is beyond the scope of this bibliography.

j291 ———. *The Army Boys on the Firing Line; or, Holding Back the German Drive*. New York: George Sully & Co., 1919. 216p.

The third story in the Army Boys Series which relates the adventures of Frank, Bart, Tom, and Billy with the American forces in France as they withstand the repeated attacks of the Germans. Filled with their characteristic and brave adventures.

j292 Rolt-Wheeler, Francis William. *The Wonder of War at Sea*. Boston: Lothrop, Lee & Shepard, 1919. 376p.

Jed, the hero, is the son of an American fisherman whose trawler was sunk in British waters in 1914 by a German mine. Jed is picked up by a British destroyer and soon proves to be a most useful addition to the crew. As a result, he is able to observe many naval battles which prove to be disastrous to the German navy. Eventually Jed witnesses the collapse of the enemy's naval forces in the surrender of the German fleet on November 21, 1918. Aside from the story of Jed's adventures, the book goes into detail on the different types of mines, depth bombs, naval and anti-aircraft guns, superdreadnoughts, destroyers, submarine-defense tactics, etc. By and large the book is a patriotic testimonial to the accomplishments of the British navy in wartime.

j293 ———. *The Wonder of War in the Holy Land*. Boston: Lothrop, Lee & Shepard, 1919. 368p.

Recounts the flight of an American archaeologist and his son from their digs at the ancient site of Babylon, in order to escape the Arab tribes, the Turks, and their German allies during World War I. About the war in this part of the world, the author remarked in the preface to his novel, "Old campaigns between the Children of Israel and the Philistines were studied by generals as guides to modern strategy, and soldiers suddenly found the Bible as real a book to them as though it dealt with their native towns."

j294 [Russell, Mary Annette (Beauchamp) Russell, Countess]. *Christopher and Columbus*, by the author of *Elizabeth and Her German Garden*. London: The Macmillan Co., 1919. 500p.; Garden City, N.Y.: Doubleday, Page & Co., 1919. 435p.

Anna-Rose and Anna-Felicitas Twinkler, two charming and irrepressible 17-year-old twins of a German father and a British mother, are now orphaned. They leave Germany at the approach of the war and are sent to relatives in England, then to America. Eventually they get to California. The twins refer to themselves as Christopher and Columbus since they consider themselves discoverers of America. An honorable and helpful millionaire bachelor whom they meet on shipboard befriends them and introduces them to America and American culture. The reviewer in *The New York Times* called the tale "nonchalantly preposterous, and entirely delightful." There is no reason to dispute the first half of this description.

j295 Sheppard, William Henry Crispin. *Don Hale with the Flying Squadron*. Philadelphia: Penn. Pub. Co., 1919. 308p.

Don has decided to resign from the Red Cross ambulance corps and enter pilot training in the famous Lafayette Escadrille. The story begins with Don and George Glenn, his good friend, arriving at the famous training camp. Don and his friends are traced through the rigorous flight-school experiences and then as qualified aviators in the air war over the front lines. There are the usual standard encounters with spies and their espionage conspiracies combined with plenty of air-combat descriptions. The famous German Red Baron and his squadron of daredevil pilots are featured. After an air mission behind the German lines Don is involved in a terrific storm that forces him off his return course and tests to the limit his ability and resourcefulness as a combat pilot. The tale concludes with Don and two of his aviator friends under arrest by the French secret service for unspecified offenses. A trial ensues and, of course, Don and his friends are found not guilty. At the end Don receives, along with several others, the French Croix de Guerre for his extraordinary efforts. He now decides to be transferred to the American air service. This is the more interesting adventure of the first three Don Hale books, although they are all cut of the same cloth, as are the vast majority of juvenile stories about the war.

j296 ———. *Don Hale with the Yanks*. Philadelphia: Penn Pub. Co., 1919. 314p.

The final volume of this juvenile series. Don is now a member of the American air corps with the rank of lieutenant. There is a detailed description of the American airdrome, its planes and equipment, its everyday operation, and the activities of the men. George Glenn has transferred along with Don, and the two are soon deeply involved in air missions. Although the plot elements are different, the flying experiences tend to be similar if not identical to many of those in the previous story. Chapters that are historical essays on the course and strategy of the war are interspersed within the fictional narrative. Most of the action concerns air warfare except for Don's search for George after he crashes in no-man's-land, which offers some details on the ground war in the trenches and on the battlefield. On another occasion Don and a fellow pilot crash in enemy territory and manage to avoid capture by dressing as peasants and finally escaping in the famous enemy "Blackbird" airplane in a race back to the American lines. The story ends with Don and his friends safe and sound.

* Sherwood, Elmer (pseud. of Samuel Lewenkrohn). *Ted Marsh on an Important Mission*. Racine: Whitman, 1919.

The Lucky juvenile stories were all reissued under the *Ted Marsh* ... titles. This Ted Marsh tale was originally published as *Lucky on an Important Mission*. Refer to *Lucky, the Young Soldier* for additional information (item j130).

j297 Strang, Herbert (pseud.). *Tom Willoughby's Scouts; a Story of the War in German East Africa*. London: H. Milford, 1919. 297p.

Not seen.

j298 Stratemeyer, Edward. *Dave Porter's War Honors; or, At the Front with the Fighting Engineers*. Boston: Lothrop, Lee & Shepard, 1919. 308p.

The fifteenth tale in the Dave Porter Series of juvenile stories. This one continues Dave's activities with the fighting engineers at the French front and involves gas attacks, air battles, acts of bravery in battle, Dave's battle wound and hospital stay, his military award, and his experiences with machine-gun attacks, as prisoner of war, and all the other heroics so commonplace in most of the stories for boys cranked out by the Stratemeyer enterprise. This series is composed primarily of didactic tales using Dave Porter and his chums as exemplars of the manly, all-American virtues. This title concludes Dave's adventures in the war.

Juvenile Novels 421

j299 Stuart, Gordon (pseud. of George Neser Madison). *The Boy Scouts of the Air with Pershing*. Chicago: Reilly & Lee, 1919. 256p.

Jerry and Tod are air-support pilots with the First Army of Pershing in the Argonne Forest during the autumn of 1918. Not only do they literally skim the treetops, bombing and strafing German machine-gun nests; they also are involved in nearly every phase of the air war--night bombing missions, dropping spies over the lines, fierce dogfights and so forth. Spies seem to be all over the front and behind the Allied lines. There is a horrendous bombardment by the Big Bertha guns of the Germans. The boys find a message in a toy balloon that floats over the lines. It is a cry for help from a young boy called Jules. Although this technique is a popular German trick, they decide to embark on a humanitarian mission to investigate and perhaps rescue this unknown Jules. Jules turns out to be a small boy whom the scouts eventually are able to reunite with his mother in Paris. The story ends during the final days of the war with the boys looking forward to returning home. A typical "gee whiz" war story.

j300 Tarkington, Booth. *Ramsey Milholland*. Garden City, N.Y.: Doubleday, Page & Co., 1919. 218p.

A story of the war's effect on youth, seen through the experiences of an average American boy and girl. Ramsey Milholland, partway through his university schooling, enlists in the army and goes to France, and Dora Yocum, of pacifist disposition, eventually becomes convinced of the "rightness" of the war, and becomes a Red Cross worker at home.

j301 Tomlinson, Everett Titsworth. *Sergeant Ted Cole, United States Marines*. Boston: Houghton Mifflin Co., 1919. 319p.

Describes the heroism of the marines in the Château-Thierry area in France in 1918. Ted Cole and his marine buddies demonstrate battlefield bravery and a determination to push forward in spite of the heavy fire of some of the best German troops. Details of this wartime adventure tale are based on many actual accounts of the war. This is a typical juvenile story seemingly written to whip up patriotic spirits and pride in the achievements of the marines over there. The book begins in June of

1917 with the decision of Ted Cole and his friend Hans Mentz to enlist in the marines after graduation from high school. They are traced through basic training at Paris Island. The author provides details and illustrations of actual enlistment papers, training exercises, the sea journey to France, and experiences in the trenches and on the battlefields.

j302   Tomlinson, Paul Greene. *Bob Cook and the Winged Messenger.* New York: Barse & Hopkins, 1919. 250p.

The setting is the American army in the trenches of France. There is a considerable use of carrier pigeons to carry messages for the Allies as well as for German spies. The narrative consists of the chatty dialogue of Bob Cook and his buddies at the front, their daily concerns and activities, and heroic war experiences against the foe. There are plenty of the usual charges across no-man's-land, enemy captures, bayonet combat, and all the rest of the standard warfront activities covered in the run-of-the-mill juvenile war literature. The possible exception is the love and romance of Arthur and Madeleine La Ferre, who turns out to be an unwilling victim in a German spy plot with French conspirators. The story ends as the armistice is signed and everyone celebrates.

j303   Trent, Martha. *Phoebe Marshal; Somewhere in Canada.* New York: Barse & Hopkins, 1919. 221p.

The story is set principally in the small Canadian village of Billancourt and in France during the Great War. Phoebe is the heroine and only nurse assigned to a convalescent hospital for Canadian soldiers. There is considerable comment on the local Indians both as background and as minor characters in the village. The plot describes the social relationships of Phoebe and her friends with the new company of tank soldiers stationed there. Phoebe discovers a badly wounded Canadian soldier tied to a tree in the woods. The captain of the tank company rushes off in search of clues to this mystery and discovers a secret German submarine base which has engaged some of the local Indians to carry drums of oil ashore for storage. No sooner is Captain Struthers captured than Phoebe arrives with a tank crew who manage to capture the submarine crew and destroy the German U-boat. After this adventure Struthers and the tank company are sent to France and Phoebe receives word that her brother has been badly wounded. She decides to leave for the hospital in France, but the wounded man she visits is not her brother. She takes a train to visit another hospital but it is bombed. In the wreckage she discovers a dead passenger who turns out to be the German spy from her village in Canada. Secret documents are hidden on his body and she volunteers to take them to the appropriate military authorities. She now locates her wounded brother and the story has a happy ending as they prepare to return home to Canada. There is a moderately romantic interest between Phoebe and Captain Struthers. All in all, this is a milder version of the typical boys' series novel but written for girls.

j304 Vandercook, Margaret O'Bannon (Womack). *The Red Cross Girls with the U.S. Marines.* Philadelphia: John C. Winston Co., 1919.

Not seen.

j305 Van Dyne, Edith (pseud. of Lyman Frank Baum). *Mary Louise Adopts a Soldier.* Chicago: Reilly & Lee, 1919. 233p.

Not seen.

j306 Wallace, Dillon. *John Adney, Ambulance Driver.* Chicago: A.C. McClurg & Co., 1919. 304p.

The hero is a seventeen-year-old boy who has just arrived friendless and alone in New York City. With only fifteen cents to his name he accidentally meets a Mr. Smith, the second steward of an English passenger liner, who buys John his dinner and arranges a job for him on the boat. The only hitch is that John must deliver a package once they dock in London. John is naive and agrees, thinking he is part of a British secret-agent mission. He is not too many days at sea before his suspicions arise about what he has agreed to do. The entire matter is eventually cleared up in London in an encounter with a Lieutenant Blake who turns out to be with the British secret service. The steward disappears and when the ship leaves for New York it is soon torpedoed and sunk. The U-boat shells the defenseless survivors and John is wounded. As the sub surfaces John and his friend, Bronk, decide to resist and Bronk lassos the German officer and drags him into the water. Meanwhile two American destroyers race up and the sub is destroyed. John and Bronk end up in a French hospital.

After they recover they decide to join the American Volunteer Ambulance Corps. This leads to a series of incredible adventures in the trenches and on the battlefields. John ends up again in the hospital, receives the Croix de Guerre from a French general, and when the first American troops arrive, is reunited with his brother. This is one of the few juvenile stories that makes some effort to describe the nature of the deaths and mutilations caused by the shelling both at sea and on the battlefield. A decided level or two above the series novels for boys written by such authors as Durston, Ralphson, et al.

j307A Westerman, Percy Francis. *A Sub and a Submarine*. London: Blackie & Son, 1919. 256p.

Not seen.

j308 ―――. *The Thick of the Fray at Zeebrugge, April, 1918*. London: Blackie & Son, 1919. 256p.

Not seen; however, it deals with the Zeebrugge-Ostend raids in 1918.

j309 ―――. *Winning His Wings, a Story of the R.A.F.* London: Blackie & Son, 1919. 288p.

Not seen.

j310 Winfield, Arthur M. (pseud. of Edward Stratemeyer). *The Rover Boys under Canvas; or, The Mystery of the Wrecked Submarine*. New York: Grosset & Dunlap, 1919. 310p.

Describes the adventures of the four sons of the original Rover Boys: Dick, Tom, and Sam. It is the only story of the series that is involved with the war. Andy, Randy, Jack, and Fred are attending Colby Hall military school when the time comes for the annual encampment of the school. The four boys and some of their schoolmates become mixed up in the mystery surrounding a wrecked German submarine and German spies, though about two thirds of the novel deals with their normal school activities. This is a juvenile story mainly addressed to preteen boys and falls clearly into the "gee whiz" juvenile category. Literary ability and quality are obviously not elements to be found in this genre.

j311 Young, Clarence (pseud.; Stratemeyer Syndicate). *The Motor Boys on the Firing Line; or, Ned, Bob and Jerry Fighting for Uncle Sam.* New York: Cupples & Leon, 1919. 356p.

Not seen.

1920

j312 Beach, Charles Amory. *Air Service Boys over the Atlantic; or, The Longest Flight on Record.* New York: George Sully & Co., 1920. 218p.

The novel takes place in the fall of 1918, chronicling the war exploits of three young United States airmen as they engage in battle with German aircraft. After considerable combat the three flyers depart on leave to claim an inheritance in Virginia. Their trip involves a successful crossing of the Atlantic by plane, though to make the crossing successful they had to land on an iceberg for repairs. A "gee whiz" story.

j313 Bishop, Austin. *Bob Thorpe, Sky Fighter in Italy.* New York: Harcourt, Brace and Howe, 1920. 275p.

An informative thriller. The author was a pilot in the war and evokes the excitement of air combat as well as the every-day activities of the men between missions.

j314 Bishop, Giles, Jr. *The Marines Have Landed.* Philadelphia: Penn. Pub. Co., 1920. 356p.

Not seen.

j315 Botsford, Charles Alexander. *In the Trenches.* Philadelphia: Penn. Pub. Co., 1920. 307p.

A story for boys, based on an actual news dispatch: "On the afternoon of the 21st we gained a small local success. We advanced our line on a front of 600 yards, and gained all our objectives. Our estimated casualties of all ranks were 48. We took 133 prisoners." It is the author's purpose to show what really happened on such an occasion. The author has written a series of war-adventure stories for boys to instill a sense of duty and patriotism. There is accurate descriptive information on equipment, weapons, trench construction,

and front-line warfare. The story offers a vivid and
probably quite realistic picture of the war and some of
its terrible front-line conditions and activities.
Otherwise, this is the usual juvenile novel.

j316A Bridges, Thomas Charles. *The Secret of the Baltic*.
London & Glasgow: Collins' Clear-type Press, 1920(?).
230p.

Not seen.

j317B Davidson, Halsey. *Navy Boys on Special Service; or,
Guarding the Floating Treasury*. New York: George
Sully & Co., 1920. 216p. [Reissued by Equitable in
1930 as *Deep Sea Boys on Special Service*....]

Not seen.

j318   Dawson, Coningsby William. *The Little House*. London:
John Lane Co., 1920. 127p.

The little house of this tale is given the role of
narrator of all that occurs within its walls. As a
result, the author has tended to create a quasi-fairy-
tale atmosphere. In any case, it is a very old and empty
little house which stands on Doll's House Square in
London. The house becomes extremely frightened from
the nights of air raids and bombings; however, not so
frightened that it refuses to give shelter to people who
are also afraid. One night a "little lady who needed
to be loved but did not know it" entered with her two
children. Later a wounded army officer who needed rest
and a haven from the air raids also arrives. The officer shortly returns and he and the "little lady" receive
all the love they need from each other. Of course, the
little house is delighted with its contribution to this
state of affairs.

j319   Driscoll, James R. *The Brighton Boys in the Argonne
Forest*. Philadelphia: John C. Winston Co., 1920.
235p.

Lieutenant Herbert Whitcomb of the 28th Division is
with his former schoolmate Don Richards in the Red Cross
ambulance service. Together with ten other American
soldiers they hold off and outwit a vastly greater number
of Germans in a section of the Argonne Forest, as well
as capture a German spy who has infiltrated the American
army.

j320　Flower, Jessie Graham. *Grace Harlowe Overseas.* Philadelphia: Henry Altemus Co., 1920. 255p.

The first of the six titles which constitute the author's Grace Harlowe Overseas Series. This series follows a previous series entitled The College Girls Series, also featuring Grace Harlowe. These stories were written especially for high-school and college-age girls. Grace goes with the Overton College Red Cross Unit to France where she serves her country by aiding the American army forces. The story views the war from the perspective of a young girl and contains the usual spy mysteries, front-line fighting, and behind-the-lines activities one might expect in this type of juvenile adventure literature. It also exhibits a good dose of patriotic war propaganda for the all-American girl. (The sixth title of the series, *Grace Harlowe with the American Army on the Rhine*, deals with Germany after the Armistice and is not within the scope of this bibliography.)

j321　————. *Grace Harlowe with the Marines at Chateau Thierry.* Philadelphia: Henry Altemus Co., 1920. 255p.

Not seen.

j322　————. *Grace Harlowe with the Red Cross in France.* Philadelphia: Henry Altemus Co., 1920. 255p.

Not seen.

j323　————. *Grace Harlowe with the U.S. Troops in the Argonne.* Philadelphia: Henry Altemus Co., 1920. 255p.

j324　————. *Grace Harlowe with the Yankee Shock Boys at St. Quentin.* Philadelphia: Henry Altemus Co., 1920. 255p.

Grace and her friend Elfreda are with the Red Cross ambulance corps at the front. The American army is planning a big push against the Germans on their Hindenburg line. Grace has a deep suspicion of Germans and of all things German, including "German Kulture." Her ambulance is shelled and wrecked, but Grace and Elfreda escape injury and the approaching enemy troops by hiding under the flooring of a nearby barn. When the Germans burn the barn down the girls make a mad dash for freedom, but Elfreda is captured. Grace seizes a rifle and attacks the Germans holding Elfreda and succeeds in escaping with her from the clutches of the enemy. This is just one of a number of heroic and characteristic adventures of Grace at the front. The plot contains the standard elements of spies, battlefield narrow escapes, artillery bombardments, and all the usual action counterpointed by the cool and collected temperament of Grace. She aids and serves the wounded soldiers in field hospitals and behind the lines in a sequence of brave exploits equivalent to those of the opposite sex in the boys' series novels on the war. At the end Grace is a "captain" and receives the American Distinguished Service Cross for her "pluck and unparalleled heroism," and the Armistice is signed. A stereotyped juvenile series for girls equal to any written for boys in terms of the characteristic exploits and brave deeds of the leading characters.

j325 Havard, Aline. *Captain Lucy's Flying Ace*. Philadelphia: Penn. Pub. Co., 1920. 302p.

Details the further adventures of Lucy Gordon in the European war theater as she continues in her service for the war effort. This time she is in a refugee children's hospital in Normandy. When she is sent to the devastated area of Port-Saint-Aignan to rescue other refugee children, Lucy aids in the unravelling of an espionage plot which takes her behind the German lines.

j326 Kay, Ross. *The Underground Spy*. New York: Barse & Hopkins, 1920. 234p.

The ninth and final story in the Big War Series. It is late in 1918. Lieutenants Leon and Earl Platt observe the Blue Cross people who treat exhausted and wounded war horses at an animal hospital in France. They are asked to join a small scout group and soon make a new friend of Jessie Tiger, an American Indian serving with the American Expeditionary Forces. Earl and Jessie rig up a false tree trunk listening post to scout the Germans, while Leon and some others discover a long unoccupied tunnel. Plenty of scenes of no-man's-land, combat struggles, etc. When the Armistice is signed, Leon and his buddies search for Earl among the prisoners. Earl is eventually discovered and the story concludes with their happy reunion. There is a didactic chapter on how and why the war began. The Germans are painted as single-dimensional caricatures. A simplistic story of adventure and heroics for boys.

j327   Ralphson, George Harvey. *Over There with the Yanks in the Argonne Forest*. Chicago: M.A. Donohue, 1920. 246p.

A bit of everything appears in this juvenile tale. The story begins in New York with the announcement of the sinking of the *Lusitania*. Clyde's brother Clint who is on a tour of Germany decides to enlist secretly in the French ambulance corps. Clyde is involved in a German spy plot at his father's steel mill in Brooklyn. A New York broker and family friend, Fehler, is heavily implicated in the German spy organization. Clyde later joins the Red Cross ambulance service and when the U.S. declares war on Germany both brothers enlist in the American army in France and fight in the Baccarat sector of Lorraine, the Aisne River, and the Argonne Forest. The plot ends with the signing of the Armistice.

j328   Sawyer, Ruth. *Leerie*. New York: Harper & Brothers, 1920. 309p.

A sentimental and improbable love story written primarily for girls and young women. Leerie is a nurse who has a loving touch that endears her to all of her patients. This is especially the case with Peter Brook, so much so that they make plans to be married. But just before this happy event, Leerie feels a great call to go to France and do her duty, and this she does. Peter, left behind, also decides to go. Naturally, their varied experiences in war service and helping others provide deep satisfaction. She now knows that Peter and she have a relationship truly for all time.

j329   Terhune, Albert Payson. *Bruce*. New York: E.P. Dutton & Co., 1920. 204p.

An animal story about a collie called Bruce, a "hopelessly awkward and senseless pup," who is eventually trained to carry messages and becomes a courier dog during the war. In carrying messages Bruce saves regiments from danger and even uncovers a German spy masquerading as a Red Cross nurse. Ultimately Bruce is wounded and returned home to the United States.

1921

* Durston, George (pseud.). *The Boy Scout Automobilists*. Akron, Ohio: Saalfield Pub. Co., 1921.

A later reprint with a different title and author of the first half of *The Boy Scouts with King George* ... by Robert Maitland (item j42).

* ———. *The Boy Scout Aviators*. Akron, Ohio: Saalfield Pub. Co., 1921.

A later reprint with a different title of *The Boy Scouts with King George* ... (item j42).

* ———. *The Boy Scout Aviators*. Akron, Ohio: Saalfield Pub. Co., 1921.

A later reprint with a different author and title of the second half of *The Boy Scouts with King George* ... (item j42).

* ———. *The Boy Scout Fire Fighters*. Akron, Ohio: Saalfield Pub. Co., 1921.

A later reprint with a different title of the first half of *The Boy Scouts Under Fire in France* ... (item j174).

* ———. *The Boy Scout Pathfinders*. Akron, Ohio: Saalfield Pub. Co., 1921.

A later reprint with a different title of the second half of *The Boy Scouts Under Fire in France* ... (item j174).

* ———. *The Boy Scouts Afloat*. Akron, Ohio: Saalfield Pub. Co., 1921.

A later reprint with a different title of *The Boy Scouts Under the Stars and Stripes* ... by the same author (item j175).

* ———. *The Boy Scouts Afloat*. Akron, Ohio: Saalfield Pub. Co., 1921.

A later reprint with a different title of the second half of *The Boy Scouts Under the Stars and Stripes* ... (item j175).

Juvenile Novels   431

*   ———. *The Boy Scout's Challenge*. Akron, Ohio: Saalfield Pub. Co., 1921.

A later reprint with a different title and author of the first half of *The Boy Scouts with the Allies* ... by Robert Maitland (item j43).

*   ———. *The Boy Scout's Champion Recruit*. Akron Ohio: Saalfield Pub. Co., 1921.

A later reprint with a different title of the first half of *The Boy Scouts Under the Red Cross* ... (item j79).

*   ———. *The Boy Scout's Defiance*. Akron, Ohio: Saalfield Pub. Co., 1921.

A later reprint with a different title of the second half of *The Boy Scouts Under the Red Cross* ... (item j79).

*   ———. *The Boy Scouts in Camp*. Akron, Ohio: Saalfield Pub. Co., 1921.

A later reprint with a different title of the first half of *The Boy Scouts in the War Zone* ... (item j255).

*   ———. *The Boy Scouts in Camp*. Akron, Ohio: Saalfield Pub. Co., 1921.

A later reprint with a different title of *The Boy Scouts in the War Zone* ... (item j255).

*   ———. *The Boy Scouts on the Trail*. Akron, Ohio: Saalfield Pub. Co., 1921.

A later reprint with a different title of the first half of *The Boy Scouts Under the Stars and Stripes* ... (item j175).

*   ———. *The Boy Scouts on the Trail*. Akron, Ohio: Saalfield Pub. Co., 1921.

A later reprint with a different title of *The Boy Scouts with the Allies* ... by Robert Maitland (item j43).

*   ———. *The Boy Scouts to the Rescue.* Akron, Ohio: Saalfield Pub. Co., 1921.

   A later reprint with a different title of *The Boy Scouts Under Fire in France* ... by the same author (item j174).

*   ———. *The Boy Scouts to the Rescue.* Akron, Ohio: Saalfield Pub. Co., 1921.

   A later reprint with a different title of the second half of *The Boy Scouts in the War Zone* ... (item j255).

*   ———. *The Boy Scout's Victory.* Akron, Ohio: Saalfield Pub. Co., 1921.

   A later reprint with a different author and title of the second half of *The Boy Scouts with the Allies* ... by Robert Maitland (item j43).

*   ———. *The Boy Scouts' Victory.* Akron, Ohio: Saalfield Pub. Co., 1921.

   A later reprint with a different title of *The Boy Scouts Under the Red Cross* ... by the same author (item j79).

*   Griggs, Edward (pseud.). *A Boy Scout Hero.* Akron, Ohio: Saalfield Pub. Co., 1921.

   A later reprint with a different author and title of the second half of *The Boy Scouts Under the Red Cross* ... by George Durston (item j79).

*   ———. *A Boy Scout Mystery.* Akron, Ohio: Saalfield Pub. Co., 1921.

   A later reprint with a different author and title of the second half of *The Boy Scouts Under the Stars and Stripes* ... by George Durston (item j175).

*   ———. *A Boy Scout on the Trail.* Akron, Ohio: Saalfield Pub. Co., 1921.

   A later reprint with a different author and title of the first half of *The Boy Scouts Under the Stars and Stripes* ... by George Durston (item j175).

*   ———. *A Boy Scout Patriot.* Akron, Ohio: Saalfield Pub. Co., 1921.

    A later reprint with a different author and title of the first half of *The Boys Scouts Under the Red Cross* ... by George Durston (item j79).

*   ———. *A Boy Scout's Adventure.* Akron, Ohio: Saalfield Pub. Co., 1921.

    A later reprint with a different author and title of the first half of *The Boy Scouts Under Fire in France* ... by George Durston (item j174).

*   ———. *A Boy Scout's Chance.* Akron, Ohio: Saalfield Pub. Co., 1921.

    A later reprint with a different author and title of the second half of *The Boy Scouts with the Allies* ... by Robert Maitland (item j43).

*   ———. *A Boy Scout's Courage.* Akron, Ohio: Saalfield Pub. Co., 1921.

    A later reprint with a different author and title of the second half of *The Boy Scouts with King George* ... by Robert Maitland (item j42).

*   ———. *A Boy Scout's Daring.* Akron, Ohio: Saalfield Pub. Co., 1921.

    A later reprint with a different author and title of the first half of *The Boy Scouts with King George* ... by Robert Maitland (item j42).

*   ———. *A Boy Scout's Destiny.* Akron, Ohio: Saalfield Pub. Co., 1921.

    A later reprint with a different author and title of the second half of *The Boy Scouts Under Fire in France* ... by George Durston (item j174).

*   ———. *A Boy Scout's Holiday.* Akron, Ohio: Saalfield Pub. Co., 1921.

    A later reprint with a different author and title of the first half of *The Boy Scouts with the Allies* ... by Robert Maitland (item j43).

*   ———. *A Boy Scout's Struggle.* Akron, Ohio: Saalfield Pub. Co., 1921.

A later reprint with a different author and title of the first half of *The Boy Scouts in the War Zone* ... by George Durston (item j255).

*   ———. *A Boy Scout's Success.* Akron, Ohio: Saalfield Pub. Co., 1921.

A later reprint with a different author and title of the second half of *The Boy Scouts in the War Zone* ... by George Durston (item j255).

j330   Havard, Aline. *Captain Lucy in the Home Sector.* Philadelphia: Penn. Pub. Co., 1921. 306p.

The last of four juvenile books concerning the adventures of a young girl of an American military family in Germany during and after the war. This book relates the girl's part in uncovering a plot to re-establish the German monarchy.

j331   Turpin, Edna Henry Lee. *The Old Mine's Secret.* New York: The Macmillan Co., 1921. 288p.

The setting is a southern town in the United States in which the children serve the war effort by growing war gardens and participating in Red Cross work. One of the boys convinces his comrades that reopening a silver mine in the community would be of more significance to the war effort. A spy incident plays a minor part in the novel.

1922

j332   Bishop, Giles, Jr. *Lieutenant Comstock, U.S. Marine.* Philadelphia: Penn. Pub. Co., 1922. 363p.

Not seen.

j333   ———. *The Marines have Advanced.* Philadelphia: Penn. Pub. Co., 1922. 393p.

This tale covers the adventures of Dick Comstock and his friends during the period from 1914 to about 1917, shortly after the U.S. enters the war. The character of

Dick is cast in the mold of the super-patriotic, all-American boy who is a zealous and competent leader as well as an enthusiastic participant in the causes of his country. The book describes Marine activities in camp, their engineering techniques, and provides a history of the corps, etc. The Marines are sent to Santo Domingo and Monte Cristi after General Huerta's soldiers arrest some American sailors from the U.S.S. *Dolphin* in Tampico. The activities of German agents and spies in Mexico are described as well as many of the Marine expeditions in Latin America. In the last chapter the U.S. joins the war and Dick and his buddies travel by troopship to France where they arrive to the overwhelming cheers of the French people. This is a patriotic juvenile story for boys with special didactic emphasis on the history and activities of the Marines.

j334 Driggs, Laurence La Tourette. *Arnold Adair with the English Aces; Being the Further Flying Adventures of an American Aviator*. Boston: Little, Brown & Co., 1922. 321p.

This is the sequel to *The Adventures of Arnold Adair, American Ace* (item j168). Arnold has now returned from the States to England where he intends to join the British Royal Air Force with the help of a family friend, Colonel Hull. London is now experiencing German air raids and Adair immediately is able to join the British in repulsing the attacks. The novel describes the conditions in wartime London as well as the camaraderie among the British officers of the Independent Fighting Squadron. Adair joins this group as they go on to numerous air adventures over the war zones of France and Germany. The novel provides some detail on the tactics of air fighting, strafing, and bombing along the front lines. A romantic interest is introduced in the person of Lady Joan and Duncan Stuart, an English ace. There is an attempt to describe the English social system and its relationships, especially as it involved the English airmen. Some drama is created with the rivalry of the German baron flying ace and his challenges to the English. The story concludes on a sentimental but happy note. The author writes in a fairly modern style characteristic of and somewhat similar to that of Arch Whitehouse. There is a somewhat greater sense of drama and the realities of war and flying than exist in much of this type of young adult fiction.

j335 Hamilton, Frederick Spencer. *P.J. the Secret Service Boy: being a Record of Some of the Holiday Adventures of Mr. Philip John Davenants in 1914 and 1915 During the Great War.* London: Thomas Nelson & Sons, 1922. 367p.

Introduces the exploits of fifteen-year-old Philip John Davenant who becomes an interpreter for his father's friend Cyril Ambrose, Assistant Commissioner at Scotland Yard at the beginning of World War I, and helps to uncover several espionage plans of Germans masquerading as friendly aliens in England.

1923

j336 Bishop, Giles, Jr. *Captain Comstock U.S.M.C.* Philadelphia: Penn. Pub. Co., 1923. 358p.

This is the fourth and final story of the activities of Dick Comstock of the U.S. Marines. The book can be characterized as a "gee whiz" adventure-war tale for boys. The setting is the battlefields of France and the author has based the main elements of his story on historical facts. The novel promotes the concept of the clean, upright, and patriotic military officer. Dick is promoted to captain and soon experiences the problems and challenges of his command at the front, beginning with Belleau Wood. Naturally, he is a born leader. Written by a former marine general, the story doesn't mince words on the rigors and dangers of front-line action. The story also tends to glorify the strength and character of the Marines in action. The plot involves the rescue of civilians, encounters with Germans, the mystery of Lieutenant Reddy Doyle and Suzette, and the final happy return of Dick and his friends to the U.S.

j337 Hamilton, Frederick Spencer. *More About P.J., the Secret Service Boy.* London: Thomas Nelson & Sons, 1923. 330p.

Not seen.

j338 Humphreys, Eliza Margaret J. (Gollan) von (pseud.: Rita). *The Ungrown-ups.* New York: G.P. Putnam's Sons, 1923. 382p.

Reveals a picture of the home front during the great

Juvenile Novels 437

war. Philistia, the chief character, is observed from her childhood years into her adolescence. The war years have turned her days into a period of home drudgery and hand labor with an underdevelopment of many of her qualities and an overdevelopment of others. Eventually she visits a wealthy household in the city which is engaged in all the more exciting aspects of war work on the home front, e.g., benefits, entertainments, etc. This experience demonstrates to her what has been lacking in her life and what is much more preferable. This is the major point of the story, along with several reconciliations and mutual understandings among the members of her family. The novel is in the form of a young girl's diary.

1925

j339 Snell, Roy Judson. *Skimmer the Daring; Including Skimmer and His Thrilling Adventures.* new ed. Chicago: Albert Whitman, 1925. 382p.

Not seen.

1927

* Appleton, Victor (pseud.; Stratemeyer Syndicate). *The Movie Boys' War Spectacle; or, The Film that Won the Prize.* Garden City, N.Y.: Garden City Pub. Co., 1927. 210p.

A reprint with a slightly different title of *The Motion Picture Chums' War Spectacle* ... (item j64).

* Durston, George (pseud.). *A Boy Scout on Duty.* Akron, Ohio: Saalfield Pub. Co., 1927.

A later reprint with a different author and title of *The Boy Scouts with King George* ... by Robert Maitland (item j42).

* ———. *A Boy Scout's Bravery.* Akron, Ohio: Saalfield Pub. Co., 1927.

A later reprint with a different author and title of *The Boy Scouts with the Allies* ... by Robert Maitland (item j43).

* ———. *A Boy Scout's Campaign*. Akron, Ohio: Saalfield Pub. Co., 1927.

A later reprint with a different title of the author's *The Boy Scouts Under Fire in France* ... (item j174).

* ———. *A Boy Scout's Discovery*. Akron, Ohio: Saalfield Pub. Co., 1927.

A later reprint of *The Boy Scouts Under the Stars and Stripes* ... (item j175), by the same author.

* ———. *A Boy Scout's Mission*. Akron, Ohio: Saalfield Pub. Co., 1927.

A later reprint with a different title of the author's *The Boy Scouts in the War Zone* ... (item j255).

* ———. *A Boy Scout's Secret*. Akron, Ohio: Saalfield Pub. Co., 1927.

A later reprint of *The Boy Scouts Under the Red Cross* ... by the same author (item j79).

j340 Mukerji, Dhan Gopal. *Gay-Neck, the Story of a Pigeon*. New York: E.P. Dutton & Co., 1927. 197p.

Chitra-griva or Gay-Neck is a carrier pigeon born in India. The first part of the novel deals with his training and adventures in India. The second part relates his activities in the European war. The story is written with charm and freshness and is especially appropriate for children as well as any adult interested in bird lore and especially the use of carrier pigeons in wartime.

1928

j341 Clarke, Covington (pseud. of Clarke Venable). *For Valor*. Chicago: Reilly & Lee, 1928. 264p.

Traces the career of "Red" McGee, an American boy who accompanies his older brother to England to enlist in the British air force. When his brother is shot down, Red joins the Royal Flying Corps. The novel recounts his training as a cadet and follows his progress over the battle lines in France, detailing many aerial dogfights.

Juvenile Novels 439

j342 Whiting, John Downes. *S.O.S.: A Story of the World War at Sea*. San Francisco: Lantern Press; Gelber, Lilienthal, 1928. 302p.

The story of Hugh Canfield, a boy from Maine who joins the Naval Reserve radio corps during the war. The novel recounts Hugh's experiences at sea, in France, and with the Coast Guard service off the coast of Maine. One of the better written juvenile books dealing with the war.

1929

j343 Clarke, Covington (pseud. of Clarke Venable). *Aces Up*. Chicago: Reilly & Lee, 1929. 262p.

Presents the further adventures of Lieutenant "Red" McGee and Buzz Larkin, American pilots in the R.A.F., who appeared in the author's *For Valor* (item j341). McGee and Larkin are repatriated to the American air force when the United States enters the war. The story covers aerial dogfights over the western front and recounts a story of counterespionage.

1930

j344AB Bridges, Thomas Charles. *With Beatty in Jutland*. London & Glasgow: Collins' Clear-type Press, 1930(?).

Not seen.

j345 Darling, Esther (Birdsall). *Navarre of the North*. Garden City, N.Y.: Doubleday, Doran & Co., 1930. 268p.

A dog story for boys and girls. Navarre is an Eskimo wolf dog rescued by young Paul Barran from a cruel master. The first portion of the book takes place in Alaska, but when Paul goes to war in France Navarre goes with him. There the dog rescues a wounded officer and is awarded the Croix de Guerre.

* Davidson, Halsey. *Deep Sea Boys After a Submarine; or, Protecting the Giant Convoy*. New York: Equitable, 1930. 88p.

Originally published in 1918 with the title *Navy Boys after the Submarines*. See item j163 for the complete annotation.

*   ———. *Deep Sea Boys at the big Surrender; or, Rounding up the German Fleet*. New York: Equitable, 1930. 90p.

This is the same story published in 1919 as the *Navy Boys at the Big Surrender*.... See item j248 for complete annotation.

*   ———. *Deep Sea Boys Behind the Big Guns; or, Sinking the German U-boats*. New York: Equitable, 1930. 92p.

Published originally in 1918 with the title *Navy Boys Behind the Big Guns*.... See item j164 for complete annotation.

*   ———. *Deep Sea Boys Chasing a Sea Raider; or, Landing a Million Dollar Prize*. New York: Equitable, 1930. 90p.

Originally published in 1918 with the title *Navy Boys Chasing a Sea Raider*.... See item j165 for complete annotation.

*   ———. *Deep Sea Boys on Special Service; or, Guarding the Floating Treasure*. New York: Equitable, 1930. 85p.

Originally published in 1920 with the title *Navy Boys on Special Service; or, Guarding the Floating Treasury*. See item j317.

*   ———. *Deep Sea Boys to the Rescue; or, Answering the Wireless Call for Help*. New York: Equitable, 1930. 89p.

Originally published in 1919 under the title *Navy Boys to the Rescue*.... See item j249 for complete annotation.

j346   Driggs, Laurence La Tourette. *On Secret Air Service*. Boston: Little, Brown & Co., 1930. 324p.

A story of intrigue as the Allied forces and the Germans vie with one another to discover and use the other's military secrets. The novel concerns the exploits of three young officers of the Allied air forces, Lieutenant Edmond Martin of Luxemburg, Captain Arnold Adair, and Captain Horace Starr, as they become involved in ferrying secret service men behind the German lines.

Juvenile Novels

j347 Rohan, Jack. *Rags: The Story of a Dog Who Went to War.*
New York: Harper & Brothers, 1930. 242p.

The story of Donovan, an American sergeant, and his nondescript dog. Both find one another in Montmartre during a blackout in Paris. Instantly adopted as a mascot, the dog Rags accompanies his new friend to the front to share his battle experiences and contribute valuable service in delivering written messages in the Meuse-Argonne sector when men could not get through. Wounded together, Rags and his sergeant are conveyed to the same hospital where they recover together. At the end the still disabled Donovan and Rags return home to the United States on the same ship and travel to Fort Sheridan near Chicago where Donovan is hospitalized. After Donovan's death, Rags is adopted by a military family at Fort Sheridan.

j348 Vale, Edmund. *Roc; a Dog's-eye View of War.* London: J.M. Dent & Sons, 1930. 177p.; New York: E.P. Dutton & Co., 1930. 178p.

Roc, a red setter, is the pet of a soldier and the mascot of a Highland regiment. When the regiment is ordered out and Roc's master is killed, the dog is taken over by "Big Brown," a gunnery officer, who relates Roc's war experiences on the western front. The author has created a believable story for children.

1931

j349 Quirk, Leslie W. *Jimmy Goes to War.* Boston: Little, Brown & Co., 1931. 295p.

An autobiographical novel closely based upon the war experiences of the author. The story covers the period from August 15, 1917, through the end of the war. At the beginning Jimmy is planning to go to Columbia University as he learns of the enlistments of his tutor and a close friend. After he enters the university, he visits his friend on board a ship soon to leave for France. The boat departs before Jimmy is aware of the warning bell and he is on his way with the others to Liverpool. Jimmy soon changes his mind and decides to enlist for service in France as an American Field Service ambulance driver. When he gets to Paris his friend is soon off with the Lafayette Escadrille while Jimmy ends up in the Reserve

Mallet as a supply truck driver. This novel can be considered the story of the Reserve Mallet activities during the war. The narrative recounts the rigors, hazards, and everyday life of the support troops as they brave the bombardments, attacks, and incredible difficulties of transporting ammunition, shells, and other supplies to the front lines. Their one unusual feat was the transportation of tanks from Rheim to Lor in order to force the Germans out of their secure positions and aid the Allies' push to the Rhine. The story concludes with the Armistice and Jimmy's safe return home. This can be considered a juvenile novel of sorts. The emotional growth through the experience of the war changes him into a man. The writing has ability and compels some interest.

1932

j350 Burtis, Thomson. *Daredevils of the Air*. New York: Grosset & Dunlap, 1932. 215p.

The first title of the four in the author's Air Combat Series of stories for boys. The hero is Lieutenant Rudford Riley who is the leader of The Phantom Five, a small group of pilots on special duty with the Royal Flying Corps. The action occurs during the early days of the war and involves all kinds of exploits in the air over the front lines in France. Since the author was a pilot during the war, it is apparent that his experiences count heavily in the adventures of Lieutenant Riley and his friends. The book still holds a certain amount of interest for boys, much as the novels of Arch Whitehouse described elsewhere in this bibliography.

j351 ———. *Four Aces*. New York: Grosset & Dunlap, 1932. 216p.

This second title in the Air Combat Series continues the career and adventures of Rudford Riley and his friends and associates. (All of the titles in this series tend to be similar in plot and characterization.) When this story begins, Rud Riley has spent two years, from the Dardanelles region to the North Sea, flying as a scout to protect a photo reconnaissance aircraft. The other principal character is the crazy daredevil flyer, Jerry Lacy, called the "Manhattan Madman." The action starts with an air battle with the von Huff circus, a famous group of German pilots. Rud and several other pilots are sent to the Italian front to run bombing missions. Two mysterious murders occur at the base, with implications of Mafia involvement. Rud is wounded and after two months in the hospital is sent back to the western front where he joins the Special Flight "A" group in a photographic mission over the German lines. The book briefly explores the problems of military discipline, officer jealousy and rivalry, and the debilitating effect of a spit-and-polish martinet commander. An action-packed war story for boys.

j352 ———. *Wing for Wing*. New York: Grosset & Dunlap, 1932. 212p.

The third in a series of four novels in the author's Air Combat Series that employs very much the same cast of characters. (See the novels of Arch Whitehouse for similar tales written in recent years.) The main characters are Major Rudford Riley, Lieutenant Colonel Stormy Lake, Colonel ("Squads Right") Shafer, the base commander, and several others in the 31st Pursuit Squadron. The action consists mainly of air flights and daredevil battles over the western front, especially with the famous German Red Devil Squadron of Baron von Baer. Two mysterious murders occur at the base, and a supposed informer by the name of Private Greene saves the day by tricking the members of the Red Devil Squadron in an improbable escapade. This is more of a mystery and adventure story than strictly a tale of front-line combat, air or ground. It is a step above most of the juvenile novels written about the war.

1933

j353 Burtis, Thomson. *Flying Blackbirds*. New York: Grosset & Dunlap, 1933. 242p.

The fourth and final story in the author's Air Combat Series. The plot continues with many of the principal characters from the previous books but especially Lieutenant Colonel Stormy Lake and the Baron von Baer, commander of the famous German Red Devils. The flying Blackbirds are a squadron of handpicked daredevil pilots led by Stormy Lake who all continue their efforts (as related in *Wing for Wing*, item j352) to destroy or capture all of the Red Devils, especially the daring von Baer.

The plot is filled with the usual air battle scenes and near crashes. One characteristic of all four titles in this series is the sense of honor and verbal commitment exhibited by both the German and Allied pilots. War in the trenches was certainly hell, but the war in the air seems to be an entirely different, almost detached, war of gentlemen or knights in gossamer armor.

1935

j354 Adams, Eustace Lane. *Doomed Demons*. New York: Grosset & Dunlap, 1935. 210p.

Recounts the exploits of the airmen stationed at the United States Naval Air Base at Souilly-sur-Mer in France, who, under the command of Lieutenant commander "Bull" Meehan, are designated to clear the English Channel of German U-boats. Young pilot Ensign Jimmy Deal, the daredevil of the station, when shot down behind German lines, returns in a captured prize, a German Gotha. He also rescues the French Admiral Criseneuf, as well as his own commander, when they are shot down at sea. He then goes to destroy the canal lock at Ostende, thereby bottling up the German U-boats in the canal between Ostende and Bruges, the U-boats' repair base.

1936

j355 Adams, Eustace Lane. *Wings of the Navy*. New York: Grosset & Dunlap, 1936. 211p.

Recounts the exploits of three American naval seaplane pilots whose escapades on blimp patrol as well as seaplane duty result in the capture of two U-boats. On another occasion they rescue their squadron's captain who has been downed behind enemy lines.

1937

j356 Adams, Eustace Lane. *War Wings*. New York: Grosset & Dunlap, 1937. 216p.

Recounts the further adventures of pilot Ensign Jimmy Deal of the United States Naval Air Station at Souilly-sur-Mer. Among his exploits is landing a captured Fokker

amid the firing of the guns of his own base. Another
incident involves duty on the front-line trenches with
the doughboys. When the Army requested that a Navy man
become acquainted with the trenches which the Navy was
supporting with fire support, Jimmy volunteers, and while
on this temporary duty he helps to foil an attempt to
mine the American trenches.

1939

j357 Aspden, Don. *Mike of Company D*. New York: Charles
Scribner's Sons, 1939. 261p.

An animal story about Mike, a dog who is adopted as
mascot by a company of soldiers after following his
civilian master, Shorty, into the service. Mike gets
overseas as contraband when the soldiers go to Europe
and into the front-line trenches.

j358 Seredy, Kate. *The Singing Tree*. New York: Viking Press,
1939. 247p.

The setting is a farm in Hungary during the years 1914-
1918. The main characters are Kate and Jancsi, children
of the farm's owner, Marton Nagy, who has left for the
war. Jancsi is left in charge of the farm with his
mother. The farm eventually shelters relatives and
friends of the family, five German war orphans and six
Russian prisoners who help with the work. An underlying
theme is racial tolerance, and that all men are brothers.
A home-front tale for boys and girls with a serious
message. (A sequel to the author's *The Good Master*.)

1940

j359 Salten, Felix (pseud. of Sigmund Salzmann). *Renni, the
Rescuer: A Dog of the Battlefield*. Translated by
Kenneth C. Kaufman. Indianapolis: Bobbs-Merrill Co.,
1940. 326p.

Another war animal story by the author of the famous
Bambi story for children. Renni is a shepherd dog
trained by an easygoing young man who prefers not to
use force in the discipline of animals. This pays off
by the complete trust of the dog in his master. Later
in France when they both are sent to the battlefields,

Renni performs heroic acts of canine bravery that testify eloquently to the patient and loving training of the dog. The author seems to have little or no understanding of the nature of war and neither do the characters whom he has created.

1942

j360   Downey, Fairfax Davis. *War Horse*. New York: Dodd, Mead & Co., 1942. 236p.

Follows the adventures of Santa Barbara, a chestnut-colored, western mare, rounded up on the plains of Texas and sent to the Kansas City Remount Depot for shipment to France as a cavalry mount. The book details the story of Sergeant Jim Thomas, a Texas cowboy who had herded the horses. He joins the army to remain with and train Santa Barbara and finally to return with the animal to Texas. Santa Barbara sees rugged action on the German front. This is a fictionalized version of many of the events involving a horse belonging to a sergeant in Major Downey's regiment at the front in France.

1964

j361   Tiemann, Philip W. *No Slacker, 1917-1918. A Chronical of the War at Home*. New York: Vantage Press, 1964. 141p.

Tells the story of Dave Page, a 16-year-old boy in 1917. Too young for the military, yet eager to perform what he considered was his duty to his country, Dave joined the Home Militia which protected such vital local establishments as waterworks. The final chapter begins with Dave's 18th birthday, the day he enlists in the United States Army. In his foreword the author indicates the novel's close connection with historical events: "Dave Page's experiences are presented as fiction, but they are basically a historically accurate picture of a young suburbanite's view of what went on both before and following our entry into 'the war to end war.'"

1966

j362 Peyton, K.M. (pseud. of Kathleen Wendy Peyton and Michael Peyton). *Thunder in the Sky*. Cleveland, Ohio: The World Publishing Co., 1966. 158p.

The main character, Sam Goodrich, is a 14-year-old who works on a barge ("The Flower of Ipswich") transporting ammunition to France from England. Sam discovers that the barge's commanding officer, Bunyard, is pro-German and that Sam's 17-year-old bargemate brother, Gil, has become involved in spy activity for Germany to earn extra money. Referring to the deep conflicts of the main adolescent characters, the *London Times Literary Supplement* reviewer praised the novel: "It is doubtful whether, ten years ago, a story embracing so much of the pain of life, and so frank about the nature of near-adult emotion, would have been published for young readers. Now it comes like an enfrancisement...."

j363 Whitehouse, Arch (pseud. of Arthur George Joseph Whitehouse). *The Ace from Arizona, Frank Luke, the Hun Killer*. New York: Award Books, 1966. 223p.

Not seen.

1967

j364 Coombs, Charles Ira. *Frank Luke, Balloon Buster*. New York: Harper & Brothers, 1967. 256p.

A novel based on the life of a famous American flying ace of the war who spent only a fortnight in combat but managed to shoot down more than twenty enemy balloons and airplanes. Intended for the juvenile market.

j365 Whitehouse, Arch (pseud. of Arthur George Joseph Whitehouse). *Scarlet Streamers*. New York: G.P. Putnam's Sons, 1967. 126p.

The second novel in the author's adventure series of juvenile novels dealing with the exploits of the Lafayette Escadrille. The two other novels are *Spies with Wings* (item j366) and *The Laughing Falcon* (item j367). In this tale two young American fliers contend for the leadership of the famous Escadrille group. The story relates the dogfights, military intrigues, and personal conflicts in this well-known flying group. Sous-lt. Harry Wilson, who was recently promoted to a command position in the French air service, only requires his pilots to go on reconnaissance and defensive missions. However, Bill Arnold, Wilson's challenger, still sees the sky as a new front for the war and disobediently involves himself in spectacular air skirmishes with the Germans. His rebellion soon comes to threaten his friendship with Harry as well as his very life. The story is based on the author's own experiences in the war and demonstrates considerable historical accuracy in the descriptions of how the air war was conducted.

j366 ———. *Spies with Wings*. New York: G.P. Putnam's Sons, 1967. 156p.

Not seen.

1969

j367 Whitehouse, Arch (pseud. of Arthur George Joseph Whitehouse). *The Laughing Falcon*. New York: G.P. Putnam's Sons, 1969. 157p.

The third novel in the author's series of stories based on the history and exploits of the Lafayette Escadrille. (The two previous titles are *Spies with Wings*, item j366, and *Scarlet Streamers*, item j365.) George Dumont, Captain Pitt, and the other members of the Escadrille are puzzled by the mysterious appearances of a pilot they call the Laughing Falcon who flies a different aircraft on each occasion and has recently rescued some of the American pilots in trouble. Grateful to this mysterious protector, the Escadrille men indulge in some detective work and the resulting clues point to either of two young men. But the puzzle increases when the rescuer next appears and fires on members of the Escadrille. This is followed by an air chase, and the Falcon is captured and reveals the secret of his mission--he is a German air observer in disguise. A juvenile tale that portrays truthfully conditions, situations, and the drama of World War I air combat.

1972

j368 Cooper, Gordon. *A Time in a City*. London: Oxford University Press, 1972. 160p.

A juvenile story about a young girl named Kate in domestic service in England during the war. Reminiscent of the television series "Upstairs, Downstairs," it relates some of the involvement of the gentry and their sons with the war, although most of the book deals with daily life in the servants' quarters. Just before the end of the story Kate meets a young soldier from her own village. The book is primarily the story of Kate's adjustment to a new home and her new tasks as a kitchen maid in wartime England.

1975

j369 Farmer, Penelope. *August the Fourth*. Berkeley, California: Parnassus Press, 1975. 46p.

A sensitive children's book describing the impact of the war. Four children go off on a picnic in Wiltshire on the day England declares war and get into trouble with their parents. The parents react in an unexpected way because the war has changed everything. Older brothers go to enlist and a trainload of soldiers passes the village. It all seems very exciting to the children, but one girl, writing about the events of this day two years later, describes how different it all turned out to be.

1978

j370 du Bois, William Pene. *The Forbidden Forest*. New York: Harper & Row, 1978. 56p.

A Big Bertha, the gargantuan cannon of the Germans, is installed in "The Forbidden Forest" area of Germany. The huge gun is capable of shelling Paris, 80 miles distant. Into this forest escape two unlikely companions, a boxing kangaroo called Lady Adelaide and a bulldog with the name of Buckingham. There they discover the Germans preparing to shell Paris. The cannon misfires and the shell does enormous damage to German defenses, resulting in the end of the war, while Buckingham and Lady Adelaide, together with her boxing partner, Spider Max, escape to France.

Bibliography of Critical Materials

BIBLIOGRAPHY OF CRITICAL MATERIALS

This is a listing of the more important critical references dealing with the novels of World War I. All of the standard sources have been examined for possible citations, e.g., the *Annual Bibliography of English Language and Literature*, the annual bibliography of the Modern Language Association, *Readers' Guide to Periodical Literature*, *Humanities Index* (preceded by *Social Sciences & Humanities Index* and the *International Index*), *British Humanities Index*, *Subject Index to Periodicals*, *Canadian Periodical Index*, *Catholic Periodical & Literature Index*, *Essay & General Literature Index*, and other possible sources such as the *Subject Guide to Books in Print 1978*, *NUC: Books, Subjects,* and the *United States Catalog 1928*, and all of the *CBI* volumes to date.

Indeed, we also carefully checked all notes, critical lists, and bibliographies in books written on the novels of the Great War. There has been a deliberate attempt to be comprehensive in this coverage of English-language criticism. Wherever possible the cited indices and bibliographies have been examined to 1978 or the latest published volume available, i.e., 1974 for the *Annual Bibliography of English Language and Literature* and 1977 for the *MLA International Bibliography*. The journal literature in most cases offers either substantial critical analysis or a contemporary view that we consider of some interest for the serious student of World War I fiction.

BOOKS

Aichinger, Peter. *The American Soldier in Fiction, 1880-1963: A History of Attitudes Toward Warfare and the Military Establishment.* Ames: Iowa State University Press, 1975. 143p.

Aldridge, John W. *After the Lost Generation: A Critical Study of the Writers of Two Wars.* New York: McGraw-Hill, 1951. 263p.

Allen, W.E. "A Literary Aftermath." *Promise of Greatness: The War of 1914-1918*. Edited by George A. Panichas. New York: John Day Co., 1968, pp. 503-515.

Beach, Joseph Warren. *American Fiction, 1920-1940*. New York: The Macmillan Co., 1941. 371p.

Bergonzi, Bernard. *Heroes' Twilight: A Study of the Literature of the Great War*. New York: Coward-McCann, 1965. 235p.

Bostock, John Knight. *Some Well-known German War Novels, 1914-1930*. Oxford: Blackwell, 1931. 25p.

Brooks, Van Wyck. "Parvenne Intellectuals." *Sketches in Criticism*. New York: E.P. Dutton & Co., 1932, pp. 51-54.

Butterfield, Herbert. *The Historical Novel; An Essay*. New York: The Macmillan Co., 1924. 113p.

Cadogan, Mary, and Patricia Craig. *Women & Children First: The Fiction of Two Wars*. London: Victor Gollancz, 1978. 301p.

Chesterton, G.K. "On War Books." *End of the Armistice*. New York: Sheed & Ward, 1940, pp. 191-197.

Clarke, Ian Frederick. *Voices Prophesying War, 1763-1984*. London: Oxford University Press, 1966. 254p.

Connor, James Richard. "Pen and Sword: World War I Novels in America, 1916-1941." Ph.D. dissertation, University of Wisconsin, 1961. 415p.

Cooperman, Stanley Roy. "Expectation and Impact in the Post-World War I Novel of Protest." Ph.D. dissertation, Indiana University, 1962. 373p.

―――. *World War I and the American Novel*. Baltimore: The Johns Hopkins Press, 1967. 273p.

Cowley, Malcolm. "The Other War." *A Second Flowering: Works and Days of the Lost Generation*. New York: Viking Press, 1973, pp. 3-18.

―――. "War Novels: After Two Wars." *Modern American Fiction*. Edited by A. Walton Litz. New York: Oxford University Press, 1963, pp. 296-314.

Critoph, Gerald E. "The American Literary Reaction to World War I." Ph.D. dissertation, University of Pennsylvania, 1957. 425p.

Cru, Jean N. *War Books: A Study of Historical Criticism*. San Diego: San Diego State University Press, 1976. 194p.

Dawson, Loleta I., and Marion Davis Huntting. *European War Fiction in English; And Personal Narratives; Bibliographies*. Boston: F.W. Faxon Co., 1921. 120p.

Dickinson, James Franklin. "The Treatment of Military Heroism in the French War Novel." Ph.D. dissertation, New York University, 1950. 233p.

Dolan, Paul J. *Of War and War's Alarms: Fiction and Politics in the Modern World*. New York: The Free Press, 1976. 192p.

Eisinger, Chester E. "The War Novel." *Fiction of the Forties*. Chicago: University of Chicago Press, 1963, pp. 21-61.

Evans, Benjamin Ifor. *English Literature Between the Wars*. London: Methuen & Co., 1949. 133p.

Falls, Cyril Bentham. *The Great War*. New York: G.P. Putnam's Sons, 1959. 447p. (Title in England: *The First World War*.)

———. *War Books: A Critical Guide*. London: Peter Davies, 1930. 318p.

Feigenbaum, Lawrence H. "War as Viewed by the Postwar Novelists of World Wars I and II." Ph.D. dissertation, New York University, 1950. 308p.

Fiedler, Leslie Aaron. *Love and Death in the American Novel*. New York: Criterion Books, 1960. 603p. Rev. ed. New York: Stein and Day, 1966. 512p.

Field, Frank. *Three French Writers and the Great War: Barbusse, Drieu la Rochelle, Bernanos: Studies in the Rise of Communism and Fascism*. Cambridge: Cambridge University Press, 1975. 212p.

Frierson, William Coleman. "Diffusion, 1929-1940." *English Novel in Transition, 1885-1940*. Norman: University of Oklahoma Press, 1942, pp. 279-322.

Frohock, Wilbur Merrill. *The Novel of Violence in America.*
   2d ed., rev. & enl. Dallas: Southern Methodist University
   Press, 1958. 238p.

Fuller, Edmund. *Man in Modern Fiction; Some Minority Opinion
   on Contemporary American Writing.* New York: Random House,
   1958. 171p.

Fussell, Paul. *The Great War and Modern Memory.* New York:
   Oxford University Press, 1975. 363p.

Galsworthy, John. "Literature and the War." *Another Sheaf.*
   New York: Charles Scribner's Sons, 1919, pp. 263-269.

Geismar, Maxwell. *Writers in Crisis: The American Novel Between
   Two Wars.* Boston: Houghton Mifflin Co., 1942. 299p.

Genthe, Charles V. *American War Narratives, 1917-1918: A Study
   and Bibliography.* New York: David Lewis, 1969. 194p.

Gibson, Robert. "The First World War and the Literary Consciousness." *French Literature and Its Background*, Vol. 6,
   The Twentieth Century. Edited by John Cruickshank. London:
   Oxford University Press, 1970, pp. 55-72.

Gordon, Ambrose. *The Invisible Tent; The War Novels of Ford
   Madox Ford.* Austin: University of Texas Press, 1964.
   153p.

Gosse, Edmund William. "War and Literature." *Inter Arma;
   Being Essays Written in Time of War.* New York: Charles
   Scribner's Sons, 1916, pp. 1-38.

Greever, Garland. *War Writing; A Handbook of Rhetoric, with
   Specimens.* New York: Century Co., 1919. 383p.

Greicus, M.S. *Prose Writers of World War I.* Writers and
   Their Work, no. 231. London: Longmans for the British
   Council, 1973. 49p.

Hartwick, Harry. *The Foreground of American Fiction.* New
   York: American Book Co., 1934. 447p.

Hatcher, Harlan Henthorne. "War Generation." *Creating the
   Modern American Novel.* New York: Farrar & Rinehart, 1935,
   pp. 221-233.

Bibliography of Critical Materials

Healey, Robert C. "Novelists of the War: A Bunch of the Dispossessed." *Fifty Years of the American Novel: A Christian Appraisal.* Edited by Harold C. Gardiner. New York: Charles Scribner's Sons, 1951, pp. 257-271.

Hewett-Thayer, Harvey Waterman. "Novel of the Great War." *Modern German Novel; A Series of Studies and Appreciations.* Boston: Marshall Jones Co., 1924, pp. 214-253.

Hoffman, Frederick J. *The Mortal No: Death and the Modern Imagination.* Princeton: Princeton University Press, 1964. 507p.

———. "The Novel of World War I." *Promise of Greatness; The War of 1914-1918.* Edited by George A. Panichas. New York: John Day Co., 1968, pp. 516-527.

———. *The Twenties.* 2d ed. New York: Collier Books, 1962. 516p.

Istas, Helen R. "French and German Attitudes Toward the First World War as Reflected in Novels and Memoirs, 1914-1938." Ph.D. dissertation, Indiana University, 1952. 133p.

Jones, Peter Gaylord. "The Developing Voice: An Appraisal of the Modern American War Novel." Ph.D. dissertation, New York University, 1970. 437p.

———. *War and the Novelists; Appraising the American War Novel.* Columbia: University of Missouri Press, 1976. 260p.

Klein, Holger, editor. *The First World War in Fiction; A Collection of Critical Essays.* London: The Macmillan Co., 1976. 246p.

Klotz, Marvin. "The Imitation of War, 1800-1900: Realism in the American War Novel." Ph.D. dissertation, New York University, 1959. 314p.

Leed, Eric J. *No Man's Land: Combat & Identity in World War I.* Cambridge: Cambridge University Press, 1979. 257p.

Lenrow, Elbert. *Reader's Guide to Prose Fiction.* New York: D. Appleton-Century Co., 1940. 371p.

Lewis, Wyndham. "The War Writers; Excerpt from 'The Old Gang and the New Gang.'" *Enemy Salvoes; Selected Literary Criticism.* New York: Barnes & Noble, 1976, pp. 212-216.

Lilacs, Gyorgy. *The Historical Novel*. London: Merlin Press, 1962. 363p.

Löhrke, Eugene W., editor. *Armageddon: The World War in Literature*. New York: Peter Smith, 1930. 820p.

McGarry, Daniel D., and S.H. White. *Historical Fiction Guide*. Metuchen, N.J.: Scarecrow, 1963. 628p.

MacLeish, Archibald. *Irresponsibles; A Declaration*. New York: Duell, Sloan and Pearce, 1940. 34p.

March, John Leslie. "A Circle of Meaning: American Novelists Face the Military Necessity." Ph.D. dissertation, University of Pennsylvania, 1959. 579p.

Miller, Wayne Charles. "The American Military Novel: A Critical and Social History." Ph.D. dissertation, New York University, 1968. 730p.

―――――. *An Armed America: A History of the American Military Novel*. New York: New York University Press, 1970. 204p.

Morgan, Charles. *Reflections in a Mirror*, second series. London: The Macmillan Co., 1946, pp. 195-212.

Muller, Herbert J. *Modern Fiction: A Study in Values*. New York: McGraw-Hill, 1964, c.1937. 447p.

Oldsey, Bernard Stanley. "Aspects of Combat in the Novel, 1900-1950." Ph.D. dissertation, Pennsylvania State University, 1956. 307p.

Panichas, George A., editor. *Promise of Greatness: The War of 1914-1918*. New York: John Day Co., 1968. 572p.

Pattee, Fred. *The New American Literature, 1890-1930*. New York: Century Co., 1930. 507p.

Pfeiler, William K. *War and the German Mind: The Testimony of Men of Fiction Who Fought at the Front*. New York: Columbia University Press, 1941. 349p.

Phipps, Frank Thomas. "The Image of War in America, 1891-1917: A Study of a Literary Theme and Its Cultural Origins and Analogues." Ph.D. dissertation, Ohio State University, 1953. 275p.

Bibliography of Critical Materials 459

Postman, Harry. "The American Citizen-Soldier: A Sociological Analysis of War Novels." Ph.D. dissertation, Columbia University, 1957. 689p.

Priestley, J.B. "Brief Interlude." *Literature and Western Man*. New York: Harper & Brothers, 1960, pp. 370-375.

Read, Herbert. "The Failure of War Books." *A Coat of Many Colours*. Rev. ed. London: Routledge & Kegan Paul, 1957, pp. 72-76.

Rutherford, Andrew. "The Common Man as Hero: Literature of the Western Front." *The Literature of War: Five Studies in Heroic Virtue*. New York: Barnes & Noble, 1978, pp. 64-112.

Schinz, Albert. *French Literature of the Great War*. New York: D. Appleton & Co., 1920. 433p.

Spindler, Russell S. *The Military Novel*. Wisconsin: U.S. Armed Forces Institute, 1964. 178p.

Swinnerton, Frank. *The Georgian Literary Scene, 1910-1935; A Panorama*. 6th ed., rev. London: Hutchinson & Co., 1950. 415p.

Taylor, William Arthur. *Historical Fiction*. Folcroft, Pa.: Folcroft Library Editions, 1975, c.1957, 48p.

Tomlinson, Henry Major. "Authors and Soldiers." *Waiting for Daylight*. New York: Alfred A. Knopf, 1922, pp. 80-87.

Van Doren, Carl. *The American Novel, 1789-1939*. Rev. and Enl. New York: The Macmillan Co., 1940. 406p.

Ward, A.C. *The Nineteen-Twenties: Literature and Ideas in the Post-War Decade*. London: Methuen & Co., 1930. 222p.

West, Herbert Faulkner. "Literature of War." *Mind on the Wing; a Book for Readers and Collectors*. New York: Coward-McCann, 1947, pp. 204-248.

Williamson, Henry. "Reality in War Literature." *The Linhay on the Downs*. London: Faber & Faber, 1934, pp. 224-262.

Winther, Sophus Keith. *The Realistic War Novel*. (University of Washington Chapbooks, no. 35.) Seattle: University of Washington Bookstore, 1930. 35p.

Winwar, Frances (pseud.). "World War and the Arts." *War in the Twentieth Century*. Edited by Willard Walter Waller. New York: Random House, 1940, pp. 192-232.

Wohl, Robert. *The Generation of 1914*. Cambridge: Harvard University Press, 1979. 307p.

Woods, Dorothea Eleanor. "French Literature and Peace, 1919-1939." Ph.D. dissertation, University of Illinois, 1957. 269p.

ARTICLES

Barnett, Corelli. "A Military Historian's View of the Literature of the Great War." *Essays by Divers Hands*, 36 (1970), 1-18.

Berendsohn, Walter Arthur. "War Memories in Literature." *Christian Science Monitor Weekly Magazine*, (July 24, 1934), 10.

Bergonzi, Bernard. "Before 1914: Writers and Threat of War." *Critical Quarterly*, 6 (1964), 126-134.

―――. "Words of War." *Guardian*, (March 5, 1964), 8.

"Best Sellers in the Last War." *Publishers Weekly*, 136 (September 9, 1939), 879-880.

Blyton, William Joseph. "Response to Crisis: Some Contrasts from English Literature." *Quarterly Review*, 277 (July 1941), 105-114.

Canby, Henry S. "Modern War." *Saturday Review of Literature*, 5 (June 8, 1929), 1087-1089.

―――. "War and Literature." *Saturday Review of Literature*, 24 (September 20, 1941), 8.

―――. "War Books and 'All Our Yesterdays.'" *Golden Book*, 11 (March 1930), 94-96.

―――. "War or Peace in Literature." *Saturday Review of Literature*, 8 (April 9, 1932), 645-647.

Cohen, J.M. "The Earth is Hungry: Literature of the First War." *Listener*, 74 (November 11, 1965), 753-755.

Bibliography of Critical Materials

Cooperman, Stanley. "Of War and Man." *Nation*, 180 (July 23, 1955), 80.

Cowley, Malcolm. "Ambulance Service." *New Republic*, 72 (November 2, 1932), 325-328.

―――. "Two Wars--and Two Generations." *New York Times Book Review*, (July 25, 1948), 1.

D., F.M. "Submarine and Air-bomber Fiction." *Southern Literary Messenger*, 2 (June 1940), 361-362.

Davis, Elmer Holmes. "Apocalyptic Literature." *Saturday Review of Literature*, 10 (April 21, 1943), 641-643.

"Does War Produce Literature?" *Literary Digest* 99 (December 15, 1928), 25-26.

Dougherty, Lewis A. "When the Novel Came Marching Home." *San Francisco Quarterly*, 2 (May 1936), 13-26.

Edwards, Oliver. "The Writers' War." (London) *Times*, (November 19, 1964), 16.

Eisinger, Chester E. "The American War Novel: An Affirming Flame." *Pacific Spectator*, 9 (1955), 272-288.

Fay, Sidney. "War Literature." *The Literary Review (Evening Post)*, (October 23, 1920), 30.

Feeney, L. "Something of War and Its Effects on Literature." *America*, 61 (September 16, 1939), 547-548.

Fenton, Charles A. "A Literary Fracture of World War I." *American Quarterly*, 12 (Summer 1960), 119-132.

―――. "The Writers Who Came Out of the War." *Saturday Review*, (August 3, 1957), 5-7.

Fiedler, Leslie. "The Anti-war Novel and the Good Soldier Schweik." *Ramparts*, 1 (January 1963), 43-48.

Gardiner, H. "Mars and the Muses in 1917." *America*, 68 (October 31, 1942), 101-102. Discussion, 68 (December 5, 1942), 241-242; 68 (January 2, 1943), 353-354.

Gribble, Francis. "Has the War Killed Literature?" *The New World*, (April 21, 1921), 409-413.

Gruber, Helmut. "Neue Sachlichkeit and the World War." *German Life & Letters*, 20 (January 1967), 138-149.

"A Guide to American Literature Written During World War I." *Saturday Review of Literature*, 9 (October 22, 1932), 197.

Gummere, Francis B. "War and Romance." *Atlantic Monthly*, 126 (October 1920), 490-496.

Hagboldt, Peter Herman. "Ethical and Social Problems in the German War Novel." *Journal of English & Germanic Philology*, 32 (January 1933), 21-32.

Herrick, Robert. "War and American Literature." *Dial*, 64 (1918), 7-8.

Hindle, Wilfred H. "War Books and Peace Propaganda." *Bookman* (London), 81 (December 1931), 158-160.

Horrox, Lewis. "Literature and War." *Hibbert Journal*, 38 (April 1940), 342-354.

Howard, Michael. "Back to All That." *New Statesman*, 55 (January 11, 1958), 46.

Johnston, John Hubert. "David Jones: The Heroic Vision." *Review of Politics*, 24 (January 1962), 62-87.

Jones, D.A.N. "The War Game." *New York Review of Books*, (October 26, 1967), 20-23.

Kahn, Lothar. "The Jewish Soldier in Modern Fiction." *American Judaism*, 9 (1960), 12-13, 30-31.

Kaye, F.B. "Puritanism, Literature, and the War." *New Republic*, 25 (December 15, 1920), 64-67.

Kazin, Alfred. "Mindless Young Militants; The Hero-victims of the American War Novels." *Commentary*, 6 (December 1948), 495-501.

Kermode, Frank. "The Words of Two Wars." *Daily Telegraph* (London), (August 30, 1975), 7.

Kitchin, Laurence. "Snobs' Wars." *Listener*, 80 (November 21, 1968), 679-681.

Lewisohn, Ludwig. "The Crisis of the Novel." *Yale Review*, 20 (1933), 533-544.

Loveman, Amy. "The War in Fiction." *Saturday Review of Literature*, 11 (March 9, 1935), 542.

Marston, John. "Fifteen Years After." *Cornhill Magazine*, 150 (August 1934), 213-224.

Morris, Lloyd. "Heritage of a Generation of Novelists." *New York Herald Tribune Book Review*, (September 25, 1949), 74.

Munson, Gorham. "The Fledgling Years, 1916-1924." *Sewanee Review*, 40 (1932), 24-54.

Partridge, Eric. "The War Comes into Its Own." *The Window*, 1 (January 1930), 72-104.

―――. "The War Continues." *The Window*, 1 (April 1930), 62-85.

Potter, Stephen. "Plan of Attack." *Spectator*, 213 (July 31, 1964), 156.

Press, John. "Charles Sorley." *Review of English Literature*, 7 (April 1966), 43-60.

Pritchett, V.S. "First Person Singular in War Fiction." *New Statesman and Nation*, 23 (May 2, 1942), 291.

Rahv, Philip. "The Cult of Experience in American Writing." *Partisan Review*, 7 (1940), 412-424.

Roscoe, Burton. "What They Read During the Last War." *Saturday Review of Literature*, 20 (September 23, 1939), 3-4, 12-16.

"Reading and Fighting." *Saturday Review of Literature*, 6 (April 12 1930), 913; Payson, H. "War and Peace; Reply to...." 7 (August 30, 1930), 90.

Remenyi, Joseph. "The Psychology of War Literature." *Sewanee Review*, 52 (January 1944), 137-147.

Rickmers, C. Mabel. "A German on German War Literature; A Review of *Die forderung des tages....*" *Bookman* (London), 81 (October 1931), 52-53.

Sabo, Leslie, Jr. "Making of a Doughboy." *Free World*, 8 (August 1944), 177-179.

Sassoon, Siegfried Lorraine. "Dynasts in War-time." *Spectator*, 168 (February 6, 1942), 127-128.

Schröter, Klaus. "Chauvinism and Its Tradition: German Writers at the Outbreak of the First World War." *Germanic Review*, 43 (March 1968), 120-135.

Smith, William J. "The War Novel." *Commonweal*, 64 (May 11, 1956), 146-149.

Stewart, Randall. "American Literature Between the Wars." *South Atlantic Quarterly*, 44 (1945), 371-383.

Stromberg, R.N. "The Intellectuals and the Coming of War in 1914." *Journal of European Studies*, 3 (June 1973), 109-122.

Taylor, Mark. "Novels of War Novels?" *Commonweal*, 104 (September 2, 1977), 566-571.

Titterton, L.H. "War Comes Back to Fiction." *Independent* (Boston), 116 (March 27, 1926), 359-360.

Tomlinson, Henry Major. "War Books." *Criterion*, 9 (April 1930), 402-419.

―――. "War Books." *Yale Review*, 19 (March 1930), 447-465.

"Tonic of War Books." *Literary Digest*, 104 (March 22, 1930), 21.

Van Abbe, Derek. "Clio in the Underworld." *German Life & Letters*, 16 (January 1963), 128-135.

Van Doren, Carl. "American Realism." *New Republic*, 34 (March 21, 1923), 107-109.

―――. "Post-war: The Literary 20's." *Harper's*, 173 (1936), 148-156.

Van Doren, Mark. "The Art of American Fiction." *Nation*, 137 (April 25, 1934), 471-473.

Walcutt, Charles C. "Fear Motifs in the Literature Between the Wars." *South Atlantic Quarterly*, 46 (April 1947), 227-238.

Bibliography of Critical Materials 465

Waldmeir, Joseph. "Novelists of Two Wars." *Nation*, 87 (November 1, 1958), 304-307.

"War Books and War." *Spectator*, 144 (May 10, 1930), 773-774.

"War Books That Go Too Far." *Literary Digest*, 106 (July 12, 1930), 16.

"War's Effect on Literature." *Literary Digest*, 49 (December 26, 1914), 1277-1278.

"War's Reaction on Literature." *Nation*, 99 (December 31, 1914), 765.

Waugh, Arthur. "Literature and War." *Fortnightly Review*, 102 (November 1914), 766-767.

Whipple, Leon. "Mosaic of War." *Survey*, 64 (April 1, 1930), 34-35.

Wilkinson, Clennell. "Back to All That." *London Mercury*, 22 (October 1930), 539-546.

―――. "Real Thing." *London Mercury*, 21 (February 1930), 338-342.

―――. "Recent War Books." *London Mercury*, 21 (January 1930), 236-242.

Williamson, Henry. "Reality in War Literature." *London Mercury*, 19 (January 1929), 295-304.

Willoughby, D. "French Novels of the War." *Saturday Review* (London), 150 (August 23, 1930), 224-225.

Wilson, N. "Ernst Stadler and Charles Peguy: Notes on the Fiction and Facts of a Relationship." *Modern Language Review*, 57 (October 1962), 551-555.

Yaffle (pseud.). "Brighter Realism; A Plea for Nicer and Better War Books." *Living Age*, 337 (February 1, 1930), 697-699.

Young, Thomas Daniel. "Kind of Centering." *Georgia Review*, 28 (Spring 1974), 58-82.

Indexes

AUTHOR INDEX

(Citations to, for example, *1919 or *j1919 refer to asterisked items within the year 1919 in, respectively, the adult and juvenile sections of the bibliography.)

Abdullah, Achmed 302, 303, 692
Acland, Peregrine 548
Adams, Eustace Lane j354, j355, j356
Adams, Samuel Hopkins 304
Aldington, Richard 549, 586
Allain, Marcel 305
Allen, Alice Maude 647
Altsheler, Joseph Alexander 10, 11, 12
Alverdes, Paul 550
Alford, James Church 13
Ames, Franklin T. j8, j9, j230
Ammers-Kueller, Jo van 52
Anand, Mulk Raj 755
Anderson, Robert Gordon 185
Andreev, Leonid Nikolaevich 112
Andrews, Mary Raymond (Shipman) 14, 186 461
Angellotti, Marion Polk 187
Appleton, Victor j64B, j143, j144, j231, j232, *j1927
Arundel, Louis j10
Ashton, Winifred 211
Aspden, Don j357
Atherton, Gertrude Franklin (Horn) 188
Atkinson, Eleanor j145
Aumonier, Stacy 306
Austin, Oscar Phelps j108
Ayres, Ruby Mildred 15

Bacheller, Irving Addison 189
Bailey, Irene Temple 190

Bailey, Paul 885
Baldwin, May Irene j65
Ball, Eustace Hale 528
Balmer, Edwin j233
Barbour, Ralph Henry j146, j234, j235
Barbusse, Henri 113, 307
Barney, J. Stewart 16
Barretto, Larry 551
Bartimeus 114
Bartlett, Stephen 727
Bartlett, Vernon 587
Barton, George 308
Baskerville, Beatrice C. 191
Bates, Gordon j147, j148, j149, j236, j237
Bates, Sylvia Chatfield 53
Battersby, Henry Francis Prevost 309
Baum, L. Frank j214, j305
Baxter, Arthur Beverley 414
Bazin, René François Nicolas Marie 415
Beach, Charles Amory j150, j151, j152, j238, j239, j312
Beach, Rex Ellingwood 310
Bee, David 816
Beebe, Elswyth Thane (Ricker) 777, 779
Begbie, Harold 311
Beith, John Hay 454
Bell, John Joy 17, 54
Bell, John Keble 149, 351
Bellah, James Warner 529
Benjamin, Rene 55
Bennet, Robert Ames 192

Bennett, Arnold 193, 194, 500
Bennett, Rolf j11AB, j66AB j67A
Benoit, Pierre 588
Bensen, Arthur Christopher 70
Benson, Edward 56, 57, 195
Benson, Stella 115
Benstead, Charles Richard 589
Berger, Marcel 58, 196, 312, 476
Berger, Maude 196
Bernard, Marguerite j153
Bertram, Cyril Anthony 552
Bertrand, Adrien 313
Bevan, Tom j68A, j109A
Bindloss, Harold 59
Birmingham, George A. 18
Bishop, Austin j240, j313
Bishop, George Bernard Hamilton 60
Bishop, Giles j314, j332, j333, j336
Black, Alexander 314
Blaine, John *j1916, *j1918, *j1919
Blake, George 553
Blaker, Richard 590
Blankfort, Michael 729, 821
Blasco Ibáñez, Vicente 197, 198, 315
Bleneau, Adele 19
Blighton, Frank Harris 39
Boggs, Winifred 118
Boileau, Ethel 591
Bond, Aimee 199, 316
Boot, Douglas 684
Borden, Mary 447
Borel, Marguerite 257
Borgese, Giuseppe Antonio 477
Botcharsky, Sophie, & Florida Pier 643
Botsford, Charles Alexander 317, 448, j154, j315
Bottome, Phyllis 116, 318
Bourget, Paul Charles Joseph 61

Bower, B.M. 319
Bower, John Graham 244
Bowes, Joseph 200, 320, 416
Boyd, James 702
Boyd, Martin 806
Boyd, Thomas 478
Boylesve, Rene 201
Bradley, Mary (Hastings) 20
Brandau, Hermann 661
Brehm, Bruno 662, 693
Brereton, Frederick j1, j12, j69, j70, j71, j110, j111, j155, j156, j157, j241, j242
Bridge, Ann 784
Bridges, Thomas Charles j13A, j112A, j316A, j344AB
Bridges, Victor 21
Briffault, Robert Stephen 730
Brittain, Vera Mary 715
Broch, Hermann 663
Broger, Karl 592
Brooks, Edna j158, j159, j243
Brophy, John 530, 694
Brown, Alice 321
Brown, Demetra Vace 322
Brown, George Rothwell 117
Brown, Kenneth 322
Brown, William Perry j193, j194, j281
Bruce, Keith 756
Buchan, John 22, 323, 685, *1919
Buckrose, J.E. 202
Bunker, Annie Crosby 417
Burgess, Anthony 807
Burke, Edward 118
Burley, Andrew S. j244, j245, j246
Burr, Anna Robeson (Brown) 449
Burrage, Alfred McLelland 592a

Burtis, Thomson j350, j351, j352, j353
Butler, Eliza 783
Byrne, Donn 1

Cable, Boyd 119
Cahill, James Semple 483
Caine, Thomen Henry Hall 479
Cameron, Ian 874
Cammaerts, Emile j160
Cammaerts, Tita j160
Campbell, R.W. 23, 24, 62, 120, 203, 204, 324
Campbell, William Edward March 686
Canaway, William 827
Canfield, Dorothy 593
Canfield, Mrs. Flavia A. j247
Cannan, Gilbert 325, 450
Capy, Marcelle 664
Carter, Herbert j72, j113
Cass, F. Delysle j55
Castle, Agnes (Sweetman) 25, 26, 205
Castle, Egerton 25, 26, 205
Cather, Willa Sibert 462
Celine, Louis-Ferdinand 695, 787
Chack, Paul 531
Chambe, René 644
Chambers, Robert William 27, 63, 121, 122, 206, 326, 327
Chamson, André 554
Chapman, Allen j161
Chartres, Annie (Vivanti) 123
Chase, Josephine j147, j148, j149, j236, j237
Child, Philip 731
Childs, James Rives 665
Cholmondeley, Alice 124
Clarke, Covington j341, j343
Clevely, Hugh 811
Cloete, Stuart 837
Clouston, Joseph Storer 125, 207

Cobb, Frank *j1915, *j1916, *j1918, *j1919
Cobb, Geoffrey Belton 64
Cobb, Humphrey 703
Cobb, Thomas 208
Cocteau, Jean 491
Cogswell, A.M. 463
Cohn, Clara (Viebig) 464
Coles, Cyril Henry 757
Coles, Manning 757
Colette 594
Comfort, Will Levington 28
Commander 209
Conkling, Roscoe E. 758
Connor, Ralph 126, 328
Cook, W. Victor 329
Cooke, Marjorie Benton 210
Coombs, Charles Ira 832, j364
Cooper, Gordon j368
Copplestone, Bennett j73, 127, 330
Corby, Alan 732
Cosic, Dobrica 871, 886
Cowan, Louise Henry 484
Cowen, William Joyce 696, 716
Cradock, Fanny 865
Cradock, Phyllis 865
Cretin, Roger Auguste 714
Crocker, Arthur 704
Crockett, Sherman j14, j74, j75, j114, j162
Crosby, Barbara 732
Crosland, Thomas William Hodgson 29
Cule, W.E. 30
Cummings, E.E. 465

Daly, Victor 666
Dana, Mercedes 466
Dane, Clemence 211
Dark, Sidney 128
Darling, Esther Birdsall j345
Darlington, William Aubrey Cecil 331

Davidson, Halsey j163, j164, j165, j248, j249, j317B, *j1930
Davignon, Henri 212
Daviot, Gordon 555
Davis, Clyde Brion 773
Davis, Richard Harding 129
Davis, Robert H. 9
Dawson, Coningsby William 332, 556, 595, j318
Dawson, Warrington Francis 451
Dawson, William James 213
Deane, Peter 492
De Crespigny, Charles Norris Williamson 65
Deeping, Warwick 214, 717
Degee, Oliver 751
Dehan, Richard 215
De Hart, Horace Peter Biddle j49, j50, j51, j52, j93, j94, j125, j126, j195, j196, j282, j283.
Delafield, E.M. 216
De La Pasture, Edmée Elizabeth Monica 216
Delderfield, Ronald Frederick 849
de Montherlant, Henry 808
Dent, Walter Redvers 596
De Pourtales, Guy 742
De Selincourt, Hugh 66
Destouches, Louis Ferdinand 695, 787
Deval, Jacques 597
Dilas, Milovan 812
Dillon, Mary C. (Johnson) 217, 333
Diver, Katherine Helen Maud (Marshall) 130, 218
Divine, Charles 512
Dix, Beulah Marie 67
Dodd, Frank W. 31
Dodge, Henry Irving 219
Doolittle, Hilda 800
Dorgelés, Roland 418
Dorling, Henry Taprell 104, 334, 690, j133

Dos Passos, John Roderigo, Jr. 419, 452, 667, *1945
Downey, Fairfax Davis j360
Drake, Robert L. j15, j16, j17, j18, j19, j20, j76, j115, j166, j167, j250
Driggs, Laurence La Tourette j168, j334, j346
Driscoll, James R. j169, j170, j171, j172, j173, j251, j252, j253, j319
Du Bois, Mary Constance j254
Du Bois, William Pene j370
Dunbar, Ruth 335
Durston, George j77, j78, j79, j80, j174, j175, j255, *j1921, *j1927
Dwinger, Edwin Erich 668
Dyer, Walter Alden j20, 256

Eddis, F.E. 220
Edgar, George 68
Edgar, Josephine 872
Elliot, Robert 803
Ellis, Julie 887
Ellsberg, Edward 645, 669
Emerson, Alice B. j176, j177, j257
Empey, Arthur Guy 513
Erichsen, Erich Anton 131
Erskine, Laurie York 598
Ervine, St. John Greer 132
Evans, Alan 873
Ewart, Ernest 119
Ewart, Wilfrid Herbert 453

Fallas, Carl 788
Farigoule, Louis 750
Farmer, Penelope j369
Faulkner, William 501, 789
Federn, Karl 599
Ferguson, John 133
Ferraro, Agnese 336
Fetterless, Arthur 69, 221

Findley, Timothy 866
Fiske, James *j1915, *j1916, *j1918, *j1919
Fitzhugh, Percy Keese j178, j179, j180, j181, j258
Flatau, Dorota 222
Fleming, Guy 134
Flower, Jessie Graham J320, j321, j322, j323, j324
Foote, Mary (Hallock) 337
Ford, Ford Madox 485, 493, 502, 532, *1950
Forester, Cecil Scott 557, 705, 718, 782
Forward, Charles Walter j21
Fowler, Guy 600
Fox, Edward Lyell 135
Frank, Leonhard 558
Frankau, Gilbert 420, 706
Fredenburgh, Theodore 601
French, Alice 179
French, Allen 136
Frenssen, Gustav 602
Frey, Alexander Moriz 603
Frooks, Dorothy 338
Frothingham, Eugenia Brooks 223
Fulcher, Paul Milton 604

G., H.L. 70
Galsworthy, John 339
Gambier, Kenyon 340
Gann, Ernest K. 828
Garis, Howard Roger j22
Gatlin, Dana 224
Gavin, Catherine Irvine 834
George, Walter Lionel 341
Géraldy, Paul 137
Gibbon, John Murray 225
Gibbs, Arthur Hamilton 503, 605
Gibbs, George Fort 32, 138, 342, 421
Gibbs, Philip Hamilton 422, 494, 707
Giesy, John Ulrich 33, 226
Gijsen, Marnix 860a

Gilbreath, Olive 227
Gilson, Charles James L. 228
Giono, Jean 838
Glaeser, Ernst 559
Glasgow, Ellen Anderson Gholson 343
Godfrey, George L. 646
Godwin, George Stanley 606
Goldfrap, John Henry j4B, j37, j38, j47, j48, j88, j122
Goldring, Douglas 139
Goodridge Roberts, Theodore 467
Gordon, Charles William 126, 328
Gorman, Herbert Sherman 697
Goss, Warren Lee j259
Gould, Nat (Nathaniel) 140
Grabenhorst, Georg 560
Graham, Stephen 708
Grant, Allan j23, j24, j25, j26, 278
Gratacap, Louis Page 141
Graves, Armagaard Karl 2
Graves, Clotilde, Inez Mary 215
Greene, Homer Flag j116
Grey, Zane 229
Grierson, Francis D. 230
Griggs, Edward *j1921
Gristwood, Arthur Donald 514
Guest, Carmel (Goldsmid) 533
Guiches, Gustave 231
Guilloux, Louis 719
Gull, Cyril Arthur Edward Ranger 47, 48
Gurner, Ronald 607

Haines, Donal Hamilton 344
Hale, Beatrice (Forbes-Robertson) 71
Hale, Harry j27
Hale, Marice Rutledge (Gibson) 172
Hales, Alfred Greenwood 142, 143

Hall, James 572
Hamilton, Cicely Mary 345
Hamilton, Frederick Spencer
    j28, j29, j80, j335, j337
Hamilton, Mary Agnes 72, 608
Hamilton, Robert W. 144
Hancock, Harrie Irving j81, j82, j83, j84, j260, j261, j262, j263, j264
Hanley, James 609, 743
Hannah, Ian Campbell 73
Hannay, James Owen 18
Hardy, Jocelyn Lee 709
Harraden, Beatrice 232
Harris, Credo Fitch 233
Harris, John 804, 850, 867
Harrison, Charles Yale 610
Harrison, Henry Sydnor 468
Harrison, Sarah 888
Hasek, Jaroslav 611
Haskell, Edward F. 766
Havard, Aline j182, j265, j325, j330
Havens, Allen 647
Hay, David 829
Hay, Ian 454
Hay-Newton, F. 145
Hayes, Clair Wallace j30, j31, j32, j33, j85, j86, j117, j118, j119, j183, j266, j267, j268
Hayes, Harold Melvin 423
Heinz, Max 612
Hellier, F. 74
Hemingway, Ernest 561
Hemingway, Hetty 146
Hennessy, Max 867
Hepburne, Melissa 875
Herbert, Alan Patrick 346
Herrick, Robert 75
Heth, Edward Harris 733
Higgins, Aileen Cleveland j34B
Hill, Grace Livingston 347, 348
Hill, Herbert 720
Hill, Susan 847

Hilton, James 767
Hinkson, Pamela 670
Hirst, George 839
Hobson, Laura Z. 817
Hocking, Joseph 3, 34, 147
Hodson, James Lansdale 562, 792
Hogue, Oliver 349
Holmes, Wilfred Jay 759
Holt, Lee 234
Hopkins, William John 148
Hornibrook, Isabel Katherine j184, j269
Horsley, Reginald Ernest j120A
Howard, Berthyl 350
Howard, Keble 149, 351
Howard, Mary 872
Huard, Frances 352
Hudson, Alec 759
Huebsch, Edward 876
Hueffer, Oliver Madox 613
Hughes, Rupert 235, 353
Humphreys, Eliza M.J. (Gollan) j338
Hunter, Evan 840
Hunter, Jack D. 818
Hurrell, Francis Gordon 236
Hutchinson, Arthur Stuart-Menteth 768
Hutchinson, Ray Coryton 744
Hutchison, Graham Seton 581, 677
Hutter, Catherine 777
Huzard, Antoinette de Bergevin 413
Hyde, Robin 721

Imbrie, Walter McLaren 424
Inchbold, A. Cunnick 425
Ingram, Archibald Kenneth 515
Isham, Frederick Stewart 237

Jack, Donald Lamont 809, 855, 861, *1976

Author Index 475

Jackson, Charles Tenney j185, j186
Jacob, Naomi Ellington 710
Jacobsen, Norman 269
James, William R. 238, j270, j271, j272, j273
Jameson, Annie Edith (Foster) 202
Jameson, Margaret Storm 504
Janes, Henry P. 76
Jasper, Philip j274, j275, j276, j277
Jeans, Thomas Tendron 35, 150
Jenkin, A.M.N. 354, 524
Jenkins, Burris Atkins 239
Jenkins, Herbert George 355, 525
Jenkins, Robin 876a
Jennings, John Edward, Jr. 813
Jepson, Edgar 426
Jerome, Jerome Klapka 356
Johannsen, Ernst 614
Johns, William Earl 671
Johnson, David 801
Johnson, Owen McMahon 455
Johnston, Annie Fellows j187
Johnston, Jennifer 859
Johnston, William Andrew 357
Jones, David Michael 734
Jones, Doris Egerton 240, 358
Jones, J. 889

Kaplan, De Witte 411
Kauffman, Reginald Wright 358
Kay, Ross j2, j3, j35, j36, j87, j121, j188, j278, j326
Kaye-Smith, Sheila 241
Keable, Robert 456
Keel, Frederick Bolton 615
Kehoe, Thomas Joseph 242
Kelland, Clarence Budington 359, 360
Kellerman, Bernhard 495

Kelley, Ethel May 243
Kelly, Thomas Howard 427
Kenneally, Thomas 862
Kennedy, William Anthony 361
Kessel, Joseph 534, 814, *1928
Kimber, Hugh 516
King, Basil 151, 362, 363
King, Rufus Gunn 760
Kinross, Albert 496
Kirk, Laurence 616
Kitchin, Frederick Harcourt 127, 330, j73
Klareich, Lee 735
Klaxon 244
Knipe, Alden Arthur j279
Knipe, Emilie j279
Koppen, Edlef 648
Kreutz, Rudolf Jeremias 364
Kubiny, Victor von 428
Kummer, Frederic Arnold 76, 365
Kyne, Peter Bernard 517

L., C.E. 77
Laing, Janet 245, 366
Lang, William 367
Lathrop, Loren Andrews 340
Lathrop, William Addison 368
Latzko, Adolf Andreas 369
Laughlin, Clara Elizabeth 469
Lawrence, David Herbert 480
Lawton, Wilbur j4B, j37B, j38B, j50, j88B, j122
Lazo, Hector 698
Leake, R.E. 246
Lebedeff, Ivan 761
Leblanc, Maurice 4, 78, 152
Lee, Albert j89
Lee, Jeanette Barbour (Perry) 247
Lee, John Alexander 736, 868
Lee, Mary 563
Lefèvre, Paul 137

Leigh, James 649
Leighton, Robert j90
Lengyel, Emil 650
LeQueux, William 5, 36, 79, 80, 153, 154
Lernet-Holenia, Alexander Maria 722
Le Roux, Hughes 248
Leslie, Henrietta 617
Levin, Meyer 851
Lewenkrohn, Samuel j129, j130
Lewis, Gladys A. 370
Lewys, George 370
Lincoln, Natalie Sumner 249
Lister, Frederick William 779
Locke, William John 81, 155, 156, 429
Löhrke, Eugene William 564
Long, Helen Beecher 250
Lorenz, Helmut 618
Lowndes, Marie Adelaide (Belloc) 37, 82, 83, 252
Lucas, Anna M. 749
Lucas, Edward Verrall 84
Lutes, Della (Thompson) 253
Lutz, Grace Livingston Hill 347, 348
Lyman, Edward Branch j123
Lynn, Escott 38, 85, 254, 371, 430, 457
Lyons, Albert Michael Neil 372

Macaulay, Rose 86
MacDonald, Philip 518
MacGill, Patrick 87, 157, 255
MacGrath, Harold 373
Machen, Arthur 158
Mack, Charles E. 535
Mackenzie, Compton 374, 505, 536, 565, 737
Mackintosh, Elizabeth 555
MacLean, Charles Agnew 39
MacLennan, John Hugh 769
MacNichol, Shaw 497
Madison, George Neser j59, j205, j299

Maher, Richard Aumerle 375
Maher, Stephen John 256
Mahon, Terence 566
Maitland, Robert j39, j40, j41, j42, j43, j44
Malone, Paul Bernard 762
Malpass, Eric Lawson 873a
Malraux, André 458, 785
Mann, Francis Oscar 672
Mann, Leonard 673
Manning, Adelaide Francis Oke 757
Manning, Frederic 567
Mansfield, Charlotte 159
Marbo, Camille 257
March, William 687
Margerison, John S. 258, 259, j280
Markovits, Rodion 569
Marlow, Ralph j45, j46, j91
Marshall, Archibald 40, 376
Marshall, Arthur Hammond 40, 376
Marshall, Bruce 790
Marshall, William Leonard 843
Martin, Mabel (Wood) 519
Martin du Gard, Roger 763
Mason, Alfred Edward Woodley 431
Mason, Grace (Sartwell) 377, 378
Masters, John 852, 877, 891
Maugham, William Somerset 537
Maurois, André 379, 458
Maxwell, William Babington 380
McCann, Hugh Wray 822
McCarthy, Justin Huntly 381
McClure, Robert E. 506
McCutcheon, George Barr 260
McDonald, Roger 890
McFee, William 470, 619
McGrath, Harold 373
McKee, Ruth Eleanor 745
McKenna, Marthe (Cnokaert) 711

Author Index

McKenna, Stephen 160, 161, 382
McNeile, Herman Cyril 395
Meersch, Maxence van der 738
Merrill, Lewis C. 786
Meynell, Wilfrid 6, 88
Milholland, Ray 723
Miller, Patrick 486
Millin, Sarah Gertrude (Liebson) 823
Mitchelson, Austin 863
Molesworth, Guilford Lindsey 162
Montague, Charles Edward 507
Montague, Margaret 89, 383, 432, 433, 487
Moore, Henry Charles j92
Morris, Gouverneur 261
Morris, Suzanne 878
Morris, Walter Frederick 569, 620
Morton, Guy Eugene 262
Morton, John Bingham 384
Mottram, Ralph Hale 488, 498, 508, *1927
Moulton, Hugh Fletcher 621
Mukerji, Dhan Goapl j340
Münch, Paul Georg 90
Mundy, Talbot 91, 92, 263
Munthe, Axel Martin Fredrik 93
Myrivilis, Stratis (Strates Myribeles) 869

Nadaud, Marcel 264, 385
Nason, Leonard Hastings 509, 538, 570, 622, 651
Nazhivin, Ivan Federovich 571
Newberry, Perry 520
Newman, Bernard 623, 712, 724
Newton, Wilfrid Douglas 7, 265
Nexo, Martin Andersen 687
Noble, Edward 521

Nordhoff, Charles Bernard 572
Nylen, Irene 434

O'Donovan, Gerald 435
Odum, Howard Washington 573
O'Flaherty, Liam 574
Olden, Balder 624
O'Malley, Mary Dolling 784
Oppenheim, Edward Phillips 41, 94, 266, 267, 386, 436, 437
Osmond, Robert William 795
Owen, Walter 652

P., K.S. 163
Padover, Saul Kussiel 674
Pakington, Humphrey 781
Paletta, Filippo 688
Palmer, Frederick 8, 95
Palmer, John Leslie 96
Palmer, Lilli 892
Paretti, Sandra 879
Parker, Ellanore J. 770, 793
Parker, Thomas Drayton j189
Parry, D.H. 164
Patchin, Frank Gee (Glines) j190, j191
Paul, Elliot Harold 625
Payne, Donald Gordon 874
Payson, Howard j47, j48
Pennell, Elizabeth (Robins) 165
Perkins, Lucy (Fitch) j192
Perry, William B. j193, j194, j281
Pertwee, Roland 626
Peyton, K.M. j362
Peyton, Kathleen Wendy j362
Phillpotts, Eden 166
Pier, Arthur Stanwood j124, 268
Pier, Florida 643
Pierson, Jane Susanna 167
Pilpel, Robert H. 880
Platt, Edward 403, 404
Plivier, Theodor 653, 689

Plowman, Stephanie 844
Pollock, Channing 510
Poole, Ernest 438
Poore, Ida Margaret 439
Pope, Marion Manville 168
Porter, Horace j49, j50, j51, j52, j93, j94, j125, j126, j195, j196, j282, j283
Prévost, Marcel 97
Private 19022 566
Pulleyne, Douglas 522
Putnam, Nina (Wilcox) 269

"Q" 42
Quiller-Couch, Arthur Thomas 42
Quirk, Leslie j349

Radziwill, Catherine (Rzewuska) 410
Ralphson, George Harvey j53, j54, j95, j96, j284, j285, j286, j287, j289, j327
Randall, Homer j197, j198, j289, j290, j291
Rathbone, Irene 675
Rathborne, St. George j72, j113
Raymond, Diana 824
Raymond, Ernest 471, 627, 798
Rebreanu, Liviu 628
Reeman, Douglas E. 815, 825
Reeve, Arthur Benjamin 43
Remarque, Erich Maria 575
Renn, Ludwig 576
Reynés-Monlaur, Marie 169
Richard, Hetty L.H. 146
Richards, H. Grahame 170
Richmond, Grace Louise (Smith) 270, 387
Rickard, Jessie Louisa (Moore) 98, 271, 388
Ridge, William Pett 171
Rinehart, Mary (Roberts) 272, 273, 389
Ritchie, Lewis A. Da Costa 114

Rixon, Anne Lovisa 764
Roberts, Cecil Edric Mornington 676
Roberts, Leslie 629
Robins, Elizabeth 390
Robinson, Derek 848
Robinson, Eliot Harlow 440
Roche, Arthur Somers 391
Rock, Phillip 881
Rohan, Jack j347
Rolland, Romain 459, 472, 523
Rolt-Wheeler, Francis William j127, j199, j292, j293
Romains, Jules 750
Rosner, Karl Peter 473
Roth, Amelia M.A. 392
Roth, Joseph 881a
Ruck, Berta 44, 274, 393, j97
Rudolf, Robert De Montjoie 394
Russell, Mary Annette (Beauchamp) Countess 124, j294
Rutledge, Marice 172

Sabsay, Nahum 746
Saffron, Robert 882
Salten, Felix j359
Sapper 395
Sassoon, Siegfried Lorraine 539, 630, 725, *1937
Saunders, John Monk 524
Sawyer, Ruth j328
Saxon, Peter 841
Sayler, H.L. j55
Scanlon, William T. 577
Schauwecker, Franz 578, 631, 747
Schem, Lida Clara 441
Schickele, Rene 540
Schindel, Bayard 579
Scholefield, Alan 860, 864
Schultz, Walter C. 726
Schulz, Emil 580
Schutze, Gladys Henrietta (Raphael) 616

Scott, John Reed 99
Sedgwick, Anne Douglas 460
Seredy, Kate j358
Sergeey-TSenski, Sergei Nikolaevich 775
Serrell, Edith j153
Seton, Graham 581, 677
Shaler, Robert j56, j200, j201
Shanks, Edward Buxton 396
Shaw, Frank Hubert j98
Shears, Sarah 882a
Shedd, Margaret 833
Sheehan, Perley Poore 9, 173
Shepherd, William Gunn 275
Sheppard, William Henry Crispin j128, j202, j295, j296
Sherman, Malcolm Clarke 810
Sherman, V.T. *j1915
Sherriff, Robert Cedric 632
Sherwood, Elmer j129, j130, *j1917, *j1919
Sherwood, Margaret Pollock 100
Shneur, Zalman 774
Sholokhov, Mikhail 699
Sidgwick, Cecily (Ullmann) 174, 276
Sidgwick, Ethel 277
Simson, Eric Andrew 615
Sinclair, Bertha Muzzay 319
Sinclair, May 101, 175, 442
Sinclair, Upton Beall 397, 765
Sitwell, Edith 739
Slade, Gurney 727
Sladen, Douglas Brooke Wheelton 45, 102
Sleath, Frederick 398, 443
Smith, Arthur Douglas Howden j23, j24, j25, j26, 278
Smith, Bertha (Whitridge) 131
Smith, Frederick Escreet 830

Smith, Gene 893
Smith, Helen Zenna 633
Smith, Wilbur A. 835
Snaith, John Collins 176, 399, 400
Snell, Roy Judson j339
Snow, Francis Haffkine 678
Solzhenitsyn, Alexander Isaevich 853
Springs, Elliott White 634, 654
Sproul, Albert Cliff 279, 280
Spurr, Jack 177
Stallings, Laurence 489
Stancu, Zaharia 842
Stander, Siegfried 854
Stanley, Dorothy 281
Stanley, W. 894
Stanley, William 856
Staples, Reginald Thomas 869, 883
Stead, Francis Herbert 178
Steele, Daniel 655
Stern, Gladys Bronwyn 401
Sterrett, Frances Roberta 282
Stevens, James 525
Stevens, Robert Tyler 870, 883
Stevenson, Burton Egbert 46, *1915
Stevenson, William 895
Stilgebauer, Edward 103, 283
Stoker, Alan 873
Stone, A. 284
Storm, Julie 819
Stowell, Gordon 582
Strang, Herbert j5, j57, j58, j99, j100, j132, j203, j297
Stratemeyer, Edward j204, j298, j311
Strathern, Paul 857
Streatfeild, Noel 679
Strong, Charles S. 680

Strunsky, Simeon 285
Stuart, Gordon j59, j205, j299
Sturgis, Granville Forbes 444
Sullivan, Mary Agnes 336
Szabo, Pal 681

Taffrail 104, 334, 690, j133
Tarbell, Ida Minerva 402
Tarkington, Booth j300
Terhune, Albert Payson j329
Thane, Elswyth 778, 780
Thanet, Octave 179
Tharaud, Jean 490
Tharaud, Jérôme 490
Theiss, Lewis Edwin j206
Thomas, Adrienne 656
Thompson, Edward John 526, 635, 682
Thompson, Sylvia 511
Thorndike, Jeanie Paine 771
Thorne, Guy 47, 48
Thurston, Ernest Temple 286, 541
Tiemann, Philip W. j361
Tilden, Freeman 287
Tilsley, W.V. 657
Tinayre, Marcelle 105
Tolstoy, Aleksei Nikolaevich 481, 776, *1925
Tomlinson, Everett Titsworth j301
Tomlinson, Henry Major 542, 636
Tomlinson, Paul Greene j134, j207, j208, j302
Tousseul, Jean 751
Tracy, Louis 106, 180
Train, Arthur Cheney 288
Tremaine, Herbert 181
Trent, Martha j209, j210, j211, j212, j213, j303
Trent, Paul 403, 404
Trevor, Elleston 845
Trites, William Budd 583

Troyat, Henri 796
Trumbo, Dalton 752
Tucker, William J. 772
Turiansky, Osyp 713
Turpin, Edna Henry Lee j331

Ulrich, Charles Kenmore 405
Unruh, Fritz von 543
Utechin, Nicholas 863

Vachell, Horace Annesley 289
Vale, Edmund j348
Valentine, Douglas 290, 406, 407
Vallotton, Benjamin 182, 291
Van Dyke, Henry 408
Van Dyne, Edith j214, j305
Van Zandt, Earl Christian 409
Vance, Louis Joseph 292
Vandercook, Margaret O'Bannon (Womack) j101, j102, j103, j104, j135, j136, j215, j216, j217, j304
Vane, George 445
Vassili, Paul 410
Veer, Willem De 49
Venable, Clarke 527, j340, j341, j343
Vercel, Roger 714, 740
Vring, Georg von der 544

Waddell, William Freeland 50
Waldo, Nigel 293
Wallace, Dillon j306
Walpole, Hugh Seymour 107
Ward, Kenneth j137, j138, j139, j140, j141
Ward, Mary Augusta (Arnold) 183, 294
Waring, Lily Florence 831

Author Index

Warner, William Henry 411
Warr, Charles Laing 108
Washburn, Claude Carlos 474
Wassermann, Jakob 499
Watson, Frederick 446
Watts, Mary (Stanbery) 295
Webster, Frank V. j60
Welcome, John 884
Wells, Carolyn j218
Wells, Herbert George 109, 184
Wendler, Otto Bernhard 638
Wertenbaker, Lael 820
West, Rebecca 296
Westerman, Percy Francis j6AB, j7AB, j61AB, j62A, j105A, j106AB, j142A, j219, j220A, j221AB, j222A, j223AC, j224A, j225A, j226A, j307A, j308, j309
Weston, George 584
Wharton, Edith Newbold (Jones) 297, 482
Wharton, James B. 545
Wheen, Arthur Wesley 585
White, Antonia 782a
Whitehill, Dorothy j227
Whitehouse, Arch (Arthur George Joseph) 826, 836, 846, 858, j362, j363, j364, j365, j366, j367
Whiting, John Downes j342
Widdemer, Margaret j228
Wiley, Hugh 546
Wilke, Karl 658
Wilkinson, Iris Guiver 721
Williams, George Valentine 290, 406, 407
Williamson, Alice Muriel (Livingston) 51, 65, 298
Williamson, Charles Norris 51, 65, 298
Williamson, Henry 639, 791, 794, 797, 799, 802
Wilson, Theodora 110, 741
Winder, Francis Arnold 640
Winfield, Arthur M. j310

Wise, Jennings Cropper 641
Wittlin, Jozef 753
Witwer, Harry Charles 299, 412
Wolff, William A. j39, j40, j41, j42, j43, j44
Woolf, Virginia (Stephen) 475
Wren, Percival Christopher 754
Wylie, Ida Alena Ross 300
Wyndham, Horace 111
Wynee, May j107A

Yardley, Herbert Osborn 700
Yeates, Victor M. 701
Youd, Christopher Samuel 805
Young, Clarence j229, 311
Young, Florence Ethel 301
Young, Francis Brett 642
Yver, Colette 413

Zander, Harry William 691
Zerbe, Alvin Sylvester j63
Zerbe, James j63
Zilahy, Lajos 659
Zweig, Arnold 547, 683, 728, 748

TITLE INDEX

(Asterisked items in the bibliography are cited as, for example, Buchan*1919, giving author and year.)

According to Her Light 466
The Ace from Arizona j363
Ace of the Argonne 832
Aces Up j343
Across the Black Waters 755
Adrienne Toner 460
The Adventures of Arnold Adair j168
The Adventures of Lieut. Lawless, R.N. j11AB
Adventures of Richard Hannay Buchan*1919
Afraid 128
The African Queen 705
The Age of Death 843
The Air Scout j2
Air Service Boys Flying for France j150
Air Service Boys Flying for Victory j238
Air Service Boys in the Big Battle j239
Air Service Boys over the Atlantic j312
Air Service Boys over the Enemy's Lines j151
Air Service Boys over the Rhine j152
Air-man and the Tramp 247
An Airman's Wife 197
Airship Boys in the Great War j55
Alf's Button 331
Alice Blythe j209
All Else is Folly 548
All for a Scrap of Paper 3
All for His Country 33
All Our Yesterdays 636
All Quiet on the Western Front 575
All Roads Lead to Calvary 356
The Alpha Raid 864
Amazing Interlude 272
Amazing Years 171
The Amazon 625
The Ambassador's Trunk 308
The Ambulance Driver 760
Amelie and Pierre 796

The American 333
The American Heart 338
American Pep 284
Amnesia 749
And Quiet Flows the Don 699
And the Captain Answered 179
Annette of the Argonne 79
Annie's Boys 882a
The Anvil 602
The Anzac War Trail With the Light Horse in Sinai 320
Apartment Next Door 357
Arches of the Years 591
The Armoured Cruiser 747
The Armoured-car Scouts j155
The Army Boys in France j197
The Army Boys in the Big Drive j289
The Army Boys in the French Trenches j198
The Army Boys Marching into Germany j290
The Army Boys on the Firing Line j291
Arnold Adair with the English Aces j334
Ashenden 537
At All Costs 586
At Grips with the Turk j69
At His Country's Call j89
At Plattsburg 136
At the Defense of Pittsburgh j81
At the Fall of Warsaw Fiske*j1915
At the Front 448
At the Sign of the Sword 36
The Audacious Adventures of Miles McConaughy 278
August 1914 853
August the Fourth j369
Aunt Sarah and the War 6
The Aussie Crusaders with Allenby in Palestine 416
Australia Hops In 704
Aw Hell! 527
Axelle 588

Balkan Monastery 708
Banks of Colne 166
The Barbarian 60
Barbarians 121
Barbed Wire Entanglements 762
Barbed-wire Grant of the Engineers j270
The Barber of Putney 384
Barometer Rising 769
Baron Fritz 599
Barrage Fire Barnes of the Field Artillery j271

Title Index

Battle Days 221
The Battle Months of George Daurella 67
Battle Stations 759
The Battleship Boys on the Sky Patrol j190
The Battleship Boys with the Adriatic Chasers j191
Battling on the Somme j121
Beatrice Ashleigh 301
Before the Curtain Falls 665
Before the Wind 245
Behind the Barrage 640
Behind the Enemy's Lines 279
Behind the German Lines 153
Behind the Lines 620
Behind the Scenes of Destiny 483
Behold the Fire 821
The Belfry 101
The Belgians to the Front Fiske*j1915
Belinda of the Red Cross 144
Bellary Bay 884
Beloved Stranger 558
Ben, the Battle Horse j256
Benoit Castain 97
Between the Days 497
Between the Lines in Belgium j8
Between the Lines in France j9
Between the Lines on the American Front j230
Between Two Gods 168
Between White and Red 668
Bid Me to Live 800
The Big Five Motorcycle Boys at the Front j45
The Big Five Motorcycle Boys on the Battle Line j91
The Big Five Motorcycle Boys Under Fire j46
Billy Barcroft, R.N.A.S. j219
Birds of a Feather 385
The Bitter End 530
Bitter Victory 719
The Black Drop 321
The Black Stone 342
Blighty 423
Blind 438
Blind Alley... 341
The Blond Beast 192
The Blonde Countess 700
Blood Relations 707
The Blue Max 818
"Blue Peter" 403
The Boardman Family 295
Bob Cook and the German Air Fleet j207

Bob Cook and the German Spy   j134
Bob Cook and the Winged Messenger   j302
Bob Cook's Brother in the Trenches   j208
Bob Thorpe, Sky Fighter in Italy   j313
Bob Thorpe, Sky Fighter in the Lafayette Flying Corps   j240
The Bomb-Shell   4
Bonds in Common   646
The Borderer   59
The Box with the Broken Seals   386
The Boy Allies at Jutland   j115
The Boy Allies at Liege   j30
The Boy Allies at Verdun   j117
The Boy Allies in Great Peril   j85
The Boy Allies in the Balkan Campaign   j86
The Boy Allies in the Baltic   j76
The Boy Allies in the Trenches   j31
The Boy Allies on the Firing Line   j32
The Boy Allies on the North Sea Patrol   j15
The Boy Allies on the Somme   j118
The Boy Allies under the Sea   j16
The Boy Allies under the Stars and Stripes   j119
The Boy Allies under Two Flags   j17
The Boy Allies with Haig in Flanders   j183
The Boy Allies with Marshal Foch   j266
The Boy Allies with Pershing in France   j267
The Boy Allies with the Cossacks   j33
The Boy Allies with the Flying Squadron   j18
The Boy Allies with the Great Advance   j268
The Boy Allies with the Submarine D-32   j166
The Boy Allies with the Terror of the Seas   j19
The Boy Allies with the Victorious Fleets   j250
The Boy Allies with Uncle Sam's Cruisers   j167
Boy of Bruges   j160
The Boy Scout Automobilists   Durston*j1921, j42
The Boy Scout Aviators   Durston*j1921, j42
The Boy Scout Fire Fighters   Durston*j1921, j174
A Boy Scout Hero   Griggs*j1921, j79
A Boy Scout Mystery   Griggs*j1921, j175
A Boy Scout on Duty   Durston*j1927, j42
A Boy Scout on the Trail   Griggs*j1921, j175
The Boy Scout Pathfinders   Durston*j1921, j174
A Boy Scout Patriot   Griggs*j1921, j79
A Boy Scout's Adventure   Griggs*j1921, j174
A Boy Scout's Bravery   Durston*j1927, j43
A Boy Scout's Campaign   Durston*j1927, j174
The Boy Scout's Challenge   Durston*j1921, j43

Title Index 487

The Boy Scout's Champion Recruit Durston*j1921, j79
A Boy Scout's Chance Griggs*j1921, j43
A Boy Scout's Courage Griggs*j1921, j42
A Boy Scout's Daring Griggs*j1921, j42
The Boy Scout's Defiance Durston*j1921, j79
A Boy Scout's Destiny Griggs*j1921, j174
A Boy Scout's Discovery Durston*j1927, j175
A Boy Scout's Holiday Griggs*j1921, j43
A Boy Scout's Mission Durston*j1927, j255
A Boy Scout's Secret Durston*j1927, j79
A Boy Scout's Struggle Griggs*j1921, j255
A Boy Scout's Success Griggs*j1921, j255
The Boy Scout's Victory Durston*j1921
The Boy Scouts Afloat Durston*j1921, j175
The Boy Scouts Afoot in France j113
The Boy Scouts at Liege j39
The Boy Scouts at Mobilization Camp j200
The Boy Scouts Before Belgrade j40
The Boy Scouts Call to Arms j201
The Boy Scouts in Belgium j53
The Boy Scouts in Camp Durston*j1921, j255
The Boy Scouts in England Blaine*j1916
The Boy Scouts in Europe Blaine*j1916
The Boy Scouts in France Blaine*j1916
The Boy Scouts in Front of Warsaw j77
The Boy Scouts in Germany Blaine*j1916
The Boy Scouts in Italy Blaine*j1916
The Boy Scouts in Russia Blaine*j1916
The Boy Scouts in Servia Blaine*j1916
The Boy Scouts in the Netherlands Blaine*j1916
Boy Scouts in the North Sea j54
The Boy Scouts in the War Zone j255
The Boy Scouts in Turkey Blaine*j1916
The Boy Scouts of the Air in Belgium j59
The Boy Scouts of the Air on the French Front j205
The Boy Scouts of the Air with Pershing j299
The Boy Scouts of the Field Hospital j56
The Boy Scouts on a Submarine Blaine*j1918, j175
The Boy Scouts on the Belgium Battlefields j47
The Boy Scouts on the Trail Durston*j1921, j175
The Boy Scouts on the Western Front Blaine*j1919, j174
The Boy Scouts on War Trails in Belgium j72
The Boy Scouts to the Rescue Durston*j1921, j174, j255
The Boy Scouts under Fire in France j174
The Boy Scouts under the Kaiser, or Karl Adler's Devotion j41
The Boy Scouts under the Kaiser; or, the Uhlans in Peril j95

The Boy Scouts under the Red Cross   j79
The Boy Scouts under the Stars and Stripes   j175
The Boy Scouts with Joffre   Blaine*j1919, j255
The Boy Scouts with Joffre; or, In the Trenches in Belgium
    Sherman*j1915, j53
The Boy Scouts with King George   j42
The Boy Scouts with the Allies   j43
The Boy Scouts with the Allies in France   j48
The Boy Scouts with the Cossacks, or Fred Waring's Service
    j44
Boy Scouts with the Cossacks; or, Poland Recaptured   j96
The Boy Scouts' Test   j78
The Boy Scouts' Victory   Durston*j1921, j43, j79
The Boy Volunteers on the Belgian Front   j137
The Boy Volunteers with the American Infantry   j138
The Boy Volunteers with the British Artillery   j139
The Boy Volunteers with the French Airmen   j140
The Boy Volunteers with the Submarine Fleet   j141
The Boy with Wings   44
Bretherton, Khaki or Field-grey?   569
The Brighton Boys at Château Thierry   j251
The Brighton Boys at St. Mihiel   j252
The Brighton Boys in the Argonne Forest   j319
The Brighton Boys in the Radio Service   j169
The Brighton Boys in the Submarine Fleet   j170
The Brighton Boys in the Trenches   j171
The Brighton Boys with the Battle Fleet   j172
The Brighton Boys with the Engineers at Cantigny   j253
The Brighton Boys with the Flying Corps.   j173
The Broken Soldier and the Maid of France   408
Brown Brethren   157
Brown on Resolution   557
Bruce   j329
Brusilov's Breakthrough   755
The Builders   343
The Burning Spear   339
Burton of the Flying Corps   j99
Bury Him Among Kings   845

Cab of the Sleeping Horse   99
Cadet of Belgium   j23
Call of the Soil   313
The Call to the Colors   j185
The Cameliers   349
The Camels are Coming   671
The Camp Fire Girls behind the Lines   j215
Camp Fire Girls in War and Peace   j269
The Camp Fire Girls on the Field of Honor   j216

Captain Calamity   j66AB
Captain Comstock   j336
Captain Conan   714
Captain Lucy and Lieutenant Bob   j182
Captain Lucy in France   j265
Captain Lucy in the Home Sector   j330
Captain Lucy's Flying Ace   j325
Captain Marraday's Marriage   208
Captain Zillner   364
Carl and Anna   558
Carry On!   j132
The Case of Sergeant Grischa   547
Catherine Joins Up   656
Cattle Car Express   650
The Cavalry Goes Through   623
The Cavalry Went Through   623
Chalmers Comes Back   476
Chances   605
Changing Winds   132
The Charmed American   370
Chevrons   509
Children of Fate   172
Children of No Man's Land   401
Christine   124
Christopher and Columbus   j294
City of Comrades   362
Civilian into Soldier   736
The Clammer and the Submarine   148
Class of 1902   559
Clear the Decks   209
Clerambault   459
Cloud Nineteen   894
The Clutch of Circumstances   210
The Cockerel   352
Cognac Hill 512
Cold Feet   566
Colonials in Khaki   74
The Coming   176
The Coming of the Dawn   167
Command   470
Commander Lawless, V.C.   j67A
Common Cause   304
Company K   686
The Complete Memoirs of George Sherston   Sassoon*1937
Comrade Rosalie   j254
Comrades   217
Comrades Ever   457
Comrades of the Clouds   598

The Confessions of a Little Man During the Great Days   112
Conscript Mother   75
Conscript 'Tich'   177
Contact   634
The Convictions of Christopher Sterling   311
A Corporal Once   622
Corp'ral Kelly of the Fightin' Fifth   238
Countess   872
Cousins German   613
Covenant with Death   804
The Crime at Vanderlynden's   508
The Cross Bearers   603
The Cross of Carl   652
The Cross of Fire   185
Crowning an Ideal   417
The Crowning of a King   748
The Cup of Fury   353
Cupid in Oilskins   54
Curse of Magira   816
The Curtain of Steel   334

Damascus Lies North   682
Dangerous Days   389
Daredevils of the Air   j350
The Dark Forest   107
The Dark Moment   784
The Dark Star   122
Darkness and Dawn   481, 776
Daughters of Hecuba   464
Dave Darrin after the Mine Layers   j260
Dave Darrin and the German Submarines   j261
Dave Darrin on Mediterranean Service   j262
Dave Porter Under Fire   j204
Dave Porter's War Honors   j298
The Dawn Patrol   600
The Day of Wrath   106
Daylight in a Dream   783
The Days of Wrath   106
Dead Yesterday   72
Dearer Than Life   34
Death of a Hero   549
Debatable Ground   401
Deep Sea Boys After a Submarine   Davidson*j1930, j163
Deep Sea Boys at the Big Surrender   Davidson*j1930, j248
Deep Sea Boys Behind the Big Guns   Davidson*j1930, j164
Deep Sea Boys Chasing a Sea Raider   Davidson*j1930, j165
Deep Sea Boys on Special Service   Davidson*j1930, j317
Deep Sea Boys to the Rescue   Davidson*j1930, j249

Title Index

Deep Soundings 732
The Deepening Stream 593
Deer [*sic*] Godchild j153
The Demon Device 882
Demon's Dawn 831
The Desert of Wheat 229
The Deserter 129
Destroyer Doings 258
The Devil in Harbour 834
Devil's Cradle 276
Devil's Paw 436
Digger Tourists 756
The Dispatch-Riders j61AB
Dodging the North Sea Mines j35
Don Hale in the War Zone j128
Don Hale Over There j202
Don Hale with the Flying Squadron j295
Don Hale with the Yanks j296
Donald and Helen 120
Doomed Demons j354
Dorothy V.A.D. and the Doctor 203
Double Duty 726
Double Traitor 41
The Dough Boys 255
Douglas Romance 102
Downfall 774
The Dragon-flies 344
The Dreadnought of the Air j6AB
Dreadnoughts of the Dogger j90
The Dream 808
A Dreamer Under Arms 236
Drink to Yesterday 757
Drums Afar 225
The Dupe 159

The Eagle's Height 803
The Earthquake 288
Echoes of Flanders 108
The Edge of Doom 309
Education Before Verdun 728
Elizabeth's Campaign 294
The Emden 813
An Emperor in the Dock 49
The End 141
The End of a Dream 354
Enemies of Women 197
The Enemy 510
The Enemy Within 262

England to America 432
An English Girl in Serbia   j107A
The Enlisting Wife 270
The Enormous Room 465
Entente Upon the Seas 531
Ermytage and the Curate 463
Esmeralda 269
Europa in Limbo 730
Everyman's Land 298
Everything is Thunder 709
Extremes Meet 536
Eye of the Lion 820
The Eyes of the Blind 391

Faber 499
A Fable 789
Facing the German Foe Fiske*j1915
Fairy Gold 505
Falcons of France 572
False Faces 292
A Farewell to Arms 561
The Feet of the Young Men 181
Fergus Lamont 876a
The Fiery Way 578
Fifty Feet Under the Sea j24
Fighting in France j87
Fighting in the Alps Fiske*j1915
Fighting in the Clouds for France Fiske*j1915
Fighting Livingstons 651
The Fighting Mascot 242
The Fighting Starkleys 467
Fighting the U-boat Menace Fiske*1918, j175
Fighting the Zeppelins j25
Fighting with French j57
Fighting with the U.S. Army 317
Find the Angels 29
The Finding of Nora 223
Fire of Green Boughs 271
Firebrand of Bolshevism 410
The Firefly of France 187
Fires of Faith 405
First Encounter 419, Dos Passos*1945
First Papers 817
First the Blade 211
The Flag j116
Flesh in Armour 673
Flight Errant 616
Flight From Bucharest 870

The Flower of the Land 770
The Flowers of the Field 888
Flying Black Birds j353
Flying Poilu 264
Follow the Leader 773
For the Freedom of the Seas j146
For Valor j341
The Forbidden Forest j370
Forced to Fight 131
Forest of Swords 10
The Forest of the Hanged 628
The Fortress 854
The Fortune 139
Fortunes of War j234
Forward Ho! 520
Four Aces j351
Four Days 146
The Four Horsemen of the Apocalypse 198
Four Infantrymen 614
The Four Roads 241
A Fox Under My Cloak 794
Frank Forester j58
Frank Luke, Balloon Buster j364
The French Twins j192
Fritz Strafers j220A
Frogs Die in Earnest 684
From Baseball to Boches 299
From the Nile to the Tigris j156
Fugitives from Passion 595
The Full Measure of Devotion 224
The Furnace 631

"G.B." 569
A Gamble with Death 842
Garland of Valour 811
Gaspard the Poilu 55
Gay-Neck 340
The General 718
General Bramble 458
Generals Die in Bed 610
Georgina's Service Stars j187
The German Prisoner 609
German Spy 724
The German Spy, a Present-day Story 5
The Ghosts of Africa 895
The Gift 383
The Gift of Paul Clermont 451
Ginger 111

Ginger and McGlusky 142
Girl from Alsace 46
The Girl He Left Behind 250
The Girl Philippa 63
The Girls at His Billet j97
Glamour 380
The Glory and the Dream 795
The Glory is Departed 722
God and Tony Hewitt 496
God Have Mercy on Us! 577
God's Sparrows 731
Gog, the Story of an Officer and Gentlemen 69
Going West 363
Golden Pilgrimage 579
The Golden Triangle 152
The Golden Virgin 797
Good Old Anna 37
The Good Soldier: Schweik 611
Goodbye, Dear England 823
Goshawk Squadron 848
Gossamer 18
Gossip from the Forest 862
Grace Harlowe Overseas j320
Grace Harlowe with the Marines at Chateau Thierry j321
Grace Harlowe with the Red Cross in France j322
Grace Harlowe with the U.S. Troops in the Argonne j323
Grace Harlowe with the Yankee Shock Boys at St. Quentin j324
Grapes of Wrath 119
The Great Crusade 641
The Great Desire 314
The Great Destroyer 661
The Great Impersonation 437
Green and Gay 234
Greenmantle 22
Grey Dawn--Red Night 562
Grey Fish 329
The Grey Seas of Jutland 827
Grope Carries On 672
The Ground-swell 337
Guests of Summer 604
Guignol's Band 787
Gunboat and Gunrunners 35
Gunpowder Stewart of the Naval Militia j272
Guns of Europe 11

H.M.S. Edinburgh 244
"H.M.S. Saracen" 825
Halt! Who's There? 88

Title Index

The Hampton Women 887
He Looked for a City 768
Heart of Alsace 291
Heart of War 891
An Heiress in Name Only 392
Helen Carey j210
Hell Dock 31
Hellbirds 863
A Helluva War 513
Her Country 186
Her Privates We 567, Private 19022*1930
Here's Luck! 546
Here's to the Day! 39
A Hero of Liege j5
High Heart 151
Higher Command 648
The Highflyers 359
The Hills of Desire 375
Hindenburg's March into London 90
Hira Singh 263
Hira Singh's Tale 263
His Daughter 261
His German Wife 45
His Soul Goes Marching On 461
His Wife's Job 377
History of Button Hill 582
The Holiday Adventures of Mr. P.J. Davenant j28
Hollow Sea 743
Honour Come Back-- 710
Honourable Estate 715
Honours of War 68
Hope of the House 25
Horses in the Sky 551
Hosannah Tree 833
Hosts of the Air 12
The Hounds of Spring 511
The House of Baltazar 429
The House of Courage 388
The House of Death 476
The House on Charles Street 449
How Dear is Life 791
How Many Miles to Babylon? 859
How They Did It 435
How Young They Die 837
How Young They Died 837
The Hungry Hundred 259
Hunting Down the Spy Cobb*j1916
Hunting the U Boats j120A

Hushed Up at the German Headquarters   154
The Hyphen   441

I Live Under a Black Sun   739
I Met a Man   729
Illusion   542
The Imposter   491
In Araby Orion   635
In Arms for Russia   228
In Defence of Paris   j26
In God's Land   687
In Khaki for the King   38
In Parenthesis   734
In Pawn to a Throne   322
In Russian Trenches   Fiske*j1915
In Secret   326
In the Battle for New York   j82
In the Company of Eagles   828
In the Fire of the Furnace   58
In the Trenches   j315
The Invader's Son   361
Invasion   738
Invasion '14   738
The Invasion of the United States   j83
Irene to the Rescue   j65
The Iron Cross   13
It Happened "Over There"   239
"It's a Great War"   563
It's Me Again   861

Jack Race Air Scout   j27
Jacob's Room   475
Jamesie   277
Jean Clarambaux   751
Jeanne-Marie's Triumph   469
Jed's Boy   j259
Jesting Army   627
Jim Redlake   642
Jimmie Higgins   397
Jimmie the Sixth   282
Jimmy Goes to War   j349
Jimmy May in the Fighting Line   j186
Jitny and the Boys   j73
John Adney, Ambulance Driver   j306
John Brown: Confessions of a New Army Cadet   324
John Dene of Toronto   355
Johnny Got His Gun   752
Johnstone of the Border   59

Title Index

Joining the Colors   j154
Journey to the End of the Night   695
Journey's End   632
The Judgment of Peace   369

The Kaiser Goes; The Generals Remain   689
Kaiser's Coolies   653
Kangaroo   480
The Kangaroo Marines   23
Karen   276
Katrin Becomes a Soldier   656
The Keepers of the Narrow Seas   j220A
Keeping Secrets   878
Keeping Up With William   189
The Khaki Boys at Camp Sterling   j147
The Khaki Boys at the Front   j148
The Khaki Boys Fighting to Win   j236
The Khaki Boys on the Way   j149
The Khaki Boys Over the Top   j237
The Khaki Girls at Windsor Barracks   j243
The Khaki Girls Behind the Lines   j158
The Khaki Girls of the Motor Corps   j159
Khaki: How Tredick Got into the War   287
Kif   555
A Killing for the Hawks   830
The King   473
King--of the Khyber Rifles   91
Kingdom of the Blind   94
King's Men   96
The Kinsmen Know How to Die   643
Kissing Kin   780
Knights of the Air   254

L.P.M.: The End of the Great War   16
Labels   503
The Lad with Wings   44
The Ladies' Road   670
Lads of the Lothians   430
Lament for Adonis   682
Lament for Agnes   860a
Lance   766
The Land Lay Waiting   793
Land-girl's Love Story   393
Larry Dexter in Belgium   j22
Last of the Grenvilles   330
Last Post   532
The Last Raider   815
The Last Shot   8

The Last Summer of Mata Hari 876
The Last Weapon 110
The Laughing Falcon j367
The Laughing Girl 206
Lawrence in the Blue 727
Leerie j328
Legends 424
Legion of Dishonor 761
The Legion of the Condemned 528
Lena 740
Let the Day Perish 674
Letters of a V.A.D. 246
Lieutenant Comstock, U.S. Marine j332
A Life at Stake 312
Life in the Tomb 869
Life Without End 677
Light 307
The Light Above the Cross-roads 98
The Light Heart 778
Lilies, White and Red 352
Lilla 82
The Lingering Faun 519
The Lion at Sea 867
Lion in the Evening 860
Little Comrade 46
Little England 241
The Little House j318
Little House in Wartime 26
The Little Moment of Happiness 360
A Little Princess of the Stars and Stripes j34B
A Lively Bit of the Front j221AB
A London Lot 372
The Lonely Warrior 474
The Long Mountain 839
The Long Trick 114
The Long Walk of Samba Diouf 490
Lord Raingo 500
Loretto 612
The Lost Naval Papers 127
Lost Shadows 713
The Lost Traveller 782a
Love and the Crescent 425
Love and the Loveless 799
Love Lane 399
Love of an Unknown Soldier 251
Love Time in Picardy 368
The Lovers 165
Love's Inferno 103

Title Index

Lucia Rudini j211
Lucky on an Important Mission Sherwood*j1917, j130
Lucky, the Young Navy Man j129
Lucky, the Young Soldier j130

Madeleine 819
Mademoiselle Prune 352
The Magic Ship 879
Magnificat 660
The Maid of Mirabelle 440
The Major 126
Making the Last Stand for Old Glory j84
Man and His Lesson 380
A Man Could Stand up 502
The Man From God's Country 487
The Man From Scapa Flow 690
The Man From the Clouds 207
The Man in the White Slicker 570
Man on Horseback 302
The Man the Devil Didn't Want 754
The Man Who Survived 257
Man with Four Lives 896
Man with the Club Foot 290
The Man with the Lamp 366
Man's Highest Duty 434
The Map of Days 591
Mare Nostrum 315
Maria Capponi 540
Marieken de Bruin j212
The Marines Have Advanced j333
The Marines Have Landed j314
The Marne 297
Mary Louise Adopts a Soldier j305
Mary Louise and the Liberty Girls j214
Mattock 525
McGlusky's Great Adventure 143
Me Among the Ruins 861, Jack*1976
Meanwhile; a Packet of Letters 70
Medal Without Bar 590
The Medici Fountain 814
Memoirs of a Fox-Hunting Man 539
Memoirs of an Infantry Officer 630
Men Pass 664
Me'ow Jones, Belgian Refugee Cat j123
Messages of Love 805
The Messenger 390
Michael 56
The Middle Parts of Fortune 567

Midshipman Rex Carew, V.C.   j280
Mike   56
Mike of Company D   j357
Mildmay Park   444
Mimi   226
Minniglen   205
Mirabelle of Pampeluna   413
Miss Amerikanka   227
Miss Pim's Camouflage   281
"Missing"   183
Mr. Britling Sees It Through   109
Mr. Mann   428
Mr. Standfast   323
Mr. Sterling Sticks it Out   311
Mrs. Fischer's War   617
Mitsou   594
Mixed Division   62
A Modern Girl   583
Montenegro   812
Moonlit Way   327
More About P.J., the Secret Service Boy   j337
Mother and Son   523
Mothers of Men   411
The Motion Picture Chums' War Spectacle   j64B
The Motor Boys in the Army   j229
The Motor Boys on the Firing Line   j311
The Motorboat Boys Down the Danube; or, Caught in the Whirlpool of War   j10
The Motorboat Boys Down the Danube; or, Four Chums Abroad   j10
The Movie Boys' War Spectacle   Appleton*j1927, j64
The Moving Picture Boys on French Battlefields   j231
The Moving Picture Boys on the War Front   j143
Moving Waters   521
Mufti   395
The Mustering of the Hawks   850
My Airman Over There   199
My Boy in Khaki   253
My Country   117
My Enemy, My Love   883
My Kingdom for a Grave   844
My Wife   118
My-Man   77

The Natural Man   486
The Nature of the Beast   286
A Naval Adventuress   404
A Naval Venture   150
Navarre of the North   j345

Title Index 501

Navy Boys after the Submarines   j163
Navy Boys at the Big Surrender   j248
Navy Boys Behind the Big Guns   j164
Navy Boys Chasing a Sea Raider   j165
Navy Boys on Special Service   j317B
Navy Boys to the Rescue   j249
Nest-builder   71
Never Without You   692
The New Gethsemane   135
Nicky-Nan, Reservist   42
The Night Cometh   61
Nine Holiday Adventures of Mr. P.J. Davenant in the Year
   1915   j80
1915   890
1919   667
Ninety-six Hours' Leave   160
The Ninth of November   495
No Hero--This   717
No Man's Land   587
No More Parades   493
No More War   178
No Names, No Pack Drill   678
No Slacker, 1917-1918   j361
No Through Road   829
Nomads in Flanders   649
Non-Combatants and Others   86
The Noonday Sword   824
North of Suez   619
Not All Ashes   772
Not Only War   666
Not So Quiet   633
Not to the Strong   771
Now, God Be Thanked   877
Number 70, Berlin   80
Nurse Benson   381
The Nursery (Banks of Colne)   166
Nurse's Story in Which Reality Meets Romance   19

The Ocean Wireless Boys and the Naval Code   j37B
The Ocean Wireless Boys of the Iceberg Patrol   j38B
The Ocean Wireless Boys on the Atlantic   j4B
The Ocean Wireless Boys on the Pacific   j88
The Ocean Wireless Boys on War Swept Seas   j122
Of Water and the Spirit   89
Off With the Old Love   134
Okewood of the Secret Service   406
The Old Blood   95
The Old Indispensables   396

The Old Mine's Secret   j331
The Old Order Changeth   40
Old Soldiers   885
Oliver Hastings   85
On Board the Mine-Laying Cruiser Fiske*j1915
On Land and Sea at the Dardanelles   j13A
On Secret Air Service   j346
On Some Fair Morning   777
On the Field of Honor   248
On the Road to Bagdad   j110
On Virgin Soil   624
One Man's Initiation   419
One Man's War   857
One of Ours   462
One Spring in Picardy   856
Only a Dog   j131
Only Fade Away   790
Ordeal by Fire   58
Other Ranks   657
Otto Babendiek   602
Our Fatal Shadows   816
Our Jackies with the Fleet   j193
Our Pilots in the Air   j194
Our Sammies in the Trenches   j281
Our Young Aeroplane Scouts at the Marne   j282
Our Young Aeroplane Scouts at Verdun   j125
Our Young Aeroplane Scouts Fighting to the Finish   j195
Our Young Aeroplane Scouts in at the Victory   j283
Our Young Aeroplane Scouts in England   j93
Our Young Aeroplane Scouts in France and Belgium   j49
Our Young Aeroplane Scouts in Germany   j50
Our Young Aeroplane Scouts in Italy   j94
Our Young Aeroplane Scouts in Russia   j51
Our Young Aeroplane Scouts in the Balkans   j126
Our Young Aeroplane Scouts in the War Zone   j196
Our Young Aeroplane Scouts in Turkey   j52
Out of Darkness   515
Out of the War?   252
The Outrage   123
Over Here   243
Over There with Pershing's Heroes at Cantigny   j284
Over There with the Canadians at Vimy Ridge   j285
Over There with the Doughboys at St. Mihiel   j286
Over There with the Engineers at Cambrai   j287
Over There with the Marines at Chateau Thierry   j288
Over There with the Yanks in the Argonne Forest   j327
Overshadowed   564

Title Index

P.J., the Secret Service Boy j335
A Pair of Vagabonds 316
Pandora's Young Men 446
Paper Prison 754
Parade's End Ford*1950
Parson's Nine 679
The Parts Men Play 414
Pass Guard at Ypres 607
The Passing Bells 881
Passion's Sweet Sacrifice 875
Passport Invisible 173
Passport to Hell 721
The Path of Glory 553
Paths of Glory 703
The Patriot and the Spies 50
Patriot's Progress 639
Patrol 518
Patty-bride j218
Paul Clermont's Story and My Own 451
Pawns Count 266
The Peculiar Major 351
People of the Plains 681
Peter Jackson 420
Peter Jameson 420
Phoebe Marshal j303
Pierre and Joseph 415
Pierre and Luce 472
Pierrot j20
Pigboats 645
Pillbox 17 592
Pilot and Observer 534
Pincher Martin 104
Pink Roses 325
The Plattsburgers j124
Playboy Squadron 846
The Playground of Satan 191
Plumes 489
"Poilu" j145
Polly Sees the World at War j227
Pollyooly Dances 426
Portrait of a Spy 541
The Potter Boys in the Front Line Trenches Cobb*j1919, j174
The Potter Boys Under Old Glory Cobb*j1918, j175
The Potter Boys with the Tanks Cobb*j1919, j255
Potterat and the War 182
The Power of Love in the World War 688
The Pretty Lady 193
Prince of the Captivity 685

Prisoner Halm 658
Private Angelo Ferraro, U.S.N.G. 336
Private Gaspard 55
Private Spud Tamson 24
Private Suhren 544
Private Wire to Washington 373
Professor Latimer's Progress 285
Promenade in Champagne 801
Pugs and Peacocks 450
The Pure in Heart 534
Pursuit 626

Quaker-born 73
The Querrils 306
The Quiet Shore 798

Rachel Fitzpatrick 439
Rags j347
The Raider 813
Ralph on the Army Train j161
Ramsey Milholland j300
Randall and the River of Time 782
Random Harvest 767
Rank and Riches 40
Rasputin 571
The Ravi Lancers 852
Reach to Eternity 886
Records of a Rectory Garden 163
Red and Black 387
Red Cross & Iron Cross 93
Red Cross Barge 83
The Red Cross Girls Afloat with the Flag j217
The Red Cross Girls in Belgium j101
The Red Cross Girls in the British Trenches j102
The Red Cross Girls on the French Firing Line j103
The Red Cross Girls with the Italian Army j135
The Red Cross Girls with the Russian Army j104
The Red Cross Girls with the Stars and Stripes j136
The Red Cross Girls with the U.S. Marines j304
Red Fleece 28
The Red Horizon 87
The Red Planet 155
Red Signal 347
The Redlakes 642
The Refugee Family j247
Renni, the Rescuer j359
Retreat 589
Retreat From Death 720

Title Index

Return of the Brute 574
Return of the Soldier 296
Return to the Wood 792
The Revellers 180
Richard Chatterton, V.C. 15
The Rider in Khaki 140
The Rise and Fall of Carol Banks 654
Rising of the Tide 402
Road to Calvary 776, 481
The Road to Calvary 481, 776
Robin Linnet 57
ROC; A Dog's-eye View of War j348
Rogue by Compulsion 21
Roll River 702
The Roll-call 194
The Romantic 442
Rough Justice 507
Rough Road 156
Rounding Up the Raider j105A
Roux the Bandit 554
The Rover Boys under Canvas j310
Rube 477
Ruth Fielding at the War Front j176
Ruth Fielding Homeward Bound j257
Ruth Fielding in the Red Cross j177
Ruth of the U.S.A. j233

S.O.S. j342
Sacrifice 105
Saint Mary's Village Through the Eyes of an Unknown Soldier Who Lived On 788
Saint Teresa 468
Salt of the Earth 174
Salt of the Earth! 753
San Fairy Ann 516
Scar That Tripled 275
Scarlet Streamers j365
Schlump 580
Scout Drake in War Time j184
Scouting the Balkans in a Motor Boat Sherman*j1915
Sea Fights, 1914-1918 531
A Sea Lawyer's Log 367
The Sea-Girt Fortress j7AB
The Search 348
Search for the Spy j3
The Second Coming 76
The Second Fiddle 116
The Secret Battle 346

The Secret Battleplane j106AB
The Secret Hand 407
Secret History 51
Secret History Revealed by Lady Peggy O'Malley 51
The Secret of the Baltic j316A
The Secret of the Marne 196
The Secret Sea-Plane 47
Secret Service Submarine 48
The Secret Wireless j206
Secret Witness 138
The Secrets of the German War Office 2
Sergeant Eadie 538
Sergt. Spud Tamson, v.c. 204
Sergeant Ted Cole j301
A Servant of Reality 318
The Settlers 851
Seven Days in the Line 615
The Seventh Vial 443
The Shadow of Rosalie Burnes 378
Shadows 170
Shadows Around the Lake 742
Shelled by an Unseen Foe Fiske*j1916
Sherston's Progress 725
The Ship of Death 283
Shock Troops 810
Shot with Crimson 260
Shout at the Devil 835
Show Me Death! 596
Siberian Garrison 568
The Silence of Colonel Bramble 379
The Silent Legion 202
The Silent Prophet 881a
Simon Called Peter 456
The Singing Tree j358
Single Handed 557
The Single Star 230
Sir Harry 376
Sister Clare 169
The Sister of a Certain Soldier 256
Sixty-four, Ninety-four! 498
Skimmer the Daring j339
The Sky Pilot in No Man's Land 328
The Sleepwalkers 663
Smashing the Hindenburg Line j278
A Smile a Minute 412
The Smiths in War Time 149
Sniper Jackson 398
Snow Trenches 655

Title Index

Soldier 868
Soldier of Life 66
Soldiers--and Women 638
Soldiers Both 231
Soldiers March! 601
Soldier's Pay 501
Soldiers' Women 638
Some Do Not 485
Some Found Adventure 506
Some Further Adventures of Mr. P.J. Davenant j29
Somewhere in Scotland 145
The Somme, Including also The Coward 514
A Son at the Front 482
The Son Decides 268
Sonia: Between Two Worlds 161
Sonia Married 382
Sons 840
The Sons of Cain 529
Soul of a Bishop 184
The Soul of Susan Yellam 289
South Wind of Love 737
Spanish Farm 488, Mottram*1927
Spears Against Us 676
Special Providence 608
The Spectre of Masuria 680
Spies 280
Spies with Wings j366
Splendid Chance 20
Splendid Outcast 421
The Splinter Fleet of the Otranto Barrage 723
Spy 712
The Spy in Black 125
A Spy of the Huns 162
The Spy on the Submarine j189
A Spy was Born 711
Squad 545
Squadron Forty-Four 826
Squadron Shilling 836
Stand to Arms 64
The Standard 722
Stealthy Terror 133
Stepdaughters of War 633
Still a Woman 644
The Strange Case of Gunner Rawley 620
Strange Meeting 847
The Strong Hours 218
The Sub j133
A Sub and a Submarine j307A

Sub of the R.N.R.   j62A
The Submarine Hunters   j222A
Submerged   669
Summer 1914   763
The Summons   431
The Sunken Fleet   618
Suzy   697
The Swallow   335
The Sword Falls   552
Sylvia & Michael   374

Taps   698
Tasker Jevons   101
Ted Marsh on an Important Mission   Sherwood*j1919, j130
Tell England   471
The Terror   158
Test of Scarlet   332
A Test to Destruction   802
Testament   744
That Damn Jew   758
That Goldheim   220
That Was the End   693
That Which Hath Wings   215
That's Me in the Middle   855
These Men, Thy Friends   526
They Also Serve   517
They Call It Patriotism   662
They Gave Him a Gun   716
They Knew How to Die   643
Thick of the Fray at Zeebrugge   j308
Thirteen Years in Hell   691
This is the End   115
This, My Son   522
Thomas the Imposter   491
Those Strange Years   741
Three Against Fate   608
Three Cheers for Me   809
Three Couriers   565
Three Daughters   745
Three Englishmen   706
Three Kingdoms   504
Three Live Ghosts   237
Three Soldiers   452
The Three Strings   249
The Three Things   14
Through Blazes For Love   735
Through Hell to Peace   1
Through the Enemy's Lines   j100

Through the Wheat   478
Through Tunnels and Canyons Roared a Train   746
Thunder at Dawn   873
Thunder Bird   319
Thunder in the Sky   j362
Thy Son Liveth   30
A Time in a City   j368
A Time of Death   871
A Time to Embrace   892
The Tin Soldier   190
To Serve Them All My Days   849
To the Fore with the Tanks!   j223AC
To the Honor of the Fleet   880
To the Slaughterhouse   838
Told with a Drum   733
Tom Slade, Motorcycle Dispatch-bearer   j178
Tom Slade on a Transport   j179
Tom Slade with the Boys Over There   j180
Tom Slade with the Colors   j181
Tom Slade with the Flying Corps   j258
Tom Swift and his Air Scout   j232
Tom Swift and his War Tank   j144
Tom Willoughby's Scouts   j297
Tommy and the Maid of Athens   147
Tommy of the Tanks   371
Too Fat to Fight   310
The Tortoise   447
Towards Morning   300
Trail of the Beast   303
The Trap   647
Trapped   484
A Tree May Fall   889
The Tree of Heaven   175
Trench-mates in France   j63
Trooper Sharpe of the First Cavalry   j273
Twenty-three and a Half Hours' Leave   273
Two American Boys Aboard a Submersible   j114
Two American Boys in the French War Trenches   j74
Two American Boys with Pershing in France   j162
Two American Boys with the Allied Armies   j14
Two American Boys with the Dardanelles Battle Fleet   j75
Two Black Crows in the A.E.F.   535
Two Boys of the Battleship   j60
The Two Crossings of Madge Swalue   212
Two Masters   585
Two Prisoners   659

Unchanging Quest   494

Uncle Sam of Freedom Ridge   433
Uncle Sam's Army Boys in Italy   j244
Uncle Sam's Army Boys in Khaki Under Canvas   j245
Uncle Sam's Army Boys on the Rhine   j246
Uncle Sam's Boy at War   j108
Uncle Sam's Boys Smash the Germans   j263
Uncle Sam's Boys with Pershing's Troops at the Front   j264
Uncle Sam's Navy Boys Afloat   j274
Uncle Sam's Navy Boys in Action   j275
Uncle Sam's Navy Boys with the Marines   j276
Uncle Sam's Navy Boys with the Submarine Chasers   j277
Unconquered   130
The Undefeated   400
Under Fire for Serbia   Fiske*j1915
Under Fire: The Story of a Squad   113
Under Foch's Command   j157
Under French's Command   j12
Under Haig in Flanders   j111
Under Jellicoe's Command   j92
Under the Blue Cross   j21
Under the White Ensign   j224A
Under the Yankee Ensign   j235
The Underground Spy   j326
Unfeeling Sky   841
The Ungrown-ups   j338
The Unknown Soldier   556, 587
The Unpardonable Sin   235
Up and Down   195
Urgent Private Affairs   621
"Utmost Fish!"   822

Vae Victus   123
Valerie Duval   j213
Valour   214
Verdun   750
The Vermilion Box   84
Victorious   358
The Victors   492
The Vintage   53
Vive la France   j279

W Plan   581
Wallflowers   293
The Walnut Trees of Altenburg   785
The Wanting Seed   807
War   7, 576
The War and Elizabeth   294
War Birds and Lady Birds   654

Title Index

War Cache 265
War Comes to Castle Rising 865
The War Eagle 213
War Horse j360
War Is War 592a
The War, Madame ... 137
War Nurse 637
The War Terror 43
The War Wedding 65
War Wings j356
The War Zone of the Kaiser Sherman*j1915
War's Rosary 350
The Wars 866
The War-Workers 216
The Wasted Generation 455
A Watch-Dog of the North Sea j142A
The Waters of Strife 445
The Way of Revelation 453
The Way of Sacrifice 543
"We Are French!" 9
We That Were Young 675
The Web 365
Wee Macgregor Enlists 17
What Outfit, Buddy? 427
When Blackbirds Sing 806
When the Gods Laughed 629
Where Are My Legions 893
Where the Path Breaks 65
Where the Souls of Men Are Calling 233
Where Your Heart Is 232
Where Your Treasure Is 232
The Whistler's Room 550
The White Horse and the Red-haired Girl 340
The White Morning 188
Who Goes There? 27, 88
Whom the Gods Love 786
Why Stay We Here? 606
William--An Englishman 345
Willing Horse 454
Wilmshurst of the Frontier Force j225A
The Wiltons in War Time 394
The Wind Brings Up the Rain 873a
Wind that Blows 779
The Winds of the World 92
Wing for Wing j352
Winged Victory 701
Wings 524
Wings for the Chariots 858

Wings of Destiny 584
Wings of the Navy j355
Wings on My Feet 573
Winning His Wings j309
Winning in the Air Cobb*j1915
Winning the War Cross Cobb*j1916
Winona's War Farm j228
With Allenby in Palestine j241
With Beatty in Jutland j344AB
With Beatty in the North Sea j112A
With Beatty off Jutland j226A
With Cossack and Car in Galicia j109A
With French at the Front j1
With Haig at the Front j68A
With Haig on the Somme 164, j203
With Jellicoe in the North Sea j98
With Joffre at Verdun j70
With Joffre on the Battle Line j36
With Our Russian Allies j71
With Pershing at the Front j188
With Pershing in France Fiske*j1919, j174
With Soul on Fire 565
With the Allies to the Rhine j242
With the Hero of the Marne Fiske*j1919, j255
Woman of Knockaloe 479
Woman of Mystery 78
Wonder of War at Sea j292
Wonder of War in the Air j127
The Wonder of War in the Holy Land j293
The Wonder of War on Land j199
The Wonderful Year 81
Wooden Crosses 418
Wooden Swords 597
The World Went Mad 694
World's End 765
Worn Doorstep 100
Wounded Souls 422

Yank--the Crusader 409
The Year Between 240
Years for Rachel 274
Yellow Document 305
The Yellow Dog 219
Yellow Dove 32
Yellow English 222
The Yellow Pigeon 533
Yellow Souls 222
Yesterday and Today 764

Title Index

You No Longer Count   201
The Young Anzacs   200
The Young Eagles   874
Young Lion of Flanders   52
Young William Washbourne   781
Young Woman of 1914   683

Zeppelin's Passenger   267
Zero Hour   560

Ref
Z
5917
W33
H33

MAY 1 0 1982